ANNUAL EDITIONS

READINGS IN

AMERICAN HISTORY

Historians Writing and Written About

Brooks Adams
Henry Adams
Selig Adler
Robert C. Alberts
Donald G. Alexander
Thomas B. Alexander
Norman C. Amaker
Robert Hardy Andrews
Jules Archer

Bernard Bailyn
George Bancroft
Lowell John Bean
Charles Beard
Mary Beard
Carl Becker
Lee Benson
Barton Bernstein
Robert Beverley
John W. Blassingame
Daniel Boorstin
William Bradford
James MacGregor Burns

Bruce Catton
David M. Chalmers
Edward Channing
Noam Chomsky
Winston Churchill
Warren Cohen
Henry Steele Commager
Joseph R. Conlin
Rupert Costo
Avery Craven
Herbert Croly
Joseph P. Cullen
Richard N. Current

Vine Deloria, Jr.
Bernard DeVoto
David Donald
Martin B. Duberman
Melvyn Dubofsky
W. E. B. DuBois
William A. Dunning

Gerald G. Eggert
Arthur Ekrich, Jr.

David Hackett Fisher
D. F. Fleming
Jack D. Forbes
John Hope Franklin
Frank Freidel

John Kenneth Galbraith
Lloyd Gardner
Eugene D. Genovese

Marvin E. Gettlemen
Edward Gibbon
Estelle Gilson
Saul Gilson

Andrew Hacker
Louis Halle
Virginia Van der Veer Hamilton
Oscar Handlin
Robert L. Heilbroner
John Higham
Richard Hofstadter
David Horowitz
Joseph Kinsey Howard
Emmet John Hughes
Harold Melvin Hyman

Walter Jarrett
Manfred Jonas
Alvin M. Josephy, Jr.

Morton Keller
George F. Kennan
Gabriel Kolko
Aileen Kraditor

Walter LaFeber
Ann Lane
Christopher Lasch
Michael A. Lebowitz
Jesse Lemisch
Gerda Lerner
N. Gordon Levin
Stewart Levine
George Lewis
Leon Litwak
Nancy O. Lurie
Staughton Lynd

Richard K. MacMaster
Robert James Maddox
Karl Marx
Cotton Mather
Ernest May
Thomas J. McCormick
Perry Miller
Barrington Moore, Jr.
Samuel Eliot Morison
John Lothrop Motley

Allan Nevins
Roy F. Nichols
Michael Novak

Walter Oakes
William O'Neill

Henry M. Pachter

Robert R. Palmer
Francis Parkman
Thomas G. Paterson
Dexter Perkins
Kevin P. Phillips
U. B. Phillips
Norman Pollack
David Potter
Thomas Pressly

Benjamin Quarles

James G. Randall
Edwin O. Reischauer
Peggy Robbins
James I. Robertson, Jr.

Arthur M. Schlesinger, Jr.
David M. Shoup
Joel H. Silbey
Francis Butler Simkins
Don Elton Smith
Henry Nash Smith
John Smith
Robert Sobel
Oswald Spengler
Kenneth Stampp
Stan Steiner
Wilson Sullivan
Charles S. Sydnor

Charles Tansill
Stephan A. Thernstrom
Hugh Thomas
Arnold Toynbee
Lionel Trilling
Leon Trotsky
Frederick Jackson Turner
William M. Tuttle

Irwin Unger

Alden T. Vaughan
Virgil J. Vogel

Richard C. Wade
Joseph Frazier Wall
Ronald Walters
Richard J. Walton
James Weinstein
Bell I. Wiley
William Appleman Williams
John Wiltz
C. Vann Woodward
W. E. Woodward

Howard Zinn

ANNUAL EDITIONS

READINGS IN

AMERICAN HISTORY

Annual Editions
the dushkin publishing group, inc.
Guilford, Connecticut

FORTHCOMING ANNUAL EDITIONS

Accounting	Geography
American Government	Geology
American Studies	Health
Anthropology	Marketing
Art Appreciation	Mathematics
Art History	Music Appreciation
Astronomy	Music History
Biology	Philosophy
Botany	Physical Education
Business	Physical Science
Career Education	Political Science
Chemistry	Psychology
Computer Science	Religion
Earth Science	Sociology
Economics	Speech
Education	Western Civilization
Engineering	World History
English Composition	Zoology

Copyright © 1972 by the Dushkin Publishing Group, Inc.,
Guilford, Connecticut.

Library of Congress Catalog Card Number: 74-187540

Manufactured by Kingsport Press, Inc., Kingsport, Tennessee
First Printing

Preface

In the broadest sense this book is, and must be, revisionist history. Why? Not just because this age has made obsolete Fourth of July oratory in praise of American progress. Not just because the smug satisfaction of "consensus" history does not square with the facts of racial, class, and cultural antagonisms. And not just because it is no longer axiomatic that America is "the last, best hope of mankind." This is revisionist history because in the space of a decade Americans have found themselves staring down the gun barrels that killed a President, an aspirant for that same office, a black pacifist leader, three civil rights leaders, and students at Jackson and Kent State. It is revisionist history because men have landed on the moon, because flames have ripped through Watts and Detroit, because many Americans have questioned and abandoned "the American way of life." It is revisionist because of the unending horror and tragedy of Vietnam. In short, it is revisionist because there is a new urgency to know the meaning of the past. Where is the United States as a nation? How did it get there? What sort of future has the past made likely?

The writing of good history has never been the province of academics alone. Historical insight is as accessible to the amateur as it is to the professional. The politician, the journalist, the general, the jurist—each has a unique vantage point from which to view events. But it is the sustained efforts of the nation's leading news magazines, historical journals, and journals of opinion that bring author and public together. The staffs of these journals maintain and encourage high standards of historical scholarship and fine writing, and, most important, promote meaningful dialogue and controversy.

Most students rightly expect that American history courses will help them understand not only the past but also the forces of the present that shape their lives. Thus, when we began to plan this book of readings, we selected three kinds of articles from the thousands available. The first were those that probed current historiographical issues. These debates are of more than scholarly interest, for the way a nation sees its history is the way it will think and act. The second were those that explored largely neglected but vitally important aspects of American experience. Thus, throughout the book there are a number of articles dealing with racial conflict, dissent, the relationship between the sexes, violence, power, technology, and the environment. Finally, we devoted a special section to the future. The future can be predicted reasonably only by some kind of extrapolation from the past. Or putting it in T. S. Eliot's phrase, time past and time present are both "present in time future."

In order to maximize the usefulness of these readings for students taking the introductory survey course, we have provided a Topical Map at the front of the book, which consists of a succinct topical outline of American History and a correlated and cross-referenced topic guide indexing the material in the readings themselves.

Terry Chase
PUBLISHER

Contents

4. Civil War and Reconstruction

5. Industrialization, Empire, and Argument

6.   Inside Twentieth-Century America

7.   The Uses of American Power in the Twentieth Century

8. Probing the Future

Topic Outline

Topical Map

The **Topical Map** is an accessing device in two parts.

Part One, the **Topic Outline**, relates the principles and problems of American history to the basic structure of the field as it's taught in most introductory courses. The outline makes it possible for you to see how each basic topic is related to others within the field.

Part Two, the **Topic Guide**, shows where items in the outline appear in this Annual Edition. The guide makes it possible for you to find any topic wherever it forms an important part of the discussion anywhere in these 61 articles.

I. Political History
Colonial America
American Revolution
  Declaration of Independence
  Articles of Confederation
  Constitution
  Bill of Rights
Federalist Era
  Democratic Party
Civil War
  Sectionalism
  Republican Party
  Secession
  Emancipation Proclamation
Reconstruction
Gilded Age
  Bossism
Populism and Progressivism
  Socialism
World War I
Interwar Era
New Deal
Politics after World War II
  New Frontier
  New Left
Politics: Alternatives for the Future

II. Military History
American Revolution
War of 1812
Indian Wars
Mexican War
Civil War
Spanish-American War
Latin American Intervention
World War I
World War II
Nuremberg Tribunal
Korean War
Vietnam War

III. Diplomatic History
American Revolution
Louisiana Purchase
War of 1812
Monroe Doctrine
Manifest Destiny
Civil War
Alaska Purchase
Spanish-American War
Latin American Intervention
Open Door Policy
World War I
League of Nations
Pacifism
Isolationism
Protectionism
Good Neighbor Policy
World War II
Marshall Plan
Truman Doctrine
Point Four Program
Alliance for Progress
Nixon Doctrine

IV. Economic History
Capitalism
Commerce
Depression
Finance
Foreign Aid
Industry
Inflation
Keynesian Economics
Labor Movement
Wage and Price Controls.

V. Social History
Abolition Movement
Blacks: The Struggle for Rights
Communications Media
Counterculture
Education
Enlightenment in America
Immigration
The Indian
Industrialization
Intellectual Life
Nationalism
Plessy v. Ferguson
Pollution
Population Explosion
Prohibition
Protest Movements
Puritanism
Radicalism
Science and Technology
Slavery
Socialism
Urbanization
Women's Role
Women's Liberation Movement
Youth and Alienation

VI. Historiography
Consensus Historians
New Nationalists
Progressive Historians
Radical Historians
Revisionists

Topic Guide

ANNUAL EDITIONS
READINGS IN
AMERICAN HISTORY

1 New Directions for Hist

Most historians would agree that each generation must rewrite history to some degree. But to what degree? Certain contemporary historians—broadly known as revisionists, radicals, or historians of the New Left—want to explain the extraordinary tapestry of American history in a fashion that speaks to the political, social, economic, and cultural demands of the present. They are busy writing new views of the past as well as playing new roles in the present. Beginning with the meeting of the American Historical Association in New York City in 1969, the radicals have increasingly gone on the offensive against consensus history, which tends to stress the success of the American pluralistic past. The debate has captured increasing attention from the press and the public, because it reflects the highly inflammable political and cultural divisions within American society itself. Historians, high priests of the American past, have sought to determine whether America is in need of a second revolution because it is and has been a sick society or whether America ought to be cleansed of the venom infused into the body politic by the naysayers. There are positions between these extremes, but on campuses across the country the conflict between consensus historians and radicals has resulted in the firing of academics on the charge that radicals use the university as political recruiting grounds.

The articles in this section have been selected to portray the intellectual underpinnings of the debate. "The Spirit of '70," a *Newsweek* cover story, is an extended interview with six of the nation's most prestigious and outspoken historians—Richard Hofstadter, Andrew Hacker , Eugene Genovese, Daniel Boorstin, Staughton Lynd, and Arthur Schlesinger, Jr. Their assessment of where we are and where we seem to be headed varies from Genovese's fear of a "massive breakdown" to Boorstin's chiding diagnosis of "national hypochondria." Their widely divergent interpretations of the meaning of the American past reflect the intellectual and ideological ferment throughout the historical profession. The second essay, from *Time Magazine*, "Revisionism: A New Angry Look at the American Past," is followed by David Donald's "Radical Historians on the Move." Next, in "The Americanization of History," Henry Steele Commager, an "Establishment" figure with a gift for trenchant criticism of the Establishment, sounds the clarion call for the uniqueness and promise of American history. "Here," he writes, "is the most original contribution to historical thought ever to come out of the New World: History is not exhausted. In a New World, the world may begin anew." Next is one of the last pieces written by the late Richard Hofstadter for the *Columbia Forum*. In "The Importance of Comity in American History," Hofstadter argues a middle position: consensus history and radical history alike allow their penchant for simplicity to distort historical complexity. Complexity, says Hofstadter, while it rules out "that hope of ultimate and glorious triumph," has its comforts. "In an age when so much of our literature is infused with nihilism, and other social disciplines are driven toward narrow positivistic inquiry, history may remain the most humanizing among the arts."

However divided historians are about American history as a whole, few would any longer argue that revision of America's racial history is long overdue. Yet this agreement itself does not make the revision a reality, as John Blassingame's "Black Studies: An Intellectual Crisis" and Alvin Josephy's "Indians in History" make abundantly clear.

Newsweek

The Spirit of '70

Six Historians on the 'American Crisis'

July 6, 1970 / 50 cents

The Spirit of '70

Six Historians Reflect on What Ails the American Spirit

[The Fourth of July] shall be constantly celebrated by the delivery of a Publick Oration . . . in which the Orator shall consider the feelings, manners and principles which led to this great National Event as well as the important and happy effects whether general or domestick which already have and will forever continue to flow from the Auspicious Epoch.
—*An act of the Boston town meeting, 1783*

We will still have oratory on this 194th birthday of the American nation. We will fly flags and pop firecrackers and stand on a thousand Main Streets watching bands and baton twirlers strut by. We will be reassured again that we are still one people beloved of God and the bearers of hope to the world. Yet something is plainly and poignantly wanting in our Fourth of July devotions this year. We are not very comfortable with pessimism, but we have just passed through an anxious spring into an uncertain summer, and the American present does not seem quite so auspicious to us as the American past always has. We have become more painfully conscious of what pulls us apart than what holds us together, and some of our most sober public and private men are concerned for our common future.

This Independence Day finds the nation in a recession of the spirit—a psychic downturn so pronounced that the mood may in itself constitute a kind of American crisis. In the pages that follow, six prominent American historians examine that malaise; their assessments of its genesis, its depth and its meaning vary widely, but none of them doubts that the country is in some sort of trouble with itself. The riptides of contemporary history have estranged Americans one from another by age, by race, even by class in ways Karl Marx could not have imagined: the hard-hat, union-label workingman at the barricades in Wall Street defending The System against its own mutinous children. The flag itself, the very symbol of America's indivisibility, has become for some of her citizens a weapon of controversy.

America has had grievous problems before, of course; some of them, as the essays in these pages point out, have depressed the nation profoundly, and one of them, in the middle of the last century, actually plunged her into civil war. What seems now to have corroded is America's ancient faith that she can not only endure but prevail—that her people can, by skill, application and the grace of God, master any ill and move on to greater glory. "The United States," Prof. Richard Hofstadter once wrote, "was the only country in the world that began with perfection and aspired to progress." The idea was no doubt delusive, but it sustained America through wars, panics, madnesses, internal upheavals and sundry other hard times; it even helped her progress by nourishing her belief that she could.

Today, however, doubt is common currency in the Republic. The Eisenhower '50s softened some of the nation's divisions and veiled others, and the early Kennedy-Johnson years rekindled some of the old confidence that America could indeed master her own imperfections and the world's. But the reduced new Spirit of '70 has been stealing up on America over half a decade or more of war, inflation, ghetto turmoil, campus uprisings and political assassination. Lyndon Johnson in his last years was no longer able to inspire the nation; Richard Nixon has only occasionally made the attempt. America's dissonances have come to seem louder and less manageable than they had ever been. The left prophesies repression, the right, anarchy. And the center, where most of America still lives, labors merely to be heard.

The essays that follow agree only that something ails the American soul; they diverge on what the trouble is and on how the nation is to live through it. Perhaps the gloomiest among them, although he specifically rejects the word, is Cornell's Andrew Hacker, a Republican and relatively speaking a conservative, who believes that the American era is dying in a wash of sybaritism. The two leftmost of the six historians, Eugene D. Genovese and Staughton Lynd, are ironically rather less inclined to view the illness as terminal. Genovese, a Marxist, and Lynd, a "resistance" activist, both see the contradictions of capitalism as the real root of the malaise—and democratic socialism as the path to salvation.

The others are less absolute, but no less concerned. Daniel Boorstin of the Smithsonian Institution, a centrist with admirers in the Nixon Administration, believes that the *crise* is largely neurotic —that what Americans are really suffering is a case of national "hypochondria" about everything from war to poverty to the quality of their drinking water. Arthur M. Schlesinger Jr., a liberal and a Democrat, believes that the sheer pell-mell velocity of history in a technological age has compounded all the nation's old problems, created new ones and so deeply unsettled us. Columbia's Hofstadter, who styles himself a '30s-vintage "radical liberal," is disturbed by

'The U.S. began with perfection and aspired to progress'

We hold these truths: America's Founding Fathers sign the Declaration of Independence, 1776

the psychic rootlessness of the young and its impact on the larger society.

Some partisan critics tend to blame the dispirited state of the union on Mr. Nixon, as its presiding officer, and on Spiro Agnew, John Mitchell and others of his agents. The judgment is no doubt unjust; the President inherited the war, the inflation, the racial crisis and at least the beginnings of the malaise. But it still falls to him to try to dispel it, and his efforts thus far have been neither sustained nor sustaining. In St. Louis last week, he delivered a classical American booster speech to an ecstatic convention of the Jaycees. "It is time to stand up and speak about what is right about America," proclaimed the President, a sometime Jaycee himself. ". . . We should love America. But let us love her not because she is rich and not because she is strong [but] because America is a good country and we are going to make her better." The Jaycees gave him a whooping, whistling, standing ovation.

Mr. Nixon spoke out of an older Fourth of July tradition—the ritual celebration of the spirit that created the Republic, tamed and settled the continent and made the whole world its theater of action. The message is still a powerful one, profoundly appealing to the American psyche. The Spirit of '70 evoked in the following pages is a diminished counterpoint to those old themes. America's pre-eminent virtue, if her historians are right, may prove to be neither her wealth nor her grandeur but her hardihood. Americans may not reconstruct The System as completely or as radically as Lynd and Genovese propose; they may never recover those Spartan gifts of citizenship mourned by Boorstin and Hacker; they may only incompletely master the headlong rush of history described by Schlesinger. But they are a durable and a resilient race, and, while the modesty of it may take some getting used to, they may just, as Richard Hofstadter suggests, muddle through.

—PETER GOLDMAN

'It is time to stand up and speak about what is right about America'

'The Age Of Rubbish'

RICHARD HOFSTADTER

Richard Hofstadter, 53, is De Witt Clinton Professor of American History at Columbia University. His works include "The American Political Tradition" and "The Paranoid Style in American Politics."

At his request, Professor Hofstadter's contribution is in the form of an interview with Newsweek editors.

Q. Is America experiencing a crisis of the spirit?

A. It seems to me that if there is any kind of civic experience that constitutes a crisis of the spirit, this crisis does go that deep. One element of importance is a decided crisis in the sense of vocation among young people. This is a vital factor in the situation, whose importance will become clearer as time goes on. It has been developing for quite a while—it goes back to the time when people spoke of them as beatniks and comes down through hippiedom, and the widespread alienation among the young.

I would look at it this way: we are living in a culture that is remarkably secular. Religion just doesn't play the role it used to play, and this is particularly true for people under 40 in this society. When a very strong religious bond is missing there are a few other things that can hold the culture together. One of them is a very strong sense of institutional loyalty, such as some people have for universities, for example, and others even for business corporations. Another, and I think a far more important one, is a sense of vocation—a very strong desire to do something in particular and to do it well—it may be anything from carpentry to being a Supreme Court judge. But the desire to perform well, the feeling of craftsmanship, the sense of vocation, which has been quite intense in this society for a long time, has, it seems to me, begun to fade in the last ten, perhaps twenty, years. And it seems to be fading faster and faster.

Young people don't have anything that they want to do. Our culture hasn't been able to perpetuate from one generation to the next, as it used to, the desire to do this or that or the other thing, and I think this is one of the roots of the dissatisfaction in college. Students keep saying that they don't know why they are there. They are less disposed than they used to be to keep order partly because the sense that they are leading a purposeful life has gone. They have the feeling that they are being processed, that they don't have any say about their lives. The truth is that all too often they haven't decided what they want their lives to say.

I think this vocational crisis spills over into a desire among people who have an activist disposition—for those who aren't passive, who don't go in for the drug culture as an essential solution—to find their existential values in politics. And to my mind that's very dangerous. It's dangerous on the political right. You can see it in people who years ago would have been plain, simple, ordinary fundamentalists; now they want a world crusade against "atheistic Communism." But you also see it on the left—and that's more conspicuous now—among young people who give you an existential rationale for acts of incivility, force or violence. As they see it, you don't have to explain your goals, you don't have to explain your program, or even have one. The act is self-sufficient because you can't see beyond it. This I think is a very dangerous way of thinking, because when you try to get existential values out of politics, which has to do really with wholly different things, I think you're heading for an increase in fanaticism. Now, whether this decline in the sense of vocation is going to be reversed, I really can't say.

Q. Are there any historical parallels to the current American mood?

Culver Pictures   UPI
Henry Adams   **Spiro Agnew**

The crest: Martin Luther King at the March on Washington, 1963

A. I don't see any satisfactory historical parallels in our national experience. In European history, the period of the Protestant Reformation is perhaps the closest parallel. Of course, there have been great moments of generalized despair—look at the way in which the nerves of England were shattered by the terrible losses in the trenches during the first world war. But you didn't quite find this failure in people to want to do some satisfying work. In fact, the current mood is so rare that one might reasonably hope that it's likely to be transient.

Q. Do you think the psychic condition of the young is the most significant aspect of the national malaise?
A. Well, there are several salient aspects. You have a major urban crisis. You have the alienation of the young. Still more important, you have the question of race, and you have a cruel and unnecessary war. And it seems to me to be a staggering parcel of questions for one society to have to tackle at one time. I think that's the thing that puts this period beyond parallel in our own history. The 1850s and 1860s, which also hung on an unresolved question of race, may mark the other worst crisis that we've had. But it seems to me not to have had so many elements of difficulty. The society then was really growing and thriving in lots of ways. It foundered over its inability to solve this problem, but it picked itself up and went on after a ghastly war. The 1930s were also simpler than our own time because you had a crisis that was single in nature—the crisis of the Depression. Today we have a multilateral crisis which I see as quite unique.

Q. In those earlier situations, were we as a nation as uncertain as we seem to be today about whether we can solve our problems?
A. Well, I suppose that there have always been some people who had the same sort of uncertainties that you hear people sounding now. You know Henry Adams, and half the intellectuals of the 1890s, if not more than half, were very disturbed about the

Young people don't have anything that they want to do

New York Public Library

At the eve of war: Raid on a Boston antislavery rally, 1860

condition of the country then. And since this is a country of frustrated elites, you get echoes of this kind of disappointment ringing down through our history, at least from the early nineteenth century on. But, I don't suppose there was any age in which you had such a mass consensus of intellectuals on their own alienation as you have in this period. We have witnessed the emergence of what Lionel Trilling has called "the adversary culture," and almost every intellectual seems to be conscripted into it. There's not much dialogue left in the fashionable intellectual community between those who are alienated from the society and those who are prepared to make an intelligent defense of it. Almost the entire intellectual community is lost in dissent, so to speak. Radicalism is irresistibly chic. All this may end with the war, but I wouldn't count on its ending among the young.

I think they have to be surprised in some tremendous way before their thinking can change very much. My generation was surprised by a number of things—by the Nazi-Soviet pact; by the way we won the war, not by conducting it in brilliant political or revolutionary ways, but by the sheer weight of metal and organization. We were surprised by the fact that instead of having a tremendous depression after the war, which those of us who were mature in the '30s thought surely was coming, we entered upon one of the great boom periods of history. I don't think that young people now are going to have their minds changed very much by arguments. They have to be profoundly surprised by something before they will begin to reconsider their experience.

Q. Is there something fundamental to American life in the current appeal of Spiro Agnew?
A. Agnew didn't create the silent-majority sentiment, he's merely catering to it. It has been stimulated to the danger point by certain kinds of flamboyant, extremist tactics of a conspicuous minority of dissenters in the last five years or so. There are many more people in this country who are disturbed by and who intensely dislike young people—college students mainly—than there are hawks. There's simply a staggering amount of dislike of the college

young according to a recent Gallup poll. The activist young operate from elitist premises which they themselves aren't aware of, but which working people are acutely aware of. The kids ask for two weeks off for conducting political activities, or to go on a pass-fail basis at the end of the term because so few of them have completed their work. People who work in offices and on assembly lines can't negotiate such arrangements, but if they could, they'd certainly have to sacrifice their salaries. The kids implicitly assume a certain kind of indulgence that other types of people in this society don't get. This is intensely resented. The kids dislike the idea that they're thinking and acting as an elite, but they are.

Their elitism is based on moral indignation against most of the rest of us. They see the country preaching democracy and practicing racism, as they would call it. They also see the horrors of the war, and these things make up their sense of what the country is. They have very little sense that anything precedes all this, or that there are parallel failures in the history of other nations. Also the sense that there has been anything positive accomplished in this country is not very vivid with them. The activists don't seem to regard their elders as really bad, but as shallow and demoralized by their material well-being. They are in some degree right about that. And they don't want to be like their parents or their teachers. But they find no appealing alternative models either, and that's where their sense of vocation suffers. What do you do if you don't want to be like your successful commuting lawyer father who lives in Westchester in a split-level house, comes home tired, and looks at television all evening? And they have a sort of alternative style or culture of their own. They have rock instead of jazz, they have pot instead of alcohol. They feel they're living in a completely different world. And they are.

Q. There's a lot of talk of revolution among the young. Do you think there is any authentic revolutionary feeling involved?
A. The talk is awfully loose. I was raised in the 1930s, on a more severe brand of Marxism. I always thought of a revolutionary as being a kind of professional, which was the way Lenin and Trotsky practiced it. This too is a vocation, and I think most of those who sloganize about revolution don't really have this vocation either. They do have strong impulsive moral responses to this or that event. They have an honest desire to do something right away. But the consistent work, the study, the application, the risk-taking, that goes into the making of a Lenin or a Rosa Luxemburg or any number of other classic revolutionary figures don't seem to me to be present among many of them. What you have, in place of revolutionaries, are clowns like Abbie Hoffman and Jerry Rubin.

Q. Is our sense of ourselves as a country diminishing?
A. I think that part of our trouble is that our sense of ourselves hasn't diminished as much as it ought to. We've now been a world power—an imperial power, let's say—for 70 years and we still have this "never lost a war" complex which haunted Johnson and now haunts Nixon—he made reference to it in his Cambodian speech. And the notion has never settled in here that it is a normal thing in the history of a mature major country that it must meet equal, opposite and adversary force of some kind or another,

have an occasional setback, have a check, set a limit to its aspirations, and, if it exceeds them be punished for it. We were raised in a country whose theater of action was for so long a limited one, basically the Western Hemisphere. In this limited theater we always got our way sooner or later, mostly sooner, and mostly very cheaply, against the Indians, Mexicans, the Spaniards, the English only when they were busy with Napoleon. It never seems to have dawned on us that you can finally move into a theater of action so big that you can't ever have that kind of quick and easy supremacy. This explains to some degree the extraordinary hysteria we had over the Korean War. Just after having fought and won a major war, people thought that we were going to go back to the quiet life, and they became hysterical when they saw there was a situation which seemed to require still another effort. And in Vietnam, even more now.

Q. How authentic is the danger of repression that we hear so much about today?

A. The ultimate danger is very real, but a lot of the talk about repression as a current and existing reality will only make matters worse. One of America's outstanding characteristics is that for a society that is in so much trouble, and has so many reasons for agitation on war and racial justice, it has remarkably little repressive apparatus and is remarkably open to peaceful dissent. Those who yell about repression and try to tell us that America is already Fascist simply have no idea of what they are talking about.

The possibility that repression may eventually increase and become really very serious is another matter. There is good reason for anxiety on that count. But this society has had less repression in recent years than at most times in its past, and less repression than all but a handful of other societies on the surface of the globe. "Repression" is one of those imbecile catchwords of our era like genocide and imperialism that have had all the meaning washed out of them.

What we do have is a complete inefficiency in handling certain kinds of problems that I should think would make other peoples laugh. In any other major country it would be impossible for any organization, white or black, to accumulate arms and then spend a lot of time threatening, perhaps very idly, to kill the police, because in almost any other society the law would not permit them to keep arms, the police would have no reason to take them seriously, and there would be no such hideous business as you had in the murderous raid on the Black Panthers in Chicago. But this is a wide-open society. In most places any maniac can carry a gun or own a gun, and this, it seems to me, points to the real nature of our problem—a lack of rational organization rather than an excess of planned repression. The business at Kent State was a perfect case in point: you had total incompetence and a bunch of confused young National Guardsmen, probably just as confused as the kids they shot at.

Q. Do you see any encouraging signs in the current American atmosphere, and what would you say are the negative aspects?

A. Well, I don't see any positive aspects other than the fact—though it is often denied—that the blacks have gained quite a good deal from their agitation of the last several years. Unless there is a violent

UPI

The crash: Jobless men in New York, 1930

reversal, the day may come when people will look back on the '60s as a period of great black advance, as a very decisive turning point. Otherwise I can't see much that is positive coming out of this period. If I get around to writing a general history of the recent past, I'm going to call the chapter on the '60s "The Age of Rubbish." I think we'll be lucky to get out of this situation without further polarization and a strong right-wing reaction. I'm not worried that the radical young or the blacks are going to make a revolution. I am worried that we could be driven into a terrible new phase of reaction. I don't predict it. I would predict the contrary, if I had to predict. But that is the thing we should all be concerned about. And if we get out without such a reaction I would say we had muddled through.

Q. You have no doubt that this is a bad time?

A. Oh, I have no doubt that it's a bad time, and it's not over yet.

To be good soldiers: Lyndon Newsweek—Wally McNamee
Johnson decorates Vietnam heroes, 1968

'We Will Meet As Enemies'

ANDREW HACKER

Andrew Hacker, 40, is a professor in the Department of Government at Cornell University. His works include "Political Theory: Philosophy, Ideology, Science" and "The End of the American Era."

We cannot bring ourselves to make personal sacrifices

The malaise of the American spirit cannot be blamed on wrongheaded policies, inept administrations, or even an inability to understand the dimensions of our current discontents. The reasons are more fundamental—I would say historical—arising from the kind of people we have become. I have called our time "the end of the American era" because as individuals we no longer possess the qualities upon which citizenship depends. To be specific: we cannot bring ourselves to make the personal sacrifices required to sustain domestic order or international authority.

We have, in short, become a loose aggregation of private persons who give higher priority to our personal pleasures than to collective endeavors. Americans no longer display that spirit which transforms a people into a citizenry and turns territory into a nation. There eventually arrives a time when a preoccupation with self-centered concerns deflects a population from public obligations, when a willingness to be governed stands less in evidence. We have reached that time.

Current anxieties over our Asian involvement are only symptomatic. Even so, they reveal a good deal about our character. Let me remark upon a few aspects of our behavior connected with this venture.

While it may not be a role many of us desire, most nations have achieved greatness through their military conquests. But such success calls for citizens who are willing to die without questioning the mission in which they are enlisted. However, only a diminishing minority of Americans—and particularly young Americans—still possess the purblind patriotism which induces soldiers to take the risks which

produce battlefield results. To be sure, Vietnam has witnessed instances of American valor. Yet my reading of the rosters of medal winners shows them most usually to be small-town boys—again a dwindling segment of our total population. It should be clear by now that the average Viet Cong is a braver fighting man, readier to battle to the end for a purpose he holds dear. And the Viet Cong, or others like them, will be our enemies for many years to come.

Whole classes of Americans have taken every opportunity to avoid active service, not excluding campus conservatives who stretch out their deferrals and non-college youths who join the National Guard. While in some part this avoidance may stem from disapproval of the war, it also derives from a widespread unwillingness to forgo the comforts of civilian life. In short, more and more Americans are turning too sybaritic to be good soldiers. Nor is it realistic to suppose that at some future time they will suspend their sophistication and rally to the recruiting stations. (How many Americans would actually volunteer to fight for Israel's survival or South Africa's blacks, let alone for Thailand and the Philippines?)

But even if we pull out of Southeast Asia—an unlikely eventuality—I see no prospect of our mobilizing resources for domestic reconstruction. We will continue to maintain an expensive military establishment, if only to gird ourselves for future Vietnams. (We may well be sending troops into Northeast Brazil before this decade is over.) So long as we feel we have a responsibility to police the world, or believe that every foreign flare-up endangers our security, further overseas expeditions cannot be ruled out.

Moreover, were we to reduce military outlays, the traditional American antipathy to taxes would create pressure for cutting public expenditures—so we can catch up with our purchases of snowmobiles, swimming pools, second homes and similar artifacts of indulgence. As John Kenneth Galbraith pointed out long ago, we measure prosperity by the expansiveness of our private purchases. I may *know* that the several hundred dollars I spent on eating out ought to be levied for social rehabilitation. But neither I nor anyone I know has written his congressman asking that his taxes be raised by an appreciable margin.

For my own part, I am wary of historical analogies. The last time I read Oswald Spengler was twenty years ago, and I was never able to get all the way through Arnold Toynbee. The image of civilizations as cyclical may make sense to Europeans, but my mentality is too American to see history so schematically. Nevertheless I do believe that every nation has a history, a process most vividly reflected in the character of its inhabitants at any point in time.

Some writers have replied that Great Britain lost most of America in a colonial war and then went on to a century of industrial and international splendor; or that Russia suffered ignoble defeat from Japan and then Germany, yet proceeded to raise itself as a new society. But despite those setbacks, the British and Russian populations at that time consisted chiefly of peasants and proletarians willing to enlist themselves in a national endeavor. Americans are past that point. Thus when I speak of the decline of America's spirit, I refer principally to the changes which have occurred in us as individuals. My life is far more pleasant and much more interesting than that my grandparents knew. But these opportunities for enjoyment have undermined my ability to be the kind of citizen my grandfather could be.

James Reston recently remarked, "I have never known a time when we have faced the basic problems of the human condition so frontally." To this I would add that an awareness of problems need not lead to their solution. Indeed, too much comprehension can have the opposite effect. More and more of us are now part-time sociologists: we have no difficulty in dilating on all manner of crises ranging from poverty and civil liberties to pollution and violent crime. Whether in conferences, committee meetings, or cocktail parties, we talk endlessly about fatherless families, generation gaps, sexual inadequacy, bad architecture, racial intolerance, subjugated women, bureaucratic bungling, the need for community and the demise of the American spirit. We are literate, knowledgeable, and as correct as any society has ever been in its assessment of its dislocations.

Yet as one who might have contributed to this understanding—I have taught college students for fifteen years—I realize that sociological sophistication seldom prompts individuals to eschew personal pleasures so as to make society a better place. I am not unaware of the young law graduates working in poverty storefronts instead of Wall Street. They have my total respect, and I only wish that more young people would take jobs as prison guards or nurses in mental or municipal hospitals. Yet I am not persuaded that these terms of altruistic enlistment add up to a new trend. I wonder what this new generation will be doing ten years from now. Will the enthusiasts currently teaching in Bedford-Stuyvesant send their own children into those classrooms?

I foresee the rest of this century as a dangerous time, during which we will continue in our accustomed ways. We will claim to want new styles of leadership, overlooking our own inability to serve as followers in any but the most marginal of ways. I expect that I will enjoy myself as a consumer and a private person. But once we walk out of our own doors we will suffer increasing discomforts. In part these will consist of physical inconveniences such as congested highways and airports, silent telephones and absence of electricity, a polluted atmosphere and a brutalized landscape. But the greater irritant will be from fellow citizens of classes, races, ages and sexes different from our own, whose demands for new rights and expanded recognition will threaten our own security and self-esteem.

We can no longer be a single nation, possessed of a common spirit. Neither "class struggle" nor "civil war" entirely describes the contours of this discord. Suffice it to say that increasingly we will encounter one another as enemies, that as individuals we stand more vulnerable to the abrasions we effect on each other. Some of us will flee, to further suburbs and hoped-for havens. Others will literally fight, in the streets or through subterranean subversion. And many more will see their morale shattered, their confidence destroyed, their anxieties deepening.

Still, I do not regard this as a "gloomy" assessment, or a "pessimistic" prognosis—labels most reviewers have affixed to my ideas. Terms such as these only obscure the issues. I write as a student of America's history, of its people, of its contemporary condition. The only service I can provide is to indicate how we have arrived at our current perplexities, and why the options open to us are so narrowly limited.

'A Massive Breakdown'

EUGENE D. GENOVESE

Eugene D. Genovese, 40, chairman of the Department of History at the University of Rochester, is the author of "The Political Economy of Slavery" and "The World the Slaveholders Made."

When a growing portion of the nation's youth loudly proclaims its defection from everything; when even the most traditional and conservative campuses seethe with perpetual turmoil; when two successive Presidents worry about a credibility gap (a polite way of saying that a significant number of Americans consider their President a liar); when black people find themselves trapped between failure of a promised integration and white resistance to black control of black communities; when white people generally split between those who feel guilty about the blacks and those who unashamedly hate them—two variations, although not to be equated, of old-fashioned white racism; when the richest nation in world history cannot keep its water and air clean, much less eliminate poverty; when great cities are acknowledged to be ungovernable, not to mention unlivable; when the country is racked with fear, foreboding, and hopelessness—then we had better declare a state of spiritual crisis, for the alternative would be to declare that irrationality, decadence, and disorder constitute our normal and preferred national condition.

The United States has gone through rough times before, but the present crisis has no genuine predecessors. The spiritual crises of the mid-nineteenth

Charles Phelps Cushing

The old glory: Gen. Winfield Scott takes Mexico City, 1847

century, highlighted by a long and bloody sectional war, are certainly not to be minimized. But today, for the first time, the country faces a massive breakdown, manifested in every section, class and stratum, in faith in its ideals, institutions and prospects.

Today, a large number of Americans publicly proclaim that their country is fighting an unjust and immoral war and is committing acts that qualify as war crimes. These Americans are, of course, a minority even of the antiwar public, and their existence as a sizable group is not unprecedented—consider, for example, the hostile reaction at home to the Mexican War. But the steady augmentation of their numbers warns of a deeper malaise.

Vietnam must seem like God's abandonment of His people

Perhaps even more striking is the vast number who oppose the war on other than moral grounds and who may very well already constitute a majority of the nation. At first glance these people direct only strategic and tactical criticisms and wish simply to admit a particular miscarriage of foreign policy; on the surface no great moral issue arises from their dissent. But Americans have never before admitted that our country could be beaten, much less beaten by a ragged army of non-white guerrillas. The demand to recognize defeat and stop playing God could and should be interpreted as a healthy national awakening to the limits of power—an inevitable and welcome stage in the maturation of a great world power. But Americans have never believed that we could be beaten in anything; that some problems might not be immediately soluble or indeed soluble at all; that a national cause as just as ours could ever be abandoned by God.

It is no accident that so many who begin by urging a tactical reconsideration in Vietnam end by denouncing the war as a crime. Americans have always believed that we are invincible precisely because we are God's chosen and the bearers of His morality to the world. For those infected with two centuries or more of self-righteous chauvinism, our debacle in Vietnam must call into question our national cause and—even in this secular age—seem like God's abandonment of His people in the wake of their succumbing to the sins of pride and avarice. Thus, even those who speak for Realpolitik, including the most cynical and opportunist, have unwittingly contribut-

ed to the breakdown of an increasingly brittle and shoddy spiritual façade.

The disillusionment with the war could not, however, by itself have caused our celebrated sense of national virtue and omnipotence to crumble so quickly. Had it not intersected with the racial crisis, the decay of our cities, the rising tide of official and popular violence, and the other manifestations of our having to contend with a ruling class (how else should we describe the handful who have a stranglehold on the nation's wealth and access to power?) that has neither the will nor ability to rule effectively, its effects would surely have been muted and protracted. When, for example, we think of our spiritual condition, we usually think first of the defection, political and cultural, of our youth. But our youth, in turning their backs on the values of their parents, schools and communities, respond to much more than the war, and it is difficult to believe that an end to the war will bring an end to their defection.

Both young and old, in different and sometimes opposing ways, have been shaken by the exposure of an enormous gap between our national pretensions and our national practice: an egalitarian society cannot keep its pledge of racial integration after more than fifteen years of sustained efforts; a democratic society suffers one President after another who is elected on a platform of ending a war each immediately proceeds to escalate; a constitutional political order sees nothing wrong with having Presidents Truman, Eisenhower, Kennedy, Johnson and Nixon wage war without the Congressional declaration required by the Constitution; a peace-loving society creates the greatest military machine in world history and permits its requirements to take priority over all others and indeed to crush all hopes of adequate response to pressing social ills; an idealistic and affluent society (in fact, a society that has historically identified its idealism with its affluence) is unable to demonstrate that any of its ideals are compatible with an affluence based on a commitment to the ethos and economic practice of the marketplace.

Young people respond, as do their elders, to the inability of so rich and powerful a country to solve its deepest problems. Their elders, having fought their way through depression and world war to a decent standard of living, which they once considered proof of their own moral virtue, respond with fear and confusion. Young people, who have little or no investment of their own lives in the material conditions on which they have been raised, are psychologically in a much better condition to take a hard and sometimes brutal view of the quality of life their parents' struggle has purchased.

The simultaneous disasters in Asia and at home have exposed several decades of systematic deception, which the self-deception of the 1950s cult of affluence and suburbia has come to symbolize. From Truman to Nixon we have been told of the splendors and achievements of our capitalist economy, which ostensibly has cured the inherent ills revealed during the Great Depression. Only one or two small details were left out. Even the much-revered John F. Kennedy never thought it necessary to mention that this splendor has rested on the creation of an enormous war machine that has effectively blocked commitments to housing, education, safety, transportation, health and other requirements of human welfare.

FOR DEMOCRACY AND THE FREEDOM OF THE SEAS

ENLIST IN THE NAVY

Authenticated News

First in war: A Navy recruiting poster, circa 1917

Nor has anyone in the government bothered to point out that the same Keynesian controls on which the prevention of a major depression depend have a few small side effects, such as a severe inflationary burden on large portions of the working and middle classes.

The deception in foreign policy has been much worse, but it was not until the 1960s that we had a generation sufficiently removed from the happy days of Harry Truman and Joseph McCarthy to laugh when they were told that America was leading something called the free world against a monolithic Communist empire that was somehow on the verge of fratricidal war. In the past, it had been easy enough to convince the American public that Thieus and Kys were defending the freedom of their own people and ours; that periodic interventions from Guatemala to Iran to the Congo were altogether altruistic, in contradistinction to such nasty Soviet interventions as those in Hungary and Czechoslovakia; that the wanton murder of 500,000 "Communists" by a pro-Western government in Indonesia was none of our business, but that we should all be outraged and ready to protest against the Soviet Union's unwillingness to permit free emigration of Jews; or that Chiang Kai-shek rightfully represented China in the United Nations. Indeed, so anesthetized had Americans become, so accustomed to believing in sheer lying as some Orwellian truth, that the country was stunned when young people started laughing.

The crisis is indeed spiritual, but its root lies in the palpable failure of our vaunted capitalist social system. It should not be necessary, even in these crazy times, to defend the genuine achievements of our national culture, among which we may find a profound commitment to personal freedom, political participation and social justice. But so long as the defense of capitalism in its corporate and oligopolistic phase and its political and military priorities takes precedence over those values and simultaneously remains confused with them, no solution will be possible. The spiritual crisis can only be resolved through the creation of a political movement capable of realizing our national ideals by the reordering of our economic and social priorities through the restructuring of our economy.

The decline and fall of the Roman Empire took 400 years or so; in the interim a great civilization slipped further and further into decadence, degradation and despair. Perhaps a benevolent God will grant our civilization as much time, but no one should count on it. If we fail to generate a political movement of national reconstruction, the existing order may last in this country for a long time, but it is now clear that it will never be able to quench the revolutionary flames now engulfing the earth.

The great political and moral problem for the world as a whole is the reconciliation of socialism, which has increasingly become the banner of the oppressed peoples of Asia, Africa and Latin America, with personal freedom and the tradition of free and rational criticism that have been the glories of Western civilization. Only the West can effect that reconciliation, and the West can do nothing without the United States. If, therefore, we fail here, we shall guarantee the death of the most precious parts of our hard-won heritage and—ironically—contribute to the victory of a totalitarian socialism everywhere.

The way it was: Police masked against the flu in Seattle, 1918

'A Case of Hypochondria'

DANIEL J. BOORSTIN

Boorstin

Daniel J. Boorstin, 55, is now director of the National Museum of Science and Technology at the Smithsonian Institution. He is writing a multivolume study of "The Americans."

Our inventive, up-to-the-minute, wealthy democracy makes new tests of the human spirit. Our very instruments of education, of information and of "progress" make it harder every day for us to keep our bearings in the larger universe, in the stream of history and the whole world of peoples who feel strong ties to their past. A new price of our American standard of living is our imprisonment in the present.

That imprisonment tempts us to a morbid preoccupation with ourselves, and so induces hypochondria. That, the dictionary tells us, is "an abnormal condition characterized by a depressed emotional state and imaginary ill health; excessive worry or talk about one's health." We think we are the beginning and the end of the world. And as a result we get our nation and our lives, our strengths and our ailments, quite out of focus.

We will not be on the way to curing our national hypochondria unless we first accept the unfashionable possibility that many of our national ills are imaginary and that others may not be as serious as we imagine. Unless we begin to believe that we won't be dead before morning, we may not be up to the daily tasks of a healthy life.

We are overwhelmed by the instant moment—headlined in this morning's newspaper and flashed on this hour's newscast. As a result we can't see the whole real world around us. We don't see the actual condition of our long-lived body-national. And so we can't see clearly whatever may be the real ailments from which we actually suffer.

In a word, we have lost our sense of history. In our schools, the story of our nation has been displaced by "social studies"—which is the study of what ails *us*. In our churches the effort to see man *sub specie aeternitatis* has been displaced by the "social gospel"—which is the polemic against the supposed special evils of our time. Our book publishers and literary reviewers no longer seek the timeless and the durable, but spend most of their efforts in fruitless search for *à la mode* "social commentary"—which they pray won't be out of date when the issue goes to press in two weeks or when the manuscript becomes a book in six months. Our merchandizers frantically devise their 1970½ models (when will the 1970¾'s arrive?) which will cease to be voguish when their sequels appear three months hence. Nei-

We have wandered out of history

The utopians: The Oneida Community of Free Lovers, 1870 . . .

Culver Pictures

ther our classroom lessons nor our sermons nor our books nor the things we live with nor the houses we live in are any longer strong ties to our past. We have become a nation of short-term doomsayers.

Without the materials of historical comparison, having lost our traditional respect for the wisdom of ancestors and the culture of kindred nations, we are left with nothing but abstractions, nothing but baseless utopias to compare ourselves with. No wonder, then, that so many of our distraught citizens libel us as the worst nation in the world, or the bane of human history (as some of our noisiest young people and a few disoriented Negroes tell us). For we have wandered out of history. And all in the name of virtue and social conscience!

We have lost interest in the real examples from the human past which alone can help us shape standards of the humanly possible. So we compare ours with a mythical Trouble-Free World, where all mankind was at peace. We talk about the War in Vietnam as if it were the first war in American history—or at least the first to which many Americans were opposed. We contemn our nation for not yet

having attained perfect justice, and we forget that ours is the most motley and miscellaneous great nation of history—the first to use the full force of law and constitutions and to enlist the vast majority of its citizens in a strenuous quest for justice for all races and ages and religions.

We flagellate ourselves as "poverty ridden"—by comparison only with some mythical time when there was no bottom 20 per cent in the economic scale. We sputter against The Polluted Environment—as if it was invented in the age of the automobile. We compare our smoggy air not with the odor of horsedung and the plague of flies and the smells of garbage and human excrement which filled cities in the past, but with the honeysuckle perfumes of some nonexistent City Beautiful. We forget that even if the water in many cities today is not as spring-pure nor as palatable as we would like, for most of history the water of the cities (and of the countryside) was undrinkable. We reproach ourselves for the ills of disease and malnourishment, and forget that until recently enteritis and measles and whooping cough, diphtheria and typhoid, were killing diseases of childhood, puerperal fever plagued mothers in childbirth, polio was a summer monster.

Flooded by screaming headlines and hourly televised "news" melodramas of dissent and "revolution," we haunt ourselves with the illusory ideal of some "who'e nation" which had a deep and outspoken "faith" in its "values."

We become so obsessed by where we are that we forget where we came from and how we got here. No wonder that we begin to lack the courage to confront the normal ills of modern history's most diverse, growing, burbling Nation of Nations.

Our national hypochondria is compounded by distinctively American characteristics. The American belief in speed, which led us to build railroads farther and faster than any other nation, to invent "quick-lunch" and self-service to save that terrible ten-minute wait, to build automobiles and highways so we can commute at 70 miles an hour, which made us a nation of instant cities, instant coffee, TV-dinners, and instant everything, has bred in us a colossal impatience. Any social problem that can't be solved instantly by money and legislation seems fatal. Our appliances and our buildings and our very lives seem out of date even before they are ready for occupancy. What can't be done right now seems hardly worth doing at all.

Some of these current attitudes are themselves the late-twentieth-century perversions of the old American Booster Spirit, which has had no precise parallel anywhere else. Totalitarian nations have been marked by their obsession with "planning"— with five-year plans and ten-year plans. But planning expresses willingness to accept a sharp distinction between present and future, between the way things are and the way they might be. And that distinction has never been too popular in the U.S.A. The nineteenth-century Boosters of Western cities defended their extravagant boasts by saying there was no reason to wait, if you were actually bragging only about things that were certain to happen. To them the beauties of Oleopolis or Gopher City were none the less real simply because "they had not yet gone through the formality of taking place."

This Booster-Vagueness has always made Americans wonderfully unpedantic about the distinction between the present and the future. The amiable vagueness, which once gave an optimistic nineteenth-century America the energy and the hope to go on, still survives. But in a hypochondriac twentieth-century America its effects can be disastrous. Now that very same extravagant vagueness leads some Americans to believe that every battle is Armageddon—and that the battle is already lost. And that the nation is none the less dead simply because the national demise "has not yet gone through the formality of taking place."

An immigrant nation, without an established religion and without political dogma, had to depend heavily on its sense of a shared past (and a shared future). American history itself was an antidote to dogmatism and utopianism. It proved that a nation did not need to be altogether one thing or another. Federalism was a way of combining local control with national government. Ethnic pluralism was a way of allowing people to keep as much as they wanted of their Old World language, religion and cuisine—to live among themselves as much as they wished. The immigrant was not compelled either to keep or to abandon his Old World identity. Free public schools, and the American innovations of the free high school and the public college, tried to have standards and yet give everybody the same commodity. The nation aimed to preserve "free private enterprise" (freer and on a larger scale than anywhere else) and yet to provide social security, farm price supports and other insurances against the free market. On a priori grounds, each and all of these would have seemed impossible, and they were all messy, philosophically speaking.

The best antidote, then, against ruthless absolutes and simple-minded utopias has been American history itself. But that history becomes more and more inaccessible when the technology and institutions of our time imprison us in the present. How can we escape the prison?

First, we must awaken our desire to escape. To do this we must abandon the prevalent belief in the superior wisdom of the ignorant. Unless we give up the voguish reverence for youth and for the "culturally deprived," unless we cease to look to the vulgar community as arbiters of our schools, of our art and literature, and of all our culture, we will never have the will to de-provincialize our minds. We must make every effort to reverse the trend in our schools and colleges—to move away from the "relevant" and toward the cosmopolitanizing, the humanizing and the unfamiliar. Education is learning what you didn't even know you didn't know. The last thing the able young Negro needs is "black studies"—which simply re-enforces the unfortunate narrowness of his experience and confines him in *his* provincial present. We all need more ancient history, more medieval history, more of the history and culture of Asia and Africa.

Then, we must enlarge and widen and deepen what we mean by our history. The preoccupation with politics which has been the bane of the history classroom fosters the unreasonable notions that today governments are the root of all good and evil. The self-righteous effort by self-styled prophets of self-vaunted new "schools" of history would make history a mere tool of contemporary polemics, and so destroy the reason for exploring our past. They would make men of all other ages into the slaves of our conceit—to be used only for our purposes. We must make our history more total by incorporating the past that people lived but that historians have not talked much about. In the United States this means an effort to make more of the history of immigrants, of the history of technology, of the history of everyday life, of business and advertising and housing and eating and drinking and clothing. Democratizing our history does not mean perverting it to the current needs of demagogic or "revolutionary" politics. It does mean enlarging its once-pedantic scope to include the whole spectrum of the ways of life of men and women.

When we allow ourselves to be imprisoned in the present, to be obsessed by the "relevant," we show too little respect for ourselves and our possibilities. We assume that we can properly judge our capacities by the peculiar tests of our own day. But we must look into the whole Historical Catalogue of man's possibilities. To be really persuaded that

Bob Fitch—Black Star

. . . and a northern California hippie commune, 1970

things can be otherwise, we must see how and when and why they have actually been otherwise.

To revive our sense of history is surely no panacea for current ills. But it surely is a palliative. It may help us discover what is now curable, may help us define the timetable of the possible, and so help us become something that we are not. If history cannot give us panaceas, it is the best possible cure of the yen for panaceas. And the only proven antidote for utopianism.

"The voice of the intellect," observed Sigmund Freud (who did not underestimate the role of the irrational) in 1928, "is a soft one, but it does not rest until it has gained a hearing. Ultimately, after endlessly repeated rebuffs, it succeeds. This is one of the few points in which one may be optimistic about the future of mankind." Beneath the strident voice of the present we must try to hear the insistent whisper of reason. It does not sound "with it." It speaks only to the attentive listener. It speaks a language always unfamiliar and often archaic. It speaks the language of all past times and places, which is the language of history.

How can we escape the prison?

Lynd

'Again–Don't Tread on Me'

STAUGHTON LYND

Staughton Lynd, 40, has taught at Spelman College and Yale. His books include "Class Conflict, Slavery and the United States Constitution" and "The Intellectual Origins of American Radicalism."

It is misleading to speak of the condition of the "American spirit" or of "psychic recession" in America as a nation. There are and always have been different, conflicting groups in American society which experienced life quite differently at the same point in time. The spiritual crisis of the American Indian or of the Afro-American throughout the past 350 years is something deeper and more grave than anything undergone by white Americans. Historians know relatively little even about what life felt like for the working-class white: for seamen and tenant farmers at the time of the American Revolution, for the immigrant Irish laborers on whose bodies (Thoreau said) were laid the tracks of American railroads, for the Eastern European steelworkers who worked twelve hours a day and 24 hours every other Sunday in Pittsburgh and Gary. Generalizations about national character and national spirit are usually extrapolations from documentary evidence produced by the affluent articulate, and should be suspect for this reason.

There *is* a crisis in American society, however. It is fundamentally economic, not spiritual, but it expresses itself secondarily in the realm of psyche and spirit. And no doubt certain generalizations—"alienation," for instance—do produce an incomplete description of the quite different spiritual crises experienced by different classes, races, and age groups. My friend David Harris, a draft resister, writes from a Federal penitentiary:

"It seems one of the characteristics of the insanity consuming America is that no experience is actively shared. The operational identities, the fantasies, the frustrations and all the hurts are collected in individual sockets that eventually deny any other reality and demand, in sheer desperation, to be recognized."

Doubtless George Wallace and Eldridge Cleaver could each find a part of himself in those words. But the description is too general to get at the reality of either man, or of the parts of American society they personify.

So it is superficial and falsely ponderous to speak of a crisis in the American spirit. Equally spurious is the tendency to select a single aspect of the present crisis and mechanically compare it to some counterpart phenomenon in the past. Of course it is true that the nation was at least as deeply divided in the years before the Civil War as it is today, and that after the Civil War there was an era of assassinations and industrial conflict resembling the period of racial conflict since World War II, and that young people were disillusioned and rebellious in other times, too. Comparisons of this kind nurture the implicit

The place to begin is the failure of the New Deal

thesis that since there have been crises before, the good old American ship of state will also weather the storms of the present. There are some people who would be ritually repeating this adage as the waters closed over their heads.

To be helpful, analysis must avoid murky psychological generalizations and must deal with the specific character of the present crisis as a whole.

The place to begin, in my opinion, is the failure of the New Deal to overcome the Depression of the 1930s. Richard Hofstadter emphasized this 25 years ago in his "The American Political Tradition." It has recently been stressed again by Howard Zinn and Barton Bernstein. Zinn writes:

"When the reform energies of the New Deal began to wane around 1939 . . . the nation was back to its normal state: a permanent army of unemployed; twenty or thirty million poverty-ridden people effectively blocked from public view by a huge, prosperous, and fervently consuming middle class; a tremendously efficient yet wasteful productive apparatus that was efficient because it could produce limitless supplies of what it decided to produce, and wasteful because what it decided to produce was not based on what was most needed by society but on what was most profitable to business."

Bernstein concurs. The number of unemployed in 1939 was still about half the number out of work in

DONT TREAD ON ME

The first resisters: A battle flag, circa 1776

1933. And: "The liberal reforms of the New Deal did not transform the American system; they conserved and protected American corporate capitalism . . . There was no significant redistribution of power in American society."

The New Deal did not overcome unemployment but World War II did. What Roosevelt had failed to accomplish in his capacity as Dr. New Deal he achieved in his role as Dr. Win The War. And the important thing is this, that ever since then American prosperity has depended on massive public defense spending in a "permanent war economy." Walter Oakes coined the phrase in an article written for Politics magazine in 1944. Said Oakes: "The fact is that the capitalist system cannot stand the strain of another siege of unemployment comparable to 1930-1940 . . . The traditional methods . . . will not be followed." Oakes was brilliantly right. Business opinion overcame its antipathy to public works so long as the product was military, because only in this way could a recurrence of the Depression be forestalled.

I believe this to be the key fact from which the current crisis is derived. Also important is the increase in overseas private investment, now roughly ten times greater than at the end of World War II. This fact underlies American foreign policy since the 1940s just as huge government spending on "defense" is the basis of domestic policy. But the relative importance of the two economic facts, public defense spending and private investment overseas, is clear. Overseas economic expansion has helped the American economy but defense spending—the welfare program of the rich—has become essential to it.

At least as important as the export of capital and goods to other countries is the effort to make the domestic market bigger through advertising. Perhaps it could be said of nineteenth-century capitalism that it made approximately what people needed (although it did not distribute its product to those who needed it most). The situation now is that human needs are manufactured by advertising and then products of dubious social utility made "in response to demand." Thus car fins, changing women's fashions, and what young people denounce as the "plasticity" of American life. Thus also the role of TV and other instrumentalities of mass culture. People who talk about "America's spiritual crisis" see TV as a symbol. They show how violence is packaged and sold on the screen so that it is experienced as intensely immediate but also distant and artificial at the same time, with the result that a generation is readied to kill without feeling, and to have Vietnam brought into its living room without crying out in horror and stopping the war. What is not enough emphasized is that TV as a cultural phenomenon is the result of TV as an advertising medium. Mass culture is only the filler between commercials.

The overseas imperialism of Coca-Cola and napalm is accompanied by a "domestic imperialism" which tries to make people buy things which they don't really need. Yet neither of these sales programs solves the problem. The productive capacity of the American economy dwarfs the ability of people either abroad or at home to absorb its products at a profit. The fundamental way in which the United States has tried to deal with its ability to produce is by war, or more precisely, by a condition of permanent war-readiness which year by year increases the probability that wars will occur.

Because our economy is dedicated to the production of plasticity and lethal junk, young men and women grow up in America not believing that adult society has useful work it needs them to get done. Paul Goodman describes in "Growing Up Absurd" how in modern America there is no initiation to adulthood, how adolescence ceases to be an apprenticeship to becoming a full citizen, because there are so few grown-up jobs now which a person can respect himself for doing. The root of delinquency and rebelliousness in all their forms is unemployment but this unemployment is more than an absence of a pay check, it is also the absence of useful work. Most Americans are out of work even when they are making a good living. They put money on the table but use only a fraction of their human capacity in getting it. Work for most Americans may no longer be dirty, but it is still boring, humiliating, and unworthy of what man might be. The young are right to rebel against an adulthood which insults them.

Education tries to shape the young for this unmanly and inhuman adult work-life, and so itself becomes a target. The rapid expansion of higher ed-

ucation since the end of World War II came about because of technological change in industry. Automatized and computerized industry requires more and more young men and women who have white-collar skills but behave with the docility expected of blue-collar workers. The thrust of the multiversity in which so many of our 7 million college students are trained is toward skilled obedience. The student, like the worker he is intended to become, uses his mind as well as his hands, but not creatively, not at his own initiative, still within limits set by orders coming down from above. That is what modern capitalist industry is like and so that is what modern higher education is like, too. And the students tell those who give them orders to practice being foremen on someone else. In their own words, they refuse to be bent, folded, spindled, and mutilated.

Those who tell us that the crisis of America is a crisis of authority are, in a sense somewhat different than they imagine, absolutely right. In choosing to forestall depression by war spending, the United States has made the larger choice to respond to change with violence. Rather than moving with life, like a gardener or a teacher, our society rigidly confronts life like a policeman. Repression and authoritarianism are on the rise in America because at its highest levels the society insists that things stay the way they have been, remain in a form familiar and amenable to control: this society believes it is better (for other people) to be dead than different. And so in every institution, at every age, in every meeting of those with more power and those with less, there is indeed a crisis of law and order. The people who talk most about it are those who have the power, hence the law and order, and feel no need for change. They—and I am talking not of George Wallace but of the Ivy League graduates in Wall Street and government—are apparently prepared to destroy the world rather than let it become something which they don't run.

What they fear, when all is said and done, is socialism: management of the economy not by corporation executives selected by other corporation execu-

Students refuse to be bent, folded, spindled and mutilated

Bettmann Archive

The first blood: The Boston Massacre, 1770

tives but democratically, by the people. The danger as perceived from Harvard Square, the Yale Green, and their various extensions is that incompetent common people in Mozambique or Muncie might take the rhetoric of the Declaration of Independence seriously and try to run the economy themselves. To prevent this, an outcome which they perceive not as the end to their accustomed power and profits but as the end to freedom, God, country, and motherhood, the decent young scions of the governing class are prepared to use any means. Marx was more right than he could have imagined when he said that the choice was between socialism and barbarism.

If America can stay democratic it will become socialist

This choice is likely to present itself as a struggle for democracy. Cold-war ideology has led us to suppose that the choice for socialism means dictatorship, while capitalism, whatever its other handicaps, is free. Of course it is perfectly true that socialism can mean dictatorship. But the historically emergent problem which I see dominating the next generation in this country, say from 1970 to the year 2000, is the struggle to preserve and extend American democracy against repression from the right (both the genteel right of the Northeast, and the rougher Southwestern variety with which the former will reluctantly ally). If America can stay democratic I believe it will become socialist. In the struggle to keep it democratic, a coalition may be formed which will have the power to make it socialist. Huey Long once said that if Fascism came to the United States it would call itself democratic. If socialism is to come, it will have to be democratic; and if democracy is to be preserved and extended, Americans will have to open their minds in a new way to what democracy would mean if applied to the economy.

Earlier, I criticized the practice of drawing comparisons between single aspects of the present and the past. Let me in closing refer to the one total moment of the American past which I think has some essential resemblance to our present situation.

We are learning to say No

A consequence of the permanent war economy has been the concentration of decisions over life and death in the hands of one man, the President, and the growing sense on the part of the American people (left and right) that government in Washington is almost a foreign power, an invader rather than a protector. We have rightly come to feel, not that we run the government, but that it runs us and we protect ourselves as best we can. The labels are different, but in effect we begin to perceive our government as a constitutional monarchy, and a capricious one at that.

Accordingly, the American Revolution which the nation will shortly commemorate jumps back into focus. The process of that revolution was of everescalating resistance to arbitrary power, which the people did not control, but could only petition and say No to. So today, having petitioned all too often, we are learning the salutary habit of saying No. Confronted by the authority of the Selective Service System (in a permanent war economy induction is the initiation to adulthood), of armed policemen like those who shot down unarmed "rioters" in the Boston Massacre, of a dozen contemporary variants of the customs officer without a search warrant, the contemptuous governor, and the king who would not hear, an increasing number of the American people are taking the best page from their history and responding: Don't tread on me.

'The Velocity Of History'

ARTHUR M. SCHLESINGER JR.

Arthur M. Schlesinger Jr., 52, is Albert Schweitzer Professor of Humanities at the City University of New York and chronicler of the ages of Jackson, Roosevelt and Kennedy. He served on JFK's staff.

America is unquestionably experiencing an extreme crisis of confidence. And this crisis is unquestionably not illusory, even if it coexists with affluence, social gains and scientific miracles. It is a crisis with many sources; but none is more important, I think, than the incessant and irreversible increase in the rate of social change.

Henry Adams was the first American historian to note the transcendent significance of the ever accelerating velocity of history. "The world did not [just] double or treble its movement between 1800 and 1900," he wrote in 1909, "but, measured by any standard known to science—by horsepower, calories, volts, mass in any shape—the tension and vibration and so-called progression of society were fully a thousand times greater in 1900 than in 1800." Hurried on by the cumulative momentum of science and technology, the tension and vibration of society in 1970 are incalculably greater than they were when Adams wrote. Nor, pending some radical change in human values or capabilities, can we expect the rate of change to slow down at all in the

Bettmann Archive

A new deal: FDR campaign song, 1936

foreseeable future.

This increase in the velocity of history dominates all aspects of contemporary life. First of all, it is responsible for the unprecedented instability of the world in which we live. Science and technology make, dissolve, rebuild and enlarge our environment every week; and the world alters more in a decade than it used to alter in centuries. This has meant the disappearance of familiar landmarks and guideposts that stabilized life for earlier generations. It has meant that children, knowing how different their own lives will be, can no longer look to parents as models and authorities. Change is always scary; uncharted, uncontrolled change can be deeply demoralizing. It is no wonder that we moderns feel forever disoriented and off balance; unsure of our ideas and institutions; unsure of our relations to others, to society and to history; unsure of our own purpose and identity.

The onward roar of science and technology has other consequences. A second springs from the paradox that the very machinery civilization has evolved to create abundance for the mass also creates anxiety for the individual. The high-technology society is above all the society of the great organization. In advanced nations, the great organizations—of government, of industry, of education, of research, of communications, of transport, of labor, of marketing—become the units of social energy. These great organizations, as Professor Galbraith points out, generate a life, world and truth of their own; in all areas, the sovereignty of the consumer begins to yield to the sovereignty of the producer; and, in the shadow of these towering structures, the contemporary individual feels puny and helpless. Indeed, no social emotion is more widespread today than the conviction of personal powerlessness, the sense of being beset, beleaguered and persecuted. It extends not only to Black Panthers and members of the Students for a Democratic Society but also to businessmen, publishers, generals and (as we have recently come to observe) Vice Presidents.

A third consequence springs from the technological process itself. For the inner logic of science and technology is rushing us on from the mechanical into the electronic age—into the fantastic new epoch of electronic informational systems and electronic mechanisms of control, the age foreshadowed by television and the computer. One need not be a devout McLuhanite to recognize the force of Marshall McLuhan's argument that history is profoundly affected by changes in the means of communication. There can be little doubt that the electronic age will have penetrating effects not just on the structure and processes of society but on the very reflexes of individual perception. Already television, by its collectiveness and simultaneity, has fostered an intense desire for political self-expression and visibility, as it has spread the habit of instant reaction and stimulated the hope of instant results.

The accelerating velocity of history has, of course, a multitude of other effects. Improved methods of medical care and nutrition have produced the population crisis; and the growth and redistribution of population have produced the urban crisis. The feverish increase in the gross national product first consumes precious natural resources and then discharges filth and poison into water and air; hence the ecologi-

The new technology: The Philadelphia Centennial, 1876

cal crisis. Nor can one omit the extraordinary moral revolution which makes our contemporary society reject as intolerable conditions of poverty, discrimination and oppression that mankind had endured for centuries.

All these factors, as they have risen in intensity and desperation, are placing increasing strain on inherited ideas, institutions and values. The old ways by which we reared, educated, employed and governed our people seem to make less and less sense. Half a century ago Henry Adams wrote, "Every historian—sometimes unconsciously but always inevitably—must have put to himself the question: How long . . . could an outworn social system last?" This is a question which historians—and citizens—must consider very intently today.

If this analysis is correct, then the crisis we face is a good deal deeper than simply the anguish over the ghastly folly of Vietnam. For that matter, it is a good deal deeper than is imagined by those who trace all iniquities to the existence of private profit and corporate capitalism. For the acceleration of social change creates its problems without regard to systems of ownership or ideology. The great organization, for example, dominates Communist as much as it does democratic states. Indeed, more so; for the more centralized the ownership and the more absolutist the ideology, the greater the tyranny of organization. The individual stands his better chance in societies where power is reasonably distributed and diversified and where ideas are in free and open competition.

If the crisis seems today more acute in the United States than anywhere else, it is not because of the character of our economic system; it is because the revolutions wrought by science and technology have gone farther here than anywhere else. As the nation at the extreme frontier of technological development, America has been the first to experience the unremitting shock and disruptive intensity of accelerated change. The crises we are living through are the crises of modernity. Every nation, as it begins to reach a comparable state of technical de-

Schlesinger

The present turmoil may be the price of progress

velopment, will have to undergo comparable crises.

Is the contemporary crisis more profound than other crises in our history? This seems to me an unanswerable question, because a crisis surmounted always seems less terrible than a crisis in being. One cannot say that we are in more danger today than during the Civil War, for example, or during the Great Depression, or during the second world war. One can only say that we met the earlier challenges —and have not yet met this one. And one can add that in earlier crises in our history the quality of our national leadership seemed much more adequate to the magnitude of the challenge.

What Lincoln brought to the Civil War, what Franklin Roosevelt brought to the Great Depression and the second world war, were, above all, an intense imaginative understanding of the nature of the crisis, perceived in the full sweep of history, with a bold instinct for innovation and a determination to mobilize and apply social intelligence and a compassionate sense of human tragedy. It was this embracing vision that gave particular policies their meaning and strength and inspired the American people to rise to their obligations and opportunities. Today, alas, our national leadership hardly seems aware of the fact we are in a crisis; in fact, it hardly appears to know what is going on in America and the world. It is feeble and frightened, intellectually mediocre, devoid of elevation and understanding, fearful of experiment, without a sense of the past or a sense of the future. This is one reason why our crisis of confidence is so acute. It is as if James Buchanan were fighting the Civil War or Herbert Hoover the Great Depression.

The basic task is to control and humanize the forces of change in order to prevent them from tearing our society apart. Our nation is in a state of incipient fragmentation; and the urgent need (along with ending the war) is a national reconstruction that will bring the estranged and excluded groups into full membership in our national community. This means social justice as well as racial justice; it means a far broader measure of participation in our great organizations and institutions; it means the determination to enable all Americans to achieve a sense of function, purpose and potency in our national life. And it means leadership in every area which greatly and generously conceives its responsibility and its hope.

I do not accept the thesis of the inexorable decline of America. No one can doubt that our nation is in trouble. But the present turmoil may be less the proof of decay than the price of progress. The cutting edge of science and technology has sliced through ancient verities and accustomed institutions; it has raised up new questions, new elites, new insistences, new confrontations. As the process has gathered momentum, the immediate result has been—was almost bound to be—social and moral confusion, frustration, fear, violence. Yet the turmoil, the confusion, even the violence may well be the birth pangs of a new epoch in the history of man. If we can develop the intelligence, the will and the leadership to absorb, digest and control the consequences of accelerated technological change, we can avoid the fate of internal demoralization and disintegration—and perhaps offer an example that will help other nations soon to struggle with similar problems and will, in time, restore American influence in the world.

But, as Herbert Croly wrote 60 years ago, we can no longer conceive the promise of American life "as a consummation which will take care of itself . . . as destined to automatic fulfillment." We face a daunting task—still not a bad one for all that. Emerson said, "if there is any period one would desire to be born in—is it not the era of revolution when the old and the new stand side by side and admit of being compared; when all the energies of man are searched by fear and hope; when the historic glories of the old can be compensated by the rich possibilites of the new era? This time like all times is a very good one if one but knows what to do with it."

Revisionism: A New, Angry Look at the American Past

EVERY epoch recreates its own concept of the past. As the climate of opinion shifts over the course of a generation, so do historians' views of history. A series of events as related by one historian may be altered beyond recognition by a later one. Such is the case with American history today. Traditional notions of the past are being brusquely challenged from the left by a group known as revisionists who emphasize not the homogeneity and accomplishments of the American heritage but its massive dislocations and conflicts. Though forming a diffuse movement rather than a well-defined school, they have a growing influence on the study of history; at last December's meeting of the American Historical Association, their candidate for president, Staughton Lynd, the ex-Yale professor who now works with Radical Organizer Saul Alinsky, received nearly one-third of the vote.

The revisionists have a particular quarrel with the dominant scholarly voice of the recent past: what they call "consensus history," as exemplified by such diverse writers as Richard Hofstadter of Columbia, Daniel Boorstin of the Smithsonian Institution, Henry Nash Smith of the University of California at Berkeley, and George Kennan of the Institute for Advanced Study at Princeton. The consensus historians, who came to maturity during World War II and the early years of the cold war, exhibit an understandable hostility to totalitarianism in their writings. By contrast, they emphasize the spirit of compromise and accommodation in American history. Compared with the violence that racked the Old World, the New seems to them refreshingly free of sustained class and sectional strife. They feel that the pluralism of American life has blurred ideological divisions between rich and poor, between agrarians and urbanites. They are friendly to the realistic practicing politician and denigrate the self-righteous crusading reformer.

In place of this relatively benign view of America, the revisionists have portrayed a land of teeming passions and deep-seated, almost irreconcilable disagreements. Some revisionists accept the class-warfare theories of Karl Marx; most of them owe a considerable debt to Progressive Historian Charles Beard, who interpreted the American past as an economic struggle between haves and have-nots. Since most revisionists took part in the civil rights or antiwar movements of the past decade, they make an easy transition to a study of previous periods of intense struggle: the Revolution, the Civil War, the Populist revolt, the efforts of labor to gain recognition. Compared with the America summarized in contemporary textbooks, theirs is indeed another country.

Viewpoint of the Masses

The weakness of consensus history, argue many revisionists, is that it is elitist. It reflects the viewpoint of the political and economic establishments that left the most voluminous records. Revisionists concentrate instead on writing history, in the words of Roosevelt University's Jesse Lemisch, "from the bottom up." This presents problems of its own: the masses do not leave much in the way of records. Nonetheless, Revisionist Stephan Thernstrom of Brandeis University was able to overcome this obstacle in his *Poverty and Progress*, by making an imaginative use of U.S. census reports. Generalizing from shifts in population, occupation and income in a typical Massachusetts industrial town, he concludes that there was much less social mobility in 19th century America than is commonly assumed. Few laborers repeated the Horatio Alger story and moved out of

their class, although in the course of a generation some rose within it. Only a high rate of movement between towns, says Thernstrom, prevented the development of a permanent proletariat in the European fashion. Similarly, Revisionist Leon Litwak of San Francisco State College combed newspapers, letters and legislative records of pre-Civil War days for his *North of Slavery*, which contends that anti-black prejudice existed on a much wider scale than has been suspected. Litwak found less racism in the South than in the North and West, where many localities enacted laws to keep Negroes out. Americans outside the South objected to the spread of slavery not so much because they thought it was evil as because they were terrified that the despised black man would move to their part of the country.

Doctrinaire of the Center

Many historians have viewed the Civil War as a tragic, unnecessary accident; Revisionist Eugene Genovese of the University of Rochester regards it as the inevitable clash of two highly developed and mutually exclusive class structures. In *The Political Economy of Slavery* and *The World the Slaveholders Made*, Genovese characterizes the "slavocracy" as a self-contained culture with an authentic life-style and ideology of its own. He berates even his mentor, Karl Marx, for failing to understand that the Southern "way of life" served as more than a veneer for the exploitation of the black man. It seems anomalous for a Marxist to offer a defense of the old South, but the strength of Genovese is that he believes in respecting the enemy. He feels that the admirable qualities of Southern statesmen, from Thomas Jefferson to Robert E. Lee, were inseparable from the tradition that produced them. "If we blind ourselves to everything noble, virtuous, honest, decent and selfless in a ruling class," Genovese asks, "how do we account for its hegemony?"

LYND

Consensus historians have generally given high marks to the "Progressive Era" of Theodore Roosevelt and Woodrow Wilson, and to F.D.R.'s New Deal, for accomplishing significant reform within a democratic framework. The revisionists are not willing to concede so much. To Gabriel Kolko of the State University of New York at Buffalo, the Progressive Era represented not the bridling of predatory big business by the Federal Government but rather the capture of Government by business. In *The Triumph of Conservatism*, Kolko argues that most Government regulation was enacted at the behest of leading corporations, which wanted railroad legislation, meat inspection or fair-trade laws to save them from increasingly anarchic competition. They lost no time gaining control of regulatory commissions like the ICC that were intended to supervise their activities.

In one of the revisionist attacks on the New Deal, *The Conservative Achievements of Liberal Reform*, Bernard Bernstein of Stanford criticizes F.D.R. for inviting big business to take part in such governmental enterprises as the NRA, which gave capitalists a power over federal policy that they had never enjoyed before. It was only when threatened politically by Huey Long that Roosevelt moved to the left, and urged higher taxes, Social Security and a system of unemployment compensation. The scourge of big business, concludes Bernstein, was nothing more than a "doctrinaire of the center."

It is almost axiomatic with consensus historians that violent revolutions do more harm than good. But in the best revisionist work to date, *Social Origins of Dictatorship and Democracy*, Barrington Moore Jr. of Harvard makes a strong case for the necessity of revolution. Without such a revolution in its past, he declares, a nation cannot achieve industrial democracy. Revolution is necessary to destroy the reactionary power of the agricultural interests that impede modernization: both large landholders and peasantry. Because Germany and Japan had no revolution, landowners were able to combine with industrialists in both countries to take power. Since democratic forces were too weak to challenge this union, it eventually culminated in fascism. In Russia and China, on the other hand, an untamed peasantry became the backbone of another successful authoritarian movement: Communism. But the Puritan revolution in England and the 1789 revolution in France effectively crippled the agricultural powers and opened the way for modernization along democratic lines.

The one social revolution in the U.S.—the Civil War—succeeded only partially, according to Moore. The radical reconstructionists failed to win the land redistribution in the South that would have assured the ex-slaves their freedom. Still, the power of the landowners was sufficiently reduced to prevent them from later joining with Northern capitalists to impose a form of totalitarianism on the U.S. Considering the horrors attendant upon revolution from below (Communism) and revolution from above (fascism), Moore prescribes revolution only as a last resort, and under certain specific conditions.

The most debatable revisionist reinterpretations have involved American foreign affairs. The U.S., revisionists say, has become the imperialistic aggressor of the cold war, while the Soviet Union, even under Stalin, is seen as essentially cautious and realistic. In *The Tragedy of American Diplomacy* and more recently in *The Roots of the Modern American Empire*, William Appleman Williams —perhaps the longest-practicing revisionist—contends that the American pursuit of an open-door policy has brought it into conflict with nations around the world. Williams interprets every act of U.S. diplomacy in the light of his neo-Marxist conviction that capitalism must always expand in search of new markets. Thus the U.S., while claiming to be championing Chinese integrity against the Japanese invasion of Manchuria, was only interested in China as a source of trade. This economic compulsion eventually led to war with Japan, says Williams. In relentless application of this same principle, other revisionists find American capitalist cupidity behind the decisions to go to war in Korea and Viet Nam—a clear example of twisting the facts to fit the theory.

While minimizing the vices of the totalitarian leaders, Cold War revisionists invariably exaggerate the shortcomings of American statesmen. This requires something approaching a conspiracy theory of history. How else explain the fact that U.S. leaders are always doing what they say they are not doing? D. F. Fleming, professor emeritus of Vanderbilt University (*The Cold War and Its Origins*), and David Horowitz (*Empire and Revolution*), onetime director of research for the Bertrand Russell Peace Foundation, accuse the U.S. of having followed a deliberate policy of intimidating Russia. As evidence, they cite events from the Allied intervention in the Russian civil war of 1918-21 to America's rigorous opposition to the expansion of Russia into Eastern Europe at the end of World War II. According to the revisionists, Russia after the war was not being aggressive, but simply establishing security within its normal sphere of influence. The ruthless, bloody way in which the Soviets imposed their rule is blithely brushed over by the re-

DAN BERNSTEIN

MOORE

visionists. Intimations of conspiracy are liberally sprinkled throughout *American Power and the New Mandarins* by M.I.T.'s linguist-turned-historian Noam Chomsky. He attributes the Viet Nam War to the machinations of amoral technocrats who slavishly serve the repressive U.S. social order.

Marx argued that the rightful goal of philosophy was not merely to study society but to change it. Similarly, the revisionists seek what they term a "usable past"—which means, in effect, a past that supports their present political convictions. The evidence suggests that they have overused the past. Their understandable anguish over the Viet Nam War has led them to condemn American participation in other wars; too readily, they find a link of culpability stretching from one conflict to the next. In so far as they tend to disregard history that does not serve their needs, they are anti-historical. Thus, when Staughton Lynd, in *Intellectual Origins of American Radicalism*, combs American history to establish a tradition of radicals who shared his vision of a noncapitalist, decentralized society, he plucks out Tom Paine, Lloyd Garrison and Henry David Thoreau as fellow ideologues. This is not history but polemics.

Many revisionists impose too strict a pattern on the chaos of history. By concentrating on inexorable social and economic forces, they do not make sufficient allowance for political, cultural and psychological factors. The accidental in history too often eludes them. The American Revolution, for example, was not necessarily the inevitable product of contending social forces. In his *Origins of American Politics*, Bernard Bailyn points out that the colonial leaders, misled by radical British publicists, developed an almost paranoid fear that the British Crown was adding to its power when in reality that power was waning. This misreading of the times contributed significantly to the movement for independence.

Limits of Economics

A rigid theory of economics is insufficient to explain the behavior of democratic statesmen like F.D.R. and Truman. No doubt these Presidents were interested in the preservation and expansion of American markets. But their foreign policies were determined by other, more significant factors—among them a legitimate and noneconomic desire to maintain a balance of power in the world, without which peace is not possible. They were also subject to a variety of domestic pressures, not all of which can be defined in economic terms. As Hofstadter argues in defense of F.D.R.'s prewar policies, "his undeniably devious leadership at certain moments reflected not his Caesaristic aspirations but the difficulties of a democratic politician confronting the force and unhampered initiative of Caesaristic powers"—meaning fascist Japan and Germany. The point equally well applies to later U.S. Presidents confronting Soviet Russia.

AP

GENOVESE

It is in the nature of radicalism not to be able to live at peace with the past. History does not prove very comforting to those who yearn for utopian change. That is one reason, no doubt, why the revisionists—with the exception of Moore—have not written works equal to the best of the consensus school. It seems to be true that conservatives—men with a fondness for the past—write the better history; witness Gibbon, Spengler, Henry Adams. The revisionists have a valid point: If the past is not usable, then what is its value? In the deft hands of Moore or Genovese, Marxian class analysis exposes strata of human experience that were not apparent to previous historians. But history is too rich and varied to yield its secrets to one method alone. The revisionists who ultimately endure will be historians first, revisionists second.

Radical Historians on the Move

By DAVID DONALD

Mr. Donald, author of "Charles Sumner and the Coming of the Civil War," teaches history at Johns Hopkins. His "Charles Sumner and the Rights of Man" will be published in November.

Just after Christmas last year, the American Historical Association experienced an attempted revolution. It would be hard to think of a less likely setting for subversion than the sedate parlors of the Sheraton Park and Shoreham Hotels in Washington. Most of the 7,000 historians who came to this 84th annual convention expected to meet old friends, to look for jobs for themselves or their graduate students, and perhaps to listen to an occasional paper on, say, "Pre-Columbian Contacts with the New World" or "Ethnic Influences on Austro-American Relations, 1885."

Instead, they spent most of their time and energy in business meetings, where the "Radical Caucus" tried to overthrow the "Establishment" and take over the Association. For the first time in history there was a contest for the presidency. Though the "Establishment" candidate, Robert R. Palmer, professor of history at Yale University, won, a third of the votes went to the Radical nominee, Staughton Lynd, who failed to receive tenure at Yale. Historians bitterly debated Radical resolutions calling for an end to the war in Vietnam and the immediate withdrawal of American troops. These were finally rejected, but by the narrow vote of 647 to 611. As the exhausted scholars ended their convention, Radicals were already planning for the 1970 meeting in Boston. Counting upon massive support there from the Harvard, M.I.T. and Boston University graduate students, one Radical remarked as he left Washington: "I don't envy Mr. Robert R. Palmer."

By next December Radicals may pick a more important target than the staid and powerless American Historical Association, but the discontent underlying their abortive revolution is not likely to disappear. During the past five years many of the ablest and most articulate young historians of the United States have become increasingly unhappy. In a broad sense the sources of their dissatisfaction are those which have produced alienation and rebelliousness throughout our society: the continuing war in Vietnam; the oppression of our black population; the blighting of our cities; the inanities of our politics — in short, the debasement of the quality of American life.

As historians, however, they have some special grievances and a special sense of urgency. They agree with C. Vann Woodward, the outgoing president of the American Historical Association, that "history as currently written is bland, banal or Philistine, that it is often morally obtuse, esthetically archaic and intellectually insipid." They accuse their predecessors of contributing to our present crisis by promulgating a cheerily optimistic view of the American past. Their chief enemies are the "Consensus" historians—as they label the middle-aged leaders of the profession—whose writings minimize political, social and economic conflict in American history and stress the beliefs and experiences which most of our people have shared.

Radicals tend to forget that Consensus historiography was never a unified theory; its practitioners ranged from Richard Hofstadter, who incisively criticized "The American Political Tradition" (1948), to Daniel Boorstin, who rejoiced that "The Genius of American Politics" (1953) lay in our indifference to ideology. The new generation of historians sweepingly condemns all Consensus scholars for accepting, and even eulogizing, a society where poverty is tolerated because it is presumed to be transient; where racial discrimination is permissible because it too will pass away; where political conflict is muted, since everybody agrees upon everything; and where foreign adventurism is acceptable, since politics stops at the water's edge.

Mostly young men in their thirties and early forties, the Radical historians are openly scornful of their predecessors for pursuing safe academic careers. For many of them, social involvement is more important than academic tenure. Most are activists, veterans of good causes. Lynd and Howard Zinn, both of whom taught by choice at Spelman College, a predominantly Negro institution, participated in the civil-rights movement in the South during its most dangerous days. Eugene Genovese risked his job at Rutgers

University, and subsequently became a major issue in New Jersey politics, by publicly announcing that he favored a victory of the Vietcong. Gabriel Kolko headed a drive to ban classified military research from the University of Pennsylvania campus, where he then taught, and in May, 1967, presented a bitter indictment of our Vietnam policy before the International War Crimes Tribunal in Stockholm.

Though it is tempting to label all these discontented historians members of the "New Left," they are united less by ideology than by opposition to the status quo. Their beliefs range from traditional liberalism through sophisticated Marxism to anarchism. The one effort to present a synthesis of their views, a collection of essays called "Toward a New Past" (1968), which Barton J. Bernstein of Stanford University edited, shows that they disagree with each other as often as with more traditional historians. It is dangerous to speak even of "schools" of Radical history, because today's friends may tomorrow be locked in deadly doctrinal conflict, yet it is possible to point out some types of Radical history and to name some of the principal Radical historians.

The young historian most completely disenchanted with his profession is Martin B. **Duberman, who is at the age of 39 a professor at Princeton University. With his undergraduate degree from Yale and his doctorate from Harvard, with his dull, important book (which won a Bancroft Prize) on dull, important Charles Francis Adams, and his second, elegantly written biography of James Russell Lowell, Duberman would seem a predestined member of the historical establishment. Yet the man's appearance suggests how imperfectly he fits his chosen professional role. Duberman has the face of a poet, and it is hard to imagine this brooding, anxious young man lecturing on, say, the Webster-Ashburton Treaty or the Dingley Tariff.**

Duberman constantly worries about his social function as historian, and his most recent book, "The Uncompleted Past" (1969) reveals his increasing discontent. Believing that historians, looking for a common denominator among groups of men, lose sight of the uniqueness of the individual, he chose instead to become a biographer. After completing his studies of Adams and Lowell, how-

ever, he concluded that it is impossible to re-create even one historical figure; the best biography can describe but never explain. Still hoping that there is something to be gained from a study of the past, Duberman confesses that he is "more hardpressed than ever to spell out in any concrete way the nature of those insights."

So despairing are Duberman's views that some reviewers have assumed that "The Uncompleted Past" is his valedictory to the historical profession. This, he protests, is not the case. He is, and will remain, a historian, but a historian who almost takes pride in the irrelevancy of his professional work. Just as he lives in New York City but teaches in Princeton, so will he continue to write plays (like the moving documentary, "In White America") and to grind out history. At the point in his career where the traditional historian announces that he is beginning what he hopes will be his major work, Duberman says that his next historical project will be a study of the experimental college and community, Black Mountain.

Equally radical in rejecting the historical profession is Lee Benson, professor of history at the University of Pennsylvania. Benson's criticisms, are, however, almost the exact opposite of Duberman's. The trouble with history, Benson argues, is not the impossibility of recapturing the past but the laziness and slovenliness of historians. A gregarious extrovert and a nonstop talker, he has dedicated himself to reforming his profession by making history a science.

Benson sneers at what he calls "impressionistic" history — i. e., history written from such conventional sources as newspaper accounts, autobiographies and manuscript letters. Trained in the gritty facts of economic history at Cornell, he trusts only such objective data as census compilations and voting returns. During his several years at Columbia's Bureau of Applied Social Research, Benson gained greater confidence in statistical techniques and larger contempt for literary or narrative history. A specialist in the history of the period before the Civil War, he dismisses the work of his predecessors—Allan Nevins, Bruce Catton, Avery Craven, Roy F. Nichols and J. G. Randall—as "trivial." "Perhaps no other phenomenon has had so many man-years of scholarship devoted to it as the American Civil

War," he remarks in a recent issue of Daedalus; but "nothing meaningful has emerged" from the "incredible amount of resources and intelligence and effort expended in this field."

It is not certain that much more has emerged from Benson's own researches. His most important book, "The Concept of Jacksonian Democracy" (1961), was initially received as a model of methodological sophistication—partly, perhaps, because it was written in impenetrable language and because it was peppered with figures and tables, which most historians do not understand. But Benson himself subsequently admitted that his statistical procedures were crude and that even these were imperfectly reported in his book. Besides, his data bore little relationship to his conclusions. Even repeated fail to show how Benson thought his detailed account of New York elections in the 1840's proved that the so-called Age of Jackson was instead an Age of Equalitarianism produced by the Transportation Revolution.

Benson's call for scientific history has attracted a number of followers, and it is yet too early to render a final verdict on the value of their quantitative studies. For instance, through massive computerization of thousands of Congressional roll-call votes, Thomas B. Alexander's "Sectional Stress and Party Strength" (1967) and Joel H. Silbey's "Shrine of Party" (1967) independently confirm the traditional view that pre-Civil War statesmen were increasingly torn between party loyalty and sectional allegiance. Quantification is, of course, a politically neutral technique, and those who practice it are readings not necessarily identified with any leftist protest movement. The vogue of statistical history is, however, impressive evidence that many other historians share Benson's radical dissatisfaction with history as conventionally written.

A very different sort of dissatisfaction is that voiced by Eugene Genovese, the learned Marxist who is now chairman of the history department at the University of Rochester. Lively and intense, so full of ideas that his words pour out in a torrent, Genovese is a veteran of a score of dialectical wars at Brooklyn College, where he was an undergraduate, and at the age of 39 has become one of the most formidable debaters in the historical profession. Usually mild-mannered, he becomes furious when

Drawings by Marty Norman.

his Marxism is confused with Stalinism; his doctrines, like his name, are of Italian derivation, for he draws heavily upon the writings of Antonio Gramsci, a founder of the Italian Communist party, whom he considers "the greatest Western Marxist theorist of our century."

Scorning simple economic determinism, Genovese adheres to a sophisticated materialistic interpretation of history, which stresses the interplay between the economic foundations of a society, its social structure and its value systems. He feels that his network of interrelationships is torn apart when a historian tries to judge, rather than to understand, the past. In writing of the Old South, he deplores the "moral absolutism" which leads some historians to condemn Southern whites because they owned Negroes. Instead, the historian ought "to recognize that the Southern slaveholders had their own code of morals and adhered to it," that they were "honorable men who defended principle" in the Civil War.

Genovese and several other young historians generally identified with him—Aileen Kraditor of Sir George Williams University, Marvin E. Gettleman of Brooklyn Polytechnic Institute, and Ann Lane of Douglass College—have done much to make Marxism academically respectable again, but they have not yet produced a sweeping new interpretation of the American past. Much of Genovese's work on the Old South is quite traditional; he freely admits that his conclusions are often close to those of U. B. Phillips, the Southern white historian whom liberals label a racist. Though there is much that is original in Genovese's "Political Economy of Slavery" (1965), that brilliantly argued book rests upon the unproved assumption that the Old South was a pre-capitalistic society. Genovese's second book, "The World the Slaveholders Made" (1970), is even more explicitly intended "to defend the claims of the Marxian interpretation of history." If it is not entirely persuasive in arguing that slavery was more a matter of class than of race, it is nevertheless more lively and provocative than most of the dreary books recently published on Black History.

A lonely figure among Radical historians is Gabriel Kolko, now professor at the State University of New York at Buffalo. Rarely appearing at historical conventions, rarely contributing to the little magazines of the left, Kolko is an impressively productive scholar. At the age of 37 he has published five books—two of them prior to his doctoral dissertation. Acknowledging a profound intellectual debt to Marx—and, more particularly, to Barrington Moore, the resident Marxist theoretician at Harvard—Kolko follows an independent line, for

he believes that "the American experience extends well beyond Marx's economic categories, and his political theory is entirely inadequate." Precisely what this means Kolko demonstrated in "The Triumph of Conservatism" (1963) and "Railroads and Regulation" (1965), two studies of the Progressive era. Though most historians have written of Progressivism as a ·movement of middle-class reformers to regulate corporate monopoly, Kolko argues that it was business itself that sought Federal regulation, partly to escape Populist legislation by the state legislatures, chiefly to rationalize its own economic order. The Progressive period, then, marks the triumph of big business.

Ever since the days of Theodore Roosevelt and Woodrow Wilson corporate monopoly has been not "just another interest group in American life, but . . . the keystone of power which defines the essential preconditions and functions of the larger American social order."

In more recent books Kolko has tried to demonstrate how these economic interests have shaped American foreign policy. "The Politics of War" (1968), for example, traces in minute detail the direction American diplomacy took between 1943 and 1945. Behind every move Kolko discovers efforts of the Government "to protect and advance American economic power in the control of the world economy." For instance, the massive program of foreign aid since World War II was essentially "a means of subsidizing American interests while extending American power in the world economy."

An admirer of Thorstein Veblen, Kolko writes in a style that could be taken for a parody of the master's. A fairly typical Kolko sentence runs: "If, in the last analysis, the structure of power can only be understood in the context in which it functions and the goals American power seeks to attain, the fact that the magnitude of such a vast description requires a full history of twentieth century America should not deter social analysts from highlighting the larger contours of the growth of modern American bureaucracies, if only to make the crucial point that these bureaucratic structures are less the source of power than the means by which others direct power in America for predetermined purposes."

When one cuts through the jargon, he discovers that Kolko writes a simplified, almost schematic, version of history. Correctly stressing that many businessmen in the Progressive years accepted and even favored certain kinds of Federal regulation, he slights those Progressive programs designed to promote social justice. Kolko also practices a double standard of historical morality. He is so intensely American that he holds the United States Government to a rigorous accounting; he blasts the "fashionable tendency" to see our errors as the consequence of ignorance, misunderstanding, or incompetence on the part of our statesmen and argues that there are no historical accidents. Toward other nations he is more tolerant, and he is willing to believe that the Russian massacre of 10,000 Poles at Katyn was "the exception not the rule."

In contrast to Kolko's schematic view of American history is the work of Radical scholars strongly influenced by anarchism and pacifism. Staughton Lynd may serve as a representative of this group, though many of its members strongly dissent from some of his views. Such disagreement

does not at all distress Lynd, whose boyish bearing and carelessly ruffled hair make him look a decade younger than his 41 years, for he thrives on controversy. The son of Robert and Helen Lynd, authors of the famous sociological studies of "Middletown," Staughton Lynd has since his days at the Fieldston School in the Bronx been debating his political principles with himself, in what he calls a continuing "dialogue between the hard-boiled centralizer and the sensitive anarchist, the Commissar and the Yogi, the Marxist and the pacifist." With equal vigor he debates with others, whether to the left or right of his own position.

Much of Lynd's historical writing is an elaborate effort to prove that his is an indigenous form of radicalism deriving from a long American tradition. His most important book, "Intellectual Origins of American Radicalism" (1968), traces his own ideas to the English "Commonwealthmen" of the 18th century, to American Revolutionists like Tom Paine, and to the abolitionists. Thoreau is his hero. Just as the New England Transcendentalist practiced "anarcho-pacifism" by refusing to pay taxes for the unjust war with Mexico, so

Lynd withheld a part of his income tax that would have helped support our war in Vietnam. Just as Thoreau practiced "revolutionary socialism" when he supported John Brown's raid, so Lynd helped organize the civil-rights movement in Mississippi.

Other Radical historians share Lynd's need to discover a usable American past, even when they do not share all his enthusiasms. Jesse Lemish, for instance, looks to the common man for the leavening spirit of radicalism, and he believes he has found strong evidence of it among common seamen at the time of the American Revolution. In Lemish's call for further "histories of the inarticulate" the Radicals link hands with the advocates of Black History; both groups of historians emphasize evidence of rebelliousness among Southern slaves. Michael A. Lebowitz has discovered true radicalism among the Jacksonians; his thesis, he freely admits is not proved but neither "has it been properly tested." Along with Lynd, Duberman and Kraditor admire the abolitionists.

In "The Populist Response to Industrial America" (1962), Norman Pollack pictures the discontented farmers of the 1890's not as frustrated hicks but as sophisticated critics of the capitalist system. James Weinstein sees in Eugene V. Debs and other leaders of the old Socialist party of America the true prophets of present-day discontent, and Melvyn Dubofsky's "We Shall Be All" (1969) rehabilitates the radical reputation of the "Wobblies." Describing the early days of S.N.C.C. (1964), Howard Zinn hopes the civil-rights movement will lead to "a fundamental restructuring of the economic system of the United States, a change far beyond Fair Deals and New Deals and other temporary aids."

At their best these Radical studies in American history are able and intelligent, and they have illuminated some forgotten corners of our past and rehabilitated some long-neglected men of good will. Judged by any standard, Lynd himself is a historian of extraordinary ability, and it is a disgrace to the profession that he does not hold an appointment at a major university. Yet, taken as a whole, the work of these Radical scholars fails to carry conviction; these books leave unshaken the Consensus historian's argument that most Americans throughout our history have been contented participants in the capitalist system. As Genovese observes, this searching for Radical ancestors often amounts to "mere sentimentalism." Genovese adds that even Lynd is often

writing "not history at all . . . but a political testament with historical references added to establish a pedigree."

Genovese's remarks suggest one reason why Radical history has been slow in finding acceptance: Radical historians spend much of their time tearing each other apart. They engage in endless debates in Liberation, Dissent and the now defunct Studies on the Left; and The New York Review of Books has become a bloody amphitheater for their internecine quarrels. Genovese and Lynd, in particular, have for years been locked in fierce controversy over both the nature of history and the role of the historical profession. Saved by the Rutgers tenure system from a right-wing assault, Genovese wants the university to remain a place of free inquiry, where scholars can be unaffected by either conservative repression or leftist "obscurantism, egocentric pseudo-existentialism, and abstract moralizing."

Lynd, who lost his job at Yale and subsequently was barred from teaching at several Illinois colleges, has no such love for the university, which he fears as "a marvelously effective instrument for making us middle-class men"; he thinks the Radical historian must be an activist, with "a foot solidly off campus." This same disagreement split the Radicals at the American Historical Association in December. Lynd was chosen by the Radical Caucus as its nominee; Genovese denounced these Radicals and urged the Association to "put them down, put them down hard, and put them down for once and for all."

Radical historians also make too much of their differences with scholars of the older generation. In fact, Radical and Consensus historians often complement, rather than contradict, each other. One can, for instance, believe with Lynd that there were genuinely Radical thinkers during the Revo-

lutionary era and still consider the Revolution as an essentially conservative movement. Duberman's picture of abolitionists happy and well-adjusted in their good works supplements the Consensus explanation that these reformers came from an old patrician class losing its function in urban, industrial New England. Kolko's analysis of Progressivism is largely compatible with Hofstadter's; both men view the differences between Wilson and T. R. as superficial, and both hold that neither Democrats nor Republicans seriously challenged the dominance of business.

Despite these self-imposed handicaps, Radical historians are beginning to have a significant influence upon their profession. They have stimulated new attention to American intellectual history, a subject nearly moribund for the past decade. For instance, Christopher Lasch's "New Radicalism in America" (1965) is a stimulating reappraisal of Progressive thinkers like Jane Addams and Herbert Croly. Deftly interrelating the psychological origins of the Progressives' ideas and the social goals they hoped to achieve, Lasch shows both the humanitarian impulses behind their reforms and the blueprints for social control that often resulted from their activities.

Radical historians have also given new importance to the study of American diplomacy. It is they—not the older scholars of the "Establishment"—who have written the basic books, resting upon massive research, on the last three decades of our foreign relations. One does not have to accept Kolko's interpretations to find "The Politics of War" an instructive account of how American foreign policy was formulated. Equally useful, and better balanced, is Walter La Feber's "America, Russia, and the Cold War" (1967), which covers the years from 1945 through 1966.

Much of this Radical work on foreign policy was stimulated by the example of William Appleman Williams, formerly of the University of Wisconsin, where many of these young historians did their graduate work. Like Williams, the Radicals usually do research only in American archives, and they concentrate on showing how United States policy was formed. As a result, Henry Pachter has observed, their monographs frequently tend "to attribute too much of what happened in the last 80 years to American initiatives. *We* did this, *we* did that—as though diplomacy was not an interaction of many powers." Dean Ernest May of Harvard points out that this single-archive approach to diplomatic history often leads to another kind of distortion: "those historians who concern themselves exclusively with American events tend also to be those who are on the hunt for villains."

But Radical writing on foreign policy also shares the great strengths of Williams's best books—notably "The Tragedy of American Diplomacy" (1959), which has exerted great influence. Unwilling to write conventional diplomatic history, chronicling what one clerk wrote to another, Williams has constantly stressed the interrelationship of domestic and foreign policy. He tries to show how internal pressures resulting from industrialization and economic development have shaped American diplomacy. Some of the best recent monographs on United States foreign policy — La Feber's "New Empire" (1963), N. Gordon Levin's "Woodrow Wilson and World Politics" (1968), Lloyd Gardner's "Economic Aspects of New Deal Diplomacy" (1964) and Thomas J. McCormick's "China Market" (1967) — explore and test Williams's thesis. Even the historian averse to the essentially economic interpretation underlying such studies must commend the effort to relate our foreign policy to our total national experience.

Most important of all, Radicals have aroused new interest in the writing and reading of American history. All too often conventional historians have been engaged in what Richard Drinnon, a young Radical, calls "a kind of mindless confrontation of the documents," and their work is tediously meaningless, both to themselves and to their few readers. The dissenting historians, on the other hand, feel that they are engaged in an important and challenging undertaking. Insisting that the United States has had a complex history, they demand that we explore roads not taken, that we harken to voices long unheard. Passionately, even stridently, they warn their elders against confusing objectivity with a defense of the status quo. They call upon the scholar and the teacher to be not merely a recorder but — like our greatest historians, from Bancroft to Beard—a social critic.

Doubtless the Radicals ask too much. They would like historians to combine the sensitivity of Duberman, the methodological clarity of Benson, the theoretical sophistication of Genovese, the industry of Kolko and the activist-idealism of Lynd. A profession composed, by and large, of hardworking rather than brilliant men cannot meet such standards, and the Radical historians themselves are thus far more distinguished for promise than performance. By the time they reach middle age, they may discover that their grasp has exceeded their reach. But by that time, they too will be old fogeys, waiting to be overturned by a new generation of revisionists. ∎

THE AMERICANIZATION OF HISTORY

Jefferson read the same accounts that Adams had and drew from them the same moral lessons. But here the two parted company.

HENRY STEELE COMMAGER

It is all very distant now and, in an age of technical history, almost alien—a concern for the happiness of man, the progress of society, and the prosperity of the Commonwealth; the belief that the New World opened a new chapter in history, that man was in control of his own destiny, that virtue was the distinguishing character of a republic, and that collectively the American people could achieve virtue. These were the principles and hopes that inspired the achievement of independence, the founding of the nation, and the advancement of science and learning, and that provided posterity with the materials by which it could know its forebears.

If we inquire into the historical philosophy and vision of the generation that founded the American nation, however, we are met at the threshold by what seems to us a paradox: the contrast between the formal political and formal historical writing of the American Enlightenment. The generation that gave us the most profound and eloquent political treatises of our literature, from the Declaration of Independence and *Common Sense* to the debates in the Federal Convention and the *Federalist Papers,* gave us not a single formal historical work that anyone but a scholar can remember or an antiquarian would read, except as an act of piety. Of all that generation only the grotesque Parson Weems wrote histories that survive, and most would acknowledge that he was not really a historian at all and that he really belongs to the era of romanticism, not the Enlightenment.

Yet no other generation has been so preoccupied, we might say so obsessed, with history as that of the Founding Fathers. Turn where you will in the writings of these statesmen and you are launched on the seas of history—often, it must be admitted, the Aegean and the Mediterranean Seas. History, wrote Ben Franklin, would:

give occasion to expatiate on the advantage of civil orders and constitutions; how men and their properties are protected by joining in societies and establishing government; their industry encouraged and rewarded; arts invented, and life made more comfortable; the advantages of liberty, mischiefs of licentiousness, benefits arising from good laws, and from a due execution of justice, etc. . . .

Jefferson, too, was confident that history was essential to wisdom and statesmanship. It taught the young, he observed, the virtues of freedom:

By apprizing them of the past it will enable them to judge of the future; it will avail them of the experience of other times and nations; it will qualify them as judges of the actions and designs of men; it will enable them to know ambition under every disguise . . . and, knowing it, to defeat its views.

It is clear at once that the generation of the Enlightenment, European and American alike, thought of history not as we customarily think of it—the reconstruction of the past—but as a moral enterprise. Perhaps it was not history at all; let us call it philosophy and be done with it. They had no use for the pedantry of the annalists and the erudites; they would have had little interest in the research of a Niebuhr or a Ranke, who addressed themselves to what actually happened. They were, in short, in the great tradition of historical thinking and writing—the tradition that stretches almost unbroken from Herodotus to Gibbon: history as philosophy.

In the ancient world the philosophy had been predominantly secular; in the Middle Ages, it was philosophy as a revelation of God's purpose with man; after the seventeenth century it once again became, covertly if not always overtly, secular. Bolingbroke put it with wonderful succinctness when he said that history is philosophy teaching by examples—and what was this but a restatement of the axiom of Dionysius of Halicarnassus? This was Voltaire's notion of history, Voltaire who towered above all of his contemporaries, and it was Montesquieu's, too —Montesquieu of the *Grandeur and Decadence.* It was Abbé Raynal's idea of history, and that of Turgot and his tragic disciple Condorcet, of the Swiss Johannes Müller, who inspired Schiller's *William Tell,* of the Dane Ludvig Holberg, who wrote *Universal History,* and of the great Gibbon, the only one who can be called a professional historian.

It was all history as philosophy, not history as fact. "Let us begin by laying facts aside," wrote Rousseau in his *Dissertation on the Inequality of Mankind,* and this is pretty much what all of them did, all but Gibbon anyway. In America, perhaps especially in America, it was morality that was important, not facts; it was wisdom and justice and virtue. Here is one of the signers, the eminent Dr. Benjamin Rush, urging the trustees of the new Dickinson College to exchange a set of the *Journals of the House of Commons* for books on mathematics. "It would distress me," he wrote, "to hear that a student at Dickinson College had ever wasted half an hour in examining even their title pages. He would find nothing in them but such things as a scholar and a gentleman should strive to forget!" Just before the Revolution, John Adams praised Mr. Macaulay's *History of England,* because "it is calculated . . . to bestow the reward of virtue, praise, upon the generous and worthy only . . . No charms of eloquence can atone for the want of this *exact historical morality.*" And a few months later, young Thomas Jefferson was writing that he "considered history as a moral exercise." It was, he added, "interchangeable with fiction" in inculcating moral lessons.

How could the philosophers so confidently rely on history to provide lessons that would be relevant to their own times and problems? It was easy enough. We have learned to distrust all analogies taken from remote times or different societies, but to the Enlightenment no societies were different and no times remote. After all, mankind was everywhere the same. Hume said it once and for all: "Mankind are so much the same in all times and places that history informs us of nothing new or strange. . . . Its chief use is only to discover the constant and universal principles of human nature."

Constant and *universal*—those are the key words. If history was not everywhere the same, human nature was, and it was human nature that the philosophs studied. That is why they could move with ease from Greece and Rome to China or Peru. That is why Leibniz could recommend Chinese as the universal language and his disciple Christian Wolff assert that the teachings of Confucius were quite as acceptable as those of Jesus—a heresy for which he was promptly banished from Prussia by an indignant monarch. That is why Diderot could go to Tahiti for lessons that Bougainville failed to teach, and Dr. Johnson to Abyssinia. That is why the philosophs had so little interest in individuals as such, only in individuals as a type, and why the Enlightenment produced so few good biographies—Boswell was, of course, a romantic, as was Parson Weems. That is why artists insisted on depersonalizing their historical characters, dressing them all in Roman togas or, perhaps, in nothing—even the practical Franklin wished to be painted "with a gown for his dress and a Roman head." Said Sir Joshua Reynolds, who knew everything: "A history painter paints man in general; a portrait painter a particular man, and consequently a defective model." That is why the eighteenth century—outside England anyway—delighted in the nude, for if you are going to portray Man in General, then away with clothing, which was always of time and place. The human body, after all, was the same in every clime and age. How wonderfully apt was the astonished cry of the boy Benjamin West when they took him to see the Apollo Belvedere: "My God, how like a Mohawk Indian!"

Thus the Founding Fathers could confidently draw from their study of history—chiefly Greek, Roman, and English—moral lessons that were applicable to their own day. But now we come to something that still has the power to excite us. All read the same history; all drew from its examples much the same body of conclusions. But here what we may call the school of John Adams and the school of Jefferson parted company, and their disagreement is basic to an understanding of the two men, and an understanding of the way in which the American Enlightenment differed from the European.

In his interpretation of history, Adams belonged to the Old World, not the New. As he surveyed history—a survey that covered more than a score of societies—he found men and governments everywhere the same. Men were creatures of greed, ambition, vanity, passion; all were animated by an ungovernable lust for power; all governments tended to tyranny. And from this reading of history Adams drew conclusions that he thought were inescapable. If human nature and government were everywhere the same, what reason was there to suppose, or even to hope, that they would be different in America? Adams looked about him and concluded that indeed they were not different, and the moral lesson that he then drew from history was clear and simple: the supreme task of statesmanship was to contrive so many checks and balances that the innate depravity of men would be frustrated.

But then we have Jefferson—and he was not alone, to be sure, having been anticipated by Thomas Paine and supported by Joseph Priestley and others of the American Philosophical Society clique—with a very different interpretation. He had read the same histories that Adams had read, and drew from them the same moral lessons. But beyond this he would not go. He challenged Adams, and the whole body of Enlightenment thought, on the central issue of the application of historical laws to America, and into this challenge we can read the beginnings not only of Americanism but of American romanticism.

Where Adams saw history as retrospective, Jefferson saw it as prospective. Adams took for granted that Americans were prisoners of the past, doomed forever to repeat the errors of the past. But Jefferson was confident that man was not the prisoner of history, but might triumph over history; that he was not condemned forever to repeat the errors of the past but could avoid them; that human nature was not always the same, but that in a new and favorable environment—physical, political, and cultural—human nature itself would change.

Here is the most original contribution to historical thought ever to come out of the New World: History is not exhausted. In a New World, the world may begin anew.

It was not puritanism; Jefferson had no use for the sifted-grain thesis, for he thought all grain was potentially good. It was not millennialism—Philip Freneau with his boast that "Paradise anew shall flourish, no second Adam lost"—for Jefferson did not believe in original sin, and perhaps not in any sin not the product of law or religion. There was exultation, to be sure, and hope—"I like the dreams of the future better than the history of the past," Jefferson wrote to Adams, who was not much given to dreams. But as with most of Jefferson's ideas, those about history were firmly rooted in logic and experience. Never before had man been vouchsafed a chance to achieve the good life, under favorable auspices. Nature was abundant and, for the most part, beneficent. Man was master of his environment, and where that environment was not beneficent science could change it—just what Lester Ward was to say almost a century later in his stunning refutation of Herbert Spencer. Government was part of environment, and men flourished in freedom as they could not in tyranny, flourished in peace as they could not in war. Learning and science—now to be the possession of all the people—would teach wisdom and confer happiness. In such an environment the lessons of the past were irrelevant, or were there only as a warning.

Not content with rejecting the lessons of the past, the Jeffersonians added a new dimension to the idea of progress, Americanizing that idea, as it were, just as they had Americanized the character of history by making it do service for the future rather than for the past. Progress was a darling notion of the Enlightenment, but progress as the philosophs imagined it was a narrow and elitist concept—the advance of arts and letters and the sciences, the conquest of superstition and tyranny. Americans—we cannot assign this feeling to any one group or school so general was it—democratized and vulgarized the idea. Progress was the welfare of the common man; it was not merely something to delight members of the academies or the courts; it was something to improve the standards of living. It was not merely the avoidance of ancient evils—that could be taken for granted—it was the achievement of positive good. Thus the Americans took progress away from the utopianists—the fiction writers and the imaginary kingdom-contrivers such as Thomas More or Campanella or St. Pierre or Holberg—and placed it squarely in America. They not only democratized it, they realized it, and all the philosophs in the Old World acknowledged that Utopia was indeed America and differed only on whether it was to be found in Pennsylvania or in Connecticut.

Yes, it is all very distant now, and we are in a time of disillusionment, one that questions the value of history, the relevance of the past, and the achievement of the Founding Fathers. Let us conclude with a passage from one of the letters of Thomas Paine, who so wonderfully combined the spirit of rationalism with romanticism. He had no sense of history — Edmund Burke made that clear in his *Reflections*—but he had a feeling for the future denied the great Burke:

A thousand years hence, perhaps in less, America may be what Europe is now. The innocence of her character that won the hearts of all nations in her favor may sound like a romance, and her inimitable virtue as if it had never been. . . . The ruin of that liberty which thousands bled for or struggled to obtain may just furnish materials for a village tale.

When we contemplate the fall of empires and the extinction of the nations of the ancient world, we see but little to excite our regret than the mouldering ruins of pompous palaces, magnificent museums, lofty pyramids, and walls and towers of the most costly workmanship. But when the empire of America shall fall, the subject for contemplative sorrow will be infinitely greater than crumbling brass and marble can inspire. It will not then be said, here stood a temple of vast antiquity, here rose a Babel of invisible heighth, or there a palace of sumptuous extravagance, but here, ah painful thought, the noblest work of human wisdom, the grand scene of human glory, the fair cause of freedom, rose and fell.

MEN AND IDEAS

THE IMPORTANCE OF COMITY IN AMERICAN HISTORY

RICHARD HOFSTADTER

■ *Professor Richard Hofstadter, of Columbia University, who died in New York on Saturday, October 24, 1970, was one of the most eloquent and influential historians writing in the English language during the last quarter century.*

—JACK POLE

"It may seem strange," a foreign observer has suggested, "that American historians should be moved to take sides over the very question of whether there are any sides to take." Even after 15 years the controversial hyperbole that so often comes with a new idea has not entirely disappeared. A few of the embattled younger historians still seem to imagine that they are being asked to see the American past as stripped of all significant conflict and to accept a historical rationale for political tameness or passivity by denying the reality of past and present issues.

It is indeed true that consensus history arose at a moment of conservative retrospect in our national history, and that such a moment was more conducive than periods of political radicalism to a reconsideration of Progressive history. It is also true that there are moments in consensus writing that seem to warrant the suspicions of radical historians. For example, when Daniel Boorstin asks us to regard with what seems to many of us an excessive satisfaction, the pragmatic mindlessness that he finds characteristic of American society, or when he asks us all too baldly to celebrate "the marvelous success and vitality of our institutions," we begin to feel a twinge of that irritation with the consensus idea that John Higham gave vent to some years ago. But if the essentially political revulsion from consensus history has some warrant, it is still no more than a marginal consideration. In any case, it rests upon certain intellectual confusions. It is always possible, but not, I think, desirable, to find too simple an identification between past and present problems—a conclusion to which Charles Beard's book on the Constitution stands as permanent testimony. To take a strong stand for Negro rights today, for example, it is not necessary to find a long history of effective slave rebellions; to be deeply concerned over the problem of poverty, it is not necessary to show either that we have degenerated from an idyllic past or, for that matter, that poverty in the past was much worse than we ever imagined it. Again, it is a mistake to assume that the consensus idea is intrinsically a *prescriptive* one which commits us to this or that particular arrangement. It is a part of the *descriptive* task of the historian or political scientist to find and account for the elements of consensus in any situation, but he is not required to endorse what he finds. He may analyze society in functional terms, but this does not require him to assume that no arrangements are

Excerpted from *The Progressive Historians* by Richard Hofstadter, Knopf, 1968, © Richard Hofstadter. Reprinted in *The Columbia Forum*, Winter 1970, Vol. XIII, No. 4.

dysfunctional. If the matter is seen this way, I believe it will be understood that the idea of consensus is not intrinsically linked to ideological conservatism. In its origins I believe it owed almost as much to Marx as to Tocqueville, and I find it hard to believe that any realistic Marxist historian could fail to be struck at many points by the pervasively liberal-bourgeois character of American society in the past.

Many aspects of our history, indeed, seem to yield to a "left" consensus interpretation, and some radical historians have in fact begun to see it that way. Presumably, insofar as the idea of consensus has permanent validity, it will be detachable from any particular political tendency and will prove to be usable from more than one point of view. Irwin Unger pointed out that some of the New Left historians have already begun to make use of the notion of Left consensus ("The 'New Left' and American History," *American Historical Review*, 72 [1967], 1251-3). My own assertion of consensus history in 1948 had its sources in the Marxism of the 1930s. Political struggles, as manifested in the major parties, I argued, had "always been bounded by the horizons of property and enterprise. . . . American traditions . . . show a strong bias in favor of equalitarian democracy, but it has been a democracy in cupidity rather than a democracy of fraternity" (*The American Political Tradition, vii.*).

Finally, I see little point in denying that, for all its limitations, consensus as a general view of American history had certain distinct, if transitional merits. Coming when it did, it was an indispensable corrective force as well as an insight of much positive value. To the degree that the consensus school returned to the Turnerian theme of American uniqueness, it began to confront the problem Turner glimpsed but did not really try to cope with—the task of getting this theme into its necessary comparative frame. Above all, the consensus historians rediscovered the differentness of our history, reasserted a regard for its niceties after it had undergone too many simplifications, saw its continuities after its discontinuities had been grossly exaggerated, returned to an understanding of its pragmatic and pluralistic character, and forced us to think about the importance of those things Americans did not have to argue about.

Once all this has been granted, I think the important ground on which consensus as a general theory of American history should be quarreled with is not its supposed political implications but its intrinsic limitations *as history*. Having come into being as a corrective, the idea of consensus as an interpretative principle has the status of an essentially negative proposition. It demarcates some of the limits of conflict in American history, and underlines some other difficulties in the historical legacy of the Progressives, but as a positive principle it does not go very far. As J. R. Pole has put it, "The idea of consensus was useful as a direction-finder. It is not an explanation." It has somewhat the same relation to historical writing as an appropriate frame has to a painting: it sets the boundaries of the scene and enables us to see where the picture breaks off and the alien environment begins; but it does not provide the foreground or the action, the interest or the pleasure, the consummation itself, whether analytical or esthetic. It has been developed as a counter-assertion more than as an empirical tool. Sociologists and political scientists have also been interested in the phenomenon of consensus, and it is instructive to see how they approach it. They have asked such down-to-earth questions as: How much agreement is required for an effective consensus? Whose participation in a consensus really counts? Who is excluded from the consensus? Who refuses to enter it? To what extent are the alleged consensual ideas of the American system —its preconceptions, for instance, about basic political rights—actually shared by the mass public? (So far as the masses are concerned, what we call consensus is often little more than apathy.) Their questions and their answers are, of course, mainly contemporary, and they have the advantage of opinion poll data as well as the usual descriptive apparatus of the historian. But they raise some interesting questions about the past; they are acutely aware of the complex texture of apathy and irrationality that holds a political society together, and they help us to realize how incidental for many purposes are explicitly formulated theoretical commitments.

Consensus is certainly an idea of some uses, but it will be more fruitful when it is taken not as a satisfactory general theory or as an answer but as a whole set of new questions about the extent to which agreement prevails in a society, who in fact takes part in it, and how it is arrived at. We can distinguish, for example, the constitutional consensus, which exists when an effectively overwhelming majority of the politically active public accepts the legitimacy of the legal-constitutional order in which it finds itself. One can also speak of a policy consensus, which exists when an issue moves, at least for a time and perhaps permanently, out of the area of significant controversy. Americans now of middle age can remember how social security passed in no more than 20 years from the status of an almost visionary social reform to a controversial issue, and then to an established consensual position.

Finally, there is a subtler, more intangible, but vital kind of moral consensus that I would call comity. Comity exists in a society to the degree that those enlisted in its contending interests have a basic minimal regard for each other: one party or interest seeks the defeat of an opposing interest on matters of policy, but at the same time seeks to avoid crushing the opposition, denying the legitimacy of its existence or its values, or inflicting upon it extreme and gratuitous humiliations beyond the substance of the gains that are being sought. The basic humanity of the opposition is not forgotten; civility is not abandoned; the sense that a community life must be carried on after the acerbic issues of the moment have been fought over and won is seldom very far out of mind; an awareness that the opposition will someday be the government is always present. The reality and the value of comity can best be appreciated when we contemplate a society in which it is almost completely lacking—for example Spanish political culture on the eve of the civil war of the 1930s as we find it portrayed in the opening chapters of Hugh Thomas's brilliant history, *The Spanish Civil War*. In Spain the center dwindled and fell apart, and the extremes were occupied by reactionaries, lay and clerical, and radicals or nihilists with burning anticlerical passions; neither side had more than the faintest residual sense of the humanity of the other. Where Spain might be taken as the example of a society that failed to develop comity, the Weimar Republic is a case history of its gradual, but accelerating, breakdown.

The waxing and waning phases of comity shed considerable light on American history. The period of the Revolution, which drove out or silenced Americans of Loyalist persuasion and united most politically active Americans in a common cause, brought about a high measure of comity that was of great value in helping them surmount the difficult problems of political organization and real antagonisms of interest. Even the debates over the Constitution, sharp though they were, did not destroy it. But during the 1790s the political leaders, prodded by their particularist passions, groping uncertainly and not always successfully toward the still ill-formulated principle of legitimate opposition, and embroiled to a remarkable degree in the material and ideological issues arising out of the French Revolution and the ensuing war, entered upon a brief period of violent political emotion in which comity dwindled and a disruption of the Union seemed possible. Having once survived it, they made their way slowly out of this situation, and the period during which the second American party

system grew and flourished was one of predominant comity, in which the gift for conciliation became highly developed. The story of the 1850s, however, is one of the steady dissipation of comity, climaxed by the coming of the Civil War. Not all groups were equally or fully included in the system. Catholics felt themselves to be outsiders, and won acceptance only very slowly and by degrees. The so-called new immigrants during the period of post-Civil War industrialization were in the same position, and finally found their incorporation in the system of comity only in the twentieth century. Negroes have never been given a real part in the covenant of comity. A great deal of the severity of our present crisis arises from the fact that they have not been able to fight or bargain their way in, and they have learned to find their exclusion intolerable.

One of the greatest difficulties that confront the interpretative historian is that he must not just steer clear of ideas that seem false but must refrain from overextending those that are true. There is nothing in the idea of consensus, to be sure, which requires that we deny the reality of conflict. Yet I think it is a valid comment on the limits of consensus history to insist that in one form or another conflict finally does remain, and ought to remain, somewhere near the center of our focus of attention. Our attention to conflict is not just a requirement of the drama of all truly interesting history—that is to say, a requirement of historical esthetics—but also a necessity of historical knowledge. History deals with change, and in change conflict is a necessary, and indeed a functional, ingredient. It is one thing to say that a school of historians has overstressed a certain type of conflict or has misconceived social alignments, but another to write conflictless history. Americans, it is true, have not had to debate in any very serious way the merits of popular government or private property, or the grand systems of European political theorists. But they have had a steady diet of major political controversy, and we do not have to look very hard to find conflict in our history. The American nation was born in an age of almost constant stress and crisis that lasted from 1763 to 1788, during which its people experienced a dozen years of agitation over imperial policies, several more years of warfare and harassment, and during this time were stirred by intense debates over new state constitutions and two new federal constitutions. Afterward, about once in each generation they endured a crisis of real and troubling severity. The Union was in some danger of division during 1798-1801; it was in serious trouble during the years 1807-14 and again in 1832. It was racked by such grave differences in the 1850s that it finally broke in two. It went through a touchy crisis again in Reconstruction, climaxed by the events of 1876-77. It was deeply disturbed in the 1890s and again in the 1930s. And now, in the 1960s, it is in the midst of a dangerous major crisis the outcome of which I hesitate to try to predict. Surely these episodes evoke a record of significant conflict to which we cannot expect to do justice if we write our history in terms of the question whether or not Americans were disagreeing with John Locke.

There are three major areas in which a history of the United States organized around the guiding idea of consensus breaks down: first, I believe it cannot do justice to the genuinely revolutionary aspects of the American Revolution; second, it is quite helpless and irrelevant on the Civil War and the issues related to it; and finally, it disposes us to turn away from one of the most significant facts of American social life—the racial, ethnic, and religious conflict with which our history is saturated.

I would not propose to lose what is valid in the insight into America's happy circumstance of having been "born free," of not having to throw off the incubus of a feudal tradition and feudal establishments; nor would I quarrel with the perception that on some counts American thought in the Revolutionary era had a remarkably legalist and traditionalist—that is to say, conservative—cast. Certainly the pattern of the American Revolution was different from that of the Puritan, French, and Russian revolutions. But will it do to conclude that since Americans were in this sense born free, they had no revolution at all? Oddly enough, I believe our answer to this question will be clearer and more exact if it is properly equivocal. If we conclude that the American Revolution lacked a true revolutionary character because of the traditionalism of its *ideas*, we may miss a vital point. This Revolution represented the inheritance of the most radical ideas in Western civilization: the Protestant Reformation, the Puritan Revolution, the Glorious Revolution, the whole tradition of English dissent and radical criticism. Taken out of its parochial setting, it was the agency of some explosively radical ideas; not only because of its threat to the principle of legitimacy and to colonialism but also because it took the demand for popular government out of the realm of slogans and rallying cries and showed that it was actually susceptible to being translated into living institutions and being made to work. If our test for a revolution is the formation of a radically new ideological system, or regicide, or a widespread lethal terror, the American Revolution will not quali-

fy. But if our criterion is the accelerated redistribution of power among social classes or among various social types, a pragmatic disrespect for vested interests, the rapid introduction of profoundly important constitutional changes, we must reconsider it. The Tories may have been almost as devoted to Locke as the revolutionaries, but perhaps as many as 60,000 of them found what the revolutionaries stood for to be so intolerable that they left the American states never to return, and thousands of others risked their reputations, fortunes, and lives to fight against it. It does seem to have made an effective difference; and Washington's generation, looking back over the years of battle, sacrifice, and turmoil from 1763 to 1801, would surely have been puzzled at efforts to portray their age as one of bland unity. People who are "born free" may have to make remarkable exertions to stay that way.

Yet many Americans were born in slavery. And the phenomena of slavery and race—everything associated with the Civil War and its aftermath—have had to be incorporated sideways and almost by stealth into the consensus view of our history. Even more than the Revolution, the Civil War has been a stumbling block for the consensus theorists, as it was for their Progressive predecessors. The Progressives, with their disposition to set "democratic" agrarian against capitalist and to play down the issues of slavery and race that cut across this alignment, usually failed to confront the importance of slaveholding leadership in American democracy; and their tendency to see the issues of the Civil War and Reconstruction as a struggle between agrarianism and capitalism led them to some stark oversimplifications and to underplaying the moral and intellectual side of the struggle.

I am struck too by the importance of those kinds of conflicts which the Progressive historians lost sight of in their emphasis upon the polarized opposition of classes, and which the consensus theorists also neglect in their concern to deny the Progressives: the ethnic, racial, religious, moral conflicts with which American life is permeated. Certainly American history, even without feudalism and socialism, has been far from bland. In fact, a magnificent book could be written on violence in American life—the story of our early mobs and rebellions; the long, ruthless struggle with the Indian; our filibustering expeditions; our slave insurrections; our burned convents and mobbed abolitionists and lynched Wobblies; our sporadic, furiously militant Homesteads, Pullmans, and Patersons; our race lynchings, race riots, and ghetto riots; our organized gangsterism; our needless wars. What can, of course, raise such a book above the level of a mere description of certain sensational aspects of our history is the need to explain why the extraordinary American penchant for violence has been so sporadic, channeled, and controlled that it has usually bled itself out in the isolated, the local, and the partial, instead of coalescing into major social movements. How do we explain why, long before this country had a large, militant organized labor force, it had some of the bitterest and most violent strikes in the history of international labor movements? Why, without organized militarism or an established and influential military caste, have we so loved generals in politics? Why have we entered with such casual impulsiveness into wars with England, Mexico, Spain, and North Vietnam?

With the instructive effects of the debate over consensus history behind us, we can return to the assessment of conflict in American life and thought without going straight back to the arms of the Progressives. We can avoid what made them most vulnerable: their sometimes too exclusive reliance on geographical or economic forces, their disposition to polarize, to simplify, to see history as the work of abstract universals, to see past conflicts as direct analogues of present conflicts, their reductionist stress on motives, their tendency toward Manichaeanism, their occasional drift toward conspiratorial interpretations of events. We can do more justice to the role of parties and other institutions; we are in a position to write more sophisticated accounts of types of conflict they ignored; we will almost certainly be able to do better with the complex issues of slavery and race. We can achieve a better and fuller understanding of the importance of ideas than Beard and Turner did, and in dealing with ideas we can achieve a much clearer sense of their historical and institutional settings and their actual functions than was possible for Parrington's generation.

As more and more historians become aware that conflict and consensus require each other and are bound up in a kind of dialectic of their own, the question whether we should stress one or the other may recede to a marginal place, and give way to other issues that are at stake: the dualism of the Progressives as against the tendency of their successors to see so many forces at work that historical explanation seems to dissolve; the renewed interest in the argument over the effectiveness of ideas and states of mind, the tendency to take more account of the symbolic aspects of politics, the search for new methods. But as one looks at the productive historiographical arguments of the past two decades, one cannot fail to see that historians are responding in their own way to the sense of crisis that is so pervasive in our time. Here the issue is an old one: they are troubled about their own role and function, caught between their desire to count in the world and their desire to understand it. On one side their passion for understanding points back to the old interest in detachment, in neutrality, in critical history and the scientific ideal. But the terrible urgency of our political problems points in another direction, plays upon their pragmatic impulse, their desire to get out of history some lessons that will be of use to the world. And at this point we seem closer than we might have imagined to Bancroft, and to his contemporaries among the romantic historians who believed that they were finding instructive moral lessons in history. Beard himself appears not quite so far from Bancroft as he would have thought, at least at the beginning of his career; but he went a significant step further, and in proposing not just to draw general moral lessons about the direction and meaning of history but to forge specific recommendations for policy upon which he believed the life and death of American democracy depended, he became our supreme tragic example of the activist mind in history.

It will always be possible to argue over these two views of the historian's role—and in the end most historians will be persuaded less by the arguments than by the dictates of their temperaments. In the American temperament there is a powerful bias toward accepting the pragmatic demand upon history: it is hard for us to believe that there is such a thing as a truth that cannot be made useful. The urgency of our national problems seems to demand, more than ever, that the historian have something to say that will help us, and the publisher's puff on the jacket of almost every historical work of any consequence tries to suggest its relevance to the present. Against this, the professional case for detachment seems at first overwhelmingly strong. Most of us think we have other and better criteria of a historical work than its usefulness as a source of battle cries or slogans, even in the best of causes. Unlike economics and sociology, history is not, in the jargon of our time, a policy science, and rather than deploring this as a limitation, we may seize upon it as a luxury. Again, it is easy to point to the dangers of committed history, of which Beard provides so poignant an example. The activist historian who thinks he is deriving his policy from his history may in fact be deriving his history from his policy, and may be driven to commit the cardinal sin of the historical writer: he may lose his respect for the integrity, the independence, the pastness, of the past.

Such are the risks; and yet let us not deceive ourselves: the case for the historian *engagé*—and I mean here the case for him *as a historian,* not as a public force—also has its strength. It is not just that great histories have been written—witness Churchill and Trotsky in our age—by embattled participants. We must go beyond this to admit that, while there are few instances of historical insight in the direct and immediate service of public policy, there are innumerable instances of a vital connection between strong public concerns and distinguished historical work. The marvelous vitality that French historiography has derived from the controversial heritage of the French Revolution is a case in point. But the leading interpreters of America have also been, in this extended sense of the word, *engagé*—they have been committed to the historical realization of certain civic values, even in some cases to specific ends. At their worst they may stray into a culpable present-mindedness, like Beard striking at the stale constitutionalism of 1913 through the Constitution of 1787, or Parrington assimilating Roger Williams and Thomas Hooker to the democratic insurgency of the Progressive era. But this present-mindedness, though it has been responsible for major errors, has often brought with it a major access of new insight—bearing error and distortion not in arbitrary solitude but in a kind of fertile if illicit union with intellectual discovery. At their best, the interpretative historians have gone to the past with some passionate concern for the future; and somehow—the examples of Tocqueville and Henry Adams may encourage us—they have produced from the inner tensions of their minds an equipoise that enables them to superimpose upon their commitment a measure of detachment about the past, even to reconcile themselves to having knowledge without power.

The great fear that animates the most feverishly committed historians is that our continual rediscovery of the complexity of social interests, the variety of roles and motives of political leaders, the unintended consequences of political actions, the valid interests that have so often been sacrificed in the pursuit of other equally valid interests, may give us not only a keener sense of the structural complexity of our society in the past, but also a sense of the moral complexity of social action that will lead us toward political immobility. Since a keen sense of history begets a feeling of social responsibility and a need to act, this is not necessarily the case; but history does seem inconsistent with the coarser rallying cries of politics. Hence I suppose we may expect that the very idea of complexity will itself come under fire once again, and that it will become important for a whole generation to argue that most things in life and in history are not complex but really quite simple. This demand I do not think the study of history can gratify. As practiced by mature minds, history forces us to be aware not only of complexity but of defeat and failure: it tends to deny that high sense of expectation, that hope of ultimate and glorious triumph, that sustains good combatants. There may be comfort in it still. In an age when so much of our literature is infused with nihilism, and other social disciplines are driven toward narrow positivistic inquiry, history may remain the most humanizing among the arts.

Black Studies: An Intellectual Crisis

JOHN W. BLASSINGAME

○ JOHN W. BLASSINGAME is assistant editor of the Booker T. Washington Papers and lecturer in history at the University of Maryland. Mr. Blassingame gave this talk last spring to the faculty of the College of Arts and Sciences there.

I T IS PRESUMPTUOUS OF ANYONE to pretend to speak authoritatively on such a new development as black studies. At the end of a year fraught with the armed occupation of campus buildings and racial riots among students, I may rightfully be assigned to the camp of the foolhardy for attempting to speak on the rapidly escalating demands for increased attention to black people.

Black studies is such an emotionally loaded concept that most universities have had great difficulty in establishing programs. First of all, colleges started considering such programs at a time when the Negro community is furiously debating its place in American society. This, in itself, is not new. Generally, however, this is the first time that whites have seriously considered the debate worth noting. Consequently, they are often overwhelmed by the force of the demands, confused by the rhetoric, and unsure of the legitimate intellectual response.

The first problem that one encounters in surveying black studies programs around the country is the confusion over objectives. In fact, most people who write these proposals never include objectives, goals or the justification for such programs. Instead, such ambiguous terms as "need," "demand," "relevance," or "such a program needs no justification" are used. It is inconceivable that

Reprinted from THE AMERICAN SCHOLAR, Volume 38, Number 4, Autumn, 1969. Copyright © 1969 by John Blassingame. By permission of the author.

any other kind of program could be established with so little thought being given to long-range goals. When I have asked college teachers around the country why they are establishing black studies, the usual answer has been that the black students demand them. When I ask black students what are the goals of Afro-American studies, I often get a blank stare. In one committee meeting on black studies at a university in Washington, D.C., a Negro student demanded that thirty new courses be offered next year and a black studies department be created. When a faculty member asked what the objectives of the department would be, the student replied, "How do you expect me, a freshman, to know?" and stormed out of the conference room.

There is often great confusion over objectives and contradictory patterns in the programs. Reacting to student demands for "relevance," a number of colleges have combined social service concepts with traditional academic pursuits. In spite of the fact that neither students nor faculty know what the students mean by "relevance," some effort is made to give students some contact with, or skills they can ostensibly carry back to, the black community. Few of them try to find out what the black community thinks is "relevant" to its needs. Then, too, such an objective clearly reveals other inconsistencies in goals. Although established at predominantly white universities apparently for all students, no consideration is given to the "relevance" of the programs to the white community. Of course, some blacks and whites argue that such programs are intended solely for Negro students.

Black students have demanded that black studies, above all else, should be "relevant" to their needs. As far as one can determine, the programs are supposed to give them pride, a sense of personal worth, and the tools for restructuring society. The attempts to fulfill the last objective are often the most confusing and contradictory aspects of the programs. Rarely is there much thought about what is needed to restructure society. Many students apparently forget that it is still true that the first requirement in any struggle is to know your enemy. What blacks need more than anything else is much more sophisticated knowledge about American society. It is not enough to know that "whitey" has been, and is, oppressing blacks; most Negroes do not have to go to college to learn that. Instead, Negroes must study business practices, high finance, labor law and practices, judicial procedures, consumer practices and the communications media.

Armed with this knowledge, blacks would know which of the interlocking corporations to boycott or buy stock in to bring about meaningful change in their economic position. Knowledge of labor unions may enable blacks to break down the almost invulnerable conspiracy to prevent blacks from earning a living that is based on the tripod of nepotism, political corruption, and prejudice. With serious study we may learn that injunctions, boycotts, campaigns for open shops in union states, government-operated apprenticeship programs, application of conspiracy laws, and other devices may force the unions to loosen their stranglehold on the black worker. While a study of the law may convince us that it is a device for oppression of the poor, we may find enough loopholes in it to afford some degree of protection to the weak. Investigation of law enforcement practices may permit Americans to regain civilian control over our quasi-military, autonomous police. A clearer understanding of the communications media may enable us not only to increase black representation in the publishing, radio, television and advertising fields, but to change white attitudes toward blacks and to create a more favorable image of blacks in the communications media. These are the things that are most "relevant" to the black community.

For many white colleges, faced with the demand to lower admission standards to take in more black students, black studies represents a "soft" program that these students can pass. While I believe that it is criminal for any college to admit poorly prepared students without establishing academic support programs to help them, I do not think there is any predominantly white college that has the experience or the will to do this. If they are serious in their endeavors to establish academic support programs for poorly prepared students, they will have to turn for advice to predominantly Negro colleges, which have had a great deal more experience in this area. Even so, a program that lacks academic respectability is of no use at all to black students and is certainly irrelevant to the black community.

The reasoning behind many of the black studies programs is more sinister than I have indicated. It is clear that in many cases predominantly white schools have deliberately organized ill-conceived programs because they are intended solely for Negro students. In short, a number of institutions are not seriously committed to Afro-American studies. Some professors at one of the leading universities in the country will approve, without question, any proposal for black studies because they say "it's only for the niggers." At a time when most traditional departments in state universities find it difficult to operate on a million dollar annual budget, black studies programs are established with a budget of less than a quarter of a million dollars to use for teaching personnel *and* a plethora of community action programs. Many colleges are not seriously committed to black studies because they feel the demand will die out shortly. Consequently, rather than setting aside university funds to establish the programs, they turn to foundations for support. This, of course, is not conducive to long-term planning. As our experience with Latin American studies reveals, the cycle of foundation interest in such programs is, at most, ten years. The cycle for black studies, I predict, will be even shorter. The foundation money is likely to dry up very quickly when Mao Tse-tung perfects his intercontinental ballistic missile—then, we will embark on Chinese studies.

The lack of commitment extends beyond inadequate financial support to far more serious realms. The most serious is the elimination of any required standards for teachers. While I accept many of the complaints against the traditional academic degrees, it is clear that Urban League officials and local black preachers are not, in very many cases, prepared to teach the college level courses in black studies that they have been assigned. Similarly, while I share the general arrogance of college teachers who feel they can teach anything in their general field, it is too late for most of us to retool quickly to teach topics we have ignored for twenty and thirty years. Yet, because of the lack of commitment and the urgent demand, many colleges are hiring all manner of people to teach black-oriented courses, especially if they are black. Social workers, graduate students who have just embarked on their graduate careers, high school teachers, principals, and practically anyone who looks black or has mentioned Negroes in an article, book or seminar paper are hired to teach Afro-American courses.

These poorly prepared teachers are hired in some cases to discredit the whole program. Given such teachers and in the face of such designs, black and white students are justified in running the teachers out of the classrooms as they have done in many cases.

Generally, Negro students have demanded that black instructors teach black-oriented courses. In many ways I sympathize with them. Having faced unprepared white teachers who have sometimes had to get their reading lists from the black students and who have not learned that Negro is spelled with an "e" instead of an "i," the black students are skeptical. Besides, they reason, it was the white scholar who, by his writing and teaching, made the Negro the "invisible man" of American scholarship. It is certainly asking a lot to expect one to accept cheerfully a man who has continuously embezzled from him his pride, culture, history and manhood for more than four hundred years.

In spite of these considerations, the black students often go too far. All white teachers are not racists. I submit that some of them have more "soul" than some blacks. "Blackness," in all its shades, represents no mystical guarantee of an "understanding" of the black man's problems, life or culture. Neither color nor earnestness but training must be the test applied to any teacher. Since many black students suffer from contact earlier with poorly trained teachers, it is more of a disservice to them than to white students to add more ill-prepared instructors at the last stage of their education. Yet, in their fervor to find black teachers, Negro students ignore the possible crippling effects of hiring simply *any* black man. They have often suggested teachers whom no administrator, regardless of his designs, could accept. For example, a group of black students in one college suggested that a Negro graduate student who had not completed a year of graduate study be hired to teach a Negro history course. Upon investigation, it was discovered that the student in question had already flunked out of graduate school during the first semester.

The black students, however, must be applauded for forcing predominantly white colleges to come to grips with their discriminatory hiring practices. Still, the revolution in this area will fall short if Negro students only demand black teachers for black-oriented subjects. Instead, they must broaden their demands into other areas. How many blacks do we have teaching mathematics, biology, engineering or law at predominantly white schools? Faculty desegregation must expand into these areas if the black scholar is not to end up in an intellectual straitjacket where he is restricted to black-oriented subjects.

The threat to black intellectuals is real. Not only do the black students demand that the teachers in black studies programs be Negroes, they also want them to have the right shade of "blackness." In essence, this means that the black scholar must have the right ideological leanings. As some of us succumb to the persuasive arguments to hop on the treadmill and try to keep up with the mercurial changes in the black "party line," serious scholarship is likely to suffer. It is in this regard that the control of black studies programs by black students is most dangerous. Black scholars being considered for positions in these programs must not only gain the approval by the faculty of their academic credentials, they must also kowtow to the black students. On one occasion a friend of mine, after receiving faculty approval of his appointment at one college, was required to pay obeisance to the black students. Flamboyant by nature, he went home, donned flowing African robes, returned, wowed the students and received the appointment. The case of another black scholar was more tragic. After being approved by the faculty, he went before the black students to prove his ideological fitness. When he opened his remarks to them by pointing out that he had a white wife, the students rejected him. In spite of his qualifications he was not hired.

I do not mean to imply by the preceding remarks that I reject student involvement in decisions that affect their lives. On the contrary, I feel that we must do much more in this direction. In no case, however, should student control go so far as to restrict the intellectual freedom of the scholar. Even if one wants to push "black realism," this is not the way to do it. Black intellectuals have worked so long and hard in their fight against the white intellectual establishment, often publishing their own books when white publishers rejected them because they were unorthodox, that they do not want manumission from their white masters only to be enslaved by black masters. In short, while we support student involvement, we reject it for black studies until the same degree of student control is extended to other areas.

Often, when the Negro scholar escapes the ideological snare of the black students, he faces the almost equally dangerous trap of being overworked by his white colleagues. Frequently, because he is one of few blacks on the faculty, presidents and deans use him as a flying troubleshooter to defang militant students. Inevitably, he is appointed to every committee that is related in any way to Negroes (and the list of them seems limitless). Then, too, the Negro scholar is expected to serve as father-confessor, counselor, success model, substitute parent, general dispenser of pablum to overwrought black students, and all-around authority on the "Negro problem." Consequently, the Negro scholar finds himself more overworked than when he taught fifteen hours a week in a predominantly Negro school. The danger in all of this is that black scholars may find that they have almost no time for research and writing. Few students and administrators realize that by requiring an inordinate amount of work from black scholars they are seriously crippling them in their efforts to find out more about the black experience.

Few students seem to realize that their demands for black faculty are causing raids of major proportions on the faculties of Negro colleges. Of course, some students have insisted that their schools raid only other white colleges. The impact of the current raiding practices (and they are likely to increase) on the Negro colleges is not clear. On the one hand, predominantly white colleges are finding that it is not easy to entice Negro faculty away from places they have been for several years. Many black professors disdain the offers because they do not feel the predominantly white colleges will follow through later on promotions. Others argue that they were told to go and teach "their people" ten years ago and to hell with the white schools that have suddenly discovered them. Where were they ten years ago when they were really needed? Many black professors refuse the offers because they realize that their white colleagues will not respect their academic credentials.

In spite of all the hue and cry from black college administrators, the raids have had a salutary effect on the position of the black faculty member. Deans are suddenly discovering that they can add $5,000 to an instructor's salary at the same time that they cut his teaching load by six hours. Since he is now the rarest gem in the academic marketplace, the black teacher is rapidly approaching parity with his white colleagues in the perquisites of the profession. In many cases, black administrators have used the raiding as a lever to pry more money out of reluctant state legislatures for teaching salaries.

The demands of black students for separate, autonomous black studies departments, separate social centers and dormitories have been a godsend to white racists engulfed by the liberal wave of the last ten years. Ivy League Ku Klux Klansmen applaud and vigorously support such demands. The immediate capitulation of white colleges to such demands is understandable: they support their traditional beliefs and practices. Take Harvard, for example. When a Negro graduate of Harvard, Roscoe Conkling Bruce, tried to reserve a room in the freshman dormitory for his son in 1923, President A. Lawrence Lowell refused the request. He wrote Bruce:

I am sorry to have to tell you that in the freshman halls we have felt from the beginning the necessity of excluding Negroes. I am sure you will understand why we have thought it impossible to compel the two races to live together.

In April of the same year the Board of Overseers of Harvard voted unanimously that "men of the white and Negro races shall not be compelled to live together."

By endorsing the shibboleths of "self-determination," many

white intellectuals are really supporting a recrudescence of "separate but equal" facilities. In this regard, black students can appreciably close the generation gap by asking their parents what separate facilities mean in practice. Few of them have forgotten that a separate railroad car meant uncomfortable, dilapidated, filthy, rarely cleaned cars where black women were insulted by drunken white hooligans. Separate residential areas meant, and still do mean, unventilated, rarely heated, overcrowded, unpainted apartments with high rents, few city services, consistent violation of housing codes by unfeeling landlords who go unpunished by city officials, and black men and women dying of tuberculosis and in firetraps, and black babies dying from rat bites.

When it has been possible for whites to give Negroes separate educational facilities, this has been done with enthusiasm. The result has always been disastrous. Separate facilities have never been equal. It is incomprehensible that black students can trust what they call the "white power structure" to provide separate but equal facilities at the same time that the current administration, as conservative as it is, has found that several Southern states are still offering separate but unequal education to blacks and whites. The evidence of this is overwhelming. A cursory check of state expenditures to black and white colleges supports the charge. How can blacks receive an equal education in Florida when the state expenditures for white colleges were twenty-seven times larger than appropriations for Negro colleges in 1963? For those who eschew research, an on-the-site investigation would be instructive. Who can compare the small cinderblock buildings of Southern University in New Orleans with the shiny, commodious brick buildings of Louisiana State University right down the street and believe that separate facilities can be equal?

Are predominantly white colleges any more justified in bowing to the demand of black students for separate social facilities and black roommates than they are for bowing to the same demands of white students? The answer is an unequivocal no. Instead, they must react the way Columbia University did in 1924 when a group of white students threatened to leave a dormitory because a Negro student was admitted. Dean Hawkes spoke for the faculty when he asserted: "If any student finds his surroundings uncongenial, there is no need for him to stay in Farnald Hall or anywhere else at the University."

I understand the very persuasive arguments of many black students that they need these separate facilities for emotional reinforcement. I sympathize with them but reject their argument. I have read too many autobiographies of black men who studied at white institutions when racism was much more violently overt and when they were much more deprived educationally and culturally than any of these students are, to accept their facile arguments. Often the lone student at Yale, Harvard, Oberlin, Iowa State and other colleges, these men succeeded in spite of the lack of organized programs of emotional reinforcement.

A number of predominantly white colleges have not only utilized black studies to set up separate social facilities for blacks, they have also organized all-black classes for their Negro students. When the black students at a California college complained that they were being used as resource persons in a "Racism in America" course, a separate all-black section was established with a black psychologist as the teacher. The reaction of the students to the course was mixed. One group told me that it was a great course because the teacher required no reading; allegedly, since all of the blacks understood white racism, they simply met and "rapped" with each other. The more astute students described the course as a "bull session" where everybody "got down on whitey."

While some California schools have retrograded further than most colleges, many of the others are not far behind. Even when these programs have been open to all students, the belligerent attitudes of the black students have often scared white students away. To the historian all of this is reminiscent of the treatment of black students when many white schools were first desegregated. Many contemporary black students are in these colleges because earlier black men were not even allowed in the classroom with their white classmates when they desegregated white colleges. Is it fair to the memory of men like this for black students to turn their college educations into "bull sessions" that they could have had without going to college?

Inadvertently, the white colleges are reinforcing the growth of apartheid in America, denying black and white students the opportunity to learn to understand all people, and approving the denial of social equality to Negroes. America's predominantly white colleges can follow one of two paths. The current separatist ideologies fostered by black studies plans can only lead to more Negro students feeling like one black Columbia University student who wrote in 1967: "I feel compelled to announce the fact that Columbia College will never be integrated. If half, or even three-quarters of the College population were black, there would still exist two separate and basically unrelated student communities . . ." Another student at Columbia indicated the other direction. He asserted that at Columbia, "Acutely aware of the white-problem-in-America as I am, as prejudiced toward my own people as I am, I have still found individuals—not black—whom I can respect, admire, and even love."

I realize that any new program may initially encounter many problems. Those that I outlined above, however, can be avoided. The Negro community has too much at stake—its very existence—for the college community, again, to miss an opportunity to begin to end the centuries of neglect and repression of blacks in America. Black studies is too serious an intellectual sphere, has too many exciting possibilities of finally liberating the racially shackled American mind, for intellectuals to shirk their responsibility to organize academically respectable programs. This possibility of curricular innovation must not be used to establish totally different programs, segregated entirely from traditional schemes. Instead, we must take advantage of this opportunity to enrich the educational experiences of all students and teach them to think and to understand more clearly the problems of their age. While we may make our admissions procedures more logical in an effort to find more Negro students, they must be required, whether in black studies or in any other program, to meet the requirements that all other students must meet to graduate. The black community has suffered too much already from the "Negro degrees" given to us in the past by predominantly white colleges.

I do not mean to imply by the remarks made above that the growing maze of black studies programs has been developed only for sinister reasons. In all probability most of the individuals establishing and supporting them have been sincere. But goaded by the emotional demands of black students and pushed by a growing sense of guilt at having fiddled while America burned, many white intellectuals have organized instant programs of little worth. Characteristically, intellectuals, frustrated by their inactive lives, often want to propose fuzzy plans for the immediate eradication of ills. In this instance they have been hamstrung by two things. On the one hand, the guilt they feel for having contributed to the perpetuation of racism in America causes them to clutch frantically at any straw that may atone for their sins. On the other, they are forced by the masterful rhetorical play on this guilt by black students to accept the most far-reaching and often unworkable plans for a total restructuring of American society. The key to the dilemma is the rhetoric of the black students.

Adopting the classic political technique of demanding more

than one is willing to accept, black students discovered very quickly that white intellectuals actually believed that their demands were nonnegotiable. Consequently, white intellectuals have established programs that are, in many instances, practically closed to white students, are soothing to their consciences because they seek to provide services to the black community that only the state can provide, are organized and controlled by students, are contrary to the logical pattern of existing programs, are based solely on emotional rather than intellectual needs, are designed to perpetuate the white myth that Negroes cannot compete on an equal basis, are suited to contemporary problems rather than equipping students to propose new solutions to the ever-changing nature of proscriptions against blacks in America, and permit Negroes to learn about themselves at the expense of knowledge about the larger American society with which they must battle. Such programs represent poor preparation indeed for black men who must survive in a white society.

The most serious effect of student rhetoric on black studies programs is undoubtedly the white acceptance of the demand for combining community action, academic and counseling programs. I agree with the students that the university cannot fulfill its *raison d'être* by ignoring community needs. Similarly, I feel that some students, in the best tradition of Rousseau, should have first-hand knowledge of the community in which they live. To provide this through community action programs is, of course, an enormous undertaking. A few years ago when Howard University officials adopted a community action program for the Washington census tract with the worst social problems, they found that the $400,000 they invested in the program made little impact. The problems encountered in our mini-war on poverty are also instructive in this regard. The poverty program with its well-meaning, paternalistic, relatively well-financed activities has not only in many cases been less than beneficial, but has often been positively destructive, to the black community. In light of the desire of blacks to "do their own thing," how are we to react to another series of paternalistic programs directed by people in the so-called "white power structure"?

Such programs can, of course, be highly successful. First, however, they must be much more carefully planned than most of those I have seen. One gets the vague impression upon reading many of the proposals that a horde of idealistic black, and maybe white, students are going to be let loose on the black community. Black men and women have played in this scene many times before. Nothing could be more self-defeating. A few weeks ago I watched a team of young, highly committed, but wholly undirected VISTA workers unintentionally insult blacks in their first public contact with them in a small rural Louisiana community. In light of the tensions in urban areas, community action programs must be well organized, carefully planned, and amply funded. They must, in addition, involve community leaders in the initial planning stages of the programs.

One question that apparently never arises in connection with this aspect of black studies proposals is how much community involvement students actually want. Are contemporary students *that* different from those of my own generation? Do they really have that much time after studying? In many cases investigation has shown that at the same time that students demand more community action programs they rarely participate in those that the colleges have already established.

While the lack of serious thought behind many of these programs can be hidden by skipping over objectives and using glittering generalities in regard to the community action arm, all of the confusion, guilt and sinister designs are revealed in the list of courses. All of the proposals begin by hiding the colleges' sins behind grandiose claims about the number of black-oriented or related courses they already offer. Many of these are often very tangentially related to blacks under the broadest conception possible. The revelations about the nature of the programs, however, are in the new courses. I realize the variations on a black theme may be endless, but I am frankly amazed as I read the list of some new courses. While it may be possible to teach a course on the "Afro-American on the Frontier," I have serious doubts about the course proposed for one black studies program entitled "The Sociology of Black Sports." And although we have done very little research on the Negro family, it may be possible to teach a course on the subject. But can we, as one college proposes, offer one course on "The Black Family in the Urban Environment" and another one on "The Black Family in the Rural Environment"? What in the world is the course proposed in a California state college entitled "Relevant Recreation in the Ghetto"? This same school must have had a deeply disturbed home economist on its black studies committee, for it also proposed that one of the relevant courses for the Afro-American program should be "The Selection and Preparation of Soul Food."

That delectable tidbit indicates clearly the slim intellectual base of many programs. Even when the programs have not been this shallow, they have often been planned with little thought of what is going on in the American educational establishment. The contemporary revolution in public school textbooks, the burgeoning summer institutes, and rapid changes in public school offerings are bound to catch up with many college-level black studies programs in the next few years. The number of courses one takes is irrelevant if the reading list and general information are the same as that one received in high school. After all, the thrill of hearing Crispus Attucks praised in the first grade, rediscovered in the eighth, revived in the twelfth, and finally "evaluated" in college is just as deadening as our annual peregrinations with Columbus. Dry rot is already surfacing in some programs. Some students find that the "Introductory Seminar in Afro-American Studies" often exhausts the books and articles the teachers in their other courses are able to find. Strangely enough, the reading list for the "Sociology of Race Relations" is often identical to the one for "The Afro-American in American History." The toleration level of students for this kind of shallowness is understandably low.

While all of the problems I have indicated place black studies in serious jeopardy, they are not insurmountable. To overcome these obstacles we have to plot new courses for black studies. First, the programs should be rationally organized, fitted into the total pattern of university offerings, be directed to the needs of all students, amply funded, and as intellectually respectable as any other college program. The same qualifications should be required of teachers, the same work of students, and there should be clearly stated objectives, as there are in other academic programs. Community action programs must be separated from academic programs and adequately financed, staffed and truly related to community needs. Finally, if any of these programs is to succeed, we must break out of our airtight cage of guilt and emotionalism to the open arena where we can establish a meaningful dialogue on black studies.

Indians in History

The white man's books speak with forked tongue

Alvin M. Josephy, Jr.

Mr. Josephy, a vice president of American Heritage,
is the author of three distinguished books about Indians.
His new book, *The Artist Was a Young Man:
The Life Story of Peter Rindisbacher,*
has just been published by the
Amon Carter Museum in Fort Worth.

It is only eighty years, less than the life-span of men and women still alive, since the so-called Battle of Wounded Knee in December, 1890. That massacre, in which some three hundred American Indian men, women, and children were slaughtered on the plains of South Dakota by the raking fire of Hotchkiss guns, ended the last desperate struggle for freedom by the Sioux people and brought to a close within our country what most Indians realize—and what historians must inevitably realize—was the military conquest of one race by another, begun in the Caribbean four hundred years before when Columbus landed on San Salvador Island. The historical significance of the long, armed conflict not only is still with us but is at the root of much of the understanding of the American past and present.

From the beginning, American Indians, their cultures, life-styles, values, and history, have been closely interwoven with the course of the white man's affairs. Much of our culture and many of our attitudes about ourselves and peoples in the rest of the world reflect the Indian-white contact. Yet the true nature of the Indian's role is almost unknown to the non-Indian.

Almost twenty years ago Bernard DeVoto put his finger on one of the wellsprings of the problem. "Most of American history," he wrote, in an introduction to Joseph Kinsey Howard's *Strange Empire,* "has been written as if history were a function solely of white culture—in spite of the fact that till well into the nineteenth century the Indians were one of the principal determinants of historical events. . . . Disregarding Parkman's great example, American historians have made shockingly little effort to understand the life, the societies, the cultures, the thinking, and the feelings of Indians, and

disastrously little effort to understand how all these affected white men and their societies."

A perceptive study done recently by Virgil J. Vogel, an assistant professor of history at Chicago City College, underscores what DeVoto wrote in 1952, and what is still pertinent today. Vogel examined more than one hundred major works on American history, many of them used as influential sources by other historians, and concluded that, as a body, they obliterated, defamed, disparaged, and disembodied the American Indian, creating and perpetuating false impressions about him and producing "deformed" history by not relating accurately or in proper proportion his role in our past.

The blackout of information about the Indians Vogel found particularly disturbing. As a case in point, he examined the historical treatment of the Trail of Tears, the forced removal of more than 125,000 Indians from the Southeast during the Administrations of Andrew Jackson and Martin Van Buren, a cruel and tensely controversial episode that occurred in defiance of the Supreme Court, cost the lives of thousands of Indians, and brought hardship, suffering, and ruin to tens of thousands of others. Debate over the infamous removal policy racked the nation for a decade, pitted the President of the United States in a dramatic confrontation with the Chief Justice of the Supreme Court, increased conflict between North and South, and added to the States Rights and Nullification embers smoldering in the South prior to the Civil War.

Yet Vogel found few, and then usually little more than passing, references to the entire episode in the histories he examined. Edward Channing's *History of the United States,* W. E. Woodward's *A New American History,* Carl Becker's *The United States, Experiment in Democracy,* Francis Butler

Simkins' *The South, Old and New,* and Charles and Mary Beard's *The Making of American Civilization, Basic History of the United States,* and *The Rise of American Civilization* were among the many general histories that either totally ignored mention of the removal policy or failed to tell what happened to the Indians. Even Arthur M. Schlesinger, Jr.'s, full-length, Pulitzer Prize-winning treatment of that particular period, *The Age of Jackson,* included not a single word about the Indians' Trail of Tears.

Defamation and disparagement of the Indians, calling attention to their faults and none of their virtues, ignoring or denying their contributions, and condemning them to an inferior, or even subhuman, species in intelligence and adaptability, colored almost every work of history that Vogel encountered. Many historians termed them dirty, lazy, brutish, unproductive, and on a level with wild beasts.

Vogel found the theme of denigration continuing unabashedly even into modern-day works, whose author added patent untruths about the Indians. "The Indians had no bona fide medicine to speak of," wrote Alden T. Vaughan in *New England Frontier* (in fact, Vogel pointed out, the Indians of North America used about 150 medicines which were later included in the *U. S. Pharmacopeia* and *National Formulary,* and the Indians of Latin America contributed about fifty more). "American civilization . . . owed very little to the aborigines of the New World," commented Richard N. Current and his collaborators, T. Harry Williams and Frank Freidel, in their *American History, A Survey:* ". . . none had any conception of the wheel." (False: the wheel was known in Middle America and was used on children's toys.)

Research beyond Vogel's work will provide anyone willing to make the effort with abundant examples to add to his list. The storehouse of sectional, state, cultural, intellectual, and specialized histories shows, almost without exception, the same sort of treatment of Indians. Typical of such works is Charles S. Sydnor's *The Development of Southern Sectionalism 1819–1848,* whose stated purpose was to present a "full and impartial study of the South and its part in American history." In the text's 399 pages, there are only four brief references to the political and legal contest between the federal and state governments over the Indians' presence in the South and none at all to the Indian peoples themselves or to what happened to them. The word Cherokee appears three times in the volume, but not in the index, and there are no references to works on Indian affairs in the otherwise ample bibliography. Similarly, Perry Miller's two volumes on the New England mind in the sev-

enteenth century almost entirely ignore the Indians' presence among the Puritans. The work carries as a frontispiece in both volumes an early New England woodcut view of Boston, with a benign-looking Indian looming prominently in the foreground as if symbolizing the presence and influence of Indians in New England colonial life. In the text the Indian is given short shrift, even though it is a study of the century that saw the great King Philip's War threaten the presence *of the white man* in New England.

Major works such as these, resting on original research that gives them authority, set the tone and attitude for lowlier but more numerous studies. In recent years, they too—elementary, high school, and college textbooks, readers, and teachers' guides— have begun to come under scrutiny. In an article which appeared last fall in *The Indian Historian,* a respected and authoritative journal of Indian history published in San Francisco by Indian scholars, Lowell John Bean, an anthropology professor at California State College, Hayward, tore apart a children's text used in the fourth grade in the California public school system, analyzing and correcting a multitude of inaccuracies, distortions, untruths, half-truths, omissions, and stereotyped images of California Indians, and concluded, "What distortions of truth are passed on from one reader to another in California's public schools? What distortions of self-image are being acquired by California's Indian children who are exposed to this book . . . ? The children and their teachers have every right to expect a book such as this to represent the truth. This type of literature must not go unchallenged."

Among Indians themselves, as might be expected, dissatisfaction with histories and school textbooks is not new. In 1965, Rupert Costo, a California Cahuilla Indian scholar, wrote in *The Indian Historian,* "No matter who he may be, the Indian backs away in disgust and horror from most textbooks used to teach children American history."

As far back as 1928, Indians living in Chicago and grouped in an organization known as the Grand Council Fire of American Indians addressed a Memorial to William Hale Thompson, the Chicago mayor, who was then criticizing school books for being pro-British. "We do not know if school histories are pro-British," the Indians said, "but we do know that they are unjust to the life of our people—the American Indian. . . . History books teach that Indians were murderers—is it murder to fight in self-defense? Indians killed white men, because white men took their lands, ruined their hunting grounds, burned their forests, destroyed their buffalo. . . . White men who rise to protect their property are called patriots—Indians who do the same are called murderers. White men call the Indians treacherous—but no mention is made of broken treaties on the part of the white man. . . . White men called Indians thieves—and yet we lived in frail skin lodges and needed no locks or iron bars. White men called Indians savages. What is civilization? Its marks are a noble religion and philosophy, original arts, stirring music, rich story and legend. We had these . . . . Tell your children of the friendly acts of Indians to the white people who first settled here. . . . The Indian has long been hurt by these unfair books. We ask only that our story be told in fairness."

For many years, California Indian scholars working with the editors of *The Indian Historian* have been engaged in a professional program of evaluating and criticizing books used in the California school system and elsewhere. "Our Committee read 15 basic and supplementary textbooks," an interim report said. "Not one was free from error and misrepresentation. At least three should be replaced as quickly as possible. All others need extensive revision."

In recent years, non-Indian agencies, often under pressure from Indian groups, have begun to make their own studies. Their results, as of last year, were noted in a report on the status of Indian education issued in the fall of 1969 by a subcommittee of the U. S. Senate Committee on Labor and Public Welfare. "A report prepared for the subcommittee by the University of Alaska showed that: 1) Twenty widely used texts contain no mention of Alaska Natives at all. . . ; 2) Although some textbooks provide some coverage of the Alaskan Eskimo, very few even mention Indians; and 3) Many texts at the elementary and secondary level contain serious and often demeaning inaccuracies in their treatment of the Alaskan Native.

"A similar study by the University of Idaho," the subcommittee's report went on, "found Indians continually depicted as inarticulate, backward, unable to adjust to modern Euro-American culture, sly, vicious, barbaric, superstitious and destined to extinction. Minnesota has for years been using an elementary school social studies text which depicts Indians as lazy savages capable of doing little more than hunting, fishing, and harvesting wild rice. California, with its progressive public school program, found in a study of 43 texts used in fourth, fifth, and eighth grades that hardly any mention at all was made of the American Indian's contribution or of his role in the colonial period, gold rush era or mission period of California history, and, when mentioned, the reference was usually distorted or misinterpreted." The states cited, it might be noted, all have large populations of Indian children being taught about their ancestors from these books. At the same time, in New York, the Association on American Indian Affairs, an Indian-interest group supported by contributions principally from non-Indians, analyzed high school textbooks used throughout the country and found that only one in the seventy-five examined was adequate in its treatment of Indians.

What is "adequate" in the historic treatment of Indians? One criterion, certainly, is to treat history accurately and whole, giving fair and balanced attention to all the groups of humans who were involved. The idea is not unique, and, indeed, is being given strong voice today by blacks and other minority groups about the telling of their own roles in American and world history. In the case of the Indians, it means giving proper representation to their side of history and to their presence and achievements in the Western Hemisphere before the "discovery" by Columbus; their spiritual beliefs, social and political organizations; their patriotic motives in fighting to save their homelands and existence; their foods, medicines, utensils, articles of clothing, means of transportation, words, ideas of government, liberty, and the individual worth and dignity of man, much of it bequeathed to the white man by the Iroquois, Delaware, and other tribes. It means conveying an understanding that the so-called "savages" were actually in harmony with nature and their environment; that they had perfect levels of social and political organization, completely right for the size of each group; that they possessed rich and sophisticated cultural heritages that included music, dance, arts, crafts, and lore; and that their values encompassed many that we wish today for modern civilization.

It means, moreover, removing blinders about aspects of Indian-white relations that add perspectives to American history as a whole, such as the Indians' original friendship, everywhere, toward whites; the slave-catchers and others who turned them against whites even before the first settlers arrived; the great Indian war for religious freedom in New Mexico in 1680, when the Pueblos drove all Spaniards out of that region; the organization of the League of the Iroquois and its impact on the political thinking of the English colonists; the struggle of Tecumseh in the early nineteenth century to create an Indian state which might eventually have joined the United States; the victory of Little Turtle and his Indian allies over General Arthur St. Clair in 1791 in which some 600 U. S. troops lost their lives, more than twice the number Custer lost at the Little Big Horn; and the federal government's use of Christian churches to run the

Indian reservations in the 1870s (a startling example of the joining of church and state in the United States).

"We are the bad guys who burned the wagon trains," said Vine Deloria, Jr., a Standing Rock Sioux Indian in his book *Custer Died for Your Sins,* an eloquent statement of the problems the white man has made for the Indians. That enduring image of the raiding, war-whooping Indian still dominates textbooks, novels, movies, and television programs. But back in 1883, Sarah Winnemucca, a Northern Paiute Indian woman from Nevada who had received education in the white men's schools, told in her book *Life Among the Paiutes* how the Indian families were so afraid of the hostile white men streaming through their land in covered wagons that, though they had to get from one side of the trail to the other, they hid during the day and crossed only at night. A new image?

The telling of history straight and whole—as it was—about the Indians, so that we see them as real societies of fathers of families, mothers afraid for their children, patriots, statesmen, wise men, cowards, lovers, and fools (not all men were braves and not all spokesmen were chiefs), implies acceptance of concepts and points of view that not all historians will recognize or welcome.

Since the days of Jamestown and Plymouth, and the writings of John Smith and William Bradford, the relating of American history by white historians has reflected their own Western-civilization-based point of view, as well might have been expected, but what they wrote has also been self-serving. The frontier Indian, resisting white expansion and domination, *had* to be a skulking savage. To the seeker of his land, he *had* to be an aimless nomad. To the exploiter, he *had* to be irresponsible and drunken. To the civilizer, he *had* to be lazy. Even the romantic, the poet, and the philosopher had to give the Indian a false image: to them he was the noble child of nature. To almost no one could he be real.

Today, the historian who wishes to convey a better sense of the true history of Indians has little reliable historical literature on which to draw. Three and a half centuries of telling American history from the point of view of the intruder, moving from East to West across the continent in the wake of "discoverers," "explorers," "openers of the country," provide scant groundwork for a new approach. The answer, so far, seems to be to tack on, as a sort of preface prior to discussing "The Age of Discovery," an appreciative survey of 25,000 years of Indian history in the Western Hemisphere before the coming of the white man, and then to touch base conscientiously with the Indians as often as appears correct through the main body of the text.

This approach was followed by Samuel Eliot Morison and Henry Steele Commager's *The Growth of the American Republic* with enough success to win praise from Vogel as "perhaps the most nearly flawless college text" from the point of view of its attention to Indians. Still, the work—though indeed a monumental improvement over most other general histories in its treatment of the Indians—is inexact in many archaeological and anthropological details which, were they errors in history, would not be tolerated by the authors, and the principal body of the text contains enough other flaws to make clear the dimensions of the wilderness in which the historian must wander when he genuinely seeks learning on Indian matters.

He must examine colonial, territorial, War Department, Indian Bureau, and other governmental agency archival records, with which he will feel comfortable, but he must also pore through the very valuable historical researches that accompanied Indian claims cases. He must become familiar with the pertinent diaries, logbooks, letters, and other writings of explorers, trappers, traders, missionaries, artists, soldiers, miners, settlers, and government agents, some of them French, some Spanish, some English, many of them obscure, but all of them potential suppliers of new insights, as well as information, about the Indians with whom they came in contact.

He must learn the versions and lore of the tribes themselves, listen to the oral history of those who kept the records from generation to generation, and read the published and unpublished writings of Indians who tell, truer than most historians have been willing to believe, what really happened, at least on the Indian side. Books like *Black Elk Speaks,* a narrative history of the Oglala Sioux told by an Oglala holy man; *Cheyenne Memories,* a Northern Cheyenne history written by a Cheyenne scholar, John Stands In Timber; and *Two Leggings,* the narrative of a nineteenth-century Crow, relate better than any white man's account could, the thinking and feelings of the people of those tribes that made them act and react as they did during the turbulent period of the Plains wars. Written without the benefit of the perspectives of these books, chapters on the history of those wars—and there have been plenty of such works that reflect only the white man's point of view about what the Indians did and why—must inevitably be deficient. Finally, and perhaps most important of all, the historian will have to enter the door of other disciplines, drawing particularly on the great mass of archaeological and ethnological studies that are already available, and becoming, in the process, enough of an ethnohistorian to make the

Indians three-dimensional and understandable when he writes about them.

There are now some 750,000 Indians and Eskimos in the United States, and many of their children are attending schools and colleges where they are subjected to the use of insulting books. Their high dropout rates, self-hatred, a suicide rate far in excess of the national average, and their lack of motivation can be traced in great part to the feelings of disgrace and humiliation they suffer from their continual confrontation with stereotype thinking about them.

From the point of view of the American people as a whole, the damage is just as serious. The problems we have created for the Indians continue to defy solution because we do not know their history or their true nature. To our detriment, we do not know what they might be able to teach us about conservation, the rearing of children, psychosomatic medicine, and the attainment of harmonious and ordered lives. And we fail utterly to appreciate how knowledge of our mistakes in our treatment of the Indians might now help us in our relations with other peoples in the world.

Fortunately, a number of correctives to the long centuries of blackouts, distortions, and misinformation are beginning to appear. More and better books, written by Indians and non-Indians, and explaining the historic causes of present-day problems, are beginning to appear. Notable among them are Vine Deloria, Jr.'s, *Custer Died for Your Sins,* Stan Steiner's *The New Indians,* the Citizens Advocate Center's *Our Brother's Keeper,* Jack D. Forbes's *The Indian in America's Past,* and Stewart Levine's and Nancy O. Lurie's *The American Indian Today.* Even the field of fiction has struck newly realistic notes for the Indian with Thomas Berger's *Little Big Man* (now being made into a movie, with Indians playing most of the Indian roles) and the Pulitzer Prize novel for 1969, *House Made of Dawn,* by N. Scott Momaday.

In the mass communications field, the television industry, with its endless stock portrayals of Indians that never existed, has many sins to live down, including a series that glorified Custer, which pressure by angry Indians two years ago forced the offending network to cancel. But in its journalistic programs filmed on Indian reservations, its discussion panels on Indian affairs, and its documentaries that are beginning to deal with Indian history, television is starting to make amends. One of TV's outstanding ventures is a documentary history of the Cherokees' Trail of Tears, the first of a projected series of four programs on Indians produced by National Educational Television for countrywide showing. Filmed on the same sites in the South where the history occurred, the film stars Johnny Cash, himself a descendant of Cherokees, playing the role of John Ross, the principal chief of the Cherokee nation during the time of the tribe's forced removal to the West. The drama of the program is matched by the faithfulness with which it re-creates the true history of what happened to the Indians.

At the same time, Indians themselves are beginning to research and write their own tribal histories, principally for the use of their people and for the schools on their reservations or in the states in which the reservations are located. Programs for such histories, undertaken by Indian scholars and sometimes aided by non-Indian historians and anthropologists, are under way among the Poncas, Choctaws, Pawnees, Blackfeet, Navajo, Rosebud Sioux, and Quinaults, among other tribes, while in various cities and on Alcatraz Island, which the Indians occupied in dramatic fashion last November, groups of Indians who have lived urbanized existences and come from many different tribes have created Indian cultural centers to teach their own people Indian history, language, and culture.

Demands by Indians and various of their organizations, including the National Congress of American Indians and the National Indian Youth Council, have also stirred many universities into new activities. With a $500,000 annual grant from the Doris Duke Foundation, six of them—the universities of Utah, Arizona, Illinois, New Mexico, Oklahoma, and South Dakota—embarked several years ago on an ambitious Indian oral-history program, sending interviewers with tape recorders onto reservations to record the legends, lore, and histories from the Indians themselves. Transcripts from the tapes already run into thousands of manuscript pages and will provide the raw materials for many history books of the future. In addition, courses in Indian studies and revised courses in American history that include a fuller and fairer treatment of the American Indian are being included in the curriculum of many colleges and universities. Perhaps the most important milestone was reached in March at Princeton University, with the holding of a four-day convocation of American Indian scholars under the auspices of the American Indian Historical Society and funded by a grant from the Ford Foundation. The Indian participants, who came from Canada, Mexico, and South America, and the United States, met with the determination that "the leadership and authority of the American Indian in all fields affecting our history, culture, economic improvement and social development must be asserted if any progress is to be attained by our people." In a series of panels, the participants read and discussed papers that ranged in subject from "Philosophy of the American Indian and Relation to the Modern World" to "Modern Psychology and Child Development: The Native American Case." The meeting was all-Indian; whites were limited to a few academic and professional observers.

On the elementary and high school level, also, new winds are blowing. In Montana, as an example, the histories of the tribes in that state are being added to the curriculum of the public school system, largely under the guidance of John Woodenleg, a former tribal chairman of the Northern Cheyenne Indians and a descendant of a Cheyenne leader at the Battle of Little Big Horn.

Finally, the last few years have seen a prolifera-tion of Indian newspapers and magazines, written, edited, and published by Indians on reservations and in various cities, and carrying articles on Indian history and lore, as well as news about Indian affairs. Designed primarily to be read by Indians, they have attracted the attention of many whites also, and some of them enjoy large national circulations among non-Indian readers.

"It is up to us to write the final chapter of the American Indian upon this continent," wrote Vine Deloria, Jr. Perhaps that is the way it will happen. But for the present there is plenty of work to do, by Indians and non-Indians laboring together, to set straight the chapters already written. □

The early history of the United States must recount how, in a remarkable short period of time, a handful of colonies precariously pitched in the wilderness was transformed into a dynamic republic. That transformation demanded imagination, heroism, and sacrifice; it was also propelled by greed, intolerance, and hypocrisy. Americans have been quite willing to recognize the latter faults as characterizing the colonial efforts of England, France, Holland, and Spain while retaining for themselves the sole proprietorship of the former virtues. It is not surprising, therefore, that a more open-minded inspection of the facts has led to viewing early American history as an amalgam of the virtuous and the detestable. Each of the articles in this section sheds some light on the vice-virtue dichotomy that was the founding of this nation.

The religious fervor with which many groups of colonists were imbued has been generally accepted as part of the American heritage, but the intolerance that fervor engendered is little known. In the first selection, "Mary Dyer: Conscientious Dissenter," Don Elton Smith probes the collision of the Quaker conscience of Mary Dyer with the religious strictures of Puritan Boston. Mary Dyer's actions and those of the people of Puritan Boston deserve pondering, for both represent qualities that have coexisted within the American mind down to the present.

Joseph Cullen's "Indentured Servants" is a reminder that the history of American labor began as a mixed bag of promise and exploitation. There can be no doubt that for many, seven years of indentured serviture were a fair price to pay for freedom from the penury and social immobility that generally characterized the poorer classes of European society. There can also be little doubt that indentured serviture was often a callous way of inducing labor into the American wilderness.

Another view of moral equivocation is provided by Richard MacMaster's "Anti-Slavery and the American Revolution." Here he inspects the critical years from 1771 to 1780 in which a white upper class (read "Founding Fathers") contemplated but ultimately rejected the full emancipation and equality of its black underclass (read "Slaves"). The question is still to be fully resolved.

That there are strong parallels between the debate in the United States over the Vietnam War and the debate among Great Britain's ruling classes over the American Revolution is perhaps more than "A Curiosity of History," as Estelle and Saul Gilson have titled their article on this fascinating comparison. Perhaps Americans, having been among the first to initiate the age of nationalistic revolt, should not be surprised that the practice, the agony, and the ultimate consequences of this revolt have yet to go out of fashion.

The final selection is a little-known but revealing story of the ratification of the Constitution in Pennsylvania. In "Don't Put off until Tomorrow What You Can Ram through Today," Robert Alberts provides a ring-side seat in the chambers of Pennsylvania's state legislature from which to watch the pro-Constitution Federalists railroad ratification past the anti-Constitution Democrats. The scene is an absorbing one and goes a long way toward clothing the Founding Fathers in the garb of rough-and-tumble politics of which the celestial light of their success has so often robbed them.

MARY DYER: CONSCIENTIOUS DISSENTER

Jailed for nothing more than attempting to pass through Massachusetts, Mary Dyer spent the rest of her life protesting bigotry—and was jailed, tried, and hanged for her dissent!

by Don Elton Smith

Massachusetts Quakers were jailed, fined—even whipped!

A native Californian and published writer, Don Elton Smith is a student of American history at Claremont Graduate School and is currently working on his first book.

Mary Dyer did not arrive in Boston harbor in July, 1657, as a conscientious dissenter. But her introduction there to the discriminatory and punitive legislation directed against Quakers surely awakened in her the dormant potentialities for it. She and Ann Burden, who came from England on the same ship, were the first members of the Society of Friends (as Quakers were properly called) to come into the Bay Colony following the passage of the anti-Quaker law of October 14, 1656. By the authority of that statute the two women were arrested and imprisoned. So began Mary Dyer's struggle for the repeal of the statutes directed against the Friends. Her persistent attempts to publicly protest what she termed an "unrighteous law" were ended only by her execution three years later.

The repressive legislation enacted by the General Court of Massachusetts had been the result of the Puritan reaction to Friends' missionary activity begun in the Bay Colony the previous year. The Puritan leaders had had earlier reports of the Society of Friends and the enthusiasm and persistence of their witness in England and Barbados. To the Puritan, the Quaker expounded the rankest of heresies: God spoke directly to the man who waited quietly and expectantly for His word.

This was not merely doctrine to the Quaker, but his personal experience. "As I walked after the plough," wrote one English Friend, "I was filled with the Love and the Presence of the Living God which did Ravish my heart when I felt it; ... the Word of the Lord came to me in a still small voice, which I did hear perfectly, saying to me, in the Secret of my Heart and Conscience, 'I have ordained Thee a Prophet unto the Nations.'"

Such sentiments were anathema to Puritan divines, who held that all revelation was in the Bible, that they alone were capable of interpreting Scripture, and that, therefore, only they could declare the will of God. The

From *Mankind*, May 1970. Reprinted from Mankind Magazine, copyright © 1970 by Mankind Publishing Co.

doctrine of the Inner Light was an obvious challenge to their authority. On the other side of the dispute, the Friends of that age were not content to let their lives speak quietly of their faith. They attacked with vividness of phrase and remorseful energy what they termed a hireling ministry.

The first Quaker missionaries to Massachusetts, two English women named Ann Austin and Mary Fischer, arrived in Boston in July, 1656. The Puritan leaders were appalled that such people had come to their colony where there had been established, in their view, a model Christian community destined to be a light to all the world. As the Reverend John Norton expressed it: "The visible-political churches, church officers, church worship and administrations are Gospel-institutions, appointed by Christ, to continue to the end of the world. . . . After New England hath now shined twenty years and more, like a light upon a Hill," could Quaker anarchism be allowed to undermine and destroy it?

It was clear to the Puritan leaders that some effective measure of control had to be introduced. Without any statutory authority, Deputy-Governor Richard Bellingham ordered the women seized before they could leave

William Robinson, Marmaduke Stephenson, and Mary Dyer on their way to the gallows. Mary Dyer was saved   only to be executed later.

the ship. They were arrested, searched, and jailed incommunicado. An imposition of a five pound fine was ordered upon any that should speak to them. Their books, some one hundred volumes, were burned in the market place by the hangman. Stripped naked in the

jail so their bodies might be examined for witch marks, they were "barbarously mis-used" according to one chronicler. So detained for five weeks they were at last sent to Barbados, minus their bedding and Bibles which the jailer retained for his "fees."

On August 7, two days after they had sailed, nine more evangelizing Friends arrived. They also were arrested and warned by Governor John Endicott not to break the colony's ecclesiastical laws. But when he was asked to let them read a copy of those laws, he denied the request. The prisoners were held in close confinement for eleven weeks until transportation was arranged to return them to England.

Nor was the Puritan magistrates' problem solely one of keeping out Quaker intruders. Among church members of the Commonwealth there were indications that more than a few minds were sympathetic to the Quaker position. Nicholas Upsall of Boston had tried to save the Quaker books from burning. He had bribed the jailer to allow him to send food to the imprisoned Friends. Lawrence and Cassandra Southwick, a grave and aged couple of Salem, gave hospitality to Quaker visitors and became the nucleus of a little circle of Friends.

There is an interesting passage in Cotton Mather's ecclesiastical history of New England, *The Magnalia,* that suggests a native Quakerism: "I can tell the world that the first Quakers that ever were in the world were certain fanaticks here in our town of Salem, who held forth almost all the fancies and whimsies which a few years after were broached by them that were so called in England, with whom yet none of ours had the least communication."

Perhaps even more worrisome to the magistrates was the appeal that the Quaker message might have among the more deprived residents of the Bay Colony. They were uncomfortably aware of the existence of social discontent. More than once did Reverend Norton warn about the danger of Quakers, pointing out "the suitableness of their doctrine unto discontented, seditious, factious, and tumultuous spirits, especially if pressed with poverty or a suffering condition. . . ."

This was the situation that led the General Court on October 14, 1656, to pass the first act against Quakers—the statute applied to Mary Dyer and Ann Burden the following July. It provided penalties for three distinct groups of violators. Members of the Society of Friends who dared to come within the jurisdiction of the Commonwealth were to be whipped and then jailed until they could be expelled. Ship captains responsible for bringing Quakers to the colony were to be fined one hundred pounds. Residents of Massachusetts who were found guilty of defense of Quaker opinions, were to be fined forty shillings for a first offense, four pounds for a second, and were to be banished for a third offense.

Only by chance were Mary Dyer and her ship companion, Ann Burden, the first Friends to arrive in the Bay Colony after this enactment. The two Quaker women had not come to Massachusetts as missionaries, nor had they heard of the passage of the repressive legislation. Mary Dyer was merely passing through the colony, while Ann Burden had come to settle the estate of her deceased husband who had been a citizen of Boston.

Apparently because of these very circumstances, the women escaped the prescribed whippings. Ann Burden's goods were confiscated and shipped to Barbados for sale and she was forced to return on the ship by which she had come. Mary Dyer was held in prison until her husband came from Rhode Island and promised to prevent her from speaking to anyone until they were beyond the Massachusetts boundary. The Dyers returned to their home, but Boston was to see more of Mary Dyer.

Conscientious dissenters of the present day often testify that public witness strengthens their convictions and their resolution more than any other preparation or act. How much significance can be attributed to Mary Dyer's first skirmish with the anti-Quaker legislation of Massachusetts? To be jailed for nothing more than attempting to pass through the colony must have made the unreasonableness of that law's application vivid to her. Her jail experience must have made her keenly aware of the starkness of confinement that other prisoners of unjust laws suffered. But the most cogent point is that Mary Dyer's character is of greater significance than her experience. It was not so much what had *happened* to her that tempered her resolve as her *attitude* toward her experience. Almost twenty years earlier in her life she had given dramatic evidence of that character.

It was the year 1635 when Mary Dyer and her milliner husband, William, had moved from New Exchange, London, to settle in Boston. They were members of the Boston church of John Wilson and John Cotton when, in the following year, Anne Hutchinson had begun the meetings that led to her defiance of ministerial authority. Both William and Mary Dyer were implicated in the Hutchinson affair. When the Reverend Wheelwright was condemned, William Dyer signed a protest petition and as a result was disfranchised and disarmed. And, in 1638, when Anne Hutchinson walked out of the meetinghouse for the last time after hearing her sentence of banishment read, Mary Dyer got up, took her hand, and walked out with her.

John Winthrop, governor of Massachusetts and historian of the colony, made the observation that Mary Dyer was "notoriously infected with Mrs. Hutchinson's errors, and very censorious and troublesome, she being of a very proud spirit, and much addicted to revelations." Certainly Mary Dyer displayed a strong sense of loyalty to those whom she felt were unjustly accused. She had the courage to identify herself with them and to dissent publicly from prevailing opinion.

The Dyers, as a result of the Hutchinson episode, had

been banished and had gone to Newport, Rhode Island, with a number of others who were out of harmony with Massachusetts theology. William held a number of

CULVER PICTURES

official positions there and became Attorney-General of the colony in 1649. He and Mary went to England in 1651 — William, in all likelihood, to attend to legal affairs of the colony. When he returned, Mary remained in England. She became acquainted with some of the English Quakers who were experiencing growing persecution at that time. Again she identified herself with the oppressed, joining the Society of Friends and becoming, soon afterward, a recognized minister. She returned to Rhode Island, as has been described, in 1657.

Threats of violence are not effective against the convictions of conscience. Whippings and hangings, it is said, set an example, but they argue a contrary case as well. The nobler spirits of men are evoked by the specter of suffering and they ally themselves with the sufferer. Upon that principle more than one persecuted people has flourished. The Puritans discovered their harsh treatment drew Quakers from without and created them within Massachusetts.

Following Mary Dyer's brief detention in Boston, there were visits to Massachusetts Bay and Plymouth colonies by other Quakers. Eleven crossed the Atlantic in the ship *Woodhouse* in the summer of 1657. It was a curious little ship, built by Robert Fowler, a Quaker convert who had undertaken the project in response to an inner command. It was far too small a craft for ocean travel, yet its builder was impressed that the God of the waters could guide it, as He had directed Noah's Ark. The ship's log, now in the Devonshire House Library, London, provides a remarkable account of the successful navigation of the Atlantic by little more than prayer: "we regarding neither latitude nor longitude (sic), but kept to our Line which was and is our Leader, Guide, and Rule."

Operating from Rhode Island, the Friends made repeated trips into the northern colonies, holding meetings and gaining adherents. Regular Quaker worship began to be held in Salem in the homes of members, even though the magistrates levied fines on the local attenders. Under this steady financial attrition, Lawrence and Cassandra Southwick were harried and fined into a state of poverty and finally banished. Their two children, having no estates to cover their fines, were ordered sold into slavery, but no ship captain was found willing to transport them to Virginia or Barbados for that purpose. Although the intruding Quakers were apprehended, thoroughly whipped, and expelled from the colony, they soon reappeared. Considering the fact that these whippings were customarily laid on with a two-handed whip of three cords, knotted, and thick as a finger, such persistence must have seemed like the ultimate in pig-headed stubbornness to the exasperated magistrates.

The failure of these fines and punishments to stamp out the Friends' activity led the General Court to pass a more stringent law in October, 1657. It provided that if Quakers returned after banishment they were to suffer, for succeeding visits, the loss of one ear, then the other, and finally to have the tongue bored. Women, however, were to be whipped rather than lose their ears. For the third offense they would receive the same treatment as that prescribed for the men. Anyone giving lodging to a Friend was to be fined at the rate of forty shillings per hour of lodging granted. The following May another law provided for a ten shilling fine for profession by any resident of Quaker ways, by either speaking, writing, or attending meetings.

In the months that followed, three of the Friends had their right ears cut off. William Brend was given one hundred and seventeen blows on his bare back with a tarred rope, which the Reverend John Norton thought was fair enough, since Brend had "endeavoured to beat the gospel ordinances black and blue." The townsfolk thought differently, however, and rising public indignation compelled the authorities to summon a physician to try to save the unfortunate Quaker's life, and within a week all the Friends were released from prison.

Thereupon the clergy of the colony, led by Reverend Norton, pressed for a law which prescribed hanging for Quakers returning after being banished. The General Court was seriously divided on such an extreme measure

and it was uncertain that a majority could be convinced of its necessity. As it happened, when a vote was forced, the measure passed 13-12, but only through the failure to summon one of the members, Deacon Wozel.

Wozel was ill that October day and had stayed home. He had requested that he be sent for if a vote was to be taken, as he (and other opponents) were against it on the grounds that a death sentence without a jury trial was against the law of England. To allay these feelings and to avoid possible dissension, in view of the measure's narrow majority, an amendment for trial by jury was added. It was a mockery of English law, however, since the only question the jury was to consider was whether the defendant was a Quaker, a point the defendants readily affirmed.

The General Court issued a statement to justify their position. The colony is like a family, the Court declared, and just as one must protect a family by keeping out of its household the dangerous company of people infected with contagious and mortal disease, so they must defend the Commonwealth. If such people intrude into a household and cannot be kept out, then they may be killed. The colony, they said, was their home; anybody who broke into it might properly be slain in self-defense. Thomas Prince, the successor of the Pilgrim, William Bradford, as Governor of Plymouth, added his own justification, opining that in his conscience, "the Quakers were such a people that deserved to be destroyed, they, their wives and children, their houses and lands, without pity or mercy." Out of this climate of opinion among those of the governing class came these four laws passed in a two year period, in an attempt to drive Quakers from Massachusetts.

Friends gave prayerful consideration to these laws of Massachusetts and the suffering that it brought to men and women who sought no more than to obey an inward leading of the Spirit in their worship of God and witness to men. Four who felt an inner command to go to the Bay Colony were Marmaduke Stephenson, William Robinson, Patience Scott, and Mary Dyer. Stephenson was a Yorkshire farmer who, coming on a religious mission to Barbados, had heard of the enactment of the capital penalty and had hastened to New England. Robinson was one of the *Woodhouse* voyagers. Patience Scott was a niece of Anne Hutchinson, only eleven years old and yet, as she felt, under the "moving of the Lord to bear her testimony against the persecuting spirit."

Together these four walked from Rhode Island to Massachusetts, were apprehended, and brought before the Court of Assistants on September 12, 1659. The accused claimed the right as peaceable and loyal subjects of England to travel throughout her dominions. The Court would not recognize such a contention. On a warrant signed by Edward Rawson, the Friends were

The whipping of Quakers at the cart's tail in Boston. Massachusetts passed the anti-Quaker law on October 14, 1656.

banished and warned they would be hanged if they returned. The men set out for Salem and remained in the Massachusetts area. Patience Scott and Mary Dyer returned to Rhode Island.

But Mary Dyer came back to Boston on October 8 and was imprisoned. Writing from her cell, she addressed the General Court: "Whereas I am by many charged with the Guiltiness of my own Blood; if you mean, in my coming to Boston, I am therein clear, and justified by the Lord, in whose will I came....

"I have no self ends, the Lord knoweth, for if my Life were freely granted by you, it would not avail me, nor could I expect it of you, so long as I should daily hear or see the Sufferings of these people, my dear Brethren and Seed, with whom my life is bound up, as I have done these two years; ....

"Was ever the like Laws heard of, among a People that profess Christ come in the Flesh? And have such no other Weapons, but such laws ...? Of whom take you Counsel? Search with the Light of Christ in ye, and it will show you of whom, as it hath done me and many more, who have been disobedient and deceived, as now you are; ....

"If you neither hear nor obey the Lord nor his Servants, yet will he send more of his Servants among you, so that your end shall be frustrated, that think to restrain them, you call Cursed Quakers, from coming among you, by any thing you can do to them; ....

"In Love and in the Spirit of Meekness I again beseech you, for I have no Enmity to the Persons of any; but you shall know, that God will not be mocked but what you sow, that shall ye reap from him ... Even so be it, faith."

Robinson and Stephenson were apprehended on October 13. Ten other Friends had also come to Boston in the month following the banishment. On October 19, Mary Dyer, Robinson, and Stephenson came before the Court. Asked why they had come to Massachusetts, they answered, "In obedience to the call of the Lord." Governor Endicott hesitated and ordered the prisoners back to the jail. The next day he called them back and, after disclaiming any desire for their death, sentenced them as follows: "Hearken, you shall be led back to the place from whence you came and from thence to the place of execution, to be hanged on the gallows till you are dead."

"The will of the Lord be done," said Mary Dyer.

"Take her away, Marshal," said the Governor.

"Yea, joyfully shall I go," she said.

The execution was set for October 27. In the intervening days the imprisoned Friends sought to speak of God to passersby until they were moved into a low, dark room where they could not see the people. Then they worshiped quietly together.

The community was stirred by the death sentence. A great crowd turned out for the execution, so large that the bridge at North End broke under the weight of those returning home. Marshal Michaelson and Captain James Oliver led the prisoners on the march from jail to the gallows. They were accompanied by two hundred armed men, besides many horsemen, and drums were beat as they marched to prevent the condemned from addressing the populace. Perhaps the authorities were uncertain as to public opinion. The three Quakers walked hand in hand, Mary Dyer between the men.

"Are you not ashamed to walk thus between two young men?" Marshal Edward Nicholson taunted.

"No," the resolute woman replied. "It is an honor of the greatest joy I can enjoy in this world. No eye can see, no ear can hear, no tongue can speak, no heart can understand the sweet incomes and refreshings of the Spirit of the Lord which now I enjoy."

The gallows is traditionally said to have been the "great tree" which, until 1876, stood beside the Frog Pond on Boston Common. The prisoner, after the noose was fitted to his neck, climbed the tree by a ladder and then the ladder was pulled away. In this way William Robinson and Marmaduke Stephenson died. Stephenson's last words were, "We suffer not as evil-doers, but for conscience sake."

Mary Dyer climbed the ladder, her arms and legs were bound and her face was covered with a handkerchief loaned by her former pastor, Reverend Wilson. Only then was she told of her "reprieve." In fact, her death sentence had been feigned from the beginning. The General Court had received pleas from the governors of Connecticut and of Acadia and Nova Scotia not to hang the Quakers. Mary Dyer's son had begged for his mother's life. Whether it was these pleas or a consideration for the temper of the local populace that proved most influential is not clear. At any rate, the Court had decided not to hang her, as is shown by the Colonial Records of October 18, 1659, the day *before* sentence was pronounced: "It is ordered that the said Mary Dyer shall have liberty for forty-eight hours to depart out of this Jurisdiction, after which time, being found therein, she is to be forthwith executed. And it is further ordered that she shall be carried to the place of execution and there stand upon the Gallows with a rope about her neck until the Rest be executed, and then to return to the prison and remain as aforesaid."

Mary Dyer protested that she ought not live if the wicked laws were not annulled. Again she appealed to the magistrates and churchmen with the authority which she felt had been given her, yet with humility: "In obedience to the Lord whom I serve ... I can do no less than once more to warn you, to put away the Evil of your Doings, and kiss his Son, the Light in you, before his Wrath be kindled in you; ... and if these things be not so, then say, 'There hath been no Prophet from the Lord sent amongst you;' tho' we be nothing, yet it is His Pleasure, by Things that are not, to bring to nought Things that are."

As for the reprieve, she said she submitted, "finding

nothing from the Lord to the contrary, that I may know what his Pleasure and Counsel is concerning me, on whom I wait therefore, for he is my Life, and the length of my Days; and as I said before, I came at his Command, and go at his Command." The next day she was put on horseback and sent off to Rhode Island. She had faced Massachusetts law a second time, had made an unequivocal stand against it, but the issue was not yet resolved.

After passing the winter at Shelter Island in Long Island Sound, Mary Dyer departed in the middle of May for Massachusetts. The law of banishment on pain of death was still in force. Its atrociousness was still to be brought home to the men in authority. That, Mary Dyer was convinced, was her work. John Taylor, a Friend from York, England, who was visiting the island during her stay there, wrote: "She said that she must go and desire the repeal of that wicked law against God's people and offer up her life there."

She arrived in Boston on May 21, 1660, and was brought before the Governor on the thirtieth. Endicott, having secured her own word that she was indeed the same Mary Dyer and a Quaker, again passed sentence of death upon her. "This is no more than what thou saidst before," observed the dissenter. "But now," replied the Governor, "it is to be executed. Therefore prepare yourself to-morrow morning at nine o'clock."

Mary Dyer answered him solemnly: "I came in obedience to the will of God at your last General Court, desiring you to repeal your unrighteous laws of banishment on pain of death; and that same is my word now, and earnest request, although I told you that if you refused to repeal them, the Lord would send others of His servants to witness against them."

"Are you a prophetess?" jeered Endicott. But she had scarcely begun to answer when he ordered her taken away.

Reverend John Wilson urged her to repentence on the fateful morning. "Nay, man, I am not now to repent," she replied. Captain Webb remarked that she was guilty of her own blood, since she had returned deliberately and with full knowledge of the law. "Nay," was her rejoinder, "I came to keep Blood-guiltiness from *you*, desiring you to repeal the unrighteous and unjust Law of Banishment upon Pain of Death, made against the innocent Servants of the Lord. . . ." Would she have any of the people pray for her? She said she wanted the prayers of "all the people of God."

As she stood on the ladder of the gallows with the noose around her neck, she was given the opportunity to save herself. If she would promise to leave Massachusetts and never return, she might walk away from that spot. "Nay, I cannot," was her reply. "In obedience to the will of the Lord God I came and in His will I abide faithful to death." Firm in the conviction of her faith and of her mission to Congregational Massachusetts, Mary Dyer was hanged on May 31, 1660.

One more Friend, William Leddra, was hanged the next spring. Twenty-seven others were under sentence but escaped the gallows. Word of the executions had reached King Charles and he had directed that those accused of capital crimes were to be sent to England for trial. The Commonwealth thereupon changed its tactics and ordered savage whippings instead of hanging.

One historian (Brooks Adams) had judged that the Massachusetts magistrates could not have continued the executions even if the King had not intervened. Popular indignation had made it impossible to execute Wenlock Christison, who had been condemned. Even the whippings were checked by public opinion. John Greenleaf Whittier's poem, "How the Women Went from Dover," graphically portrays the constable and citizens of one Massachusetts town refusing to countenance the cruel whipping of three Quaker women. The last persecution of Friends in New England ended in 1677.

Whether or not the magistrates of Massachusetts would have been forced to abandon executions of the Quakers even without the King's intervention, it is clear the undergirding impulse of the reform stemmed fundamentally from the willingness of the few resolute Friends to non-violently challenge the moral validity of the statute by exposing themselves to its application. The same attitude toward the subsequent whippings resulted at last in toleration of Quakers and Quaker meetings.

For Americans, deeply disturbed by the current rash of protests, Mary Dyer stands as a model of the conscientious dissenter. She stood not for the rights of one faction, but of all men. Her faith embraced the interrelatedness of all men through an omnipresent God. She could not undertake, therefore, to destroy her enemies but sought to reconcile them through her personal acceptance of suffering in behalf of her principles. Believing in Brotherhood, she was certain that reconciliation would come if only she were faithful to Truth as God revealed it to her.

By accepting the violence that the government of Massachusetts chose to employ to enforce conformity to their norms of behavior, she pressed the magistrates to face the implications of their position. She helped break the odious laws and the system of enforcing conformity by giving her life in a demonstration to the public of the inhuman character of the system. Concurrently, she and the other Quaker martyrs showed clearly the ineffectiveness of violence as a tool of suppression when it is countered with the conscientious dissent of even a few committed men and women.

Indentured Servants

Most colonials got to America by trading seven years of servitude for passage across the Atlantic.

Joseph P. Cullen

Joseph P. Cullen, a regular contributor and consulting editor for this magazine, is in the National Park Service, formerly a historian now director of public relations in the southeastern jurisdiction.

IN 1607 three English ships arrived safely at Jamestown, Virginia to found the first permanent English colony in the New World. Most of the passengers, other than the officers and "gentlemen," were indentured to work for the Virginia Company for seven years in return for their passage and keep. At the end of that period they could either return to England or take up land for themselves in Virginia and work for the company as free laborers. Despite the hardships suffered by the colonists in those early years and the high mortality rate, some elected to remain.

It soon became evident, however, that the success of the infant colony depended on more people settling there than the Company's system provided. In a country where land was cheap and plentiful and resources abundant, the paramount need was for a large labor supply. Consequently, a system was adopted whereby people coming from Europe could be indentured to individuals as well as to the Company. As an inducement to the colonists in the early years, for each indentured servant they brought in they were granted a "head-right" of fifty acres of land free.

To many English tenant farmers struggling for maintenance on borrowed land, and to the laborers starving under low wages and miserable living conditions, the opportunity to migrate to the New World as an indentured servant came as a welcome release. And although the practice of granting fifty acres to the importer, and generally to the servant at the end of his period of indenture, gradually died out

with availability of cheap land, the system survived for many years and was, in fact, the principal means of peopling the English colonies.

IN 1619 eight ships brought 1,261 new settlers to Jamestown, increasing the population to approximately 2,400 people. Many of these newcomers were

From *American History Illustrated*, April 1967. Reproduced through the courtesy of The National Historical Society, publishers of AMERICAN HISTORY *Illustrated*, 206 Hanover Street, Gettysburg, Pa. 17325. Published 10 times a year.

indentured servants, each of whom signed a contract to work for a master for a specified number of years, usually three to five, in return for his passage and room and board in the New World, after which he would be given a certain amount of clothes and other provisions to help him begin life on his own, along with various amounts of land if he so desired. One servant wrote that his indenture called for "a pigg to be payd at every years end and in the end of the term to have a Convenient lott," along with "three suits of apparel and six shirts." Another was to receive " meat, drink, lodging and apparell, and double apparell at the end of the term."

In those early years few single women came over indentured, and most of those who did were used as domestic servants until they married, but the supply never could meet the demand despite all attempts

This drawing by W. L. Sheppard of the first settlers of Jamestown, Va. illustrates the unwillingness of the gentleman adventurers to dirty their hands in manual labor. Indentured servants seemed a logical answer to such labor problems. ("Pioneers of America")

to encourage emigration. "The Women that go over . . . as Servants," wrote one contemporary, "have the best luck as in any place in the World besides, for they are no sooner on shoar than they are courted into ... Matrimony."

In 1619 the Virginia Company sent ninety young women to become wives of the planters. These were the first of many groups of "younge, handsome, and honestly educated maydes" sent across the Atlantic for this purpose. They were not indentured, however, but were placed in respectable homes until they "happened upon good matches."

That same year a notorious Dutch slaver stopped at the little colony and exchanged twenty Negroes, including two women, for desperately needed provision. As slavery did not then exist in Virginia either by law or custom, some authorities maintain that these people were indentured servants, not slaves, and when their time was up they became free settlers the same as everyone else.

AS THE colony grew and prospered, the number of indentured servants continually increased. Out of almost 5,000 settlers in 1635, about half had arrived indentured to furnish the necessary labor to tame the wilderness into farms and plantations. By 1671 the number had grown to 6,000 and ten years later there were 15,000 indentured workers in Virginia alone. With the gradual development of the other colonies the demand increased proportionately, and it is generally estimated that indentured servants comprised over 60 percent of all immigrants into the colonies down to 1776.

With the increased demand came abuses and irregularities, however. In 1665 the captain of the ship *Recovery* complained that his only cargo on leaving England was forty passengers, "persons utterly useless to this Kingdom, but rather destructive in their idle course of life." The English courts adopted the policy of transporting felons from the jails and lewd women from houses of correction to the New World to be rid of them, and the demand being so great the plantation owners did not hesitate to accept them. Political prisoners and prisoners of war were also often sent abroad. Unscrupulous captains and crews kidnapped many to be sold to the highest bidder in America. Many of these were being pursued by the law for one reason or another, but the kidnappers generally concentrated on the young, the inexperienced, and the friendless, who were usually lured into taverns and then seized and carried forcibly aboard ship.

MANY of those kidnapped it was claimed were "felons condemned to death, sturdy beggars, gipsies, and other incorrigible rogues, poor and idle debauched persons." Historian Beverley, in his famous

"The History and Present State of Virginia" published in London in 1705, stated that "though the greedy planter will always buy them yet it is to be feared they will be very injurious to the country which has already suffered many murders and robberies."

Many of these were not really criminals, however, in the modern sense of the word. Some had been imprisoned for unpaid debts, while others were guilty of nothing more than stealing a loaf of bread to feed a starving child, or public drunkenness, and there was great demand for them on the part of honest and scrupulous planters. For example, the great distances that necessarily separated plantations made most of them inaccessible to such schools as were established in the southern colonies. Consequently, in many cases plantation owners secured these convicts as indentured servants to be special tutors to their children, particularly if they were well versed in

Early settlers bound for the New World. (Engraved from a drawing by Howard Pyle, in "Harper's Magazine," November 1882.)

Latin, as was often the case. One contemporary observer reported that two-thirds of the schoolmasters in Maryland just before the Revolution were indentured servants of one kind or another. Tradition has it that George Washington "had no other education than reading, writing, and accounts," which were taught him "by a convict servant whom his father had bought as a schoolmaster."

THE establishment of the Royal African Company in 1662, however, with its encouragement and official support of slavery, doomed the indentured servant system in the southern colonies when the tobacco and cotton crops demanded a huge supply of cheap labor which the system could not produce. And slavery also had other major economic advantages. The slave was owned for life, not just a few years, so he would not have to be continually replaced; all offspring also belonged to the master for life, so the slaves could be bred like animals and the supply thereby increased at relatively little cost; if necessary they could be sold, usually for a profit; and because of their color could be detected more easily if they ran away. Consequently, by 1800 there were virtually no indentured servants in the South.

In the Middle and New England colonies, however, where slavery was not economically feasible, there was a strong demand for indentured servants, particularly during the first half of the 18th century. Massachusetts in 1710 passed an act offering 40 shillings a head to any captain who brought in a male servant from age 8 to 25. Particularly needed were skilled workers such as experienced seamen, carpenters, blacksmiths, silversmiths, coopers, weavers, and bricklayers. Consequently Europeans came by the thousands, particularly Germans, who freely bonded themselves for a number of years in return for learning a trade or even just the language and customs of the new country. Between 1737 and 1746 sixty-seven ships landed 15,000 Germans at Philadelphia alone. Many had sufficient money to pay the passage, but instead saved it to use after their indentures had been served. One contemporary observer noted:

> Many of the Germans who come hither bring money enough with them to pay their passage, but prefer to be sold, hoping that during their servitude they may get a knowledge of the language and character of the country and its life, that they may the better be able to consider what they shall do when they have gotten their liberty . . . They launch forth, and, by dint of sobriety, rigid parsimony, and the most persevering industry, they commonly succeed.

He also noted that the "Scotch are frugal and laborious, but their wives cannot work so hard as German women," and the "Irish do not prosper so well; they love to drink and to quarrel; they seem, besides, to labor under a greater degree of ignorance in husbandry than the others."

AS THE country continued to develop, the demand for apprentices, house servants, farmhands, laborers, settlers for lands the speculators had secured also increased, and with this increased demand came dishonest schemes and abuses. Many who left their homes for the New World started with funds for passage and a little more to live on when they arrived. But for some reason there seems to have been more profit for unscrupulous agents and captains in selling the immigrants upon arrival than in simply transporting them as paying passengers. Consequently, various frauds and deceptions were practiced to relieve the ignorant and unsuspecting of their money at the embarkation points. Their belongings were often stolen outright; they were lured into taverns and robbed; they were subjected to exorbitant charges or sold passage on nonexistent ships; with the result that the only way they could get to America was to

Arrival of the young women at Jamestown in 1621. (Drawing by Howard Pyle originally published in "Harper's Magazine" April 1883.)

agree to sell themselves to pay their passage.

It was remarkable that any of them survived the crossing. Packed into unsafe and unsanitary ships "like so many herrings," they died by the score. The horrible conditions existing aboard many of these floating hells equaled those of the infamous "middle passage" for the African slave trade. Food was totally inadequate and often so rotten as to be inedible. Any unusual delay due to storm or calm threatened death by starvation or thirst. In many instances the immigrants fought for the bodies of rats and mice in order to stay alive. On at least one ship cannibalism was resorted to and the bodies of six dead humans were consumed before another vessel brought relief to the maddened passengers.

DISEASE and sickness were rife in the filthy holds of the ships as dysentery, smallpox, and typhus swept through them. In one ship 250 out of 400 died; in another 350 out of 400; and in another 250 out of 312. The statistics indicate that in 1711, for example, only one out of three survived the crossing.

This high mortality often caused extra hardship for many of the survivors, as all passengers, living

or dead, had to be paid for if possible before the ships' captains would release the immigrants. Thus it was not unusual to see a widow sold to pay for her husband's passage as well as her own, meaning she would have to serve double the normal time of indenture. Children were sold to pay for deceased or unwell parents. Consequently, families were often broken up, just as in the slave trade, never to meet again.

Those fortunate enough to survive the sea passage, however, generally found that the opportunities available to them made the sacrifices worthwhile. In most cases they were well treated. As one observer noted: "There is no master but will allow his servant a parcel of clear ground to plant some tobacco in for himself, which he may husband at those many idle times he hath allowed him, and not prejudice but rejoice his master to see it."

Most of them, particularly in the early years in the South, lived on average farms of from 300-400 acres and cultivated them side by side with the owner and his family. They were generally regarded as members of the family and treated as such; when their indenture was worked out, they might become neighbors of their former owners, although many pushed on farther west as the coastal areas become more populated and land more expensive. In the northern colonies, where they served mostly as house servants and apprentices, they were also usually treated fairly, and after becoming freemen had every opportunity to succeed. A good example was Paul Revere, whose father had come to Massachusetts as an indentured servant.

THEY were also protected by laws. Most of the colonies passed legislation to improve the legal position of the indentured servant and to safeguard his social condition. Generally, corporal punishment was limited and servants had the right to take complaints against their masters into court. An early statute provided that if any servant had just cause for complaint against his master or mistress for "harsh or unchristianlike usage or otherways for want of diet," he could bring his complaint to the nearest justice of the peace. Another required that "every master shall provide for his servants complete dyett, clothing and lodging, and that he shall not exceed the bounds of moderation in correcting them beyond the meritt of their offences."

And these laws were not ignored. Sometimes the servants were taken away from cruel masters or mistresses without compensation and the employers were forbidden to own servants again. In rare cases the masters were jailed for brutality. "The servants," stated one observer, "live more like Freemen than the most Mechanick Apprentices of London, wanting for nothing that is convenient and necessary, and ac-

cording to their several capacities, are extraordinary well used and respected."

Despite all this, just as in the South, the system could not furnish the northern colonies with the necessary labor supply, particularly the skilled labor so desperately needed. Skilled craftsmen, even in Europe, were usually not financially helpless and if they did migrate they could generally afford to pay their own passage and come as freemen. Also, by 1770 the colonists found it cheaper to hire native-born youngsters as apprentices, rather than pay the passage for indentured servants. As a result, and particularly after the Revolution with its emphasis on equality, the system gradually died out and by the early 19th century had virtually ceased to exist in the North.

Threshing grain with flails—the method used during Colonial days, and one of the chores of indentured servants. From a drawing by F. O. C. Darley in "Scribner's Monthly."

THAT some of the indentured servants caused serious problems is unquestionable. Running away was the most common offense, particularly among the kidnapped class and the prisoners sent here against their wills. But also among the lists of runaway servants were to be found tailors, clothiers, carpenters, and other skilled workers. If caught, they had to serve double their time and were often whipped and branded. Few were ever captured, however, and many became highway robbers and criminals of some sort, or settled around the docks in the cities to prey upon newly arrived immigrants. Here they joined with the penniless, sick, and disabled who could go no farther even had they so desired, and created the first slums in the country.

The presence of both slaves and indentured servants in the southern colonies almost of necessity led to some sexual immorality. With white male servants working in the fields side by side with Negresses and deprived of association with white women of their own class, it was inevitable that many would yield to temptation and create the first of the mulatto class in America. Such intercourse was forbidden by law, but as all children born to slaves were also slaves, it is doubtful that the masters were overly concerned.

Children born to female indentured servants, however, were born free and punishment here was usually swift and sure, particularly if the father was a Negro. Often the woman was punished by public whipping and forced to serve another full term of indenture. If the father was white, most colonies required the servant "in regard to the losse and trouble her master doth sustain by her having a bastard shall serve two years after her time by indenture is expired."

Regardless of the problems, however, the system of indentured servants filled a dire need in the early years of the New World. Such persons supplied much of the labor necessary for development and growth and in turn became a market themselves for the goods produced by the young nation. With their help the population from 1691 to 1763 increased almost seven times, and instead of the original scattered settlements there was now almost one continuous settlement from Maine to Georgia. They played a major role in pushing the frontier ever westward across the backcountry and even over the mountains, and they carried with them a strong spirit of independence and self-reliance as well as a lack of respect for a government three thousand miles east across the ocean that had done little to help or protect them. They carried with them the seeds of the American Revolution.

Anti-Slavery and the American Revolution
A Crack in the Liberty Bell

Richard K. MacMaster

THE AMERICAN REVOLUTION occurred at a time when critics of Negro slavery were advancing proposals for its abolition. Granville Sharp, John Wesley, Anthony Benezet, and other abolitionists published pamphlet attacks on slavery and concerted their strategy in regular correspondence across the Atlantic. Lord Mansfield's decision in the Somerset case in 1772 gave British foes of slavery a major victory and stimulated fresh efforts in the American Colonies.

The American Revolution retarded the anti-slavery cause. The partial emancipation proclamation issued by John Murray, Earl of Dunmore, as Governor of Virginia, was even alleged as one of the reasons for independence in 1776. Americans defended their rebellion with appeals to the natural rights of men to liberty and property, but they deliberately excluded persons of African descent held as slaves from a share in these inherent rights. In frank debates in the Virginia Convention and in the Continental Congress in 1776, the leaders of the new nation interpreted their charters of liberty in this sense. Some Americans argued that Congress or the state governments should make provision for a gradual emancipation of Negro slaves. They cited the ringing words of the Declaration of Independence

First published in the October 1971 issue of 'History Today.'

in presenting their case for liberty and drew on the prevailing notions of natural rights to strengthen their argument against slavery. These abolitionists remained outside the main currents of American thought in the era of the Revolution. They conceived of slavery as a moral evil to be rooted out of the land in a time of national crisis.

The contradiction between liberty and slavery did not escape the minds of the men who shaped the American Revolution. In the debates that carried the Continental Colonies closer to separation from the British Empire, the two terms stood in sharp opposition to one another. Pamphleteers and newspaper essayists marshalled examples from Sparta and Rome to prove that slavery violated essential human rights. Most Americans expressed an abhorrence for slavery, as an abstract concept. No one called for the testimony of the Pompeys and Catos at work in the corn-fields as to the relative merits of slavery and freedom. 'I have often thought that we should have been more strenuous in our Opposition to

ministerial Tyranny, had we not been conscious that we ourselves were absolute Tyrants, and held Numbers of poor Souls in the most abject and endless State of Slavery,' observed a correspondent of the *Virginia Gazette* in 1771. Others saw the same link that led logically from arguments for an inherent right to liberty to arguments for an end to chattel slavery. Some did phrase the case for liberty in terms that unmistakably included their own slaves, but many chose to restrict their concept of freedom to exclude Black bondmen. The Revolutionary generation as a whole denied that American liberty and African slavery were incompatible, but the essential contradiction remained unresolved in American society.

On May 15th, 1776, delegates from nearly every county in Virginia assembled in the chamber of the House of Burgesses at the Capitol in Williamsburg to decide on independence. It was a constant topic in the hallways of the Capitol and in the smoky taprooms of the Williamsburg

July 4th, 1776; 'In the Declaration of Independence Jefferson acknowledged that African slaves had rights to life and liberty, which were violated by the British merchant who carried them to Virginia for sale'. After the painting by John Trumbull. Jefferson (centre) flanked by Franklin and Hancock

From *Critical Period of American History, 1783-1789* by J. Fiske; New York 1898

GEORGE MASON, *1725-1792, whose original draft of the Declaration, it was argued, 'could only be the prelude to a general emancipation of slaves'. Portrait by Herbert Walsh*

taverns, but for two weeks the Virginia Convention had discussed more trivial matters before publicly debating the issue that was on every delegate's lips. Edmund Pendleton, President of the Convention, agreed in advance that Thomas Nelson would present a resolution calling for complete and final separation from Great Britain, and that Patrick Henry would speak in favour of the motion. The delegates heard Nelson's resolve with a sense of relief and listened eagerly to Henry's long oration. 'He entered into no subtlety of reasoning,' Edmund Randolph recalled, 'but was roused by the now apparent spirit of the people, as a pillar of fire, which, notwithstanding the darkness of the prospect, would conduct to the promised land. He inflamed and was followed by the Convention.' Only one delegate, Robert Carter Nicholas, voted against the overwhelming majority who favoured independence. The thing was done. The first great point was settled. Virginia instructed her dele-

gates in Congress 'to propose to that respectable body to declare the United Colonies free and independent States'.

The Virginians then took up the issue of precisely what sort of free and independent state they wanted, and appointed a committee to prepare 'a Declaration of Rights, and such a plan of Government as will be most likely to maintain peace and order'.

George Mason of Gunston Hall, a delegate from Fairfax County, arrived in Williamsburg two days after this important vote. Confined at home by a crippling attack of the gout, he sensed the drift that the Convention would take and sketched out his own thoughts on the issues facing them. Mason was added to the committee as soon as he took his seat. 'We are now going upon the most important of all Subjects – Government', Mason exulted to his old friend Richard Henry Lee. He expected 'a thousand ridiculous and impracticable proposals' from his colleagues on the committee, but he found the task exhilarating. He worked incessantly on the project for several days, and, when the committee held its next session, Mason presented them with a draft Declaration of Rights.

As his first principle, Mason wrote: 'That all men are born equally free and independent, and have certain inherent natural Rights, of which they cannot by any Compact, deprive or divest their Posterity; among which are the Enjoyment of Life and Liberty, with the Means of acquiring and possessing Property, and pursuing and obtaining Happiness and Safety.' The committee accepted Mason's draft and authorized its publication in the *Virginia Gazette* of June 1st, 1776. It was quickly reprinted and spread up and down the Atlantic seaboard in the version endorsed by the committee.

If the committee members agreed on the substance of the Declaration of Rights, certain members of the Convention argued that Mason's opening phrases could only be the prelude to a general emancipation of slaves. They were so adamant in their opposition to Mason's choice of words that they blocked debate on any other part of the Declaration of Rights for several days. Thomas Ludwell Lee complained to his brother that 'A certain set of Aristocrats . . . have to this time kept us at bay on the first line, which declares all men to be born equally free and independent'. Robert Carter Nicholas led the attack on Mason's draft and he spoke for a substantial number of delegates who were unwilling to grant equal rights of liberty and property to their own slaves. It was evident that the Declaration of Rights could not pass the Virginia Convention in its original form. Mason had to accept a compromise that amounted to a surrender. The Convention amended the Declaration of Rights to affirm 'That all men are by nature equally free and independent, and have certain inherent rights, of which, *when they enter into a state of society*, they cannot, by any compact, deprive or divest their posterity'.

The Virginia Convention deliberately chose this short phrase to exclude Blacks from the purview of the Declaration of Rights. No one would seriously argue that slaves were not men, so that Mason's original phrase could be construed as an assertion of their right to liberty. No one would seriously argue that slaves had entered into a state of society in Virginia, and therefore slaves had no natural rights. The Declaration of Rights asserted that a man had a natural right to acquire property in slaves, but slaves had no just claim to their own freedom. The social compact could be as safely invoked to deny the rights of men as to ground the case for liberty.

Although the debate on this turn of phrase consumed several days, there is no official transcript of the exchange. Edmund Randolph recalled the gist of the reply made by Mason and his supporters on the floor of the Convention. 'It was answered, perhaps with too great an indifference to futurity, and not without inconsistency, that with arms in our hands, asserting the general rights of man, we ought not to be too nice and too much restricted in the delineation of them, but that slaves not being constituent members of our society could never pretend to any benefit from such a maxim'. If Randolph's memory was correct, neither George Mason nor his critics ever intended that slaves should be included in a theory of natural rights. His opponents directed their fire at a straw man, when they depicted his Declaration of Rights as a prelude to social convulsion. In adding the phrase, 'when they enter into a state of society', the full Convention clarified and made explicit the sense in which Mason's words were generally understood.

When Thomas Jefferson penned the first draft of the Declaration of Independence, he had access to copies of the Virginia Declaration of Rights in the version presented by the committee to the Convention and published in the Philadelphia newspapers. He obviously drew on Mason's first article for the ringing assertion, 'We hold these truths to be self-evident, that all men are created equal, that they are endowed by their Creator with certain inalienable rights, that among these are Life, Liberty and the pursuit of Happiness'.

Jefferson and his colleagues in the Continental Congress were also aware of the stormy debate in the Virginia Convention over the opening words of the Declaration of Rights. Jefferson's phrases seemed the more provocative, for he made no saving allusion to the social compact in his assertion of the equality and natural rights of all men. Since his prologue failed to set a similar debate in motion, it is unlikely that his sweeping declaration of first principles was generally understood as a promise of enfranchisement to slaves. Jefferson's context subtly altered the application of his self-evident truths.

From his proclamation of basic human rights, Jefferson proceeded to indict King George III for his infringement of the natural rights of his American subjects. His bill of particulars reached an emotional crescendo with a presentment of the King as personally responsible for the horrors of the African slave trade, and for the threat of servile insurrection in the American Colonies. He charged the monarch with waging war on human nature, 'violating its most sacred rights of life and liberty in the persons of a distant people who had never offended him, captivating and carrying them into slavery in another hemisphere, or to incur miserable death in their transportation thither'. If the King had not himself carried slaves across the Atlantic, he had nonetheless 'prostituted his negative for suppressing every legislative attempt to prohibit or to restrain this execrable commerce'. By allowing Lord Dunmore, the Governor of Virginia, to promise freedom to any slave or indentured servant who enlisted in the British service, the King was encouraging slaves to rebel, 'and to purchase that liberty of which *he* deprived them, by murdering the people upon whom *he* also obtruded them'.

In his first rough sketch of the Declaration of Independence, Jefferson made the same points more succinctly. He condemned George III for 'prompting our negroes to rise in arms against us; those very negroes whom by an inhuman use of his negative he hath refused us permission to exclude by law'.

Jefferson had discussed the slave trade in a pamphlet published in 1774 as *A Summary View of the Rights of British America*. As in his drafts of the Declaration of Independence, Jefferson roundly condemned the slave trade, but absolved his fellow Americans from complicity in violating the rights of human nature, since slavery had been 'unhappily introduced in their infant state' by British merchants. The Colonists looked to a day when slavery could be abolished and longed to cut off further importations as a necessary first step. The King thwarted the repeated attempts of the Colonial Assemblies to tax the slave trade, 'thus preferring the immediate advantages of a few British corsairs to the lasting interests of the American states, and to the rights of human nature deeply wounded by this infamous practice'.

In the Declaration of Independence Jefferson acknowledged that African slaves had rights to life and liberty, which were violated by the British merchant who carried them to Virginia for sale. The slave in the American Colonies, deprived of his liberty, had no right to regain his lost freedom by resisting his American master. Jefferson stigmatized this rebellion as a crime. Their American owners had not deprived them of liberty. Master and slave were alike victims of British avarice. The Liverpool merchant, with the connivance of King and Parliament, had introduced slaves into His Majesty's dominions. The slave had been wronged, yet he should seek redress, not from his master, but from the British King. With this tortuous logic, one could maintain the natural rights of all men to liberty and still defend the system of slavery.

Jefferson's entire section on the slave trade and servile insurrection did not survive the debate on the Declaration of Independence in Congress. Jefferson wrote afterwards that Congress struck out the passage 'in complaisance to South Carolina and Georgia, who had never attempted to restrain the importation of slaves, and who on the contrary still wished to continue it'.

Condemnation of the African slave trade was quite common in the Chesapeake Colonies, as the efforts made by the Maryland and Virginia legislatures to curb it with a prohibitive tax

By courtesy of Liverpool Public Libraries

Future slaves assembled on a quayside; water-colour by B. Reading, 1780

indicate. Many factors entered into this opposition, and slave-holding Virginia planters wrote and voted against the slave trade, without seeing any inconsistency in their position. Opposition to the slave trade was much weaker in the Carolinas and Georgia. Rice-planters were not so well supplied with slaves as their neighbours in the Chesapeake tobacco region. The South Carolina legislature had attempted to tax the slave trade in 1764 so as to limit the number of slaves brought into the colony and reduce the danger of insurrection. Fear of slave revolts, rather than humanitarian motives, governed most opposition to the slave trade in the plantation colonies.

Congress deleted Jefferson's strictures on the slave trade in deference to a small minority of delegates. Defenders of the slave trade would not presumably accept a theory of natural rights offering liberty to their slaves, but the debate did not go that far. Delegates who had publicly condemned the slave trade were quick to yield the point. A condemnation of the African slave trade, excised out of regard to slave traders, made no appreciable difference in presenting the case for American liberty.

A few days after the adoption of the Declaration of Independence, Congress began consideration of the Articles of Confederation that would bind the free and independent states into a permanent union. On July 25th, 1776, the members of Congress debated the status of slaves, and concluded that slaves were no more than their owner's property. Critics of slavery, as well as its defenders, agreed on this point. They had few kind words for slavery, but they would not extend the rights of men to slaves. Edward Rutledge of South Carolina looked to the day when slavery would disappear. William Hooper of North Carolina agreed with Rutledge that slavery was an unprofitable burden on the Southern economy. Thomas Lynch of South Carolina grudgingly excused it as the only labour system available to the rice-planters. No one effectively challenged the point made by Samuel Chase of Maryland that slaves were property, like cattle and sheep. Benjamin Franklin dryly suggested that sheep were less likely to raise an insurrection against their masters. John Adams of Massachusetts acknowledged that slaves were properly the wealth of their masters, but argued that slaves and free labourers equally constituted the wealth of the state. Here, if ever, the Continental Congress had opportunity to denounce slavery as a violation of the rights they had so recently declared inalienable. Instead, the debate turned on the relative productivity of free and slave labour. This debate created a deep rift between Northern and Southern delegations, and threatened to break up the Congress. At issue in this sectional split was not slavery, for all the states admitted property in slaves in 1776, but relative numbers of slaves. The proportion of slaves to free inhabitants was much higher in South Carolina than in Massachusetts, and consequently South Carolinians would have to pay a proportionately higher tax to support the national government. Slave-owning delegates from New York debated with slave-owning delegates from Maryland on this issue, but they were in full agreement on the more fundamental point.

The leading men of the American Revolution saw the right to acquire, possess, and protect property as a fundamental one in a free society. A healthy respect for the sanctity of private property characterized the turbulent decade before the American Colonies declared themselves free and independent. Liberty and property were inseparable. The Boston Tea Party in 1773 shocked many Americans. Virginians declared that they stood solidly with the Bostonians in defence of their rights, but insisted that the East India Company be indemnified. The tea, after all, was private property. Samuel Chase and the Annapolis Committee of Safety were swift to denounce the burning of the *Peggy Stewart* as mob violence.

The Revolutionary generation sought to make liberty and property secure against the encroachments of Parliament. They intended to preserve the traditional rights of Englishmen and the forms of government that their ancestors had nurtured in the American wilderness. They never aimed at shaking their society to its foundations. When Virginia gave Jefferson, Madison, and Mason authority to revise the laws of the Old Dominion, they agreed at their first meeting to make as few changes as possible. No sweeping revision according to a visionary plan, but the elimination of errors and ambiguities in the existing laws was the task they set for themselves. The new state constitutions preserved nearly all the local institutions of the colony without alteration. Such fundamental rights as the security of property in slaves would scarcely be challenged, when the constitution-makers were reluctant to tamper with the prerogatives of a sheriff or to reapportion the electoral districts of the lower house.

There were some men who believed that slavery should be abolished as one of the first acts of the new nation. The Reverend William Gordon, pastor of the Third Congregational Church in Roxbury, Massachusetts, hoped that the Massachusetts constitution would go further than other states had gone in protecting the rights of men. 'The Virginians begin their Declaration of Rights with saying "that *all* men are born *equally free and independent*, and have certain inherent natural rights of which they cannot, by any compact, divest their posterity; among which are the enjoyment of life and *liberty*",' Gordon observed. 'The Congress declare that they "hold these truths to be self-evident, that *all* men are created *equal*, that they are endowed by their Creator with certain *inalienable rights*, that among these are life, *liberty* and pursuit of happiness". The Continent has rung with affirmations of the like import. If these, Gentlemen, are our genuine liberty that their bondmen should go free.

The abolitionists drew egalitarian arguments out of the Declaration of Independence and scored the inconsistency of their neighbours in limiting these natural rights, in practice, to white men. Their own attitudes owed little to the rhetoric of the Revolution, but they found in this rhetoric a ready weapon for their own cause.

The Reverend Samuel Hopkins of Newport, Rhode Island, published *A Dialogue Concerning the Slavery of the Africans* in 1776 and dedicated it to the Honourable Members of the Continental Congress. He pointed out to them the 'inconsistence of promoting the slavery of the Africans, at the same time we are asserting our own civil liberty' and of 'holding so many thousands of blacks in slavery, who have an equal right to freedom with ourselves'. Hopkins had long denounced the sinfulness of slavery in a town that flourished on the profits of the slave trade. His anti-slavery attitude was deeply rooted in his theology. As the pupil and interpreter of Jonathan Edwards, he had developed the idea that true virtue consisted in universal benevolence and given it particular application to his most oppressed brethren, the Black slaves.

Hopkins warned Americans in 1776 that slavery was 'a sin which God is now testifying against in

From *Critical Period in American History*

THOMAS JEFFERSON, *1743-1826; after a portrait by St Memin*

sentiments, and we are not provoking the Deity, by acting hypocritically to serve a turn, let us apply earnestly and heartily to the extirpation of slavery from among ourselves. Let the State allow of nothing beyond servitude for a stipulated number of years, and that only seven or eight, when persons are of age: and let the descendants of the Africans born among us be viewed as free-born; and be wholly at their own disposal when one and twenty.'

David Cooper, a New Jersey Quaker, also commented bitterly on the Declaration of Independence. He wrote: 'If these solemn truths, uttered at such an awful crisis, are *self-evident*: unless we can shew that the African race are not *men*, words can hardly express the amazement which naturally arises on reflecting, that the very people who make these pompous declarations are slave-holders, and, by their legislative conduct, tell us, that these blessings were only meant to be the rights of *whitemen*.'

These men, and others like them, hit on the great paradox of the American Revolution. With arms in their hands, asserting the general rights of men, the Americans of this generation were not prepared to argue from their own claims to

TO BE SOLD, on board the Ship *Bance-Island*, on tuesday the 6th of *May* next, at *Ashley-Ferry*; a choice cargo of about 250 fine healthy NEGROES, just arrived from the Windward & Rice Coast. —The utmost care has already been taken, and shall be continued, to keep them free from the least danger of being infected with the SMALL-POX, no boat having been on board, and all other communication with people from *Charles-Town* prevented.

Austin, Laurens, & Appleby.

N. B. Full one Half of the above Negroes have had the SMALL-POX in their own Country. .

An advertisement of a sale of slaves, published during the latter years of the eighteenth century

the calamities he has brought upon us'. It was necessary to cast out 'the accursed thing which is among us', William Gordon declared, if the Americans looked for deliverance from their enemies. 'Is it not an iniquity which separates us from our God, that we continue to hold in bondage the Africans ? Is not this the crying sin of America ?'

These New Englanders were not alone in calling for a reformation of morals, if the new nation was not to be carried down by the burden of its own evil-doing. 'We in Connecticut have girded on the outward garment of sack-cloth and ashes;' observed a petition to the Connecticut Assembly for the abolition of slavery, 'but we have forgot to keep that fast which the Lord himself has chosen, we have not undone the heavy burdens, nor have we let the oppressed go free.' Daniel Byrnes, a Delaware Quaker, issued an appeal to his neighbours to free their slaves. 'How can any have the confidence to put up their addresses to a God of impartial justice, and ask of him success in a struggle for freedom, who at the same time are keeping others in a state of abject slavery?' Thomas Rankin, one of Wesley's lay preachers in Maryland, told members of the Continental Congress 'what a farce it was for them to contend for liberty, when they themselves kept some hundreds of thousands of poor blacks in most cruel bondage'. Elhanan Winchester and John Leland preached against slave-owning as among the 'abominations which greatly prevail in this country, and which threaten it with ruin and desolation, unless repentance and reformation prevent', and urged Virginia and South Carolina Baptists to liberate their slaves.

Denunciations of slavery thundered from 'New Light' Congregational and Presbyterian pulpits from Massachusetts to the South Carolina back-country. Evangelical clergymen penned pamphlets and newspaper essays against slavery, borrowing as freely from Montesquieu as from Whitefield's sermons to support their cause. The sinfulness of slavery became a commonplace of Evangelical thought. The Ketoctin Baptist Association in Virginia refused to admit slave-owners. The Methodists throughout the American Colonies adopted a rule against slavery in 1780. Eager converts like Harry Dorsey Gough in Maryland and Robert Carter in Virginia liberated hundreds of slaves at a stroke of the pen.

The Quakers had already begun to set their slaves free on the eve of the American Revolution. They petitioned the state legislatures in Virginia and North Carolina to make legal provision for the manumission of slaves. They succeeded in obtaining such a law in North Carolina in 1777, only to have it overturned by men who expressed fear that a free Black population would endanger the safety of the state in case of invasion by the British Army. A series of Quaker petitions in Virginia went unheard until 1782, when Friend Edward Stabler told the Virginia Assembly of slaves freed by Quakers without any legal document to prove their right to freedom, who were then sold into slavery by the State of Virginia to pay the militia fines levied on their former owners.

Anthony Benezet, a Philadelphia Quaker, reprinted and circulated anti-slavery writings of all kinds, and the Quaker Meetings assessed their members to provide copies of his pamphlets for the perusal of state and national legislators.

In Pennsylvania, where Quakers were most numerous, the state legislature abolished slavery in 1780. Although Friends had often petitioned for abolition, they had little to do with the passage of this bill. George Bryan, a Presbyterian from Dublin, and General Daniel Roberdeau, a close friend of Whitefield, shepherded the bill through a legislature dominated by Scotch-Irish Presbyterians. Bryan urged its passage in newspaper essays that defended abolition on Scriptural grounds, addressed to fellow Presbyterians in the south-western part of Pennsylvania.

The abolition of slavery did not proceed any further during the American Revolution. Black men petitioned for an end to slavery in Massachusetts and Connecticut without success. 'We have turned a deaf ear to the cries of the oppressed; and this law which supports Oppression reaches through the whole of these United States' a New England abolitionist noted gloomily in 1780. The Massachusetts Constitution of 1780, which repeated George Mason's declaration of the natural right of all men to liberty, made no provision for the abolition of slavery.

By the time that George Washington was inaugurated as the first President of the United States in 1789, abolitionists had succeeded in ending slavery only in New England and Pennsylvania. Abolition societies, composed principally of Quakers, regularly petitioned the legislatures of New York, New Jersey, Delaware, Maryland, Virginia, and North Carolina. Methodists circulated anti-slavery tracts and the Presbyterian Synod of the Carolinas periodically listened to ministers who believed that slavery was inherently sinful. One of these Presbyterian abolitionists, the Reverend David Rice, led the fight to keep slavery out of the new state of Kentucky and lost the battle.

If the American Revolution brought a sense of the equal rights of all men to life and liberty, or a broadened humanitarian outlook, its impact was certainly uneven. The leadership of the anti-slavery crusade belonged rather to country parsons and Quaker shopkeepers than to the men who framed the national charters of liberty.

Men who were already convinced of the moral evil of slavery attempted to enlist the popular idea of natural rights in their own cause and broaden their appeal. In this endeavour, they were partially successful. Hopkins brooded on the failure of the American Revolution to live up to its ideals, but they were largely ideals he had imposed on it. The Evangelical crusade against slavery converted few who were not already convinced of the justice of its cause. By 1789 a substantial number of Americans were convinced that slavery was absolutely evil, while others saw it as a labour system no more immoral than any other. The sin of slavery would be a central theme of abolitionist thought thereafter. A debate in the first Congress over a Quaker petition for a general emancipation might as easily have been a debate over the Kansas-Nebraska Act, with tempers rising, sectional lines drawn, and an appeal to a higher morality than the charters of the new nation.

A Curiosity of History

The thing that hath been, it is that which shall be;
and that which is done is that which shall be done:
and there is no new thing under the sun.

ESTELLE AND SAUL GILSON

○ ESTELLE GILSON, who has just completed her first novel, has published articles in *Opera News* and *Saturday Review*. SAUL GILSON practices internal medicine in New York City. His poetry has appeared in "little" magazines.

IF THERE WAS NO NEW THING under the sun before the birth of Christ, what has historical man experienced since? Is nothing unique? Horace wrote in 20 B.C. that "many poets, cultivating their genius with unkempt beard and dirty nails, despise work, withdraw from society and shun baths and barbers." Today, two thousand years later, the one hundredth generation of unwashed poetasters parade their flowing locks and revel in the derision of their elders.

Knowing history, we yet seemed doomed to repeat it. For history is a record of successive dooms whose lessons are as ambiguous and obscure as any Delphic utterance. Learn from the past? Coleridge said: "Passion and party blind our eyes and the light experience gives is a lantern on the stern which shines only on the waves behind us." History is just there—an ocean of experience into which our wake gradually disappears.

Consider, for example, the American experience with the Vietnam war. Surely we did not learn from the French disaster, nor did we learn from a similar experience recorded in our own tongue and of which we were the cause. Two hundred years ago the American Revolution brought to Great Britain dissension, repression and turmoil that could read as do the topics of our times.

For Credibility Gap

Read Horace Walpole in 1777: "Eleven months ago I thought America subdued; and a fortnight ago, it was as little likely to be subdued as ever. We, the people, know little of the truth . . . for General Howe's retreat produced despair; the taking of one post has given confidence. If you ask me what I believe . . . nothing but what is past—and perhaps have not heard a quarter of that." And again in 1781, "I wonder you are not cured of being sanguine or rather of believing the magnificent lies that every trifling advantage gives birth to."

For Domestic Opposition to the War

Here is Walpole again in 1777: "We have been horribly the aggressors."

And William Pitt: "I rejoice that America has resisted." And later, "If I were an American, as I am an Englishman, while a foreign troop was landed in my country, I never would lay down my arms . . . never, never, never . . . you cannot conquer America."

Edmund Burke: "Nothing less will content me than Whole America."

Edward Gibbon: "I shall scarcely give my consent to exhaust still further the finest country in the World in the prosecution of a war from whence no reasonable man entertains any hopes of success. It is better to be humbled than ruined."

William Cowper: "I think it [the American War] bids fair to be the ruin of the country . . . I cannot look upon the circumstances of this country, without being persuaded that I discern in them an entanglement and perplexity that I have never met with in the history of any other. . . . If we pursue the war, it is because we are desperate: it is plunging and sinking year after year into still greater depths of calamity. If we relinquish it, the remedy is equally desperate . . . either way we are undone."

James Boswell: "I am growing more and more an American. I think our ministers are mad in undertaking this desperate war."

Even the favoring of revolutionaries over one's own brethren in uniform is not unique to us today. Winston Churchill, in his history of the times, wrote: "There was gloating over every setback and disaster to the British cause," and some British peers took a "parricide joy" in the loss of British troops and ships.

The Quest for Peace

You may read King George III, but whose voice do you hear? "I should think it the greatest instance among the many I have met with of ingratitude and injustice, if it could be supposed, that any Man in my Dominions more ardently desired the restoration of Peace and solid happiness in every part of this Empire, than I do, there is no personal Sacrifice I could not readily yield for so desirable an object, but at the same time no inclination to get out of the present difficulties which certainly keep my mind very far from a state of ease, can incline me to enter into what I look upon as the distruction [sic] of the Empire."

But here is Cowper again: "If people leave off fighting, peace follows, of course. I wish they would withdraw the forces and put an end to the squabble."

Walpole writes that the administration is ". . . persisting in a mere point of honor," for it has rejected "all proposals of accommodation offered by the Opposition" and "delayed offering terms themselves till they knew it was too late. . . . For what are we now really at war? . . . to stave off for a year perhaps, a peace that must proclaim our nakedness and impotence. . . . The ministers were too sanguine making war. I hope they will not be too timid of making peace." Later, he wrote, "My wishes are limited now to peace, I care not what sort of peace; the longer it is deferred, the worse it must be."

On the Destruction and Expense of the War

King George said, "I have heard . . . drop that the advantages to be gained by this contest could never repay the expence, I owne that let any War be ever so successful if persons will set down and weigh the Expenses they will find as in the last that it has impoverished the State, enriched individuals, and perhaps raised the Name only of the Conquerors, but this is only weighing such events in the Scale of a Tradesman behind his Counter; it is necessary for those in the Station it has pleased Divine Providence to place me to weigh whether expences though very great are not sometimes necessary to prevent what might be ruinous to a Country than the loss of money."

Among those who read the scales differently, however, we have Walpole again: "The distance of the war augments its horrors almost as much as its expense. . . . The destruction of twenty-four thousand lives on their own side and the Lord knows how many thousands on t'other, with the burning of towns, desolation of the country and the expense of above thirty millions of money. . . . Whatever puts an end to the American War will save the lives of thousands . . . millions of money too. If glory compensates such sacrifices, I never heard that disgraces and disappointments were palliatives." In 1780 he wrote, "You hear, on the Continent, but too much of our barbarity; the only way in which we have yet shown our power."

Cowper, too: "Perseverance will only enfeeble us more; we cannot recover the colonies by war . . . crushed as we are under an enormous public debt that the public credit can at no rate carry much longer . . . the consequence is sure. . . ."

Perhaps you have wondered why the King thought that the loss of money and lives must be weighed against future consequences.

The Domino Theory

"Step by step the demands of America have risen—independence is their object . . . every man not willing to sacrifice every object to a *momentary* and inglorious Peace must concurr with me in thinking that this Country can never submit. . . . Should America succeed, the West Indies must follow them . . . Ireland would soon follow . . . then this Island would be reduced to itself and soon would be a poor Island indeed. . . . Consequently, this Country has but one Sensible, one great line to follow, the being ever ready to make Peace when to be obtained without submitting to terms that in their consequence must anihilate [sic] this Empire, and with firmness to make every effort to deserve Success."

Meanwhile, Back on the Home Front

While the Administration tried to create favor for its war policy, rebellion and dissension increased. Walpole worried about it: "I am almost afraid that there will be a larger military spirit than is wholesome for our constitution. France will have done us hurt enough, if she has turned us into generals instead of senators. . . . The nation is not yet alienated from the Court, but it is growing so enough for any calamity to have violent effects. Any internal disturbance would advance the hostile designs of France." Later, he wrote, "Foreign enemies seldom destroy a country, and then only by total conquest. In my opinion the subversion of a happy constitution, which is only effected by domestic enemies, is a worse evil, certainly a more permanent and more mortifying one, than defeats by strangers."

In 1776 Samuel Johnson noted "the magistrates dare not call the guards for fear of being hanged. The guards will not come for fear of being given up [to] the blind rage of popular juries."

And Steven Watson, in his *Reign of King George III*, describes similar circumstances contributing to the riot of 1780.

Backlash for Law and Order

The riot was instigated by Lord George Gordon. According to Watson, "young men like Gordon who drank success to America were not unnaturally considered by most of their seniors to be little better than traitors" as were those politicians whose only hope of attaining power depended upon a British defeat. Gordon, under thirty, and a member of Parliament, was wild, flighty, hated Lord North, the prime minister, yet refused to cooperate with the Opposition. His influence as self-appointed leader of a protestant organization was considered inconsequential. But on June 2, 1780, Gordon marched at the head of a procession formed to pressure the Commons into accepting his group's petitions. Encouraged by Gordon's haranguing, crowds attempted to attack Parliament. By nightfall they had shifted their activities from Westminster to London, from shouting to arson, and the riot, which was to continue for more than a full week, was under way. Uncontrollable mobs burned homes and businesses, attacked the

Bank of England, and broke open every prison, recruiting the former inmates to their ranks. Many ransacked and burned distilleries, and drunken rioters burned to death where they fell.

London was at the mercy of the mob. Troops who were called out could not fire into the crowds until a magistrate had read the riot act, but magisterial sanction was not easily obtained—in part, as Watson puts it, because the magistrates "did not want to rank themselves with those who repressed the ebullience of a free-spirited city . . . in part . . . because they feared reprisals from the mob against their own personal property." Indeed, there were such reprisals; magistrates and wardens continually released previously arrested rioters.

It was only after the King and the Privy Council ordered the military to disregard the city magistrates, to suppress the riots and restore public order, that the mob was finally beaten. More than four hundred and fifty people were killed or wounded before London returned to normal. Now, horrified Londoners and country gentlemen condemned all mob action; aldermen sought credit for preserving law and order; and, as Watson states, "the swing back to Lord North as a safe man . . . increased in speed and weight."

Restoration of Peace or a Massacre by Troops?

Now read Fanny Burney on June 9, 1780: "A private letter . . . brought word this morning that much slaughter has been made by the military among the mob. Never, I am sure, can any set of wretches less deserve quarter or pity; yet it is impossible not to shudder at hearing of their destruction. Nothing less, however, would do; they were too outrageous and powerful for civil power . . . . Now, if after all the intolerable provocation by the mob, after all the leniency and forbearance of the ministry, we shall by and by hear that this firing was a massacre . . . will it not be villainous and horrible? And yet as soon as safety is secured, by this means alone all now agree it can be secured—nothing would less surprise me than to hear the seekers of popularity make this assertion."

And there it is—eighteenth-century England or twentieth-century America? Dissension, taxes, riots, bigotry, domino theory, alienation, militarism, backlash. Surely, in our present mess we have heard no glad tidings. Is it permissible to be heartened by England's survival even into the Welfare State? It would be nice if from this encapsulated fragment of the past we could infer that we will eventually solve our problems. But there are too many variables beyond our knowledge and control.

Perhaps, then, the best we can derive from these quotations is some social psychotherapy that will enable us to be a little more objective, to avoid the long, inscrutable view, to recognize helplessness and entrapment of position instead of villainy, and to hear our prophets of doom with the necessary grain of salt.

Societies, even as individuals, are doomed; only the timetable is uncertain.

Business of the Highest Magnitude

OR

DON'T PUT OFF UNTIL TOMORROW WHAT YOU CAN RAM THROUGH TODAY

ROBERT C. ALBERTS

The high-flown political skullduggery described in this article was discovered by Robert C. Alberts in doing research for his most recent book, The Golden Voyage: The Life and Times of William Bingham, 1752–1804, *published by Houghton Mifflin in 1969. Mr. Alberts is now Contributing Editor of this magazine.*

Dr. Benjamin Rush believed the hand of God must have been involved in the noble work. John Adams, writing from Grosvenor Square, London, called it the greatest single effort of national deliberation, and perhaps the greatest exertion of human understanding, the world had ever seen. A great many people, however, held a con-

trary view, and in the fall of 1787 their opposition made it seem likely that the proposed Constitution of the United States would not be forwarded to the states by the Continental Congress, or, if forwarded, would not be ratified by the American people.

Opposition was especially intense in Pennsylvania, the only state with a well-developed, statewide two-party system. The Pennsylvania Democrats (Antifederalists) were efficiently organized; they controlled the state militia and the mobs in most cities; and they were led by a group of uncompromising idealogues who were determined that their state would not ratify the new Constitution. Both the Democrats and the pro-Constitution Federalists knew that Pennsylvania was the pivotal state and that the fight there would be an influential and perhaps decisive factor in the larger national contest. The struggle that ensued has not often been equalled in this country for bitterness, violence, vehemence of debate, or political high comedy.

The Constitutional Convention completed its work on September 17, after sixteen weeks of almost daily sessions. The engrossed Constitution, signed by thirty-nine delegates from twelve states, was sent forthwith to the Congress in New York City. With it went a covering letter from General George Washington, written, it is thought, by Gouverneur Morris of Pennsylvania. A resolution of the Convention asked the Congress to submit the Constitution for ratification, not, as expected, to the state legislatures, but to a convention of delegates popularly chosen in each state, and convened solely for that purpose.

The next day Benjamin Franklin led the Pennsylvania delegation to the second floor of the State House in Philadelphia to appear before the Pennsylvania House of Assembly. General Thomas Mifflin, Speaker and one of the delegates, read the Constitution aloud. When he finished, the citizens standing in the rear of the chamber broke into applause. On Wednesday the Constitution was printed in full in the *Packet*, the *Journal*, and the *Independent Gazetteer or Chronicle of Freedom*, and thereafter in others of the country's eighty-odd newspapers. It was distributed in Pennsylvania as a pamphlet, with five hundred copies in the German language for the benefit of the state's large German-speaking population.

The first public response seemed to be favorable, but the Democrats were bursting with protest. Speaking "for the present and future ages—the cause of liberty and mankind," they went to work with handbills and pamphlets, with squibs and speeches, with articles and letters in the papers, in meetings and in exchanges in the boarding houses and taverns. To Democrats the new Constitution was the product of "as deep and wicked a conspiracy as ever was invented in the darkest ages against the liberties of a free people," and it "would surely result in a monarchy or a tyrannical aristocracy," and perhaps in civil war. They voiced these major objections:

1. Congress had instructed the Convention delegates to recommend possible amendments to the Articles of Confederation and Perpetual Union. Instead, meeting behind locked doors in a "dark conclave," they had willfully written a plan for an entirely new form of government.

2. Their Constitution would annihilate the present confederation of coequal states, where the sovereign power should properly reside, and substitute for it a consolidated national government. The authority of the states would be grievously curbed if not obliterated. The ability of the new Congress to impose internal taxes and duties at its pleasure would undercut the taxing powers of the individual state legislatures.

3. Unprotected by their state governments, the citizens would be at the mercy of the central government. There was no bill of rights; liberty of the press, habeas corpus, and religious toleration were not assured; trial by jury was abolished in civil cases; and there was no prohibition

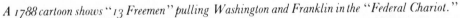

A 1788 cartoon shows "13 Freemen" pulling Washington and Franklin in the "Federal Chariot."

AMERICAN ANTIQUARIAN SOCIETY

of a standing army in time of peace.

4. The government of three branches, this "triple-headed monster," was unworkable. The President was too powerful, the Vice President "a needless and dangerous officer," the Senate too aristocratical, the House too small to represent the people, the jurisdiction of the Supreme Court too extensive. The country was too large to be ruled under the principles of liberty by a consolidated government.

5. The whole proposition was extravagant and would bankrupt the nation.

The more zealous Pennsylvania Democrats pounded hard on those objections and added several others of their own. For one thing, none of the eight Pennsylvania delegates to the Convention had been Democrats, and none had come from the six counties beyond the western mountains, where, among Scotch-Irish and German immigrant farmer-frontiersmen, the chief opposition to the Constitution lay. For another, the Democrats would lose jobs, power, and their control over the Pennsylvania militia. For a third, they would probably see the repeal of their ultrademocratic (and unworkable) state constitution. Without having bothered with the formality of a popular vote, they had imposed this constitution on the state in the turmoil of 1776, and they held it to be a model for other states and nations to follow. (Much of it was written by James Cannon, a mathematics professor at the College of Philadelphia who seems to have been somewhat ahead of his time. He tried but failed to include an article reading, "That an enormous proportion of property vested in a few individuals is dangerous to the rights, and destructive of the common happiness, of mankind; and therefore every free state hath a right by its laws to discourage the possession of such property.")

In New York, the Continental Congress had been unable to muster a quorum of seven states throughout the summer, but on Thursday, September 20, attendance picked up and the members took under consideration the new frame of government that had been placed before them. The assent of nine of the thirteen states was required for approval.

Pennsylvania's Federalist congressmen, under the leadership of William Bingham, a wealthy Philadelphia merchant and banker, pushed hard through a week-long debate to forward the Constitution with an affirmative and unanimous endorsement. Richard Henry Lee of Virginia, leading a strong minority, spoke of "essential alterations" and of the need to call another constitutional convention. He moved that a bill of rights and a long list of amendments be added, and he proposed a resolution stating that the new plan of government be submitted to the existing state legislatures rather than to state conventions assembled solely for that purpose. The minority then offered to forward the plan to the states for consideration, but with the warning that the Convention had acted improperly in producing it and with a reprimand

to the delegates. The two sides worked for a suitable compromise.

Back in Philadelphia, without waiting for formal word from the Continental Congress, Democrats and Federalists prepared for a mighty struggle in the House of Assembly. The Democratic minority planned a delaying action. The House had resolved to adjourn sine die on Saturday, September 29. Delay would carry the issue over to a new Assembly to be elected five weeks later. Democrats might win a majority in that body and thus have the votes to defeat a call for a state convention—if the Congress really did send the Constitution forward. Or they might elect a majority of anti-Constitution delegates in the convention—if one had to be called. Defeat of the Constitution in Pennsylvania, or delay in calling a state convention, would strengthen the anti-Constitution forces in the twelve other states.

The Federalists not only wanted the Constitution to be ratified in Pennsylvania; they also wanted their state to be the first to act. That would strengthen the movement in the other states. It would take advantage of the early wave of sentiment in favor of the Constitution and give the western farmers less time to find fault with it. It would allow the Democratic leaders the least opportunity to return to their inland counties and organize the opposition. And early ratification would give Pennsylvania a leg up on placing the new seat of government near Philadelphia, where it obviously belonged.

The Federalists drew up a plan designed to take their opponents by surprise. They would make a motion for a state convention on Friday morning, one day before adjournment, and attempt to rush it through before the Democrats could recover. The procedure was irregular, perhaps, since the Congress had not yet *asked* for a convention, but the issue was vital and the cause was just.

William Bingham arranged to send news from New York by dispatch riders who would change horses at frequent posts along the ninety-mile route.

On Friday morning, September 28, every Federalist member was in his seat. After the House attended to some routine business, George Clymer, merchant of Philadelphia, signer of the Declaration of Independence and one of the framers of the new federal Constitution, rose in place. The members, he said suavely, could not have forgotten a business of the highest magnitude that had been recommended to their attention by the federal Convention. He was persuaded that they would readily concur in taking the necessary measures, and therefore he had prepared a resolution to that end.

His resolution was promptly seconded by Gerardus Wynkoop, who sat for Bucks County.

Robert Whitehill, member from Cumberland County, one of the authors of the ultrademocratic Pennsylvania constitution, rose to object. The members, he said, ought to have time to consider the subject. He moved, there-

Order of Procession,

In honor of the establishment of the CONSTITUTION of the United States.

To parade precisely at Eight o'Clock in the Morning, of FRIDAY, the 4th of JULY, 1788, proceeding along Third-street to Callowhill-street; thence to Fourth-street; down Fourth-street to Market-street; thence to the Grounds in Front of Bush-hill.

I.
AN Officer, with twelve Axe-men, in frocks and caps.

II.
The City Troop of Light-Horse, commanded by Colonel Miles.

III.
INDEPENDENCE.
John Nixon, Esq; on horseback, bearing the staff and cap of Liberty—The words, " 4th July, 1776," in gold letters, pendant from the staff.

IV.
Four Pieces of Artillery, with a detachment from the Train, commanded by Captains Morrell and Fisher.

V.
ALLIANCE WITH FRANCE.
Thomas Fitzsimons, Esq; on horseback, carrying a flag, white ground, having three fleurs-de lys and thirteen stars in union, over the words " 6th February, 1778," in gold letters.

VI.
Corps of Light-Infantry, commanded by Capt. Claypoole, from the 1st regiment.

VII.
DEFINITIVE TREATY OF PEACE.
George Clymer, Esq; on horseback, carrying a staff, adorned with olive and laurel, the words " 3d September, 1783," in gold letters, pendant from the staff.

VIII.
Col. John Shee, on horseback, carrying a flag, blue field, with a laurel and an olive wreath over the words— " WASHINGTON, THE FRIEND OF " HIS COUNTRY"—in silver letters—the staff adorned with olive and laurel.

IX.
The City Troop of Light Dragoons, commanded by Major W. Jackson.

X.
Richard Bache, Esq; on horseback, as a Herald, attended by a trumpet, proclaiming a New Æra— the words " NEW ÆRA," in gold letters, pendant from the Herald's staff, and the following lines,
Peace o'er our land her olive wand extends,
And white rob'd Innocence from Heaven descends;
The crimes and frauds of Anarchy shall fail,
Returning Justice lifts again her scale.

XI.
The Hon. Peter Muhlenberg, Esq; Vice-President of Pennsylvania, on horseback, carrying a flag, blue field, emblazoned—the words " 17th September, 1787," in silver letters, on the flag.

XII.
Band of Music.

XIII.
The Honorable Chief-Justice M'Kean,
The Hon. Judge Atlee,   The Hon. Judge Rush, (in their Robes of Office)
In an ornamented Car, drawn by six horses, bearing the CONSTITUTION, framed, fixed on a staff, crowned with the Cap of Liberty—the words— " THE PEOPLE," in gold letters, on the staff, immediately under the Constitution.

XIV.
Corps of Light-Infantry, commanded by Capt. Heysham, from the 3d regiment.

XV.
Ten Gentlemen, representing the States that have adopted the Foederal Constitution, viz.
1. Duncan Ingraham, Esq;   New-Hampshire,
2. Jonathan Williams, jun. Esq;   Massachusetts,
3. Jared Ingersoll, Esq;   Connecticut,
4. Hon. Chief Justice Brearley,   New-Jersey,
5. James Wilson, Esq;   Pennsylvania,
6. Col. Thomas Robinson,   Delaware,
7. Hon. J. E. Howard, Esq;   Maryland,
8. Col. Febiger,   Virginia,
9. W. Ward Burrows, Esq;   South-Carolina,
10. George Meade, Esq;   Georgia.
Bearing distinguishing flags and walking arm in arm, emblematic of Union.

XVI.
Colonel William Williams, in armour, on horseback, bearing a Shield, emblazoned with the arms of the United States.

XVII.
The Montgomery county Troop of Light-Horse, commanded by James Morris, Esquire.

XVIII.
An ornamented Car, drawn by four horses, bearing Captain Thomas Bell, carrying the Flag of The United States,—Monsieur Barbé de Marbois, Flag of France,—Mr. Hennekin, Flag of The United Netherlands,—Mr. Helstad, Flag of Sweden,—Mr. Lock, Flag of Prussia,—Thomas Barclay, Esquire, Flag of Morocco,—States in alliance with America.

XIX.
The Judge, Register, Marshal, and other Officers of the Court of Admiralty, with their insignia.

XX.
Wardens of the Port, and Tonnage Officers.

XXI.
Collector of the Custom, and Naval Officer.

XXII.
The Surveyor-General, Receiver-General, Secretary, and other Officers of the Land Office.

XXIII.
Register, Recorder of Deeds, and Comptroller-General.

XXIV.
Peter Baynton, Esq; and Colonel Isaac Melcher, as an American and an Indian, smoaking the Calumet of Peace, in a carriage drawn by two horses.

XXV.
GRAND FOEDERAL EDIFICE, on a carriage drawn by ten horses, containing Messrs. Hilary Baker, George Latimore, John Wharton, John Nesbitt, Samuel Morris, John Brown, Track Francis, Joseph Anthony, John Chaloner and Peter Oswi, citizens of the Union.
Attended by the House-carpenters.

XXVI.
Corps of Light Infantry, commanded by Captain Rose, 5th regiment.

XXVII.
The Agricultural Society, headed by their President, S. Powel, Esq;

XXVIII.
The Farmers, headed by Richard Peters, Richard Willing, Samuel Meredith, Isaac Warner, George Gray, William Peltz, ——Burkhart and Charles Willing, with ploughs, &c.

XXIX.
The Manufacturing Society, with the spinning and carding machines, looms, &c. headed by Robert Hare, Esq;

Corps of Light Infantry, commanded by Capt. Robinson, from the 6th regiment.

The Marine Society, with their insignia.

The Foederal Ship, The UNION, commanded by John Green, Esq; Captain S. Smith, W. Belchar and Mr. Mercer, Lieutenants, with a proper crew of Officers and Seamen.

The Pilots of the Port, with a Pilot Boat.

Boat Builders, with a Barge.

The Ship-carpenters, Sail-makers, Rope-makers, Block-makers and Riggers.

The Merchants and Traders of the city and liberties of Philadelphia, headed by Thomas Willing, Esq; with their insignia—followed by the Merchants Clerks.

Corps of Light Infantry, commanded by Capt. Sproat, from the 4th regiment.

TRADES and PROFESSIONS.

XXX.
1. Cordwainers.

XXXI.
2. Coach-painters.

XXXII.
3. Cabinet and Chair-makers.

XXXIII.
4. Brick-makers.

XXXIV.
5. Painters.

XXXV.
6. Porters.

XXXVI.
7. Watch-makers.

XXXVII.
8. Fringe and Ribband Weavers.

XXXVIII.
9. Bricklayers.

XXXIX.
10. Taylors.

XL.
11. Instrument-makers, Turners and Windsor Chair-makers.

XLI.
12. Carvers and Gilders.

XLII.
13. Coopers.

XLIII.
14. Plane-makers.

XLIV.
15. Whip Manufacturers.

XLV.
16. Black-smiths, White-smiths, Nail-smiths and Bell-hangers.

XLVI.
17. Coach-makers.

XLVII.
18. Potters.

XLVIII.
19. Hatters.

XLIX.
20. Wheel-wrights.

L.
21. Tin-plate Workers.

LI.
22. Skinners, Breeches-makers and Glovers.

LII.
23. Tallow-chandlers.

LIII.
24. Butchers.

LIV.
25. Printers, Stationers and Book-binders.

LV.
26. Saddlers.

LVI.
27. Stone-cutters.

LVII.
28. Bakers.

LVIII.
29. Gun-smiths.

LIX.
30. Copper-smiths.

LX.
31. Gold-smiths, Silver-smiths and Jewellers.

LXI.
32. Distillers.

LXII.
33. Tobacconists.

LXIII.
34. Brass-founders.

LXIV.
35. Stocking Manufacturers.

LXV.
36. Curriers.

LXVI.
37. Druggists.

LXVII.
38. Upholsterers.

LXVIII.
39. Sugar-refiners.

LXIX.
40. Brewers.

LXX.
41. Peruke-makers and Barbers.

LXXI.
42. Ship-chandlers.

LXXII.
43. Engravers.

LXXIII.
44. Plaisterers.

Corps of Light Infantry, commanded by Capt. Ross, from the 3d regiment.

The Civil and Military Officers of Congress in the City.

His Excellency the PRESIDENT, and the SUPREME EXECUTIVE COUNCIL.

The Justices of the Common Pleas and the Magistrates.

Sheriff and Coroner, on horseback.

City Wardens.

Constables and Watchmen.

The gentlemen of the Bar, headed by the Honorable Edward Shippen, Esquire, President of the Common Pleas, and William Bradford, Esquire, Attorney-General, followed by the Students of Law.

The Clergy of the different denominations.

The College of Physicians, headed by their President, Dr. Redman.

Students of the University, headed by the Vice-Provost, and of other Schools, headed by their respective Principals, Professors, Masters and Tutors.

The County Troop of Light Horse, commanded by Major W. Macpherson, bringing up the rear of the the whole.
Major Fullerton to attend the right wing——Colonel Mentges the left wing.

On the UNION GREEN, at Bush-hill, Mr. WILSON will deliver an Oration, suited to the day; after which a Collation will be prepared for the company.

The following gentlemen, distinguished by a white feather in the hat, are Superintendants of the procession. General Mifflin, General Stewart, Colonel Proctor, Colonel Gurney, Major Moore, Major Lenox, Mr. Peter Brown, Colonel Will, Colonel Marsh.

To add to the entertainment of the day, ten vessels will be prepared and paraded as follows, one representing New-Hampshire, opposite the Northern-Liberties,—the next for Massachusetts, opposite Vine-street,—Connecticut, opposite Race-street,—New-Jersey, Arch—Pennsylvania, Market—Delaware, Chesnut—Maryland, Walnut—Virginia, Spruce—South-Carolina, Pine—and Georgia, South-street. The RISING SUN, under the command of Captain Philip Brown, will be anchored off Market-street, and superbly dressed. At night she will be handsomely illuminated.

By Order of the Committee of Arrangement,
Francis Hopkinson, Chairman.

Philadelphia: Printed by HALL and SELLERS.

In Philadelphia this "Order of Procession" outlined that city's joyful parade to celebrate the new Constitution. After a glorious array of patriotic floats marched representatives of the "Trades and Professions."

fore, to postpone consideration until the afternoon session.

Thomas Fitzsimons (City of Philadelphia), one of the signers of the federal Constitution, declared that the business was of the highest consequence. The only object of consideration was not the merits of the new Constitution, but solely whether the election of delegates should be held. It was the general wish of the people that the House should go forward in the matter.

William Findley (Westmoreland County), Ulster-born, former weaver and teacher, now a farmer and Democratic leader, agreed that the subject was important. It was so important, indeed, that the House should go into it with deliberation. It was so important that the members should not be surprised into it.

Daniel Clymer (Berks County), cousin of George, said (in extract): "I have heard, Sir, that only four or five leading party-men in this city are against it, whose names I should be glad to know, that their characters might be examined; for I am confident they will be hereafter ashamed to show their faces among the good people whose future prosperity they wish to blast in the bud. Let them be careful, lest they draw upon themselves the odium of that people who have long indulged their rioting upon public favor."

Findley: "The gentleman from Berks has spoken warmly against opposing the present measure in a manner as if intended to prevent men from speaking their minds. He has charged some leading characters in this city with giving opposition; if he means me as one of them—"

Daniel Clymer (addressing the Speaker): "No, Sir, upon my honor, I did not mean him."

Findley: "Well, then, I don't consider that part of his speech as addressed to the House, but merely to the gallery."

Daniel Clymer: "The measure will be adopted; for it is too generally agreeable, and too highly recommended, to be assassinated by the hand of intrigue and cabal."

Whitehill: "The gentlemen that have brought forward this motion must have some design. Why not allow time to consider it? I believe if time is allowed, we shall be able to show that this is not the proper time for calling a convention; and I don't know any reason there can be for driving it down our throats, without an hour's preparation."

George Clymer: "To hesitate upon this proposition will give a very unfavorable aspect to a measure on which our future happiness, nay, I may also say, our future existence, as a nation, depends."

Hugh Henry Brackenridge of Westmoreland County, Princeton graduate, former schoolteacher and chaplain in the Revolutionary Army, now a lawyer, author, and wit, was the only member from the western counties and the only Democrat to support the Constitution actively. He rose to express the view that, "from its magnitude and importance," the members surely must have re-flected for some days on the matter. In his opinion they were as well prepared now to determine upon the principle as they would be after having eaten their dinner.

Whitehill: "Congress ought to send forward the plan before we do anything at all in this matter. For of what use was sending it forward to them, unless we meant to wait their determination? Now as these measures are not recommended by Congress, why should we take them up? Why should we take up a thing which does not exist? Is it not better to go safely on the business, and let it lie over till the next House? When we have adjourned, let our constituents think of it, and instruct their representatives to consider of the plan proper to be pursued. Will not the next House be able to determine as we are?"

Daniel Clymer: "The Constitution lately presented to you [was] framed by the collective wisdom of a continent, centered in a venerable band of patriots, worthies, heroes, legislators and philosophers—the admiration of a world. No longer shall thirty thousand [Philadelphians] engage all our attention—all our efforts to procure happiness. No!—The extended embrace of fraternal love shall enclose three millions, and ere fifty years are elapsed, thirty millions, as a band of brothers!

"As this subject is now before us, let us not hesitate, but eagerly embrace the glorious opportunity of being foremost in its adoption. Let us not hesitate, because it is damping the ardor with which it should be pursued. Sir, it is throwing cold water on the flame that warms the breast of every friend of liberty, and every patriot who wishes this country to acquire that respect to which she is justly entitled."

The question was put: Would the House agree to postpone consideration of the matter? It was defeated.

George Clymer spoke to the real Federalist concern. "If this House order a convention," he said, "it may be deliberated and decided some time in November, [1787], and the Constitution may be acted under by December. But if it is left over to the next House, it will inevitably be procrastinated until December, 1788."

The Federalists began to cry, "Question! Question!" and a vote was taken on the resolution: Would the House agree to elect delegates and call a state convention? It was carried 43 to 19.

Whitehill then moved that the session adjourn until four o'clock that afternoon, at which time, he said, they might decide the lesser issues of time and place of the election of delegates and the holding of the convention.

Undoubtedly, congratulations were exchanged, and there was much joking at the Federalists' luncheon tables at how smoothly everything had been managed and how clearly the victory had been won. But when the session resumed at four o'clock, the Federalists were astounded to find not one of the nineteen Democratic members in his seat. With forty-four members present, the House was two votes short of a quorum—which meant that no business could be conducted.

Mr. Wynkoop observed that the missing members

The center building in this 1790 engraving was Pennsylvania's State House, where the acrimonious debate described in this article took place. In the nineteenth century, Philadelphians started calling the remodelled building Independence Hall.

were those who had given opposition that morning, and he suspected that they had conspired to absent themselves. He moved that the sergeant at arms be ordered to fetch them. The sergeant accordingly was dispatched. When he returned, he was examined at the bar of the House.

Speaker: "Well, Sergeant, have you seen the absent members?"

The sergeant replied that he had seen seventeen members at Major Boyd's boarding house on Sixth Street.

Speaker: "What did you say to them?"

Sergeant: "I told the gentlemen that the Speaker and the House had sent for them, and says they, 'There is no House.'"

Speaker: "Did you let them know they were desired to attend?"

Sergeant: "Yes, Sir, but they told me they could not attend this afternoon, for they had not made up their minds yet."

Daniel Clymer: "How is that?"

Sergeant: "They had not made up their minds this afternoon to wait on you."

Speaker: "Who told you this?"

Sergeant: "Mr. Whitehill told me first."

Clymer: "Who told you afterward?"

Sergeant: "Mr. Clarke said they must go *electioneering* now."

Clymer: "Was there no private citizens there?"

Sergeant: "No, Sir."

Clymer: "There was none then, but *men in public offices?*"

Sergeant: "No."

Clymer: "Did you hear of any one willing to come?"

Sergeant: "No, Sir."

The Federalists, outwitted, baffled, and angry at this breach of trust, debated what to do next. If no business could be conducted, the Assembly would be forced to adjourn the next day without naming a date for selecting delegates or for holding the convention. Mr. Wynkoop declared, "I would be glad to know, if there is no way to compel men, who deserted from the duty they owed their country, to a performance of it, when they were within reach of the House. If there is not, then *God be merciful to us!!!*"

A search of the books revealed no regulation compelling an absent member to attend, the only penalty being loss of one third of a day's pay for each absence. The Speaker declared a recess until nine thirty the following morning.

Federalists discussed the affair in homes and taverns throughout the evening, with liberal abuse for the nineteen recalcitrant members and much speculation about what the minority would do when the Assembly reconvened. The Democratic leaders worked through the night behind locked doors at Major Boyd's; they were preparing an address to their constituents in which they set forth their objections to the new plan of government.

When General Mifflin took the chair on Saturday morning, the minority members were again absent and again no quorum could be declared.

George Clymer presented to the House a packet of documents he had received from New York in the early morning. It contained, he said, a resolution of Congress, passed unanimously, requesting the legislature of each state to put the proposed Constitution to a vote of a popularly elected convention. This had been signed the day before, and Mr. William Bingham had forwarded it to him by express rider, "having chosen this mode in preference to the ordinary conveyance by post." The resolution was read aloud.

Fortified by this new evidence of regularity, the Speaker again sent the sergeant at arms to find the missing members and request their attendance, this time accompanied by the assistant clerk carrying the resolution of Congress. They returned to report that they had seen a dozen of the members in various places and had delivered the message and shown them the resolution. Mr. Findley had "mended his pace" and escaped; others had declared they would not attend; one said he would consider the matter and do what he thought just.

In the meantime word had spread around the city that the Democrats had "absconded" from their duties at the Assembly. A crowd of men gathered, and as time passed they grew impatient. They marched off in search of any two absent members, and the path led straight to Major Boyd's boarding house. There they found two Democrats: James McCalmont of Franklin County and Jacob Miley of Dauphin. Both men had been militia officers in

This ode of celebration, written by Francis Hopkinson for Philadelphia's Constitution parade, was tossed out among the marchers and borne aloft by pigeons released from one of the floats.

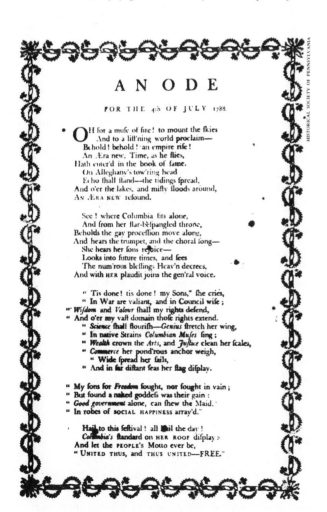

the Revolution. McCalmont, fifty, a major, had a distinguished record as a frontier scout and Indian fighter; he had been famous for his speed in running and his ability to reload a musket or rifle while in full flight or pursuit.

Several of the crowd entered and read the congressional resolution aloud. McCalmont and Miley refused to budge. When that information was conveyed to those waiting outside, they shouted imprecations, smashed windows with stones, broke down the front door, and stormed into the house. McCalmont and Miley were collared, dragged from the premises, and pushed and pulled through the streets to the State House. General Mifflin, hearing a commotion outside and suspecting the reason, discreetly absented himself for a while from the chamber. The two men, their clothes dirtied and torn, their faces white with anger, were thrust onto the floor of the House and escorted to their seats. The clerk wrote in his minutes, in what must be considered something of an understatement, "The Speaker left the chair, and in a few minutes Mr. James McCalmont and Mr. Jacob Miley entered the House. The Speaker resumed the chair, and the roll was called." Both men answered to their names or were declared present by others. With forty-six members on the floor the Speaker declared a quorum.

McCalmont rose to protest that he had been brought into the Assembly room by force, contrary to his wishes, by a number of citizens he did not know. He asked to be dismissed from the House.

Fitzsimons replied that he would be glad to know if any member of the House had been guilty of forcing the gentleman from his determination to absent himself. If so, the House should mark such conduct with its disapprobation, he said.

Brackenridge added: "If the member has been conducted by the citizens of Philadelphia to his seat in the legislature, and they have not treated him with the respect and veneration he deserves, it must lie with him to obtain satisfaction, but not with us. How he came here can form no part of our enquiry. Whether his friends brought him (and I should think they could not be his enemies who would compel him to do his duty and avoid wrong), I say, Sir, whether his friends brought him, or by the influence of good advice persuaded him to come, and he did come; or whether to ease his difficulty in walking to this room they brought him in a sedan chair, or by whatever ways or means he introduced himself among us, all we are to know is that he is here, and it only remains for us to decide whether he shall have leave of absence."

McCalmont: "I desire that the rules may be read, and I will agree to stand by the decision of the House."

The rules were read, and they were found to state that "every member who did not answer on calling the roll should pay two shillings and six pence, or, if there was not a quorum without him, five shillings."

McCalmont rose, took some loose silver from his pocket, held it out, and said, "Well, Sir, here is your five shillings to let me go."

The crowd gathered behind the railing roared with laughter. The Speaker declared that the person appointed to receive fines was not in his place, and that even if he had been, the member should not pay a fine. McCalmont had not broken the rule, the Speaker said. He had appeared and answered to his name and therefore could keep his money.

Mr. Robinson of Philadelphia County, though a Federalist, had some uneasy qualms of conscience. He opined that the House had no authority to detain the member as though he were in prison. Mr. Wynkoop expressed his amazement at this solicitude for a member who had absconded "from his duty at the bar of the House." Mr. McCalmont declared that he had to answer for his conduct at a more important bar than that of the House.

Fitzsimons was stern. He declared that he was a true friend to good order and decorum, but that he believed the gentleman's complaint was not to be redressed by the House of Assembly. The member himself had trespassed, Fitzsimons said; McCalmont had perhaps offered the greatest indignity to the legislature of Pennsylvania that could be offered. He had tendered a pittance, a fine of five shillings, in order to be permitted to destroy the business, if not the good government, of the state. The member was now present, Fitzsimons said, and should stay, not only on constitutional grounds, but from the law of nature that would not suffer any body to destroy its own existence prematurely.

Robinson: "Suppose the House determine that he shall not leave, and yet he should attempt to withdraw. Certainly you will not lock your doors."

Fitzsimons: "Yes, Sir, if no other method could retain him."

A moment later McCalmont rose and made a dash for the door. The crowd yelled, "Stop him!" and those about the door barred his way. McCalmont returned to his seat.

The Speaker put the question: "Shall Mr. McCalmont have leave of absence?" It was voted "almost unanimously in the negative."

Brackenridge then moved that the delegates to the state convention be elected on the first Tuesday in November. McCalmont objected that this was much too early and moved the last Tuesday in December. His motion failed. He moved the third Tuesday in December, then the second Tuesday, with the same result. He moved that the site of the convention be moved from Philadelphia to Carlisle, but he was not upheld. He moved that the change be made to Lancaster and was enthusiastically supported by the member from Lancaster. Fifteen members voted for Lancaster in a defeated motion.

The formal resolution was now put: That the election of delegates be held on November 6, 1787, and that the convention meet in the State House in Philadelphia on the third Tuesday in November. It was passed by a vote of 44 to 2. The Federalists had won their victory. The Assembly adjourned. McCalmont and Miley were released.

In the campaign that followed for election of delegates, Democrats and Federalists attacked one another with arguments and invective and sometimes with clubs, stones, and fists.

October 5, 1787: The first of twenty-four letters of "Centinel" (sentinel of the people's liberties) appeared in the *Gazetteer*. These papers, running through the next fourteen months, still of undetermined authorship, were the Democratic counterpart of the eighty-five papers (*The Federalist*) produced by "Publius" in New York. Centinel attacked Publius on many points and brilliantly set forth the Democratic case against the Constitution, the "harpies of power," and "the wealthy and ambitious, who in every community think they have a right to lord it over their fellow creatures." The treatment accorded McCalmont and Miley, Centinel said, showed what would happen to free citizens under the Federalist Constitution.

October 6: At a public meeting in the State House yard, James Wilson cogently answered the Democratic arguments point by point, and in so doing assumed the role of the country's most effective proponent of the Constitution in debate. His speech was widely distributed, reprinted, copied, and quoted. The Democrats attacked it as a "train of pitiful sophistries and evasions," compared Wilson (unfavorably) with Tiberius, Caligula, and Nero, and charged that he was "strongly tainted with the spirit of *high aristocracy.*"

November 6: The Federalists scored an overwhelming victory in the election of delegates, losing only the six western counties. Their majority was 2 to 1, or 46 convention votes to 23. Elated at their victory, several dozen Federalists gathered on election night before Major Boyd's, reviled the "damned rascals" housed therein, flung stones through the newly repaired windows, and broke the door with large rocks.

November 21: The convention convened in the State House. The delegates spent the first week arguing about procedure. James Wilson distinguished himself with five powerful, if somewhat florid, speeches. Robert Whitehill, the Democrat from Cumberland County, submitted fifteen proposed amendments to the Constitution as a bill of rights. They were ignored. On a number of occasions the members were close to physical assault on one another.

December 7: Delaware ratified the Constitution, won over by the compromise that gave the small states equal representation in the Senate (the Constitution's only irrevocable article). John Smilie of Fayette County, who with Whitehill and Findley was leading the fight against ratification in the Pennsylvania convention, sneered that Delaware had "reaped the honor of having first surrendered the liberties of the people."

December 12: Pennsylvania became the second state—and the first large state—"to assent to and ratify" the Constitution. The vote was, predictably, 46 to 23. A transcript of the convention proceedings was made for publication, but the Federalists persuaded the court printer to release only the Federalist speeches.

December 13: The delegates marched in procession to the Court House at Market and Second streets, accompanied by members of the new Assembly, state and city officials, and other local dignitaries. The ratification was read from a balcony to a great gathering of citizens. The city bells rang out, and thirteen cannons fired salvos.

December 18: The defeated Democratic delegates issued a pamphlet titled *Reasons for Dissent* and mailed a copy to every printer in the country. No copies were delivered. Democrats charged that they were destroyed by "the sons of power" who controlled the Pennsylvania post-office system.

December 27: Federalists in Carlisle, a Scotch-Irish town of three hundred houses in the Cumberland Valley some 120 miles west of Philadelphia, staged a public celebration in honor of the ratification. They procured James Wilson for an oration, dragged a cannon to the public square, and heaped up a great stack of barrels for a bonfire. Antifederalists charged the crowd, upset the barrels, spiked the cannon, burned a copy of the Constitution, and began to beat Wilson with bludgeons. An old soldier saved his life by throwing himself over the body and taking the blows until help came.

Two days of riots followed. John Montgomery, venerable Federalist, one of the founders of Dickinson College in Carlisle five years earlier, wrote to a friend, "They are violent on both sides. . . . We [Federalists] are in a very disagreeable unhapey situation in this place nothing ever happned so bad amongst us neaghbours pass each other without speaking."

June 21, 1788: The Constitution became law and the United States a new nation with ratification by New Hampshire, the ninth state.

July 4: Philadelphia mounted an all-day celebration to mark the day of Independence and the forming of the new Union. Some five thousand marched or rode in a Federal Procession a mile and a half long. All the trades, crafts, and professions were represented, many of them with elaborate floats, in a spectacle such as no American had ever seen before. High point of the procession was a structure called the "New Roof or Grand Fœderal Ediface," 36 feet high, drawn by ten white horses. Benjamin Rush called the Ediface "truly sublime" and observed approvingly that of the thousands who took part in the ceremonies that day, very few engaged in quarrels and almost no one was intoxicated.

On an open field at the parade's end, James Wilson, standing on the Grand Ediface, delivered the Fourth of July oration. Some of his passages were drowned out by the ill-timed firing of thirteen cannons on vessels anchored in the Delaware, but his soaring closing words were loud and clear: "PEACE walks *serene* and *unalarmed* over all the unmolested regions—while LIBERTY, VIRTUE, and RELIGION go hand in hand harmoniously *protecting, enlivening,* and *exalting* all! HAPPY COUNTRY, MAY THY HAPPINESS BE PERPETUAL!"

* * *

The Pennsylvania Democrats made their peace with the new form of government. Within two years they got the Bill of Rights they had fought for: ten amendments to the Constitution that were remarkably like the amendments Robert Whitehill had vainly offered to the Pennsylvania state convention. James McCalmont became a judge, and Jacob Miley a representative, under the new Pennsylvania constitution. Robert Whitehill served four terms and John Smilie served eight terms in the House of Representatives of the United States. William Findley served eleven terms, and in one of them, in 1795, he moved the creation of the first standing congressional committee—a body of honest representatives called the Ways and Means Committee, formed to keep a sharp eye on the financial operations of a Federalist administration.

3 National Consolidation Expansion

All too often American history seems to be a succession of leaps from one glory-filled war to the next. The Revolutionary War and the Civil War are etched upon the nation's mind, but the history in between (including the nearly disastrous War of 1812) often seems hazy and disjointed. This section inspects some of the most salient aspects of the period from the end of the War for Independence through the War of 1812. These were crucial years for the young republic. Westward expansion, with its extermination of and deceitful treaty making with the American Indian, developed a momentum that was to carry the nation to the shores of the Pacific. The growth of business vastly accelerated the development of American capitalism. Finally, a prolonged confrontation with England witnessed not only the first attempts to restrict the constitutional liberties guaranteed by the Bill of Rights but also the burning of the nation's capital by an invading force and the near-secession of the New England from the Union.

Independence opened up new horizons for investment; it also demanded the creation of new financial institutions to facilitate the transactions of an economy experiencing rapid capitalistic development. "William Duer and the Origins of the New York Stock Exchange" by Robert Sobel depicts the unstable world of those who participated in the first bull and bear markets of the emerging investments business.

The next article, "One Way to Deal with Dissent" by Robert Hardy Andrews, retells the tale of the Alien and Sedition Acts—one of Congress' rare instances of writing laws that expressly contravened freedoms guaranteed by the first ten amendments of the Constitution.

"Tecumseh: The First Advocate of Red Power" by Walter Jarrett takes us westward to the Plains to witness the relentless advance of white Americans and the concomitant destruction of Indian cultures. Had Tecumseh's remarkable leadership of an Indian federation dedicated to repulsing the white invader materialized as an effective fighting force, American history might well have taken a different course. In any event, Tecumseh is a reminder that American Indians did not first conceive of Red Power in the 1960s.

The War of 1812 was the creation of congressional war hawks against the wishes of James Madison, the nation's fourth President. In those days the power of the executive was comparatively weak, and the military-industrial complex nonexistent. In short, Madison was forced into war with only the bravado of militiamen eager to take Canada to aid him. The result was nearly disastrous.

The first article on that war, "Dolley Madison and the Burning of Washington" by Elswyth Thane, reveals the extraordinary cool of the nation's first lady as well as the fragility of American power. The stiffening resolve of American nationalism despite serious defeats might help explain why the nationalism of small countries sprouts rather than wilts when confronted with the supposedly overwhelming might of the superpowers.

The next article, Wilson Sullivan's "Secession: Shadow and Substance," explores another facet of that strange war—the nation's first serious flirtation with secession. It may surprise northern ears to listen as Massachusetts Congressman Josiah Quincy says, "As it will be the right of us all, so it will be the duty of some, to prepare definitely for separation; amicably if they can, violently if they must." Fortunately, the Hartford Convention, meeting in protest against a war that had crippled New England's commerce, never took the final step of secession.

In 1814, the Treaty of Ghent largely restored the status quo between England and the United States. What it did not recognize formally was that the nation had successfully passed through one of its shakiest periods. Its existence in the shark-infested waters of international politics was secure, the Constitution had been affirmed, and unity was restored and strenghtened.

William Duer and the Origins of the New York Stock Exchange

by Robert Sobel

Awarded a fellow of the Columbia University of Seminar in Early American History, Robert Sobel is associate professor of history at the New College of Hofstra. He is also the author of several books, including *Prosperity on Margin: The Stock Market in the 1920s.*

New York in 1792 was a bustling but small city. Boys would fish off the Hudson piers at Rector Street and report large catches of lobster and crab. Collect Pond, a short walk from Chambers Street, was a favorite ice-skating place, which was reached in wintry days by sleigh rides from the Bowery. The city was dirty, as were most urban centers of the time, but the sanitation department — thirty-five scavengers and a host of pigs — did their jobs as best they could.

The pigs were kept near Bunker Hill, off Broadway near Grand Street, an area which in the summer and fall was used for bull-baiting and other manly sports.

In this diorama the first investors met under the Buttonwood tree at 68 Wall Street to buy and trade securities and bank notes.

Mayor Richard Varick, an incurable optimist, looked forward to the day when the area might have to be relocated, due to the increase in the city's population. In 1792 there were some thirty-four thousand New Yorkers, few of whom lived above what is now Canal Street.

New York was one of the busiest ports in the nation, and in 1794 it would pass Philadelphia in total tonnage handled. The wharfs were fed by a good system of dirt roads and the Hudson River. Bowery Road was the major land route, with Bull's Head Tavern on Bayard Street the last stop for drovers bringing their cattle to slaughter.

Chatham Street and Broadway was New York's busiest intersection. St. Paul's Church was on one corner and a theatre and park on another. A few blocks away were a group of boarding houses used by Columbia College students, as well as by those who worked at the municipal jail, the city hospital, and the almshouse, which were also nearby.

Trinity Church, at the head of Wall Street, was a major municipal landmark, and the street itself the center of the city's business district. Alexander Hamilton had lived on Wall Street a few years earlier when the capital was in New York. City Hall was nearby — it had been used earlier as Federal Hall, the temporary seat of government — and municipal functionaries jostled with merchants and lottery ticket sellers in the several coffeehouses on the east side of the street, which ended in what was appropriately called Coffee House Wharf. The area smelled of coffee, indigo, chocolate, sugar, spices, fruits — all of which were either exported or imported by Wall Street.

The government was in Philadelphia in 1792, but former Assistant Secretary of the Treasury William Duer remained in New York. One of the social arbiters of the city, Duer kept a fine home presided over by his wife, Kitty, the daughter of Revolutionary War General Lord Sterling. A political power, Duer had arranged for the leasing of Washington's home while the President was in the city, had been one of those asked by Hamilton to write an essay in the *Federalist Papers* (which was not printed), and was a leading light in Federalist circles. Some thought the bright young man might one day be considered for the presidency itself!

Although interested in politics and involved in society, Duer's major interests were in business and speculation. He was in charge at Parker & Duer, Duer & Parker, and William Duer & Co., all engaged in land speculation and commerce. His name was one of those respected in London and Paris banking circles, at a time when few Americans were considered capable of large-scale business ventures. Duer would be a guiding force in the Scioto Company, a major land combine, and the Society for Useful Manufactures, the first attempt at a permanent manufacturing complex. Duer had the connections, abilities, funds, and desire to participate in speculations. A major opportunity for profit presented itself in 1792, and Duer grabbed at it with both hands.

The major speculative items in 1792 were government bonds and stock in new banks. In order to finance the new constitutional government, Secretary of the Treasury Hamilton had proposed a series of bond issues two years earlier. With Washington's aid, he was able to pursuade Congress to pass the Funding Act of 1790, which provided for the issuance of federal bonds to be exchanged for Continental and Confederate obligations.

Three types of securities were sold: six percent bonds which bore interest from the date of issue; six percents which would begin to pay interest ten years after issuance; and three percent bonds. By the end of the year, some $62 million of these bonds were sold, and the "sixes," "threes," and "six deferred" were traded both in America and Europe. In 1791 they were joined by the "B.U.S.'s." The Bank of the United States, proposed by Hamilton, endorsed by Washington, and approved by Congress, was capitalized at $10 million (25,000 shares of $400 par value), and traded in whole, half, and quarter shares.

Although some shares were traded in Philadelphia and New York in 1791, most transactions were handled by Americans for European interests. The bonds and B.U.S. stock were hot speculative items. Since the stability of the new government was in doubt, the issues sold at a discount. Should the United States fail, they would be worthless; should the new government succeed, they would appreciate in value.

Hope & Company of Amsterdam, Daniel Crommelin & Company, with branches throughout the Netherlands, the Société Gallo-Américaine of Paris, Etienne Clavière of Genoa, and other European houses were deep in speculation in these issues by late 1791. But they could not act intelligently without information, preferably of the "inside" variety from one with important connections. They would need American agents to handle transactions. These agents would have to be free to make decisions on the spot, and so would have to be partners, people with shares in the enterprise. William Duer filled the qualifications admirably.

As early as 1788, Parker & Duer acted as American agent for Etienne Clavière and some London firms. Van Staphorts & Hubbard and Willinks & Stadinski joined soon after. Brissot de Warville, their emissary to America, reported that Duer was one of the best speculators he had ever met. "It is difficult to unite to a great facility in calculation, more extensive views and a quicker penetration into the most complicated projects. To these qualities he joins goodness of heart; and it is to his obliging character, and his zeal, that I owe much valuable information on the finances of this country, which I shall communicate hereafter." By 1791, the combine was deep in speculation in land, bills, and, most important, government bonds and B.U.S. stock.

Speculation in government obligations, called "scrip" in the slang of the day, reached new highs in 1791. "Scripponomy," "Scriptophobia," and "Scriptomania" were terms used by conservative newspapers to describe it. "The Scriptophobia is at full height," wrote the *New York Journal and Patriotic Register;* "It has risen like a rocket — like a rocket it will burst with a crack — then down drops the rocket stick." A reader of the newspaper protested, "O that I had but cash — how soon would I have a finger in the pie!"

James Madison wrote Thomas Jefferson of the bull market, reporting that "stock and script the sole domestic subjects of conversation . . . speculations . . . carried on with money borrowed at from two and a half per cent a month to one per cent a week." And the *New York Daily Gazette* of August 13, 1791, printed one of the many poems inspired by the rush to buy securities:

SPECULATION
What magic this among the people,
That swells a may-pole to a steeple?
Touched by the wand of speculation,
A frenzy runs through all the nation;
For soon or late, so truth advises,
Things must assume their proper sizes —
And sure as death all mortal trips,
Thousands will rue the name of SCRIPTS.

Through all this, Duer reigned as king of speculators, making a reputation as well as a fortune. Then, during the last week of the year, he acted to institutionalize his new role. Meeting with Alexander Macomb, a

William Duer (above, left) was a member of the Continental Congress and Assistant Secretary of the Treasury before he became involved in speculative ventures. Although he was to die in debtors' prison William Duer was the man most instrumental in the founding of the New York Stock Exchange. Alexander Hamilton (left), Secretary of the Treasury, foresaw the possibility of a market crash due to overinvestment and he warned his friend Duer, "My friendship for you, and my concern for the public cause, were both alarmed." With the signing of the Corre's Hotel Pact in 1792 the New York Stock Exchange was formed and soon afterward stock at $200 a share was sold to raise money to buy the land and construct the Tontine Coffee-House (above) on the corner of Wall and Water streets. Neither the Pact nor the Tontine would have been possible without William Duer and his securities speculation companies. Duer probably exercised more control over the stock market than any other individual before or since.

wealthy New Yorker like himself, Duer formed what has come to be known as the "Six Per Cent Club." The two men and their partners would pool their resources to speculate in the six percent bonds and whatever other securities interested them. The Club would disband on December 31, 1792, at which time the profits would be distributed according to shares. Thus was born the first native-born American securities pool.

The Club had been formed just in time to participate in the next stage of the bull market — speculation in shares of new banks. The Tammany Bank, the Million Bank, and others were announced early in 1792, and were quickly oversubscribed. The Tammany, capitalized at $200,000 divided into 4,000 shares, received subscriptions for 21,740 shares a few hours after being first offered on January 18, and similar situations existed with other institutions. "Bancophobia" replaced scriptomania as the "in" word along Wall Street in New York and Chestnut Street in Philadelphia.

Again, the conservative newspapers were concerned, especially with the sharp rise in price for the Bank of New York. "More banks may certainly assist gambling, and enable adventurers the longer to swim on the fluctuating waves of speculation," thought a reader of the *New York Daily Advertiser.*

Alexander Hamilton was both concerned and delighted with the interest in stocks and scrip. Higher prices would mean greater confidence in American securities, and this would ease his tasks in borrowing money from Europeans. On the other hand, he feared the bull market would end in a crash. Writing to William Seton, cashier of the Bank of New York, he complained of "these extravagant sallies of speculation," which "do injury to the government, and to the whole system of public credit, but disgusting all sober citizens, and giving a wild air to every thing."

Hamilton realized his old friend, William Duer, was behind many of the manipulations, and he wrote to him, warning of disaster. He told Duer not to overstep himself, for this could bring ruination. "I feared lest it might carry you further than was consistent either with your own safety or the public good. My friendship for you, and my concern for the public cause, were both alarmed." But Duer continued his operations, although he assured Hamilton that all was well.

The rapid and sudden increase in securities trading created a difficult situation for those who handled such transactions. In the past, bankers, tradesmen, lottery ticket sellers, merchants, and others would handle stocks and bonds as a sideline, to be held for investment or sold if and when a good price was to be had. By early 1791, interest in securities had risen to the point where a more or less continual market was needed.

The natural place for such a market was Wall Street in New York and Chestnut Street in Philadelphia. The latter place would seem the more likely location for the larger market. It was the home of the national government as well as the seat of the Bank of the United States. But it lacked a figure like William Duer, and so interest became focused on New York.

In the summer of 1791, trading took place in the street, where individuals with securities to sell would search out those who wished to buy, and vice versa. Then, as the colder weather of winter approached, the traders moved indoors, to several of the taverns along Wall Street. This created a difficulty, however. What if you wanted to buy B.U.S. stock, but no one in Merchant's Coffee House had any to sell? On the other hand, there might be a merchant or banker in another coffeehouse or tavern who wanted to sell, but had no buyer. How could the two be brought together? Clearly, a central market was badly needed.

Attempts were made that winter to solve this problem. Commodities such as sugar and tobacco were bought and sold at auctions. Why not have similar auctions for stocks and bonds? Several appeared in the latter part of 1791, and they advertised in the many New York papers their locations and times.

Usually, the auctions were held shortly after the midday meal. Sellers would deposit their securities with the auctioneer, who would then call them off for the buyers. Most transactions were made on time, with money and security exchanged sixty days after the contract was made. By early 1792 there were a dozen or so such auctions in the city, most of them around Wall Street, and some auctioneers were so busy that they had to schedule two sessions, one in the morning, the other in the afternoon.

This system created more problems than it solved. In the first place, the auctions were held at the same time, and the potential buyer and seller might be at different locations — as had been the case earlier — and the transaction lost. But more important, the new system placed both buyer and seller at the mercy of the auctioneers, who had formed a guild-like combine to periodically raise their fees. Clearly such a situation could not be tolerated.

On March 11, 1792, the following advertisement appeared in *Louden's Register* and other newspapers: "The Stock Exchange office is opened at No. 22 Wall Street for the accommodation of the dealers in Stock, and in which Public Sales will be held daily at noon as usual in rotation by A. L. Bleeker & Sons, J. Pintard, McEvers and Barclay, Cortland & Ferrers, and Jay & Sutton."

These firms, leading brokers all, had combined their forces to combat the auctioneers. From that time on, they would hold their own auction and do away with the hated commissions. Considering the size of their auction, they believed it would soon put the others out of business.

The new auction was an immediate success, and the participants next considered putting their association into a more permanent form. On May 17, they gathered at Corre's Hotel and signed an agreement which established what amounted to a brokers' guild: "We, the subscribers, brokers for the purchase and sale of public stocks, do hereby solemnly promise and pledge ourselves to each other that we will not buy or sell from this date, for any person whatsoever, any kind of public stocks at a less rate than one-quarter of one per cent commission on the specie value, and that we will give preference to each other in our negotiations." The Corre's Hotel Pact is usually considered the basic document which organized the New York Stock Exchange.

Soon after, the brokers decided to build their own coffeehouse and exchange. A subscription for 203 shares of stock at $200 a share was quickly raised, the money used to buy land and construct the Tontine Coffee House at the corner of Wall and Water streets.

The Pact and the Tontine would not have been possible were it not for William Duer. It was Duer who made a securities market necessary by sparking the investment and speculation bull market of 1792, and it was Duer who made New York, and not Philadelphia, the central city of American securities. But Duer did not sign the Corre's Hotel Pact, nor was he a member of the Tontine. By then, he was otherwise occupied.

As buyers and sellers rushed to and fro from auctions in March, William Duer would sit in his Wall Street office, ordering purchases and sales, organizing new ventures, and in general building what he hoped would become a major fortune. By early March, Duer was playing both sides of the market at the same time. He would buy in conjunction with one syndicate, and sell with another. Since he controlled both groups, he would act in such a way as to maximize his gains. Never before or since has a single individual exercised so much control over the market. Perhaps this was the reason that Duer lost his head.

By the second week in March, he started to believe his own propaganda, and was convinced the market would rise indefinitely. Accordingly, he plunged in on the bull side, signing several large purchase orders for bank stock. The money would not be payable for several days, and by then, thought Duer, the stock prices will have risen so high that he would have a handsome profit without having committed a cent.

But prices did not rise; instead they leveled off, and then started to decline, crowding the auctions with worried sellers and a few hopeful buyers. On March 6, the six percents had sold for 24 shillings, 4½ pence; by March 15, the price had fallen to 21 shillings, 4 pence, and other issues fell similar amounts. Money

dried up on Wall Street and elsewhere, and Duer was unable to borrow funds to cover his debts.

At the same time, discrepancies were uncovered in his accounts. Comptroller of the Treasury Oliver Wolcott informed Duer that he owed the government almost a quarter of a million dollars from the time he was Assistant Secretary of Treasury.

Duer ran from one friend to another, contacting all his associates, with no luck; he could not raise money for either his shortages or his stock contracts. In desperation, he wrote to Hamilton, pleading for aid. But before an answer could arrive in New York, Duer was finished. "I am now secure from my enemies, and feeling the purity of my heart defy the world." Thus, Duer assured an associate, Walter Livingston, that all was well. It was March 22. Within twenty-four hours, the master speculator would be taken to debtors' prison.

The next week saw the first major financial panic in American history, an event for which the brokers' auction at No. 22 Wall Street had not been prepared. The office was jammed with sellers and individuals, seeking credit or loans. John Pintard, a founder of the auction and one of the city's leading figures, was also involved in speculation; he fled to New Jersey. The leader of one of New York's first families, Walter Livingston, ran from door to door declaring his solvency.

Pierre de Peyster was more realistic. He owned a Duer note and meant to collect. He ran to the prison, and confronted Duer with a brace of dueling pistols. Pay me now, he cried, or be prepared to defend your honor! Duer paid de Peyster $1,500, and the challenger left.

The panic was short-lived, ending when Hamilton threw his resources of the Treasury behind selected government issues. As the brokers met in Corre's Hotel that May prosperity had returned. The National Gazette reported that there were few signs of the March disaster left. "The shock of the time was very severe, but of short continuance." Stocks were rising, "credit is again revived — and prosperity once more approaches in sight." Pintard was back in the city, and a wiser Livingston again was looking for investments. Duer was in jail, where he would remain until his death on May 7, 1799.

It snowed on January 1, 1793, and the skaters at Collect Pond were obliged to return to their homes. Ice formed on the Hudson, and small boys cut holes and poked their lines into the frigid water, searching for fish. Jefferson had estimated that more than $5 million had been wiped out in the panic, but there were no signs of it that day. On the surface at least, the city was the same as it had been a year earlier when Duer formed the Six Per Cent Club. But there was one major difference. The cornerstone had been laid for the Tontine Coffee House, the first home of the New York Stock Exchange, which was made possible by William Duer, and remains his most significant contribution. ♣

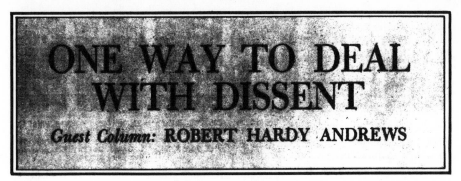

ONE WAY TO DEAL WITH DISSENT

Guest Column: ROBERT HARDY ANDREWS

Losses in an undeclared and unpopular war mounted shockingly. So did taxes and living costs. So did dissent and its by-product, dissension. With a national election just around the corner, Ins joined Outs in crying that the country could not endure another four years of the wrong man in the White House. The angry incumbent fought back, insisting he knew best, but could not bridge a widening credibility gap. Whatever he said or did, there was catcalling in Congress and turmoil in the street. Doves outdid Hawks in vehemence and violence. Exercise of inalienable American rights to write, speak, and march in protest against administration policies, foreign or domestic, had gone about as far as it could go, short of confrontation at the barricades. That was the state of affairs in 1798.

The Constitution and the Bill of Rights were barely ten years old. Only two men had held the reins of presidential power, revocably entrusted to them by the sovereign electorate. The first, George Washington, Father of His Country, nursed soul wounds in bitter voluntary retirement at Mount Vernon, complaining bewildered, "I have been vilified in such exaggerated and indecent terms as could scarcely be applied to a common pickpocket." His successor, previously his resentful Vice President ("My country in its wisdom has consigned me to the most insignificant office that ever the invention of man contrived."), having inherited a whirlwind, reaped a hurricane. And proud, petulant, unpredictable John Adams dealt with dissent and dissenters — and committed political

suicide — by signing the Alien and Sedition Acts. So doing, he set off a chain reaction that continues, in some degree at least, in our more enlightened times.

John Quincy Adams said a generation later that his father's last-ditch challenge to minorities coalescing into an opposition majority "was an ineffectual attempt to extinguish the fire of defamation; it operated like oil upon the flames." Jefferson, writing in 1807 when he thought the Second American Revolution was won and over, capsuled what had gone before. "History in general only informs us what bad government is." But Patrick Henry, heroic against autocracy when in 1775 he made history with "Give me liberty, or give me death!" saw matters differently in 1798, and was echoed by many when he declared that although the acts were probably unconstitutional by letter of the law, that was unimportant as long as they kept the Republicans from seizing the helm of the ship of state.

There were three Alien Acts. The first lengthened waiting time for admission to American citizenship from five to fourteen years. The second empowered the President to arrest or expel from the United States, without trial, any alien regarded as "dangerous to the public peace and safety." The third provided for imprisonment or deportation of subjects, of any foreign power with which the United States might be at war. It did not require a declaration of war *per se.* Taken together the three acts made it possible to muzzle and if need be wipe out the anti-administration press, since most of its editors could be classed as "aliens" at the pleasure of the ruling Federalist Party — under deliberately vague definitions buried in small print.

There were other targets. Where Irish Catholics were allowed to vote at all, they voted against the government in the Irish tradition. Samuel Dexter, a Federalist Senator from Massachusetts, demanded deportation of Irish immigrants flooding New England on the claim that clearly they were all subjects of an unfriendly foreign power. James Madison, attempting to exercise his own right of dissent, argued that "Many Irish proved themselves loyal Americans in 1776," but was shouted down. Concurrently, there were charges that Fisher Ames, a Massachusetts Congressman, had been elected "only due to the votes of Negroes . . . smuggled in under a very lax mode of conducting the elections." However this was dropped when second thought brought up the point that deporting Negroes would deprive their owners of valuable property. But as for Frenchmen, whether refugees from the Terror or agents of the Directory then ruling France, all were lumped under, "Good riddance of bad rubbish."

In 1793 George Washington had proclaimed that the United States would forever maintain neutrality "when European nations quarrel." In his farewell address — which Alexander Hamilton, whose word was law to Federalists, did not deny he had written—Washington warned against foreign entanglements. But in 1798 the Federalist majority Congress suspended relations with France, abrogated treaties under which France had helped win American independence, and authorized American privateers "to seize French ships preying on American commerce." That Great Britain also preyed was passed over. Washington was dragooned into accepting titular command of a new army "for defence against France," actually raised by Hamilton.

John Adams owed his place to Hamilton. His Secretary of War, McHenry, was Hamilton's appointee. He knew how much sound and how little real fury there had been in the Whisky Insurrection in 1794, when at Hamilton's insistence Washington called up 15,000 militiamen from four states, and Hamilton marched them into Pennsylvania to force farmers to pay federal taxes on homemade whisky (Washington's spelling) that was their only barter crop. On that occasion, Hamilton had supervened the courts, ruling that "Every man may of right apprehend a traitor" and ordering his officers to ignore judicial process and "summarily take hold of all who are worth the trouble." Prodded along by bayonets, a hundred and fifty prisoners were paraded in Philadelphia with placards lettered *Insurgent* stuck in their hats. Two were sentenced to death. Washington pardoned all, and the first army Hamilton had led disintegrated overnight. But now he led another.

"Adams knew," says one authority, "that Hamilton's officers talked in 1798 of a military coup in 1799 if not before. He knew Hamilton had dreams of being the American Napoleon, invading and conquering Louisiana, Texas, Mexico, and points south. He knew his chances for a second term were already dubious at best. Yet stubbornly, crankily, persistently, he sought the peace his party leaders did not want." He had one uninvited helper, a Pennsylvania physician and politician, Dr. George Logan, who had once made plows for Madison. On his own initiative and at his own expense, Logan went to France on a private peace mission. He claimed encouraging response, and was credited in some quarters with "strengthening Adams in his no-war resolve" (though of course Adams would have denied he needed anyone's assistance). But when word of Logan's negotiations leaked out, Hawks screamed, and the Federalist majority in Congress pushed through the Logan Act forbidding any private citizen to undertake diplomatic negotiations without official authority. (One wonders when, if ever, the Logan Act might be invoked against unofficial delegations talking peace in Hanoi.)

John Adams loved being President. It was gospel to him that no other American could do as much as well and wisely for his country. Taking his oath of office in 1797, he muttered dourly that "There never was a democracy that did not commit suicide." This had been variously interpreted. On the internal evidence, he seems to have meant that he did not propose to let "democracy" wreck the well ordered Establishment which he had proposed, in his *Defence of the Constitution* published in 1787, should be headed by a Senate comprising only "the rich, the well-born, and the able." In point of fact, the word "democracy" did not appear in the Declaration of Independence, or the Constitution, or any of the first state constitutions. Even the word "republic" troubled the Founding Fathers. The Constitution did not officially declare the new nation to be a republic.

Adams was President because he polled seventy-one electoral votes to sixty-eight for Thomas Jefferson. Jefferson as Vice President, loathed and feared by Federalists, was slowly assembling a party of his own which gradually came to be called Republican. Merging into it one or two at a time were forty-two societies formed to crystallize opposition to the Federalist monolith. Of these, fifteen called themselves "Democratic," twenty-five preferred the more conservative "Republican," and two chose the middle of the road as hyphenate "Democrat-Republicans." (In fact the party Jefferson founded kept "Republican" as its name until 1844, when for the first time it declared itself to be "the Democratic Party of this Union." (To George Washington, any opposition party, whatever name it chose, was anathema. His denunciation of "certain self-created societies," in his last annual message to Congress, was taken in his successors' times to mean that "ordinary people have no right to come together for political purposes." Quite clearly this was how John Adams felt.

So it was not necessarily mere panic and passion that caused him to make the greatest mistake in his storm-tossed political career, when, while he let the Alien Acts go unenforced, he unleashed suppression of free speech and press and assembly. Signed into law in June, 1798, and limited in duration to March 3, 1801, "and not to be removed" — thus covering only the period during which for the first time the party in power faced organized opposition at the polls — the Sedition Act was frankly designed to destroy the Republican Party. Perhaps surprisingly, Alexander Hamilton took no hand in framing it. "Let us," he said, "not establish a tyranny." But once the act was law, he took the lead in enforcing it.

Suddenly, it was a crime "to write, print, utter or publish any false, scandalous, and malicious writings against the Government of the United States, either House of Congress, or the President," or "to stir up sedition or opposition to any lawful act of Congress or the President," or "to aid the designs of any foreign power against the United States." In original draft, the act had gone much farther. As it stood, it imposed fines up to $5,000, prison sentences of from six months to five years, on anyone who might "unlawfully combine or conspire to oppose any measures of the Government of the United States . . . or to intimidate or prevent any person holding a place or office from undertaking, performing or executing his trust or duty." Punishment could be even more severe for anyone who might "counsel, advise or attempt to procure any insurrection, riot, or unlawful assembly."

News traveled slowly in most cases, but not in this instance. Almost overnight the country knew it was no longer safe to speak freely, from any viewpoint not approved by constituted authority. Appeal to the Supreme Court was unthinkable. Justice Samuel Chase, raging against followers of Thomas Jefferson, ordered federal marshals "not to put any of those creatures called Democrats on any jury." Judges denounced Jefferson and Madison from the bench as "apostles of atheism, anarchy, bloodshed, and plunder." Knowing their fate if they were hauled into court, dozens of dissenters fled to Canada. Madison spoke out bravely, declaring that the Constitution specified exactly the four crimes for which Congress could fix punishment, that criminal libel was not one of these, and that the First

Amendment forbade Congress to pass any law restricting freedom of speech or of the press. "To the press alone, chequered as it is with abuses, the world is indebted for all the triumphs which have been gained by reason and humanity over error and oppression." Fine words, but no editors dared to publish them. Within weeks, twenty-four of them were arrested.

David Brown, a soldier under Washington at Valley Forge, put up a liberty pole in his front yard and prayed publicly for "peace and retirement of the President." Arrested, he was sentenced to pay a $400 fine and serve eighteen months in prison. Jedediah Peck, a circuit-riding minister, presumed to pray that the President might realize his errors and was dragged from Otsego to New York, two hundred miles, in manacles. Matthew Lyon of Vermont, who bore the double onus of being an Irish Catholic and a declared Jeffersonian, had fought in Congress with a Federalist, Griswold — Lyon with fireplace tongs, Griswold with a club. Efforts to expel both from the House failed. But now Griswold was avenged by the Sedition Act.

That Congress usurped power "to create crimes and inflict punishment," Madison wrote to Jefferson, "turns loose upon us the utmost invention of insatiable malice and ambition." A lesser figure would have gone to jail for this. But Madison and Jefferson stood too tall to be touched, at least not yet. Justice Chase called for indictment of an editor who quoted Jefferson. "A licentious press is the bane of freedom." Justice Iredell ordered a Federal Grand Jury to denounce Congressman Cabell of Maryland for sending a letter to his constituents in which he urged them to vote Republican. This was under a Sedition Act provision that banned comment on officeholders "with intent to bring them into disrepute."

But backlash had set in. "Instead of fastening the Federalist grip on the government, the Act laid them open to attack in the name of American liberty." Convinced the Federalists drove toward permanent autocracy, Jefferson launched underground resistance. His dispassionate analysis of the situation as he saw it went by courier to Kentucky, re-

cently admitted to the Union. There the Kentucky Legislature passed resolutions branding the Alien and Sedition Acts "contrary to the Constitution, therefore null and void." Thus for the first time a state declared that when federal government exceeded its constitutional powers, states had a right to call a halt. Soon after, a second Kentucky Resolution spelled out in so many words the doctrine of *States' Rights and Nullification*.

Still victory was not easy for the party of dissent. "Do you imagine," a Federalist spokesman demanded, "that the industrious and orderly people of New England will ever suffer themselves to be governed by an impious philosopher imposed on them by Virginia influence?" At Yale, its president, Timothy Dwight, warned all right-thinking patriots that "The outlaws of Europe, the fugitives from the pillory and the gallows, have undertaken to assist our own abandoned citizens in the pleasing work of destroying the nation!" It remained for John Adams himself to put Jefferson in his place as President. Napoleon ruled now in France, and Adams was able to deal sensibly with him. "I want nothing on my tombstone," Adams said, "but 'Here lies John Adams who took upon himself the responsibility for peace with France.'" He had finished Federalism by signing the Alien and Sedition Acts. Now by ending the war that had never been declared, "He left Hamilton and the others who were looking forward to a career in military glory with no more excuse to claim they were the nation's saviours."

Hamilton and the Federalists could not drop Adams as their party's official candidate. But Hamilton wrote to his party leaders: "My mind is made up. I will never again be responsible to Adams by my direct support." From a printer sworn to secrecy, he ordered many copies of his *A Letter from Alexander Hamilton, Concerning the Public Conduct and Private Character of John Adams, Esquire, President of the United States*. Intended for *sub rosa* circulation in the Deep South, so late in the campaign that word of it could not get back to Adams until voting was over, it outlined arrangements by which a few more votes for President would go to Charles

Cotesworth Pinckney, a Federalist wheelhorse, than to Adams, while the people would be led to believe they chose electors who would give Adams a second term. He could be counted on to resign, if Pinckney finished ahead of him.

The plan might have worked, but for Aaron Burr and the letter that went astray. "The story goes that Burr, who was ever an early riser, was walking in the streets near General Hamilton's house, when he met a boy carrying a covered basket. 'What have you there, my lad?' asked Burr. 'Pamphlets for General Hamilton,' the boy replied, unaware of their importance. Burr glanced at one, and saw what prize had been thrown into his hands. 'Now,' said Burr, 'I have Hamilton hollow!'"

The letter was published immediately. Adams recorded in his diary: "If the single purpose had been to defeat the President, no more propitious moment could have been chosen. One thing I know, that Cicero was not sacrificed to the vengeance of Antony, with unfeeling selfishness, more egregiously than John Adams was to the unbridled ambition of that bastard son of a Scots peddler, Alexander Hamilton."

Hard words. But no one invoked the Sedition Act, against Adams, or Hamilton, or Burr who had hoisted both on Hamilton's petard. States until then tacitly committed to Pinckney cast their electoral votes instead for Jefferson and Burr. Seeing their party monolith crumbling, Federalists practised commonsense politics, by getting out from under while they could.

But the Second American Revolution — as Jefferson called it — was not over. A few votes gone the wrong way in New York would have given Adams re-election, in spite of his own party's withdrawal of support. However, Aaron Burr had wrested control of New York from Hamilton, largely by transforming Tammany Hall from a drinking club of Revolutionary veterans into a vote-delivering machine. Burr delivered New York — ostensibly to Jefferson. Balloting for President was by first and second choice. There were sixty-five votes for Adams, seventy-three for Jefferson — and seventy-three for Burr. Under electoral procedure as then in effect, this left it for the House of Representatives to break the tie, and Federalists controlled the House. But Hamilton no longer controlled the Federalists. Deserters, playing *Save himself who can,* made overtures to Burr, the man Hamilton hated most. For whatever reason — and there is still no agreement among historians as to his actual motives, whether sinister or sincere — Burr refused to purchase a victory by taking Federalists into his Tammany-based legion.

Amidst threats of New England secession, word that militia was on the march in Virginia and the Carolinas, strengthening possibility of civil war that would split the Union, the House voted again and again. The tie remained unbroken. Then, finally, Bayard of Maryland swung over to Jefferson. John Adams would not wait in the White House to welcome its new tenant. In almost his last act as President, he did

what would make the Supreme Court supreme indeed, in interpreting the Constitution, by making John Marshall its Chief Justice. Then he went home to eat his heart out, as Washington had done before him, as other Presidents have done since down through the generations. The two party system was enshrined. Now erstwhile Outs were Ins and would entrench themselves in power as persistently as Federalists had done until the Great Change.

Doing this took too much maneuvering. Republicans now in the majority in the House impeached Justice Chase. By narrow margin, conservatives, who had cheered when Chase highhandedly set law aside and even went beyond provisions of the Sedition Act, managed to acquit him in the Senate. But Chase was finished anyhow; John Marshall made that clear. Both

sides found it the course of common sense to pass the Twelfth Amendment which prescribes that electors shall vote separately for President and Vice President — thus to prevent the danger of another tie (and also, some political scientists believe, to lessen likelihood of recourse again to the kind of politics that produced the Alien and Sedition Acts of 1798).

There was public celebration, but also there was some loud mourning when in March, 1801, the Sedition Act died quietly. The Alien Acts were repealed in April, 1802. In retrospect, Thomas Jefferson summed up in 1807: "History in general only informs us what bad government is." Whether in the history to which his apothegm referred there was a lesson that posterity might do well to think about, is for posterity to decide.

TECUMSEH
The First Advocate of Red Power

by Walter Jarrett

Walter Jarrett has published several articles in MANKIND and is a frequent contributor to other American publications. He was one of the writers selected recently to develop a textbook for college level American Indian Studies programs.

If the present day advocates of Red Power and Pan-Indianism need an idol they need search no further than the great Shawnee Chief Tecumseh. Realizing that the contact of white and Indian civi-

lizations always meant the eventual supremacy of the white, with the decay and destruction of the Indian, Tecumseh attempted to block the white advance into the old Northwest Territory by forming a federation of Indian tribes that reached all the way from Alabama to Minnesota and from Kansas to New England—and almost succeeded. ❖❖❖ Born in Ohio in the spring of 1768, Tecumseh was the son of the Shawnee chief Pucksinwah, head of the Kispokotha sept, or clan. His mother was named Methotasa (early writers incorrectly referred to her as a Creek or Cherokee) and at the time of Tecumseh's birth his parents were on their way to an important council at Chillicothe, located at the present site of Oldtown, Greene County, Ohio, three miles north of the county seat, Xenia. For five years the various septs of the Shawnee had been meeting at Chillicothe at intervals in an effort to determine what the Shawnee should do, as a nation, about the whites who, despite treaties forbidding it,

From *Mankind*, April 1971. Reprinted from Mankind Magazine, copyright © 1971 by Mankind Publishing Co.

*Lowawluwaysica, Tecumseh's brother who called himself
"The Shawnee Prophet," disobeyed the great Indian leader and
destroyed all hopes of an all-Indian confederation at Tippecanoe.
Blackhoof, a Shawnee chief, was one of the first to recognize
Tecumseh's remarkable qualifications for leadership.*

were crossing the mountains to the east and spilling into
lands used by that tribe.

When Tecumseh was six years of age, his father was
killed by a white hunting party. Thereafter, the young
boy was guided and trained by his older brother, Chiksika. He was taught Shawnee history, traditions and the
codes of the tribe. As was the custom, Tecumseh had
to commit these matters to perfect memory and learn
to repeat them verbatim. From his mother and older
sister, Tecumapese, the young Indian learned the value
of patience and the need for pity for those without
power, and that cruelty for the sake of cruelty, whether
to animals or man, degraded a person. By the time he
was eight years old, Tecumseh was already exhibiting
signs of leadership. By this time the Americans were
already establishing settlements in the traditional hunting grounds of the Shawnee — Can-tuc-kee (Kentucky)
— and the Shawnee, like other tribes of the old Northwest, increasingly realized that their total elimination
was not far distant if they did not fight back. The ever-
increasing number of whites were driving off the game
and taking possession of the land. Far away in Washington, the government of the whites continued to give
lip service to the fiction of Indian independence and
land ownership, but the Indian was more impressed by
the rapidity with which the whites obtained any area
they coveted. No opposition short of war seemed to have
the least chance of damming the white flood. And in
the spring of 1777, the Shawnee, under the leadership of
Tecumseh's godfather, Black Fish, went to war against
the settlers of Kentucky. It was to be a war without
end for the Shawnee, who were supported by the British,
who desired to retain the lucrative Great Lakes fur
trade and were glad to help the Indians keep the aggressive American frontiersmen as far from Canada as
possible. The Indians preferred trading with the British
to trading with the Americans and felt no danger from
Canadian expansion.

As the Shawnee war waged on, year after year, other
tribes occasionally joined them in battle against the
Americans. The Indians, even those who had been
friendly toward the whites in the beginning, were becoming resentful of the way in which they suffered at
the hands of the white men. They were cheated at
trading posts after being plied with whiskey until their
reasoning powers were gone. An Indian might trade
a year's catch of furs for a few trinkets and a little bad
whiskey. He gave the trinkets to his wife and drank
the whiskey and was left with nothing but a heavy head
to show for a year's work. Too, the white man's diseases
wrecked havoc among the Indians with whom they
came into contact along the advancing frontier. Such
was the world in which Tecumseh grew up.

In the spring of 1779, the situation grew so bad for
the Shawnees that the nation split up and hundreds
of men, women and children left the homeland in Ohio
and moved across the Mississippi, hoping to find peace

there — and relief from the constant war. But Black Fish, Chiksika, and the white chief, Blue Jacket, remained behind. Of course, Tecumseh and the rest of his family stayed in Ohio with his brother, Chiksika.

In the spring of 1783, Tecumseh took part in his first battle against the whites, and at the age of fifteen, outshone even the ablest warriors of the Shawnee. He killed four men in the fight and helped Chiksika kill another. The most any other Shawnee killed in the battle was two. One white was taken prisoner. Later, at the Shawnee camp he was burned alive. Tecumseh found the torture and burning of the prisoner so revolting that, without any voice in tribal matters as of yet, he protested. In an impassioned speech he pointed out that such cruelty was unworthy of real men, of Shawnees, and swore that never again would he take part in the torture of any living creature, man or animal, nor would he consider as friend any man who allowed himself to take part in anything so degrading. The vigorous manner and eloquence with which he spoke so impressed his companions that they agreed with him not to repeat the act. Tecumseh never altered his resolution. Time and again he protected women and children from his infuriated followers. Years later, at the battle of Fort Meigs, a party of Americans were captured by the British and Indians. Although the Americans had surrendered as prisoners of war, they were herded into an outdoor pen and the British General, Henry A. Procter, gave the Indians leave to select any man each of the prisoners and kill him in any manner desired. The Indians were firing point blank into the huddled Americans, others were being selected and tomahawked in cold blood when Tecumseh arrived on the scene. Slamming to a halt, leaping from his mount and brandishing his war club, he rushed to the aid of an American, Colonel John Dudley. Two Indians had grabbed him, one had jerked his head back by the hair and the other was just about to stab him. Tecumseh knocked the knife-wielder aside and ordered the other to turn the prisoner loose. Instead, the Indian whipped out his knife and cut Dudley's throat, severing the jugular vein. Tecumseh struck the Indian a blow on the head with his club, killing him. Tecumseh then ordered the other Indians to stop the slaughter, which they did, then addressed them scathingly, calling them cowards and saying that he would slay anyone who harmed another prisoner. Turning to Procter, he asked, "Why have you allowed this massacre?"

"Sir," replied Procter, "your Indians cannot be commanded."

"Begone," was the angry reply of the outraged Tecumseh. "You are unfit to command. Go, put on petticoats."

Tecumseh put the remaining prisoners under the guard of four warriors, warning them that if any more were killed or abused, all four would be executed. He then ordered the others to mount up and follow him

back to the battle where brave men, not cowards, were needed.

When Chiksika was killed in battle in April, 1788, there was no question of Tecumseh's taking over the command of the remaining Kispokotha Shawnee who were then fighting against the whites with the Cherokees. The occasion was so automatic that no vote had to be taken. Time and time again the young Tecumseh led his band to victory. He was possessed with an uncanny knack of assessing any situation in an instant and acting immediately in a manner which at once swung the scales in his favor. The Shawnees realized that no one else approached his qualifications for leadership.

Tecumseh watched the advance of the whites and the progressive deterioration of the Indians with an ever-growing surge of anger. He was certain in his own mind that the land belonged to the Indian tribes forever, no matter by what show of legality it might be taken away from them, and that they could cling to their culture and traditions. From the east the tide of whites was ever-increasing, moving toward the lands west of the Ohio river and filling up the Kentucky hunting grounds where the once great herds of buffalo were now becoming scarce. It is not known when the idea of banding the Indians into a vast confederation to drive the white invaders back again beyond the Ohio and the mountains occurred to Tecumseh. But he was still a young man when he concluded that the only possible method of opposing the white advance successfully was to obtain the cooperation of all the Indians and to have them act in concert.

By 1794, Tecumseh found himself with a large number of followers. Tall, handsome and modest, he refrained from boasting of his own prowess, being content to let others boast of him and let his actions speak for themselves. It was in the spring of that year that Tecumseh moved the members of his sept to the banks of Deer Creek in the vicinity of present London, Ohio, and several hundred members of other septs, most of whom were young men, followed him, seeing in Tecumseh the makings of a great new chief. Everything the young chief did turned out well — with two exceptions. One was allowing his younger brother, Lowawluwaysica — who would become known as the Prophet — to assume second in command of his following. Where Tecumseh was tall and perfectly proportioned, his brother was a head shorter and ugly; where Tecumseh was gentle and good-natured, Lowawluwaysica was devious and surly — and would eventually destroy his brother's plans for an Indian confederation.

Tecumseh's second mistake was marrying the Peckuwe maiden, Monetohse. While she was slender and attractive, she was also demanding and found fault in everything her husband did. While Tecumseh was able to overlook her behavior toward himself, he could not overlook the fact that she neglected to care for his son, born two years after the marriage. He invoked an ancient Shawnee marital law and dissolved their marriage, sent Monetohse back to her parents in disgrace, and placed his son in charge of his older sister, Tecumapese.

On August 20, 1794, General Anthony Wayne, commanding an American army, defeated a large Indian force on the banks of the Maumee river in Ohio. In the battle, Tecumseh, leading a party, was with the advance which met the attack of the American infantry. The defeat of the Indians on the Maumee pro-duced an entire change in the relations between the Indians and the Americans and led to treaty negotiations.

Tecumseh refused to have any part of the peace treaty signed at Fort Greenville in August, 1795, between the whites and representatives of various Indian tribes as a result of the defeat administered by Anthony Wayne. The treaty gave the whites twenty-five thousand square miles of Indian territory as well as sixteen tracts *within* lands left to the Indians for government reservations. Representatives of the twelve tribes who attended the

At the battle of Fort Meigs, the British general, Henry A. Procter, gave the Indians leave to select American prisoners and kill them in any manner desired. The Indians were firing point blank into the huddled Americans when Tecumseh arrived on the scene. Slamming to a halt and leaping from his horse, he brandished his war club and rushed to the aid of the prisoners, killing one Indian and ordering the others to stop the slaughter. The great Shawnee chief then addressed his followers scathingly, calling them cowards and saying that he would personally kill anyone who harmed another prisoner. Turning to the "civilized" General Procter, Tecumseh told him that he was not fit to lead men and should "go put on petticoats."

UPI PHOTO

treaty conference were given $1,666 for each tribe and promised an annual allowance of $825! As far as Tecumseh was concerned it was out and out thievery of Indian lands and any agreement with the whites was worthless. Upon being told of the terms of the agreement by the white Shawnee chief, Blue Jacket, Tecumseh said: "My heart is a stone: heavy with sadness for my people; cold with the knowledge that no treaty will keep whites out of our lands; hard with the determination to resist as long as I live and breathe. Now we are weak and many of our people are afraid. But hear me; a single twig breaks, but the bundle of twigs is strong. Someday I will embrace our brother tribes and draw them into a bundle and together we will win our country back from the whites."

The Treaty of Greenville brought peace to the Ohio land and the settlement of Ohio by whites began in earnest. William Henry Harrison was given command of Fort Washington and charged with protecting the new white settlers as the Shawnee land became checkered with new farms.

A short time after the signing of the Greenville Treaty, Tecumseh took a new wife, an older woman named Mamate. Mamate gave birth to a son in the summer of 1796 and died soon afterwards. The new baby was named Nay-tha-way-nah and given to Tecumapese to care for. Perhaps the birth of his second son reminded Tecumseh that the place of his own birth was already the site of a white farm. He became determined to win back the land that rightfully belonged to the Shawnee. Too, the plan of an Indian confederation was never far from his mind and the way to just such a confederation was shown to him when the Delawares, who had been pushed out of lands given to them by treaty time and time again, came to him in 1798. The Delawares had heard much of the young Shawnee chief who was so strong in all ways. Would Tecumseh come and bring his Shawnees to live with the Delawares and lead them too? Tecumseh would and led his followers into Indiana territory to join the Delawares. Within a year other Ohio tribes had come under Tecumseh's sphere of influence, impressed not only with his reputation for fairness and proven ability to lead men, but also with the eloquence with which he held audiences spellbound.

Soon after joining the Delawares, Tecumseh began traveling and addressing councils of various Indian tribes in an effort to bring them into what he saw as a powerful amalgamation of Indian strength and power. He traveled to the council fires of what remained of the Iroquois Confederation in the east; nearer home he spoke to the Wyandots, the Potawatomies and others. The Hurons, Ottawas and Chippewas, Winnebagos, Foxes, Sacs, Menominees of Michigan, Wisconsin, and Canada would hear him, as would the Sioux, Mandans and Cheyennes west of the Mississippi; in the south the Natchez and Choctaws of Mississippi,

traditional enemies, sat down together in council with him, as did the Creeks, the Seminoles, Chickasaws, Alabamas, the Biloxis and his old friends, the Cherokees. He urged the Indians to prohibit the consumption of any alcoholic beverages and the smoking of marijuana, to study closely and seriously the ways of the whites, to break all alliances existing between themselves and the whites, and to take no part in the white man's fight with other whites.

Too, he encouraged the Indians to appear weak, to swallow their pride and fall back, and under no pretext take up arms against the whites until the time was ready, the time when all Indians would take up the fight together. For that fight, Tecumseh told them, he would give the sign. It would be a sign that would come to all the tribes on the same day and at the same time. Tecumseh hoped that when the time came the whites would vacate the Indian lands west of the mountains peacefully but if they would not then the great wave of Indians from all tribes, fighting together, would sweep across the land and destroy the whites to the last man.

Meanwhile, William Henry Harrison had pulled political strings to have himself appointed governor of Indiana. He arrived at his new post in early 1801 and soon began new land acquisitions by negotiations with the Indians. In 1802-1803, another million acres were added to lands available for white settlement. Other treaties followed, and the resulting Indian resentment was attributed by Harrison to British influence. Harrison had little sympathy for the Indians and was convinced that the only possible way to deal satisfactorily with them was to destroy them. He had visions of himself as a great conqueror of Indian lands and mapped out grandiose campaigns and felt that all he needed was an opportunity to exhibit his abilities as a strategist. He was not yet aware of Tecumseh, but the Indian leader was very aware of William Henry Harrison.

Tecumseh continued to travel, recruiting tribe after tribe to join his confederation and give their aid when the great sign was given. When he spoke of the great sign he never failed to awe his audience. When the period of waiting was over, he told them, and tribal unification had been completed, he would stamp his foot and the earth would tremble and roar. He promised that great trees would fall, streams would change their courses and run backwards and lakes would be swallowed up into the earth and elsewhere new lakes would appear. The sign would shake men everywhere to their very bones like nothing they had ever known before. But when it came they were told to drop their hunting bows, their hoes, leaving their fields and camps and assemble across the lake from the fort of Detroit. On that day tribes would cease to exist. They would all be Indians, one people united forever for the good of all!

In the summer of 1802, Tecumseh preached his

message across the northeast, in Vermont and Massachusetts, two years later he was in Minnesota talking to the Sioux. Everywhere he went he carried the same message and when he left it was with the assurance that another tribe would join him when the time came. In 1805, Tecumseh and Lowawluwaysica, who now called himself the Shawnee Prophet, established a new village near Fort Greenville that was not a Shawnee village but an *Indian* village where all Indians, regardless of tribe, were welcomed. A year later, William Henry Harrison became aware of Tecumseh's activities and wrote a letter to the Delawares in which he accused them of pursuing a "dark, thorny" path by following the "pretended prophet" and asked them to call upon the Shawnee Prophet and demand that he show some sign of his powers. A party of forty Delawares did call upon the Prophet who, frightened, turned to Tecumseh and asked what he must do. Tecumseh pointed out that he could foretell what would happen just as their brother Chiksika and their father Pucksinwah had been able to do. The fact that Tecumseh was the true prophet was known only to himself, his brother and others close to the family. Tecumseh allowed everyone else to think that his younger brother could foretell the future. Tecumseh instructed his brother to tell the Delawares that fifty days from that day the sky would turn black at high noon, the night creatures would stir and the stars would shine. The Shawnee Prophet did as he was told and, of course, was credited with predicting the eclipse. Unfortunately, the Shawnee Prophet forgot that his brother was the true prophet as he enjoyed his new-found fame.

Meanwhile, Tecumseh became friends with a family of whites named Galloway and one of his greatest joys was discussing, at length, matters of politics, religion, ethics and such with James Galloway. Galloway had a fine library with which the Indian chief acquainted himself, *Hamlet* becoming his favorite tale. Tecumseh could speak English quite well, but while he could read and write the white man's language, he was not fluent enough to read the more difficult books in the Galloway library. James Galloway's daughter, Rebecca, offered to help him. She spent many hours teaching the Shawnee chief, who was then thirty-eight years of age. In the spring of 1808, when she turned seventeen, Tecumseh asked for Rebecca's hand in marriage. Rebecca thought over the marriage proposal for a month and then agreed to marry Tecumseh, with whom she was in love, but only if he would adopt her people's mode of life and dress. He thought over her request for a month, then returned and told her that to do as she wanted would lose him the respect and leadership of his people. Rebecca Galloway wept when Tecumseh took leave of her for the last time.

That same year Tecumseh had his first interview with William Henry Harrison. He promised Harrison peace if the United States did not make further treaties involving land cessions and added that if such cessions were made, he would form an alliance with the English and make war on the Americans. Harrison dismissed Tecumseh's request as preposterous. A year later the two men met again but by this time events made peace impossible. Illinois Territory was created, leaving Indiana with its present boundaries. Harrison received permission from the secretary of war to buy more Indian land; the purchase of 2,500,000 acres in the fall of 1809 increased the number and wrath of Indians hostile to the United States. While Tecumseh maintained that the Indians held the land in common, that no one tribe owned this or that territory, Harrison couldn't

The death of Tecumseh. At least four Americans claimed the honor of having killed the great Shawnee chief on October 5, 1813.

agree with him less and pointed out that had the Great Spirit intended to make one nation of the Indians, he would not have put different languages into their heads, but would have taught them all to speak alike. Tecumseh replied bitterly that no one tribe had the right to give away or sell what belonged to all and not until the United States agreed to cease purchasing lands from Indians and restored the lands recently bought, would peace be possible. Pointing to the moon that had risen on the council, Governor Harrison said that the moon would sooner fall to the earth than the United States would give up the lands. "Then," said Tecumseh, "I suppose that you and I will have to fight it out."

Another council was held in August, 1810 between Tecumseh and Harrison that was just as fruitless. Describing the arrival of Tecumseh at the conference, Captain George R. Floyd, commanding officer of Fort Knox, wrote: " . . . they were headed by the brother of the Prophet, Tecumseh, who perhaps is one of the finest looking men I ever saw — about six feet high, straight, with large, fine features, and altogether a daring, bold looking fellow."

The next day this "daring, bold looking fellow" let Harrison know for the last time that he meant business. The meeting got started on a bad note when Harrison told Tecumseh that, "Your father wishes you to take a chair." The very idea of the governor calling himself "your father" was repugnant to Tecumseh.

Tecumseh spoke first and pointed out that he felt that the Americans were trying to force the red people to do some injury to the whites so the latter would have an excuse to war on the Indians and that they were "continually driving the red people; when, at last, you will drive them into the Great Lakes, where they can't either stand or walk." The Shawnee chief ended with a threat: "We shall have a great council, at which all the tribes will be present, when we shall show to those who sold that they had no right to the claim that they set up; and we will see what will be done to those chiefs that did sell the land to you. I am not alone in this determination; it is the determination of all the warriors and red people who listen to me. I now wish *you* to listen to me. If you do not, it will appear as if you wished me to kill all the chiefs that sold you the land. I tell you so because I am authorized by all the tribes to do so. I am the head of them all! I am a warrior and all the warriors will meet together in two or three moons from this. Then I will call for those chiefs that sold you the land and shall know what to do with them. If you do not restore the land, you will have a hand in killing them."

As for confidence in yet another treaty with the whites, Tecumseh asked: "How can we have confidence in the white people? When Jesus Christ came on earth, you killed him and nailed him to a cross . . ."

Harrison's reply was as highhanded as ever and caused the followers of Tecumseh to bring out their arms. They were stilled by the chief and left the council. Another council in July of the next year ended much the same way.

Autumn of 1811 found Tecumseh in the south addressing councils of Cherokees, Seminoles, Choctaws and Chickasaws; autumn of 1811 found William Henry Harrison planning to attack Tecumseh's Tippecanoe village in his absence. Harrison gathered 1000 men, mostly volunteers, and with a well-planned campaign already formulated, prepared to annihilate his unsuspecting enemies — an act that he forgot to report to the president. He left Vincennes on September 26, 1811, and moved directly up the Wabash, paused long enough to build Fort Harrison on the present site of Terre Haute, and on the night of November 6, encamped on Tippecanoe Creek. Before leaving, Tecumseh had warned his followers, and especially his brother, the Shawnee Prophet, to avoid battle with the whites at all costs. At long last he could see the fulfillment of his years of work: the Indian confederation now actually existed and the time for war was almost at hand.

That night the Prophet sent a deputation of three men to Harrison and it was settled that the terms of peace were to be arranged the next day. But the next morning, under orders from the Prophet, who told them that they would not only be victorious but that he had rendered the bullets of the white men to be harmless when fired against them, the Indians treacherously attacked the Americans. The conflict was fierce and bloody with the Indians rushing boldly and openly to clinch with the enemy. The Prophet perched himself on a hill nearby and chanted a war song — but not for long. When messengers raced to him to say that the Indians were dying in a most natural way, he urged them on, then deserted them. When the warriors saw that the fire of the whites was just as lethal as ever and that the Prophet had fled, they became demoralized and retreated. The white casualties were 61 killed and 127 wounded; the Indian losses were unknown. Harrison immediately dispatched messengers to the East with reports of an overwhelming defeat of the Indians. In later years there was much controversy as to whether or not Harrison had actually won. He had avoided rout and repulsed the Indians, but he also found it necessary to retreat almost immediately. But the fact that the Indians had fought and had not won an overwhelming victory all but ruined Tecumseh and dashed the Indian confederation on the very eve of its birth.

Tecumseh arrived back at Tippecanoe only four days after the fateful battle, his face as frozen as stone. Shaking his brother, fallen and disgraced, by the hair until his nose began to bleed, he told him that death was too good, too easy, for him. In a day he had destroyed what it had taken Tecumseh a decade to build. The Prophet was drummed out of the camp. He was no longer an Indian, he no longer existed.

As Tecumseh had predicted, the earth did shake. On December 16, 1811, a deep, terrifying rumble was felt in the south of Canada. Trees fell and huge rocks toppled. Lake Michigan and Lake Erie trembled and great waves broke on the shores, though the day was windless. In the west the earth shuddered so fiercely that great herds of bison staggered to their feet and stampeded, and in the south whole forests fell. In Missouri the town of New Madrid was destroyed, the Mississippi River turned and flowed backwards. The earthquake lasted for two days and filled the atmosphere with choking dust. A second struck on January 23 and a third hit four days later. The fourth and worst quake came on February 13 and lasted for an hour. It did more damage than the other three combined. Many of those that had deserted Tecumseh's cause reconsidered, for this was very strong medicine, but it was too late. The defeat at Tippecanoe had taken the ardor for war out of too many of his followers.

Those that remained faithful followed Tecumseh into the British service in the War of 1812, which broke out immediately. But Tecumseh, commissioned as a major-general, was doomed to continued disaster. The English commander, General Henry Procter, was incompetent, and in all the qualities of real manhood, the inferior to his Indian ally. After the battle of Put-in-Bay, on Lake Erie, he started to retreat. Tecumseh protested and was induced to go on only by the promise that winter supplies would be delivered a few miles up the Thames. It was on this stream that Procter finally determined to make a stand, but at the onset of the action he retreated with his red coats, leaving the Indians to bear the brunt of the battle. On October 5, 1813, as he had predicted before the battle, Tecumseh was killed. Only one person at the site of the battle could identify the Shawnee chief and that was the Kentucky frontiersman, Simon Kenton. While at least four Americans claimed the honor of having killed Tecumseh, as far as is known Kenton never identified his body.

But there on the banks of a quiet Canadian stream, thirty-five miles from Detroit, the great Tecumseh, statesman, diplomat, a man devoted to the cause of his people and yet a humble and modest intellectual, found an unmarked grave. The Indians lost their greatest leader, the whites won the West. ✤

DOLLEY MADISON AND THE BURNING OF WASHINGTON

The First Lady fled Washington three hours before the British entered the city.

by Elswyth Thane

Elswyth Thane has been writing professionally for more than thirty years and is recognized as an authority on colonial America. Her books include biographical works on George and Martha Washington, *Potomac Squire and Washington's Lady*, as well as *Mount Vernon: The Legacy*.

The present situation of the world is indeed without parallel, and that of our own country is full of difficulties." It has a familiar sound. But this was James Madison, speaking at his inauguration in 1809.

Thomas Jefferson returned to Washington from his home at Monticello to witness the ceremony, which took place in what is now known as the Statuary Hall of the Capitol, which was then fitted with drapes and desks as the debating chamber of the House. Madison had inherited from his predecessor a very touchy state of affairs between the infant United States and the European Powers who were already at war with each other in the eternal quarrel between France and England. Other nations might in their own interests take one side or the other, but the United States found itself caught right in the middle and bullied by both of them.

From *Mankind*, July 1970. Reprinted from Mankind Magazine, copyright © 1970 by Elswyth Thane.

With James Monroe acting as Secretary of State, and Jefferson coaching from the sidelines, the new President adopted a precarious policy of maintaining peace with an old ally, France, at the expense of strained relations with an old enemy, England. The Prince Regent had recently taken over the Government from the aged, almost insane George III, but he retained his father's Ministry.

The American Minister in London resigned and came home, as his colleague in Paris had already done, though the astute French Minister, Louis Sérurier, was still busy in Washington on France's behalf. The slow communications of the period prolonged the negotiations and led the uninformed to suppose that Madison was weak and undecided, and that his policies were influenced by his associates from day to day. But Sérurier knew Madison by hard experience, and he reported briefly to Paris: "Mr. Madison governs by himself."

Since Bonaparte had put his brother Joseph on the puppet throne of Spain, the possibility existed that he intended to make Spanish Florida another Louisiana, and this roused the perpetual American dread of either France or England as an aggressive near neighbor on the southern half of the American continent. As far back as 1808, Jefferson had expressed a desire to exclude all European influence from this hemisphere. In January, 1811, Madison issued a proclamation which foreshadowed what in 1824 would become known as the Monroe Doctrine — in which he stated that "the United States could not see without serious inquietude any part of a neighboring territory . . . pass from the hands of Spain into those of any other foreign power." Florida was to remain a sore point until 1819.

The general belief that the British in Canada were involved in a conspiracy with the Indians against United States' westward expansion increased the hostility be-

Following the burning of Washington, the British moved on to Baltimore and landed a force of nine thousand. General Robert Ross was killed in the first skirmish.

tween the two nations. In the autumn of 1811 the battle of Tippecanoe on the Wabash River worsened relations with the bloody victory of William Henry Harrison over the Shawnee chief Tecumseh. The British persisted in its reckless blockade of American ports, seizing American ships and cargos, and carrying off seamen from the crews to serve under the British flag on the pretense that they were deserters from the British forces.

The 12th Congress, which met in November, 1811, was "in confusion and perplexity," and Jefferson was quoted as saying that it had three choices: embargo, war, or submission to piracy against its ships at sea. No one contemplated the third. Embargo, which not even Jefferson had been able to enforce, was universally detested for its strangling effect on American trade with Europe. New England, which had suffered most from Jefferson's embargo experiment in 1807, openly preferred war — or threatened secession. The choice was, therefore, between war with France and war with England, with some reckless advocates for a triangular war with both.

The least warlike of men, scholarly, frail in health, of a gentle, reflective nature, Madison might have succeeded somehow in threading his diplomatic way through the recurrent crises if it had not been for England's obstinate, bungling, inexcusable interference with American commerce at sea. But in April, 1812, Madison's message to Congress requested an immediate embargo for sixty days, which was extended to ninety days by Congress. At the same time it gave him the power to call up one hundred thousand militia for a limited period of time.

The assassination of the British Prime Minister Spencer Perceval in London opened the way for concessions or a change of policy by the British Government, but the news of Perceval's death did not reach Washington in time. On the 4th of June, 1812, the House declared war on England by a vote of 79 to 49. On the 17th the Senate voted for war, 19 to 13.

Once again, after years of peace and growing prosperity, the New World faced the Old on its own ground, as before, with untrained troops and a very limited navy. Since England was already entangled in a war with Bonaparte on the Continent, it was obvious that she could not commit her full force to a new conflict across the Atlantic.

Popular opinion in America was violently divided, and in New England where merchant shipowners wanted only to appease England and save their trade abroad, the embargo was as unpopular as it had been in Jefferson's time. Federalists spoke bitterly of "Mr. Madison's war," and accused the President of partiality towards the French, whose behavior at sea was almost as provocative as England's.

The nearest British were in Canada, and the Tippe-

canoe affair still rankled, so preparations were made at Washington to invade Canada from Lake Champlain and Detroit. The Indians, of course, joined with the British, and the Canadian campaign soon became a disaster for the United States. Commodore Oliver Perry's decisive victory over a British fleet on Lake Erie in September, 1813, was the only consolation.

By his declaration of war in June of 1812, Madison had risked the loss of a second term, as it was an election year. A campaign of violent abuse was launched against him, in which the sober, abstemious man was accused of drunkenness after dinner, the use of opium "for pains in his teeth," and other frivolous fabrications. But in the confused and divided state of the Congress and the country these were actually believed and handed on, in the frantic attempt to discredit him.

When November came and the ballots were counted, Madison won an easy victory over DeWitt Clinton of New York, nephew of the Vice-President, who had recently died in office. Elbridge Gerry became Vice-President. Madison retained Monroe as Secretary of State. The country may not have liked the idea of war, but it believed in Madison.

The city of Washington itself had no military or strategic importance. It lay in the "Y" formed by the union of the Potomac and the Anacostia rivers, or Eastern Branch. A creek called the Tiber flowed westward along the base of Capitol Hill through a marshy woodland. Alexandria, eight miles down the Potomac, was a much better and a long established seaport. People inclined to whistle in the dark were mistakenly convinced that invasion by the British, if it came, must start at Boston, where the Federalist majority would welcome and possibly aid the enemy.

Instead, early in 1813, Admiral Sir George Cockburn brought his ships boldly into Chesapeake Bay, from where British officers in thin disguise were able to circulate in the streets and taverns, and were sometimes entertained by stubbornly disaffected Americans, even while villages and farms along the shore were being raided for supplies and burned for resisting the foraging parties. The British also had every opportunity to buy American newspapers and hire spies to report American preparations for defense, or the lack of them.

In the summer of 1813 Madison was attacked by the dread Potomac malaria, which carried with it a high fever and other symptoms so serious that it was said "his life hung on his nursing." His devoted wife, Dolley, never left that to anyone else, and gave him the most constant care, cheerful, competent, and comforting, hiding from him her own alarm and fatigue.

Those were days of tension and uncertainty in the nation's capital, and she was almost alone in the White

House during this frightening time, while the President lay dangerously ill and the British menaced the city. Madison's secretary, Edward Coles, who was always Dolley's mainstay, was absent in Philadelphia, also ill, and her son by her first husband, had been sent abroad to further his education.

"And now if I could I would describe to you the fears and alarms that circulate around me," Dolley wrote to Coles in May. "For the last week all the city and Georgetown (except the Cabinet) have expected a visit from the enemy, and were not lacking in their expressions of terror and reproach. We are making considerable efforts for defense. The Fort is being repaired, and five hundred militia, with perhaps as many regulars, are to be stationed on the Green near the Windmill. The twenty tents look well in my eyes, who have always been an advocate for fighting when assailed, though a

The reputation of British Admiral Sir George Cockburn caused Americans to flee their homes as he proceeded toward Washington. Earlier, Cockburn had sacked and burned the small town of Havre de Grace, Maryland, with a vengeance that caused even the officers under Admiral Cockburn's command to remonstrate.

Quaker. I therefore keep the old Tunisian sabre within reach.

"One of our generals has discovered a plan of the British," she continued, "to land as many chosen rogues as they can about fourteen miles below Alexandria in the night, so that they can be on hand to burn the President's house and offices. I do not tremble at this, but feel hurt that the Admiral (of Havre de Grace memory) should send me word that he would make his bow at my drawing-room soon...."

This reference to Havre de Grace, a small town in Maryland at the head of the Bay where the Susquehanna flows into it, arose from the most notorious raid yet perpetrated by Admiral Cockburn's men. The Admiral himself had taken part in this outrage, to the extent of carrying off a handsome coach valued at $1000, in which he intended to ride through Washington after he had captured the city, and a sofa which caught his fancy and was seized from a private house which had been set on fire.

His seamen roamed at will through the helpless town, appropriating furniture, silver, and horses before burning the houses and stables. Most of the militia were absent at rural homes in a false security, and Havre de Grace was pillaged and fired until even the British officers under Cockburn's command remonstrated.

Baltimore, which lay where the Patapsco River emp-

tied into the Bay below Havre de Grace, was known to be well defended, and had set up relays of mounted couriers to carry the alarm, and the British left it alone. Washington itself was guarded—after a fashion—by the unfinished Fort Warburton, later called Fort Washington, on the east shore of the Potomac below Alexandria. Fire from the guns at the fort would have raked any enemy ship coming up the Bay towards the capital, and earthworks were being thrown up along the waterfront.

"We have been in a state of perturbation here for a long time," Dolley wrote to Edward Coles from the White House. "The depredations of the enemy approaching within twenty miles of the city and the disaffected [Americans] making incessant difficulties for the Government. Such a place as this has become! I cannot describe it. I wish for my part we were in Philadelphia. The people here do not deserve that I should prefer Washington. Among the other exclamations and threats, they say that if Mr. Madison attempts to move from this house in case of an attack they will stop him and that he shall *fall with it!* I am determined to stay with him. Our preparations for defense, by some means or other, are constantly retarded; but the small force the British have in the Bay will never venture nearer than at present, twenty-three miles."

The expected attack did not come then, for the British fleet fell back down the Bay to attack Norfolk and Hampton at the mouth of the James River. There Cockburn's men acted with even greater brutality than at Havre de Grace, on the word of a British officer named Napier, whose diary recorded that "every act of rapine and plunder" was encouraged, and the women trapped in the captured towns suffered rape and gunshot wounds.

Cockburn was a noisy swaggerer, brutal even by the rough standards of the navy of his day, and his name was detested throughout America. He settled down for the winter of 1813-14 at a house on the Georgia coast, from where he threatened to liberate and arm the slaves against their white masters.

By the time Madison was convalescent, Washington was no longer directly menaced, and he took up his burden of work again, while Dolley, as the nation's hostess and first lady, resumed her usual social program to show that no one was nervous and to maintain the morale of the city. For three weeks she had nursed her husband night and day, sometimes with despair, and she wrote Coles that now that Madison would get well she felt as though she might herself die from fatigue.

A New Year's Day reception at the White House was now an established custom, and in 1814 it was as brilliant as in happier times. But there was a dark undercurrent of apprehension, and a Washington matron wrote to her mother that "a plan might be carried into execution, and without a miracle, of seizing the Presi-

dent and Secretaries with only fifty or a hundred men, and rendering this nation a laughing-stock to every other in the world."

At a Cabinet meeting in July, 1814, Madison placed the defense of the capital in the hands of General John Armstrong, who was Secretary of War, and General William Winder, a debonair Maryland lawyer with very little military experience. Armstrong had fought as a young man in the army of the Revolution, but since then had failed to distinguish himself in the Canadian campaign in 1812. Winder had also taken part in the Canadian disaster, and had spent some time as a prisoner at Quebec.

Both men proved to be a bad choice, but Madison had very little to choose from at the time and was no soldier himself. Most of the Revolutionary War heroes were aged or dead, and there was no precedent for the situation in which Madison found himself — one with which George Washington could have dealt decisively and doubtless with success.

A personal hostility between Armstrong and Secretary of State Monroe, and Armstrong's expressed desire to see an end to "the Virginia dynasty" in Government, was a serious complication. Monroe met Armstrong's gruff bad manners with an icy courtesy. The amiable Winder had few qualifications for organizing an army and a staff.

Meanwhile, a British army from the Peninsular War in Spain had been freed from combat by Bonaparte's abdication, and could be dispatched to America by Wellington under the command of General Robert Ross, an able, disciplined professional soldier. These experienced troops were joined by others at Bermuda, and another British squadron of frigates under Admiral Cochrane arrived there to transport Ross's force to the American seaboard.

On August 17, 1814, the ships passed by the Potomac and reached the mouth of the Patuxent River, the next waterway of any size opening into the Chesapeake Bay north of the Potomac. Marines and Ross's veteran line regiments began landing the next day at the little town of Benedict in Maryland, which was as far up the river as the transports could go, and only about thirty miles overland from Washington. At the same time Cockburn returned to the Chesapeake with his marines and began committing new outrages on the Virginia shore of the Potomac.

Ross, having served under Wellington's discipline in Spain, forbade pillage and maintained order around Benedict, in contrast to Cockburn's plundering habits. Ross had no animals, so the men dragged the big guns ashore by long ropes.

They found the town of Benedict deserted — because of Havre de Grace — and the troops met no resistance although under a blistering August sun they established a camp on shore and began to form their brigades in preparation for their march toward the capital. On the morning of the 18th a foaming horse brought a messenger to Washington from Point Lookout at the mouth of the Potomac, to inform the astonished War Department that the British were landing an army east of the city, and not from the Potomac side as might have been expected.

Calm as Dolley contrived to remain, after the shocking news of the landing at Benedict became known in Washington, the city went into panic. Everyone thronged into the streets or began to collect their most precious household goods for flight. Couriers on sweating horses rode out to urge the state governors to summon the unwilling militia, most of which never appeared. Stories of the horrors at Havre de Grace and Norfolk were revived, and induced many men of substance to send their women and children westward across Rock Creek to Georgetown and even beyond, to Frederick in the Maryland hills.

Rumors of the size of the invading force were exaggerated, and the dusty roads west and north of the capital were soon crawling with refugees who had heard of Cockburn's methods in an occupied town. The horse-drawn stages setting out for New York and Boston were filled with frightened passengers who spread the alarm as they went. To Dolley Madison, who could remember when yellow fever had emptied the city of Philadelphia in 1793, the scenes of disorder and heedless flight were hideously familiar. Plague or war. War or plague. It was the same.

The Cabinet, an island of false calm, conferred at the White House while the enemy disposed itself in leisurely professional style for its march on the capital. Monroe's experience of Revolutionary days, when he had fought in General Washington's army at Trenton and Princeton, caused him to offer to mount a horse and ride out with a small escort towards the British camp at Benedict to reconnoiter, and Madison gratefully agreed. Thus it was that a Cabinet member with no military rank became a volunteer scout on horseback, in place of the commanding officer or the Secretary of War, whose business it conceivably was.

Winder was active enough in his showy way, rushing about on horseback to oversee the local defenses instead of sitting down to plan an organized campaign to beat off the invading army. Under his direction, earthworks dating from the Havre de Grace alarm two years before were repaired and extended.

The District of Columbia militia were ordered to mobilize at the foot of Capitol Hill on the night of the 19th under Winder's command. Many of them reported for duty without guns, uniforms, or military equipment of any kind, and they were sent away again to provide themselves with weapons, "if only with butcher knives."

By Saturday morning, the 20th, when Monroe from behind the screen of a pine forest was observing Ross's men around Benedict, some militia had again assembled in Washington city, and they presented an encouraging sight to the obstinate optimists who wrote for the newspapers, and the valiant women who like Dolley Madison were determined to stay with their men in the city.

Nevertheless, the banks prepared to move their specie inland, and the State Department clerks began to fill large linen sacks with their files and records, while Armstrong from his office in the same building remarked that these precautions looked to him "like unnecessary alarm."

Wagons which should have carried rations to the military camp which Winder had established at a place called Woodyard in Maryland, between Washington and Benedict, were commandeered to transport government papers across the Potomac into Virginia, where they were placed under guard in an unoccupied house in Leesburg. Otherwise, many valuable Revolutionary documents, Congressional records and secret journals, George Washington's commission and wartime correspondence, laws, treaties, and diplomatic records, all would have perished.

Armstrong remained paralyzed by his own unfounded conviction that the British had no intention of coming to Washington. What, he would inquire blandly, could they want with Washington when Baltimore was nearby, a valuable port and a full-grown, flourishing city worth taking? But Baltimore had its defenses. And Washington was the capital. He could not see the difference.

Winder was calling frantically for volunteers, but few responded. Monroe arrived at Winder's camp at Woodyard, and his dispatches from there to the President told of the advance in a marching column of about four thousand red-coated British regulars towards Bladensburg, on the very doorstep of Washington.

Bladensburg was a small Maryland town just outside of the District of Columbia line, whose main street ended in a bridge over the Eastern Branch, where a road leading into Washington began. The decision was taken to defend this bridge, which lay only six miles from the eastern edge of the city. It occurred to no one in command that it would have been far simpler to blow it up at once.

On Monday, the 22nd of August, Madison collected a small party, including Armstrong, Secretary of the Navy William Jones, and Attorney General Richard Rush, and rode with them out across the Navy Yard Bridge into Maryland. There was some idea that the presence among them of the President himself might encourage the throng of ill-fed, disorganized milita,

volunteers, sailors, and regulars, who sent up a ragged, half-hearted cheer when he was recognized. He spent that night at Winder's camp, which was said to resemble "a race-course or a fair" more than a military base, and he reviewed the straggling ranks of the makeshift army the next morning.

It was believed that the British, who had advanced as far as Upper Marlborough, would first try to seize Annapolis as a base for their operations to attack either Baltimore or Washington. This foolish guess seemed to allow plenty of time for the Americans to assemble and position their untrained forces. When Madison left the Woodyard camp about 2 p.m. to return to Washington with Armstrong, Rush, and their small escort, he did not know that Ross was already marching from Upper Marlborough and was then only three miles behind them.

When Winder discovered that the British were actually on the move towards him, he made a running retreat into Washington with his men, and set up a temporary camp near the Navy Yard. He then showed up at the White House to explain that he had feared a night attack on his unprepared army, and had thought best to remove it from Ross's path. He had, however, divided his forces in order to leave about twenty-five hundred men under General Tobias Stansbury of Maryland to defend the bridge at Bladensburg. His own men were exhausted from the hasty retreat in intense heat, a summer temperature which the British were also unaccustomed to, and many of them had dropped in their tracks.

Monroe remained with Stansbury's militia at Bladensburg—he had hardly been out of the saddle for three days. At midnight of the 23rd, a scribbled note from him was delivered at the White House: "The enemy are in full march for Washington. Have the materials prepared to destroy the bridges. You had better remove the records." This was advice which should have come from the Secretary of War, but the Secretary of State was the better soldier.

The last night the Madisons were to spend at the White House was a sleepless one.

At 11 a.m. on Wednesday the 24th, Armstrong was still dithering around in Washington when Winder reluctantly moved his men out from the Navy Yard to a point at Old Fields (now Forestville, Maryland) several miles nearer Washington than his deserted position at Woodyard, which had been occupied by the British bivouac the night before. From Old Fields he intended to support Stansbury at Bladensburg. Madison ordered Armstrong to follow Winder with the militia which had so far remained idle at Washington, and this removed from the city its last defenders visible to the inhabitants.

An hour later the President, with a brace of borrowed duelling pistols buckled around his waist, rode out after them with three companions, one of whom was the faithful Rush. He left Dolley in the White House surrounded by her terrified but loyal servants.

The heat was oppressive that day, as only Potomac heat can be, and a rumor ran through the streets that the water supply had been poisoned. Dolley hurried from room to room, gathering the Presidential silver, the best clocks and ornaments, and those of Madison's personal papers and treasured books which she thought it essential to preserve. A letter from her to her married sister Anna Cutts, begun on the Tuesday, and finished the next day, gives a vivid picture of what the President's wife went through while awaiting further news from him:

Dear Sister:

My husband left me yesterday to join General Winder. He inquired anxiously whether I had courage or firmness to remain in the President's House until his return on the morrow, and on my assurance that I had no fear but for him and the success of our army, he left, beseeching me to take care of myself, and of the Cabinet papers, public and private. I have since received two dispatches from him, written with a pencil. The last is alarming, because he desires that I should be ready at a moment's warning to enter my carriage and leave the city; that the enemy seemed stronger than had at first been reported, and it might happen that they would reach the city with the intention of destroying it. I am accordingly ready; I have pressed as many Cabinet papers into trunks as to fill one carriage; our private property must be sacrificed, as it is impossible to procure wagons for its transportation. I am determined not to go myself until I see Mr. Madison safe, so that he can accompany me, as I hear of much hostility towards him.

Disaffection stalks around us. My friends and acquaintances are all gone, even Colonel C. with his hundred men who were stationed as a guard in this enclosure. French John [the White House butler] with his usual activity and resolution offers to spike the cannon at the gate and lay a train of powder which would blow up the British, should they enter the house. To the last proposition I positively object, without being able to make him understand why all advantages in war may not be taken.

Wednesday morning, twelve o'clock — Since sunrise I have been turning my spy-glass in every direction, and watching with unwearied anxiety, hoping to discover the approach of my dear husband and his friends; but alas! I can only descry groups of military, wandering in all directions, as if there was a lack of arms, or of spirit to fight for their own firesides.

Three o'clock.—Will you believe it, my sister? We have had a battle, or skirmish, near Bladensburg, and here I am still, within sound of the cannon! Mr. Madison comes not. May God protect us! Two messengers, covered with dust, came to bid me fly; but here I mean to wait for him.... At this late hour a wagon has been procured, and I have had it filled with plate and the most valuable portable articles belonging to the house. Whether it will reach its destination, the Bank of Maryland, or fall into the hands of the British soldiery, events must determine.

Our kind friend Mr. Carroll has come to hasten my departure, and is in a very bad humor with me because I insist on waiting till the large picture of General Washington is secured, and it requires to be unscrewed from the wall. This process was found to be too tedious for these perilous moments; I have ordered the frame to be broken, and the canvas taken out. It is done! and the precious portrait is placed in the hands of two gentlemen of New York for safekeeping. And now, dear sister, I must leave this house, or the retreating army will make me a prisoner in it by filling up the road I am to take. When I shall write again to you, or where I shall be tomorrow, I cannot tell!

DOLLEY.

It is interesting that to Dolley the danger was of being made prisoner by the retreating American army's flight along her escape route, and not by the invading British, who were so close behind.

The devoted French steward, John Sioussat, was the last to leave the White House, after he had seen Dolley off safely in her carriage, accompanied by her faithful maid Sukey and followed by the wagonload of portable valuables which he had helped her assemble, and of which she soon lost sight. In order to make room for what she considered national property, she left behind almost everything. Her personal luggage and expensive wardrobe, imported footwear, headgear, and the trinkets which were her especial delight were all sacrificed. Sioussat carried her pet macaw to the house of a friend before locking the doors of the White House and depositing the key with the French Minister, whose flag would be respected by the invaders.

Following the President, as she could not, on the morning of the 24th when he took the road to Winder's camp below Bladensburg, we find him with Monroe, from whom he learned that the British, having spent the night in Woodyard, were just entering the town of Bladensburg from the opposite direction. Winder and Armstrong were nowhere to be seen, but Winder's men had at last been joined by Stansbury's so that a semblance of resistance at the bridge was thought possible and some artillery was posted there. There was no decisive leadership and no discipline among the raw

Dolley Madison's flight from Washington. Filling a cart with plate and portable valuables which she considered national property (including a large portrait of George Washington), Dolley Madison, accompanied by her maid Sukey, left the city a mere three hours before the first of the British troops entered.

American forces, which resulted in a conflict of orders, and a lack of confidence naturally prevailed.

Ignorant of the exact location and extent of the American position, Madison and Rush rode right through the militia lines and out the other side, before they were warned by a startled scout that they had come within gunshot of the British, who were approaching just over the hill, and that the President was in danger of being taken prisoner by the enemy. They turned back in some haste then and encountered Armstrong, Winder, and Monroe, who urged Madison to return to Washington at once.

The British had begun letting off their terrifying rockets, some of which fell and exploded nearby. The noise and flash of these unaimed missiles created panic among the militia and the mob of civilian spectators who had rashly ridden out from Washington to see the battle.

The result was a general stampede back towards the city, while Ross led his red column across the Bladensburg bridge, taking heavy casualties from the hidden artillery on the American side. His seasoned troops stood the fire, and set up their skirmish lines on the west, or Washington bank of the river, which caused the Americans there to desert their guns and flee. This "battle" was later derisively known as "the Bladensburg races."

Both Armstrong and Winder arrived at Capitol Hill in Washington ahead of their troops—they had horses—and Monroe overtook them there while the retreating militia flowed past them towards Georgetown, sometimes stopping to steal food and loot their own city along the way. This was the disorganized mob which Dolley had feared would cut off her own retreat. Nobody knew where the President was by now, but he was thought by Monroe to be at the White House.

Meanwhile, Colonel Charles Carroll had finally prevailed upon Dolley, almost by force, to allow herself to be removed from in front of the British army. If she had been caught in its advance she would have suffered indignities if not actual danger when the city was occupied by the victorious troops. Her capture would have caused her husband untold anxiety and humiliation. It had been arranged that she should await him at Carroll's house in Georgetown, where the family of Secretary of the Navy Jones had already taken refuge.

The record of the ensuing days, and the whereabouts of the Madisons during that time, is still obscure, and many picturesque legends have grown up around their adventures while the British were in possession of Washington. Most of these stories are contradictory or will not bear scrutiny, but it appears that Madison reached the White House only minutes after his wife had left it, and he was persuaded by Rush and Colonel John Mason, who never left his side, that she was in safe hands and that he must at all costs save himself from humiliating capture.

He rode with them to a tavern at Falls Church in Virginia, west and south of Washington, and from there to Salona, the home of the Reverend William Maffitt, where he spent the night, hoping that Dolley would be found and brought to him. But in the hurry and confusion messages miscarried or were never sent, and unknown to him Dolley was only a mile or so away at Rokeby, the home of her friend Mrs. Matilda Love Lee.

Mrs. Lee recorded that "a number of city people took refuge at my house the night the British took Washington. Mr. Madison had gone further up the country. Early in the evening Mr. Monroe came by my house to look for Mr. Madison; as Mr. Monroe was so weary I gave him his supper and asked him if he thought I was safe where I was for the night. 'Madam,' he said, 'as safe as if you were in the Allegheny Mountains.'"

And so she was, but Mr. Monroe took a good deal upon himself to say so. None of them knew that the President was only a few minutes' ride away at Salona.

The British entered Washington down Maryland Avenue at twilight on the 24th of August, 1814, to find most of the houses closed and deserted, and the streets almost empty. The infamous Admiral Cockburn rode in beside Ross, urging him to burn the city to the ground, which went against Ross's disciplined inclination. As they came into sight of the Capitol at the end of Maryland Avenue, a single volley was fired from a house at the corner of 2nd Street. It struck Ross's horse, which fell dead beneath him.

A search of the house proved it to be deserted and no guns were found in it, but the triumphal entry had been marred and Ross gave the order for the house to be burned. It was the first fire set by the British that historic day.

Ross led his troops — an advance guard of about two hundred men, to take possession of a national capital — to an open field east of the Capitol Building, about where the Library of Congress now stands, and a rough camp was established there. No one appeared who had the authority to negotiate with him for the surrender of the undefended city. Cockburn was roaring destruction and hellfire, and Ross — still unable to believe in so easy a conquest — took a detachment of soldiers to the Capitol Building as darkness fell.

His men fired into the windows, shattering the glass, but there was no sign of life within. The locks were then shot off the doors and the two wings were searched for sharpshooters.

None were found, but kegs of gunpowder were set in the wooden passage or rope-walk connecting the two legislative chambers (the Rotunda had not yet been built to connect them), and when the powder exploded into fire the troops piled up books and papers and broken furniture along with some tar barrels found in the House and Senate chambers, and kindled them, too. The old shingle roof caught rapidly, and the wooden floors fed the blaze, which burned so fiercely that some of the marble columns cracked and crumbled in the heat.

Ross and Cockburn gathered their men to proceed down Pennsylvania Avenue towards the White House. In the oncoming darkness lit by the blazing Capitol, the Navy Yard was seen to be also in flames, set by its own commandant in retreat, under order from Navy Secretary Jones, to prevent the British from seizing the ammunition, stores, and equipment there.

The British march by torchlight down tree-shrouded Pennsylvania Avenue was a parade without drumbeat or bugle, and even the tramp of the soldiers' feet was muffled by the deep dust of the roadway. The few houses along the way were dark, shuttered, and empty.

Arriving at the White House, the troops with Cockburn's approval broke open the door and roamed through the rooms, smashing or carrying off whatever caught their eye. The Admiral himself took a cushion from what he assumed was Mrs. Madison's chair, with a few vulgar remarks, and encouraged the men to help themselves to Madison's fine cellar of wines, and the provisions with which the house was stocked.

The French Minister, Sérurier, who remained in Washington throughout the invasion, protected by his flag, recorded that as his house was near the President's, he feared for its safety when he saw British soldiers approaching with lighted torches. He hastened out to ask for a guard to be placed around his residence, and found Ross in the oval drawing-room where the President's household goods were being stacked in a pile to be burned. His request for protection was granted, with Ross's compliments.

About midnight, when everything of value had been confiscated into the soldiers' knapsacks and pockets, or destroyed by their gun-butts, and the cellar and larder had been emptied, they went from room to room with their torches, setting fire to the draperies at the windows and whatever could be tossed into piles to feed the blaze. All Dolley's new furniture, all her fine yellow damask and red velvet and imported rugs and crystal chandeliers, the gowns and headdresses she had left in the cupboards, many of Madison's valuable books, were consumed as the flames burst through the broken windows and licked up the outside of the house.

Ross and Cockburn then made their way to a tavern near the Treasury Building, ordered supper from the frightened landlady, and ate it by the light of the conflagration. They spent the night in a house in Carroll Row east of the Capitol, whose owner was forced to give them hospitality. All that night the sky over Washington glowed red from the holocaust, which was visible to the Madisons from their separate refuges, appearing to be much worse than it was, for private property had been respected by Ross except for those houses suspected of concealing snipers.

The next morning, in the humid August heat and fitful winds which precede a tropical storm, the invaders rekindled their smoldering fire at the Treasury Building, set the State and War Department Building blazing, and burned the offices of the *National Intelligence*, a newspaper whose editorials had long offended them.

THE FALL of WASHINGTON — or Maddy in Full Flight

"Maddy in Full Flight," a London newspaper cartoon satirizing President James Madison's flight from the American capital—as well as French-American friendship.

That same morning Madison rode back to the tavern at Falls Church, hoping to find his wife there, but returned to Salona without her. The fires still burned in Washington under a black pall of smoke which hung on the heavy air between the gusts which heralded a coming hurricane. On the afternoon of the 25th a violent storm swept in over the city, bringing torrential rains which gradually quenched the flames its high winds had fanned.

Ross was aware by now that outraged American forces were rallying in the countryside, lacking only leadership, and he was a long way from his ships. He had decided to withdraw to Benedict on the night of the 25th, but before he could do so the tornado struck the city, forcing everyone to take whatever shelter he could find.

A British account said that "the most tremendous hurricane ever remembered by the inhabitants broke over Washington the day after the conflagration. Roofs of houses were torn off and carried into the air like sheets of paper, while the rain that accompanied it was like the rushing of a cataract. This lasted for two hours without intermission, during which many of the houses spared by us were blown down, and thirty of our men and as many more of the inhabitants were buried beneath their ruins. Two cannons standing upon a bit of rising ground were fairly lifted up into the air and carried several yards to the rear."

The British camp in the field on Capitol Hill was a shambles of soaked tents, provisions, and equipment, much of which was blown away entirely. After the storm had finally abated about nine p.m. the last British pickets were called in and the retreat to Benedict began, back across the Bladensburg battlefield where many of the dead and wounded still lay, and on through Upper Marlborough, till they reached their landing-place on the Patuxent. They had occupied Washington almost exactly twenty-four hours.

The storm was, of course, providential, as it put out the fires and discouraged further marauding by the British. It also caught a multitude of homeless refugees on the roads and drenched their poor possessions they had thought to save by flight. It overtook Madison on his way from Salona to Wiley's Tavern near Great Falls, where he had at last learned that Dolley had gone in the hope of finding him.

He took refuge from the hurricane at a house along the way, and then resumed his journey, to be reunited with his distracted wife at Wiley's. The men of the party discussed taking the women and children on to Frederick for safety, but changed their minds when a muddy courier arrived with the news that the British were evacuating Washington and drawing back towards their ships at Benedict. Madison thought it was his duty to return to the capital at once. Dolley was to remain at Wiley's until he sent her word that it was safe for her to join him.

He was sixty-three years old, always in frail health, and he had been on horseback for four days most of the time in a state of acute anxiety. But so far from the accusation that he had fled from Washington thinking only of his own safety, he had wisely recognized the necessity of preventing the capture of the American President by the enemy, and provided in every possible way for the safety of others in his party before setting out again almost alone to the ravaged city.

He accumulated a sizable escort as he went, and the word of his intention was passed ahead of him. Riding roundabout from Montgomery Courthouse—from where a small force of reassembled militia had just set out for Baltimore with Winder — he spent the night of the 26th at the house of Mrs. Henrietta Bentley in the little Quaker village of Brookeville. A young woman who had also found refuge there described the scene at the Bentley house that evening:

"Just at bed-time the President arrived, and all hands went to work to prepare supper and lodgings for him, his companions, and guards. Beds were spread in the parlor, as the house was filled, and guards were placed round the house during the night. . . . The fires they kindled and the lights within the tents had a beautiful appearance. All the villagers, gentlemen and ladies, young and old, thronged to see the President. He was tranquil as usual, and though much distressed by the dreadful event which had taken place, was not dis- spirited."

Madison sent off express riders the same night to summon Monroe from an army bivouac, and Armstrong from his Frederick refuge, requesting them to meet him in Washington. The next morning he sent word to Dolley that the enemy were retreating on board their ships, and that he and Rush — his faithful companion still — were leaving at once for Washington.

"You will of course take the same resolution," he added, with full confidence in her courage and devotion. "I know not where we are to hide our heads, but shall look for a place on my arrival. Mr. Rush offers us his house in the Six Buildings. Perhaps I may fall in with Mr. Cutts and have the benefit of his advice."

Mr. Cutts had married Dolley's favorite sister Anna, and was living with his family in the house on F Street which had been the Madisons' home before they moved to the White House. Madison knew they would be wel- come there. He was not yet fully aware that everything he and Dolley had in the world, except the plantation called Montpellier in the Virginia mountains, had been reduced to ashes.

Madison and Monroe reached the devastated capital about five o'clock on the afternoon of the 27th. The British had departed in such haste that they had left about a hundred of their wounded behind them at a makeshift hospital in Carroll Row. A citizens' com- mittee had buried nearly as many British dead. General Winder, arriving outside Baltimore with a small force of militia, estimated the American dead at about two hundred.

The President's party had not been long at Rush's house when a thunder of cannon began down the river, seeming to indicate a naval attack on Fort Washington from the Potomac after all. The Fort was at once blown up and deserted by its defenders, and a British detachment of frigates and rocket-ships under Captain James Gordon in the *Seahorse* proceeded unhindered towards Alexandria. Early on the morning of the 29th they were plundering the wharves and warehouses of that undefended city.

In the absence of both Winder and Armstrong, the President asked Monroe to take charge of Washington. Madison then with some members of his Cabinet rode out to inspect the damage in the city and plan a defense against a possible new invasion from the Potomac side.

The Cutts family had returned from their Maryland refuge to the house on F Street, and the President paused there to write a note to Dolley. He advised her to remain at Wiley's until further notice, as a landing by the British from the river below Washington would only force her to flee again. But by the time he returned to the house after a tour of inspection at the ruined Navy Yard, Dolley had already arrived at her sister's home. She had set out at once on receiving his letter from Brookeville.

The F Street house became temporary presidential headquarters and a guard was set up around it. Friends and neighbors who had remained in Washington and witnessed the brief British occupation soon called on Dolley to exchange adventures, and there was laughter over the teacups in a strange sense of anti-climax now that the British were actually gone from the streets— whatever they might intend to do next.

The ease with which Alexandria had succumbed led to the expectation that Georgetown might be next, and the Baltimore defenses were also being strengthened. Its harbor was protected by Fort McHenry at the mouth of the Patapsco River, but Ross had given out his intention of setting up his winter headquarters in that prosperous city, which was more than ready to accept the challenge.

In Washington public opinion had now swung around to support Madison, though there were still some people who laid the blame for Washington's inadequate defense on his shoulders, and there had been various threats against him, so his casual presence among the troops and citizens at work repairing the waterfront defenses at Georgetown caused some concern for his personal safety.

When Secretary of War Armstrong finally appeared there himself, he was openly denounced for his witless conduct at the time of the Benedict landing. Charles Carroll, who happened to encounter him at the new fortifications, loudly refused to take his proffered hand, and there was a general resolve not to serve under his orders again.

This was communicated to Madison as he was riding back to the F Street house with Rush and another companion. He replied with his usual calm deliberation that the contingency of Armstrong's remaining in command would not arise. The next day Armstrong resigned, at the President's request, protesting that the criticism of him was inspired by intrigue and falsehood.

Madison felt his own responsibilities very keenly as Chief executive and Commander-in-Chief, and realized too late that the Secretary of War should have been dismissed as soon as what Madison later called "his objectionable peculiarities" became obvious at the time of the Benedict landing.

Both the Capitol and the White House, at opposite ends of Pennsylvania Avenue, were fire-gutted, smoke-blackened ruins, whose outer walls still stood. A temporary government was set up in the Patent Office on F Street between 8th and 9th. The building had been spared by the British torches, but was damaged by the hurricane.

The first impression that Washington as a city had been wiped out by the fire prevailed for several days, until it gradually became apparent that the chief harm was to the main public buildings only. The gloomy opinion that Washington could never again be the seat of government soon gave way to optimism, although Philadelphia rose to the occasion with an urgent invitation for the Government to establish itself there, where many people had always thought it belonged.

Madison and Monroe were already at work, Monroe combining in his single efficient person the offices of Secretary of State and acting Secretary of War. The Government departments whose quarters had been destroyed settled into cramped quarters in whatever private houses were available for rent; the banks re-

opened for business; and entertaining by the habitual hostesses began to revive—the chief topic of conversation being rival tales of terror and presence of mind during the occupation experience.

In the general exodus from Washington when the British first landed at Benedict the French Minister Sérurier, whose diplomatic immunity proved very useful to his friends, had been persuaded by the Tayloe family of Mount Airy, Virginia, to give the protection of his flag to their beautiful Washington residence known as the Octagon House. This handsome dwelling stood on New York Avenue at 18th Street, and had been built about 1798, regardless of expense, by one of William Thornton's finest designs.

Sérurier had established the French Embassy there, and he now offered the undamaged house to the President as a more roomy and convenient executive residence than F Street. The offer was gratefully accepted, with Colonel Tayloe's approval. And with the various departments scattered about in whatever temporary quarters they could find, the business of government was resumed.

The British Army was again aboard its ships, not badly hurt by its adventure in Washington, and there was still considerable alarm as to where it would strike next. On September 11 word reached Washington by fast courier that fifty British vessels had arrived at the mouth of the Patapsco River fourteen miles below Baltimore. The city's defenses were organized under the competent General Samuel Smith, and the remnants of Winder's Bladensburg army had arrived there.

Hulks had been sunk below Fort McHenry to block the channel, and just in time. The British landed a force of some nine thousand soldiers and marines for an overland assault from North Point, where a road led into the city. They were met by Smith's militia, who had marched out half way the night before. General Ross was killed in the first skirmish, and there is a touching tradition that he had only time to speak his wife's name as he fell back into the arms of his aides. He died there by the roadside. His men soon retreated to their ships, having discovered that the American militia could still be effective if properly led.

Admiral Cockburn had boasted that he could take Fort McHenry in a couple of hours, but it withstood twenty-five hours of steady bombardment from the river, even though its guns were outranged. During that long night of September 13, 1814, a young Maryland lawyer named Frances Scott Key stood at the rail of a ship offshore and watched "the rockets' red glare, and the bombs bursting in air" over the Fort, while its battered flag still flew.

He had been sent under a white flag of truce with a companion to negotiate with Admiral Cochrane for the release of a well-known physician who had been taken prisoner at Upper Marlborough during the British retreat from Washington, and all three Americans were detained until daybreak lest they carry information ashore. Convinced of failure at last, the British finally put Key and his companions ashore, and withdrew down the river. They had lost Ross; the American militia under Smith's leadership had stood their ground; and Fort McHenry had not surrendered.

The words scribbled by Key on the back of a letter were carried to a printer in Baltimore. As "The Bombardment of Fort McHenry" they were first published as a broadside, with the direction that they could be sung to the air of "Anacreon in Heaven," and were heard thus for the first time at a tavern in Baltimore, where a young actor named Durang stood on a chair to render them to an enthusiastic crowd. Despite the somewhat difficult tune, "The Star-Spangled Banner" was soon familiar in every one of the eighteen United States.

By mid-October, 1814, the British fleet had withdrawn from the Chesapeake Bay entirely, and sailed for Jamaica for repairs, taking the army with it. This move seemed to indicate that the next attack would be launched at New Orleans, for the control of the Mississippi.

Meanwhile, the 1815 New Year's Day reception was held at the Octagon House, with Dolley Madison a radiant hostess in a new gown of rose-colored satin trimmed with ermine, with white ostrich plumes in her headdress. A week later, Andrew Jackson at New Orleans inflicted an overwhelming defeat and terrible losses on a veteran British army which had rashly attempted a frontal assault in unfamiliar terrain.

On February 14, 1815, the Octagon House was brilliantly lighted, with a band playing and wine flowing freely, to celebrate the arrival of a courier from Ghent with the Treaty which finally ended the war of 1812. Madison was suddenly popular again, and people spoke of "Mr. Madison's peace." The Madisons never returned to the White House, which was restored on the original plans as closely as possible, even to the famous oval rooms, and reopened to the public for the 1819 New Year's Day reception when James Monroe was President.

SECESSION:
Shadow and Substance

WILSON SULLIVAN

Wilson Sullivan is a Presidential biographer and contributed the biographies of Presidents Washington, Jefferson, Van Buren, Lincoln, Grant, Theodore Roosevelt, Franklin D. Roosevelt, and Lyndon B. Johnson for *The American Heritage Pictorial History of the Presidents of the United States*. He is also an editorial contributor and critic for *Saturday Review*. Sullivan is a graduate of Harvard and lives in New Jersey.

Among the more memorable comments of Senator Barry Goldwater in his bid for the Presidency was an observation that sent chills down the Eastern spine from Bar Harbor to Cape May. "Sometimes," Mr. Goldwater said, "I think this country would be better off if we could just saw off the Eastern Seaboard and let it float out to sea." This hint of welcomed secession, however casual or droll, augured ill of a man asking to lead all of the United States, and was, without doubt, a marginal, perhaps unconscious factor in his crushing defeat.

If history is to be heeded at all, the Northeast, particularly New England, should have been less than surprised by Mr. Goldwater's desire to exile from the Union those states he could not enlist in his cause. Historians are seldom challenged in their portrait of the South as the prime architect of secession. Wasn't Jefferson the first to use the term "nullification" in the Kentucky Resolutions, in which he, the greatest Federal empire-builder of them all, called it "the rightful remedy" for a Federal act that has usurped or contravened states' rights? It was not, after all, much of an ideological step from Jefferson's Resolutions to Calhoun, secession, and the Confederate States of America.

But Jefferson had only to look to New England for a precedent in the declaration of the primacy of states' rights. For it was New England, not Virginia nor South Carolina, that first posed a tangible danger of secession from the Union with the calling of the Hartford Convention in 1814. Connecticut, angered by President Madison's policy of conscription in the War of 1812, had declared itself in this

From *Mankind*, August 1969. Reprinted from Mankind Magazine, copyright © 1969 by Mankind Publishing Co.

DANIEL WEBSTER

JOSIAH QUINCY

matter "a free, sovereign, and independent state," and characterized the United States as "a confederacy [sic] of states."

The Federalists, who called the Convention, were now angry. They decried the British blockade that had crippled their shipping; Madison's failure to defend New England; the invasion of Maine; the alliance of southern planters and western farmers and expansionists who, with increased representation in Congress, had voted for the war over their op-

position. They could see in the acquisition of the Louisiana territory the march westward, the threatened American invasion of Florida, Mexico, even Canada, the end of their hegemony.

So angered was Massachusetts Congressman Josiah Quincy over statehood for Louisiana in 1812 that he threatened: "As it will be the right of us all, so it will be the duty of some, to prepare definitely for a separation; amicably if they can, violently if they must."

The British might burn the capital, occupy Detroit, and invade New York, but Daniel Webster, later a demigod of "Union," could thunder in Madison's ears: "Where is it written in the Constitution . . . that you may take children from their parents and parents from their children and compel them to fight the battles of any war in which the folly or wickedness of Government may engage it?"

Meeting in Hartford on December 15, 1814, the New England Federalists sat in secret session "for the purpose," they announced, "of devising proper measures to procure the united efforts of the commercial states, to obtain such amendments and explanations of the Constitution as will secure them from further evils."

President Madison was shocked and embittered. "No foreign foe has broken my heart," he declared. "To see the Capitol wrecked by the British does not hurt so deeply as to know sedition [sic] in New England."

Indeed, the Convention, which could not help but give aid and comfort to the British, moved perilously close to treason, moving former President John Adams to declare that its leader, George Cabot, "wants to be President of New England, sir!" And in the actions of Northern extremists there was added cause for Federal concern. Massachusetts' Governor Caleb Strong was prepared, if need be, for a separate peace with England, and John Lowell—uncle of the poet James Russell Lowell—proposed the expulsion of the West from the Union, declaring that a new federal constitution, uniting only the original 13 states, "appears to be the last hope of our country."

In one of history's supreme ironies, the South responded to threats of se-

cession with fury. The Richmond *Enquirer*, destined to be the clarion of the Confederacy, urged President Madison to invade New England, and thundered: "No man, no association of men, no state or set of states *has a right* to withdraw itself from this Union, of its own accord . . . The *majority of states*, which form this Union must consent to the withdrawal of *any one* branch of it. Until *that* consent has been obtained, any attempt to dissolve the Union, or to obstruct the efficacy of its constitutional laws, is Treason—Treason to all intents and purposes." (Note: italics are the *Enquirer's*.)

Dominated by moderates, the Convention sat on its hotheads and presented a report at once conciliatory and threatening. While it once again lamented President Madison's alleged misgovernment, it loyally noted in its report that "to attempt upon every abuse of power to change the Constitution would be to perpetuate the evils of revolution," adding carefully that "a severance of the Union by one or more States, against the will of the rest, and especially in a time of war, can be justified only by absolute necessity." But, the Convention report still insisted the states had the right in matters of Federal conscription "to interpose [their] authority" for the protection of their citizens.

More ominously, the Convention, adjourning on January 5, 1815, decided to meet again in Boston in June should the war continue and its demands not be met, the Boston convention to be invested "with such powers and instructions as the exigency of a crisis so momentous may require."

The Convention's report proved both academic and anticlimactic, for peace with Britain was achieved in the Treaty of Ghent on Christmas Eve, 1814. But the meeting at Hartford had consequences far graver than the collapse of the Federalist Party, which never wholly freed itself of the scent of treason. It set a precedent which at once abetted the Southern cause in the Civil War and lessened the credibility of the North's pious appeals for Union. Perhaps more to our point, it deepened a sectionalism, which as the campaigns of 1964 and 1968 made eloquently clear, is with us still.

4

Civil War and Reconstruction

Perhaps no era in the history of the United States provides as much evidence for the reexamination of historic events as the era of the Civil War and Reconstruction. As Richard Hofstadter pointed out in Part I, consensus history "is quite helpless and irrelevant on the Civil War and the issues related to it." Clearly there was no consensus then, and in the light of the racial divisions and confrontations of the last fifteen years, today's historians are asking if it is still reasonable to view that conflict as the war that saved the Union, freed the slaves, and then gave the Negro a new status of equality.

In "Toward a New Civil War Revisionism," John Rosenberg, after reviewing earlier interpretations, concludes that such a view is more self-serving myth than fact. Mindful of continuing racial prejudice and violence, Rosenberg arrives at the sobering conclusion that the hopes expressed in Lincoln's Gettysburg address "that these dead shall not have died in vain; that this nation, under God, shall have a new birth of freedom" simply have not been fulfilled.

In the next selection, "William Lloyd Garrison: Angry Abolitionist," Jules Archer traces Garrison's change from a moderate reformer who believed that "immediate and complete emancipation is not desirable" to the fire-eating, radical polemicist who proclaimed, "Enslave but a single human being, and the liberty of the world is in peril."

The next two articles, "Johnny Reb and Billy Yank" by Bell Wiley and "Negro Soldiers in the Civil War" by James Robertson, look at the war largely from the point of view of the foot soldier, rather than the generals who commanded him. Both authors find that the heroism of the common soldier was general and deserving of a place in history's hall of fame.

Views of Reconstruction reflect a basic controversy among historians. In "Thomas Nast and the First Reconstruction," Morton Keller follows cartoonist Nast's growing disillusionment as Reconstruction degenerated from a Radical Republican crusade dedicated to securing equality for blacks to the increasingly cynical politicking that brought Reconstruction to an end with the election of Rutherford B. Hayes in 1877. Believing in the complexity and difficulty of social change, Keller concludes that "A tougher-minded realism—alien alike to Nast's Radical Republicans and to much of the contemporary civil rights movement—may, it is true, discourage bold aspirations. But it may also prevent the wasting disillusionment that swept over Nast and is so endemic today—that comes when undue hopes are duly disappointed." In the final selection for this section, Ronald Walters examines the "Political Strategies of Reconstruction" and finds, in the famous words of Frederick Douglass, "that the liberties of the American people [in this case freed blacks] were dependent upon the ballot-box, the jury-box and the cartridge-box." In short, Reconstruction failed not because it attempted to do too much, but because white Americans would not give —and Negroes did not demand—the tools to finish the job.

Toward a New Civil War Revisionism

JOHN S. ROSENBERG

⊙ JOHN S. ROSENBERG is a graduate student in American history at Stanford University. He is currently collaborating on a documentary study of the civil rights movement.

"THE CIVIL WAR," Robert Penn Warren has written, "is our only 'felt' history—history lived in the national imagination." In a fundamental sense it was not the "Second American Revolution," as Charles Beard maintained, it was the first; "we became a nation," as Warren stated, "only with the Civil War." It is our Civil War, not our war of separation from Great Britain, which has proved more durable as the source of our national identity; it is really Lincoln the savior, not Washington the founder, who personifies America. It is not surprising, then, that the way each generation has viewed our national epic has been inextricably bound up with the way it viewed the nation. Consequently, each generation has felt impelled to reinterpret the Civil War to itself and for itself.

Two of the major influences in this continual reinterpretation have been the issues of race and war; the manner in which not only professional historians but also the public at large have viewed these twin themes has had a great deal to do with the way they understood and evaluated the Civil War. Thus, two of the major interpretations of this century were profoundly affected by contemporary attitudes toward the Negro and toward American participation in the two world wars. One was written by a generation whose outlook was heavily influenced by the war of 1917 and its aftermath and which was largely indifferent to the problems of American Negroes; the other was written by the following generation, which had learned a different lesson from its experiences with World War II and the cold war and which showed greater concern for the conditions of Negroes in this country. Since the war in Vietnam and the domestic racial crisis are having a major impact on the outlook of a new generation, it would be surprising if another interpretation of the Civil War did not emerge. It is my intention to suggest the form such a new interpretation might take.

The interpretation that came to be known as "revisionist" challenged the popular Beardian view that the Civil War resulted from an irreconcilable economic clash, and it also rejected the earlier nationalist view that the war was an inevitable conflict between slavery and freedom. The leading advocates of the revisionist position, Avery O. Craven and James G. Randall, both shared in the widespread disillusionment with war that followed World War I. "Just as Americans beginning about 1935 executed something like an about face in their interpretation of the World War," wrote Randall in 1940, "so the retelling of the Civil War is a matter of changed and changing viewpoints. In the present troubled age," he continued, "it may be of more than academic interest to re-examine the human beings of that war generation with less thought of the 'splendor of battle flags' and with more

of the sophisticated and unsentimental searchlight of reality."

Randall's writing reveals a profound disgust for war. "For the very word 'war,'" he claimed, "the realist would have to substitute some such term as 'organized murder' or 'human slaughterhouse.'" He criticized most writings about war because in them "the war is offstage in that its stench and hideousness do not appear." Although he was not as outspoken on this issue as Randall, Craven agreed that war was seldom justified. "Those who force the settlement of human problems by war," he wrote, "can expect only an unsympathetic hearing from the future. Mere desire to do 'right' is no defense at the bar of history."

The revisionists criticized the previous interpretations for assuming that the differences between the sections were irreconcilable and hence that man was incapable of avoiding the catastrophe of war. Thus, Randall's concern with "the human beings" of the war generation and Craven's criticism of "those who forced" the antagonism to the point of war reflected their belief that the war was caused by people and not by an irreconcilable conflict over basic issues. In his first major article, Craven charged that "differences—economic, social, and political—did not then [in 1825] or afterwards portend an 'irrepressible conflict' between North and South, to be settled only by bloodshed. The War Between the States in 1861-65 did not come simply because one section was agricultural and the other industrial; because one exploited free labor and the other slaves; or because a sectional majority refused to respect the constitutional rights of a minority!" Unlike Randall, Craven did believe that the sections were divided by economic interests, but he did not believe that these differences alone could have produced war.

For the revisionists to make their case that the differences between the sections were not basic enough to cause war, it was necessary for them to challenge the centrality of slavery. Randall did this by pointing out that the principal disputes were over runaway slaves and the extension of slavery into the territories. He thought that the numbers involved were too insignificant to lead to war (the census of 1860 listed eight hundred and three runaway slaves and two slaves in the Kansas territory) and that the whole question "was magnified into an issue altogether out of scale with its importance." Craven drew a distinction between slavery as a reality and slavery as a symbol. Of these two quite different slaveries, the first was economic and the second was psychological. And it was the psychological one that caused the trouble: "The first could be almost ignored in our study of sectional conflict had it not become the symbol of all sectional differences; the second leaves few pages of history from 1830 to 1860 untouched."

"Slavery," Craven thought, "was not a major economic fact in Southern life" or even the controlling factor in the life of the Negro. "The fact of his status as a slave may, in the main, be ignored. He should be thought of, first, only as a different racial element in the society. . . ." Slavery offered both advantages and disadvantages; there was little unusual about it. "What owning and being owned added to the usual relationship between employer and employee, it is difficult to say." In addition to his physical freedom and the right to drift aimlessly, Craven wrote, the slave was deprived of such things as "the dignity of responsibility and the stimulation of worry." His life partner was often chosen for him, which made his plight in that respect "as bad as that of European royalty but only a trifle worse than that of the rural whites. . . ." Slavery as a reality, then, was not really so bad and hence could not have produced a sectional conflict.

It is important to recognize the subtle but significant difference between Randall's and Craven's approach to the problem of slavery. As Professor David Potter has noted, "where Craven discounted the significance of slavery as an institution, Randall minimized its significance as an issue. One of his [Randall's] most effective arguments was his contention that, while the broad issue of freedom versus slavery may be worth a war, the issue as defined by the opposing forces in 1861 was not that broad, and was not worth a war in the form in which they defined it; for the Republicans in 1861 did not propose to emancipate the slaves, they even agreed in 1861 to guarantee slavery in the existing slave states and to return fugitive slaves to slavery."

In short, the revisionists did not believe that the war was caused by slavery or any other irreconcilable differences between the sections. Craven concluded that the conflict was made of "emotions, cultivated hostilities, and ultimately of hatred between the sections." This hatred was produced not by the wounds, which were slight, but by the salt of controversy poured on them: "Differences were but the materials with which passions worked. . . . The conflict was the work of politicians and pious cranks! The people knew little of each other as realities. They were both fighting mythical devils." Thus Craven traced the outbreak of hostilities to inept political leaders and fanatics who magnified what real divisions there were out of all proportion. "The move for an independent South which came to a climax in 1861 did not arise from permanent physical and social conditions," Craven wrote in 1939. "It sprang rather from temporary factors cultivated both without and within the section." Randall went so far as to claim that wars were never caused by basic issues. "One of the most colossal of misconceptions," he argued, "is the theory that fundamental motives produce war. The glaring and obvious fact is the artificiality of war-making agitation."

Where previous interpretations had explained the increase of emotionalism and the appearance of extremists as the result of the sectional conflict, of the historical situation itself, Craven and Randall viewed them as the cause of the conflict. The fatal crime the revisionists attributed to these "fanatics" and "demagogic politicians" was that they transformed real and concrete issues into abstractions, and hence presumably into the unreal. "What were but normal differences in the beginning of the period thus gradually became principle." Throughout revisionism runs the theme that principles, morals and abstractions were the wrench the fanatics threw into the works of democracy; the democratic process, so well equipped to handle "real" issues, was torn asunder when the dangerous and unnecessary questions of right and wrong were forced upon it. Thus, a "needless war" resulted when the "blundering generation" allowed "their short-sighted politicians, their over-zealous editors, and their pious reformers to emotionalize real and potential differences and to conjure up distorted impressions of those who dwelt in other parts of the nation." They turned "normal American conflicts" into "a struggle of civilizations."

Although the revisionists were nominally critical of the extremists in both sections, they usually reserved their most bitter condemnation for those in the North. The South is generally pictured as responding to external attack, its extremists spawned by those of the North. Craven, for example, was consistently more critical of the reformers than of the evils they were trying to correct. Claiming that the abolitionist movement "arose out of the

apprehensions engendered by changes going on in the immediate environment of the reformers," he noted that historians were becoming "less inclined to grant unstinted praise to the fanatic and [are] not certain about the value of his contribution." In fact, Craven went so far as to wonder "if the developments of history might not have been more sound without him." Randall, too, seemed to single out the abolitionists, noting that their "avenging force of puritanism in politics" was "a major cause of the conflict." But in assessing guilt for the cardinal sin of substituting abstractions for realities, Craven employed a double standard. While he believed the abolitionists guilty of introducing questions of morality into politics and converting concrete issues into principles, Craven had a warm spot in his heart for Robert E. Lee, who, we are told, "chose to yield deeply held convictions regarding immediate concrete issues in order to stand by those intangible, yet more profound values which had to do with honor, with self-respect, and with duty."

From the 1930's onward revisionism enjoyed wide acceptance in the historical profession and society at large. It partially resulted from and appealed to a general disillusionment with war, and it also reflected a disappointment and loss of faith in the United States that was prevalent among intellectuals in the depressed thirties. Many believed that the immediate results of the Civil War, and even the society they lived in, did not justify the terrible sacrifices that had been necessary to achieve them. Randall spoke of "the hateful results of the war" and claimed that "the triumph of the Union was spoiled by the manner in which victory was used." Craven looked around at the United States in 1939 and saw "Workers talking of 'wage slavery,' capitalists piling fortunes high while poverty and starvation stalk the streets. . . . To such ends did three decades of quarreling and four years of bitter warfare make substantial contributions."

As late as 1950, Kenneth Stampp, an historian who seemed to share some of the revisionists' assumptions about war, closed his study of the secession crisis with the strong implication that the Civil War had been a disaster unmitigated by the bestowal of formal freedom on the slaves. According to Stampp, the conflict had ended "with the rich richer and the slaves only half free. Nationalists," he concluded bitterly, "might rejoice that the Union was preserved. But what the Yankees achieved—for their generation at least—was a triumph not of middle-class ideals but of middle-class vices. The most striking products of their crusade were the shoddy aristocracy of the North and the ragged children of the South. Among the masses of Americans there were no victors, only the vanquished." But despite this pessimistic conclusion, Stampp maintained that "Unless the concept of 'national interest' is reevaluated, their [that of the generation of 1861] decision, their choice of war rather than peace, must be accepted as just and right."

In 1950, when Stampp wrote, there was no sign that Americans were about to reevaluate the concept, or the sanctity, of their national interest. Americans tend to view themselves as the polar opposites of their enemies. Consequently, the experience of opposition both to the total evil of Nazi Germany and to the current cold war with another system of total evil, Stalinist Russia, tended to confirm the view that the American nation, whatever its minor flaws, was the embodiment of all the noble Western values. Perhaps America was not perfect, but it was certainly better than any alternative that had appeared. Fired by the hot war against Hitler and tempered by the cold one against Stalin, a new generation came to hold attitudes about America and about war that were strikingly at odds with those held by the generation of the thirties. Thus, the Civil War came to be celebrated as a necessary step on the way to a more perfect democracy and a more powerful nation. It was now assumed without question that the very existence of the country must be protected at all costs, by any means. A generation that had sanctioned the use of atomic weapons to speed the already certain defeat of the Japanese was not likely to quarrel with the use of war as a legitimate means of securing national objectives, and certainly not as a means of preserving the nation itself.

This resurgence of patriotism and renewed acceptance of war inevitably came to be reflected in the historical profession. In his presidential address to the American Historical Association in 1951, Samuel Eliot Morison commented favorably on this shift of attitudes. "There is," he said, "a decided change of attitude toward our past, a friendly, almost affectionate attitude. . . ." He had harsh words for those historians who, "caught in the disillusion that followed World War I, ignored wars, belittled wars, taught that no war was necessary and no war did any good, even to the victor." Instead of criticizing war, Morison urged, historians should point out that "war does accomplish something, that war is better than servitude, that war has been an inescapable aspect of the human story."

These post-World War II historians, whom Professor Thomas Pressly has called the "new nationalists," had themselves supported and participated in America's involvement in what they considered a just war. Believing from their own experience that wars were caused by very real ideological conflicts, they rejected the revisionist contention that "artificial agitation" was always the primary cause. Criticizing the revisionists for ignoring moral confrontation in history, these historians stressed the necessity for moral choice, both on the part of historical actors and historians themselves. Since the intractability of evil in the world made conflict a moral necessity, those so-called "moderates" who tried to effect compromises were nothing more than appeasers. As Arthur Schlesinger, Jr., the most articulate of the new nationalists, stated the problem of conflict and compromise: "The issue here posed—what policy would have averted war—goes down to the question we formulate today [1947] in terms of appeasement or resistance." Predictably, the new nationalists vigorously denounced the Crittenden Compromise, the last major effort at sectional conciliation.

Senator Crittenden of Kentucky had proposed a series of unamendable Constitutional amendments to protect slavery in the states where it existed and in the District of Columbia, to guarantee it beneath the line of 36°30', and to exclude it above that line. According to Professor Harold Hyman, "kudos for Crittenden's formula calls for conviction that any peace is better than any war." This "ignominious capitulation" could not be preferred over the Republicans' policy of firmness "unless prejudgement exists that anything is preferable to confrontation." Schlesinger similarly rules out compromise: "A society closed in defense of evil institutions," he wrote, "creates moral differences far too profound to be solved by compromise." The revisionists, he claimed, did not face the "hard fact" that "closed and authoritarian social systems tend to create a compulsive intransigence in their own ruling groups and that these groups may respond much more to a firmness which wakens them to some sense of actuality than to a forbearance which is never great enough and always to be discounted." One is tempted to conclude that Schlesinger and Hyman share a prejudgment that, where profound moral differences exist, any war is better than any peace.

In an influential article published in *Partisan Review* in 1949, Schlesinger mounted a sustained attack against revisionism. He argued that historians need moral sensitivity as much as objectivity to understand the past. "By denying themselves insight into the moral dimension of the slavery crisis," he contended, "the revisionists denied themselves a historical understanding of the intensities that caused the slavery crisis." By failing to recognize the significance of moral outrage, in other words, the revisionists were led to false conclusions about the war's causation. "Because the revisionists felt no moral outrage themselves, they deplored as fanatics those who did feel it, or brushed aside their feelings as the artificial product of emotion and propaganda."

Reintroducing moral outrage into the historical process, Schlesinger made a persuasive argument that indignation and emotion are no more "artificial" than anything else. Since "sometimes there is no escape from the implacabilities of moral decision," the abolitionists could not refrain—and hence should not be blamed for not refraining—from vehemently attacking slavery. "If revisionism has based itself on the conviction that things would have been different if only there had been no abolitionists, it has forgotten that abolitionism was as definite and irrevocable a factor in the historical situation as was slavery itself." Revealing the influence of his own experiences, he concluded that "To say that there 'should' have been no abolitionists in America before the Civil War is about as sensible as to say that there 'should' have been no anti-Nazis in the nineteen-thirties or that there 'should' be no anti-Communists today."

But Schlesinger did more than defend the abolitionists. In addition to defending their antislavery feelings, and the actions based on them, he justified the war they helped to produce. For the revisionists, the war was "needless" and "repressible" because the sectional conflict was not fundamental or necessary but was instead the artificial product of agitation by irrational extremists and a "blundering generation" of politicians. For Schlesinger, the war was an inevitable conflict between Good and Evil. Where the revisionists claimed that the debate over slavery in the territories was an "unreal" or "magnified" one about an imaginary slave in an impossible place, Schlesinger and the new nationalists compared the territories to Poland and the South to Germany. Schlesinger, for example, argued that, "The democracies could not challenge fascism inside Germany any more than opponents of slavery could challenge slavery inside the South, but the extension of slavery, like the extension of fascism, was an act of aggression which made a moral choice inescapable." And since resistance was preferable to appeasement, war was the only moral choice: the Civil War was "an 'irrepressible conflict,'" Schlesinger wrote, "and hence a justified one."

The new nationalists substituted a commitment to the moral necessity of war for the revisionists' disillusionment with it, and they heaped praise on the abolitionists' vigorous opposition to evil in place of the revisionists' criticism of their irrational extremism. Consequently, it is not unfair to say that the new nationalists, unlike the revisionists, believed, in words made famous by Senator Goldwater in another context, that "moderation in pursuit of justice is no virtue, and extremism in defense of liberty is no vice." Or, as Oscar Handlin put it, "There surely is a difference between a fanatic for freedom and a fanatic for slavery."

Schlesinger's interpretation reflected the outlook of liberal veterans of World War II and the cold war, but a new generation that has rejected so much of the affectionate attitude toward our past noted by Morison is likely to find this liberal version of our Civil War increasingly inadequate. As we move into the second century of the post-Civil War era, the lingering plight of American Negroes and the destructive impact of American nationalism on the rest of the world seriously challenge the justification of the Civil War—that it freed the slaves and preserved the nation—and calls for a new revisionism.

This new revisionism, it must be pointed out, is not really history at all; it is a new way of *evaluating* the Civil War, not of explaining it. Most historians are not willing to engage themselves in this kind of thinking. They are willing to explore the question of whether those who participated in the war or those who lived after the war but before the present felt it was justified, but they generally are reluctant to consider whether the war was justified or unjustified on the basis of what they think of America in 1969. Even if this were acceptable behavior on the part of professional historians, ordinary citizens surely need not recognize the scholarly injunction to refrain from personally judging and evaluating the past. Especially now, when an increasing number of young people are deeply concerned with the problem of justifying war, it is worthwhile to examine the justifiability of a war nearly all Americans regard as just.

Indeed, few historians themselves recognize their own injunction not to evaluate the past; the only difference is that their evaluations are usually unconscious. As the philosopher William Dray has pointed out, the historians' debate about the inevitability of the war has really been a debate about its justifiability. The core of these disputes has not been whether the war *could* have been avoided, but whether it *should* have been. "What they are quarreling about is surely the stand to be taken on a moral issue," Dray writes. "That issue is whether war with one's fellow countrymen is a greater moral evil than acquiescence in political and economic domination, or in the continuance of an institution like chattel slavery"—or, one might add, than peaceful separation.

The former revisionists, believing as they did that the war was unjustified, purported to show that it could have been avoided, and hence they blamed the entire generation for not avoiding it. A new revisionism, however, would not attempt a new historical explanation of the war; instead, it would openly be concerned with the manner in which Americans today view it. It would not blame the men of 1861 for a catastrophe that was probably beyond their capacity to avoid. Their problem was not that they were "blundering," but that they were normal; to have avoided war under the circumstances would have been heroic. A new revisionism, then, would challenge the prevalent assumption that that catastrophe was a worthwhile and justifiable sacrifice. Thus, a new revisionism would be concerned with current attitudes and not with the old question of historical inevitability. It is one thing to recognize that historical actors in many situations cannot reasonably be expected to have acted other than they did, but it is quite another to celebrate their actions as the new nationalists do. One may differ with the revisionists and *excuse* the men of 1861 without accepting the attempt of the new nationalists to *justify* their decision. One may empathize with them—a generation hopelessly entangled in a web of nationalism and slavery—and still severely criticize those historians who today view the war as a Good Thing. One may believe, as I do, that the Civil War—or more accurately, a civil war—was unavoidable and still believe that it was a tragedy that cannot be justified either by contemporary war aims or by the results it achieved. A new revisionism, then, would not deduce justifiability from inevitability as Schlesinger does.

Since a new revisionism would be openly presentist, would be concerned with evaluation from hindsight, the issue is not whether civil war in principle is a greater moral evil than slavery or secession, but whether the actual Civil War that occurred should be justified because of what it prevented or achieved. The two issues involved were slavery and union. The new nationalists claim that the Civil War was justified to abolish one and preserve the other; a new revisionism would argue that it was not. It would argue, first, that the mere preservation of the American nation against the will of a large number of its inhabitants does not justify any sacrifices, and, second, that the limited improvement in the status of the Negro in this country was not worth the expenditure in lives required to make that improvement possible.

Generally, those who justify the Civil War do so on the grounds that it freed the slaves, not that it saved the Union. If the war had ended "prematurely," and thus left slavery intact, presumably they would not now justify it. This was the position taken by most abolitionists, a number of whom, in fact, did fear that the war would end before the slaves were freed. But there were also a number of abolitionists who remained pacifists despite their hatred of slavery, or who were not pacifists but still would not support a war for the preservation of the Union on the mere possibility that the slaves would be freed in the process. Consequently, I think the crucial question the Civil War presents today to all who are not simple nationalists is whether its results have vindicated the many abolitionists who supported it or the few who did not.

Those today who justify the war predictably claim the results have vindicated its supporters. Despite their recognition that the official war aim was merely the preservation of the Union, those abolitionists who supported the war, such as William Lloyd Garrison and Wendell Phillips, did so because of their assumption, which proved correct, that winning the war would require emancipation. Despite their previous advocacy of disunion, they did an abrupt about-face when Fort Sumter was fired on. A pacifist until the war broke out, Garrison announced after Sumter: "All my sympathies and wishes are with the government, because it is entirely in the right, and acting strictly in self-defense and for self-preservation." Accused of inconsistency, he replied, "Well, ladies and gentlemen, when I said I would not sustain the Constitution because it was 'a covenant with death and an agreement with hell,' I had no idea I would live to see death and hell secede. Hence it is that I am now with the government to enable it to constitutionally stop the further ravages of death, and to extinguish the ravishes of hell." The North, cleansed of all its corruption and left virtuous by the South's secession, was thus engaged in a noble crusade.

These abolitionists knew that the government's only purpose was to save the Union, and their abandonment of disunion was not based exclusively on regard for the Negro's welfare; after Sumter they shared in the general surge of patriotic fervor that swept the North. Thus, in his famous speech announcing support for the war, Wendell Phillips stated that he believed "in the possibility of justice, in the certainty of Union." The American flag, which he said had previously represented slavery and oppression, had come to represent "sovereignty and justice," presumably in that order. Phillips, no longer thinking there was a conflict between union and freedom, became a staunch unionist. "Do you suppose I am not Yankee enough to buy Union when I can have it at a fair price?" he asked those who accused him of compromising his principles.

There were some abolitionists, however, who either were not Yankee enough or who did not think the price of war was fair, and a new revisionism would support their position. Lydia Maria Child, one of the most sensitive and perceptive people in this group, felt there was little "of either right principle, or good feeling, at the foundation of this unanimous Union sentiment." In addition to being upset because her husband had been almost mobbed at a Union meeting for suggesting that the government should help the slaves, she was dismayed at Lincoln's stated intention of not interfering with slavery where it existed and with General Butler's offer to use his Massachusetts troops to put down any slave rebellion in Maryland. "In view of these things," she wrote, "the Union-shouts, and hurrahs for the U. S. flag, sound like fiendish mockery in my ears." George Bassett, an Illinois abolitionist, could not support the war because "It is not a war for Negro liberty, but for national despotism." In a similar vein, an ex-Garrisonian at Yale was disturbed that "Abolitionists and Disunionists of thirty years' standing should now be found lending pen and voice to uphold and urge on a war waged solely and avowedly to preserve and perpetuate the Union. . . . Is anyone so blind as to fancy that the capitalists, who last winter were mobbing Mr. Phillips, have now struck hands with him for a crusade against slavery . . . ?"

The disillusionment and despair of these abolitionists were heightened by the fact that many of their former colleagues seemed to become themselves more interested in saving the Union than in freeing the slaves. Moncure Conway, whom some Eastern abolitionists had sent to England to represent their position, learned of the swelling nationalism among his colleagues the hard way. When it was learned that he had naïvely informed the Confederate envoy that the abolitionists would withdraw their support from the war if the Confederacy would free the slaves, he was soundly denounced in the North. Repudiating their envoy, the Boston *Commonwealth* and the *National Anti-Slavery Standard* announced that "the anti-slavery men will not sanction any proposal that included a recognition of the Confederacy." Conway was so crushed when he learned that many former abolitionists would prosecute the war even if slavery were not an issue that he abandoned not only the war but the United States itself and decided to stay in England. "It never entered my mind," he wrote his wife, "that any leading anti-slavery man wd question the principle involved—wd in any way support the war simply for conquest or Union whether Liberty were or were not involved. The wholesale slaughter of men is vile enough anyway; but to slaughter them except for the holiest cause is *worse* than treason to any government that does it."

In short, there were abolitionists who thought the North's cause was less than holy. Certainly at the time there was much to support their position, for there can be no doubt that the official purpose of the war, at least initially, was exclusively to save the Union. Even the New York *Tribune* declared that "this war is in truth a war for the preservation of the Union, not for the destruction of slavery. . . . We believe that slavery has nothing to fear from a Union triumph." Lincoln stated repeatedly that he had no intention of interfering with slavery, and the widely respected Springfield (Mass.) *Republican* wrote that "If there is one point of honor upon which more than another this administration will stick, it is its pledge not to interfere with slavery in the states." As late as August, 1862, Lincoln was precise and unequivocal as to his purpose. In his famous public reply to Horace Greeley's advocacy of emancipation, the President who would be known as the Great Emancipator wrote: "My paramount objective in this struggle is to save the Union, and is not either to save or destroy slavery. If I could save the Union without freeing any slaves I would do it, and if I could save it by freeing all the slaves I would do it; and if I could save it by freeing some and leaving others alone I would also do that."

But, as we all know and as the pro-war abolitionists had predicted, Lincoln did decide that he had to free the slaves, or rather some of them, in order to save the Union (indeed, his letter to Greeley was written exactly one month after he wrote the first draft of the Emancipation Proclamation).* Even so, in retrospect it appears that those abolitionists who refused to follow Garrison and Phillips into active support of the war showed the greater

wisdom, for the motives behind abolition and the Reconstruction amendments had serious effects on the quality of freedom thereby bestowed. It was obvious to many that freedom granted purely for the purpose of military necessity would be severely limited. As Lydia Maria Child accurately predicted in 1862, before the Emancipation Proclamation had been proclaimed, "Even should [the slaves] be emancipated, merely as a 'war necessity,' everything *must* go wrong, if there is no heart or conscience on the subject."

Just as there was no conscience in emancipation, so there was little in the Reconstruction legislation. The First Reconstruction Act, as C. Vann Woodward has recently written, "was not primarily devised for the protection of Negro rights and the provision of Negro equality. Its primary purpose, however awkwardly and poorly implemented, was to put the Southern States under the control of men loyal to the Union. . . ."

Indeed, as Woodward indicates, there is a great deal of evidence to suggest that the primary concern of most Reconstruction legislators was with whites in the North, not blacks in the South. It was feared that unless the freedom of the ex-slaves was secured in the South they would swarm over the North in search of it. There is even evidence that suggests that those who drafted the Fifteenth Amendment were more concerned with securing Republican majorities in the North (where most states still refused to enfranchise Negroes) than civil rights for Negroes in the South. This is not to deny that there was some sincere support for Negro rights, but, as Woodward points out, "it was not the antislavery idealists who shaped the Fifteenth Amendment and guided it through Congress. The effective leaders of legislative action were moderates with practical political considerations in mind—particularly that thin margin of difference in partisan voting strength in certain Northern states." The Fifteenth Amendment has often been seen as the crowning success of idealistic Northern war aims. But read more carefully, as Woodward concludes, it "reveals more deviousness than clarity of purpose, more partisan needs than idealistic aims, more timidity than boldness." Thus, if we are to justify the Civil War because it led to Reconstruction, our justification must be based on the legal possibilities Reconstruction created for future generations, not what it actually achieved or even tried to achieve for the slaves, whom it only partially freed.

What little progress Negroes have been allowed to achieve has occurred almost exclusively in the past fifteen years. There is no doubt that the achievements of what Woodward calls the Second Reconstruction would have been a great deal more difficult without those of the First, but are those achievements enough to justify the ravages of our Civil War? The question is not whether Negroes are better off today than they would have been had there been no war. We may assume that they are. The question is whether the quantity and quality of freedom our society has been willing to grant is valuable enough to justify the death of one man for every six slaves who were freed. Everyone must work out his own equation for the moral calculus of war, his own formula to match ends with means. It is worth pointing out, however, that liberals generally object to sacrificing one generation for the possible benefit of the next, at least when other societies do it. It is no secret that real freedom for the Negro remained much more of a promise, or a hope, than a reality for nearly a century after the Civil War. Since Arthur Schlesinger, Jr., justified the war primarily as a noble fight for freedom, it is difficult to under-

---

* The Proclamation applied only to those areas in the South still at war with the United States, not to those under federal control. It was said at the time that Lincoln freed the slaves only where he did not have the power to do so. As the London *Spectator* dryly observed, the underlying principle was "not that a human being cannot justly own another, but that he cannot own him unless he is loyal to the United States."

stand how he could have been so optimistic about the results in 1949 when he wrote his article in *Partisan Review*. One wonders what examples of Negro freedom, what applications and affirmations of the Fourteenth Amendment, so inspired him that he was able to look with favor on a war that had sacrificed six hundred thousand lives on the altar of that freedom.

I have no illusions about the Negroes' fate had they not been freed by the war, and it could reasonably be argued that I would not question the efficacy or the morality of the war if I were black. Perhaps. But certainly there are many black militants today who feel no gratitude toward their emancipators, nor should they. They argue quite effectively that it would have been much better for all concerned if the slaves had seized their freedom rather than received it in bits and pieces as a result of quarrels among their oppressors. Our image of the "Sambo personality" and the happy, docile slave reinforces our skepticism that a successful slave revolt could have occurred, but no one can be sure of what might have been. As Eugene Genovese has pointed out, slaves in Saint Domingue were described in the same fashion as Southern Sambos, until, that is, they rose up in the greatest slave revolt in history. If, as Genovese suggests, the French Jacobins had taken power in 1790 instead of 1794 and the slaves had been freed "as the result of the vicissitudes of Jacobin-Girondist factionalism," there would now be Haitian scholars attempting to explain the black's docility in the face of oppression.

This is not, of course, to suggest that there would have been a slave rebellion, but it does suggest that we are foolish if we assume that "it couldn't happen here." Even if slavery or some modified form of oppression (but what have we had if not modified oppression?) had lasted well into the twentieth century, there is no reason to assume that it would have lasted forever. The blacks would certainly have shared in the wave of anticolonial feelings that has swept up other oppressed peoples in this century. Indeed, they are sharing in it even though supposedly freed. Even if an independent South resembled South Africa (which is unlikely since there has been cultural interdependence between the races in the South), there is room to question whether the difference between the conditions of Negro life in America and South Africa is so great as to justify over half a million deaths. Are we so accustomed to organized violence that we automatically accept without question the conclusion that the Civil War was justified even though it merely loosened the shackles of slavery? Can we be so sure that the privilege of moving from the plantation to the ghetto is worth the death and destruction of a brutal war?

It could be argued that even though emancipation has not been complete, it nevertheless was a necessary preliminary to any future progress. It is true, of course, that history will not end this year, but this bit of knowledge is of limited value in evaluating the war. The argument of future progress—that the results of emancipation are not yet known—requires an optimism about the future that America's treatment of the blacks in the past and present does not support. Moreover, the further into the future one projects this potential progress, the more difficult it becomes to argue that such progress would have been impossible but for emancipation in 1865.

Another argument against a new revisionism is that the Civil War can be justified by what it prevented, if not by what it achieved. But one need not argue that Negroes are no better off because of the war; the question is whether there has been enough real, as opposed to merely legal, improvement to justify the terrible sacrifices required to achieve it. Even admitting that the Negroes' plight has lessened, however, it is hard to say how much of that improvement is simply the seepage of industrial develop-

ment and our involvement in two world wars. And it is highly unlikely that the spread of slavery into the territories or the South's peaceful secession would have thwarted forever the development of industrialism and technology. It is possible that emancipation in 1865 speeded up the process, but that is a far different matter from saying that improvement in the Negroes' condition would have been impossible without the Civil War. It is certainly possible to imagine other paths to the present and future (or another present and future) which, although they may have been worse than the one we have followed, would not have been enough worse to make up for the many who involuntarily paid for the difference with their lives.

The only other justification for the Civil War, that it preserved the American Union, is less difficult to deal with. Ever since the Puritans attempted to build their City on a Hill, Americans have assumed that their country was morally set off from Europe; commentators on our national character have all pointed to the qualities of innocence and virtuousness, of freedom from the guilt and corruption of the Old World, in Americans' conceptions of themselves.

Robert Penn Warren has argued that this feeling of moral superiority, the "Treasury of Virtue," as he calls it, derived in large part from the experience of freeing the slaves in the Civil War. Despite the overwhelming evidence that emancipation was merely a by-product of the war, not its purpose, the doctrine of the Treasury of Virtue views the war as a purposeful crusade so full of righteousness that there was enough left over to make up for whatever small failings subsequently occurred. "From the start," Warren wrote, "America had had adequate baggage of self-righteousness and phariseeism, but with the Civil War came grace abounding. . . . From the start, Americans had a strong tendency to think of their land as the galahad among nations, and the Civil War, with its happy marriage of victory and virtue, converted this tendency into an article of faith nearly as sacrosanct as the Declaration of Independence." This assumption of American virtue, of American grace in a sinful world, was reinforced by the experience of opposition to the tyrannies of Hitler and Stalin and was reflected in much of the new nationalist historiography.

There is a great paradox in this contemporary liberal view of our history. It is well known that this hardheaded, tough-minded, pragmatic liberalism, the liberalism exemplified by Arthur Schlesinger, Jr., is rooted in the moral and philosophical assumptions associated with Reinhold Niebuhr. But along with their pessimistic view of man and tragic view of history, derived from Niebuhr, these liberals incongruously link a highly sanguine and favorable view of the United States. According to Niebuhr, it is all but impossible for societies to act morally, but according to this liberal version of our history the United States has nearly always done so. Where the Niebuhrian universe is filled with fallible men, insoluble moral problems, and complex societies where good and evil (but mostly evil) are woven inextricably together, Schlesinger's liberalism seems to see a history that reveals a virtuous, perfectible America opposing various enemies—the South, Germany, Russia—that are totally evil.

It should be pointed out that Niebuhr's disciples did not depart from his position any more than he did himself. In *Moral Man and Immoral Society* he had written that nations become even more hypocritical than usual in time of war. "In the imagination of the simple patriot the nation is not society but Society. Though its values are relative they appear . . . to be absolute. The religious instinct for the absolute is no less potent in patriotic religion than any other. The nation is always endowed with the aura of the sacred. . . ." Niebuhr is no simple patriot, but the impact of war, hot and cold, did bring him under the influence of patriotic religion. As Christopher Lasch has pointed out, Niebuhr, like many others, believed the cold war forced an ultimate choice between "Marxist despotism" and the "open society" of the West. As the leader of the "Free World," America, in short, became "Society," its values absolute, its existence sacred.

Thus, the tough-minded liberal view of the Civil War was informed by an assumption that the hard reality of evil made conflict necessary and by a commitment to the preservation of the United States at all costs. Schlesinger accused the revisionists of being "sentimentalists" who attempted to "escape from the severe demands of moral decision," who believed that "evil will be 'outmoded' by progress and that politics consequently does not impose on us the necessity for decision and for struggle." But this "realism" now seems equally sentimental for believing that total war can be moral and that America is exempt from the fallibility, self-interest, and collective egoism that Niebuhr's outlook attributes to other nations. If the revisionists were sentimentalists for putting their faith in Progress, certainly Niebuhrian liberals are equally sentimental for putting theirs in the United States. If the revisionists were optimistic for believing that the Civil War could be avoided, Schlesinger and his sympathizers are equally optimistic for believing that the forward march of American progress justifies all the sacrifices along the way.

For despite the participants in the American Celebration, the recent behavior of the United States does not inspire certainty that its preservation was worth whatever sacrifices other generations were called on to make. Arguments that nearly any amount of death and suffering one hundred years ago were justified to preserve the United States because of its moral attributes can no longer be maintained, if, indeed, they ever could. It has become clear that we are a nation like all nations, that as a Great Power we are behaving no more morally than have other Great Powers.

Since the Civil War, if not before, the pursuit of national policy has required the abandonment of many national ideals. Born on the proposition that legitimate government requires the consent of the governed, the United States nevertheless found it necessary to retain the allegiance of a substantial part of its population by force. Some of the more doctrinaire radicals of the time could not support this effort. "The same principle that has always made me an uncompromising abolitionist," said George Bassett, "now makes me an uncompromising secessionist. It is the great natural and sacred right of self-government." The radicalism of his contemporaries, however, had been replaced by an uncompromising nationalism. There is a revealing parallel between the Northern position in the Civil War and recent American interventions in other civil wars. In both cases there is a professed commitment to the principle of self-determination, but in both cases some attribute of those determining themselves invalidates the principle. In the case of the South, it was the presence of slavery; in our recent interventions, it was the presence of Communists,

supposed or real, on one side of the conflict.

Niebuhr has noted the irony involved in this compromising of ideals by both the Communists and the United States, although he thinks the Communists have jettisoned their earlier values far more willingly and completely than has the United States. "Insofar as communism tries to cover the ironic contrast between its original dreams of justice and virtue and its present realities by more and more desperate efforts to prove its tyranny to be 'democracy' and its imperialism to be the achievement of universal peace, it has already dissolved irony into pure evil."

The tyranny of our ghettoes and a "freedom" for Negroes that allows them an equal opportunity only to be killed in a cruel and unjust war have gone a long way toward dissolving America's own irony. For those who are no longer communicants in our patriotic religion, the Civil War begins to appear as a tragedy unjustified by its results. In addition to realizing that war itself is at least as evil as any human or ideological enemy, many Americans have come to deemphasize the significance of merely legal reforms, which have only a limited effect on the quality of most people's lives. Since the former revisionists were not overly concerned with the plight of the Negro, they held that a war over his status was irrational and unnecessary. The new nationalists, on the other hand, were keenly sensitive to the immorality of chattel slavery, and they were willing to justify nearly any extreme to eradicate it. But after more than a hundred years of emancipation, over a decade since the Brown decision, and several civil rights laws, it is now apparent that much more than legal change is required to constitute real progress. How naïve it now seems to justify the slaughter of six hundred thousand men for the slim reward of a formalistic and incomplete emancipation. Lydia Maria Child was right: because the nation has not demonstrated much "heart or conscience" on the subject of freedom for the ex-slaves, everything has gone wrong.

It will be apparent that a new revisionism such as the one outlined above would, like all previous interpretations of the Civil War, be firmly rooted in its own time. Consequently, it may be invalidated (indeed, one hopes it will be invalidated) by future developments: if significant gains are made by Negroes, and those gains are seen as dependent upon emancipation in 1865, then perhaps the sacrifices of the war should be regarded as justified. Thus the new revisionism may become as naïve as the new nationalists' interpretation now seems, but unfortunately it does seem appropriate for our own time. Even Lincoln can be called upon to support this view. At Gettysburg, he solemnly requested his audience to join him in resolving ". . . that these dead shall not have died in vain; that this nation, under God, shall have a new birth of freedom; and that this government of the people, by the people, for the people, shall not perish from the earth." This government did not perish from the earth, but that new birth of freedom never occurred. Sadly, we must conclude that those dead did die in vain.

WILLIAM LLOYD GARRISON: ANGRY ABOLITIONIST

Jules Archer

Jules Archer is the author of over one thousand published articles and stories as well as twelve books. His work has been translated into twelve languages, reprinted by the State Department, and adapted for television. The foregoing article is an excerpt from *Angry Abolitionist: William Lloyd Garrison* by Jules Archer, with permission of the publisher, Julian Messner, a Division of Simon & Schuster, Inc. Copyright © 1969 by Jules Archer.

The struggle of William Lloyd Garrison against not simply the institution of slavery in the United States, but against Northern hypocrisy in deploring while refusing to overturn it, has startling overtones for our own time. Garrison even denounced the white churches of America for turning their backs on the black man despite all their protestations of Christianity and the brotherhood of man — the same denunciations being heard today from black militants.

Garrison, born in Newburyport, Massachusetts, in 1805, began his career as an editor-publisher at the age of twenty-one by putting out a shoestring weekly called the Newburyport *Free Press* with printer Isaac Knapp as a partner.

After six months of unsuccessful struggle, the editors of the *Free Press* were forced to give up. In January, 1827, Garrison left for Boston, where he worked as a journeyman printer while he sought an editor's job. Unlike most young men on their own in the big city,

he shunned the taverns and sporting houses. His notions of relaxation included Bible reading and listening to fiery discourses against sin by the Reverend Lyman Beecher in the Hanover Street Church.

He jumped at the chance to print and edit a small temperance journal, the *National Philanthropist*. The crusade against alcohol, which had victimized his father and brother, was close to his heart. He also won the publisher's permission to assail other moral perils he saw in America.

His first issue as editor, appearing in January, 1828, deplored a conference of atheists called in New York City: "It is impossible to estimate the depravity and wickedness of those who . . . reject the gospel of Jesus Christ." But he was equally shocked by a gathering of Christians who met a week later to advocate going to war to enforce a more favorable boundary with Mexico.

He was indignant when the South Carolina Assembly passed a bill forbidding anyone to teach Negroes to read and write. "There is something unspeakably pitiable and alarming in the state of that society," he fumed, "where it is deemed necessary for self-preservation to seal up the mind and the intellect of man."

Northern newspapers were running sensational stories about the kidnapping of William Morgan, a renegade Freemason, presumably by Masons seeking to silence him about the society's rituals. "All this fearful commotion has arisen from the abduction of *one man*," Garrison scoffed. Who was protesting, he demanded, against the abduction of thousands of runaway slaves in the North back to the South?

"More than two millions of unhappy beings are groaning out their lives in bondage," he charged, "and scarcely a pulse quickens, or a heart leaps, or a tongue pleads in their behalf." Yet even he was not prepared to advocate instant abolition—"immediatism." He had been persuaded by Reverend Beecher and by the Reverend William E. Channing, the nation's most eloquent arbiters of morality, that peaceful, gradual emancipation was the Christian solution to slavery.

"I acknowledge that immediate and complete emancipation is not desirable," he wrote. "No rational man cherishes so wild a vision."

Garrison's paper was read in Vermont by a group of ardent Federalists eager to see John Adams elected over Andrew Jackson. They decided that Garrison was just the hard-hitting editor they needed for a pro-

From *Mankind*, February 1970. Reprinted from Mankind Magazine, copyright © 1970 by Mankind Publishing Co.

William Lloyd Garrison rose from an obscure editor-publisher to become the leading figure in the Abolitionist movement.

Adams weekly, *Journal of the Times*, to be published in Bennington. When they agreed to let him also advocate temperance, pacifism, and emancipation, he accepted their offer of a six-month contract.

In his first issue of the *Journal* he called for the formation of an anti-slavery society in Vermont, and abolition of slavery in the nation's capital. "Before God and our country," he wrote, "we give our pledge that the liberation of the enslaved African shall always be uppermost in our pursuits." In a few weeks he was demanding that every town in the twelve free states start its own anti-slavery society.

Many of the abolitionists' attacks against slavery, while radical and emotional, were justifiable. No matter what the slaveholders claimed, the conditions in the South were often severe and inhuman. Slaves were branded (below) and indiscriminately whipped (above, opposite). Devices (below, opposite), such as (A) handcuffs, (B) leg irons, (C-E) thumb screws, and (F-H) an instrument to force open closed jaws, could be found in common use throughout the South. The conditions as much as the institution itself awakened the conscience of the country.

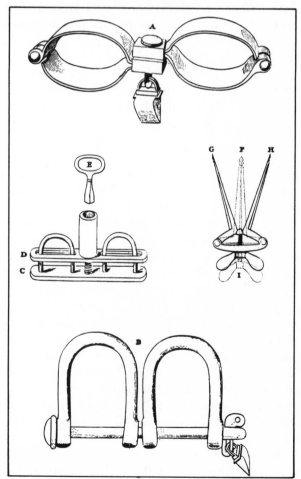

Serving the cause of John Adams, he pen-lashed Jackson both for his brutal murder of Indians in the Florida territory and for his sins as a slaveholder and slave trader. "We care not how numerous may be his supporters. To be in the minority against him would be better than to receive the commendations of a large and deluded majority!"

His growling, often sarcastic style began to create interest among other editors who read his diatribes in issues of the *Journal* they exchanged for copies of their own papers. Horace Greeley called the *Journal* "about the ablest and most interesting newspaper ever issued in Vermont."

Another editor who grew increasingly impressed with the power of Garrison's pen was Benjamin Lundy in Baltimore. In January, 1829, he set out on foot, walking all the way to Bennington to talk Garrison into joining him as co-editor of the *Genius of Universal Emancipation.*

"I need someone to put out the paper regularly as a weekly," he explained, "while I travel around, hold meetings to encourage the setting up of new anti-slavery societies and sell subscriptions. Art thou agreed, brother Garrison?"

On March 29, in his last issue of the *Journal,* Garrison announced that he had taken a new post to devote his entire effort to fighting slavery. "I trust in God," he declared, "that I may be the humble instrument of breaking at least one chain and restoring one captive to liberty: it will repay a life of severe toil."

Not all Vermonters were very sorry to see him go. One wrote to the Vermont *Gazette* applauding the departure of "My Lloyd," the pompous young prig from Massachusetts who wore silver spectacles and sounded off with "the pert loquacity of a blue jay."

The loquacious blue jay left for Boston in April, seeking a printing job that would keep him alive until August. Lundy would not be back in Baltimore until then, having gone to Haiti to resettle twelve liberated slaves. Finding work scarce, Garrison was forced to borrow money from Harriet Horton, the married daughter of his mother's old friend Martha Farnham. Loans from friends soon became an awkward but inevitable way of life for the young crusader.

If abolition was a threadbare profession, it had rewards of prestige. Boston's Congregational Society invited the young editor to give the Fourth of July address at the Park Street Church. His knees shook as he mounted the rostrum to speak to his first audience, consisting of influential clergymen, editors, and anti-slavery advocates. His voice, at first a hoarse, petrified whisper, gradually rang out like a fireball as he grew stirred by his own emotions.

"What has Christianity done, by direct effort, for our slave population?" he challenged. "Comparatively noth-ing. . . . Every Fourth of July, our Declaration of Independence is produced with a sublime indignation, to set forth the tyranny of the mother country. . . . But what a pitiful detail of grievance does this document present, in comparison with the wrongs which our slaves endure!"

Then he sent a shock wave through his listeners. "I am ashamed of my country. I am sick of . . . our hypocritical cant about the unalienable rights of man."

Garrison cried out for a religious crusade to build antislavery societies in every city of the land, freeing the slaves first in the capital, then gradually everywhere else.

It was a memorable speech, thunderously applauded.

But it was for freedom tomorrow, not freedom now, as William Goodell, another young anti-slavery editor, pointed out to him during a long walk through Boston. Garrison admitted that his position lent support to the moderates in the American Colonization Society. But it was a question of practicality. There was no other anti-slavery movement.

"Then we must make one," Goodell insisted. "As long as we support the gradual policies of the Colonizers, we condone slavery for the time being. But as moral Christians, we cannot support slavery for even a second. Nor can we accept the Colonizers' premise that the Negro is too inferior to remain in America when freed."

By the time their walk ended, Garrison was convinced that Goodell was right. "In the end we may be forced to settle for gradual abolition," he mused. "But if we insist upon freedom now, our conscience will be clear in God's eyes — and we may even hurry the dawdlers along!"

When he joined Benjamin Lundy in Baltimore in August, he confessed that his views had altered. "Since slaveholding is a sin, to advocate gradual emancipation now seems to me like asking a thief to abandon his life of crime gradually. If a thing is wrong, it should be changed *now.*"

The Quaker listened patiently, but found himself unable to accept radical abolition, fearful it would lead to violence. "However," he pointed out, "we may still edit the *Genius of Universal Emancipation* together. Thou may put thine initials to thine articles, and I will put my initials to mine, and each will bear his own burden."

Lundy's own faith in colonization was severely shaken that November. He had arranged with a shipowner for free passage to Haiti for twenty to fifty freed slaves, with support there until they could find jobs. But his announcement in the *Genius* brought only a handful of applicants. Few free slaves were eager to leave the North, and even fewer Southern slaveholders cared to free their slaves for emigration. Lundy was chagrined, but could not bring himself to accept defeat for his plan.

The anti-slavery movement was split between "gradualists" and "immediatists," and most Americans of 1829 viewed *both* as radicals. "They stir up trouble," one Pennsylvania citizen growled, "by sticking their noses into the business of the South." Their views met largely with stony indifference in the North. In an important center of slave trade like Baltimore, their lives were in danger.

The city rumbled with anger at Garrison's first piece in the *Genius* demanding immediate freedom for all slaves — and their right to stay as freedmen in the South. "Born on American soil," he told outraged Marylanders, "they are at liberty to choose their own dwelling place."

One morning a slave staggered into the office of the *Genius* and collapsed at the feet of both editors. He had been brutally whipped by an overseer for not loading a wagon fast enough. In addition to head bruises he bore thirty-seven bleeding slashes from his neck to his hips. The horrified editors hid and nursed him for two days.

Garrison sought out his master to protest, but was driven off with the threat of a hiding himself, and the slave was reclaimed. A few days later, passing the slaveholder's house, Garrison heard "the distinct application of a whip, and the shrieks of anguish." He reported bitterly to his Northern readers, "This is nothing uncommon."

He waxed sarcastic about Americans who professed to believe in the "born free and equal" clause of the Declaration of Independence, yet tolerated the slave system that made a mockery of it. His scathing attacks aroused widespread resentment North and South.

Garrison was delighted whenever he could goad a newspaper into attacking him. It was recognition, and he loved being the center of controversy. He also had a more serious motive. "Slavery will not be overthrown without excitement," he explained, "a most tremendous excitement."

Despite Lundy's warning, Garrison wrote a piece ridiculing Austin Woolfolk, the local slave trader who had given Lundy a terrible beating a few years earlier.

Woolfolk threatened vengeance. "I am not to be intimidated by the utterance of any threats, or the perpetration of any acts of violence," Garrison defied him in print. *"Dieu défend le droit."* ("God defends the right.")

Woolfolk and other Baltimore slaveholders sought to put the *Genius* out of business by pressuring its subscribers to cancel. The tolerant Lundy refused to ask Garrison to tone down his aggressive crusading. "I scattered his subscribers like pigeons," Garrison admitted with proud rue.

On the ships that transported Negroes like cattle from Baltimore to plantations in the deep South, almost one in four died en route. Garrison was shocked to learn that the *Francis*, a ship clearing Baltimore harbor with a slave cargo bound for New Orleans, was owned by a rich New Englander from his own hometown of Newburyport — Francis Todd.

Charging that the *Francis* carried seventy-five slaves chained in narrow confinement between decks, Garrison blasted Todd and his skipper, Captain Nicholas Brown, as "highway robbers and murderers."

Todd angrily filed a libel suit against Garrison and Lundy for $5,000 in damages, claiming that the slaves on the *Francis* had not been in chains and had been treated humanely. Meanwhile a Baltimore Grand Jury quickly authorized criminal proceedings against Garrison as the author of the libel.

On April 3, 1830, a jury took only fifteen minutes to find him guilty, and he was fined $100 or six months in jail. The penniless Garrison not only couldn't pay the fine, but wouldn't let any sympathizer lend him the money. Four days later he entered the Baltimore City Jail proudly.

Warden David W. Hudson was a kind and sympathetic man who permitted him considerable freedom in prison, allowing Lundy to visit him daily and even inviting Garrison to have dinner with his own family.

"Judge Brice says that you are here," Hudson reported, "only because you are ambitious of becoming a martyr."

"Tell His Honor," Garrison replied ironically, "that if his assertion be true, he is equally ambitious of gathering the faggots and applying the torch!"

Garrison joined Isaac Knapp, his old partner from the Free Press, *and in 1831 began to publish a new abolitionist newspaper* The Liberator. *The motto printed just below the masthead (left) proclaimed that "Our Country is the World, our Countrymen are all Mankind."*

The judge's charge was not without a strong core of truth. The example of the early Christian martyrs was very much in Garrison's mind when he went to jail for the blow he had struck against slavery. On his first morning behind bars he defiantly scratched an anti-slavery poem on the wall of his cell.

Fellow prisoners were curious about the twenty-four-year-old newcomer. They saw a young man with dark-brown hair, high white forehead, full sensitive lips, intent hazel eyes behind silver-rimmed spectacles, and a pale complexion that crimsoned when he was shown any appreciation or affection.

They greeted his arrival with derisive cries of "Fresh fish!" but were soon intrigued by his gentle and sympathetic manner. A tiger with his pen, Garrison was a lamb in person. Warden Hudson allowed him to visit from cell to cell as a good moral influence. Investigating inmates' grievances, he wrote letters and petitions to the Governor for them. One letter won a pardon for a highwayman sentenced for life.

The jail was frequently visited by slaveholders seeking runaway slaves who had been apprehended. One day Garrison witnessed the identification of a runaway by a master whose slave at first pretended not to know him.

"Don't you dare deny you belong to me!" the slave-owner flared. "You remember only too well the last beating I gave you — 39 lashes under the apple tree!"

"Oh, yes, I remember," the fugitive conceded bitterly. "You beat me cruelly like that often, without cause. And you never gave me enough to eat or drink. I do not want to go back with you again."

"You villain! What you want has nothing to do with it. It is only what I want that matters!"

Garrison could contain himself no longer. "Sir," he demanded, "what right have you to that poor creature?"

The Southerner blinked. "My father left him to me."

"Suppose your father had broken into a bank and stolen $10,000. Could you conscientiously keep the money?"

"Oh, an abolitionist, are you? I suppose you'd just as soon have a Negro as President. Or as a son-in-law!"

"It is not a black skin that I detest, sir," Garrison replied contemptuously, "but a black heart!"

Allowed by Warden Hudson to write letters freely, he reproached shipowner Francis Todd in Newburyport for being free to "enjoy the fruits of your crime," while Garrison was imprisoned for having served society by protesting against "a horrible traffic offensive to God."

"You have a wife," he reminded Todd. "Do you love her? You have children. If one merchant should kidnap, another sell and a third transport them to a foreign market, how would you bear this bereavement? . . . I denounced your conduct in strong language — but did

you not deserve it? Consult your Bible and your heart!"

He wrote Harriet Farnham Horton cheerfully, "I have neither broken any man's head nor picked any man's pocket, neither committed highway robbery nor fired any part of the city. Yet, true it is, I am in prison, as snug as a robin in his cage; but I sing as often, and quite as well, as I did before my wings were clipped."

A privileged martyr, hailed as a hero by fellow abolitionists, surrounded by an admiring warden and affectionate fellow prisoners, he had never enjoyed himself more.

He, a prisoner, had better and more food, could idle as he pleased, was sheltered from the rain and blazing sun, and was doctored when ill. But what of the slave?

"He gets a peck of corn . . . each week, but rarely meat or fish. . . . Rain or shine, he must toil early and late *for the benefit of another.* If he be weary, he cannot rest. . . . For the most trifling or innocent offense, he is felled to the earth or scourged on his back till it streams with blood." He added wryly, "Reflections like the foregoing turned my prison into a palace." It was powerful propaganda.

His campaign to arouse indignation over his own plight, and that of the slaves, succeeded beyond his wildest expectations. Over a hundred newspapers and periodicals ran editorials praising the young editor who had gone to jail for freedom of the press to focus national attention on the disgraceful institution of slavery.

One of his more critical admirers was Ephraim Allen, editor of the Newburyport *Herald,* with whom he had served his apprenticeship. The editor who knew him best felt that Garrison had been unfair to Francis Todd in singling the shipowner out to chastise for all the sins of the slavery system. In an editorial in the Newburyport *Herald,* Allen credited Garrison with devotion to the anti-slavery cause, but suggested caustically that "vanity . . . and eagerness for notoriety are the main springs of his devotion."

Stung, Garrison replied that if, indeed, vanity had led him to champion the cause of "the poor, degraded, miserable Africans, it is at least a harmless, and I hope . . . useful vanity. Would to God it were epidemical!"

Reconsidering, Allen felt that perhaps he had been unduly harsh toward the young crusader. He made amends with a kinder judgment in a subsequent *Herald* issue:

"We have known him from his childhood; he has been in our family and eaten at our board. Resolute in his convictions on subjects of higher importance, he may seem (and no doubt sometimes is) hasty, stubborn, and dogmatic, rash and unyielding . . . [But] he would rather be W. L. Garrison, confined as he now is in a dungeon-cell, than his tyrannical judge upon the bench which he has disgraced, or Francis Todd in the midst of the guilty splendors of ill-gotten gold."

Allen still insisted that Garrison had been too severe on Todd because most of the shipowner's cargos were freight, and he only transported slaves when business was bad.

Garrison could not resist a sly final thrust. "Surely, sir," he wrote Allen, "you do not mean to justify or palliate the *occasional* transportation of slaves?"

More and more, as time went by, he grew unwilling to make the slightest concession on moral issues. There was only absolute wrong and absolute right.

Garrison's admirers in the North sought to free him. John Greenleaf Whittier, the young poet he had discovered, was now in politics and urged Henry Clay to intervene on his behalf. Clay agreed, but before he could act Lundy received a letter from Arthur Tappan, a philanthropic New York merchant. Tappan sent $100 to pay Garrison's fine, plus another $100 to keep Lundy's paper publishing.

On June 5, 1830, after seven weeks in prison, the celebrated jailbird stepped jubilantly into the summer sunlight of Baltimore. He left for New York to thank his benefactor, whose business profits financed Bible societies, church reform movements, Negro schools, and temperance societies. Arthur Tappan and his brother Lewis had been members of the American Colonization Society until Garrison's blasts in the *Genius* had converted them to abolition.

Garrison's visit impressed the Tappan brothers. "His manly form, buoyant spirit and countenance beaming with conscious rectitude," Lewis Tappan recalled later, "were not likely to be forgotten."

Expecting to cause a sensation as a returning hometown celebrity, Garrison continued north to Newburyport. But he found little public enthusiasm for the local boy who had made good in a Baltimore jail, and no encouragement for his determination to overthrow the powerful institution of slavery. Ephraim Allen and other old friends dryly advised him to stop squandering his time and talents for no reward except "persecution, reproach and poverty." They could not shake his determination to return to Baltimore.

"But how was I to return?" he recalled later. "I had not a dollar in my pocket. . . . I was too proud to beg, and ashamed to borrow. My friends were prodigal of pity, but of nothing else." Suddenly a letter arrived from Lundy enclosing a $100 draft that had come for him from an unknown admirer. "Here Providence had again signally interfered in my behalf," he vowed, ever the true believer.

Back in Baltimore, however, he found prospects bleak for restoring the badly sagging *Genius,* now reduced to a monthly, back to a weekly. He was also aware that he and Lundy were at serious cross-purposes as to the tactics to employ against slavery. The gentle Quaker was distressed by Garrison's harsh language and personal attacks.

Garrison felt that no holds should be barred in waging God's battles. Only snarling words that exposed fang and claw could provoke the necessary national uproar.

They finally agreed it would be best to go separate ways. Not long afterwards Garrison wrote tartly, "The truth is Friend Lundy has a very irritable disposition, which is easily roused; and he finds it impossible to forgive us for venturing to question . . . his Colonization scheme."

Whenever he parted with a former friend over honest differences of opinion, Garrison's vanity compelled him to put him in the wrong for disagreeing with him.

Deciding to publish his own abolitionist paper in the nation's capital, he left for a speaking tour of the Northeast to raise funds and proselytize for abolition.

In Philadelphia he sought a minister who would let his church be used for anti-slavery lectures. But Garrison quickly found that the City of Brotherly Love had little to spare for a stormy petrel who intended to stir up trouble by attacking the American Colonization Society, to which many respectable Philadelphians belonged.

The ministers had another reason for their reluctance. Earlier that year David Walker, a Boston Negro, had

A political cartoon from Vanity Fair, *January, 1861, proclaimed "Like Meets Like" as Garrison and L. M. Keitt, a radical secessionist Congressman from South Carolina, shake hands. The caption quotes them as saying, "Well friend, at last we meet in unity to destroy 'this accursed Union.' Twas only a misunderstanding this many years—we were always one at heart."*

published a pamphlet, *Walker's Appeal,* calling upon all Southern slaves to revolt. When copies found their way below the Mason-Dixon line, Southern mayors and governors grew alarmed. The pamphlet advocated the one specter that frightened every white Southerner.

Southern port police searched ships for copies of *Walker's Appeal,* jailing and flogging any colored seaman who had one. Savannah's mayor angrily insisted that Mayor Harrison Gray Otis of Boston suppress the incendiary pamphlet. Otis replied that he did not have that power, but assured the South's mayors that he held the pamphlet in the same "deep disapprobation and abhorrence" that they did. Walker died in June, 1830, but the furor he had aroused persisted.

Northern "respectables" were anxious to avoid offending the South further by encouraging such agitators as William Lloyd Garrison. There was a "gentlemen's understanding" about such things. Northern businessmen depended upon and profited by trade with the South, and there were few Northern households which did not use the products of slave labor.

At last, however, the trustees of the Franklin Institute reluctantly agreed to let Garrison deliver his lectures there on three successive nights in August. A small crowd attended, mainly Quakers and free Negroes. Among his impressed listeners were abolitionists James and Lucretia Mott, who invited him to stay with them for several days.

He discovered that they were Hicksite Quakers — rebels against religious doctrine. Garrison was startled out of his own Baptist orthodoxy by their disdain for dogma. "If theological dogmas which I once regarded as essential to Christianity, I now repudiate as absurd and pernicious," he later confessed, "I am indebted to them for the changes."

In New Haven the only minister who would offer him the use of a pulpit was a Negro. Garrison's contempt deepened for the majority of the Northern white clergy who preached Christianity but were too fearful to practice it. He did not yet dare say in public, however, what the Motts had convinced him of in private. He needed the ministry as an ally. So he limited his attacks instead to a safer target — those who practiced slavery and called themselves Christians.

"I blush for them as countrymen," he wrote to the Reverend George Shepard from Hartford. "I know that they are not Christians; and the higher they raise their professions of patriotism or piety, the stronger is my detestation of their hypocrisy. They are dishonest and cruel — and God, and the angels, and devils . . . know that they are without excuse."

Returning to Massachusetts, he decided that Newburyport should be the first town in the state to hear his message. But his influential enemy, shipowner Francis Todd, saw to it that he was denied use of all the seaport's churches and halls. Garrison left his hometown in disgust.

"Let them answer to God and posterity for their conduct," he wrote angrily to Ephraim Allen, "for even this communication shall be read by future generations. If I had visited Newburyport to plead the cause of twenty white men in chains, every hall and every meetinghouse would have been thrown open. . . . The fact that two millions of colored beings are groaning in bondage, in this land of liberty, excites no interest nor pity!"

Going to Boston to seek an opportunity to be heard, he was rebuffed coldly by minister after minister. He was convinced that their conservative timidity alone was not the sole reason for his failure to win a rostrum. He found a prevailing contempt for Negroes, and indifference to their wrongs, as though they were something less than human.

He called upon the most powerful of all the Boston clergy, the Reverend Lyman Beecher, whose sermons Garrison had listened to reverently week after week, three years earlier. But Beecher excused himself from getting involved by explaining, "I have too many irons in the fire already."

"Then you had better let them all burn," Garrison snapped, "than to neglect your duty to the slave!"

Beecher flushed. "Your zeal is commendable, Mr. Garrison, but you are misguided." Then he sought to lure the fiery radical into abandoning attacks on the American Colonization Society for a more cautious stance. "If you will give up your fanatical notions and be guided by us"—he meant the clergy—"we will make you the Wilberforce of America." (Bishop William Wilberforce was the spokesman for moderates of the British anti-slavery movement.)

Garrison stalked out in open contempt. It was clear to him now what was wrong with the ideals of the eloquent clerical heroes he had once admired — their failure to live up to them. Appeals for help to other influential Bostonians, including Daniel Webster and the Reverend William Channing, proved equally futile.

On October 12, 1830, Garrison put an advertisement in the Boston *Courier* for a hall or meetinghouse in which he could plead the cause of the slaves. "If this application fails," he declared, "I propose to address the citizens of Boston in the open air, on the Common."

He received one offer. It came from Abner Kneeland, an unfrocked Universalist minister who had turned pantheist as head of the nature-worshiping First Society of Free Inquirers. He offered the free use of the Society's Julien Hall. Garrison, who had once denounced this sect as un-Christian, felt embarrassed and confused. Paradoxically, freethinkers who "make no pretense to evangelical piety" had made him a Christian offer, while "the religious portion of the community are indifferent to the cries of suffering humanity."

Eyre Crowe's 1853 painting "After the Sale:
Slaves Going South From Richmond" shows
the heartbreaking business of separating the
Negro families after auctioning them off.

Thanking Kneeland, Garrison spoke at Julien Hall.

Among his small audience on the night of October 15 were Lyman Beecher, who was interested in what Garrison had to say despite personal caution about sponsoring him; John Tappan, brother of Arthur and Lewis; the Reverend Samuel May, a Unitarian minister from Brooklyn, Connecticut; his cousin, Samuel E. Sewall, a Boston attorney; and May's brother-in-law, Bronson Alcott, whose daughter Louisa May was destined to become the famous author of *Little Women*.

May, Sewall, and Alcott were scions of upper-class New England families who felt displaced as leaders of Boston society by a fast-rising industrial class. Seeking a new milieu in which to establish exclusive pre-eminence, they were intrigued by the nobility of the tiny abolition movement.

May, deeply moved by Garrison's eloquence, later reported, "He, only, I believe, had had his ears so completely unstopped of 'prejudice against color' that the cries of enslaved black men and black women sounded to him as if they came from brothers and sisters."

Garrison's bitter denunciation of the American Colonization Society, as a decoy to prevent a genuine abolition movement from developing, also impressed his listeners.

"Garrison is a prophet," May told his companions enthusiastically. "He will shake our nation to the center, but he will shake slavery out of it. We ought to know him, we ought to help him. Come, let us go and give him our hands!"

Later that evening the boy who had once begged for table scraps at back doors of the rich found himself a guest in the patrician Alcott home. Until long past midnight he was still answering the questions of May, Alcott, and Sewall as to how militant it was wise for abolitionists to be.

He pointed out to his new friends that religious groups, including the Quakers, had been opposed to slavery for over two hundred years, yet in 1830 there were four times as many slaves as there had been in 1630. Didn't that now justify agitating and challenging the "respectables" and calling them harsh names, whatever the risks?

"A few white victims must be sacrificed to open the eyes of this nation and show the tyranny of our laws," he told them. "I expect and am willing to be persecuted, imprisoned and bound for advocating African rights. And I should deserve to be a slave myself if I shrunk from that duty or danger!" May was fascinated by his iron determination.

"That night," May said afterwards, "my soul was baptized in his spirit, and ever since I have been a disciple and fellow laborer of William Lloyd Garrison."

He and Sewall made arrangements for Garrison to deliver a fourth lecture at Athenaeum Hall. May, a Unitarian minister at Church Green in Cambridgeport, urged his parishioners to go to Boston to hear the "young man hitherto unknown, but who is, I believe, called of God to do a greater work for the good of our country than has been done by anyone since the Revolution. I mean William Lloyd Garrison."

Following this sermon May's father was stopped by a friend who offered sympathy. "What for?" asked May, Sr.

"I hear your son went mad at Church Green yesterday."

The encouragement Garrison had finally won in Boston decided him that here, not Washington, was the logical place to found his own abolitionist newspaper. Boston was, after all, the cultural and reform center of the America of 1830, sparked by Harvard's intellectuals. Besides, he reasoned, the timidity of New England's clergy indicated that they needed enlightenment far more than the South did just then.

Isaac Knapp, his own friend and partner on the *Free Press*, agreed to join him in publishing the new weekly. It was to be called the *Liberator*, and May and Sewall promised to drum up subscribers to keep it afloat.

Beginning with empty pockets, the partners worked as journeymen for the *Christian Examiner* in exchange for use of its type and office space. After his stint as a compositor during the day, Garrison would spend most of each night writing and setting the *Liberator* while Knapp printed it.

"We shall fare on bread and water a long time before we strike our flag," Garrison wrote Lundy. "Whether we sink or swim in this new enterprise, we shall remain the unyielding advocates of the poor slave." That iron resolve was evident in every line of the first issue, a run of only four hundred copies, which appeared on January 1, 1831.

It was a four-page affair, nine by fourteen inches, four columns to a page, with a masthead motto: "OUR COUNTRY IS THE WORLD—OUR COUNTRYMEN ARE MANKIND." In this editorial Garrison expressed his conviction of the need for a greater revolution in thinking about slavery in New England than in the South.

"I found contempt more bitter, opposition more active, detraction more relentless, prejudice more stubborn, and apathy more frozen, than among the slave owners themselves," he accused. That was why he was raising the banner of abolition *within sight of Bunker Hill and in the birth place of liberty.* He vowed unrelenting war on "the pernicious doctrine of gradual abolition," promising to fight to win for the black man in America the full rights promised him in the Declaration of Independence — rights he deserved to have not in the vague future but immediately.

"I am aware that many object to the severity of my language," Garrison acknowledged, "but is there not cause for severity? I *will be* as harsh as truth, and as uncompromising as justice. On this subject, I do not wish to think, or speak, or write, with moderation. No! no! Tell a man whose house is on fire, to give a moderate alarm; tell him to moderately rescue his wife from the hands of the ravisher; tell the mother to gradually extricate her babe from the fire into which it has fallen; — but urge me not to use moderation in a cause like the present."

He concluded with an expression of the resolution that was to shake the house of slavery until it tumbled down around the ears of Americans who tolerated it:

"I am in earnest — I will not equivocate — I will not excuse — I will not retreat a single inch — AND I WILL BE HEARD."

For four years Garrison, living in the jaws of starvation, kept the *Liberator* alive as he used it to lambaste "respectable" white America, North and South alike, with a fine impartial frenzy. By 1835 he had escalated abolition from a disdained cause for crackpots to the status of an alarming threat to the nation's stability.

People at a mass meeting in Richmond, South Carolina, insisted that Postmaster General Amos Kendall suppress "all printed papers suspected of a tendency to produce or encourage an insubordinate and insurrectionary spirit among the slaves." The Charleston postmaster wrote Kendall bluntly that he would no longer deliver abolitionist papers like the *Liberator*. The New York City postmaster joined in this defiance.

Kendall, a Massachusetts-born Jackson appointee, notified local postmasters that, while he could not *legally* countenance such refusals, he would do exactly the same if he were in their place. This encouragement to violate freedom of the press gave local postmasters — most of them politicians—the right to decide which political views they would permit local citizens to read. Bills to curb anti-slavery publications were introduced in the legislatures of Maine, New Hampshire, and Connecticut.

August brought fresh riots in New York, and in Boston mobs attacked Negroes, driving them off the streets. Visiting British abolitionist lecturer George Thompson had to go into hiding. He, Garrison, and the Tappan brothers were openly marked for assassination.

"And what has brought our country to the verge of ruin?" Garrison cried out in the *Liberator*. "THE ACCURSED SYSTEM OF SLAVERY! To sustain that system there is a general willingness to destroy LIBERTY OF SPEECH and of the PRESS, and to mob or murder all who oppose it."

Garrison demanded that Northern moderates recognize that the battle was not being fought for abolition alone, but also on higher grounds — for the civil liberties guaranteed to all Americans in the Bill of Rights.

But 1,500 Bostonians, worried by the South's anger at their city as the "viper's nest" of Garrisonian abolition, jammed into a public meeting at Faneuil Hall on August 21 to denounce those who "scatter among our Southern friends firebrands, arrows and death." Mayor Theodore Lyman presided over the meeting, and ex-Mayor Harrison Gray Otis damned the abolitionists as dangerous radicals.

Garrison sarcastically suggested that Faneuil Hall change its designation as the "Cradle of Liberty" to the "Refuge of Slavery." He deplored the "*sinful prejudices* in the high and educated classes*," knowing that such meetings would light new fires of violence in the masses.

Soon afterward an abolitionist minister was mobbed in broad daylight in Worcester. Another in New Hampshire was attacked, then arrested as a "brawler." In Connecticut a school principal supporting abolition was fired and driven out of town. Emerson and Whittier were hooted off the lecture platform when they sought to speak against slavery.

Some victims of mob spirit were more aggrieved at the Garrisonians then at the mobs for inflaming public anger by the violence of their denunciations of white conservatives in the North.

New threats against the lives of Garrison and Thompson were made daily. They were taunted with being afraid to go South and say there what they said in the North. Garrison replied that he had already done so, and had spent seven weeks in a Baltimore jail for it. If he or Thompson were to go South now, it was obvious they would be murdered. Then they would be labeled fanatics and madmen for going to their certain death.

Massachusetts Senator Peleg Sprague publicly demanded to know why abolitionists like Garrison considered Southern slavery any of their own business.

"Enslave but a single human being," Garrison replied, "and the liberty of the world is put in peril!"

October 21, 1835, proved the most unforgettable day in the life of William Lloyd Garrison. The Boston Female Anti-Slavery Society had announced an afternoon anniversary meeting at the Anti-Slavery Hall on 46 Washington Street. When a rumor spread that George Thompson would be the guest speaker, Boston was flooded with handbills offering $100 "raised by a number of patriotic citizens to reward the individual who shall first lay violent hands on Thompson, so that he may be brought to the tar-kettle before dark."

Garrison, who knew that Thompson was out of town, arrived twenty minutes early for the 3:00 p.m. meeting. He found a mob of about a hundred men milling around the building entrance, and another hundred or so lining two flights of stairs up to the third floor.

Calmly pressing his way up through the crowds, he went unrecognized until murmurs sprang up in his wake like a series of firecrackers: "That was Garrison!" He entered the hall and took his seat beside another male abolitionist scheduled to speak, C. C. Burleigh. They were the only men among twenty-five women. The mob grew increasingly surly, and some men pushed their way into the hall. Garrison faced them.

"Gentlemen," he said quietly, "perhaps you are not aware that this is a meeting of the Boston *Female* Anti-Slavery Society . . . and those only who have been invited to address them. Understanding this fact, you will not be so rude or indecorous as to thrust your presence upon this meeting."

"It's a public meeting!" snared one intruder.

"If, gentlemen, any of you *are* ladies — in disguise — why, only appraise me of the fact, give me your names, and I will introduce you to the rest of your sex. Then you can take your seats among them accordingly!"

But the surging crowd, rapidly growing to several thousand men, ripped the downstairs door off its hinges, and thrust more men into the hall. A roar went up for Thompson to be turned over to the mob. Mary Parker, President of the Society, grew frightened for the safety of Garrison and Burleigh. At her pleading they retreated into the adjacent Anti-Slavery Office, locking the door.

The women opened the meeting with a prayer, asking God to forgive the rioters besieging them. Mayor Theodore Lyman arrived on the scene, escorted by a few constables. He tried to disperse the mob by shouting that Thompson was not in Boston, but his words could not be heard in the tumult.

Meanwhile some of the mob began kicking in the lower panel of the Anti-Slavery Office. Stooping down, one man spotted Garrison sitting at a desk writing a news story of the riot. "There's Garrison!" he cried. "Out with the scoundrel!" The scoundrel turned to Burleigh.

"You may as well open the door," he said calmly, "and let them come in and do their worst."

Burleigh went out but locked the door behind him, and managed to talk the group outside the office into moving away.

Mayor Lyman, meanwhile, had shoved his way up to the third floor. "Go home, ladies, go home!" he urged.

"Mr. Lyman," said Mrs. Maria Chapman coldly, "your personal friends are the instigators of this mob. Have you ever used your personal influence with *them?*"

"I know no personal friends. . . . Indeed, ladies, you *must* retire. It is dangerous to remain!"

"If this is the last bulwark of freedom," Maria Chapman defied him, "we may as well die here as anywhere!"

But the women finally decided to adjourn the meeting to Mrs. Chapman's house. In an act of defiance, Negro and white women left arm in arm, ignoring the mob's jeers and angry threats.

A new cry went up. "Let's get Garrison!"

By this time the mob had realized Thompson was not there. No matter—Garrison would do admirably as a prize. A friend of the editor, identified only as J.R.C., managed to shove his way upstairs to the Anti-Slavery Office.

"Lloyd, this is no time for pacifist principles. We will have to fight to get you out of here alive!"

Garrison shook his head. "Do you wish to become like one of those violent and bloodthirsty men who are seeking my life? I will perish sooner than raise my hand against any man, even in self-defense. And let none of my friends resort to violence for my protection."

Mayor Lyman joined them, insisting that Garrison leave at once out a back window. At J.R.C.'s urging, he and Garrison dropped from the window onto an adjacent shed roof. The editor slipped and began plunging three flights to the ground. J.R.C.'s outstretched hand saved him.

Descending to an alley, they were spotted by the mob. They dashed into a carpenter's shop. The door was bolted behind them by the sympathetic proprietor, who motioned them upstairs to a loft as the mob stormed the shop.

"It's no use," Garrison told J.R.C. "I will go out to the mob and let them deal with me as they wish."

"No! We must avoid them as long as possible!"

He pulled Garrison upstairs and hid him behind a store of boards. A few seconds later the crowd burst into the shop and up to the second floor. J.R.C. was seized and hustled off. Garrison's hiding place was quickly discovered. Four men pulled him out and dragged him to the window, proudly exhibiting their prize to the crowd below.

"Out with him! Lynch him! *Lynch Garrison!*"

One man put a rope around his neck, and two others prepared to hang him from the window sill.

"No, wait a minute," the fourth urged. "Don't let us kill him outright. Let us give him a coat of tar and feathers, and put a black dye on his face and hands — then we will have him in his true colors!"

Roaring with laughter, the men slipped the noose from Garrison's neck down around his waist. Some were for hurling him out the window onto the heads of the mob below. But a ladder had been brought up and placed against the window.

Forced up on the window ledge, Garrison bowed ironically to the crowd below. Now he knew what it had been like for the bound victims of the French Revolution as they faced the guillotine. But he was unfrightened, even strangely happy. He trusted God;

he believed that he was right and the mob was wrong; and he considered it "a blessed privilege thus to suffer for Christ."

As he backed down the ladder to the ground, the men at the window paid out the rope as though he were a valuable but dangerous animal on a tether. Even before his foot touched the ground, hands reached for him savagely.

His trousers were ripped off, his coat torn to shreds, his shirt stripped from his body. His hat fell off and was trampled. The hooting and jeering mob dragged him by the rope down Wilson's Lane toward State Street.

His wife Helen, meanwhile, had heard what was happening and rushed to the Anti-Slavery Hall. She tried to get through the dense mob, despite the danger to the baby she was carrying, but the streets were now so jammed that passage was impossible. Word reached her that the crowd had her husband on a rope, trying to force him to recant his abolitionism.

Helen turned white. "Oh, my God!" she wept. "He will sacrifice his life before his principles!"

As the crowd dragged her husband toward the Boston Common, Wendell Phillips, a twenty-four-year-old Harvard lawyer from one of Boston's aristocratic families, looked down from his office on Court Street. Shocked at the brutal scene below, he went down into the crowd to ask what was happening.

"That's Garrison," a man replied. "They're going to hang him. Serves him right, the damned Abolitionist!"

Phillips spotted Colonel John C. Park, who belonged to his militia regiment. "Colonel," he said tensely, "why doesn't the Mayor call out the Regiment?"

Park pointed ironically to the well-dressed rioters. "The Regiment is in front of you."

That was when Wendell Phillips made up his mind to join the cause of William Lloyd Garrison. He was to become the eloquent voice of American abolition, as Garrison was its pen.

Garrison, meanwhile, continued to stumble along at the end of the pulled rope, the center of a human storm. Men ran alongside to taunt him and spit in his face. He could barely see them; he had removed his glasses to protect them, and was now practically blind without them. What disturbed him most, ironically, was the loss of his favorite hat. Wearing his martyrdom calmly, he kept his head erect, showing not the slightest trace of fear.

"They're going to hang him — for God's sake, save him!" some citizens pleaded with Mayor Lyman. The Mayor managed to relay orders to two burly brothers, Daniel and Aaron Cooley, trucking contractors. They smashed their way to Garrison's side, seized him roughly, and cast aside the rope.

"He shan't be hurt!" Daniel Cooley shouted. "Don't

hurt him — he's an American!" The implication was that it would have been all right to hang Thompson, the crowd's original target, but not a citizen, however misguided. Many in the crowd were secretly relieved, having less stomach for a gruesome lynching than the "frolic" of tar-and-feathering.

Garrison was dragged through Wilson's Lane onto State Street at the rear of the City Hall, over ground where the Boston Massacre had once taken place.

Still holding Garrison by the arms, the Cooley brothers suddenly turned and rushed him into the City Hall before they could be stopped. The crowd howled in dismay. Mayor Lyman sought to sooth the rioters with a speech as Garrison was sped upstairs to the Mayor's office. Here Sheriff Parkman provided the half-naked editor with a borrowed coat, hat, and pair of pants. The mob uproar continued.

Joining the men in his office, Lyman proposed the Everett Street jail, a mile away, as the only place in Boston where Garrison would be safe. "Will you agree to a technical charge against you of disturbing the peace?" he asked hopefully. "I'm afraid that locking you up for the night is the only way we can save you, Mr. Garrison."

"All right," the editor shrugged. He added prudently, "If it doesn't cost me anything for board or lodging!"

The problem remained of how to smuggle him the long mile to jail past the crowd outside the City Hall, which was still howling for his blood. Lyman hit on a ruse. A horse cab was ordered to draw up to the south entrance. Police cleared a passage down the steps. With a roar the mob surged to the bait. As they did, a second cab pulled up swiftly to the north entrance. Sheriff Parkman led a flying wedge out of the City Hall. He and Garrison jumped into the second carriage — but not fast enough to escape detection.

Enraged at the trick, hundreds of Bostonians raced back to the second cab and sought to drag Garrison out. By this time they had worked themselves up to a truly murderous mood. Clinging to the wheels, they flung open the doors, seized the horses and tried to cut the reins. Some threw the rope over the carriage and pulled on both ends.

As police sought vainly to beat them off, they began to upset the carriage. It tilted as the driver lashed the horses. A great surge carried it forward on two wheels, and it almost crashed on its side. Sent flying, the furious crowd gave chase. The driver cracked his whip. Men jumped up on the carriage steps. Sheriff Parkman shoved them off with a thrust of his boot. In an effort to lose the pursuers, the horses were sent along a roundabout route to the jail.

Mayor Lyman, meanwhile, managed to get to the jail in the other carriage by a direct route, pursued by part of the mob. He quickly organized a gauntlet of police to protect the entrance of Garrison into the jail. When the other carriage appeared, the mob once more rushed to seize its victim. But Garrison was quickly spirited between the lines of police to the safety of a prison cell.

Friends swiftly gathered at the jail to express relief at his narrow escape. One of his visitors was Whittier, now a member of the Massachusetts legislature.

"Sorry I can't accommodate you in my cell, John," Garrison smiled, "but if you like, I'll put in a good word for you with the Sheriff here." Admirers clustered outside the prison all evening to call encouragement to their hero through the cell window. Tired out, Garrison slept peacefully.

Rising "quite refreshed," he ate a hearty breakfast and then commemorated the occasion with a wall inscription:

"Wm. Lloyd Garrison was put into this cell Wednesday afternoon, October 21, 1835, to save him from the violence of a 'respectable and influential' mob, who sought to destroy him for preaching the abominable and dangerous doctrine that 'all men are created equal,' and that all oppression is idious in the sight of God.... Reader, let this inscription remain till the last slave in this despotic land be loosed from his fetters." It was there when the jail was torn down seventeen years later, with the slave system still to be toppled.

Isaac Knapp arrived with news that Helen was waiting for him at a secret rendezvous in Canton, Connecticut. Mob elements were guarding Boston's train and stage stations, determined to get their hands on Garrison as he tried to escape the city, so Sheriff Parkman spirited him out of jail and drove him to Canton. Helen embraced her husband gratefully, and they sped to her father's home.

In retrospect, Garrison felt icy contempt for the "gentlemen of property and standing" who had led the riot, less for what they had done to him than for their cowardly behavior toward the female abolitionists. "Mr. Thompson," he charged, "furnished a pretext for 5,000 'gentlemen' to mob 30 Christian women." He felt no great surge of gratitude toward Mayor Lyman for having saved his life.

Why had the Mayor respected the mob's demand for Thompson by pleading he was not there, instead of challenging their right to stop him from speaking? Why had Lyman appeased the mob by tearing down the anti-slavery sign? Why had he risked Garrison's life by sending him out of the City Hall a mile to jail, through the maddened crowds?

The whole affair, Garrison said, had the tacit blessings of the Boston Establishment: "It is evidently winked at by the city authorities. No efforts have been made to arrest the leading rioters. The Mayor has made no public appeal to the citizens to preserve order; nor has he given any assurance that the right of free discussion shall be enjoyed without molestation."

Garrison's struggle obviously did not end the unholy alliance of a white backlash and "law and order" city administrations. But he at least kept stinging the conscience of white America until a reluctant Lincoln signed the Emancipation Proclamation — that first step on the long, endless journey toward racial equality.

Behind him he left a special heritage for the little bands of idealists produced by every new generation. Like him, they had no need to feel powerless because they were only a small minority. If they would persist in speaking out, fearlessly, eloquently, and tirelessly against injustice, Garrison promised, they would be heard. ✤

Johnny Reb and Billy Yank

The men (and boys) who opposed each other in the American Civil War had more similarities than differences. But those differences were enough to keep our bloodiest conflict going for four years.

By Bell I. Wiley

Dr. Bell I. Wiley, one of the truly great military historians of our Nation, who is acclaimed also for his work as a teacher, editor, and publisher, has specialized on studies of military personnel, particularly of soldiers in the Civil War. He is a regular contributor to "CIVIL WAR TIMES Illustrated."

THE COMMON SOLDIERS of North and South during the American Civil War were very much alike. As a general rule they came from similar backgrounds, spoke the same language, cherished the same ideals and reacted in like manner to the hardships and perils of soldiering. They hated regimentation, found abundant fault with their officers, complained often about army rations and hoped earnestly for speedy return to civilian life. Even so, men of the opposing sides presented some notable and interesting differences.

In the first place, Billy Yanks were more often of foreign background than were their opposites in gray. During the decades preceding the Civil War several million Europeans migrated to America and because of convenience, economic opportunity, and other influences, most of them settled in the North. In 1861 there were about four million persons of alien birth living in the states adhering to the Union as against only about one fourth of a million residing in the Southern Confederacy. Because the immigrants tended to identify themselves with the section in which they settled, far more of them donned the Union blue than the Confederate gray. Probably one out of every four or five Billy Yanks was of foreign birth and only one out of every twenty or twenty-five Johnny Rebs.

On the northern side the Germans, aggregating about 200,000, were the most numerous of the foreign

groups. Next were the Irish, numbering about 150,-000, then Canadians and Englishmen each totalling about 50,000 and, down the line, lesser numbers of Scandinavians, Frenchmen, Italians, and other nationalities.

It has been estimated that 15,000 to 20,000 Irishmen marched in Confederate ranks and they apparently outnumbered any other foreign group on the Southern side. But Canada, England, France, and Italy were well represented among wearers of the gray.

ON BOTH sides most of the foreigners were enlisted men, but many served as company and field grade officers and a considerable number attained the rank of general. Forty-five of the North's 583 general officers were of foreign birth, and among them were twelve Germans and twelve Irishmen. Among the Confederacy's 425 generals, there were nine foreigners of whom five were Irish.

In both armies the foreign groups added color and variety to camp life by singing their native songs, celebrating festive days, and observing customs peculiar to their homeland. St. Patrick's Day was always

Irish-born Major General Patrick Ronayne Cleburne, CSA, killed in the bloody Battle of Franklin, November 30, 1864. (KA)

German-born Major General Peter Joseph Osterhaus. (U. S. Signal Corps photo No. 111-B-2778 in the National Archives)

From *American History Illustrated*, April 1968. Reproduced through the courtesy of The National Historical Society, publishers of AMERICAN HISTORY *Illustrated*, 206 Hanover Street, Gettysburg, Pa. 17325. Published 10 times a year.

a great occasion among Irish units, featuring horse races, athletic contests, and consumption of large quantities of alcohol. As Pat and Mike lingered at flowing bowls their pugnacious tendencies were accentuated, and before night guardhouses were crowded with men suffering from cuts, bruises, or broken bones. Indeed, St. Patrick's Day sometimes produced more casualties among sons of Erin than did encounters on the battlefield.

In combat the foreigners gave a good account of themselves. Meagher's Irish Brigade was one of the best fighting units in the Civil War. Ezra J. Warner in *Generals in Blue* rates Prussian-born Peter J. Osterhaus as "certainly the most distinguished of the foreign-born officers who served the Union," and few, if any, division commanders of any nationality on either side had a better battle record than the Confederacy's beloved Irishman, Patrick R. Cleburne.

Among native participants two groups deserving special mention were the Indians and Negroes. The Confederacy had three brigades of redmen, mostly Cherokees, Choctaws, and Seminoles. One of the Cherokees, Stand Watie, became a brigadier general. The Union Army had one brigade of Indians, most of whom were Creeks. Muster rolls of Indian units, filed in the National Archives, contain such names as Private Sweetcaller, Private Hog Shooter, Private Hog Toter, Private Flying Bird, and Lieutenant Jumper Duck. At the Battle of Honey Springs in 1864, Yankee Indians fought Rebel Indians. In combat Indians acquitted themselves well, but between battles they were poor soldiers, since they had only vague ideas of discipline and regimentation.

During the Civil War both sides enlisted Indians. This drawing shows a group of Delawares resting after a reconnaissance for the Union army somewhere in the West.

ON THE Confederate side, Negroes served almost exclusively in accessory capacities, as cooks, hostlers, musicians, and body servants. On March 13, 1865 after prolonged and acrimonious discussion the Confederate Congress passed a law authorizing recruitment of 300,000 slaves to serve as soldiers. A few companies were organized but the war ended before any of them could get into combat. It seems unreasonable to think that slaves would have fought with any enthusiasm for the perpetuation of their bondage. More than 188,000 Negroes, most of whom were ex-slaves, wore the Union blue. Despite discriminations in pay, equipment, and association with fellow soldiers, and notwithstanding the fact that they had to do far more than their share of labor and garrison duty, Negro Yanks fought well at Port Hudson, Milliken's Bend, Fort Wagner, the Crater, and other Civil War battles in which they participated.

Billy Yanks were better educated than Johnny Rebs, owing to the North's better schools and greater emphasis on public education. In some companies from the rural South, half of the men could not sign

the muster rolls. Such companies were exceptional, but so were those that did not have from one to twenty illiterates. Sergeant Major John A. Cobb of the 16th Georgia Regiment wrote a kinsman on September 8, 1861: "Paying off soldiers is a good deal like paying off negroes their cotton money . . . about one third of the men in the regiment can't write their names, so the Pay Roll has a good many X (his mark) on it, and about one half of those that write them you can't read, nor could they themselves." Among Yanks the rate of illiteracy was highest in Negro units, but the typical Union regiment seems to have had no more than a half-dozen illiterates and many had none at all. On both sides, however, spelling and grammar frequently fell far below school-room standards. In soldier letters pneumonia some-times appeared as *new mornion* or *new mony,* once as *wonst,* uneasy as *oneasy,* fought as *fit,* your as *yore* or *yourn,* and not any as *nary.* Other common usages were *tuck* for took, *purty* for pretty, *laig* for leg, and *shore* for sure. Long words were often divided, some-times with strange results. One Reb complained about the "rashens" issued by the *comma sary;* another stated that he hoped to get a *fur low* when some more *volen teares* joined the *ridge ment.* A Yank wrote that he had been marching through mud that was *nea deap.* Another reported shortly after Lincoln ordered the organization of McClellan's forces into corps: "They are deviding the army up into corpses." While reading the letter of an Illinois soldier I was puzzled by the statement "I had the camp diary a few days ago," for I had not previously found indica-

tion that Civil War organizations kept unit journals. But my confusion was cleared up by the rest of the sentence which stated "but now I am about well of it." This soldier was suffering from a malady com-monly known as the "Tennessee Quickstep."

A Yank who served under General Frederick Lander wrote in one of his letters: "Landers has the ganders." I read it just as it appeared, with a hard "g." On reflection I realized that the "g" was soft and that what the general really had was the jaundice. Landers was very unpopular with this particular Yank, so he added "I hope the old so and so dies." The next letter began: "Well old Landers is dead, and I'll bet he is down in hell pumping thunder at three cents a clap."

Soldiers in both armies frequently spelled hospital as "horsepittle," and that was a place which they abhorred almost as much as the devil himself. A Reb wrote that the hospital which served his unit "outstinks a ded horse."

BECAUSE of differences in Northern and Southern economy, Billy Yanks were more often town dwellers and factory workers than were Johnny Rebs. The contrast is vividly demonstrated in company descrip-tive rolls. The occupation columns on typical Southern rolls consist of a monotonous repetition of "farmer," while Northern rolls, except in the case of units recruited from agricultural communities, listed a wide assortment of occupations, including carpenters, clerks, coopers, shoemakers, bricklayers, printers, tinsmiths, mechanics, miners, plumbers,

ABOVE: Negro troops in Yankee blue. These are 107th U.S. Colored troops at Fort Corcoran, Washington, D. C. (LC)

A recruiting office in Boston, as sketched by Charles W. Reed, a bugler in the 9th Massachusetts Light Battery. (LC)

tailors, and boatmen. This diversity of skills among the rank and file gave the North a considerable advantage in what proved to be the first great modern war. It meant that if a wagon, steamboat, or locomotive broke down, or if a railroad needed rebuilding, or if a gun failed to function, a Northern commander could usually find close at hand soldiers who knew how to do the job.

Both during and after the war many people believed that the Confederate forces contained more boys and old men than did those of the Union. Study of descriptive rolls and other records indicates that this was an erroneous impression. There were many boys and old men on both sides. Charles Carter Hay enlisted in an Alabama regiment when he was 11 years old, and when four years later he surrendered at Appomattox he had not celebrated his 15th birthday. He had a counterpart on the Union side in the case of Johnny Clem, who began service as a drummer boy at age 9 in 1861, and who graduated to the fighting ranks after the Battle of Shiloh. E. Pollard enlisted in the 5th North Carolina Regiment at 73, but the oldest Civil War soldier apparently was 80-year-old Curtis King of the 37th Iowa, a noncombatant regiment known as the "Graybeards" because on its rolls there were 145 men who had passed

their 60th birthday. But on both sides, most soldiers were neither very young nor very old. The largest single age group were the 18-year-olds, and three-fourths of the men fell in the age bracket 18-30.

Billy Yanks manifested a livelier interest in politics than did the men whom they opposed. This was due in part to the greater literacy of the Northern soldiers and their easier access to newspapers. On the national level the nature of politics was a contributing factor. Because the Confederate Constitution provided a single term of six years for the Chief Executive, there was only one Presidential campaign in the South during the war. This was a very dull affair because Jefferson Davis had no opposition. But in the North the campaign of 1864 between Lincoln and McClellan was a hard-fought contest, and most Yanks thought that the outcome would have a great impact on the prosecution of the war. Electioneering was lively in many units, and soldiers voted in impressive numbers. When ballots were tabulated it was found that the overwhelming majority had voted for "Uncle Abe" and continuance of war until the Union was restored.

Few, if any, other campaigns generated as much enthusiasm among Billy Yanks as did the Lincoln-McClellan contest, but even in the choice of governors, Congressmen, and lesser officials, the men in blue in their letters and diaries revealed considerably more interest than did wearers of the gray.

Billy Yanks' greater involvement in politics reflected a healthier interest in things intellectual. Owing to the North's better schools, the more cosmopolitan character of its population, the more varied pattern of its economy, the presence in its borders of more large cities, the greater prosperity of its citizens, better communication, easier access to books and papers, greater freedom of thought and discussion, and sundry other advantages, Union soldiers manifested greater curiosity about things past and present than their opposites in Confederate service. Common soldiers on either side who showed a deep concern for philosophic aspects of the conflict were rare. But the North appears to have had considerably more than its share of the exceptions.

IN THEIR religious attitudes and activities Billy Yanks and Johnny Rebs manifested some notable contrasts. Letters and diaries of Southern soldiers contain more references to religion than do those of the men in blue, and Rebs were more emotional in their worship than were Billy Yanks. During the last two years of the conflict, great revivals swept over both the Eastern and Western armies of the Confederacy and men made open confessions of their sins, sought forgiveness at mourners' benches, and raised shouts of joy when relieved of the burden of

Arrival of newspapers in camp as drawn by Civil War artist Edwin Forbes. Union soldiers were better read and better informed than Confederates because of the mass distribution of Northern weeklies like "Harper's" and "Frank Leslie's."

guilt. Seasons of revival sometimes extended for several weeks as leading ministers from Richmond, New Orleans, Nashville, and other cities joined the army chaplains in promoting the cause of salvation. Revivals also took place in Northern units, but rarely did they extend beyond brigade or division. Certainly, the Union forces experienced no army-wide outbreaks of emotionalism such as occurred among Confederates.

The greater interest in religion manifested by Confederates and their greater susceptibility to revivalism was due to a combination of circumstances. The fact that Southerners were a more homogeneous people than Northerners and more often members of evangelistic sects made for greater religious zeal and emotionalism in Confederate camps. Another factor working to the same end was the South's greater ruralism. Still another factor was the example of high-ranking leaders. Robert E. Lee, Stonewall Jackson, and Leonidas Polk were deeply religious men and they showed far more interest in the spiritual welfare of their commands than did Grant, Sherman, and Sheridan. Jefferson Davis proclaimed more days of fasting and prayer and was more of a church man than was Abraham Lincoln.

The fortunes of war played a part in revivalism. The flood tides of emotionalism that swept over the Southern armies came after Vicksburg and Gettysburg, and to some extent they represent the tendency of a religiously rooted people in times of severe crises to seek supernatural deliverance from the woes that

... Johnny Reb vs. Billy Yank

ABOVE: *Typical Union infantry company. (National Archives)*

BELOW: *Confederate artillery (Palmetto Battery) near Charleston, S. C. from an 1863 photo by George S. Cook. (LC)*

beset them.

The greater religiosity of the Confederates does not seem to have produced a higher level of morality in Southern camps. Comments of soldiers, complaints of chaplains, court-martial proceedings, and monthly health reports indicate that profanity, gambling, drunkenness, fornication, and other "sins" flourished as much among Rebs as among Yanks.

THE Northern soldiers generally were of a more practical and prosaic bent of mind than were Johnny Rebs. This difference was reflected in the Northerners' greater concern for the material things of life. Billy Yanks more often engaged in buying and selling and other side activities to supplement their army pay. Their letters contain far more references to lending their earnings at interest, investing for profit, and other financial ventures than do those written by the men in gray. Admittedly, Yanks had more money to write about, but their better remuneration, important though it was, was not enough wholly to account for the difference.

Billy Yanks' letters were not so fanciful or poetic as those of Johnny Rebs, nor were they as rich in humor and banter. The Northerners did not so frequently address wives and sweethearts in endearing terms as did their Southern counterparts. Correspondence of the men in blue contains much delightful humor, but I have yet to find any matching that exemplified by the following selections from Confederate sources: A Georgia Reb wrote his wife after absence of about a year in Virginia: "If I did not write and receive letters from you, I believe that I would forgit that I was married. I don't feel much like a maryed man, but I never forgit it so far as to court enny other lady but if I should you must forgive me as I am so forgitful." Another Georgian while on tour of duty in East Tennessee wrote his spouse: "Iis, I must tell you that I have found me a Sweat hart heare. . . . I had our pitures taken with her handen me a bunch of flowers . . . she lets on like she thinks a heep of me and when I told her I was marred she took a harty cry about it . . . she ses that she entends to live singel the balance of her days." A Tar Heel wrote a male friend at home: "Thomy I want you to be a good boy and tri to take cear of the wemmen and children tell I get home and we'll all have a chance. . . . I want you to go . . . and see my wife and children but I want you to take your wife with you [when you go]."

BILLY Yanks' reasons for fighting were different from those of Johnny Rebs. Some Yanks went to war

to free the slaves. One of these was Chauncey Cooke of the 25th Wisconsin Regiment, who wrote home before he heard of Lincoln's issuance of the Emancipation Proclamation: "I have no heart in this war if the slaves cannot be free." But Cooke represented a minority. The overwhelming majority of those who donned the blue did so primarily to save the imperilled Union. Devotion to the Union found eloquent expression in some of their letters. Private Sam Croft, a youth from Pennsylvania, wrote his homefolk after a hard march in September 1861: "I have never once thought of giving out. . . . I am well, hardy, strong, and doing my country a little service. I did not come for money and good living. My Heart beats high and I am proud of being a soldier. When I look along the line of glistening bayonets with the glorious Stars and Stripes floating over them . . . I am proud and sanquine of success." Croft died at Gettysburg.

Most Rebs who commented on their individual motivation indicated that they were fighting to protect their families and homes against foreign invaders, and they envisioned the invaders as a cruel and wicked foe. "Teach my children to hate them with that bitter hatred that will never permit them to meet without seeking to destroy each other," wrote a Georgia Reb to his wife in 1862.

Georgia Private Edwin F. Jennison, died at Malvern Hill. (LC)

MANY Confederates were fighting for slavery, though this was rarely indicated in their letters. Usually they represented themselves as fighting for self-government, state rights, or "the Southern way of life." There is no doubt in my mind that most Southerners, non-slaveholders as well as planters, were earnestly desirous of maintaining slavery, not primarily as an economic system, but rather as an established and effective instrument of social control. A North Carolina private wrote a friend in 1863: "You know I am a poor man having none of the property said to be the cause of the present war. But I have a wife and some children to rase in honor and never to be put on an equality with the African race." Thus did one Reb who owned no Negroes avow that he was fighting for slavery; there were many others like him.

Billy Yanks were better fed and better clothed than Johnny Rebs. In the latter part of the war they frequently were better armed. Each side experienced ups and downs of morale, but generally speaking Confederate morale was higher than that of the Northerners during the first half of the war and lower during the second half. The nadir of Union morale came early in 1863, in the wake of Grant's reverses in Mississippi and Burnside's bloody defeat at Fredericksburg. Confederate morale plummeted after Vicksburg and Gettysburg, rose slightly in the spring and summer of 1864 and began its final unabated plunge after the re-election of Lincoln.

WHAT of the combat performance of Johnny Rebs and Billy Yanks? The Southerners apparently fought with more enthusiasm than their opponents; and, after battle, in letters to the folk at home, they wrote more vividly and in greater detail of their combat experiences. In a fight they demonstrated more of dash, elan, individual aggressiveness, and a devil-may-care quality than Billy Yanks. But the men in blue seemed to have gone about the business of fighting with greater seriousness than Johnny Rebs, and they manifested more of a group consciousness and team spirit. In other words, the Rebs thought a battle was a thrilling adventure in which each man was to a large extent on his own; to Yanks it was a formidable task requiring the earnest and coordinated exertion of all those involved—not a game-shooting experience as some Rebs seemed to regard it, but a grim and inescapable chore that ought to be performed with as much efficiency and expedition as possible.

These differences were reflected in the battle cheers of the opposing forces. Southerners charged with the "Rebel yell" on their lips. This was a wild, high-pitched, piercing "holler," inspired by a combination of excitement, fright, anger, and elation. The standard Yankee cheer, on the other hand, was a regularly intoned huzza or hurrah. The contrast between Southern and Northern cheering was the subject of much comment by participants on both sides. A Federal officer observed after the second battle of Manassas: "Our own men give three successive cheers and in concert, but theirs is a cheering without any reference to regularity of form—a continual yelling." A Union surgeon who was in The Wilderness Campaign of 1864 stated: "On our side it was a resounding, continuous hurrah, while the famous dread-inspiring "Rebel yell" was a succession of yelps staccato and shrill."

UNQUESTIONABLY Johnny Rebs made a better showing in combat during the first half of the war. This was due mainly to better leadership, particularly on the company and regimental levels. On both sides these officers were elected, and in the South, owing largely to the prevalence of the caste system, the successful candidates were usually planters or their sons—privileged persons, recognized community leaders, habituated to the direction of slaves, products of the military academies on which the region principally relied for education of its boys, and strongly indoctrinated with the spirit of *noblesse oblige*.

In the more democratic North, on the other hand, men were chosen as officers because of their effectiveness in persuading neighbors to sign up for military service. In many instances they were deficient in the essentials of leadership. By the summer of 1863, incompetent officers on both sides generally had been weeded out by resignation, dismissal, or hostile bullets. By that time also the Northerners had overcome the initial handicap of being less familiar with firearms than their opponents. During the last two years of the war, there was no discernible difference in the combat performance of Johnny Rebs and Billy Yanks. There was never any significant difference in their determination, pride, courage, devotion to cause, loyalty to comrades, and other basic qualities that go to make good soldiers. From the beginning to the end of the conflict the common soldiers of both sides acquitted themselves in a manner that merited the pride of their descendants and won for them a high standing among fighting men of all time.

Well-armed Illinois Private George W. Crane. (From Logan Collection, courtesy of Illinois State Historical Library)

NEGRO SOLDIERS IN THE CIVIL WAR

Americans of African descent made up 12 percent of Union forces. Despite prejudice against them and other handicaps, in the main they served with honor.

James I. Robertson, Jr.

Dr. James I. Robertson, Jr., professor of history at Virginia Polytechnic Institute and formerly executive secretary of the National Civil War Centennial Commission, is a regular contributor to this magazine.

LATE IN JUNE 1864, Abraham Lincoln visited the Petersburg lines of the Army of the Potomac. A climax of the President's tour came one afternoon when, accompanied by General U. S. Grant and several other officers, he rode through the camps of Negro soldiers in the XVIII Corps. Colonel Horace Porter of Grant's staff observed that "the enthusiasm of the blacks now knew no limits. They cheered, laughed, cried, sang hymns of praise, and shouted in their negro dialect, 'God bress Massa Linkum!' 'De Lord save Father Abraham!' 'De day ob jubilee am come, shuah!' They crowded about him and fondled his horse; some of them kissed his hands, while others ran off crying in triumph to their comrades that they

Assault of 2d Louisiana (Colored) Regiment on the Confederate works, Port Hudson, May 27, 1863. F. B. Schell sketch.

From *Civil War Times Illustrated*, October 1968. Reproduced through the courtesy of Historical Times, Inc., publishers of CIVIL WAR TIMES *Illustrated*, 206 Hanover Street, Gettysburg, Pa. 17325. Published 10 times a year.

had touched his clothes. The President rode with bared head; the tears had started to his eyes, and his voice was so broken by emotion that he could scarcely articulate the words of thanks and congratulations which he tried to speak to the humble and devoted men through whose ranks he rode."

For the Negro, and for Lincoln as well, this scene exemplified an unprecedented transition in American society.

THE Civil War began with no official relationship to Negroes. As an Illinois veteran later commented: "If the Negro was thought of at all [in 1861], it was only as the firebrand that had caused the conflagration, the accursed that had created enmity and bitterness between the two sections, and excited the fratricidal strife." Yet—as in the case of most wars—the motivations that began the Civil War were not the motivations that sustained it.

Freedom for the enslaved Negro was slow in becoming at least a secondary stimulus behind the Union war effort. The idea of using former slaves as soldiers was even slower, and it evolved through steppingstones of hostility, discrimination, and tragedy. As most Negro Billy Yanks painfully learned, a willingness to fight for the perpetuation of their freedom was not always greeted with acclaim by their compeers.

In the first months of the Civil War, most Federal authorities were willing to employ ex-slaves ("contrabands," they were dubbed) as laborers with the Fed-

eral armies. Yet widespread opposition existed to their being clothed, armed, and utilized as soldiers. Many Northern legislators felt that arming Negroes would be degrading for America as it would invite servile insurrections reminiscent of Nat Turner and Denmark Vesey.

A THIRD argument was biological: the Negro was an inferior being and would not, or could not, fight. A corporal in the 74th New York voiced general sentiment when he stated: "We don't want to fight side by side with the nigger. We think we are a too superior race for that." Even an early Northern missionary to the Sea Islands was moved to exclaim: "Negroes—plantation negroes, at least—will never make soldiers in one generation. Five white men could put a regiment [of them] to flight."

Other Northerners warned in 1861-1862 that white soldiers would not fight alongside Negro troops. General William T. Sherman felt it "unjust to the brave soldiers and volunteers" to place them on an equal basis with the blacks, and he added: "I cannot bring myself to trust Negroes with arms in positions of danger and trust." Even President Lincoln initially considered the idea of Negro soldiers as "more productive of evil than good."

The great host of abolitionists and humanitarians, on the other hand, saw equally compelling reasons for enlisting the freedmen. Negro units would strengthen Federal armies and, at the same time, sap the Confederacy of its manpower potential. Negro soldiers would give added meaning to American democracy. Military service would both prepare and justify the Negro for full admittance into American society. As the ex-slave Frederick Douglass eloquently stated: "Once let the black man get upon his person the brass letters, U. S., let him get an eagle on his button, and a musket on his shoulder and bullets in his pocket, and there is no power on earth which can deny that he has earned the right to citizenship in the United States."

OF THREE premature attempts made early in 1862 to organize Negro units, two met with bitter disappointment.

The first occurred in the grandiloquent "Department of the South," which actually consisted of scattered Federal toeholds along the coasts of South Carolina, Georgia, and northern Florida. Commanding this nebulous region was 60-year-old General "Black Dave" Hunter, who first incurred Lincoln's displeasure by issuing an unauthorized emancipation proclamation before the war was a year old. Then, on the first anniversary of the firing on Fort Sumter, Hunter began "recruiting" ex-slaves for a regiment.

Hunter filled his 1st South Carolina Colored Regiment through commandeering, confiscation, and impressment. A Treasury Department official who helplessly watched Hunter's tactics snarled: "Rarely has humanity been outraged by an act of more unfeeling barbarity." Yet in addition to Hunter's organizational blunders, he received no pay for the troops, no authority from Washington to muster them into service, and constant harassment from a hostile Congress.

After four months of frustration, Hunter abandoned the project. Charles Francis Adams, Jr., of the 1st Massachusetts Cavalry, wrote his father on August 10, 1862, from Hilton Head, South Carolina: "General Hunter's negro regiment was disbanded yesterday . . . Its breaking up was hailed here with great joy, for our troops have become more anti-negro than I could have imagined." However, Hunter's abortive undertaking had the value of bringing the question of using Negro troops into the open. For the remainder of 1862, the subject was constant front-page copy.

Commensurate with Hunter's scheme, General James H. Lane embarked on a similar venture in Kansas. The impetuous Lane ignored Secretary of War Edwin Stanton's warnings that only trouble would result. Lane organized his 1st Kansas Colored

Major General Benjamin F. Butler was first to conceive the idea of enlisting Negro troops into the Union armies. (KA)

Volunteers, sent them on several scouting expeditions, and allowed them to engage Confederate guerrillas in a number of minor actions. Yet it was not until well into 1863 that the Federal Government accepted the 1st Kansas Colored into service. Its members, by then proven veterans, highly resented being designated as "recruits."

THE first Negro regiment to become an official component of the U. S. Army was the hesitant creation of General Benjamin F. Butler. When in May 1862, this controversial figure took command of the occupational forces in and around New Orleans, he had a negative opinion of the notion of Negro soldiers. "By long habit and training," he asserted, the Negro has "acquired a great horror of fire-arms, sometimes ludicrous in the extreme when the weapon is in his own hand."

Nevertheless in July one of Butler's brigadiers, a Vermont abolitionist named James W. Phelps, began organizing 300 contrabands as a nucleus for what the grizzled Phelps hoped would be three regiments. Butler opposed the project. "Phelps has gone crazy," Butler wrote. "He is as mad as a March Hare on the 'nigger question.' " Growing friction between Butler and Phelps over this issue soon led to the latter's resignation. Whereupon Butler reversed his own stand and, in August, began arming 1,400 freedmen that the Louisiana government had enlisted into a militia unit in 1861. Butler's change of mind was easy to explain, wrote one Federal official. "Gen. Phelps had the start of him, while Gen. B. wanted the credit of doing the thing himself, and in his own way. And he is doing it, shrewdly and completely, as he does everything."

The recruits that Butler organized into the 1st, 2d, and 3d Regiments, Louisiana Native Guards, were all supposedly freedmen—which thus avoided the thorny issue of arming slaves. Yet, as one authority noted, "nobody inquires whether the recruit is (or has been) a slave. As a consequence the boldest and finest fugitives have enlisted."

IN August the War Department finally announced an official policy of Negro recruiting. Until that month Lincoln believed that "to arm the negroes would turn 50,000 bayonets from the loyal Border States against us that were now for us." But the war was then going badly for the Union. Many more troops were needed; and if the Emancipation Proclamation that Lincoln was about to issue was to have any meaning, Negroes had to be given the opportunity to fight for their own freedom. Thus, on August 25, General Rufus Saxton, then commanding Hunter's old Department of the

ABOVE—*Fugitive slaves like these in pencil drawing by Edwin Forbes, made near Culpeper Court House, Virginia in 1863, were often herded into regiments by zealous agents. (LC)*

South, was authorized "to arm, uniform, equip, and receive into the service of the United States, such number of volunteers of African descent as [he] may deem expedient, not exceeding 5000." In the formal Emancipation Proclamation of January 1, 1863, Lincoln broadened and gave Presidential blessing to such endeavors. Thereafter, organization of Negro units developed in earnest.

Every means of getting Negroes into the Army was employed—from inducing enlistments to conscription, bounties, and the full gamut of "persuasions." Many fugitive slaves, on entering Federal lines, were speedily herded into regiments. Agents scoured the country for Negro recruits. Some were not averse to resorting to very questionable tactics. Colored church services were frequently interrupted, "the male worshippers seeking egress through the windows." One Federal official stated that the great majority of Negro regiments were "filled by wholesale conscription . . . carried out by hunting, and in several instances shooting down the fugitives."

OBVIOUSLY the early behavior of soldiers recruited by such means was bound to be erratic if not hostile. Throughout the late 1862-early 1863 period, the city jail at Thibodeaux, Louisiana, contained dozens of Negro troops "of whose behavior there are endless complaints of burning, stealings, ravishings, and lesser crimes." Numerous authorities believed that Butler's "Louisiana Native Guards" should either be disbanded or else, stated a New Hampshire soldier, the members put "under iron rule, or to garrison some fort away from civilization."

Yet the year 1863 marked the great evolution of the American Negro soldier. This period, states Dudley T. Cornish, an authority on the subject, witnessed accomplishments that were "numerous and of outstanding importance. The recruitment of Negro soldiers [was] systematized under War Department control; officer procurement [was] regularized; centers [were] established in the North for the reception and training of Negro recruits; and in Washington the Bureau for Colored Troops [was] established to control the whole widespread machinery. The main outline of the colored troops program . . . emerged. While there were to be departures from these outlines in some details, organizational and procedural decisions made during the first half of 1863 were to serve as guideposts for the raising of Negro regiments for the rest of the war."

That the program of arming former slaves worked as well as it did was due to three factors. One was the unheralded Adjutant General of the United States, Lorenzo Thomas. This unpretentious but devoted officer agreed to become a sort of national recruiting officer for Negro units. He personally was responsible for the raising of fifty regiments, and he was the stimulus behind no less than 76,000 Negro enlistments—roughly 41 percent of the total number of Negro soldiers.

A SECOND factor was a changing attitude among high-ranking officers. In August 1863, General U. S. Grant wrote to Lincoln: "By arming the negro we have added a powerful ally. They will make good soldiers and taking them from the enemy weakens

him in the same proportion they strengthen us. I am therefore most decidedly in favor of pushing this policy. . . ." A long-critical New York *World* reporter who characterized Ben Butler's "negro Janizaries" as "worthless to their owners, worthless to our government, and good for nothing in every respect" was suddenly banished from the Norfolk, Virginia area "under pain of being put to hard, but honest, labor."

The third and perhaps most important reason for the continuing success of the Negro soldier program was the performance in 1863 of blacks in battle. They behaved and fought creditably, for both the Union and themselves. As Dr. Cornish has stated: "The test of the soldier is battle. No amount of talk can change the basic facts of war. No amount of talk could have won the Negro soldier his place in the Union Army. He had to win that place, soldier-fashion, by fighting and dying in battle." This, as will shortly be shown, the Negro willingly did.

IN spite of battle participation, however, Negro troops suffered throughout the entire Civil War from a veritable host of discriminations. The South refused to recognize them as soldiers entitled, if captured, to

BELOW—*Family worship on a plantation in South Carolina. Drawn by Frank Vizetelly, this appeared in "The Illustrated London News" on Dec. 5, 1863. Church services were sometimes broken up before scheduled by recruiters rounding up Negroes for the Army. (Copyright by "The Illustrated London News")*

A colored soldier is married with full ceremony at Vicksburg. The minister was Chaplain Warren of the Freedmen's Bureau.

the same rights and privileges accorded white troops. The North refused for two years to grant them financial status on a par with their white compatriots. In 1863 the monthly pay scale in the Federal Army ranged from $13 for a private to $21 for a sergeant major, with an additional $3.50 clothing allowance. Negro troops in any noncommissioned capacity received but $7 per month and only $3 for clothing. This unequal pay was so galling to the blacks that, in one 1864 assault, an all-Negro unit charged the Confederate works with the shout: "Three cheers for Massachusetts and seven dollars a month!"

Not until June 1864, did the Congress rectify the inequality of soldiers' pay. By then, the Negro's desire to enlist, his responsibility in caring for his family, and in some cases his devotion to duty, had been sorely impeded. In March of that year, while Negro Sergeant Stephen A. Swail of the 54th Massachusetts was winning promotion for gallantry in the field, his wife and children back home were placed in a poorhouse.

SIMILARLY, Negro soldiers were given few opportunities initially to prove their mettle in battle. In many departments their efforts were solely menial.

They were detailed to whatever heavy fatigue duty, such as railroad or fortification construction, was needed. The fact that they were soldiers of specifically designated units often carried little weight. One regiment of Negro engineers in Louisiana did nothing but dig fortifications. Two Negro cavalry regiments in Mississippi not only were mounted on mules but, more often than not, performed no dangerous feat beyond driving cattle.

Discrimination also prevailed on the officers' level. Without exception, white officers commanded Negro units. Competent officers too often declined assignments to colored regiments. In some cases, and to the disgust of the Negroes, officers were unqualified even "for the discharge of the humblest duties."

A case in point was Colonel Charles R. Drew, who was placed under arrest in Louisiana for "kicking a [Negro] private who is slow, striking and kicking a first Sgt. who is out of quarters without permission; striking with a stick a Sgt. who is from sickness unable to drill, and using . . . threats of violence toward a Private who does not face properly in saluting and who appeals to higher authority for protection against severe punishments." In quick succession thereafter, Drew gained release from arrest, won promotion, and then received the thanks of Congress for "faithful and meritorious service."

FORTUNATE for the Negro and the Union were a large number of white officers who led colored units with ability, devotion, and conscientiousness. "They met high standards of personal leadership," one scholar has asserted, "and strove night and day to look after their men, to train them as soldiers, to teach them to read and write, and by example to show them the best of the white civilization in which they were caught."

The best-known of this group were James Beecher, Norwood P. Hallowell, Thomas Wentworth Higginson, Thomas J. Morgan, Robert Gould Shaw, and Daniel Ullmann. Higginson perhaps spoke for them all when he explained why he made the switch from white to Negro troops: "I had been an abolitionist too long, and had known and loved John Brown too well, not to feel a thrill of joy at last on finding myself in the position where he only wished to be."

Many Negro soldiers doubtless felt the same way, but they were never given the chance to show it in the upper echelons of military rank.

IN several respects the most constant harassment Negro troops had to endure was open hostility from thousands of white Northern soldiers. Bell I. Wiley has shown through his exhaustive research that many Billy Yanks never ameliorated their deep-seated prejudices against the Negro. An Ohio recruit once snarled: "I don't think enough of the Nigger to go

The First Mississippi Negro Cavalry triumphantly bringing into Vicksburg dejected Confederate prisoners captured at Haines's Bluff. Reproduced from sketch by F. B. Schell. (KA)

and fight for them." After but a few months in service, a New Yorker commented: "I think the best way to settle the question of what to do with the darkies would be to shoot them." From Vicksburg, in 1864, an Illinois private wrote his brother: "I perfectly Detest the sight of them. You can't speak to them and have a civil answer. The smarter they are the worse they are."

Such hostility, Dr. Wiley illustrates, often took the form of incredibly ill treatment. In New Orleans, white soldiers and civilians sometimes attacked Negro troops, stripped them, and forced the men to return nude to their camp. A sergeant in the 27th Ohio wrote from Beaufort, South Carolina, in January 1865, that "the colored troops are very much disliked by our men & several affrays have taken place in town between them, in which the darkeys have always got the worst of it, two or three of them having been killed and several wounded." At Ship Island, Mississippi, Federal gunboats were supposed to support a landing assault by Negro units. Instead, the gunners—some of whom had had recent confrontations with the Negroes—fired at them rather than at the Confederates.

Many oppressed Negro soldiers no doubt gained a measure of solace from a favorite camp song:

So rally, boys, rally, let us never mind the past;
We had a hard road to travel, but our day is
*   coming fast,*
For God is for the right, and we have no need to
*   fear,—*
The Union must be saved by the colored
*   volunteer.*

DURING their three years' service in the Civil War, Negro soldiers participated in at least 39 major battles and 410 minor engagements. "The combat performance of the colored soldier is difficult to evaluate," Dr. Wiley has written, "because of the prejudiced character of most of the evidence on the subject. Northerners who were unfriendly to Negroes or opposed to emancipation, and nearly all Southerners, tended to belittle the colored soldiers; while antislavery zealots and commanders of colored units were inclined to close their eyes to deficiencies of the Negro fighters and exaggerate their accomplishments."

Printed works abound on the Civil War battles in which Negro troops played an active role. It is only necessary here to emphasize a half-dozen engagements highlighted by the presence of black soldiers.

The first major offensive launched by Negro troops occurred May 27, 1863, at Port Hudson, Louisiana. Some 1,080 members of the 1st and 3d Louisiana Na-

Negro soldiers mustered out. Drawing by Alfred R. Waud. (LC)

tive Guards formed the right of a Federal assaulting force against the 6,000-man Confederate garrison. The Negroes attacked without support one of the strongest natural positions along the Mississippi River. The conduct of these men, even in defeat, surprised their most vocal critics. The Negro units suffered 37 killed, 155 wounded, and 116 missing. One of the fatalities was Color Sergeant Anselmas Planciancois of the 1st Louisiana. That morning he had received the regimental flag with the statement: "Colonel, I will bring back the colors with honor or report to God the reason why." When Planciancois fell mortally wounded in the assault, he was observed by a newspaperman as having "hugged the colors to his breast."

At Milliken's Bend on June 7, 1863, the tactical situation was reversed. Only 1,100 Federals—the 20th Iowa and three small Negro regiments—were in the fort when about 1,500 Texans under General H. E. McCulloch attacked. The Confederates gained the levee behind which the Federals were posted; for about twenty minutes blacks and whites grappled in close combat with bayonets and muskets. The Negroes broke and retreated to the edge of the river. Two Federal gunboats then arrived on the scene and bombarded the Confederates into withdrawal. One Negro regiment that went into action with 300 men lost 50 killed and 80 wounded. If the conduct of the Negroes at Milliken's Bend left something to be desired, much of the fault lay in the fact—pointed out by General Grant—that they had "had but little experience in the use of fire-arms."

ONE of the most famous Negro assaults of the war took place July 18, 1863, at Fort Wagner on Morris Island, South Carolina. The unit involved was the 54th Massachusetts, "the first colored regiment of the North to go to war" and commanded by 25-year-old Robert Gould Shaw. Only fifty-one days after leaving Boston, the 54th Massachusetts was ordered to launch a 6 p.m. assault. The men had been marching through sand and swamps for most of that day. They had been two nights without rest and two days without rations. Yet the Negroes did not balk in leading a charge across three-quarters of a mile of open sand toward the Confederate earthworks.

The hand-to-hand fighting was vicious. The Federals momentarily gained a toehold in the works, but lost it after frightful casualties. Colonel Shaw and three other officers were killed; 11 officers and 135 men were wounded; another 100 men in the regiment were listed as missing and presumed dead. Of this engagement, Lieutenant Elbridge Copp of the 3d New Hampshire wrote that "language is all too tame to convey the horrors and the meaning of it all."

Barbarities marked many of the 1864 actions of which Negro troops were a part. A Confederate in the

"Emancipation Day in South Carolina." The color sergeant of 1st South Carolina (Colored) Volunteers addressing the regiment after having been presented with the Stars and Stripes at Smith's plantation, Port Royal Island, on Jan. 1, 1863. (FL)

Hinks's division of Negro infantry bringing in the guns captured at Baylor's farm near Petersburg, June 15, 1864.

4th Louisiana Cavalry went so far as to write of that period: "The feelings between our men and the negro troops, especially their officers, were intensely bitter . . . In no fight was it known beforehand whether quarter would be given."

At Olustee, Florida, in February 1864, the 8th U. S. Colored Troops lost 300 of 550 men engaged. A member of the 26th Virginia tersely summarized the battle: "The negroes saw a hard time; those who stood were shot by our men, those who ran by the Yankees. Such was the fight at Alustee."

CONGRESSIONAL claims that at Fort Pillow, Tennessee (April 12, 1864), Confederate General N. Bedford Forrest murdered 300 Negro troops in cold blood are exaggerated. Yet, in the face of valid evidence, one can hardly deny that some of the 200 Federal casualties were the victims of a massacre.

Similarly, at Poison Spring, Arkansas, a week after the "Fort Pillow Massacre," reports abounded of captured and wounded Negro soldiers being butchered. That the 1st Kansas Colored suffered there its heaviest losses—117 killed and 65 wounded—adds some credence to the charge. In an April 25, 1864, battle at Mark's Mill, Arkansas, the Southerners apparently gave little quarter to their Negro opponents. John N. Edwards of Confederate General Jo Shelby's division stated: "The battlefield was sickening to behold. No orders, threats, or commands could restrain the men from vengeance on the negroes. . . ."

At the battle of the Crater, fought July 30, 1864, near Petersburg, Virginia, General Edward Ferrero's all-Negro 4th Division of the IX Corps fell victim to incompetent leaders, demoralization among white troops whom they were supporting, a heavy loss of officers, and the concentrated fire of irate Confederates. The Negroes bolted to the rear in utter confusion. Their losses were staggering: 209 killed, 697 wounded and 421 missing. "Worse still," a Midwestern soldier alleged, "the 13th Indiana white . . . deliberately shot down many of the retreating soldiers. When I say there is a fearful mortality among the dusky heroes you will readily understand how it happened."

Entrance of the 55th Massachusetts (Colored) Regiment into Charleston, S.C., Feb. 21, 1865. Painting by Thomas Nast. (Museum of Fine Arts, Boston. Fund M. & M. Karolik, Cat. #984)

OTHER Negro soldiers, however, redeemed at Nashville the stigma of the Crater. On the second day's engagement (December 16, 1864) at the Tennessee capital, Negro units were ordered to participate in a grand assault. Their valor and total disregard for safety in the attack was such as to prompt from Confederates the retort: "We heard afterwards that they had been fed upon liquor until they were crazy drunk."

In the severe fighting, Lieutenant John S. Kendall of the 4th Louisiana recalled one particular Negro: a "hugh color-bearer who stood erect among his falling companions. His terror was apparently too great to allow him to move. He stood clinging to the flagstaff, while a hundred of our side tried in vain to hit him. The bullets whistled around him by scores. Finally one struck him and he fell. I felt a sense of compassion. He was a big, fine-looking chap. It seemed a pity."

Kendall may well have confused "terror" with heroism; for a day or two later, while riding over the ravaged battlefield, General George H. Thomas proclaimed to his fellow officers: "Gentlemen, the question is settled. Negroes will fight."

A **TOTAL** of 178,895 Negroes served as Federal soldiers in the Civil War. They were organized into 120 infantry regiments, 12 heavy artillery regiments, 10 light artillery batteries, and 7 cavalry regiments. Their numbers constituted 12 percent of the entire Federal armies. Of the total, 134,111 Negroes came from slaveholding states. Louisiana led the list with 24,052 Negro soldiers. Texas, with but 47, was at the bottom. On the Northern side, Pennsylvania contributed 8,612 Negroes to the armies, followed by New York with 4,125 and Massachusetts with 3,996.

Cumulative losses in Negro units were unusually high: 68,178 men—or more than one third of the total enrolled. Of that number, 2,751 were killed in action. The remainder succumbed to wounds and diseases. Twenty-one Negroes received the Congressional Medal of Honor. The number of Negro desertions was 14,887, or about 7 percent of the total among all Billy Yanks.

THE Negro soldier of the 1860's was neither saint nor sinner. His camp and battle behavior ultimately compared well with his white compatriots. While he exhibited a greater respect for orders and discipline, he was prone to lying, stealing, and feigning illness. As victims of discriminatory treatment throughout most of the war, the Negroes' over-all performance is deserving of high commendation. By war's end countless Federal soldiers no doubt seconded the feelings of a Wisconsin officer who, after watching a Negro regiment in action, exclaimed: "I never believed in niggers before, but by Jasus, they are hell for fighting!"

In 1892, Colonel Norwood P. Hallowell of the 55th Massachusetts (Colored) stated of Negro troops: "We called upon them in the day of our trial, when volunteering had ceased, when the draft was a partial failure, and the bounty system a senseless extravagance. They were ineligible for promotion, they were not to be treated as prisoners of war. Nothing was definite except that they could be shot and hanged as soldiers. Fortunate it is for us, as well as for them, that they were equal to the crisis; that the grand historic moment which comes to a race only once in many centuries came to them, and that they recognized it. . . ."

Years before, Abraham Lincoln had stated the case more succinctly: "And then there will be some black men who can remember that with silent tongue and clenched teeth and steady eye and well-poised bayonet they have helped mankind on to this great consummation."

THOMAS NAST
and the First Reconstruction

Morton Keller

The political cartoonist who drew the elephant and donkey as symbols of the two political parties, Thomas Nast chronicled the hopes and later the disillusions of the mid-nineteenth-century's civil rights leaders. Morton Keller, professor of history at Brandeis University and an authority on the post-Civil War era, restores to the public light this timeless and timely cartoonist in the following article.

IN THE wake of a bloody and protracted war, Americans turned their attention to the most intractable of their social problems. Influential media of news and opinion and a major political party vigorously championed Negro civil rights. But soon this movement lost its force, and foundered on the Negrophobia that darkly streaked the society. Intellectuals came to doubt that Negro political activity offered much hope of beneficial social change. Public hostility and indifference grew, and soon the politicians dropped a cause that seemed both futile and dangerous. Such was the course — of the Radical Republican movement for Negro rights after the Civil War.

Since World War II there has been a revolution in Negro civil rights that C. Vann Woodward aptly calls "the Second American Reconstruction."

But now the historical parallel has a new and ironic dimension. There is reason to fear that once again this nation will be witness to a great tragedy — a tragedy of ennobling social aspirations thwarted by indifference and hate. We face what has come to be a recurring feature of our public life: a surge of belief that we can quickly reform our society, and then an angry, wasting disillusionment when unrealistic hopes run afoul of stubborn social realities. The experience of the First Reconstruction reminds us that once before Americans ventured boldly against the labyrinthine stronghold of racial discrimination; and that once before idealism was compromised, hope deferred.

Thomas Nast's political cartoons are the best record we have of that era of American public life a century ago. He published more than 3000 drawings over the course of his career, the great majority of them in *Harper's Weekly* between 1862 and 1885. No record of that time better conveys the mood of optimism, the belief in the perfectibility of the Great Republic, that came on the heels of the Civil War. And no one more poignantly expressed the painful disillusionment with the political process that spread over important areas of public opinion in the 1870s.

It is easy to forget that post-Civil War American life was something more than Vernon Parrington's Great Barbecue, Mark Twain's Gilded Age. Nast spoke to, and for, a vast number of Americans who were ready to believe that the good society lay close at hand, and that the Republican Party was God's chosen instrument to achieve this goal. The end of the Civil War found most publicists and intellectuals in a state of euphoric optimism. Horace Greeley intoned in his New York *Tribune:* "A new world is born. . . . Never before had nation so much cause for devout Thanksgiving; never before had a people so much reason for unrestrained congratulations and the very extravagance of joy." The historian John Lothrop Motley told a friend: ". . . sometimes I wish to live twenty years longer that I may witness the magnificent gains to freedom and civilization and human progress which are sure to result from our great triumphs." James Russell Lowell found the Northern victory evidence of "the amazing strength and no less amazing steadiness of democratic institutions."

The political process, especially the Republican Party, was the instrument by which the gains of the war — national union and human freedom — would be consolidated in peacetime. George W. Curtis, the editor of *Harper's Weekly*, summed up the Radical Republican political attitude: "A hearty faith in the great principles of popular government, a generous hospitality toward new views and constant progress, a practical perception of the close relation between morals and politics, a deep conviction of the vital necessity of intelligence to a true republic will generally lead a man to act with the Republican party. . . ."

Thomas Nast was admirably suited to be the artistic spokesman for this Radical Republican spirit. He came of age with the ideological and technological conditions that made it possible for him to become the first, and perhaps the greatest, of America's political cartoonists. Born in Germany in 1840 and brought to New York in 1846, he grew up imbued with the mid-nineteenth-century belief in nationalism, liberalism, democracy, and progress. The development of the Civil War as a struggle for American nationalism and human freedom had great emotional meaning for him. During the last years of the conflict he frequently drew allegorical representations of the war's inner significance. These drawings had an enormous impact on his *Harper's Weekly* audience. His cousin-in-law, the biographer James Parton, thought that Nast's "powerful emblematic pictures" were "as much the expression of heartfelt conviction as Mr. Curtis' most impassioned editorials, or Mr. Lincoln's Gettysburg speech." Lincoln himself more pragmatically called Nast "our best recruiting sergeant. His . . . cartoons have never failed to arouse enthusiasm and patriotism, and have always seemed to come just when those articles were getting scarce."

The issues that most strongly engaged the American people before 1861 — the Revolution

1. THE IGNORANT VOTE — HONORS ARE EASY.

and Independence and, almost a century later, the debate over slavery and states' rights — evoked great words, not great pictures. Pamphlets, books, and broadsides sped over the vast country far more rapidly and less expensively than etchings, lithographs, or engravings. But in the 1850s there appeared the first devices by which an art of political commentary might flourish. *Frank Leslie's Illustrated Newspaper*, the first successful pictorial magazine in the United States, began publication in 1855. *Harper's Weekly*, which was to serve as Nast's great medium, followed in 1857. By the eve of the Civil War *Leslie's* had a circulation of over 160,000; *Harper's* had almost 100,000; and each copy had many readers. During the same years Currier & Ives lithographs, sometimes treating political topics, habituated large numbers of Americans to the pictorial representation of ideas and events. The Civil War provided the new outlets for American graphic art with their first great theme. And Thomas Nast had gifts of technique, imagination, and feeling powerful enough to reach and move the vast audience now at hand.

Inevitably Emancipation was one of Nast's wartime themes. And Negro civil rights emerged as the touchstone issue of post-war Radical Republicanism. It might seem that political expediency — the lure of Negro votes in the South and the lower North — sufficiently explains the party's commitment. But to call for Negro suffrage and other civil rights entailed political dangers as well. Negroes suffered under a heavy, and popular, burden of civil disability in most Northern states. Time and again white voters in the North made it clear that while they opposed secession and slavery, they had no desire to see Negroes enjoy the blessings of equal citizenship.

One must go beyond political considerations to understand the adherence of so many Republican politicians, journalists, and intellectuals to the cause of Negro civic equality. Men whose public lives had been taken up with the struggle against slavery and the defense of the Union were reluctant to accept a political environment where nothing divided the parties but a lust for office. To champion the cause of the Freedmen was to perpetuate the moral idealism of the war years. So at a time when racist assumptions had an important place in intellectual circles throughout the Western world and an overt Negrophobia was the prevailing sentiment among white Americans, Republican spokesmen in growing numbers supported the cause of Negro civil equality.

The Republican effort was not limited to the Radical Reconstruction governments of the South-

2. Universal Suffrage.

ern states. Party organizations in the North set out to eliminate the restrictions on Negro voting and other civil rights that encrusted their states' constitutions and statute books. Typical was the Minnesota Republican platform of 1865: "The measure of a man's political rights should be neither his religion, his birthplace, his race, his color, nor any merely physical characteristics." (Typically, too, the people of the state in 1867 rejected Negro suffrage.) Michigan Republicans in 1866 declared: "We scout and scorn . . . that political blasphemy which says, 'This is the white man's Government.' It is not the white man's Government, nor the black man's Government. It is God's Government made for man!''

Legislation approached, if it did not match, this rhetoric. Massachusetts passed the first state civil rights act a month after Appomattox; Pennsylvania followed in 1867, New York and Kansas in 1874. Other states repealed laws that restricted the movement and legal rights of Negroes. A national civil rights act in 1866 gave the Freedmen national citizenship and federal protection against state discrimination. The Fifteenth Amendment to the Constitution in 1870 authorized Congress to guarantee Negro voting everywhere. The Civil Rights Act of 1875 was the last major statement of Radical Republican racial policy. Holding that the object of legislation was "to enact great principles into law," the bill guaranteed to all the right to "full and equal enjoyment of the accommodations, advantages, facilities, and privileges of inns, public conveyances on land or water, theaters, and other places of public amusement."

As a good Republican, Nast of course had a political interest in Negro suffrage. But he viewed the mistreatment of Negroes with an indignation that rested on more than party considerations. He had a strong sense of the United States as a nation of diverse peoples, welded together by self-government and universal suffrage. (Plate 2.) The brutal repression of Negroes by an intransigent — and Democratic — South outraged his moral sensibilities. So did Northerners who reacted to Negro equality with hypocrisy or fear.

But the post-war movement for Negro civil equality had a short and stunted life. Custom and the courts quickly stripped civil rights legislation of its effective force. Southern Radical Republican governments based on Negro suffrage could not sustain themselves, and most American intellectuals and publicists took this as evidence of Negro racial inferiority.

More than the cause of Negro equality was abandoned in the 1870s. Politicians, entrepreneurs, and publicists once were bound together by a common belief in the evil of slavery and the inviolability of the Union. Now, as new issues arose

and the old ones receded, they went their separate ways. Political leaders devoted themselves increasingly to the demanding, technical business of strengthening their party organizations. Businessmen, farmers, and workingmen, struggling with the harsh depression that began in 1873, had little time for issues not germane to their immediate economic needs.

Intellectuals and journalists had growing doubts about a party system that was less and less interested in great national issues, that gave itself over so openly, and corruptly, to the niggling demands of practical business and practical politics. E. L. Godkin's *Nation*, created in 1865 to preserve in post-war America the abolitionist spirit of Radical reform, soon became the voice of the Mugwump: querulous, frustrated, disillusioned. Political novels of the seventies — Mark Twain's and Charles Dudley Warner's *The Gilded Age*, Henry Adams' *Democracy* — looked cynically at a party life that seemed to have no purpose but its own perpetuation and enrichment. John W. DeForest's *Honest John Vane* (1874), an ironic examination of the corruption of a young congressman, suggests the new mood. Vane tells an older colleague: "I thought general legislation was the big thing . . . reform, foreign relations, sectional questions, constitutional rights, and so on." "All exploded, my dear sir!" is the response. "All dead issues, as dead as the war.

3. The "Practical" Politician's Love
for the Negro.

Special legislation . . . is the sum and substance of Congressional business in our day."

Nast brilliantly portrayed the new political order as he had the old one. He made the elephant and the donkey the symbols of the major parties. With great prescience he had caught the transformation of a politics of sharp ideological confrontation into a politics of competing placemen: for no discernible ideological difference distinguished these valueless, neuter beasts from one another. But while he described the new politics, he could not accept it. In 1884 the artist of post-war Republicanism bolted his party to support the Democrat Grover Cleveland for the presidency.

Nor could Nast escape the prevailing change in racial attitudes. The cause of Negro civil rights fell victim to his increasing disenchantment with the Republican Party. He came to equate the Irish of the North and the Negroes of the South as "the ignorant vote." (Plate 1.) By the early 1880s he shared the general Northern view that Negro rights had become little more than the device of cynical politicos. (Plate 3.)

Nast lived on to 1902, bedeviled by artistic and financial insufficiency. *Harper's Weekly* observed at the time of his death: "He belongs so much to the past that the impression has naturally spread that he is an old man"; in fact, he was sixty-two. His art belonged to a brief but distinctive era, by the turn of the century only a faint (and distasteful) memory. Not until our own time could Nast's aspirations and his disappointments regain their original evocative power.

This is not to say that the generation of the Second American Reconstruction is condemned by some immutable law of history to repeat the experience of the first. But the fate of the Radical Republican commitment to Negro civil rights does suggest how evanescent are political moods in American life, and how complex and difficult is social change even in a society supposedly dedicated to the pursuit of happiness.

A tougher-minded realism — alien alike to Nast's Radical Republicans and to much of the contemporary civil rights movement — may, it is true, discourage bold aspirations. But it may also prevent the wasting disillusionment — the disillusionment that swept over Nast and is so endemic today — that comes when undue hopes are duly disappointed.

Political Strategies of the Reconstruction

In this article, the author points to the resemblance between Reconstruction times and the present. Now, as then, blacks feel the need to rely on their own group initiatives to improve their condition.

RONALD WALTERS

Ronald Walters has been an assistant professor at Syracuse University and is completing work on his doctoral degree at American University. In addition to serving as chairman of the newly formed Black Studies department at Brandeis, he holds an appointment as assistant professor of history.

IT IS SOMETIMES forgotten that we can learn about the past by paying close attention to the present. Some of the issues of the Reconstruction are particularly relevant for our times; in particular they may shed light on political strategies within the black community. The Bayard Rustin school of "coalition politics" perpetuates the myth that coalition is a relevant strategy, despite the fact that history is still waiting for it to pay off in the kind of community power which is the necessary prerequisite to any meaningful progress. A study of the Reconstruction period will help to clarify our current problem by revealing the opportunities for interracial cooperation in that era, the elements which would have been necessary to bring about that cooperation and, after it failed, the imperatives facing the black community.

Most studies of the Reconstruction period begin with a discussion of the aims of the Radical Republicans and their program. Little attention has been given to the fact that there was a community of blacks who formulated the issues adopted by the Radical politicians and that throughout the period they fought harder for change—considering their resources—than did the Congressional managers of the Reconstruction legislation.

Leon Litwack in *The Anti-Slavery Vanguard*[1] says that before the Civil War there was a split in the ranks of the abolitionists. What the movement had been witnessing, especially since 1830, was the growth of a band of militant blacks like David Walker, Martin Delaney and Henry Highland Garnett who directly challenged the right of white abolitionists like William Lloyd Garrison to speak for them. In this movement, the role of Frederick Douglass, a former slave, was central because he was the leading speaker for the abolitionists and a member of the Garrisonians. The controversy between Douglass and Garrison which finally resulted in the split between the two men was part of the same mood of independence. Doug-

[1] Ed., Martin Duberman (Princeton: Princeton University Press, 1965).

From *Current History*, November 1969. Copyright © Current History, Inc.

lass aligned himself with other black militants in pressing for the abolition of slavery and suggested that the back of the Southern "rebellion" could be broken by ending slavery in that area.

Once this objective had been attained, Douglass was faced with the question of how freedom for blacks could be maintained and protected. In his autobiography he shows his conception of the instruments necessary to protect American rights.

> I insisted that . . . to guard, protect and maintain his liberty the freed-man should have the ballot—that the liberties of the American people were dependent upon the ballot-box, the jury-box and the cartridge-box—that without these no class of people could live and flourish in this country. . . .[2]

In this same account, Douglass notes that some abolitionists, like Garrison, did not believe at first that blacks were entitled to full enfranchisement immediately after emancipation; others, like Wendell Phillips, were in favor of it. In any case, Douglass believed that a momentum must be created around this issue. The first opportunity presented itself on February 7, 1866, when President Andrew Johnson granted an interview to Douglass and several other leaders from the black community at which Douglass and George T. Downing made a case for full enfranchisement. Afterward, the President delivered a lengthy prepared statement critical of the Negro franchise which was picked up by the press. Sensing the unfair advantage in the wide dissemination given the President's statement, Douglass prepared a rebuttal statement to blunt the force of Johnson's arguments. After the House of Representatives passed a measure proposing that the issue of suffrage be left up to the individual states, Douglass and his associates petitioned the Senate not to adopt it, and lobbied to persuade key Republican politicians to oppose it.

The National Equal Rights League was formed at a meeting of the National Convention of Colored Men in Syracuse, New York, in October, 1864, and adopted Negro suffrage as an issue deserving broad support. The first meeting of the League, in Cleveland, Ohio, in 1865, called for a frontal assault on all prohibitions of freedmen's rights by suggesting the adoption of the following proposed constitutional amendment.

> That there shall be no legislation within the limits of the U.S. or territories, against any civilized portion of the inhabitants native-born or naturalized, on account of race or color, and that all such legislation now existing within said limits is anti-Republican in character, and therefore void.[3]

Under the administration of Ulysses Grant, the issue of suffrage for blacks resulted in the passage of the Fifteenth Amendment to the Constitution by both Houses of Congress. By the time this Amendment was proposed and passed, black public opinion had already clearly enunciated the issues as well as a strategy. Some of these issues were embodied in the Reconstruction Act of 1867.

In 1872, a delegation of prominent black Washingtonians carrying a petition with over 2,000 names favoring a Civil Rights Bill and a delegation of prominent blacks from Arkansas and Virginia called upon the President to request his serious attention to the pending bill. The account of this meeting, published on January 18, 1872, in the *New National Era,* a black newspaper edited by Douglass in Washington, D.C., included the petition, which mentioned the insecure position of blacks with respect to the enjoyment of the "usual accommodations, advantages, facilities, and privileges furnished by common carriers by land and water . . ." and asked correction of the "degradation" and "discrimination" which resulted.

In 1873, under the leadership of George T. Downing, a Civil Rights Convention was held, sponsored by the National Convention of Colored Men, and thereafter a Memorial was sent to the Congress which contained an eloquent and forceful plea for civil rights legislation invoking salient passages of the Constitution in its support.

These actions were bolstered by a number of petitions from state Conventions of Colored Men from Illinois, Tennessee, Mississippi, Virginia, North Carolina, Kentucky, Alabama, Georgia and Washington, D.C. All the petitions pointed to acts of injustice and asked for federal relief for the blacks as freedmen and citizens. They also exhibited deep concern with the tendency of the Reconstruction government to hasten the pace of reinvesting the former rebel Southern whites with full citizenship at the expense of the rights of blacks. They saw the acquisition of rights as the ultimate security of their new status and as a possible protection against the already advanced attempts of whites to enslave them anew.

Blacks also supported the Civil Rights Bill of 1875. Those who advocated equal suffrage made a natural connection between the vote and equal rights in all fields of citizenship including taxation, public accommodations and education.[4]

The so-called Radical Republicans, therefore, were well aware of the issues most urgent to the black community. The Radicals were responsible, through their congressional involvement, for the Reconstruction Acts, the Freedmen's Bureau and the Civil Rights Acts of 1866 and 1875; to that extent they were responsible more for the methodology of Reconstruction than for its substance. In fact, their radicalism lay in their attempts extensively to restructure the political and social life of the South. However, to realize the aims of the black community, it was necessary that the white South give some genuine consent to the plans; more important, it was absolutely necessary to have in the South the stable, effective presence of the federal power.

THE ATTEMPT AT RECONSTRUCTION

The passage of the Radical Republican program made it possible for blacks to try two practical strategies to attain their goal of equality. The first was harmonious political interaction with the white community; the second was harmonious economic interaction with white Southern labor.

When the state conventions started to meet after the war to elect officers and restructure the political processes, open suffrage made it possible for blacks to participate in the political life of the South for the first time in large numbers. There were examples of such early participation in South Carolina, where the largest percentage of blacks voted and where the largest number participated in the state legislature. In this state, there arose a remarkable class of black leaders.

Certainly few men in the South of that day had been educated abroad as was South Carolina Secretary of State Francis Cardozo (University of Glasgow and in London) or United States Congressman Robert B. Elliot (Eton College, London) and the number of black lawyers in public office was high considering the level of available opportunities (consider, for example, Samuel Lee, Richard Gleaves and Robert Elliot). Other professional men were largely self-taught and self-trained in oratorical skills, but were very effective representatives for blacks.

In Mississippi, there was a similar group of black leaders. It was said by the black Speaker of the House in Mississippi, John R. Lynch, that "of 72 counties, not more than 12 ever had colored sheriffs . . . and that in point of intelligence, capacity and honesty, the colored sheriffs would have favorably compared with the white."[5] W. E. B. Du Bois says that on the whole the Negro leadership class was generally good and in spite of the charges of corruption leveled against them the Negroes were not so corrupt as either the native pre-Reconstruction governments or as the Halls of Tammany in New York; generally they tried to make the best of situations of inherited difficulty.

In Louisiana, the pattern was much the same as blacks fought their way into positions of leadership in the state by the overwhelming effect of their numbers on the state conven-

[2] *The Life and Times of Frederick Douglass* (New York: Collier, 1962), p. 378.

[3] Herbert Aptheker, *A Documentary History of the Negro People in the United States* (New York: Citadel, 1966), Vol. 2, p. 55.

[4] James M. McPherson, *The Negro's Civil War* (New York: Vintage, 1967), Ch. 18.

[5] W. E. B. DuBois, *Black Reconstruction in America* (Chicago: Meridian, 1964), p. 447.

tion and at the ballot box.

Du Bois notes that between 1868 and 1896 "32 colored state Senators and 95 representatives served."[6] Lerone Bennett, Jr., calls Mississippi Lieutenant Governor P. B. S. Pinchback the "most practical politician black America has ever produced,"[7] and extolls the extent of his power over political life in Louisiana and the way he and his black compatriots sought to pull Louisiana out of the mire of post-Civil War chaos.

In spite of the power and influence held by black Republicans in the Southern governments, Du Bois, John Hope Franklin, Rayford Logan and others debunked the myth that blacks held absolute power in any Southern state. There was usually political cooperation between the black leaders and the non-Southern whites (the so-called carpetbaggers), although there were some Southern businessmen and politicians still represented and sharing power in every legislature in the South between 1868 and 1880. DuBois, nevertheless, relates a comment by a member of the Mississippi Legislature on the position of "colored men."

In my opinion if they had all been native southern Negroes, there would have been little cause of complaint. They often wanted to vote with Democrats on non-political questions, but could not resist the party lash. The majority of whites in both parties exhibit the same weakness.[8]

DuBois interprets this statement to mean that the basis of whatever alliance the Negroes had with the planters was economics and that politically the Negroes were caught between the revengeful Southern Democratic whites and the jealous, suspicious Northern Republicans. Nevertheless, from the standpoint of the legislation that emerged in the South during this period, it is clear that there was enough cooperation between the races at the state level, given the right conditions, to have produced a viable strategy, even though blacks did not play a fundamental role in running the governments.

THE ECONOMIC SITUATION

The economic issue for black people was as important as the political issue and had just as deep roots of concern. In 1837, a review of the economic situation of black people by the *Colored American* revealed that not one of the prominent abolitionists had any black man in a prominent position in his business. Douglass directed a stinging inquiry into the subject when he said, "What boss anti-slavery mechanic will take a black boy into his wheelright's shop, his blacksmith's shop, his joiner's shop, his cabinet shop?" It was no accident that economics was a key consideration in the Freedmen's Bureau Bill of 1865. The Radicals sought

to break up the power of the landed Southern aristocracy and thereby further weaken it politically, but they were also mindful, because of the succinctness with which the issue was put to them by blacks, that the redistribution of wealth should be of central importance.

William Still of Philadelphia noted in a speech on March 10, 1874, that the Civil Rights Bill had opened the way "for new issues" (of an economic nature) to be considered, and continued, "Landless and without capital, even [with] the Civil Rights Bill secured by the Congress of the nation, the condition of the colored man would still be pitiable, unless he is wise." But the concern with the economic situation of blacks goes back at least to the eighteenth century and the numerous petitions which were sent to colonial legislatures by blacks for relief of unfair taxation. DuBois said that all along there had been a "connection in the Negroes' mind between politics and labor."[9] In 1865, the National Equal Rights League met in Philadelphia and stressed business education for members' sons and urged Negroes to secure real estate. This theme was alive throughout the Reconstruction; in 1869 a Negro Convention was held in Louisville, Kentucky, which recommended the purchase of land by newly freed slaves.

In the South, whites resisted the drive by the Freedmen's Bureau to make small farmers out of thousands of blacks. They were willing to see (initially) the emphasis placed on black labor, not on black ownership. This temporary willingness resulted in an opportunity for blacks to try the second strategy of accommodation between black and white laboring classes in the South.

In 1869, a clear emphasis on labor developed as National Conventions of Colored Men held in Baltimore and Washington, D.C., resulted in the formation of the Negro National Labor Movement, presided over by indefatigable Frederick Douglass. At a meeting in January, 1870, the organization stated:

We would have the "poor white man" of the south, born to a heritage of poverty and degradation like his black compeer in social life, feel that labor in our organization seeks the elevation of all its sons and daughters; pledges its *united* strength not to advance the special interests of a special class; but would promote the welfare and happiness of all who "earn their bread in the sweat of their brow."[10]

THE POPULIST MOVEMENT

Such an overture was timely, for the coming Populist movement, with its emphasis on the common plight of agrarian labor regardless of color, would make it possible for blacks and whites to consider merging what had developed into two distinct labor movements. In spite of the failure of the Recon-

struction land policy, the Civil War had done much to equalize the economic status of black and white small farmers. The Populist movement, therefore, logically seemed to blacks and to whites the proper vehicle for pleading their common cause. Whites like Tom Watson were sent South to campaign openly for black support for the cause.

The possibility that a union of economic interests between poor blacks and whites might result in political dominance at the polls alarmed the Southern planter class.[11] In order to avert the impending crisis, the planters revived the specter of black "domination" of the Populist movement; this had the predictable effect of seeing the white South "close ranks" and thus close out black participation. Benjamin Quarles notes that the Southern black man become more of a scapegoat than ever as "lower class" whites attempted to divorce themselves not only from the attempt at political and economic cooperation with blacks but even from the implied *social* relations with blacks which might have been a natural consequence.[12]

THE FEDERAL ROLE

Both strategies of accommodation were doomed to failure without the element of legitimate force which has always institutionalized norms not easily accepted by a minority in American society.

Originally, the power of the federal government was the main force behind the implementation of provisions of the Freedmen's Bill. Military authority was made responsible for the enforcement of the provisions which installed the "New Order." The execution of such a policy was fraught with difficulties given the vulnerability of federal government soldiers. They openly engaged in the political life of the territories under their jurisdiction and some soldiers adopted local attitudes toward the blacks. With each act of deviation from the soldiers' basic mission, the cause of the New Order was weakened, and because from the beginning federal authority was the most powerful sanction the Freedmen's Bill provided, the failure of federal enforcement was the most serious defect in Reconstruction Plan operations.

The perceptive Douglass was aware of this possibility from the first. He argued that undue use of the federal power in enforcement of the Freedmen's Bureau Bill could make this nation and its government despotic (which he did not wish), and that the surest way to protect the rights of the freedman was to protect his basic right to vote. Somewhere in the general failure of federal power, in the political dynamics between sectional groups of Southern Democrats and Northern Republicans in the Hayes Bargain of 1876, the precious right of the black man's suffrage was

[6] *Ibid.*, p. 170.
[7] *Black Power U.S.A.*, (New York, Penguin, 1967), p. 261.
[8] Du Bois, *op. cit.*, p. 445.

[9] *Ibid.*, p. 361.
[10] Aptheker, *op. cit.*, p. 632.

[11] Benjamin Quarles, *The Negro in the Making of America* (New York: Collier, 1964), p. 146.
[12] *Ibid.*

yielded up. Furthermore, it is doubtful that at the time Douglass was analyzing this problem, he had conceived of the possibility of the election of an Andrew Johnson as President or of the rapid dissipation of the power of the Radicals in Congress. In assessing the importance of these factors, which most scholars of the period either ignore or take for granted, one should consider that John Armour Bingham (Representative, Ohio), sponsor of the Fifteenth Amendment, was not reelected in 1872; Thaddeus Stevens (Representative, Pa.), author of the Reconstruction Acts, died before 1876; William Pitt Fesenden (Representative, Maine), liberal member of the Joint Committee on Reconstruction, died in 1869; Lyman Trumbull (Senator, Ill.), backer of the Fourteenth Amendment, left Congress in 1872; and Charles Sumner (Senator, Mass.), author of innumerable efforts on behalf of the black man, died before the Civil Rights Bill of 1875 (which he spearheaded) was passed. Looking over the cast of characters in the Reconstruction drama who had left the stage, it is easy to see why the legislation which they constructed was negatively affected by their absence.

Finally, a word must be said about the way the white Southerner viewed the attempt to reconstruct his world vis-à-vis his former slave. It is possible that no amount of federal power could have permanently arrested the determination of the white South to regain ascendancy over the black man. Regardless of the superlative performance of those blacks who did participate in the political life of the South, the white South still could find little to commend in their accomplishments. This attitude is exemplified by the comments of Governor Benjamin F. Perry of South Carolina in 1867:

the fact is patent to all . . . that the Negro is utterly unfitted to exercise the highest function of a citizen. . . . We protest against this subversion of the social order, whereby an ignorant and depraved race is placed in power and influence

above the virtuous, the educated, and the refined.

He added that the "white people of S.C. would never acquiesce in Negro equality or supremacy."[13] This attitude of the white South, portrayed in the words of men like Governor Perry and in the actions of Southerners who were in secret revolt against the New Order before the ink was dry on the Emancipation Proclamation, meant that, at the least, the necessity for the application of federal power became many times more relevant to the security of the black community.

EVALUATING THE OPTIONS

The lesson which this cursory examination of the Reconstruction suggests is that if coalition is not to result in one-way exploitation each of the parties involved needs to be strong enough to avoid intellectual or physical subjugation. During the Reconstruction, the black man depended upon the strength of a stable federal presence and, to a lesser degree, upon the willingness of the white South to cooperate in the New Order. Both of these failed him miserably and, because the black was disorganized by slavery and then by emancipation, he was easily susceptible to the loss of power.

The modern version of coalition politics which has been espoused by some civil rights leaders was based on alliances between blacks and, as Stokeley Carmichael puts it, "various liberal pressure organizations in the white community — liberal reform clubs, labor unions, church groups, progressive civic groups and a large segment of the Democratic party."[14] Carmichael goes on to say that the group coalition which was supposed to influence national legislation and national social patterns failed because the specific self-interest of such allies came into conflict with

[13] Du Bois, op. cit., p. 389.
[14] Pamphlet, Toward Black Liberation, Student Nonviolent Coordinating Committee, 1967.

appeals to their decency and sense of conscience. Furthermore, he states that the major limitation of the coalition strategy was that it tended to "maintain the traditional dependence" of the black community on the good will of a community whose interests are often inimical to blacks. Such cooptation, the continuance of the master-servant relationship, will be aided if (as he says) "we do not learn from history, we are doomed to repeat it, and that is precisely the lesson of the Reconstruction."

We are living in a time curiously parallel to the Reconstruction, when again the power of the federal government needs to be marshaled on behalf of the black community to complete the job of human reconstruction. Howard Zinn travels through cities like Albany, Georgia; Selma, Alabama; Greenwood, Hattiesburg, and Yazoo City, Mississippi, analyzing the extent to which blacks may take advantage of their constitutional rights. And seeing basic rights such as voting and the use of public accommodations denied blacks by police officials, he is led to believe that some degradations will only fall by "hammer blows."[15] One of the hammer blows is the force of the black revolution and the other is the imposition of the force of the national government. In this sense, the solutions which are now posited to the problem of full citizenship for blacks have not changed significantly since the days of the Reconstruction; it is still necessary to marshal the kind of power which will force change.

Also, there is still insufficient attention given to the fact that the black community, in order to survive, must resolve the issues of Black Reconstruction. Because blacks did not have the power to resolve these issues in times past, the issues remain today and will remain until such time as the black community organizes itself to deal with them.

[15] "The Limits of Non-Violence," in Black Protest, Joanne Grant, ed. (New York: Fawcett World, 1968).

5

Industrialize

Empire

Argument

The era from the end of the Civil War to the beginning of World War I was unquestionably one of the most boisterous, energetic, and crude periods in the history of the United States. Transcontinental railroads were strung across the continent, the product of the will of robber barons and the sweat of immigrant labor. The creation of great industrial complexes, masterminded by the scions of industry and manned by Polish, Italian, Irish, Greek, and German immigrants, gave birth to a new landscape of belching smokestacks and fields furrowed by steam-driven tractors. Immigration and industrialization transformed cities into vast metropolises with towering skyscrapers, sprawling tenements, mansions for the rich, and suburbs for the well-to-do middle class. Small wonder that this era of uncontrolled expansion proved fertile ground for all the excesses of greed and corruption. Small wonder too that millions organized, protested, struck, and politicked for reform.

In some respects that period is not unlike the present one. Then as now, technological innovations brought social change at a bewildering pace, which led to widespread protest. But, as the articles in this section suggest, there is a crucial difference between the post–Civil War period and today. Reform—not revolution—was the aim of protest; optimism rather than cynicism its spirit.

In "Rise and Fall: The Age of the Bosses," William Shannon points out that "the political bosses emerged to cope with this chaotic change and growth." Only when "the great flood of bewildered foreigners was reduced to a trickle" did the usefulness of the boss come to an end. Gerald Eggert's "The Great Pullman Strike" provides another fascinating example of the ability of late nineteenth-century Americans to create and then resolve conflict, albeit bloodily, within the confines of capitalistic ideology. As Joseph Conlin points out in the next article, "The Case of the Very-American Militants," even the socialistic Industrial Workers of the World (best known as "wobblies") were far more committed to sustaining than to destroying American values. And the sensational confrontation in *McClure's Magazine* between Ida Tarbell, the muckraking lady journalist, and John D. Rockefeller's Standard Oil Company had an air of theater rather than of mortal combat about it. In "The Gentlewoman and the Robber Baron," Virginia Hamilton has portrayed one of the many remarkable women who attacked the bastions of the American male ego. Peggy Robbins recounts in "Susan B. Anthony" that the movement for equality was waged with fervor and optimism, in the belief that the Constitution meant what it said: that all men—and women—were created equal.

The idealism and perhaps the naïveté of the period are further illustrated in the next two pieces. In Joseph Wall's "The Rich Man's Burden—and How Andrew Carnegie Unloaded It," Carnegie's disbursal of his vast industrial fortune for the public benefit will probably seem curious or illogical today. In like manner, the speech of Booker T. Washington at the Atlanta Exposition, which Roger Williams describes in "The Atlanta Compromise," may well seem incomprehensible, but at the time it was widely heralded as "a platform upon which blacks and whites can stand with full justice to each other."

The foreign adventures of the United States also suggest some partial parallels with the present. "How the Panama Canal Came About" by Robert James Maddox provides an intriguing description of how President Theodore Roosevelt helped inaugurate the twentieth-century tradition of executive privilege in foreign affairs. As T R put it, "I took the Canal Zone and let Congress debate."

THE POLITICAL MACHINE I: RISE AND FALL
THE AGE of the BOSSES

They were usually corrupt and often inefficient, but the old-style politicians had their uses. Now almost all are gone

WILLIAM V. SHANNON

William V. Shannon is on the editorial board of the New York Times. *He is the author of* The American Irish *and of* The Heir Apparent, *a study of the late Senator Robert F. Kennedy, both published by Macmillan.*

The big city and the political boss grew up together in America. Bossism, with all its color and corruption and human drama, was a natural and perhaps necessary accompaniment to the rapid development of cities. The new urban communities did not grow slowly and according to plan; on the contrary, huge conglomerations of people from all over the world and from widely varying backgrounds came together suddenly, and in an unplanned, unorganized fashion fumbled their way toward communal relationships and a common identity. The political bosses emerged to cope with this chaotic change and growth. Acting out of greed, a ruthless will for mastery, and an imperfect understanding of what they were about, the bosses imposed upon these conglomerations called cities a certain feudal order and direction.

By 1890 virtually every sizable city had a political boss or was in the process of developing one. By 1950, sixty years later, almost every urban political machine was in an advanced state of obsolescence and its boss in trouble. The reason is not hard to find. Some of the cities kept growing and all of them kept changing, but the bosses, natural products of a specific era, could not grow or change beyond a certain point. The cities became essentially different, and as they did, the old-style organizations, like all organisms which cannot adapt, began to die. The dates vary from city to city. The system began earlier and died sooner in New York. Here or there, an old-timer made one last comeback. In Chicago, the organization and its boss still survive. But exceptions aside, the late nineteenth century saw the beginning, and the middle twentieth, the end, of the Age of the Bosses. What follows is a brief history of how it began, flourished, and passed away.

Soft-spoken Irish farmers from County Mayo and bearded Jews from Poland, country boys from Ohio and sturdy peasants from Calabria, gangling Swedes from near the Artic Circle and Chinese from Canton, laconic Yankees from Vermont villages and Negro freedmen putting distance between themselves and the old plantation—all these and many other varieties of human beings from every national and religious and cultural tradition poured into America's cities in the decades after the Civil War.

Rome and Alexandria in the ancient world had probably been as polyglot, but in modern times the diversity of American cities was unique. Everywhere in the Western world, cities were growing rapidly in the late nineteenth century; but the Germans from the countryside who migrated to Hamburg and Berlin, the English who moved to Birmingham and London, and the French who flocked to Paris stayed among fellow nationals. They might be mocked as country bumpkins and their clothes might be unfashionable, but everyone they met spoke the same language as themselves, observed the same religious and secular holidays, ate the same kind of food, voted—if they had the franchise at all—in the same elections, and shared the same sentiments and expectations. To move from farm or village to a big European city was an adventure, but one still remained within the reassuring circle of the known and the familiar.

In American cities, however, the newcomers had nothing in common with one another except their poverty and their hopes. They were truly "the uprooted." The foreign-born, unless they came from the British Isles, could not speak the language of their new homeland. The food, the customs, the holidays, the politics, were alien. Native Americans migrating to the cities from the countryside experienced their own kind of cultural shock: they found themselves competing not with other Americans but with recently arrived foreigners, so that despite their native birth they, too, felt displaced, strangers in their own country.

It was natural for members of each group to come together to try to find human warmth and protection in Little Italy or Cork Hill or Chinatown or Harlem. These feelings of clannish solidarity were one basis of strength for the political bosses. A man will more readily give his vote to a candidate because he is a neighbor from the old country or has some easily identifiable relationship, if only a similar name or the same religion, than because of agreement on some impersonal issue. Voters can take vicarious satisfaction from his success: "One of our boys is making good."

With so many different races and nationalities living together, however, mutual antagonisms were present, and the opportunity for hostility to flare into open violence was never far away. Ambitious, unscrupulous politicians could have exploited these antagonisms for their own political advantage, but the bosses and the political organizations which they developed did not function that way. If a man could vote and would "vote right," he was accepted, and that was the end of the matter. What lasting profit was there in attacking his religion or deriding his background?

Tammany early set the pattern of cultivating every bloc and faction and making an appeal as broad-based as possible. Of one precinct captain on the Lower East Side it was said: "He eats corned beef and kosher meat with equal nonchalance, and it's all the same to him whether he takes off his hat in the church or pulls it down over his ears in the synagogue."

Bosses elsewhere instinctively followed the same practice. George B. Cox, the turn-of-the-century Republican boss of Cincinnati, pasted together a coalition of Germans, Negroes, and old families like the Tafts and the Longworths. James M. Curley, who was mayor of Boston on and off for thirty-six years and was its closest approximation to a political boss, ran as well in the Lithuanian neighborhood of South Boston and the Italian section of East Boston as he did in the working-class Irish wards. In his last term in City Hall, he conferred minor patronage on the growing Negro community and joined the N.A.A.C.P.

The bosses organized neighborhoods, smoothed out antagonisms, arranged ethnically balanced tickets, and distributed patronage in accordance with voting strength as part of their effort to win and hold power. They blurred divisive issues and buried racial and religious hostility with blarney and buncombe. They were not aware that they were actually performing a mediating, pacifying function. They did not realize that by trying to please as many people as possible they were helping to hold raw new cities together, providing for inexperienced citizens a common meeting ground in politics and an experience in working together that would not have been available if the cities had been governed by apolitical bureaucracies. Bossism was usually corrupt and was decidedly inefficient, but in the 1960's, when antipoverty planners try to stimulate "community action organizations" to break through the apathy and disorganization of the slums, we can appreciate that the old-style machines had their usefulness.

When William Marcy Tweed, the first and most famous of the big-city bosses, died in jail in 1878, several hundred workingmen showed up for his funeral. The *Nation* wrote the following week:

Let us remember that he fell without loss of reputation among the bulk of his supporters. The bulk of the poorer voters of this city today revere his memory, and look on him as the victim of rich men's malice; as, in short, a friend of the needy who applied the public funds, with as little waste as was possible under the circumstances, to the purposes to which they ought to be applied—and that is to the making of work for the working man. The odium heaped on him in the pulpits last Sunday does not exist in the lower stratum of New York society.

This split in attitude toward political bosses between the impoverished many and the prosperous middle classes lingers today and still colors historical writing. To respectable people, the boss was an exotic, even grotesque figure. They found it hard to understand why anyone would vote for him or what the sources of his popularity were. To the urban poor, those sources were self-evident. The boss ran a kind of ramshackle welfare state. He helped the unemployed find jobs, interceded in court for boys in trouble, wrote letters home to the old country for the illiterate; he provided free coal and baskets of food to tide a widow over an emergency, and organized parades, excursions to the beach, and other forms of free entertainment. Some bosses, such as Frank Hague in Jersey City and Curley in Boston, were energetic patrons of their respective city hospitals, spending public funds lavishly on new construction, providing maternity and children's clinics, and arranging medical care for the indigent. In an era when social security, Blue Cross, unemployment compensation, and other public and private arrangements to cushion life's shocks did not exist, these benefactions from a political boss were important.

In every city, the boss had his base in the poorer, older, shabbier section of town. Historians have dubbed this section the "walking city" because it developed in the eighteenth and early nineteenth centuries, when houses and businesses were jumbled together, usually near the waterfront, and businessmen and laborers alike had to live within walking distance of their work. As transportation improved, people were able to live farther and farther from their place of work. Population dispersed in rough concentric circles: the financially most successful lived in the outer ring, where land was plentiful and the air was clean; the middle classes lived in intermediate neighborhoods; and the poorest and the latest arrivals from Europe crowded into the now-rundown neighborhoods in the center, where rents were lowest. Politics in most cities reflected a struggle between the old, boss-run wards downtown and the more prosperous neighborhoods farther out, which did not need a boss's services and which championed reform. The more skilled workingmen and the white-collar workers who lived in the intermediate neighborhoods generally held the balance of power between the machine and the reformers. A skillful boss could hold enough of these swing voters on the basis of ethnic loyalty or shared support of a particular issue. At times, he might work out alliances with business leaders who found that an understanding with a boss was literally more businesslike than dependence upon the vagaries of reform.

But always it was the poorest and most insecure who provided the boss with the base of his political power. Their only strength, as Professor Richard C. Wade of the University of Chicago has observed, was in their numbers.

These numbers were in most cases a curse; housing never caught up with demand, the job market was always flooded, the breadwinner had too many mouths to feed. Yet in politics such a liability could be turned into an asset. If the residents could be mobilized, their combined strength would be able to do what none could do alone. Soon the "boss" and the "machine" arose to organize this potential. The boss system was simply the political expression of inner city life.

At a time when many newcomers to the city were seeking unskilled work, and when many families had a precarious economic footing, the ability to dispense jobs was crucial to the bosses. First, there were jobs to be filled on the city payroll. Just as vital, and far more numerous, were jobs on municipal construction projects. When the machine controlled a city, public funds were always being spent for more schools, hospitals, libraries, courthouses, and orphanages. The growing cities had to have more sewer lines, gas lines, and waterworks, more paved streets and trolley tracks. Even if these utilities were privately owned, the managers needed the goodwill of city hall and were responsive to suggestions about whom to hire.

The payrolls of these public works projects were often padded, but to those seeking a job, it was better to be on a padded payroll than on no payroll. By contrast, the municipal reformers usually cut back on public spending, stopped projects to investigate for graft, and pruned payrolls. Middle- and upper-income taxpayers welcomed these reforms, but they were distinctly unpopular in working-class wards.

Another issue that strengthened the bosses was the regulation of the sale of liquor. Most women in the nineteenth century did not drink, and with their backing, the movement to ban entirely the manufacture and sale of liquor grew steadily stronger. It had its greatest support among Protestants with a rural or small-town background. To them the cities, with their saloons, dance halls, cheap theatres, and red-light districts, were becoming latter-day versions of Sodom and Gomorrah.

Many of the European immigrants in the cities, however, had entirely different values. Quite respectable Germans took their wives to beer gardens on Sundays. In the eyes of the Irish, keeping a "public house" was an honorable occupation. Some Irish women drank beer and saw no harm in going to the saloon or sending an older child for a bucketful—"rushing the growler," they called it. Poles, Czechs, Italians, and others also failed to share the rage of the Prohibitionists against saloons. Unable to entertain in their cramped tenements, they liked to congregate in neighborhood bars.

The machine also appealed successfully on the liquor issue to many middle-class ethnic voters who had no need of the machine's economic assistance. Thus, in New York in 1897, Tammany scored a sweeping victory over an incumbent reform administration that had tried to enforce a state law permitting only hotels to sell liquor on Sundays. As one of the city's three police commissioners, Theodore Roosevelt became famous prowling the tougher neighborhoods on the hunt for saloon violations, but on the vaudeville stage the singers were giving forth with the hit song, "I Want What I Want When I Want It!" As a character in Alfred Henry Lewis' novel *The Boss* explained it, the reformers had made a serious mistake: "They got between the people and its beer!"

In 1902, Lincoln Steffens, the muckraker who made a name for himself writing about political bossism, visited St. Louis to interview Joseph W. Folk, a crusading district attorney. "It is good businessmen that are corrupting our bad politicians," Folk told him. "It is good business that causes bad government in St. Louis." Thirty-five years later, Boss Tom Pendergast was running the entire state of Missouri on that same reciprocal relationship.

Although many factory owners could be indifferent to politics, other businessmen were dependent upon the goodwill and the efficiency of the municipal government. The railroads that wanted to build their freight terminals and extend their lines into the cities, the contractors who erected the office buildings, the banks that held mortgages on the land and loaned money for the construction, the utility and transit companies, and the department stores were all in need of licenses, franchises, rights of way, or favorable rulings from city inspectors and agencies. These were the businesses that made the big pay-offs to political bosses in cash, blocks of stock, or tips on land about to be developed.

In another sense, profound, impersonal, and not corrupt, the business community needed the boss. Because the Industrial Revolution hit this country when it was still thinly populated and most of its cities were overgrown towns, American cities expanded with astonishing speed. For example, in the single decade from 1880 to 1890, Chicago's population more than doubled, from a half million to over a million. The twin cities of Minneapolis and St. Paul tripled in size. New York City increased from a million to a million and a half; Detroit, Milwaukee, Columbus, and Cleveland grew by sixty to eighty per cent.

Municipal governments, however, were unprepared for this astonishing growth. Planning and budgeting were unknown arts. City charters had restrictive provisions envisaged for much smaller, simpler communities. The mayor and the important commissioners were usually amateurs serving a term or two as a civic duty. Authority was dispersed among numerous boards and special agencies. A typical city would have a board of police commissioners, a board of health, a board of tax assessors, a water board, and many others. The ostensible governing body was a city council or board of aldermen which might have thirty, fifty, or even a hundred members. Under these circumstances, it was difficult to get a prompt decision, harder still to co-ordinate decisions taken by different bodies acting on different premises, and easy for delays and anomalies to develop.

In theory, the cities could have met their need for increased services by municipal socialism, but the conventional wisdom condemned that as too radical, although here and there a city did experiment with publicly owned utilities. In theory also, the cities could have financed public buildings and huge projects such as water and sewer systems by frankly raising taxes or floating bonds. But both taxes and debt were no more popular then than they are now. Moreover, the laissez-faire doctrine which holds that "that government is best which governs least" was enshrined orthodoxy in America from the 1870's down to the 1930's.

As men clung to such orthodox philosophies, the structures of government became obsolete; they strained to meet unexpected demands as a swelling number of citizens in every class clamored for more services. In this climate the bosses emerged. They had no scruples about taking shortcuts through old procedures or manipulating independent boards and agencies in ways that the original city fathers had never intended. They had no inhibiting commitment to any theory of limited government. They were willing to spend, tax, and build—and to take the opprobrium along with the graft. Sometimes, like Hague in Jersey City, Curley in Boston, and Big Bill Thompson in Chicago, they got themselves elected mayor and openly assumed responsibility. More often, like Pendergast in Kansas City, Cox in Cincinnati, the leaders of Tammany, and the successive Republican bosses of Philadelphia, they held minor offices or none, stayed out of the limelight, and ran city government through their iron control of the party organization. In ruling Memphis for forty years, Ed Crump followed one pattern and then the other. Impeached on a technicality after being elected three times as mayor, Crump retreated to the back rooms and became even more powerful as the city's political boss.

What manner of men became political bosses? They were men of little education and no social background, often of immigrant parentage. A college-educated boss like Edward Flynn of The Bronx was a rarity. Bosses often began as saloonkeepers, because the saloon was a natural meeting place in poorer neighborhoods in the days before Prohibition. They were physically strong and no strangers to violence. Seventy-five years ago, most men made their living with brawn rather than brain, and a man who expected to be a leader of men had to be tough as well as shrewd. Open violence used to be common at polling places on Election Day, and gangs of repeaters roamed from one precinct to another. Although the typical boss made his way up through that roughneck system, the logic of his career led him to suppress violence. Bloody heads make bad publicity, and it is hard for any political organization to maintain a monopoly on violence. Bosses grew to prefer quieter, more lawful, less dangerous methods of control. Ballot-box stuffing and overt intimidation never disappeared entirely, but gradually they receded to the status of weapons of last resort.

Political bosses varied in their idiosyncrasies and styles. A few, like Curley, became polished orators; others, like the legendary Charles Murphy of Tammany Hall, never made speeches. They were temperate, businesslike types; among them a drunk was as rare as a Phi Beta Kappa. If they had a generic failing it was for horses and gambling. Essentially they were hardheaded men of executive temper and genuine organizing talents; many, in other circumstances and with more education, might have become successful businessmen.

They have disappeared now, most of them. Education has produced a more sophisticated electorate; it has also encouraged potential bosses to turn away from politics toward more secure, prestigious, and profitable careers. A young man who had the energy, persistence, and skill in 1899 to become a successful political boss would in 1969 go to college and end up in an executive suite.

The urban population has also changed. The great flood of bewildered foreigners has dwindled to a trickle. In place of the European immigrants of the past, today's cities receive an influx of Negroes from the rural South, Puerto Ricans, Mexicans, and the white poor from Appalachia. As they overcome the language barrier and widen their experience, the Puerto Ricans are making themselves felt in urban politics. New York City, where they are most heavily concentrated, may have a Puerto Rican mayor in the not too distant future.

But the other groups are too isolated from the rest of the community to put together a winning political coalition of have-nots. The Mexicans and the ex-hill-billies from Appalachia are isolated by their unique cultural backgrounds, the Negroes by the giant fact of their race. Inasmuch as they make up a quarter to a third of the population in many cities, are a cohesive group, and still have a high proportion of poor who have to look to government for direct help, the Negroes might have produced several bosses and functioning political machines had they been of white European ancestry. But until Negroes attain a clear numerical majority, they find it difficult to take political power in any city because various white factions are reluctant to coalesce with them.

Regardless of the race or background of the voters,

however, there are factors which work against the old-style machines. Civil service regulations make it harder to create a job or pad a payroll. Federal income taxes and federal accounting requirements make it more difficult to hide the rewards of graft. Television, public relations, and polling have created a whole new set of political techniques and undermined the personal ties and neighborhood loyalties on which the old organizations depended.

The new political style has brought an increase in municipal government efficiency and probably some decline in political corruption and misrule. But the politics of the television age puts a premium on hypocrisy. Candor has gone out the window with the spoils system. There is still a lot of self-seeking in politics and always will be. But gone are the days of Tammany's Boss Richard Croker, who when asked by an investigating committee if he was "working for his own pocket," shot back: "All the time—same as you." Today's politicians are so busy tending their images that they have become incapable of even a mildly derogatory remark such as Jim Curley's: "The term 'codfish aristocracy' is a reflection on the fish."

Curley entitled his memoirs *I'd Do It Again*. But the rough-and-tumble days when two-fisted, rough-tongued politicians came roaring out of the slums to take charge of America's young cities are not to come again.

THE GREAT PULLMAN STRIKE!

GERALD G. EGGERT

Gerald G. Eggert, an associate professor at the Pennsylvania State University, teaches American economic and labor history. For further reading, see Stanley Buder, "Pullman: An Experiment in Industrial Order and Community Planning, 1880-1930" (New York, 1967); Almont Lindsey, "The Pullman Strike" (Chicago, 1942); and the author's own "Railway Labor Disputes: The Beginnings of Federal Strike Policy" (Ann Arbor, 1967).

GEORGE MORTIMER PULLMAN, railroad sleeping car magnate, believed it possible to make high profits and at the same time provide his employees with pleasant, modern living conditions. So, in the 1880's he built a model community south of Chicago. There he located his car-building and repair shops and housed most of his employees and their families. Generously sharing his name with the town, Pullman provided his "children" — as he called them — with neat, company-owned houses set among well tended lawns and flower gardens. The town boasted a park, an artificial lake, a covered shopping arcade, a handsome church, a theater which seated a thousand, a modern school with playground, an elegant hotel, and a library. Pullman designed his town to offer hous-

From *American History Illustrated*, April 1971. Reproduced through the courtesy of The National Historical Society, publishers of AMERICAN HISTORY *Illustrated*, 206 Hanover Street, Gettysburg, Pa. 17325. Published 10 times a year.

The first meat train leaving the Chicago stockyards under escort of United States cavalry, July 10, 1894. (Coll. of LC)

ing of "character" in attractive surroundings, free from such "baneful influences" as saloons and brothels, so as to attract the "best class of mechanics" to his shops. In his community he expected workers to be contented and loyal. He also believed the town would provide them with the means to elevate and improve themselves and their children.

Pullman intended his model community to be completely self-supporting and eventually to repay the company's investment with interest. Consequently, rents in Pullman averaged 20 to 25 percent above those in nearby communities. Charges levied on the church, the arcade shops, and the theater aimed at bringing in an annual 6 percent profit. Memberships in the "public" library cost adults three dollars and children one dollar a year. Much of the produce sold at the arcade was grown on a company-owned farm which used the town's sewage for fertilizer and returned a handsome 8 percent each year to the company. In sum,

the model community, though company-dominated, was well planned, efficiently managed, attractive to most of its residents — and profitable to George M. Pullman.

Economic panic swept the Nation in 1893, creating tensions in both the Pullman shops and the model town. Although business declined sharply, Pullman determined that the 8 percent annual dividend paid on the company's stock should remain unchanged. He had made provision: Over the years the company had accumulated a profits reserve of $25,000,000 for just such contingencies. Even the salaries of company managers and foremen remained unaffected by depression. But Pullman could not protect everyone. The rank and file of his employees had to bear the brunt of necessary economies, including lower wage rates and reduced hours of employment. Wisdom might have suggested that *all* employees share the burden. The company did accept orders at a loss to provide as much work as possible, and it juggled job assignments so as to keep most employees earning something, however

The town of Pullman, looking east from the depot along the boulevard. From a photograph by F. W. Taylor. (Andrews' "The History of the Last Quarter-Century in the United States")

little. Pullman regarded these measures as generous and humanitarian. His employees saw them as devices to keep them paying the high rents which remained unchanged for company housing. Under these stresses Pullman's paternalistic experiment quickly soured.

IN early 1894 Pullman's "children" organized and affiliated with a new labor organization, the American Railway Union. On May 9 a union committee called on the employer-landlord to demand that wages be restored to the level of a year ago or that rents be lowered. Pullman replied that the company was not earning what it should, that both wages and rents were determined by supply and demand — not by his whim, and that the operations of the shops and town were completely separate. Technically this was true. The town was operated by a different corporation but in fact the same people owned and managed both.

The next morning three members of the committee were told there was no work for them that day. Assuming that the men were being eased out as punishment, the union called a strike. When the employees overwhelmingly responded, Pullman closed down. In the war of attrition that followed there was no violence and the employees won widespread sympathy. There was little doubt, however, as to which side would best be able to outlast the other. Unless the men got powerful outside assistance their strike was doomed.

EUGENE VICTOR DEBS for twenty years belonged to the Brotherhood of Locomotive Firemen and for fourteen years edited its national magazine. He watched his union suffer repeated defeats at the hands of the powerful railway companies. Particularly distressing to him was the lack of true brotherhood among railroad employees. Skilled trainmen — if union members — belonged to one of several brotherhoods according to their functions as engineers, firemen, brakemen, conductors, or switchmen. The mass of unskilled workmen remained unorganized except for a few who belonged to the Knights of Labor. Whenever one of these organizations got into a dispute with the companies, the others ignored the troubles and continued working, or joined in the strike, or supplied strikebreakers to the companies as self-interest seemed to dictate. Employee disunity provided the corporations with a potent weapon for winning strikes.

In 1893 Debs founded the American Railway Union on the principle of bringing together in a single organization all railroad employees whatever their task, skill, or function. With all railwaymen in the same union, he believed, the companies would not dare oppose their demands. Not only would the employees of a given company act in complete unison, but trained railwaymen from outside would not "scab" on their fellow unionists. Since Debs also naively believed workmen would never ask for more than simple justice, he predicted a quick end to strikes on railroads.

Deb's new union was not a year old when its testing began. In April 1894 it refused to support a wage cut ordered by the management of the Great Northern Railway. Despite the growing depression the ARU called a strike, completely paralyzed the line west of Minneapolis, and won most of its demands when the beleaguered company agreed to arbitration. Debs, who counselled no violence and carefully avoided tying up the mails, had brought the ARU through to victory. Railway workers across the land rushed to join the successful union, swelling its membership to perhaps 150,000. Four weeks after its first triumph, the organization held a national convention in Chicago.

Among the delegates were representatives from nearby Pullman. The group eloquently pleaded its case: "It is victory or death . . . to you we confide our cause . . . do not desert us as you hope not to be deserted." Delegates talked of an ARU boycott of all Pullman cars. Debs preferred to avoid a contest with the railroad companies who would be expected to resist any such boycott. Instead he suggested sending a delegation of ARU members, including Pullman employees, to the company to urge arbitration of the dispute. Company officials declined to

George M. Pullman. Though he was in general a benevolent employer, his workmen struck against him when wages failed to balance living expenses in his model community. (Coll. of LC)

discuss corporation affairs with outsiders. A second delegation, all of whom were Pullman employees, went to the same officials and were told that Mr. Pullman found nothing to arbitrate.

DEBS now faced a dilemma. The convention demanded action and would not abandon the struggling strikers from Pullman. Remembering their recent victory over the Great Northern, many were confident that the sleeping car magnate could be forced to terms. Debs was less certain. Strikes and boycotts in times of widespread unemployment were extremely risky. The young union was still relatively weak. The combined power of the Pullman Company and the Nation's railroad corporations was immense. Boycotting was of

dubious legality at best. Several states prohibited the practice outright and although no Federal statute explicitly outlawed boycotts, Federal courts in recent years had consistently enjoined them as illegal restraint of interstate commerce. A testing of these rulings might well be in order, but wisdom suggested that this was not the right time. Debs and the ARU, however, saw no alternative to boycotting except destruction of their organization. If the ARU would not assist the strikers at Pullman, could it be counted on by any of its members in time of trouble?

The convention finally resolved that if Pullman did not agree to arbitration by noon on June 26, no ARU member on any railroad line in the country would handle Pullman sleepers. Such cars would either be cut off or the trains pulling them would not be moved. The conduct of the boycott was left to Debs and other union officers, and with this decision the convention adjourned.

Debs and his associates faced a powerful, well-organized foe. The twenty-four railroad companies with terminals in Chicago included such giants as the Baltimore & Ohio, the Burlington, the Chicago & Northwestern, the Erie, the Illinois Central, the New York Central, the Pennsylvania, the Rock Island, and the Santa Fe. Their combined capitalization exceeded two billion dollars, their net earnings for the fiscal year just ended were in excess of 100 million dollars, they operated over 40,000 miles of track and employed some 220,000 men only a portion of whom were ARU members.

SOME years earlier the Chicago railroads had established an organization — the General Managers Association — for handling common problems. The GMA, among other things, fixed charges for switching, arranged loading and unloading schedules, and set common freight and passenger rates. It also dealt with railway labor problems, establishing uniform wage rates in the Chicago area.

As soon as the ARU announced its boycott, the GMA undertook countermeasures. Meeting daily throughout the crisis, the organization supplied unified

Eugene V. Debs, founder of the American Railway Union. He faced his first great test in the general strike of 1894. (LC)

leadership for the companies. At their first meeting the General Managers — a Pullman Company vice president at their side — agreed to fight the boycott. In a public statement they declared that they would not inconvenience their customers by denying them customary Pullman accommodations. The contracts under which they leased sleeping cars, they noted, obligated them to run the cars as usual or face damage suits. Finally, they added, they would not permit a labor leader, unrecognized by any of them, to dictate the make-up of their trains. They might have added — but did not — that they welcomed the opportunity to weaken or destroy the ARU. As one GMA official later testified, the companies got along very well with the existing brotherhoods and "saw no need" for a new industry-wide union which, in time, might challenge their authority.

The GMA promptly named a chairman to act as official spokesman. It authorized a standing committee to recruit strikebreakers from outside the Chicago area. The cost of fighting the ARU, it decided, would be borne equally by all member companies and it appointed a legal committee to institute actions in the courts. Looking on the boycott as essentially a managerial problem, the GMA determined to crush it by simple discipline. Any employee who refused to move cars or trains as ordered would be discharged.

Debs and his union responded by striking every line that fired ARU members. Within a few days, except in New England and the South, the Nation's railways

ground to a halt. Carloads of perishables stood hour after hour spoiling in the July sun. Passenger trains, with or without Pullman cars and whether or not carrying mail, were blocked by abandoned freights. In part because of the strike's effectiveness and in part to win public support, the companies began to refuse freight and passengers and to discontinue the regular movement of mail. Debs's offer to allow mail and emergency supplies to pass unmolested was rejected.

Almost immediately prices of meat, eggs, dairy products, and fresh fruit and vegetables rose noticeably in Chicago and in Eastern cities. Arrivals at the Chicago stockyards for the week of July 3 to 10 fell from the usual 60,000 cattle, 6,000 calves, 113,000 hogs, and 55,000 sheep to 242 cattle, 5 calves, 19 hogs, and 9,000 sheep — the latter arriving on hoof. The Nation clearly faced a national emergency. The companies probably could have outlasted the strikers and won had the strike dragged on through the summer. The public, meanwhile, would have been severely pinched for necessities. Before that happened the Federal Government intervened decisively — not to resolve the dispute but to put down the strike.

RICHARD OLNEY, Attorney General of the United States, had entered President Cleveland's second-term cabinet in 1893 with a problem. One of Boston's leading railroad lawyers, for years he served as a director and counsel of the Boston & Maine (George M. Pullman was a fellow director), and of the Boston-dominated Burlington Railroad. He was also adviser on railway matters to Benjamin P. Cheney, a director of the Santa Fe. Having no firm or partners to carry on for him, Olney feared his stint in Washington might weaken or destroy his practice. He eventually solved the problem by simply continuing to serve his leading clients. The $2,500 paid him each quarter by the Burlington alone exceeded the $8,000 salary he drew as Attorney General.

Olney violated no law, but the ethics of his arrangement were questionable. Once the Government intervened in the great strike, he found himself caught up in a flagrant conflict of interests. It seems probable, given his earlier career, the Olney would have reacted no differently to the boycott-strike had he severed all his ties to the railroads before entering public office.

Throughout the spring of 1894, Olney fought troubles on the railroads. In April, swarms of unemployed workmen in the Far West stole trains and headed them eastward. Their goal was to participate in Coxey's celebrated march on Washington to demand jobs for men needing work. The President refused to use the Army on his own authority to halt these thefts. Since most of the lines affected were in receivership, Olney, working with railroad attorneys and Federal judges, obtained injunctions prohibiting the seizure of trains that technically were property of the courts. When Coxeyites defied the injunctions and commandeered trains, the judges called upon the President for assistance. He in turn dispatched troops to enforce the orders of the courts. In May, during the Great Northern strike, the Department of Justice was asked to give a legal definition of "mail train." It ruled that *every* car which a railroad company put on a mail-carrying train was lawfully part of the mail train and as such entitled to Federal protection. Both the injunctions and the definition served Olney as useful precedents in putting down the boycott-strike in July.

When word of the pending boycott reached Washington in late June, Olney moved to thwart it. Only passenger trains had Pullman cars attached and only passenger trains carried mail. Thanks to the recent definition, the Federal Government could protect Pullman cars on passenger trains so long as the trains carried mail. Had the boycott remained a mere boycott, this tactic might have checked Debs and the ARU since they were reluctant to do battle with the Government.

BUT the boycott quickly developed into a general railway strike and protecting mail trains was not enough. Interstate commerce, too, needed unblocking. In the absence of laws against such strikes, railroad lawyers and Federal attorneys in strike-bound areas urged Olney to seek injunctions based on the Sherman Antitrust Act. Although that law originally aimed at breaking up business combinations, its prohibition against conspiracies to restrain interstate commerce could easily be stretched to cover railway strikes.

Olney wanted injunctions, but hesitated to base them on a law he regarded as of dubious constitutionality. Worsening conditions forced his hand, however, and he permitted Federal attorneys to petition for injunctions on the grounds they desired. Some people believed that court orders of themselves would end the difficulties. Olney thought not. Certain that the injunctions would be defied, he planned to use the defiance to justify sending overwhelming force to crush the strike.

On July 2, when the Federal marshal from Chicago read an injunction to a mob of 2,000 who were blocking trains at Blue Island, Illinois he was hooted and jeered. "To hell with the Government!" "To hell with the President!" "To hell with the court and injunctions!" Although the mob dispersed later that afternoon, Federal officials in Chicago the next day cited the incident as proof of the need for troops. When the telegram from Chicago, signed by two Federal attorneys, the marshal, and the judge who issued the injunction, arrived in Washington, Cleveland ordered out the troops. "We have been brought to the ragged edge of anarchy," Olney told the press, "and it is time

to see whether the law is sufficiently strong to prevent this condition of affairs." The boycott-strike no longer involved "Pullmanism" or "railroadism," he declared. It was now "a question between the American Railway Union and the Federal Government."

Governor John Peter Altgeld of Illinois vigorously protested the uninvited presence of the Army in his state's leading city. The move, he wired the President, was unnecessary since he was prepared to call out the militia when needed. The act was an unconstitutional violation of state rights, he charged. President Cleveland replied that the Army was in Illinois to enforce Federal laws and Federal court orders and needed neither requests nor permission from state officials. On the other hand, he added curtly, maintaining law and order in Illinois was Altgeld's responsibility and he urged him to see to it.

GENERAL NELSON A. MILES, commander of the forces sent to Chicago, was on vacation when the President's order arrived. Summoned to the White House, his surprising questions unnerved both Cleveland and Attorney General Olney. Miles wavered between great sympathy for the working classes and fear that if not suppressed, their anarchical doctrines and behavior would lead to bloody revolution. When placed in command, he asked if he was to go to Chicago in person. The President, taken aback, replied that he thought the general would want to be with his troops. Miles then asked whether he was to order his men to fire on rioters. Flustered, Cleveland said that

Attorney General Richard Olney was caught in a conflict of interests when the strike became wide-spread. He was serving both the Government and private railroads. (Coll. of LC)

only the person in immediate command in a given instance could make such a decision. Since Miles, who had distinguished himself in the Indian wars, did not lack courage, his strange queries may have stemmed from his political ambitions. Interested — someday — in high elective office, he apparently feared that an order to fire on citizens would be remembered and held against him.

Once in Chicago, Miles scattered his forces, sending out small detachments to support peace officers throughout the area. "Owing to the excellent discipline and great forbearance of officers and men," he cheerily reported to Washington on July 5, "serious hostilities were avoided today." Olney, according to rumor, was furious. "If Miles would do less talking to newspapers and more shooting at strikers," he said, "he would come nearer to fulfilling his mission on earth and earning his pay." Orders from Washington directed Miles to concentrate his men for forays against major demonstrations and to fire on civilians if necessary when orders to disperse were ignored.

Violence in Chicago and across the nation had been light prior to the arrival of the Army. Tensions mounted on July 4 and 5, however, and mobs — only a small portion of whom were strikers — became more aggressive. On the 6th over $340,000 worth of railroad property was burned (by contrast no more than $4,000 damage was done on any other single day of the strike) and Governor Altgeld rushed militiamen into the city. The most important skirmish occurred on July 7 when a confrontation between the Illinois guard and rioters resulted in bloodshed.

In the Chicago area alone, nearly 2,000 soldiers, 4,000 state militia, 5,000 Federal marshals, and 3,000 policemen were used to restore order and reopen the railroads. In the course of the disorders 12 civilians were fatally wounded, 515 were arrested, and 71 brought to trial for various offenses. In the Nation at large, troops — both state and Federal — and United States marshals quelled riots, broke up mobs, and freed blocked trains. By mid-July the strike was quashed. Once the strong arm of the military completed its work, the courts resumed sway and vindicated the undertaking.

EDWIN WALKER, like General Miles, was out of town when Attorney General Olney asked him to take charge of the Government's legal action in Chicago. Unlike the general, he relished his assignment. For twenty-five years Walker had been counsel in Illinois for the Chicago, Milwaukee & St. Paul Railroad (one of the lines affected by the strike) and his law partner was on the GMA's legal committee. The appointment of an attorney so close to the railroads raised eyebrows all around. "The Government might with as good grace have appointed the attorney for the Amer-ican Railway Union to represent the United States," commented Clarence Darrow, one of Debs's lawyers.

Walker worked quietly behind the scenes. Conferring openly with the GMA and secretly with Federal judges, he perfected the petition for the Chicago injunction and built up the case against Debs. He instituted civil proceedings against the ARU leader for contempt in defying the injunction, and criminal conspiracy charges before a grand jury. Eventually Debs was tried on both counts. Walker worked slowly, more concerned with final results than quick expedients. The strike over, he reported to Olney in late July that he had secured postponement of proceedings until September. "The heat was really stifling," he complained, "and the crowd of strikers present at the hearing made the air of the room intolerable." The advantage of delay, he pointed out, was that the rapidly crumbling ARU would disappear by autumn.

Walker's argument in the contempt case was completely successful, he reported to Olney. The court's decision would be delayed, however, because the judge realized fully "that not only your Department but also those representing the business interests of the entire country regard this case as a most important case." From what the judge told him, Walker inferred that the opinion would be "very carefully prepared" as the judge "evidently regards this as his opportunity."

Finding Debs guilty, the court sentenced him to six months in jail. The propriety of the injunction, which Debs's lawyers contested, the court held was fully justified under the Sherman Act. Olney was not pleased. The judge had "decided rightly enough, but upon the wrong ground." When the Attorney General himself argued the case on appeal before the Supreme Court, he completely shifted the Government's grounds. The Court must not believe that the injunction rested upon "the novel provisions of an experimental piece of legislation," he declared. The constitutional duty of the Government to regulate interstate commerce — not the Sherman Act — justified the injunction. A unanimous court upheld Olney's contentions.

Walker, meanwhile, pressed the criminal case against Debs. Darrow, Debs's attorney, skillfully turned the charge of conspiracy against the railroads and the Justice Department and called for the secret minutes of the GMA to prove his case. The minutes were produced on the judge's order, but neither Darrow nor Debs nor the jury saw them. The next day a juror fell ill and the trial was delayed. After repeated postponements the jury was dismissed. According to Debs, the jurymen crowded around him to say that so far as the matter had progressed they were convinced of his innocence.

Walker denied the story and urged Olney to authorize a new trial. "Of course, we have to take our chances with the jury," he admitted, "but certainly a mistrial will be better than dismissal of the case." Olney, satisfied with the outcome of the previous litigation, did not agree and a year later the criminal proceedings were quietly dropped.

THE great strike wrought many changes. George Pullman, embittered at the calumny heaped upon him and his model community, died in 1897. The town of Pullman was separated by court order from the Pullman Company and soon was barely distinguishable from the other drab suburban communities south of Chicago. Debs, his union fast dying, abandoned faith in the capitalistic order. By 1900 he was a leader in the Socialist party and five times was his party's candidate for President. Darrow, his lawyer, from 1894 on won fame as a pleader of unpopular causes.

Olney, at strike's end, stopped his salary from the Burlington, but remained on the company's board of directors. In November he publicly defended the right of railway employees to belong to labor unions and in early 1895 helped frame legislation providing for the voluntary arbitration of railway labor disputes under Government auspices. Completely winning President Cleveland's confidence, he became Secretary of State in June 1895, and returned to his lucrative private practice at the end of the term in 1897.

A commission appointed by President Cleveland at the end of the strike estimated the losses of the railroad companies at $5,360,000. The strikers — at the Pullman Company and on the railroads — lost $1,750,-000 in wages. Gradually the Pullman shops resumed operation and former employees, including strikers, were given preference in hiring provided only that they renounce membership in the ARU. Of the 2,700 men hired, all but 800 were old hands. Perhaps a thousand men continued the futile strike but in time were driven by necessity to find jobs in other communities. A few die-hards were eventually rehired at Pullman as openings developed. Work was no longer spread, so all employees had full-time jobs. Rent rates remained unchanged but the company made little effort to collect back rents totalling approximately $100,000.

The railroad companies, though threatening vengeance, for the most part also rehired their former employees. Only men who played too prominent a

General Nelson A. Miles, leader of the Federal troops sent to restore order in Chicago during the railroad strike. (LC)

part in the strike or were thought to be troublemakers were not re-employed. Of the tens of thousands who went out on strike only a few thousand were blacklisted and forced to seek work in other industries.

Altgeld, denouncing "government by injunction," led the attack on the Cleveland Administration at the 1896 Democratic Convention. There the party repudiated its own head and turned to William Jennings Bryan and Free Silver. General Miles, unscathed by the strike and enhanced in reputation by the Spanish-American War, savored running for President in 1900, but failed to develop a following. Edwin Walker returned briefly to private practice before retiring, and lived on till 1910.

Despite the effectiveness of the weapons forged against railway tie-ups during the strike, there were few opportunities to employ them again. Railwaymen, knowing what would happen, hesitated to strike en masse. The companies learned to work with the brotherhoods and increasingly use collective bargaining to solve labor problems. And the Government, ever reluctant to use such harsh measures, thereafter resorted to railway reform legislation whenever new crises arose.

THE CASE OF THE VERY AMERICAN MILITANTS

Notes on the IWW as a Product and a Reflection of Mainstream America

JOSEPH R. CONLIN

Joseph R. Conlin *is associate professor of history at Chico State College, Chico, California. He is author of* Bread and Roses, Too: Essays on the Wobblies *(1969);* Big Bill Haywood and the Radical Movement *(1969); and* American Antiwar Movements *(1968); and is presently collaborating with G. D. Lillibridge on* The American Experience, *to be published by Houghton Mifflin. His articles have appeared in* Studies on the Left; *the* Wisconsin Magazine of History; Science and Society; *and the* Pacific Northwest Quarterly.

T HE IWW is one of those historical phenomena about which almost everyone can rattle off an anecdote but which no one seems to understand fully. It is not that the facts are scarce. The outline of the Wobblies' story is simple enough. The union—the Industrial Workers of the World—was founded in Chicago in 1905 by a group of seasoned labor leaders and socialists. They were men who were discontented with the social conservatism of the American Federation of Labor, exemplified by Samuel Gompers' acceptance of capitalism as the ultimate economic structure of the United States. And they deplored the craft structure of the AFL as obsolete and devisive. Unfortunately, the founding fathers agreed on little else, and within a few months of its first convention, the IWW was enmeshed in factional infighting which twice split the tiny union and threatened to ruin it completely.

Somehow the IWW survived its quarrelling, and in 1909 prospects brightened. Beginning that year, the Wobblies led several dramatic and often successful strikes in eastern industrial cities. The most sensational occurred in Lawrence, Massachusetts, in early 1912, with the Wobblies wrestling a united and firmly-entrenched woolens industry to the mat. At about the same time, a series of well-publicized "Free Speech Fights" in West Coast cities, where the region's army of casual laborers passed their winters, put the IWW on the front pages and won them thousands of supporters (and enemies).

The Wobblies never quite capitalized on their eastern successes but, through the Agricultural Workers' Organization (AWO), flourished into the 1920s among the transient workers in the agricultural, construction, and lumber industries of the developing West. The union soon earned the enmity of large-scale commercial interests, newspapers, politicians, and middle-class patriotic groups, but it also had a large following due to its effective "job delegate" system of organization. Perhaps as many as five thousand unsalaried organizers followed and worked the harvests like the casual laborers they were, and organized the bindle stiffs on the job. The AWO quickly became the largest single component of the IWW and aspired to establish itself as a viable representative of the migrant workers. Those hopes were dashed. World War I intervened, and state and federal governments vied with one another to prosecute the nominally antiwar IWW into impotence. The union's leaders were imprisoned, and with the tolerated assistance of extralegal mobs, the membership was dispersed.

Ironically, it was the success of another group of revolutionaries, the Russian Bolsheviks, which sealed the IWW's fate. "The Red Dawn in the East" blinded American radicals to the unique characteristics of their own situation and diverted their energies into channels irrelevant to American conditions. By the mid-1920s the IWW had declined into a tiny cult, a state in which it survives today.

From a historical point of view the IWW has fallen victim to distortions based upon the assumption that the union was no more than an aberration. It is variously portrayed as dangerously antipathetic to American traditions, ineffective because of its extreme alienation from the greater society, or inconsequential—just a colorful ragtag bunch of poetic visionaries in a hard-nosed, practical country.

Each of these arguments has its germs of validity, but it seems a more profitable approach to the study of the IWW to show that the Wobblies were in reality more *like* than *unlike* their conventional contemporaries. The Wobblies were, after all, molded and formed by the same forces which acted in some degree upon the whole of American society. Another look at them, with emphasis on the values which they held in common with early twentieth-century Americans rather than on their differences, will reveal that the IWW moved with the American mainstream at least as often as it bucked the current.

The IWW has been classed as an aberrant movement because of charges that it sanctioned violence and sabotage, scorned political action, and violated the nation's commitment to democratic political process. Finally, the IWW has been characterized as un-American, an alien ideological import into a pragmatic country. The final point requires the least comment. With the exception of a few Italian leaders during the union's brief era in the industrial East, the IWW was headed throughout its history by natives bred in an unmistakably American milieu. The most famous of them, William D. "Big Bill" Haywood, might have sneered that his family was "so American that if traced back it would probably run to the Puritan bigots or the Cavalier pirates," but he saw fit to note his ancestry anyway. Other Wobbly leaders sported similar genealogies and for historical corroboration constantly looked to such American precedents as the Revolution, John Brown, Abraham Lincoln, and even Frederick Jackson Turner, rather than to a European revolutionary tradition. Few Wobbly membership lists survive, but police records of mass arrests of Wobblies on the West Coast shortly after 1910 show a ratio between native and foreign-born comparable to a cross-section of the region's population.

The Wobblies' reputation for violence is scarcely more valid. Former Wobbly Ralph Chaplin was correct when he blamed the interpretation of the IWW as "a conspiracy of alien arsonists and dynamiters" on historians who used the "hysterical newspaper headlines of the day as source material." As Richard Brazier, another old Wobbly, wrote, "The IWW, of course, never did have a 'good press' and we were more or less accustomed to being made the whipping boys for something we knew nothing about." A contemporary student of the IWW, sociologist Carlton Parker, observed that "some important portion of IWW terrors can be traced directly to the inarticulated public demand that the IWW news story produce a thrill." But whatever the source of the image, it was and remains a canard. Far from advocating violence, the IWW felt that violence was unnecessary and destructive to its cause. The Wobblies repeatedly urged prudence upon impulsive members and, on numerous occasions, acted positively to avert incidents. When, in January, 1909, a crowd of several thousand men threatened to attack an employment agency in Spokane, a Wobbly leader arrived just in time to cool the mob and invite it to a discussion meeting at the Wobbly Hall. There he persuaded them that *agents provocateurs* in their midst were egging them on in an effort to provide an excuse for police intervention.

The IWW did preach sabotage but defined it in terms considerably different than did the sensationalist press. Actual damage to property was one form of sabotage, the IWW admitted, but it was also the one form which the IWW shunned. (When a Wobbly paper in Spokane obliquely hinted at the violent variety in 1912, it was suspended by the national office.) The word *sabotage* derives from the French *sabots,* the clumsy wooden shoes worn by the peasants who often worked as strikebreakers. Due to their inexperience, their work was notoriously inefficient, so the French unions called upon the workers to return to their factories and work as if they were wearing *sabots* until the bosses caved in. In less connotative terms, then, sabotage was a slowdown. The Wobblies' notion of sabotage followed this definition and consisted of "striking on the job," a withdrawal of efficiency which hurt the boss "where it hurts him the most, in his

Free Speech Fights had predictable formats: street speakers berated exploitive employers, who then forced the passage and vigorous enforcement of antisoapbox ordinances. The implementation of San Diego's Ordinance No. 4660 is shown above in the Industrial Worker.

pocketbook." Another variety was *la bouche ouverte,* the "big mouth." Waiters should tell diners of their employers' chicanery in the kitchen; clerks should truthfully answer questions about inferior merchandise; and so on. John Graham described this "exact truth telling" as "delicate cruelty," but it is difficult to share his indignation.

In political America, the Wobblies are often adjudged alien to the system because of their disinterest in exerting power and effecting changes through democratic and parliamentary political procedures. It is true that the IWW as an organization, and particularly the western branch, was uninterested in political action. But this state of affairs derived less from any alienation from American traditions than from the simple reality that most western Wobblies could not vote. They were migrant workers, the nature of whose lives made them homeless men and placed them outside the political system. They could not meet the most liberal residency requirements for voting. Thus, there was no hope of using the ballot to repeal the anti-IWW ordinances in Spokane, San Diego, and a dozen other western cities.

Like most policies deriving from specific conditions, however, Wobbly nonpoliticalism varied with local circumstances. For example, the IWW and the strictly political Socialist Party in the Northwest sometimes used the same persons as their delegates; apparently the memberships overlapped. In Butte, Montana, where members of the IWW were sedentary copper miners or smelter workers rather than migrants, they apparently voted in great numbers. These Wobbly votes were likely responsible for the election of Mayor Lewis Duncan's Socialist administration in April, 1911, for after the Socialist Party repudiated the IWW, Duncan failed to be reelected in an easier contest.

But the proof of the IWW's commonality with early twentieth-century American society ultimately depends, not upon correcting the union's historical image, but upon the nature of its positive acts. The IWW's Free Speech Fights have generally been the property of the romanticizers. Between 1909, when the Wobblies first employed the tactic in Missoula, Montana, and 1916, when they abandoned the policy, the IWW staged its battles in twenty-six cities, principally in Washington, Oregon, and California. The pattern of the fights varied little from city to city. The usual precipitant was a Wobbly street-speaking campaign focused on a specific issue, often the corrupt practices of the employment agencies which casual laborers frequented. City councils responded to agency pressures with ordinances prohibiting soapbox speaking. The Los Angeles ordinance was typical:

It shall be unlawful for any person to discuss, expound, advocate, or oppose the principles or creed of any political party, partisan body, or organization, or religious denomination or sect, or *the doctrines* of any *economic* or social system in any public speech, lecture, or discourse, made or delivered in any public park in the City of Los Angeles.

The ordinances were clearly aimed at the IWW. Spokane's law exempted the Salvation Army, the only other organization much involved in street speaking. San Diego's ban was restricted to the tenderloin district, where the casual laborers congregated. And when President Taft visited Spokane during the dispute over the ordinance and spoke on the streets, a Wobbly commented sardonically:

The law. The law must be upheld. Taft can speak on the street, and pack it for blocks—yes, so tight that workmen could not get home to their dinner. He was not put in the sweat box. He was not even arrested, although the ordinance was in effect at the time. . . . Taft held up a bundle of papers and said, "This was handed me by the Chamber of Commerce, and you will have to stand for it." As it was impossible to move for two hours, we stood for it. The *Spokesman-Review* says the people don't want to have the revolutionary harangues of the IWW speakers rammed down their throats. Hundreds of people did not want the harangue of the Chamber of Commerce rammed down their throats by Taft, but they had to stand for it.

But the IWW did not "stand for it." They deliberately defied the law with the object of packing the jails beyond the city's resources to maintain them and clogging the judicial process by demanding individual trials, thus shifting the burden of enforcement from the violator to the enforcer. It was civil disobedience of the sort made famous by the civil rights demonstrators of the early 1960s.

In Missoula, where authorities were flabbergasted by the cheerful lawbreakers, the Wobblies won an easy victory. In Spokane and other cities, things were more difficult. Authorities attempted to meet mass violations with mass arrests (103 soapboxers were arrested on the first day of the Spokane fight, 500 within a month) and by torture within the city jails. Policemen beat the jailed Wobblies in Missoula. In Spokane thirty-six prisoners were forced into a Black Hole of Calcutta

The "Blanket Stiff"

He built the ROAD—
With others of his CLASS, he built the road,
Now o'er it, many a weary mile, he packs his load,
Chasing a JOB. spurred on by HUNGERS goad.
He walks and walks, and wonders why
In H——L, he built the road.

From the Industrial Worker, *April 23, 1910.*

so small that several policemen were required to close the door. Other Wobblies were moved alternately from a freezing to a steaming hot cell. In San Diego a mob kidnapped a Wobbly-sympathizer and mutilated him with lighted cigars. In Fresno men were beaten, hosed, and forced to stand knee-deep in water throughout a night.

Whether or not the IWW won its fights usually depended upon how much adverse publicity the town in question was willing to bear. Spokane's city council capitulated after the national press publicized the city's "barbarism" with lines such as a reporter's plaint that "if men had murdered my own mother, I could not see them tortured as I saw IWW men tortured in the city jail." San Diego's city fathers were sterner, and they put the Wobblies to rout.

The Free Speech Fights were certainly thrilling events, full of the color, drama, and little ironies that the Wobblies and their chroniclers were fond of. In order to pack the jails, it was necessary to place on the soapbox many Wobblies who were not polished speakers. In Spokane, one such Wobbly mounted the platform and began with the usual salutation,

"Friends and fellow workers—" This had been the signal for the police to move in and arrest the violator. But there was no policeman available, unfortunately for the unprepared Wobbly who, with a bad case of stage jitters, convulsed his audience by shouting, "Where are the cops?" The IWW solved this problem by assigning non-orators to read from the Constitution or the Declaration of Independence. In terms of propaganda, the practice carried with it the fringe benefit of having men put under arrest for reciting the basic law of the land. But nothing better illustrates the spirit in which the Wobblies carried out their serious business than a letter received in Spokane at the height of the battle:

> Ione, Ore., Jan. 7th, 1910
> FELLOW WORKER:
> A Demonstration was just held in Sheep Camp No. 1 there being three present, a herder and two dogs. The following resolutions were adopted:
> Resolved, That we send $10.00 for the free speech fight in Spokane.
> Yours for liberty,
> THOS. J. ANDERSON
> P.S.—Stay with it. I'm coming.—T. J. A.

The color surrounding the disputes is too vivid to ignore. But what, in essence, were the Free Speech Fights all about? They were certainly not revolutionary. They were joined to preserve—and to reassert on the local scene—a right which had a Constitutional amendment and a century of tradition behind it. The IWW's interest in street speaking was not even based primarily on a desire to preach revolution; they wanted the streets open for the purpose of organizing a union. "These fights were deemed necessary to organization," a Wobbly theorist wrote. "It was thought that without street meetings . . . the jobless, homeless, migratory workers could not be organized." The free-speechers in Missoula and Spokane sought to hold forth on a topic no more incendiary than the corruptions of the "job sharks," agencies which commonly defrauded casual laborers. In San Diego the Wobblies fought their battle in league with American Federation of Labor men, moderate Socialists, single-taxers, and liberals, none of whom were likely to condone anarchistic jeremiads. Hardly confrontations between wild-eyed nihilists and men of the golden mean, the IWW's Free Speech Fights might more accurately be described as disputes between defenders of traditional rights, and corrupt interests willing to trample them.

It also bears mention that the allegedly lawless IWW pursued its objectives within the spirit of the law. That is, although the union systematically violated the restrictive ordinances, it did so not with criminal intent but in order to test and repeal them, in much the same spirit as John Scopes defied the Tennessee antievolution law and the Schechter brothers the National Recovery Act. The IWW was not interested in lawbreaking as such but in demonstrating the injustice of the law through the witness of their imprisonment, and the infeasibility of the law through the disruption caused by its enforcement. If this is not the most desirable means of political expression in a stable society, neither is it antisocial. In view of the Wobblies' political impotence, it was their only alternative.

IS IT ABOUT TO STRIKE?

In 1910 trouble began to descend on Fresno by the thousands, as "footloose rebels" from all over America converged to test the ban on street speaking and fill the jails. This cartoon in the Industrial Worker *of October 1, 1910, hints at the gathering might of the IWW—and recalls with heavy-handed humor the Spokane victory in January of that year.*

The IWW affected a great deal of scorn for the law in its propaganda. Bill Haywood told a federal investigating commission that he had been plastered up with injunctions so often that he did not need a pair of pants. But in practice the IWW evinced a regard for keeping within the law which, if grudging, was also circumspect. A Washington State woman testified that she had heard speeches by every major Wobbly agitator in the region and had never heard one "advocate or teach crime." And injunction-beclothed Bill Haywood did not shy away from using the courts, injunctions, and esoteric writs of certiorari when he could benefit from them.

In view of the cynicism with which the Wobblies were prosecuted in so many of their cases, it is likely that the IWW had a more promising vision of the law than its enforcers. In fact, quite out of keeping with the reputation for recalcitrance foisted upon the Wobblies by their enemies and their historians, the IWW proved willing and often adept at negotiation and compromise. The Spokane tangle was settled on such terms. The city agreed to abrogate the obnoxious ordinance, to release all Wobblies held in violation of it, and to cease harassing the IWW's newspaper, the *Industrial Worker.* For their part, the Wobblies agreed to discontinue street speaking and demonstration until the ordinance could be officially repealed, and to withdraw several suits they had filed charging city officials with corruption. In San Diego the IWW agreed to a compromise solution worked out by a citizens' group which proscribed but did not prohibit public speeches. The plan provided for the IWW to inform the police three days in advance of all street meetings. The city council, however, rejected the plan, preferring to fight the battle to its bitter end.

To see the Wobblies as contemptuous of conventional society is to ignore their frequent solicitude for public favor and

Uncle Sam Ruled Out

"That's IWW," said Bill Haywood, making a fist, during the Paterson strike against silk manufacturers caricatured in the 1913 Solidarity.

to judge them by their unfavorable newspaper image is to lose sight of their many supporters among "respectable" and moderate elements in the population. Herman Tucker, an employee of the U.S. Forestry Department in Missoula, was an example. During the Free Speech Fight there in 1909, Tucker was watching from the window of his second-story office when a young logger was arrested on the corner below for reading from the Declaration of Independence. Although not especially sympathetic to the Wobblies, Tucker was incensed by the mockery of the arrest, rushed downstairs, mounted the vacant platform, and continued the reading. He too was arrested.

On November 5, 1916, a group of Wobblies boarded the passenger boat *Verona*, bound from Seattle to Everett, Washington, a lumber mill town from which the IWW had been forcibly expelled a short time before. When the *Verona* docked, it was confronted by an armed posse under Sheriff Donald McRae of Snohomish County, and a gunfight erupted. The *Verona* escaped into Puget Sound by snapping its shore lines, and passengers counted between five and 11 dead and 31 wounded. Many of Everett's citizens angrily blamed the incident on Sheriff McRae. Some openly expressed the hope that the IWW would return and clear the town of its legal terrorists, and some merchants felt constrained to announce that they were not members of the Commercial Club, which

backed McRae. Mayor Gill of Seattle issued an angry public attack on McRae, denouncing the sheriff's pretentious deportation of the Wobblies and accusing him of full responsibility for the massacre. Gill dramatized his partisanship by sending gifts to the Wobblies in jail.

Elmer Smith, a young lawyer in Centralia, Washington, became legal advisor to the IWW local in that city shortly before Armistice Day, 1919, when parading American Legionnaires attacked the IWW hall and, before the day was done, lynched a Wobbly still in his army uniform. Several members of the Legion were killed during the fracas, and Elmer Smith was indicted as accessory to the crime, along with ten Wobblies who had actually been present during the battle. Smith and one other defendant were acquitted, whereupon Smith devoted more than a year to organizing meetings throughout the Pacific Northwest on behalf of those still imprisoned. In 1922 he moved to California, where he continued to attack the laws and trials which made convicts of men he regarded as innocent victims.

Another forgotten facet of the IWW was that it served in many of the mining, smelter, railroad, and lumber mill towns of the West as a social organization, a workingman's fraternal lodge. Most of the time the IWW hall was used not for planning strikes but as a library and reading room, casual rendezvous, and dance hall. In a sense, the IWW was a surrogate church, a focal point for the social life of the laborers in the dismal and isolated industrial towns of the region. That is not a very colorful picture, calculated to appeal to romanticizers, but it is a facet of the IWW depicted in a dozen old photographs, and it places the union somewhere this side of un-American activities.

The IWW did not consider itself alien or irrelevant to accepted mores but assumed that it deserved support from non-proletarians. "The IWW does not give me the right to act against the common good," the *Industrial Union Bulletin* stated as early as 1907. "There is no such thing as the right to do as I please." Wobbly theorist Justus Ebert felt that progressives and liberals should support the IWW because to them "the IWW is the proletarian forerunner of the new society, the militant protestant against capitalist reaction." The claim was less a statement of fact than a plea, for Ebert added appreciatively that progressive support was frequently responsible for Wobbly successes. The Wobblies continued to appeal to the middle class. During a 1913 trial of Wobblies in Marysville, California, for incidents arising from a riot on a hop ranch near Wheatland, the IWW solicited assistance from, among other groups, the Women's Clubs of California. "As you are women," the letter read, "we are sure of your sympathy for the men now facing death and for their innocent families." It was hardly the manifesto of the cartoon-caricatured anarchist.

Nor was the statement of William D. Haywood that if the Wobblies involved in the Centralia Massacre were guilty, they should be punished. In fact, Haywood, the undisputed leader of the union by the time of World War I, effected numerous accommodations which he hoped would gain the union public acceptance, if not public favor. Realizing the havoc which patriotic passions could wreak on the union and hoping to avoid it, he urged members not to emphasize their opposition to the war and conscription but to concentrate on trade union goals. During the war, Haywood saw that potentially offensive lyrics in the IWW's *Little Red Songbook* were deleted. After the war, his assistant and confidant Ralph Chaplin tried to steer the IWW in a technocratic direction. He hoped to transform the union into something of a research bureau which would collect and publish information on the American economy, because a "high class educational program would add to the prestige of the IWW while it was under attack from so many quarters."

One of the most curious and obscure Wobbly activities during the era was the organization's tacit support of prohibition. The idea of rough-hewn Wobblies pulling alongside bluestockinged Republican dowagers and clerical conservatives in what was the safest conventional piety of the day seems preposterous if one persists in envisioning the Wobblies as nothing more than erratic Reds. The Wobblies' reasons for supporting prohibition did not differ radically from the arguments of the middle-class drys. According to C. H. Lambert, a leading California Wobbly, in 1916, prohibition would "make labor more efficient" and provide more work for members of the union. He predicted victory for two prohibition amendments then up for referendum in the state, with the implication that Wobblies would support them at the polls.

The Wobblies also regarded the saloon as the stalking ground for detectives and thugs hired to provoke strikers into brawls. During a strike against contractors laying track for the Canadian Pacific Railroad in 1913, the union ordered a boycott of the saloons. The chief of police of Grand Junction, Colorado, observed that the Wobblies of his acquaintance "will not permit a member to drink and travel with them." And the organization eventually adopted a bylaw which provided:

Any officer or employee of any part of the Industrial Workers of the World seen in public in a state of intoxication shall, upon sufficient proof, be at once removed from his position by the proper authorities having jurisdiction over such an officer or employee, and upon conviction, shall not be eligible to hold office in any part of the organization for two years thereafter.

One wonders if the American Legion had any regulations so prim.

After prohibition became a fact, the "lawless" IWW sometimes contributed its services to enforcing the law. During a strike in the Grays Harbor District of Washington in 1923, a Wobbly local informed "all bootleggers and gambling houses" that "you are hereby given notice to close up during the strike or drastic action will be taken against you." Wobblies in Portland, Spokane, and Seattle embarrassed the mayors of those cities when they offered to help close down the towns' many speakeasies. Earlier in 1923, IWW locals in Portland had a lighthearted fling when they demonstrated in protest outside a well-known "soft-drink establishment." They were arrested.

It is not the purpose of this essay to deny the Wobblies their romantic heritage and their place in the revolutionary tradition. The legends are factual as often as not, and they rank among the most exciting in the American experience. And the Wobblies were, as they said, "true blue" revolutionaries. They envisioned the total reconstruction of American society on a design which they esteemed as infinitely more democratic, equitable, and humane than what they saw around them. Perhaps the point is that in its nervous conservatism America too often dismisses its revolutionaries as bizarre by definition, forgetting that a revolutionary, utopian streak runs through the fabric of American history like a color through a plaid: sometimes dim, sometimes bold, but always a part of the design.

The Wobblies were not a curious aberration in their time and place. They evinced a commitment to traditional American liberties more edifying than their enemies'. In practice, they displayed a respect for the law which they themselves believed that they scorned. Hardly ideologues, the Wobblies were pragmatic and practical. They were buoyed by the same optimism about the future as the progressives, and they even shared in the vagaries of the time. All of which is to make a point that would be downright silly if it were not so stubbornly ignored: the Wobblies were more like their contemporaries than either party cared to admit. ଊ

The Gentlewoman and the ROBBER BARON

When Ida Tarbell set out to
probe the operations of
John D. Rockefeller's
Standard Oil Trust, it
seemed like David against
Goliath all over again

VIRGINIA VAN DER VEER HAMILTON

*Dr. Virginia Van der Veer Hamilton is an assistant professor of
history at the University of Alabama in Birmingham. She wrote
"Hugo Black and the K.K.K." for our April, 1968, issue and
is now completing a full-length biography of Mr. Justice Black.
For further reading: Success Story: The Life and Times
of S. S. McClure, by Peter Lyon (Scribner, 1963); John D.
Rockefeller: A Study in Power, by Allan Nevins (2 volumes,
Scribner, 1940); All In the Day's Work, the autobiography
of Ida M. Tarbell (Macmillan, 1939); The History of the
Standard Oil Company, by Ida M. Tarbell, abridged and
with an introduction by David M. Chalmers (Harper Torch-
books, 1966).*

One wintry morning in 1902 a prim, resolute spinster presented herself at 26 Broadway in New
York City, bastion of the powerful Standard Oil
organization. Promptly she was ushered through a maze
of empty corridors to a reception room facing an open
courtyard. As she waited, she became aware that a man
in a nearby window was observing her stealthily.

Over the next two years this unlikely visitor paid
many calls to one of the most awesome addresses in the
American financial world. Each time she saw only the
clerks who guided her, a secretary, and Henry H.
Rogers, vice president of Standard Oil. But always she
noticed the same shadowy figure watching her from the
window. Was John D. Rockefeller, master of the oil
industry, peeping at Ida Minerva Tarbell, lady journalist?

If so, Ida's turn to peep came one Sunday in 1903
when she visited the Euclid Avenue Baptist Church in
Cleveland. Feeling a little guilty about it, she had invaded Rockefeller's church for a firsthand look at the
man whose business practices she dared to castigate.
Her quarry soon appeared. At sixty-four Rockefeller
exuded power, but Ida observed that his big head had a
wet look, his nose resembled a sharp thorn, and his lips
were thin slits. Constantly, uneasily, Rockefeller peered
around the familiar congregation, but if he recognized
the stranger in its midst, he gave no sign.

Although the nation's richest man and his most persistent critic never met, their confrontation in the pages

Ida Minerva Tarbell hardly resembled her public image as the nemesis of the world's most powerful tycoon.

of *McClure's Magazine* enthralled thousands of Americans. Safe within their Victorian mansions, well-bred ladies shuddered at the audacity of one of their sex who had the spunk to describe the legendary Rockefeller as cold, ruthless, and unethical.

For eighteen installments—from November, 1902, to April, 1904—Ida's monumental "History of the Standard Oil Company" fired the indignation of middle-aged and middle-class citizens caught up in the rebellious mood of Progressivism. Politicians from statehouse legislators to Teddy Roosevelt at the White House took note of the furor. Its echoes eventually penetrated even the remote chambers of the Supreme Court.

Readers of *McClure's*, turning through their October, 1902, issue, were introduced to the sensational serial by a full-page photograph of Ida. The magazine's star writer wore a severe, high-collared white dress adorned with tucks and embroidery, and her dark hair was piled high on her head. She looked away from the camera with an air of cool detachment. Miss Tarbell, *McClure's* announced, had completed her long study of "the most perfectly developed trust in existence." Her account would begin the following month.

S. S. McClure, impulsive and mercurial, boasted that the founding of *McClure's* and the discovery of Ida Tar-

bell were his proudest achievements. In Paris in 1892 he had bounded up four flights of steps to an apartment to meet the little-known American writer. After pouring out his plans for *McClure's*, S. S. borrowed forty dollars and left. "I'll never see that money," Ida lamented, but to her relief the forty dollars was promptly repaid. Two years later Ida, serious, purposeful, and thirty-seven, joined the staff of *McClure's* in New York.

S. S. soon had reason to congratulate himself. Ida was an immediate hit with readers, who paid ten cents a copy for his lively magazine. They liked her biography of Napoleon, produced "on the gallop" in six weeks. They followed with avid interest her series on Abraham Lincoln, written after four years of painstaking research in Kentucky, Indiana, and Illinois.

As thousands of new subscribers joined his circulation lists, McClure gave Ida most of the credit. The life of Lincoln, he said, "told on our circulation as nothing ever had before." By 1900 *McClure's* was reaching 350,000 homes and was second in circulation only to its bitter rival, *Munsey's*. If McClure liked an idea, he bragged, then millions of readers would like it, too. "There's only one better editor than I am," he admitted, "and that's Frank Munsey. If he likes a thing, then everybody will like it."

Alert to the mood of his readers, McClure sensed their

concern about social and political reform. Lincoln Steffens, therefore, must check into corruption in the big cities. Ray Stannard Baker must investigate labor unions and the coal strike then going on in the anthracite fields of Pennsylvania (see "The Coal Kings Come to Judgment" in the April, 1960, AMERICAN HERITAGE). As for Ida, why not a study of one of the monopolies that frightened small businessmen? Why not, in fact, the prototype of them all? "Out with you!" S. S. commanded his talented staff. "Look, see, report."

"Don't do it, Ida," her father pleaded. "They will ruin the magazine." Others warned her of the "all-seeing eye and the all-powerful reach" of Standard Oil. If *McClure's* persisted, friends predicted, "they'll get you in the end."

Standard Oil was well aware that a popular journalist—and a female at that—was prying into its past. Executives of the corporation asked no less a public figure than Mark Twain to inquire what *McClure's* planned to publish. "You will have to ask Miss Tarbell," S. S. replied. "Would Miss Tarbell see Mr. Rogers?" Twain inquired. When her supporters heard that Ida was visiting 26 Broadway to get the company's side of its history, they were instantly suspicious. "You'll become their apologist before you get through," many prophesied.

At their first meeting Ida and Henry Rogers discovered that they had been neighbors years before in the booming oil regions of Pennsylvania, where Ida's father had made tanks and Rogers had been an independent refiner. They even recalled the beauty of a wooded ravine separating their houses. Although she decided that Henry Rogers was "as fine a pirate as ever flew his flag in Wall Street," Ida was not beguiled by nostalgic memories. She alone, she told the Standard Oil executive, would be the judge of what she wrote.

Diligent and methodical, Ida studied musty records of the many lawsuits brought against Standard Oil in the thirty years since its incorporation. Every pertinent document must be located: "somewhere, some time," Ida insisted, "a copy turns up." Rogers once suggested that Ida should meet Rockefeller himself, and somewhat apprehensively she agreed. But their meeting was never arranged.

Seeking firsthand knowledge of Standard's methods, Ida interviewed other businessmen. Reluctant though they might be, they usually responded to her firm, dignified manner. One eccentric Cleveland millionaire received her with his hat on, his feet propped on his desk, and his face buried in a newspaper. As Ida quietly began to ask questions, he placed his feet on the floor, put down the newspaper, removed his hat, and gave her his respectful attention.

Her first installment was a vivid account of the brawling, gambling spirit of pioneer days in the Pennsylvania oil country. In 1859, when they heard the exhilarating news that oil was gushing out of a well near Titusville, thousands of adventurous Americans poured into the area, and a whole series of boom towns—with names like Pit Hole, Oil City, Petroleum Center, and Rouseville—hastily sprang up. "On every rocky farm," Ida wrote, "in every poor settlement of the region, was some man whose ear was attuned to Fortune's call, and who had the daring and the energy to risk everything he possessed in an oil lease." Saloons, brothels, and dance halls catered to a drifting population of fortune seekers.

Recalling the atmosphere of her youth, Ida praised the efforts of many citizens of this rough frontier to create schools, churches, and a proper environment. Her own parents, Esther and Franklin Tarbell, had shepherded their children into respectable middle-class ways, highlighted by family picnics on Chautauqua Lake or an occasional trip to Cleveland. Crusading suffragettes visited the Tarbell home, and young Ida fell under the spell of their fervent talk. "I must be free," she vowed, "and to be free I must be a spinster." At fourteen she prayed on her knees that God would keep her from marriage.

To prepare for a career, Ida entered Allegheny College at Meadville, the lone girl in a freshman class of forty "hostile or indifferent" boys. After graduation she hoped to become a biologist, but fate and S. S. McClure decided otherwise. Now, twenty-two years later, this child of the oil regions who had elected spinsterhood and freedom was challenging the ruler of the oil industry himself.

At the close of the first chapter Ida offered her readers an enticing glimpse of the drama to come. Praising the independent oil producers, who gambled their lives and money in an uncertain new industry, she wrote:

Life ran swift and ruddy and joyous in these men. They were still young, most of them under forty, and they looked forward with all the eagerness of the young who have just learned their powers, to years of struggle and development. . . . There was nothing too good for them, nothing they did not hope and dare. But suddenly, at the very heyday of this confidence, a big hand reached out from nobody knew where, to steal their conquest and throttle their future.

The "big hand," she revealed in her next installment, was an enterprising young man with "remarkable commercial vision, a genius for seeing the possibilities in material things." As a boy of thirteen John Rockefeller discovered that lending money at 7 per cent interest was more profitable than his earlier job of digging potatoes: "It was a good thing," the boy reasoned, "to let the money be my slave." This principle, Ida told her readers, was the foundation of a great financial career.

During the Civil War, Rockefeller chose to sell produce to the Union army rather than to serve in its ranks. Before the war ended, the twenty-three-year-old merchant had foreseen greater potential in refining a new product, oil, to light the homes and lubricate the machines of America. Under his shrewd and frugal leadership his first refinery prospered. There must be no waste, Rockefeller decreed. He found a market even for the residuum that other refineries allowed to flow away into the ground. "It hurt him to see it unused," Ida wrote, "and no man had a heartier welcome from the president of the Standard Oil Company than he who would show him how to utilize any proportion of his residuum." Rather than pay a barrelmaker, Rockefeller set up his own barrel factory.

The youthful refiner got his greatest joy from a good bargain. One of those whom Ida interviewed told her that the only time he had ever seen Rockefeller enthusiastic was at the news that his firm had bought a cargo of oil much below the market price. "He bounded from his chair with a shout of joy," the man recollected, "danced up and down, hugged me, threw up his hat, acted so like a madman that I have never forgotten it."

On the basis of the large amount of oil he shipped eastward, Rockefeller began to receive the railroad rebates that Ida charged were the keystone of his future empire. She described how he and other large refiners conspired to force railroads to grant them "drawbacks," additional rebates on the shipments of their competitors. Members of this clandestine combination, known as the South Improvement Company, received a rebate of $1.06 a barrel on crude oil shipped from Cleveland to New York, plus a drawback of $1.06 on each barrel shipped by their rivals. When an independent refiner paid eighty cents a barrel to ship crude oil from the Pennsylvania fields to Cleveland, the South Improvement Company received a forty-cent-per-barrel drawback on the shipment.

This advantage, Ida charged, was used as a club over the heads of other refiners in Cleveland, forcing them to "sell or perish." His competitors wanted to keep their own businesses, Ida said, but "Mr. Rockefeller was regretful but firm. It was useless to resist, he told the hesitating; they would certainly be crushed if they did not accept his offer." When twenty-one of the twenty-six firms sold out to Rockefeller, he controlled one fifth of the nation's oil refining; "almost the entire independent oil interests of Cleveland collapsed in three months' time," Ida informed her readers. Privately an indignant Rockefeller denied Ida's version. Standard had been an angel of mercy to the Cleveland firms in distress, he told friends. "They didn't collapse," he insisted. "They had collapsed before! That's the reason they were so glad to combine their interest with ours, or take the money we offered." However, Rockefeller, who had always met criticism with lofty silence, refused to reply publicly to the articles in *McClure's*. "Not a word," he insisted. "Not a word about that misguided woman!"

But the heir to Standard Oil, John D. Rockefeller, Jr.,

was stung to a veiled defense of his father's business creation. In a speech entitled "Christianity and Business" he told members of the Y.M.C.A. at his alma mater, Brown University: "The American Beauty rose can be produced in its splendor and fragrance only by sacrificing the early buds which grow up around it." Critics of Standard Oil never let John D., Jr., forget this unfortunate metaphor. Recalling it several years later, a bishop declared from the pulpit: "A rose by any other name will smell as sweet, but the odor of that rose to me smacks strongly of crude petroleum."

If the creation of a perfect rose justified the sacrifice of other buds, could the same rationale be applied to the Standard Oil Trust? Ida's answer was a vehement No. The heroes of her serial were the independent oil "farmers" and refiners whose livelihood was threatened by Rockefeller's growing consolidation. "They believed," Ida wrote, "in independent effort—every man for himself and fair play for all. They wanted competition, loved open fight. They considered that all business should be done openly; that the railways were bound as public carriers to give equal rates; that any combination which favoured one firm or one locality at the expense of another was unjust and illegal."

The producers rose in united revolt against the South Improvement Company and the man whom they believed to be its Mephistopheles, refusing to sell oil until rail-

Ida's articles disturbed John D. Rockefeller, Jr., who defended the Standard as a "rose [that] can be produced . . . only by sacrificing the early buds which grow up around it." Angry reactions included this cartoon showing the "buds" at the feet of the senior Rockefeller as the skulls of competitors whom he had crushed.

roads agreed not to grant rebates, drawbacks, or any other special privileges. Ida remembered vividly that her own father, by then a producer himself, was one of those who had pledged not to sell.

The South Improvement Company scheme was defeated, but Rockefeller, Ida said, "had a mind which stopped by a wall, burrows under or creeps around." He next negotiated a new rebate arrangement between Standard Oil and the New York Central Railroad. In a burst of indignant prose Ida berated her protagonist:

There was no more faithful Baptist in Cleveland than he. Every enterprise of that church he had supported liberally from his youth. He gave to its poor. He visited its sick. He wept with its suffering. Moreover, he gave unostentatiously to many outside charities of whose worthiness he was satisfied. He was simple and frugal in his habits. He never went to the theatre, never drank wine. He gave much time to the training of his children, seeking to develop in them his own habits of economy and charity. Yet he was willing to strain every nerve to obtain for himself special and unjust privileges from the railroads which were bound to ruin every man in the oil business not sharing them with him.

Rockefeller's next tactic, Ida explained, was to form a national Refiners' Association to force oil producers to sell their output to a united front of refiners. To offset the power of the refiners, drillers organized a Producers' Association. The producers realized that overproduction was their curse. If they agreed to stop drilling new wells for six months and shut down their pumps for thirty days, supplies of crude oil would dwindle, and prices would rise. To the producers' surprise, Rockefeller and his fellow refiners offered them a contract for 200,000 barrels of oil at $3.25 a barrel. They signed. But when 50,000 of the 200,000 barrels had been shipped, the refiners' association broke its contract, declaring that the producers had failed to limit production and that plenty of oil was available at $2.50 a barrel. Ida placed the blame on Rockefeller for "leading them into an alliance, and at the psychological moment throwing up his contract."

One producer told Ida what it had been like to negotiate with Rockefeller, who during one meeting sat and rocked with his hands covering his eyes.

I made a speech which I guess was pretty warlike. Well, right in the middle of it, John Rockefeller stopped rocking and took down his hands and looked at me. You never saw such eyes. He took me all in, saw just how much fight he could expect from me, and I knew it, and then up went his hands and back and forth went his chair.

Month by month Ida pressed her indictment, picturing Rockefeller as a sinister conspirator obsessed with a passion to control the entire oil industry for the "holy blue barrel," as his competitors called it, of Standard

Ida's "History" helped launch an investigation of the Standard by the Bureau of Corporations in 1905–6. Its final report, given to President Theodore Roosevelt by the bureau's chief, James R. Garfield (a son of the assassinated President), called for antitrust action. Along with the Standard's Henry H. Rogers, who up to a point had co-operated with Ida, Rockefeller was glum.

Oil. He arranged for Standard to receive even more favorable rebates from major railroads. When independent operators developed a revolutionary new means of transporting oil by pipelines, the canny Rockefeller realized that this method was the shipping trend of the future. He moved into the pipeline business, driving out rivals until he controlled the entire pipeline system of the oil regions. He set up a nationwide network, paying spies to report on rival shipments, deliberately underselling his competitors, and then, having driven his rivals out of a territory, set any price he pleased.

Summarizing Rockefeller's goal, Ida wrote:

Briefly stated, his argument was this: "Controlling all refineries, I shall be the only shipper of oil. Being the only shipper, I can obtain special rates of transportation which will drive out and keep out competitors; controlling all refineries, I shall be the only buyer, and can regulate the price of crude [oil] as I can the price of refined."

The charge of spying, published in a chapter titled "Cutting to Kill," abruptly ended Ida's harmonious interviews with Henry Rogers. To substantiate her charges, *McClure's* reproduced records sent to Ida secretly by a young shipping clerk in a Standard plant. They were undercover reports from railroad agents, listing oil shipments by rival producers. On her next visit to 26 Broadway, Ida found Rogers "by no means cordial." When he asked where she got "that stuff," she replied boldly: "You know very well that I could not tell you where I got that stuff, but you know very well that it is authentic." It was their last interview.

Although the doors of Standard Oil closed to Ida, she was invited to meet an even more unexpected source of information. Frank Rockefeller summoned her secretly to Cleveland to hear his grievances against his successful brother. To help finance a shipping business, Frank had borrowed money from John D. and put up his Standard Oil stock as collateral. During the Panic of '93, when Frank was unable to meet his obligations, John D. foreclosed and took over the stock. Frank, observed Ida, was more frivolous than his brother, more generous, "not a safe man to handle money. . . . So it was a kind of obligation to the sacredness of money," she wrote, "that John Rockefeller had foreclosed on his own brother."

After chastising Rockefeller for many months, Ida produced an installment called "The Legitimate Greatness of the Standard Oil Company" in which she freely acknowledged its leader's business efficiency. Rockefeller's passion for detail and for plowing profits back into the company, she said, had resulted in a masterpiece of organization. Even the dust on the floors of his tin factories was sifted to save filings and bits of solder.

While granting Rockefeller his due, Ida could not forgive practices she considered illegitimate and debasing to business morality. His success, she feared, would tempt thousands of others to "Commercial Machiavellianism." In the wake of his growing monopoly, Ida said, Rockefeller left a trail of devastated small businesses:

Why one should love an oil refinery the outsider may not see, but to the man who had begun with one still and had seen it grow by his own energy and intelligence to ten, who now sold 500 barrels a day where he once sold five, the refinery was the dearest spot on earth save his home. . . . To ask such a man to give up his refinery was to ask him to give up the thing which, after his family, meant most in life to him.

But faced with the growing power of Standard Oil, the independents did give up. Describing one who sold out, Ida wrote that "he realized that something . . . was at work in the oil business—something resistless, silent, perfect in its might—and he sold out to that something." Along Oil Creek, she said, "the little refineries which for years had faced every difficulty with stout hearts collapsed. 'Sold out,' 'dismantled,' 'shut down,' is the melancholy record."

As dramatic proof of the fierceness of the conflict Ida devoted an entire installment to "The Buffalo Case," in which managers of a Standard affiliate in New York were convicted of conspiring to blow up a rival refinery to force it out of business. In another chapter she shocked her public by repeating the tale of Widow Backus, who declared in an affidavit that Rockefeller had fleeced her of a fair price when she sold her husband's refinery to Standard Oil. Ida said of the widow:

She had seen every effort to preserve an independent business thwarted. Rightly or wrongly, she had come to believe that a refusal to sell meant a fight with Mr. Rockefeller, that a fight meant ultimately defeat, and she gave up her business to avoid ruin.

Historians later criticized Ida for repeating the widow's tale, which was of questionable accuracy, but true or exaggerated, it made a sensational installment. Victorian ladies of comfortable means could identify with the plight of Widow Backus.

Acknowledged as "Lord of the Oil Regions" by 1879, Rockefeller controlled 90 per cent of the oil business of the nation, dominating refining, transporting, and marketing. The entire pipeline system of the Pennsylvania fields belonged to Standard. Rockefeller had achieved his goal, Ida wrote, "because he had the essential element to all great achievement, a steadfastness to purpose once conceived which nothing can crush."

To handle the affairs of his giant monopoly, Rockefeller created a new type of business organization, the trust, whereby he and eight other trustees managed the entire structure. But public resentment against the monopoly began to be reflected in a rush of legal suits. Ida reminded her readers of the 1892 ruling by the supreme court of Ohio that had resulted in dissolution of the Standard Oil Trust. It was replaced by the Standard Oil Company of New Jersey, which functioned as a holding company for the Rockefeller interests.

After eighteen chapters and almost four years of research and writing Ida and *McClure's* rested their case against John D. Rockefeller. Summing it all up, Ida told her faithful readers that they were paying more for oil under monopoly conditions than they would pay under free competition. Business opportunity in the oil industry, she said, was now limited to a few hundred men.

But there was a more serious side to it, she concluded. The ethical cost of all this should be a deep concern. "Canonize 'business success,' and men who make a success like that of the Standard Oil Trust become national heroes!" Defenders of Rockefeller might justify his methods by saying, "It's business" or "All humans are erring mortals," but Ida would not accept a moral code that "would leave our business men weeping on one another's shoulders over human frailty, while they picked one another's pockets."

In a last plea to her readers she urged them to ostracize monopolists who used unethical practices as they would ostracize unethical doctors, lawyers, or athletes, for "a thing won by breaking the rules of the game," she moralized, "is not worth the winning."

As her public exploded with wrath, *McClure's* was deluged with angry letters. Ida, readers said, was a modern Joan of Arc and "the Terror of the Trusts." Her study reminded one man of "the clarion notes of the old prophets of Israel." Another called it "the *Uncle Tom's Cabin* of today." A letter addressed to "Ida M. Tarbell, Rockefeller Station, Hades," reached her promptly.

McClure's, packed with articles by Steffens and Baker as well as with Ida's literary dynamite, thrived on its crusading zeal. But Ida was even more of a celebrity than her colleagues, and they joined in the general admiration for her work. "Ida Tarbell was the best of us," Baker admitted. In a western city a newspaper hailed the arrival of William Allen White and Ida with the headline "Celebrated Writers Here." S. S. wrote his protégée: "You are today the most generally famous woman in America."

Ida's "History" evoked even more praise when it was published as a two-volume book in 1904. "Miss Tarbell,"

Ida "a great woman historian" and "probably the most talented woman writer of history that this country has produced."

Standard, however, was not without its defenders. In Pennsylvania the Oil City *Derrick,* subsidized by the company, headlined its review: "Hysterical Woman Versus Historical Facts." A Harvard economist, Gilbert Montague, who wrote a sympathetic history of Standard's operations, termed Ida "a mere gatherer of folklore." The popular essayist Elbert Hubbard said Standard Oil was an example of "survival of the fittest" and called Ida a "literary bushwhacker" who "shot from cover and . . . shot to kill." The nickname Miss Tarbarrel was coined by Standard supporters. Even Rockefeller himself, not a notably humorous man, adopted the pun with glee.

While interest in Ida's history was at its height, new oil discoveries by wildcatters drilling deep in the Kansas plains caused a fresh boom. Standard Oil moved quickly into the new fields, threading its pipelines across prairie and farmland. But *McClure's* had reached even the remote farmers of Kansas. Populists, women's clubs, and independent oilmen vowed to keep Standard out of their fields even if they had to set up a state-owned refinery in the penitentiary. At the urging of the oilmen Ida visited the new arena. To her dismay she was received as a prophet and serenaded by oil boomers. "But here I was," she wrote later, "fifty, fagged, wanting to be let alone while I collected trustworthy information for my articles—dragged to the front as an apostle."

The news from Kansas, added to the cumulative effect of the Tarbell series, helped stir Congress to action. In February, 1905, it authorized the Bureau of Corporations to investigate the low price of crude oil, particularly in Kansas. Could the wide margin between the prices of crude and refined, a Kansas congressman asked, be attributed to the operations of a trust or conspiracy?

Enthusiastically the Bureau of Corporations dug into its assignment. In the first of three lengthy reports to Congress, it concluded that Standard "habitually" received and was still receiving secret rebates and other "unjust and illegal discriminations" from railroads. The second report charged that Standard controlled the only major pipeline serving the oil industry and that it fought would-be competitors with lawsuits, right-of-way

JOHN T. McCUTCHEON IN THE CHICAGO *Tribune,* APRIL 8, 1905

When, after the "History" appeared, Standard Oil moved in on new wells in Kansas, Kansans fought back, with a reluctant Ida as their champion. Here Rockefeller defends his policies—to the disbelief of Ida, the governor of Kansas, and Thomas W. Lawson, a muckraker of Wall Street.

said the Cleveland *Leader,* "has done more to dethrone Rockefeller in public esteem than all the preachers in the land." The New York *News* declared that "Rockefeller's very conscience is exposed by her search for truth." The Norfolk *Dispatch* and the Washington *News* proclaimed disputes, aid to railroads, and price wars. The final report accused Standard of keeping oil prices artificially high at the expense of the American consumer. Commissioner Herbert Knox Smith called for prosecution of Standard under the Sherman Antitrust Act.

The bureau's findings were not news to Ida's readers. One cartoonist pictured President Roosevelt receiving the reports on a slate bearing these words: "Standard Oil is just as naughty as Ida said it was." In the background of the cartoon was Henry Rogers, muttering to Rockefeller: "And I had my fingers crossed too."

But Roosevelt, who had originally encouraged federal legal action against Standard, became exasperated at the public vogue for the literature of exposure as other magazines and writers rushed to copy *McClure's* successful formula. Shortly after the appearance of an article in *Cosmopolitan* titled "The Treason of the Senate" an angry Roosevelt applied the term "muckrakers" to responsible and irresponsible journalists alike. Pondering the President's attack years later, Ida decided that Teddy preferred to conduct trust busting on his own and resented writers "stealing his thunder."

Meanwhile, Standard's troubles were multiplying. Three antitrust suits were brought against the corporation in state courts in 1904, four in 1905, and fourteen in 1906. Many resulted in fines or the temporary ouster of Standard from a state. The most sensational fine, $29,240,000 for 1,462 violations of the Elkins Act forbidding acceptance of rebates, was handed down by Judge Kenesaw Mountain Landis in August, 1907. Although this decision was later reversed, the "Big Fine" made Judge Landis famous and added drama to the controversy.

Once when Ida was searching for material in Indiana and Ohio, an order went out from Standard headquarters: "Simply ignore her entirely." But in the face of such mounting hostility even Standard Oil could not play the sphinx forever. The company began to give out information on its operations and employed Ivy Ledbetter Lee, an early public relations counsel, to place advertisements and friendly stories in newspapers and magazines. It ordered five thousand copies of Montague's book and distributed them to employees, ministers, libraries, teachers, and prominent citizens.

Rockefeller's own image was under such attack that a group of Congregational ministers balked at accepting his gift of $100,000 to their board of missions, calling it "tainted money." Later, to their embarrassment, they found that some of their colleagues had actually requested the gift. But the term "tainted money" briefly captured many a headline. Undeterred, Rockefeller intensified his long habit of philanthropy. Two months after the final chapter of the Standard Oil history appeared in *McClure's*, he announced gifts of one million

dollars to Yale University and ten times that amount to the General Education Board, a philanthropy in aid of higher education that he had helped to establish two years before. No one objected. Such sums, the New York *Sun* commented dryly, "deodorize themselves." When it was charged that Rockefeller was using philanthropy to silence criticism, Ida came to his defense, reminding critics that Rockefeller had been a steady giver to church and charity since boyhood. If his gifts were larger now, she pointed out, it was because his income was greater and perhaps because he sought to call public attention to the benefits reaped from Standard Oil.

John D. proved his own most effective advocate. In 1909 he published a slim book titled *Random Reminiscences of Men and Events*. Although he did not mention Ida or other critics by name, it was obvious the outcry was on Rockefeller's mind. "Just how far one is justified . . . in defending himself from attacks is a moot point," he wrote. *Random Reminiscences*, an informal account of the early career, principles, and recreations of the nation's richest man, also contained useful hints on how to give money away wisely. This little book, one Rockefeller biographer has said, "did more to make Rockefeller a human figure than tons of Sunday supplement articles."

Random Reminiscences, however, did not persuade the federal government to call off a suit charging Standard Oil with violation of the Sherman act. The case dragged through three and a half years of litigation. In 1909 a federal circuit court sustained the government's position, but Standard appealed to the Supreme Court. Many an editor invited Ida to analyze the testimony. "I could have made a good killing out of that long investigation . . ." she recalled later. "But I had no stomach for it." Weary of all the controversy, she wished only "to escape into the safe retreat of a library where I could study people long dead."

Finally, on May 15, 1911, the decision was handed down. The highest court in the land declared Standard Oil of New Jersey to be a monopoly in restraint of trade, based on unfair practices. Charging that Standard's object was "to drive others from the field and exclude them from their right to trade," the court ordered the holding company dissolved. The justices, in effect, agreed with Ida.

"The History of the Standard Oil Company" was probably the most sensational serial ever to appear in an American magazine. Allan Nevins, in his biography of Rockefeller, called it "the most spectacular success of the muckraking school of journalism, and its most enduring achievement." As a historian Ida Tarbell had her flaws. She was untrained in economics. She yearned to turn back the clock to an era of individualism in business. She was obviously partial to independent oilmen, even though she scolded them for lacking the patience and fortitude to organize effectively against Rockefeller. In her indignation she sometimes exaggerated the iniquity of her archvillain.

But at a time when strong men quailed before the Rockefeller reputation, this daughter of the oil regions, fortified by her sense of righteous morality, boldly voiced their feelings. Although small operators lost their struggle for existence, Ida carried the day in the contest for public opinion. A modern-day historian of the muck-raking era, David M. Chalmers, believes the image she fashioned of Rockefeller as a "cunning, ruthless Shylock" has not been successfully erased by a half century of Rockefeller family philanthropy. Forty years after her serial appeared, *Time* magazine credited the *McClure's* articles with bringing in a "gusher of public resentment that flowed all the way to the U. S. Supreme Court."

Was Ida's study an accurate work of historical research, or was it a subjective attack on practices of which she disapproved? Modern business historians, looking back on the "History" with the hindsight of a later era, generally substantiate her charges that Standard Oil built its monopoly upon special favors from railroads, mastery of the pipeline system, and sharp marketing

A victorious Ida Tarbell reading a pleasant headline

practices, all of which helped force small independents out of the fields and refineries.

But Ida raised a larger question: Was it better for the American oil industry to have free, albeit cutthroat, competition, or to fall under the dominance of a monopoly with the power to maintain orderly production and a profitable, if higher, price structure? It is this aspect of her account that still arouses controversy. Social historians tend to be on Ida's side, business historians to defend Rockefeller; both schools agree, however, that Ida was a pioneer business historian and that, although she worked with the crude research tools of the early 1900's and became a special pleader for her own moralistic ideas of business ethics, she presented a remarkably clear and truthful picture of the rise of Standard Oil.

Though John D. Rockefeller never met the stern spinster who judged his business morality so harshly, she and Rockefeller's son, John D., Jr., did meet at a conference called by President Wilson after World War I. The younger Rockefeller, who had once compared Standard Oil to an American Beauty rose, had become disenchanted and had made "one of the most important decisions of my life." Resigning his directorships in Standard Oil and U. S. Steel, he announced in 1910 that he would devote his life to giving away the immense sums of money that flowed from his father's business creation.

When John D., Jr., realized he was to meet Ida, he sought the advice of William Allen White. The famous Kansas editor knew the younger Rockefeller as a gentle and kindhearted person for whom Ida's book had been "an unpleasant fact which gave him something more than pause." He advised Rockefeller to meet Miss Tarbell casually and naturally; as two sensitive people they would bridge the awkward situation. After the meeting White saw John D., Jr., hurrying into the street to hail a cab for Miss Tarbell. Later he was amused to see them, placed together by some inspired host at a formal dinner, "chatting amiably . . . each trying to outdo the other in politeness."

Although Ida wrote many other books and articles, none of her later works had the impact of the Standard Oil history. In 1922 she tried to revive her interest and write a third volume on Standard. But the fire and the burning indignation that had caught a nation's attention were gone. "Repeating yourself," she decided, "is a doubtful practice."

In 1937, as Ida at eighty was writing her autobiography, John D. Rockefeller died at the age of ninety-seven. The lady who had been his nemesis lived seven more years, enjoying the tranquillity of her Connecticut farm, where she made jelly and raised peonies, lettuce, and potatoes. An interviewer who sought her out in this retreat found her characteristically self-effacing: "The proof that I am able to do anything so worthwhile as raise a potato never fails to thrill me," said the Terror of the Trusts.

Susan B. Anthony

In an era when a woman's contentment was believed to require only being kept "barefoot and pregnant," she led for years an uphill struggle to change the American mind.

By Peggy Robbins

Peggy Robbins, a frequent contributor to "AHI," is a resident of Tennessee. For more reading on Susan B. Anthony, she recommends: Constance B. Burnette, "Five for Freedom"; Rheta C. Dorr, "Susan B. Anthony: The Woman Who Changed the Mind of a Nation"; and Ida Husted Harper, "The Life and Work of Susan B. Anthony."

From *American History Illustrated*, April 1971. Reproduced through the courtesy of The National Historical Society, publishers of AMERICAN HISTORY *Illustrated*, 206 Hanover Street, Gettysburg, Pa. 17325. Published 10 times a year.

In 1900, Susan B. Anthony, "America's Number One Suffragette," retired as president of the National American Woman Suffrage Association, but the frail, gray-haired 80-year-old kept right on making appearances in behalf of what she called "the Vital Cause of Woman Suffrage." In New York City, when she appeared on stage to address a hall filled with distinguished people, her audience cheered and applauded enthusiastically. Susan turned to a companion and whispered, "What is it? What has happened?" The companion replied, "You happened, Susan Anthony." "Nonsense," the never-boastful Susan said. "They couldn't be cheering me. It's the Cause!" Whereupon, she started clapping, too—and the audience went wild with delight. They tossed flowers on the stage until Susan was standing knee-deep in them. After her speech pleading for federal legislation granting women the franchise, the applause was deafening; when it had died down, she remarked quietly, "Time brings strange changes. In this city which has just pelted me with roses I have been pelted with rotten eggs for saying the very same things I said tonight. My life has been interesting and continues to be so."

Susan Brownell Anthony, the second of six children born to Daniel and Lucy Read Anthony, began life on February 15, 1820, in Adams, Massachusetts. Daniel Anthony was a Quaker and he required that the members of his household dress as Quakers, speak as Quakers, and renounce frivolity in the manner of Quakers; but he was too independent a man, and of too liberal inclinations in some areas of human relationship, to be a true conformist. For example, he chose for his wife a playmate of his childhood, a pretty girl who not only was a Baptist but had dancing feet and a lovely singing voice. To keep her Quaker husband from being "read out of meeting," Lucy gave up her dancing and her music. She sang lullabies to her babies, but not when Quaker ears could hear.

Although Daniel was a prosperous cotton mill owner, his wife did all the household work, including farm chores, until her children grew large enough to help her. Since from eight to twelve mill hands lived with the Anthonys from time to time, there was never an end to household chores. Years later Susan expressed regret that her talented mother had not escaped from the "amiable domestic slave" class occupied by most women of her time.

When Susan was 8, Daniel moved the Anthony family to Battenville, New York, where he had acquired a partnership in a large cotton mill and a supply store for mill workers. Susan and her sister Guelma were entered in the Battenville public school in the winter of 1828. The one-room schoolhouse and the teaching methods were typical of that time: A hickory-wielding master sat at his desk near the open fireplace at the front end of the room; he devoted his energies to teaching reading, writing, and arithmetic to the boys strung out on rows of benches in front of him and almost ignored the few shivering girls seated on the bench against the back wall.

Stern-faced little Susan had insisted on being taught to read and write at home before she was 5, and now she could not be satisfied with the school work assigned her, which daily consisted of writing on her slate one sentence, such as, "Oh, may I not live in the way of sin." The day the boys started learning long division, Susan stayed after school, approached the schoolmaster's desk, and curtsied.

"Yes, Susan?" he snapped.

"Sir, may I learn long division with the boys?" she asked.

"Nonsense! Utter nonsense! What possible use could you ever have for long division?" He stood, ready to leave.

"Oh, sir, it could help me many ways. I want to learn——"

The master interrupted, "A girl needs to know how to read her Bible and count her egg money, nothing more. Go home, Susan Anthony."

Outside, Susan told Guelma what had happened. Guelma said she thought Susan should forget about learning long division, but Susan lifted her chin stubbornly and vowed, "Oh, I'll find a way." By the time the girls reached home, Susan was smiling; she'd thought of a way.

The girls in the Battenville schoolroom were allowed to come, one at a time, to a small bench near the fireplace, behind the teacher, to warm themselves. Susan arranged with the rest of the girls that she would be the one to raise her hand asking to occupy the "warming seat" just before the boys started their long division lesson. Each day she sat there behind the master, working every problem on her slate as he went over it with the boys, delighting in "advanced arithmetic." One night she astounded her father by announcing to him that she could work long division.

Susan B. Anthony had climbed the first step in a soaring life of social reform; she was to be the main strength and provide the strategy for the long and arduous campaign that emancipated modern woman.

The first year of Daniel Anthony's business operations in Battenville was unprofitable and very difficult, largely because of his refusal to sell rum and gin in the store and to hire mill workers who pledge not to drink anything stronger than cider. At a time when practically all business was transacted under the influence of "spirits," Daniel's firm opposition to intoxicating beverage in any form made the Anthony businesses at first unwelcome additions to

Battenville. But Daniel courageously stood by his principles, and the local residents gradually began to appreciate his business integrity. His store offered better merchandise at lower prices than its competitors, and Daniel was fair and considerate in his dealings with mill workers, even organizing for them a free night school which he taught himself until an instructor could be brought in.

When Susan was 12, one of the mill's spoolers—the girls who removed the spools, or bobbins, from the frames when they became full and put on empty ones—became ill and there was no one to fill in for her.

Susan volunteered to replace her.

There was just one stipulation to Susan's working in the mill as a substitute spooler: She'd have to give half of what she earned to Guelma because the older sister would have to double up on household chores with Susan away from home all day.

The next day the mill workers were surprised to see the owner's daughter at the frames, and during the following days the community buzzed with criticism of Daniel, but he ignored it. Susan worked for two weeks—from 6 a.m. until 6 p.m., six days each week—for one dollar and a half a week; she delighted in the work and was sorry she had to quit when the regular spooler returned.

As Daniel Anthony prospered he took his children out of the Battenville school and started a private school in a huge room on the upper floor of the Anthony home. It was taught during the winter months by a Quaker cousin Daniel brought to the community; summer sessions were usually taught by one of the Anthonys. Susan was the sole teacher during the summer she was 15.

The next summer Susan began a twelve-months' teaching session at a community near Battenville; she received her board and keep and five dollars a month and the "delighting opportunity for widened experience away from home." Friends and relatives of the Anthonys were shocked; it was disgraceful, they said, for Daniel to allow Susan to disobey the Quaker rule that only females who had no male relative ever left home and served as hired workers.

Susan sought her father's help in getting more formal education about the same time that the nationwide panic of 1837 began to plunge Daniel into financial reverses. At 18 she was sent to an inexpensive Quaker boarding school near Philadelphia, Miss Deborah Moulson's Academy for Young Females, where Guelma was starting her second term. For Guelma, seeking only preparation for being a proper Quaker wife, the extravagant piety required of all by the fanatical headmistress was no burden. For Susan, twelve months under the stern Quaker discipline of Deborah Moulson was deep and prolonged misery.

The brightest student by far and the only one with a desire to learn more than "homemaking," Susan did not exhibit the proper humility to satisfy Miss Moulson, and the headmistress persistently and with cruel severity crushed the girl's spirit. In later years Susan Anthony said it took a "lifetime of liberation" for her to be free of the painful inhibitions acquired during her "term" at Miss Moulson's, a year which left her pen and her voice "long mounted on stilts."

Between 1838 and 1844, Daniel Anthony operated a gristmill and a small satinet factory, both heavily mortgaged, about three miles from Battenville. The Anthonys lived in a big house that had previously served as a road tavern; its second story was a large room with "a floor laid over glass bottle bits to give more resonance to fiddling music." Daniel allowed some of the young people in the rural area to use this room for weekly "socials"; when the Society of Friends heard about this, Friend Daniel Anthony was finally "read out of Quaker meeting."

During Daniel's effort to save the gristmill and satinet factory, the whole Anthony family helped. Susan and Hannah taught school and lent their father every penny they could spare. Daniel Anthony, Jr., 16 in 1839, worked side by side with the millhands. Lucy Anthony, with the help of only the younger children, prepared meals for a dozen boarders, which included packing big noon lunch pails for them. But still Daniel Anthony lost both the mill and the factory.

During these years Susan at first served as assistant principal of a boarding school in New Rochelle, for which she received thirty dollars for each fifteen weeks of work. Later she taught in a country school for two dollars and a half a week; she held down exactly the same position for which her predecessor, a man, had been paid ten dollars a week.

In 1845 Daniel Anthony used a fund left to Lucy by her father, a fund which had for many years been entrusted to the safekeeping of Lucy's brother, Joshua Read, to make the down payment on a farm in Hardscrabble, near Rochester, New York. By this time Hannah had married and young Daniel was working in Massachusetts, so only 25-year-old Susan, 18-year-old Mary, and Merritt, a boy of 11 who was the youngest Anthony child, made the move with Daniel and Lucy. All during the slow, cold, several-days' journey by stage, canal boat, and wagon from Battenville to Hardscrabble, Susan kept thinking about how a woman was permitted no legal control over her own property, even money inherited from her father.

The farm provided both a home and a source of income for the Anthonys. Before long Daniel found employment with the New York Life Insurance Company, which was just starting in Rochester; he was a salaried member of that organization for the rest of his life.

When a letter arrived from her Uncle Joshua Read, one of the trustees of Canajoharie Academy in New York, offering her a position as head of Canajoharie's "Female Department" and suggesting she live with the Reads, whose home was near the academy, Susan speedily accepted.

Living with her non-Quaker relatives, including female cousins who danced and sang and even engaged in a little gentle flirting, Susan began to throw off her Quaker repressions. A tall, broad-shouldered young woman whose facial character was more patrician than pretty, Susan braided her heavy chestnut hair and piled it high in a coronet style quite modish at the time; she looked like a queen, her pupils said. From time to time she had suitors, but none pleased her. They drank. She said she wanted "a total abstinence man" like her father; she didn't find one.

Realizing that teaching alone no longer held enough challenge for her, she became active in a variety of "causes." At first she threw her main energy into the fight for temperance; a member of the Daughters of Temperance, she sponsored a chapter of the organization at Canajoharie and she was soon sought for organizational activities all over the state. Although not a moving speaker, she was somehow a convincing one; never an outstanding writer, she became an ever more forceful one. And she was a gifted organizer. After three years at Canajoharie

"The Age of Brass, or The Triumphs of Woman's Rights." Currier & Ives lithograph, 1869. (Reproduced courtesy of The Harry T. Peters Collection, Museum of the City of New York)

Academy, she gave up teaching to devote her full time to "social action"; in 1849 she returned to Rochester and deep involvement with the Woman's State Temperance Society of New York, the first body of its kind. She also became active in the fight against slavery, and she spoke up at every opportunity against injustices to women.

As Susan organized temperance groups, she was dismayed and disgusted to find that the men's temperance society not only refused to work with the women but actually tried to block the efforts of Susan's followers because, the men said, the women would hinder the temperance cause by involving it with the question of women's rights. About this time Susan began her fifty-year friendship with Elizabeth Cady Stanton, a social reformer five years her elder, who was the leader in the crusade for women's rights; Elizabeth had insisted that the fight for women's rights was the real fight on which their attention should be focused and that Susan was wasting too much of herself on temperance. Now Susan began to agree with Elizabeth. One of her first organized campaigns in behalf of women was a noisy one that culminated during a meeting of the New York State Teachers' Association; Susan forced through a vote that allowed female teachers to "share in all the privileges and deliberations" of the association.

By 1853 Susan was, according to one of her younger sisters, "living, breathing, eating, and sleeping women's rights." She gradually became the guiding mind of the whole crusade, spurred on by her friendship with such "rebellious women's righters" as Lucretia

Mott, Lucy Stone, Abby Kelley Foster, and Ernestine Rose. Her fellow crusaders never tired of telling how Susan, speaking to an unruly mob at a women's rights convention in New York in 1853, never flinched once even when the hisses and catcalls completely drowned out her voice.

Susan's friendship with Elizabeth Stanton had grown ever closer since the day the two had been introduced by Amelia Bloomer, a sister reformer and the wife of the Seneca Falls, New York postmaster. Susan lived much of the time in the Seneca Falls home of Elizabeth and her lawyer husband, Henry Stanton, who was active in the antislavery movement and much in demand as a speaker for that cause. The two women wrote women's rights speeches, drafted petitions, planned new organizations, and discussed further means for agitating reform—all this along with domestic chores. Susan was an old maid but Elizabeth gave birth to seven children while she crusaded. Since Elizabeth was the better speaker, and since no one could accuse *her* of being "agin the men becuz she never cotched one," she frequently campaigned while Susan stayed in Seneca Falls and looked after the Stanton children. Henry by this time was in the state legislature in Albany and was away from home much of the time. The Stanton youngsters grew up thinking Susan was their aunt. One of them later recalled that Susan and Elizabeth, working together late at night in the Stanton library, often argued so violently that their voices carried all over the big house, but that they always emerged from the library arm-in-arm for a peaceful moonlight stroll through the garden. "After an argument they never explained to each other, nor apologized, nor wept, nor went through a make-up period, as most people do."

For a few years the leaders of the "Woman Movement" dramatized their protest against constraining corsets and other "stifling apparel" by appearing in public in baggy trousers that were gathered in at the ankles—"bloomers," named for Amelia Bloomer, who advocated wearing them. It was a relative of Elizabeth Stanton's, and not Amelia, who initiated the bloomer costume, but Mrs. Bloomer publicized it in her periodical, *The Lily*, one of the first papers in America owned and edited by a woman, and the first "dedicated to purity, temperance, and woman's advance." Susan Anthony even cut short her heavy brown hair "for further effect with Bloomer dress." But it finally became apparent that the publicity of the "sensational costumes" was making many reform-minded people hesitate to join the Woman Movement; Susan reverted "with relief" to her soft, simple gray dresses and Elizabeth returned "reluctantly" to her fashionable floor-sweeping gowns.

In 1860 the first great results of the long, hard, Woman Movement occurred in New York State. In 1848 the New York Legislature had passed a Woman's Property Bill aimed at protecting the property rights of married women, but it was a weak measure prompted not by moral motives but by the anger of a few wealthy Hudson Valley farmers whose spendthrift sons-in-law had thrown away their daughters' dowries. The 1860 amendments to this law, amendments enacted as a result of the "incessant prodding and petitioning of Susan B. Anthony and her women," provided that a married woman could control her own property and her own earnings; she was granted joint guardianship of her children, with rights and privileges equal to their father's; and on becoming a widow she was given the same rights in her husband's property that, had she died, he would have had in hers. Other states followed New York in enacting "liberation legislation for women." It was a great victory for the Woman Movement, attained in spite of bitter, and often vicious, opposition. The New York *World* told its readers that "Susan B. Anthony is lean, cadaverous, and intellectual, with the proportions of a file and the voice of a hurdy-gurdy."

From 1856 until the Civil War began, Susan managed to find time from her women's rights campaigns to serve as agent for the American Antislavery Society in New York, often facing violently hostile mobs. She organized the Women's National Loyal League to urge emancipation of the Negro.

During the Civil War the fight for women's rights was suspended, except that, while Susan and Elizabeth were crusading to help the Negro, they usually added, "And free the women as well as the slaves!"

After the war Susan concentrated on winning for women the right to vote. That was, she said, the "supreme goal" of her life. When Horace Greeley, who opposed "franchising females," sneered, "Miss Anthony, are you aware that the ballot and the bullet go together? If you vote, are you also prepared to fight?" Susan answered, "Certainly, Mr. Greeley. Exactly as you fought in the last war—at the point of a goose-quill."

In the crusade for the franchise for women, Susan, in addition to making canvasses and speeches, did the work the other suffragettes did not want to do: She called conventions and then managed them; she petitioned hostile legislators and braved the opposition of whole political parties.

In late 1866, when it was learned that two constitutional amendments, one granting the franchise to Negroes and the other granting it to women, were to be submitted to popular vote in Kansas the next year, Susan and a group of her "Female Fighters for the Franchise" trekked westward and "covered Kansas

Suffragettes parade in New York City, May 6, 1912.

with spirited speeches." Both amendments were defeated, but there were 9,000 votes for woman suffrage,
only 1,000 less than for Negro suffrage, and the very
fact that 9,000 males in a single state had been persuaded to favor women voting represented a triumph
to the suffragettes. Later, Susan traveled through other
areas of the West, enduring without complaint all
sorts of privation while she made major contributions
toward securing the vote for women in several of the
new states.

From 1868 through 1870 Susan published a liberal
weekly in New York, *The Revolution,* which had the
motto, "The true republic—men, their rights and
nothing more; women, their rights and nothing less."
The Revolution demanded that the provisions of all
proposed constitutional amendments which would
give the franchise to male Negroes apply also to
women. After this and other demands of the suffragettes were ignored, Susan decided to test her right to
vote. Insisting on voting in an election in Rochester,
New York in 1873, she so confused the officials that
they allowed her, along with some suffragettes who
accompanied her, to do so.

Susan was soon arrested for "illegal voting." She'd
hardly been served with a warrant before she set out
on a lecture tour "to present a full-dress review of the
issues." While waiting for her case to come to trial,
she spoke twenty-nine times on "The Equal Right of
All Citizens to the Ballot." After each speech she
asked her audience if they thought she'd broken any
law; she was delighted that the majority of her listeners yelled back that they did not. The United States
District Attorney angrily complained that Susan had
made it impossible to select an impartial jury. She
snapped back, "Does it prejudice a jury to read and
explain to them the Constitution of the United
States?" The District Attorney had the case transferred to another county; that occasioned a delay of
twenty-two days, which Susan welcomed—that gave
her time to make twenty-one speeches on "Is It a
Crime for a Citizen of the United States to Vote?"

A newspaper reported, "No longer in the bloom of
youth—if, indeed, she ever had any bloom—hard-
featured, cold as an icicle, fluent and philosophical,
Susan B. Anthony wields more influence today than
all the beautiful and brilliant lecturers that ever
flaunted upon the platform as preachers of social
impossibilities."

Susan was found guilty of violating the law and
fined a hundred dollars. She firmly refused to pay, and
the whole thing was dropped.

Friction between Susan, president of the National Woman Suffrage Association, and Mrs. Lucy Stone, head of the American Woman Suffrage Association, had existed for some years. Lucy and some of her followers considered Susan narrow-minded and domineering, but Lucy's main objection to Susan stemmed from the latter's association with a spectacular promoter named George Francis Train. In addition to sponsoring a lecture tour in which Susan and Elizabeth Stanton participated, Train largely financed the publication of *The Revolution*. He wrote a column in the weekly which he devoted to the "necessity of greenback money." Many well-to-do citizens considered such currency a threat to sound fiscal policy. Susan endured the column as the only means of financing a paper advocating suffrage for women, a position which Lucy Stone regarded as "shocking evidence of Susan Anthony's unhinged judgment."

Mrs. Stone was not alone in denouncing the Anthony-Train association. William Lloyd Garrison, the prominent abolitionist who had often shared a lecture platform with Susan, wrote Miss Anthony he was astonished that she had "taken such leave of good sense as to be a traveling companion and associate lecturer of that crack-brained harlequin and semi-lunatic George Francis Train."

Finally, in 1889, many years after Susan had dissolved all connection with Train, she and Lucy Stone overcame their differences and the two suffrage groups united as the National American Woman Suffrage Association, with Elizabeth Stanton elected president, Susan vice-president, and Lucy Stone executive secretary. Susan served the organization as president from 1892 until 1900. During this time she supported the suffrage bills introduced before the legislatures of various states—some passed, some did not—but she campaigned hardest for a Federal woman's suffrage amendment which would be binding on all the states.

During the last decade of the 19th century Susan Anthony became a widely respected and greatly admired woman. Bouquets replaced the hurled tomatoes of earlier years; politicians sought her advice; newspapers and magazines were eager to publish anything she would write. At the Columbian Exposition of 1893 in Chicago, Susan spoke often and to huge crowds; her persistent plea that females be enfranchised through Federal legislation was consistently well received. One Chicago paper reported, "This World's Fair has absolutely set afire that amazing Susan B. Anthony and her suffragettes." It was quite different from the Philadelphia Centennial of '76,

ABOVE: Militant suffragists, with police escort, march to Capitol in Washington, April 7, 1913. Note the state banners.

during which Susan and her followers had, at first, been ignored, and then scorned.

As the years passed, Susan spoke to ever more receptive, ever more pleasantly responsive, audiences. In Washington, D.C., a large crowd of both men and women stood in tribute as she entered an auditorium; it cheered enthusiastically before she said a word. One Washington newspaper declared, "Spring is not heralded in our city by the arrival of the robin, but rather by the appearance of Miss Susan B. Anthony, a trim gray-haired lady with a red shawl about her shoulders. Miss Anthony has for some time been the inspiring symbol of the woman suffrage movement."

During the 1870's Susan began work on her *History of Woman Suffrage*, which ended up, with its fourth and final volume in 1900, as a monumentally detailed record on which several of her fellow suffragettes had collaborated.

In 1883 Susan Anthony took her first vacation; she went to Europe and was amazed to find herself famous there, particularly in England. She explained to English women that the specific objective of the woman suffrage movement was "total and complete sex equality, that women may own and possess their own souls." She went on in 1888 to organize the International Council of Women; in 1904, at the age of 84, in Berlin, Germany, she helped organize, and headed, the International Woman Suffrage Alliance.

Susan Anthony began the latter part of her life with meager financial resources; she had spent too much of the modest fees she had received for lecturing on the transportation and food needs of women who could not have attended the Woman Movement meetings without her help. When she was 70, she and her sister Mary, a retired school teacher, decided to move together into a house they had inherited in Rochester —but neither had enough money to buy furniture. As a tribute to Susan, the Political Equality League of Rochester furnished the house.

On her 86th birthday she attended a dinner in her honor in Washington and ended her remarks about women's suffrage with, "Failure is impossible!" When she died on March 13, 1906, her country flew its flags at half-mast and eulogized her as "The Champion of a Lost Cause."

Fourteen years after Susan's death, on August 26, 1920, one century after the birth of the Napoleon of Feminism, the "lost cause" was won: the Nineteenth Amendment to the Constitution—"The right of citizens of the United States to vote shall not be denied or abridged by the United States or by any State on account of sex"—was ratified, making it part of the law of the land. It was, and still is, called "The Susan B. Anthony Amendment."

The Rich Man's Burden
and how Andrew Carnegie unloaded it

JOSEPH FRAZIER WALL

Dr. Wall, professor of history and dean at Grinnell College, is the first scholar to gain access to the Carnegie papers held by the United States Steel Company. The resulting biography, Andrew Carnegie, *which will be published this month by Oxford University Press, is the basis for this article.*

On one of the last nights of the year 1868, Andrew Carnegie, who had recently moved to New York from Pittsburgh and was living with his mother in the elegant St. Nicholas Hotel, sat down at his desk to total up his various investments and his annual returns from those investments. It was an impressive statement of accomplishment for a man who, as a child of thirteen, had accompanied his parents in steerage class from Scotland to America and had found his first employment as a bobbin boy in a textile mill at $1.20 a week. Now, twenty years later, he had assets of four hundred thousand dollars and an annual income of $56,110. How gratifying it all should have been! Yet, in a curious way, it was not entirely satisfying. Carnegie had for some time realized that most of the successful men he had encountered were men with one ambition —money, and with but one talent — the ability to get it. He could not help comparing these business associates with the heroes of his childhood, Uncle Tom Morrison, Uncle George Lauder, and his father, radical Chartists who would discourse at length upon literature, history, politics, and economics.

The end of the year for a Scottish Calvinist is a time for sober reflection, for pondering upon man's sinful frailty and God's awesome majesty. Carnegie had, to be sure, never accepted the Calvinist view of either man or God, but the ethos of Scotland was bred into him. With all the introspection of a Jonathan Edwards or a John Knox, he took a hard, unpitying look at himself. Then he wrote down another kind of balance sheet to accompany his statement of business holdings:

Man must have an idol—The amassing of wealth is one of the worst species of idolitary [sic]. No idol more debasing than the worship of money. Whatever I engage in I must push inordinately therefor should I be careful to choose that life which will be the most elevating in its character. To continue much longer overwhelmed by business cares and with most of my thoughts wholly upon the way to make more money in the shortest time, must degrade me beyond hope of permanent recovery. I will resign business at thirty five . . .

Carnegie, however, did not resign business at thirty-five. For the next thirty-two years he continued to "push inordinately," and by 1900 he had built a steel empire so vast and so independently powerful that it endangered even the complex, interlocking financial world of J. P. Morgan. In February, 1901, Morgan, representing all of those interests in steel products and railroads that were threatened by Carnegie's ever-expanding empire, offered to buy Carnegie Steel and quickly accepted Carnegie's price of $480,000,000. Paying a visit to Carnegie's home, Morgan shook the Scotsman's hand and said, "Mr. Carnegie, I want to congratulate you on being the richest man in the world!"

And, during all of these years, Carnegie's note, written in 1868 and addressed to himself, had lain in his desk, undisturbed, yet ever disturbing to his self-esteem. Now with this vast fortune in first mortgage, 5 per cent gold bonds of the newly created United States Steel Corporation in his possession, Carnegie turned his full attention away from getting to giving—to debasing the idol at whose altar he had so long and so successfully worshipped. Carnegie was under no illusions about the problems that would confront him. His friend John Morley, an English statesman, had written him a month after the sale to Morgan had been consummated, "I say to you what Johnson said to Burke, when B. showed him his fine house, 'I don't envy, I do admire.' You'll have some difficulty, tho' in adapting the principles of accumulation to the business of distribution." To which Carnegie wrote in answer, "... I don't see it needs the same principles as acquisition—but it needs some of these. Tenacity and steady sailing to the haven we clear for—supreme confidence in one's own ideas, or conclusions rather, after thought —and above all, placing *use* above popularity." These were qualities of character with which Carnegie had proved himself to be well endowed, but he also showed a quality of capriciousness that often made his philanthropic gestures—or lack of them—an enigma to those soliciting him for aid.

Yet Carnegie would always believe that his philanthropic practices, like his business practices, were based upon rational, systematic principles. These principles in some respects made his task of giving more difficult but, he felt, far more socially significant and beneficial than the simple random distribution of largess. He had explained his system in a remarkable two-part essay entitled "Wealth," which appeared in the June and December, 1889, issues of the *North American Review*.

Carnegie's essay created a considerable stir when it first appeared, and deservedly so. The editor of the *North American Review*, Allen Thorndike Rice, called it the "finest article I have ever published in the Review." It was quickly picked up in Britain, where it appeared in *Pall Mall Gazette* under the title "Gospel of Wealth." It caught the attention of the reading public of two nations because of its candor, its specific proposals for the distribution of wealth, and, of course, because of its author— a well-known American millionaire who was openly critical of his own class.

The thesis of the "Gospel" was simply and boldly stated: "The problem of our age is the proper administration of wealth." To Carnegie there appeared only three alternatives by which a man of great wealth could dispose of his fortune: he could leave it to his family, he could bequeath it in his will for public purposes, or he could administer it during his lifetime for public benefit. Of the three, the least desirable both for society and for the individual was the first, and on this point Carnegie gave his oft-repeated homily on the evils of inherited wealth. The wife and daughters should be provided with moderate sources of income, he believed, but as for the sons, he felt that "The thoughtful man must shortly say, 'I would as soon leave to my son a curse as the almighty dollar,' and admit to himself that it is not the welfare of the children, but family pride, which inspires the legacies."

The second alternative, while socially more responsible, is frequently thwarted by disappointed heirs contesting the will, he wrote. Even when a philanthropic bequest is successfully carried out, "it may be said that this is only a means for the disposal of wealth, provided a man is content to wait until he is dead before he becomes of much good in the world." Carnegie approved of heavy inheritance taxes, or "death duties," to ensure society's reaping some benefits from the accumulation of wealth if either of the first two alternatives was chosen.

"There remains, then," he wrote, "only one mode of using great fortunes; but in this we have the true antidote for the temporary unequal distribution of wealth, the reconciliation of the rich and the poor—a reign of harmony.... It is founded upon the present most intense Individualism and ... under its sway we shall have an ideal State, in which the surplus wealth of the few will become, in the best sense, the property of the many, because administered for the common good, and this wealth, passing through the hands of the few, can be made a much more potent force for the elevation of our race than if distributed in small sums to the people themselves." In short, the rich man should spend his fortune during his lifetime in ways that will most effectively benefit and advance society. "This, then, is held to be the duty of the man of wealth: To set an example of modest, unostentatious living, shunning display or extravagance; to provide moderately for the legitimate wants of those dependent upon him; and, after doing so, to consider all surplus revenues which come to him simply as trust funds which he is called upon to administer ... the man of wealth thus becoming the mere trustee and agent for his poorer brethren, bringing to their service his superior wisdom, experience, and ability to administer, doing for them better than they would or could do for themselves."

In the second part of his essay, Carnegie, at the request of the editor, presented "some of the best methods of performing this duty of administering surplus wealth for the good of the people." First, the millionaire who adheres to the gospel must "take care that the purposes for which he spends it shall not have a degrading pampering tendency upon its recipients, but that his trust shall be so administered as to stimulate the best and most aspiring poor of the community to further efforts for their own improvement. It is not the irreclaimably destitute, shiftless, and worthless which it is truly beneficial or truly benevolent for the individual to attempt to reach and improve. For these there exists the refuge provided by the city or the State, where they can be sheltered, fed, clothed ... and, most important of all—where they can be isolated from the well-doing and industrious poor...."

The specific fields of philanthropy in which the wise trustee of surplus wealth would invest, according to Carnegie, were seven, listed in descending order of importance: (1) universities—the founding of universities, of

Carnegie saw to his own education with finely housed collections of books in the spacious library of his Manhattan mansion.

course, being possible only "by men enormously rich"; (2) free libraries—for Carnegie himself, he said, this "occupies first place"; (3) the founding or extension of hospitals "and other institutions connected with the alleviation of human suffering"; (4) parks; (5) halls suitable for meetings, concerts, etc; (6) "swimming baths"; and (7) churches—but only the building, not the maintenance of the church activities, which should be done by the entire congregation. "It is not expected," Carnegie added, "that there should be general concurrence as to the best possible use of surplus wealth. . . . There is room and need for all kinds of wise benefactions for the common weal."

It is fortunate that Carnegie did not expect "general concurrence" on his list of proper fields for philanthropy, for he certainly did not get it. Ministers and mission boards, in particular, were outraged to find churches seventh on the list—just after swimming baths. Artists, writers, and musicians also wanted their share of patronage, as did private schools, orphanages, and other charitable institutions.

But Carnegie's fundamental assumptions were not allowed to go unchallenged either. A sharp critique of Carnegie's gospel was offered by William Jewett Tucker, the liberal American theologian, professor of religion at Andover Theological Seminary, and later to be the distinguished president of Dartmouth College. Writing a review of "The Gospel of Wealth" in 1891 for the *Andover Review*, Tucker, as no other critic of the time did, examined the essence of Carnegie's gospel—and found it fallacious. First, Tucker pointed out, it was based upon a false assumption of inevitability. He quoted Carnegie as

saying, "We start with a condition of affairs [referring to the prevailing competitive system] under which the best interests of the race are promoted, but which inevitably gives wealth to the few." This Tucker found unacceptable. "[T]he assumption . . . that wealth is the inevitable possession of the few, and is best administered by them for the many, begs the whole question of economic justice now before society, and relegates it to the field of charity, leaving the question of the original distribution of wealth unsettled, or settled only to the satisfaction of the few. . . ."

Tucker also found fault in Carnegie's plan for the redistribution of wealth, generous and praiseworthy as it seemed to be. "Just as formerly it was contended that political power should be in the hands of the few, because it would be better administered, so now it is contended —I quote Mr. Carnegie's words, slightly transferring them, but not changing their meaning—that 'the millionaire is intrusted for the time being with a great part of the increased wealth of the community, because he can administer it for the community far better than it could or would have done for itself.' This, of course, if accepted and carried out in any complete way, becomes patronage . . . and, in the long run, society cannot afford to be patronized."

This was striking at the real inner defense line that protected Carnegie's self-esteem and provided a justification for his life. In an essay, "The Advantages of Poverty," Carnegie made one brief statement that was far more revealing of his own motivation for philanthropy than he probably ever intended or realized. In discussing the question of why the very rich should avoid extravagant living, he wrote, "they can, perhaps, also find refuge from self-questioning in the thought of the much greater portion of their means which is being spent upon others." It is the phrase "perhaps, also find refuge from self-questioning" that is the tip-off. This is the kind of refuge Carnegie must have been seeking for twenty years, ever since as a young man in 1868 he had warned himself against the degradation of money worship. But the old doubts persisted. What was really happening to an America in which one man could accumulate a fortune that ran into nine figures? Carnegie had to justify his life to himself. Unlike some of his contemporaries—Fisk, Gould, Drew—he could not accept for himself the innocent animal amorality of the freebooter, nor on the other hand could he, having rejected the tenets of orthodox religion, now retreat with John D. Rockefeller into pious Baptism and say, "The Good Lord gave me my wealth."

Carnegie must have felt that he had at last found justification for plutocracy by his gospel of wealth: a man may accumulate great wealth in a democracy, but he has a responsibility to return that wealth in a way that will not destroy society's own responsibility to preserve individual initiative. To give through the usual charitable outlets is wrong, for such charity is primarily concerned with the hopeless "submerged tenth." It keeps the weak weak and upsets the equality of opportunity. To give library buildings with the provision that the community must then furnish the books is right, for this makes available opportunities for all—it encourages the salvageable "swimming tenth" and at the same time respects the responsibility of the community. And who is better prepared for the responsible task of being steward for a nation's accumulated wealth than the man who, starting with nothing, has through his own initiative gathered in this wealth? Carnegie must have felt with the writing of his "Gospel of Wealth" that he had at last made peace

with his conscience, had at last found that "refuge from self-questioning."

He, of course, had begun to practice long before he had had a gospel to preach. That is why he was convinced that he was a "scientific philanthropist." His principles of philanthropy, he felt, were pragmatically based upon experience. His earliest philanthropic bequests, however, were based on no discernible system. Sentiment and his own idiosyncratic interests dictated his choice more than any rational philosophy. By the time his essay "Wealth" appeared in 1889, he had given a swimming bath and library to Dunfermline, the Scottish town in which he was born, a library to Braddock, Pennsylvania, and a pipe organ to the small Swedenborgian church in Allegheny, Pennsylvania, that his father and aunts had

Carnegie's first major philanthropic project was the Carnegie Institute in Pittsburgh, shown here as it looked in 1902. He envisaged the civic center as an uplifting influence on the masses, but he firmly disapproved of the undraped statues in its Statuary Hall.

attended in the 1850's. His only gift to higher education was a grant of six thousand dollars extended over a five-year period to the Western University of Pennsylvania (later to be the University of Pittsburgh). This is not a tremendously impressive list, and sentiment was clearly a major factor. But the list is interesting in its diversity. It is evident that these early gifts determined his ideas about "the best fields of philanthropy."

After the appearance of his famous essay Carnegie began in earnest to follow his own dictates. As he had indicated in "Wealth," libraries were to be his specialty in this early phase of his philanthropic career. After his first two library gifts to Dunfermline and Braddock, in which he furnished not only the library building but provided an endowment for the acquisition of books and the maintenance of the library, Carnegie would give only the building and insist upon the town's taxing itself for the books and maintenance. He was to make only three exceptions to this rule after having established it: at Duquesne and Homestead, Pennsylvania, and the borough of Carnegie, a suburb of Pittsburgh. Fifty years later, a report on the Carnegie library system by Ralph Munn, which appeared in the *Library Journal*, showed the wisdom of that rule. The only four libraries in the United States to receive an endowment from Carnegie, Munn reported, "still have exactly the same endowment which

That Carnegie enjoyed the "Hallelujah business" of receiving thanks for his benefactions is suggested by this genial scene in Worthing, England, where, arms outflung, he was accepting with delight the Freedom of the City. Freedoms were parchment scrolls, usually encased in an ornamental casket such as the one below. This charming silver-gilt casket, from Wigan, England, was presented to Carnegie in 1909 and features a suitably dignified portrait of him.

CARNEGIE DUNFERMLINE TRUST. PHOTO
COURTESY OF CARNEGIE LIBRARY. PITTSBURGH

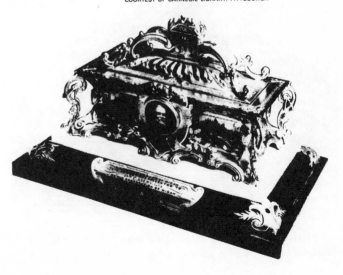

Riverside, California

In 1897 Carnegie's only child, Margaret, was born, and he bought Skibo Castle in northern Scotland as a summer home for his family.

By 1901 Carnegie needed a New York house, and he built this block-long mansion on Fifth Avenue. It cost one million dollars.

he gave them in the 1890's and the cities have firmly refused to give them any local financial support."

It was much easier at first for Carnegie to give libraries in Scotland than in the United States, for there were no taxation restrictions on British municipalities. They could tax themselves for the support of libraries, while many cities of the United States could not. Pittsburgh, for example, could not accept Carnegie's offer to provide a library building in 1881 because the city council ruled that the laws of Pennsylvania did not provide for municipal property-tax assessments to be used to maintain a free library. Shortly thereafter, however, the Pennsylvania legislature specifically provided for tax assessments for libraries, and Pittsburgh quickly requested a renewal of the offer. The renewal came multiplied several times over, for Carnegie now had in mind a great civic center, the Carnegie Institute, which would include not only an imposing library but a great museum, a music hall, and an art institute, located at the edge of Schenley Park.

This was Carnegie's first great philanthropic endeavor, and in these early days he could still allow himself the luxury of considering almost every detail, from the architectural design of the buildings to the question of nudity in the copies of classical statuary. "I strongly recommend nude to be draped since question has been raised," he wired W. M. Frew, the president of the Carnegie Library Commission. "Remember my words in speech. We should begin gently to lead people upward. I do hope nothing in gallery or hall will ever give offense to the simplest man or woman. Draping is used everywhere in Britain except in London. If we are to work genuine good we must bend and keep in touch with masses. Am very clear indeed on this question." For weeks he fussed with Frew about the names that would be carved in stone on the entablature. When he saw the proposed list in the Pittsburgh *Dispatch*, he exploded to Frew: "I cannot approve the list of names. . . . Some of the names have no business to be on the list. Imagine Dickens in and Burns out. Among painters Perugini out and Rubens in, the latter only a painter of fat, vulgar women, while a study of the pictures of Raphael will show anyone that he was really only a copyist of Perugini, whose pupil he was. Imagine Science and Franklin not there. This list for Music seems satisfactory. Palestrina rightly comes first. Have been entranced by his works, which we have heard in Rome. As I am to be in Pittsburgh very soon, I hope you will postpone action in regard to the names."

Library giving, except for so large an undertaking as the Carnegie Institute of Pittsburgh, quickly became a business, as efficient and standardized as the filling of orders for steel billets at Homestead or Duquesne. A town council would apply for a Carnegie Library, and Carnegie's secretary, James Bertram, would acknowledge the request and inform the municipal government of the specifications to be met before the grant could be made.

The town would first have to provide a site, if possible centrally located in the town. Then the governing board of the community would have to pledge an annual appropriation for books and maintenance that would amount to 10 per cent of the Carnegie gift. The size of Carnegie's gift was based upon the population of the town, usually two dollars per capita, which worked very well indeed for cities from twenty-five thousand to one hundred thousand in population. In the latter instance, for example, Carnegie would give two hundred thousand dollars for the building, and the city would pledge twenty thousand dollars a year for maintenance. But in many of the very small villages that also received gifts of libraries, the annual amount pledged in order to receive the gift might be as low as two hundred dollars a year. In fact, the only major criticism made by the Munn report of 1951 was that it would have been much better if small neighboring towns had "pooled their resources for a single library," much as communities would later do in consolidating public-school systems. From the professional librarian's point of view this is certainly a justifiable criticism, but who can say how many youths or lonely old people living in towns like Idaho Springs, Colorado, or Flora, Indiana, or Sanborn, Iowa, in those pre-radio-television days, found their only intellectual excitement or companionship in the Carnegie Free Public Library? In any event, Carnegie liked to think this was true. As he wrote to one applicant for a library building, "I believe that it outranks any other one thing that a community can do to

benefit its people. It is the never failing spring in the desert."

At first Carnegie made no attempt to provide building plans along with his grant of money for the building, leaving the architectural design to be determined by each locality. But there were so many bad buildings erected in these early years of library giving, and so many complaints from librarians who had to contend with functional problems, that Carnegie, and later the Carnegie Corporation of New York, sent out standard plans along with the monetary grant. What may have been gained in functional efficiency, however, was lost in architectural variety. Soon, in small towns all over America, there came to be an architectural style, popularly known as Carnegie Classical, that was as easily identifiable as that other standardized small-town architectural style known as Wesley Romanesque. A stranger in the community seldom had difficulty in spotting the Carnegie Library and the Methodist church, which in many towns confronted each other across the square.

The public generally believed that Carnegie insisted that his name be engraved above the front entrance of the libraries he gave. This was not true. But certainly he never objected to its being done, and, upon request, he would provide the library with a photograph of himself, which would hang in the place of honor just inside the main door. As he made clear to applicants, the one thing he did desire was "that there should be placed over the entrance to the Libraries I build a representation of the rays of a rising sun, and above 'LET THERE BE LIGHT,' and I hope you can have this on the building." Not all communities complied with this request, however. Perhaps the Methodists across the way found it a bit presumptuous for a secular institution thus to arrogate to itself Jehovah's own first command.

Carnegie frequently attended the dedication ceremonies of a major new library, particularly if it was in Britain, for there it usually meant that he would be granted the Freedom of the City, a medieval rite that he thoroughly enjoyed. He began collecting "Freedoms" in the early 1890's. The parchment scroll signifying this honor was encased in a small casket, and each town in Britain seemed to be trying to outdo its neighbor in the elaborateness of the casket design. Carnegie, who had never before been infected with the collector's mania—neither stamps nor paintings nor rare old books ever having had an appeal for him—entered into this hobby with all the zest of the most fanatic philatelist. It was a proud day when he broke the previous record, held by Gladstone, of fourteen Freedoms. He really hit top form when he received six Freedoms in six days. They came so fast, in fact, that even the London *Times*, usually so reliable, became confused and on one occasion reported that Carnegie was to receive the Freedom of Bromley-by-Bow the following week. The citizens of that small London

New York's famed Carnegie Hall would have been called simply The Music Hall but for the objection of snobbish foreign artists, Carnegie claimed.

suburb were alarmed when they read their papers on that day, for it was the first they had known about it— no casket, no parchment, nothing was prepared. The *Times* hastily carried the next day one of its few retractions. It appeared that it was Bromley, Kent, that was prepared to honor Carnegie that week.

"How dog-sick you must be of all these meetings, addresses, and Hallelujah business," Morley wrote Carnegie, who was then on one of his whirlwind collecting tours. "I shouldn't wonder at your longing for Skibo [Carnegie's castle in Scotland] and what Mr. Smith calls 'the quiet stream of self-forgetfulness'—blessed waters for all of us." But this was the kind of "quiet stream" that Carnegie never cared to fish in, and Morley's sympathy was quite wasted on him. Carnegie, for all his loudly proclaimed radical republicanism, dearly loved the pomp and circumstance of the medieval ritual—riding in an open carriage through the old twisting streets lined with crowds and flags; being met at the town hall by the Lord Mayor, resplendent in his robes and silver medallion of office, who made the formal presentation of the Freedom of the City to Carnegie. Finally came the opportunity to address the assembled crowd and to spread his gospel of wealth.

How sweet it all was! "Never so busy, never so happy," Carnegie would frequently write to his Cousin Dod or friend Morley, neither of whom could understand why he was either.

Carnegie would always insist that these shows were all for the purpose of dramatizing and publicizing the gospel of wealth, in the hope that other millionaires might be converted. As he wrote to one friend in explanation of his "Hallelujah business": "Well do I remember my apprehensions when you advocated keeping all you did quiet. *No show*. No advocacy. Only go on & do the work in a quiet way, when I knew that advertizing was essential for success, i.e. to spreading abroad what could be done. . . . Of course its disagreeable work & puts me forward as a vain trumpeter but one who isn't willing to play this part *for the good* to be done, isn't much of a man."

Carnegie enjoyed his trumpeting too obviously to convince anyone that he found it disagreeable work. The ceremonies and speeches continued, and ultimately he was to collect the Freedom of fifty-seven cities, the all-time record for Great Britain. For a time after World War II it appeared that Winston Churchill might surpass it, but he never quite equalled this total.

The flamboyant public displays of course enhanced Carnegie's already notorious reputation for being a publicity seeker. It was generally believed both in Britain and in America that he never gave a cent that was not returned to him tenfold in public adulation. Poultney Bigelow, who worked with Carnegie for the establishment of the New York Public Library system, wrote one of the harshest indictments of the philanthropist:

Never before in the history of plutocratic America had any one man purchased by mere money so much social advertising and flattery. No wonder that he felt himself infallible, when Lords temporal and spiritual courted him and hung upon his words. They wanted his money, and flattery alone could wring it from him. Ask him for aid in a small deserving case or to assist a struggling scientific explorer—that would be wasted time. He had no ears for any charity unless labelled with his name. . . . He would have given millions to Greece had she labelled the Parthenon Carnegopolis.

Such criticism, while understandable, was quite unfair, and although Carnegie generally ignored such comments, on occasion he felt it necessary to speak out. When he offered to match the six-hundred-thousand-dollar endowment of the Franklin Institute in Boston, he was greatly disturbed to receive an inquiry from Charles Eliot, president of Harvard, one of the trustees of the institute, asking if this meant that Carnegie expected the name to be changed to the Franklin-Carnegie Institute. Carnegie felt obliged to deny this at some length:

The idea of tampering with Franklin's name never entered my mind any more than when I duplicated Peter Cooper's gift of six hundred thousand. . . .

I find it difficult to avoid having gifts for new things called after the donors. Carnegie Hall New York was called by me *The Music Hall* a la Boston. Foreign artists refused to appear in "A Music Hall"—London idea. The Board changed it in my absence in Europe without consulting me. . . . "The way of the Philanthropist is hard" but I don't do anything for popularity and just please my sel'—do what I think is useful. I never reply to attacks. Altho I confess I was surprised that you should have for a moment imagined there was a man living who could dream of coupling his name with Franklin *or with any founder*.

There were many instances of Carnegie's philanthropy that, at his express order, received no publicity whatsoever. He had many people on his private pension lists, from obscure boyhood friends in Dunfermline to such celebrities as Rudyard Kipling and Booker T. Washington. The publicity he did seek and get for his gospel of wealth after 1890, however, resulted in an almost unbelievable torrent of letters from individuals requesting aid for themselves or for some project in which they were interested. His faithful secretary, James Bertram, who handled all of this correspondence, estimated that Carnegie received on the average of four to five hundred letters a day, and after the announcement of some large benefaction, this number might increase to seven hundred a day. The great majority of these letters Carnegie, of course, never saw. They came from all over the world, from writers who could not get their books published, from inventors with patents to revolutionize industry, from persons who claimed kinship with Carnegie, or simply from desperate people having no other recourse but the blind hope that a simple scrawled message to that magical name would be the open-sesame to help.

No one, however, was too important or too proud, it

would appear, to write a begging letter to Carnegie. Those letters from friends and distinguished persons he would have to see and to answer. On one day alone, he had letters from John Morley, Herbert Spencer, and William Gladstone. Morley, who never begged, had simply written a personal letter, but Spencer was begging for help for some sociological study a friend was engaged in, and Gladstone wanted Carnegie to give money to the Bodleian Library. Carnegie was impressed. "Just think," he wrote in reply to Gladstone, "one mail brought me three letters.

> One from you—Gladstone
> One from   Herbert Spencer
> One from   John Morley

I am quite set up as no other one can say this. A.C." But not set up enough to become softheaded. Carnegie politely but firmly turned down both Spencer and Gladstone.

Mark Twain, who was a frequent correspondent and who always addressed Carnegie as Saint Andrew, wrote the most delightful begging letters of all those that Carnegie received. Sometimes it would be a joke:

You seem to be in prosperity. Could you lend an admirer a dollar & a half to buy a hymn book with? God will bless you. I feel it. I know it. N.B. If there should be another application this one not to count. P.S. Don't send the hymn-book, send the money. I want to make the selection myself.

Sometimes it would be a serious request for Carnegie to enter some business venture with him or to rescue him from one in which he was already caught. Either way, he took Carnegie's refusals with good grace.

On an early spring morning in 1901, when Carnegie sailed for Europe, having sold out to Morgan and leaving behind him safely locked in a vault in Hoboken the world's largest negotiable fortune, he had some understanding of the size of the task that lay before him. Just prior to his departure he had sent to the managers of the Carnegie Company, now a subdivision of United States Steel, five million dollars of those bonds to be held in trust for the following purposes:

Income for $1 million to be spent in maintaining Libraries at Braddock, Homestead & Duquesne works.

Income from other $4 million to be applied:

1st, to provide for employees of Carnegie Company injured in service and for dependents of those killed

2nd, to provide small pensions to employees after long service, help in old age. Not to be regarded as a substitute for what the Company is already doing. . . . I make this first use of surplus wealth upon retiring from business, as an acknowledgement of the deep debt I owe to the workmen who have contributed so greatly to my success.

He also left letters granting $5,200,000 to New York City for sixty-five branch libraries throughout the five boroughs, under the same conditions as applied to all of his library gifts; and to St. Louis, one million dollars for branch libraries. Thus, by three letters written in a single day, Carnegie had given away $11,200,000. All of his previous gifts up to that date had totalled $16,363,252. But the interest on his bonds and other investments alone amounted to over fifteen million dollars a year. Carnegie knew he would have to do much better than this if he were to make any substantial cut into his vast amount of capital.

But for the next ten years Carnegie gamely ran on in a race that he had set for himself, with handicaps that were self-imposed. Library giving, which he regarded as his specialty, took care of $60,364,808 of his fortune by providing 2,509 free public libraries throughout the United States, the British Isles, Canada, New Zealand, Australia, and South Africa. But spectacularly popular as this field of philanthropy proved to be, it amounted to only one seventh of his total fortune.

The question remained: What other fields could he enter in view of the restrictions he had laid upon himself? He would not enter the medical field, for he felt that this had been pre-empted by John D. Rockefeller. Giving to churches, and particularly to missionary enterprises, was antithetical to his most fundamental beliefs. The substantial exception he made to this rule was in providing church organs—a form of philanthropy into which he rather inadvertently stumbled when he presented the organ in 1873 to the small Swedenborgian church in Allegheny. Once this gift became publicized, other requests began to come in, and soon Carnegie found himself involved in a major operation. Knowing the prejudice of Scottish Calvinists against instrumental music in church, particularly the pipe organ—"a kist fu' o' whistles"—Carnegie took a certain delight in seeing a Scottish Presbyterian church swallow its pride and ask for an organ, in the hopes that this would induce Carnegie to make other and more holy contributions to the congregation. After a time this game, however, became no longer a sport but a big business. By 1919 Carnegie had given 7,629 church organs throughout the world at a cost of $6,248,312—a chest full of whistles large enough to have impressed John Knox himself.

Still the interest on his bonds continued to accumulate, and the years of grace left to him in which to dispose of his fortune were fast slipping by. Ruling out medicine, religion, and charitable social work, he had left to him only one major field in which to dispense his largess—education. Here the need was great, the opportunities many, the demands unlimited. But Carnegie was exceedingly cautious. University presidents throughout the United States and Great Britain were more than eager to help relieve Carnegie of his money, but he remained as deaf as Ulysses' sailors to the siren calls from Harvard, Yale, Oxford, and Cambridge.

When he finally entered the field of higher education, it was by the back door, and only then by violating his own cardinal principle of not making charitable gifts to a whole class of impoverished individuals. It was Henry S. Pritchett, the president of the Massachusetts Institute of Technology, who was to open this door to Carnegie by raising the question of teachers' pensions. Like most men of very limited formal education, and particularly men of European background, Carnegie held college professors in awe. To discover that college professors might teach for several decades and not achieve a salary above four hundred dollars a year, with no provisions for retirement, was for Carnegie a shocking revelation. Office clerks at Carnegie Steel earned as much or more.

The low salaries that prevailed throughout the academic profession were of particular concern to Pritchett, who, as head of a scientific technological school, had a great deal more difficulty in recruiting able men than did the administrative officers of the traditional liberal-arts colleges. Now that many of the basic industries were following Carnegie's early example of employing chemists, physicists, and professionally trained mechanical engineers, educational institutions, even those as distinguished as M.I.T., did not find it easy to compete for personnel with companies that paid salaries three to five times higher. Another college personnel problem resulted from the fact that there were no pension plans for professors. Out of purely humanitarian concern, a college was often obliged to keep on its active teaching staff an elderly faculty member who should have been retired, thus denying a place to a young and valuable instructor. This situation further discouraged young men from going into the teaching profession.

Carnegie listened intently to Pritchett's arguments, and by the spring of the year 1905 he was ready to announce his latest philanthropic foundation, the Carnegie Teachers Pension Fund, with an endowment of ten million dollars. Under the terms of this grant as proposed by Carnegie, a board of trustees, composed of twenty-two of the leading college and university presidents in the United States and Canada, was to establish pensions for faculty in private but nonsectarian colleges and universities "under such conditions as you [the trustees] may adopt from time to time."

Had Carnegie simply set up a pension fund for all college teachers in private institutions, the trustees would have had little to do but see that there was a proper administration of the funds. It was Carnegie's strong bias against sectarianism, plus the phrase "under such conditions as you may adopt," that encouraged this able group of college administrators to set standards for higher education. The fund, at first incorporated under the laws of New York State, within a year received a national charter by act of Congress under a more appropriate name: The Carnegie Foundation for the Advancement of Teaching.

The first act of the trustees was to send out a questionnaire to 627 institutions of higher education throughout the United States and Canada, asking each college the size of its endowment, what educational standards it had established for admission and for graduation, what its relation to the state or province was, and what, if any, sectarian ties or obligations it had. Replies were received from 421 institutions, and the trustees then proceeded to establish standards for admission to the pension fund. They first decided that no school with an endowment of less than two hundred thousand dollars would be considered. No school that received a substantial portion of its operating funds from the state was eligible. No school that required a majority of its trustees to belong to a particular denomination or that had a sectarian requirement for its president, faculty, or student body, or that had a required course in a particular religious creed or sect would be eligible. Finally, no school that did not require of its students what the Carnegie board of trustees regarded as a minimum of preparation prior to admission to the college could qualify. Of the 421 original applicants, the trustees accepted only fifty-two for admission into the pension plan.

There were some surprising rejections. Northwestern and Brown universities were kept out on sectarian grounds. The University of Virginia, a private university founded by Thomas Jefferson, was eliminated because its admissions standards were too low. Of the fifty-two institutions selected, twenty-two were located in New England and New York State. Only one southern school, Tulane University, was admitted. Vanderbilt and Randolph-Macon, both of whose educational standards were acceptable, were rejected on sectarian grounds.

In those schools that had not been selected, the anguished cries and threats of faculty members shook college administrations with a violence that Carnegie and Pritchett could hardly have imagined. There were emergency sessions of boards of trustees throughout the country, and charters that had once been considered inviolate were in many places quickly changed to remove sectarian requirements. Bates College went to the state legislature of Maine and successfully pushed through a new act of incorporation that changed its former relations with the Free Baptist Church. The University of Virginia raised its standards of admission, which had an immediate impact upon secondary schools throughout Virginia and in other parts of the South. Inadvertently, Carnegie, with his pension plan, had done more in a year to advance the standards of higher education within the United States than probably any carefully conceived program to accomplish that goal could ever have done.

By 1909 it was quite apparent to anyone interested in higher education that the Carnegie Foundation had become the national unofficial accrediting agency for colleges and universities. Good teachers were accepting positions on the basis of whether or not the school was a participant in the pension fund, prospective donors used participation as a major criterion in determining the direction and size of their gifts, and the program even had an indirect effect upon admissions.

It is not surprising that schools like Northwestern and Brown should be concerned over exclusion. No president was more importunate in his demands that his faculty be included within the pension plan than was President Abram Harris of Northwestern. He even persuaded the President of the United States to come to his aid. "Northwestern is no more sectarian than Princeton," Theodore Roosevelt, with some heat, wrote Carnegie. But Northwestern would not change the provision in its charter that required a majority of its trustees to be Methodists, and not even T.R.'s big stick could force Carnegie and Pritchett to yield to sectarianism.

They did give in to the demands of the state institutions, however. In 1908 Carnegie agreed to permit state institutions, at the request of the state legislatures and governors, to participate in the pension program, and he added an additional five million dollars to the fund to accommodate these requests. This extension proved to be the undoing of the whole program. By 1915 it was apparent to the trustees that the free pension system could not be continued indefinitely. Two years later an independent legal reserve life-insurance company was created, chartered under the laws of New York State, and called the Teachers Insurance and Annuity Association of America. From 1918 on T.I.A.A. entered into contractual relationships with individual institutions of higher education and established life insurance and annuity programs for faculty and college administrators on a contributory basis. The free pension plan had proved to be infeasible within twelve years after its inauguration, but it was a noble and elevating experiment. Had a regular insurance system such as T.I.A.A. been adopted from the beginning in 1905, we should not have had the sorely needed evaluation of

"When Mr. Carnegie's money is gone." From Life, *1905.*

CULVER PICTURES

higher education that the Carnegie Fund trustees forced on the colleges and universities. The *Times* of London was quite correct in calling the foundation one of Carnegie's most significant accomplishments "in the supremely difficult art of spending large sums of money in undertakings to be of permanent advantage to the public."

By 1910 Carnegie was more than willing to agree with the *Times* as to how "supremely difficult" the art of spending was. He had given away $180,000,000 of his fortune, but he had almost the same amount still left in his possession. The capitalistic system at 5 per cent worked faster than he could. He told his good friend Elihu Root that it appeared that he would have to die in disgrace as a man of great wealth after all. Root had a simple solution. Why didn't he set up a trust, transfer the bulk of his fortune to others for them to worry about, and then die happy in a state of grace?

And so it was done. Carnegie created the Carnegie Corporation of New York in November, 1911, and transferred to it the bulk of his remaining fortune, $125,000,000, "to promote the advancement and diffusion of knowledge among the people of the United States." As United States Steel had been the supercorporation in industry, so the Carnegie Corporation of New York became the first supertrust in philanthropy.

"Now it is all settled," Carnegie wrote his Scottish solicitor, John Ross, in February, 1913. For years the newspapers of New York had run a box score on the philanthropic gifts of Carnegie vs. Rockefeller. Now the New York *Herald* printed the final score: "Carnegie, $332 million; Rockefeller, $175 million." It was no longer a contest. The public had lost interest, and so had Andrew Carnegie.

The Atlanta Compromise

Booker T. Washington's famous speech at the 1895 Cotton States Exposition was regarded as a sellout by some Negro intellectuals but as a brilliant program for progress by most whites. Either way it made the educator into a celebrity overnight.

Roger M. Williams

Booker T. Washington, advocate of racial peace. (Brown Bros.)

Roger M. Williams is "Time Magazine" bureau chief in Atlanta, Georgia. His work has appeared in a number of periodicals of national circulation.

THE Cotton States and International Exposition opened in Atlanta on a bright September day in 1895. The city's premier event since the close of the Civil War, it attracted exhibits from around the world and visitors from around the Nation. It was a colorful exhibition and a glorious tribute to Atlanta's rise from the ruins of war, and one part of it—a speech by Booker T. Washington—has achieved historical immortality.

Washington's Cotton States exposition speech, cheered loudly by both Negroes and whites, had a twin effect. It pushed Washington into the front rank of Negro leaders, and it made his prescription for Negro progress—hard work, patience, and trust in the whites—a guiding force (for a time) in American race relations. From the standpoints of popularity and influence, the speech was one of the greatest achievements of his career.

Booker Taliaferro Washington, the principal of Tuskegee Normal and Industrial Institute, was born in 1856 on a large plantation in Franklin County, Virginia. His father, he admitted candidly, was a white man who lived nearby. His slave upbringing was typically impoverished: There was no floor in the one-room cabin; there were few clothes and little food and absolutely none of the amenities of life. After Emancipation, Washington's mother took the children to West Virginia. Life was little better there, but somehow young Booker became, as he later put it, "determined to secure an education at any cost." In 1872 he went to Hampton Institute, a leading Negro vocational school. He arrived with fifty cents in his pocket and immediately fell to dusting and sweeping a recitation room to prove his fitness to be enrolled. Washington was a fine pupil. Hampton

stressed a practical education for a practical life, and he became imbued with that philosophy.

IN 1881 the Hampton principal's recommendation secured Booker T. Washington, at age 25, the top position at the newly formed Negro institute at Tuskegee, Alabama. Tuskegee under Washington became world famous and financially secure. At his death in 1915, the school had over 100 buildings and an endowment of nearly $2 million. Its academic emphasis was vocational, for Washington soon developed his Hampton-bred philosophy into a near crusade for practical education. "The education of the people of my race," he wrote, "should be directed that the greatest proportion of the mental strength of the masses be brought to bear upon the everyday, practical things of life, upon something that is needed to be done, and something which they will be permitted to do in the community in which they reside."

Washington, says the Negro historian John Hope Franklin, "believed that the Southern white had to be convinced that education of Negroes was in the true interest of the South." He realized what a dif-

From *American History Illustrated*, April 1968. Reproduced through the courtesy of The National Historical Society, publishers of AMERICAN HISTORY *Illustrated*, 206 Hanover Street, Gettysburg, Pa. 17325. Published 10 times a year.

ficult job that was. The sentiment of the South's ruling race toward Negro education was expressed in the classic statement of Mississippi's James K. Vardaman: "Why squander money on his education when the only effect is to spoil a good field hand and make an insolent cook?" Washington ignored the tirades of Vardaman and his fellow racists. He stuck to the job of building Tuskegee and promoting the goals of diligence in work and accommodation to the white South.

IN THE spring of 1895 Washington received a telegram from a group of prominent Atlantans asking that he help them secure Federal funds for an exposition in their city. He accepted, made the trip to Washington at his own expense, and appeared before the House Committee on Appropriations. His speech was brief but forceful: The Atlanta exposition represented the first great opportunity since the Civil War for the Negro to demonstrate his progress as a free member of society. Washington's plea was well received, and he stayed in Washington several extra days to help lobby for the project. A generous appropriations bill passed the committee unanimously.

The exposition directors then decided to include a Negro exhibit; their idea was not to glorify the Negro in his own right but to demonstrate the strides he had made under the Southern social system. They thought also of having a Negro speaker on the opening program. It was feared that such a move might, in the words of the official exposition history, "encourage social equality and prove offensive to the white people, and in the end unsatisfactory to the colored race," but the directors decided to invite a Negro speaker anyway. Washington was the natural choice. Not only had he helped sell the project to the House committee, he was a fine speaker, quite well known and apparently accommodating in his views on the place of the Negro in Southern society.

Washington was apprehensive about accepting an invitation to speak before such a group. No Negro ever had addressed Southern whites on an occasion of national importance. Five years later, in *Up from Slavery,* Washington recalled his concern: "It was only a few years before that time that any white man in the audience might have claimed me as his slave; and it was easily possible that some of my former owners might be present to hear me speak." He accepted, however, and was gratified to receive no directions or even hints from exposition officials as to what he should say in his speech. He had his own ideas on that score: "I was determined from the first," he later wrote in *The Story of My Life*

and Work, "not to say anything that would give undue offense to the South and thus prevent it from honoring another Negro in the future. And at the same time I was equally determined to be true to the North and to the interests of my own race." On the way to the Tuskegee train depot, he encountered a white farmer who told him, "Washington, you have spoken with success before Northern white audiences, and before Negroes in the South, but in Atlanta you will have to speak before Northern white people, Southern white people, and Negroes altogether. I fear they have got you into a pretty tight place." Washington feared the same.

NEXT morning, September 18, Washington joined the exposition's opening day procession. Crowds in holiday attire jammed the sidewalks as military units and dignitaries paraded up Peachtree Street, past the flag-draped Capital City Club and on to Piedmont Park, site of the exposition. It took three hours to reach the auditorium, and when he arrived Washington felt "as if I were about ready to collapse, and . . . that my address was not going to be a success." A white friend, who was general manager of the Southern Railroad and a trustee of Tuskegee, was so nervous about the speech and the reaction to it that he could not go into the building; instead, he paced back and forth outside. But when Washington entered the hall, he heard "vigorous cheers from the colored portion of the audience, and faint cheers from some of the white people."

The large hall was packed with people, including hundreds of Negroes, and there was a huge crowd outside unable to get in. Most of them had come primarily to hear the Negro Washington, although he was not the chief speaker of the day. That distinction went to Judge Emory Speer, who delivered a seemingly endless oration extolling America and particularly the South. Speer made one comment that bore upon Washington's subsequent remarks. "The so-called race question," he declared, "does not exist . . . the Negro has the strongest local attachment [to the South] and will remain as a race unto himself;" meanwhile, white control of local affairs would remain "unquestioned."

Victor Herbert led Gilmore's band in his own composition, "Salute to Atlanta." Then President Grover Cleveland, sitting in the library of his summer home in Massachusetts, officially opened the exposition by pressing a gold button. An electric spark flashed into Machinery Hall, starting the great engines. Lights flashed; 100 rockets exploded in the air; fountains sprayed great jets of water. The crowd sighed. The exposition was underway. On the speakers' platform were two Negroes, Washington and I. Garland Penn, commissioner of the Negro Building. Washington was introduced by former Georgia governor Rufus B. Bullock, master of ceremonies for the day, who termed him "the representative of Negro enterprise and Negro civilization." There was considerable applause, again mostly from the colored section of the audience.

WASHINGTON went straight to his subject: the role of the Negro in the South. "One third of the population of the South is of the Negro race," he said in his opening sentence. "No enterprise seeking the material, civil, or moral welfare of this section can disregard this element of our population and reach the highest success." That could have been the prologue to a warning to Southern whites to treat the Negro as a first-class citizen, but Washington was not so inclined. He was speaking not to antagonize the whites but, as he later recalled, to "cement the friendship of the races and bring about hearty cooperation between them."

His audience, white and black alike, quickly became attentive, as Washington chided his race for attempting "in the first years of our new life" to begin "at the top instead of the bottom." Then he swung into the main part of his message—the need for each race to accept the other and make its home in the South. He used a parable to put the message across. A ship lost at sea near the mouth of the Amazon River sighted another vessel and signaled for water. "Cast down your bucket where you are," came the reply. The ship in distress repeated the signal and got the same answer, so the captain cast down a bucket and pulled it up full of fresh, sweet water. "To those of my race who depend on bettering their condition in a foreign land, or who underestimate the importance of cultivating friendly relations with the Southern white man who is their next-door neighbor, I would say: 'cast down your bucket where you are'—cast it down in making friends in every manly way of the people of all races by whom we are surrounded . . .

"Our greatest danger is, that in the great leap from slavery to freedom we may overlook the fact that the masses of us are to live by the production of our hands, and fail to keep in mind that we shall prosper in proportion as we learn to dignify and glorify common labor and put brains and skill into the common occupations of life: shall prosper in proportion as we learn to draw the line between the superficial and the substantial, the ornamental gewgaws of life and the useful. No race can prosper until it learns that there is as much dignity in tilling a field as in writing a poem. It is at the bottom of life we must begin and not at the top. Nor should we permit our grievances to overshadow our opportunities."

A correspondent covering the speech for the New York *World* wrote of Washington: "The sinews stood out on his bronzed neck, and his muscular right arm swung high in the air, with a lead pencil grasped in the clinched brown fist . . . His voice rang out clear and true, and he paused impressively as he made each point. Within ten minutes the multitude was in an uproar of enthusiasm—handkerchiefs were waved, canes were flourished, hats were tossed in the air. The fairest women of Georgia stood up and cheered. It was as if the orator had bewitched them."

TO THE whites, "were I permitted," Washington said, "I would repeat what I say to my own race: 'Cast down your bucket where you are' . . . while doing this you can be sure, in the future, as you have been in the past, that you and your families will be surrounded by the most patient, faithful, law-abiding and unresentful people that the world has seen. As we have proved our loyalty to you in the past in nursing your children, watching by the sick bed of your mothers and fathers and often following them with tear-dimmed eyes to their graves, so in the future in our humble way we shall stand by you with a devotion that no foreigner can approach, ready to lay down our lives, if need be, in defense of yours, interlacing our industrial, commercial, civil, and religious life with yours in a way that shall make the interests of both races one."

Then Washington thrust his hand into the air and exclaimed: "In all things that are purely social we can be as separate as the fingers, yet one as the hand in all things essential to mutual progress." The audience greeted this declaration by rising to its feet with a burst of applause. Tears welled in the eyes of many Negro listeners, and some of them wept unashamedly. Washington, startled as he must have been by the response, remained impassive. When the tumult subsided, he cautioned whites that they "must not expect overmuch," making clear that Negroes would not expect overmuch either. "The wisest among my race," he said, in a statement that other Negroes would repeatedly turn against him, "understand that the agitation of questions of social equality is the extremest folly, and that progress in the enjoyment of all the privileges that will come to us must be the result of severe and constant struggle, rather than of artificial forcing."

That sounded like social surrender, but Washington added: "No race that has anything to contribute to the markets of the world is long in any degree

Booker T. Washington on last tour of the South, 1915. (LC)

ostracized. It is right and important that all privileges of the law be ours, but it is vastly more important that we go prepared for the exercise of these privileges. The opportunity to earn a dollar in a factory just now is worth infinitely more than the opportunity to spend a dollar in an opera house." Washington closed with a plea for ending sectional differences and assuring "absolute justice" which, "coupled with our material prosperity, will bring into our beloved South a new heaven and a new earth."

AS cheers resounded through the hall, former Governor Bullock rushed across the platform to shake and reshake the speaker's hand. Other dignitaries followed and extended their congratulations. The crowds, pressing in on Washington for a better look, became so insistent he had trouble getting out of the building. And the following morning, when he went for a walk in downtown Atlanta, he was repeatedly surrounded by people of both races who wanted to talk to and shake hands with the man who had delivered the wonderful speech.

The Atlanta *Constitution* called the speech "brilliant . . . an event in the history of the race." *Constitution* editor Clark Howell cabled a New York newspaper that it was "one of the most notable speeches, both as to character and the warmth of its reception, ever delivered to a Southern audience. The address was a revelation. The whole speech is a platform upon which blacks and whites can stand with full justice to each other." The Boston *Transcript*

noted that the speech "seems to have dwarfed all the other proceedings and the Exposition itself. The sensation that it has caused in the press has never been equalled." Negro newspapers were hardly less enchanted. The Richmond *Planet* called the speech "a magnificent effort" that places Washington "in the forefront of the representatives of our race in this country. Calm, dispassionate, logical, winning, it captivated the vast assemblage who heard it and caused a re-echoing sound of approval around the nation." Washington, rhapsodized the *Planet*, "performed with an ease that was magnetic and a grace that was divine."

Lavish praise was not confined to the South. In the North, where the old abolitionist, Radical Republican spirit was spent and where businessmen wanted a stable South in which to invest, the reaction was one of gratitude. Editorialized the New York *Tribune:* "Today when men think of American freedom they can do no better than to think of Booker T. Washington's oration at Atlanta." The *Tribune* was confusing Washington's program with true freedom for the Negro, but the vast majority of Northerners were in no mood to quibble.

A SMALL but vocal group, however, was not at all enthusiastic about Washington's speech. The group was, for the most part, composed of white liberals and Negro intellectuals, and its spokesman was William Edward Burghardt DuBois. W. E. B. DuBois was many things Booker T. Washington was not—intellectual, cuttingly brilliant, arrogant. He and his "talented tenth," the well-educated Negroes he hoped would lead the race to equality with the whites, acknowledged the necessity for efforts by the Negro at self-improvement. But they rejected Washington's strong implication that for the sake of Southern harmony the Negro should give up, as DuBois put it, "first, political power; second, insistence on civil rights; third, higher education of Negro youth."

Wrote DuBois of the Atlanta exposition address: "It startled the nation to hear a Negro advocate such a program after many decades of bitter complaint; it startled and won the applause of the South, it interested and won the admiration of the North, and after a confused murmur of protest, it silenced if it did not convert the Negroes themselves." DuBois saw in Washington "essentially the leader not of one race but of two—a compromiser between the South, the North, and the Negro." Washington's program, he charged "practically accepts the alleged inferiority of the Negro races" and preaches "a gospel of Work and Money to such an extent as apparently almost completely to overshadow the higher aims of life." To DuBois this was not only betraying the race; it was betraying the class. He gave Washington's speech a name that has endured to this day—the "Atlanta Compromise."

TODAY, in the age of the Negro revolution, the speech is considered by most civil rights activists as a sellout, a classic example of refined Uncle Tomism—portraying the Negro as deferential to the point of obsequiousness and as willing to live indefinitely in the white man's shadow. The judgment is unduly harsh, for Washington did not advocate the everlasting abandonment of the Negro's political and social rights; these would come later, he said,

after the Negro had proved himself worthy through diligent effort. It can be argued that his approach was right for his time and that a more aggressive one would have resulted in failure and perhaps bloodshed.

Yet it is certain that the Atlanta speech downplayed future gains for the sake of present accommodation and helped leave the initiative for Negro progress in the hands of Southern whites, who had their own, restrictive ideas on how much progress there should be. In so doing, the speech severely dampened Negro efforts to achieve equality for the next half century. It is tragically ironic that Booker T. Washington, a genuine American hero with the best of intentions, was the man responsible.

How The PANAMA CANAL Came About

Teddy Roosevelt lacked the patience for ordinary negotiations for the right-of-way. His short-cuts saved time and money but created grievances which remain unsettled.

Robert James Maddox

Dr. Robert James Maddox is on the faculty (History Department) of Pennsylvania State University. Source references for his study are:

Miles P. DuVal Jr., *"Cadiz to Cathay"* (Stanford, 1940).

Dwight C. Miner, *"The Fight for the Panama Route"* (New York, 1940).

Earl Harding, *"The Untold Story of Panama"* (New York, 1959).

For the most recent material, based on an examination of the Bunau-Varilla Papers, two

articles by Charles D. Ameringer *must* be read:

"The Panama Canal Lobby of Philippe Bunau-Varilla and William Nelson Cromwell, *"American Historical Review,* LXVIII (January, 1963).

"Philippe Bunau-Varilla: New Light on the Panama Canal Treaty," *Hispanic American Historical Review,* XLVI (February, 1966).

THE IDEA of connecting the Atlantic and Pacific oceans by a canal across Central America goes back to the time when Spanish explorers first realized that the much sought after natural waterway was a myth. American statesmen anticipated such a project from the early decades of the nation's existence. Not until the last few years of the 19th century, however, did the United States move to fulfill the ancient dream. Sentiment for decisive action arose during the

From *American History Illustrated*, December 1968. Reproduced through the courtesy of The National Historical Society, publishers of AMERICAN HISTORY *Illustrated*, 206 Hanover Street, Gettysburg, Pa. 17325. Published 10 times a year.

Spanish-American war when the battleship *Oregon*, stationed at Puget Sound, had to steam all the way around the tip of South America to join the Atlantic fleet for operations against Cuba. This highly publicized event, graphically demonstrating the naval and commercial advantages a canal would afford, electrified public opinion. The United States government responded quickly enough, perhaps too quickly. Its performance in acquiring the rights to build a canal brewed up a storm whose repercussions can still be felt.

Great Britain posed the first obstacle to American plans. In 1850 the two nations had signed an agreement prohibiting either from attempting to construct a canal except as a joint undertaking. Upon completion, furthermore, the passage would be left unfortified and open to ships of all nations. At a time when the British had large interests in the Caribbean and the United States was comparatively weak, these terms were the best American negotiators could get. Thirty-five years later they were unsatisfactory. American wealth and potential strength had burgeoned while Britain's involvements elsewhere—the Boer War, for instance—diminished the region's importance to her.

Opening of the Panama Canal, August 15, 1914. The SS Ancan in the west chamber of the Miraflores upper locks. (LC)

In February 1900, during the administration of William McKinley, Secretary of State John Hay and British Ambassador Lord Pauncefote concluded a treaty more appropriate to the current situation.

THE FIRST Hay-Pauncefote Treaty would have permitted the United States to construct a canal by itself, own it, and neutralize it in time of war. The pact did, however, retain the ban on fortifications. Such a restriction affronted those Americans who believed that national security and pride required a canal "Americanized" in every respect including the right to defend it. Amendments guaranteeing that right were added by the Senate, thereby rendering the treaty unacceptable to Great Britain. Hay, at first so angered by the Senate's action as to threaten resignation, reluctantly approached the British again to seek further concessions. Aided by a growing disposition in London to cooperate with the United States, he succeeded. The second Hay-Pauncefote Treaty solved the knotty problem of fortifications by the simple expedient of omitting all reference to them, thus allowing the United States to interpret the agreement as it saw fit while protecting the British government against domestic criticism of having "sold out" to Uncle Sam.

Prime movers in negotiations transferring the Panama Canal to United States ownership were (left to right) Secretary of State

John Hay, Thomas Nelson Cromwell, and Philippe Bunau-Varilla. (Photos "Dictionary of American Portraits" and LC)

Having settled the question as to who would build the canal, the next issue was where to build it. There were two feasible routes: one across Nicaragua and Costa Rica, another through the Panama region of Colombia. The Panama site had several desirable features, including shorter mileage; but it had also serious drawbacks. A French combine under the direction of Ferdinand de Lesseps, "father" of the Suez Canal, actually had begun excavations there back in the 1880's. A variety of problems, including widespread corruption, had driven the company into bankruptcy. All work had ceased by 1889 as the French public refused to subscribe further capital to what appeared a gigantic fraud. The circumstances surrounding de Lesseps' fiasco not only placed the enterprise in bad odor but also generally meant that the United States would have to deal with French stockholders (now reorganized as the New Panama Canal Company) as well as the Colombian government. Should the French place a high value on their concession—and it certainly was likely that they would try to recoup as much of their losses as possible—the additional cost might well offset Panama's physical advantages. For a considerable length of time, therefore, the consensus among government officials ran in favor of Nicaragua.

PANAMA unquestionably would have been bypassed had it not been for the work of two men: Thomas Nelson Cromwell of the Sullivan and Cromwell law firm and Philippe Bunau-Varilla, a Frenchman who had served as an engineer with the original canal company. Cromwell, whose personal charm was exceeded only by his zest for a profitable deal, became the New Company's representative in the United States to promote the Panama route. He also held stock in the Panama Railroad Company whose line, paralleling the proposed waterway, would profit hugely from a canal. Bunau-Varilla, himself a large shareholder in the New Company, seems as well to have had a genuine commitment—one might almost say an obsession—to finish the work de Lesseps had begun. Like Cromwell, Bunau-Varilla was a personable, persuasive man, dedicated to his task. Together they made a formidable pair.

At times cooperating, at times working independently, Cromwell and Bunau-Varilla carried off an exercise in lobbying which would reflect credit on the most sophisticated groups operating today. The labyrinthian paths they followed are too complex—and often too obscure—to be recounted in the space of an article. Both men had access to government officials in Congress and the administration; both used these contacts to plead, persuade, and cajole for consideration of the Panama route. There were many factors at work, of course, but the first of their many victories took place when President McKinley appointed a commission to weigh the respective merits of the two sites. They had, for the time being anyway, aroused enough interest in Panama to make it a serious alternative to Nicaragua.

IN ADDITION to their propaganda work in the United States, Cromwell and especially Bunau-Varilla kept their cause afloat by persuading the New Company to place a realistic price tag on its assets. The company's directors, at first reluctant to name any specific figure, later suggested the sum of over $109,-000,000 as a basis for arbitration. This fact the commission cited in its report (issued in December 1901) as an impediment to the Panama route. Admiral John J. Walker, chairman of the commission, specified

$40,000,000 as the concession's maximum value, stating that under no circumstances should the United States pay more. Only the strongest representations—and a trip to France by Bunau-Varilla—convinced the New Company to lower its asking price to meet Walker's estimate. This move, as much as any other, converted many people in the United States to the side of Panama.

The Panama route still had to be considered a long shot by the winter of 1901-02 despite the price reduction engineered by Bunau-Varilla. Many congressmen, including some on strategic committees, retained their preference for Nicaragua. Indeed, on January 9, 1902, the House of Representatives passed the Hepburn or Nicaragua bill with only two dissenting votes. But Panama supporters had more strength in the Senate, most notably the powerful Mark Hanna of Ohio and John C. Spooner of Wisconsin. Spooner introduced an amendment to the Hepburn bill which would have substituted Panama for Nicaragua, while Hanna through various tactics kept the House bill off the Senate floor. Meanwhile Cromwell and Bunau-Varilla kept themselves occupied clearing away possible snags with the Colombian government so as to provide pro-Panama Senators with a better case when the time came. Still, the Hepburn bill very likely would have passed the Senate without any amendments had it not been for a stroke—or strokes—of immense good luck.

FOR YEARS Bunau-Varilla had disparaged the Nicaragua route on the grounds that nearby volcanoes would endanger a canal. He had made little headway with this approach so far. Then on May 8, 1902, Mount Pelée at Martinique exploded, causing great damage and the loss of an estimated 25,000 lives. Several weeks later, on the eve of the canal debate, newspapers reported that another eruption had occurred at Mount Momotombo in Nicaragua back in March. Bunau-Varilla rushed to exploit these events. At first he distributed within the Senate press clippings of the disasters. When a pro-Nicaragua senator procured from that country's president a letter minimizing the volcanoes' importance, Bunau-Varilla countered with a true inspiration. Remembering that an issue of Nicaraguan postage stamps depicted Mount Momotombo in full eruption, he scouted up enough copies to place one in the hands of every Senator. Lest they still fail to grasp the import, he affixed each stamp to a piece of paper bearing the simple caption, "An official witness to the volcanic activity of Nicaragua." Its effects on the voting can not be ascertained with certainty but obviously Bunau-Varilla had undermined the argument that volcanoes were not a factor

President Theodore Roosevelt saw Panama Canal completed. (LC)

in Nicaragua. On June 19 the Hepburn bill *with the Spooner amendment designating Panama as the preferred site* passed the Senate.

Theodore Roosevelt sat in the White House when the Spooner amendment went through. A demented anarchist had assassinated President McKinley in September 1901. T.R. had shown strong interest in a canal for some years; like many others, he had at first supported the Nicaragua route. Careful proselytizing by Cromwell and Bunau-Varilla as well as the reduction in price agreed upon by the New Company had won him over. Given the go-ahead now by Congressional action, the Rough Rider set out to acquire canal rights forthwith. The Spooner amendment stipulated that unless an agreement could be reached in a "reasonable time," the government should turn to Nicaragua. Unwilling to see this happen, Roosevelt pressed the issue with characteristic ardor. As he intended getting elected on his own in 1904, the credit for such an accomplishment would do him no harm politically.

NEGOTIATIONS with the Colombian government began soon after passage of the Spooner amendment. But the participants stood far apart on what constituted equitable terms. The Colombians wished to achieve as favorable a financial settlement as possible while retaining effective control over the area. Hay, on the other hand, worked for a lower monetary award and also to ensure that the United States would hold large powers over the canal strip itself. For all apparent purposes the negotiations fell apart when the Colombian minister left Washington in disgust. But the redoubtable Hay refused to quit. He continued parleys with the Colombian chargé, Tomás Herrán, and by using the threat that the United States might switch to Nicaragua, bullied Herrán into signing a treaty extremely favorable to the United States.

The American Senate confirmed the Hay-Herrán Treaty on March 17, 1903—small wonder in view of its terms. Reaction in Colombia was less favorable. Colombian nationalists, incensed because the treaty virtually extinguished their sovereignty over the proposed strip, believed as well that the financial settlement was miserly. The Colombian Senate rejected the treaty on August 12 after several weeks of stormy debate. Now it looked as though the patient work of Bunau-Varilla and Cromwell had all been in vain.

Another president might have reopened talks with Colombia. Not the Rough Rider. Choosing to em-

phasize the financial question rather than the issue of sovereignty, Roosevelt convinced himself that the Colombians had acted in bad faith and were trying to blackmail the United States. Generally contemptuous of Latin Americans anyway—he sometimes referred to them privately as "Dagos"—T. R. said he refused to have any further dealings with those "foolish and homicidal corruptionists in Bogatá." Such utterances violated his motto of speaking softly; the big stick had yet to be brandished.

Fortunately, from Roosevelt's point of view, direct intervention to procure the canal site was not the only alternative to renegotiations, although he had considered it. There existed in Panama widespread dissatisfaction over the treatment that region had received at the hands of the Colombian government. Panama had been independent of Colombia in times past and a separationist movement simmered, fueled by the belief that the Colombian government ignored Panama's needs—one of which was the anticipated prosperity a canal would bring. Perhaps, if given sufficient encouragement, the Panamanians themselves would take steps to satisfy American aims —gain their independence and come to terms over the canal, thereby circumventing Bogotá altogether.

THE DEGREE to which the United States government became involved in the subsequent insurrection against Colombia has been a matter of great speculation. Some of Roosevelt's defenders assert his complete innocence in the plotting. Less charitably inclined critics have accused him of participating (through intermediaries, of course) in every detail. The truth, as it often does, lies somewhere in the middle though probably much nearer the latter version than the former. While there is no evidence to show that the administration actually took part in the conspiracy, both Roosevelt and Hay made it known to the right people that the United States would look benignly upon a revolution and could be depended upon to insure its success. That, events would show, was quite sufficient.

Cromwell and Bunau-Varilla once again assumed key roles, this time acting as intermediaries between Panamanian leaders and the Roosevelt administration. Bunau-Varilla in particular led the conspirators to believe that he had great "pull" with the American government. His claims were inflated but several shrewd predictions on his part made it seem as though he were influencing events rather than predicting them. His major contribution lay in convincing the Panamanians that the United States would back them even though the administration refused to grant any formal assurances. That this was the impression

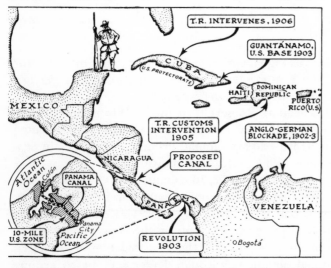

"Big Stick in the Caribbean" from "The American Pageant" by Thomas A. Bailey, third edition, 1966, D. C. Heath and Co.

Panama soldiers are shown here guarding a village on the road from Columbia. (Photograph from Keystone View Company)

Roosevelt meant to convey he made clear himself soon after the revolution. "He [Bunau-Varilla] is a very able fellow," Roosevelt said, "and it was his business to find out what he thought our government would do. . . . In fact, he would have been a very dull man had he been unable to make such a guess."

VICTORY for the rebels depended upon their ability to seize control of the two cities at either end of the rail line across the isthmus: Panama City on the Pacific and Colón on the Atlantic. What they hoped for and vitally needed was to have the United States prevent Colombian reinforcements from descending upon either point. Badly organized, poorly equipped (their major force in Panama City consisted of a fire brigade), the rebels could cope with local Colombian officials but not regular troops. The conspirators would have preferred an official promise of American assistance and a loan; Cromwell and Bunau-Varilla nevertheless emboldened them to go ahead with their plans.

The revolution itself smacked of comic opera. One slip-up almost wrecked the entire scheme. An American warship, the USS *Nashville*, dropped anchor at Colón on November 2, before the uprising took place. Orders were sent Commander John M. Hubbard of the *Nashville*, directing him to block troop landings or movements across the rail line by either side. This ostensibly neutral stance would have benefited only the rebels since the forces they possessed already were in each of the cities. Through error, however, Hubbard received his instructions *after* a battalion of Colombian troops—sent in response to rumors of an insurrection—had debarked while the American ship

stood by. Had these troops proceeded to Panama City, where the first coup was scheduled, they probably would have squashed the revolution immediately.

AMERICAN OFFICIALS of the Panama railroad, fully in sympathy with the revolution, staved off disaster. To avoid shipping the troops to Panama City as required by the railroad's charter, the superintendent sent all the available trains but one out of Colón as soon as he realized the danger. Then, offering profuse apologies, he and the conspirators persuaded the battalion commander and his staff to depart on the remaining train (consisting of an engine and a parlor car) without their men, promising that additional rolling stock would be provided the moment it became available. Leaving behind a colonel named Torres, the officers left for Panama City where they were arrested when the insurrection began later that same day, November 3.

Since Panama City lay only forty miles down the tracks, Colonel Torres, now in command of the one force which could have quelled the uprising, grew increasingly restive. The railroad superintendent, pyramiding one ingenious evasion upon another, managed to placate the colonel sufficiently to have him spend the night in Colón without a direct confrontation. Next morning the situation erupted when Torres learned of the rebellion and arrest of his superiors in Panama City. Preparing to seize control of the railroad, he sent word to the American consul in Panama City that he would kill every American there unless his battalion commander and staff were released at once. The conspirators, lacking the military strength to stop him—although Hubbard sent some Marines ashore as a last resort—had re-

Abandoned French machinery, Cristobal. (Keystone View Co.)

"The News Reaches Bogota." Cartoon by W. A. Rogers dramatizes President Roosevelt's determination to cut through red tape and get on with job of building the Panama Canal. (LC)

course to subtler means. Dipping into the Panamanian treasury, they offered Torres a sum of Colombian money worth 8,000 gold dollars to pack up his men and leave on a mail ship then sitting in harbor. To their great relief the colonel accepted their proposal.

SUPPLIED with two cases of champagne a thoughtful railroad official sent along, Torres boarded ship with his troops and sailed off the pages of history—he was never heard from again. The champagne proved his undoing according to one account. Made talkative by the unfamiliar bubbly, the story goes, Torres began boasting of his recently acquired fortune. That was a mistake. Some of his men, having themselves consumed large quantities of humbler spirits, divested the colonel of his ill-gotten gains and tossed him into the sea. Such were the wages of sin.

Success for the Panamanian revolution was assured when the Colombian battalion left Colón. Only at Panama City the day before had some shots been fired in anger. There, the unexpected arrival of three Colombian gunboats had caused understandable consternation among the rebels. Judiciously placed bribes immobilized two of the ships but the commander of the third refused to go along. Fortunately for the insurrectionaries, his courage fell short of his honesty. After firing a salvo of about a half-dozen rounds, the gunboat steamed off out of harm's way. Casualties were modest: one Chinese, presumably neutral, perished at work in his shop and a stray shell landed squarely on a donkey's hindquarters. That unfortunate creature's loyalties never have been ascertained but he (or she) may have been the revolution's only martyr.

THE REBELS, now in control of Panama's two major cities, speedily consolidated their victory. After a tumultuous celebration in which the supposedly neutral American consul took a prominent part, they set about forming a provisional government and asking recognition from the United States. Washington did not let them down. Secretary Hay immediately proclaimed *de facto* recognition of the new state which in effect notified Colombia to keep clear. Indeed, American recognition came before full details of the insurrection even reached Bogotá—before, in fact, many Panamanians learned of their own independence.

Unabashed by the haste with which he had recognized the fledgling nation, Roosevelt turned next to the important business of negotiating a satisfactory agreement over the canal site. The Panamanian minister who treated with Secretary Hay—collaborated might be a more accurate word—was none other than Philippe Bunau-Varilla himself, a French citizen who last set foot in Panama thirteen years earlier. Determined to hurry along payment for the New Company's assets, Bunau-Varilla had insisted that his appointment be one of the rewards for his assistance in mediating between the rebels and the administration. The provisional government, displeased over an arrangement they had agreed to only in desperation, sent two officials to participate in writing the treaty so as to safeguard Panamanian interests. They arrived too late. Unwilling to have anyone jeopardize the rapid conclusion of what he had fought so long to accomplish, Bunau-Varilla reached a settlement with Hay in less than five days. It is said that upon his arrival in Washington, one of the Panamanians swooned away in a dead faint when he learned what the Frenchman had done.

THE TREATY with Panama was eminently satisfactory to the United States—"disproportionately advantageous," as Hay himself admitted. Bunau-Varilla had secured the same monetary terms as provided for in the Hay-Herrán Treaty but conceded a great deal in the process. The life of the agreement was extended from ninety-nine years to "perpetuity," the canal zone was widened from six to ten miles (even farther under certain circumstances), and he granted away to the United States virtually complete authority over the strip which cut Panama in two. He signed, in other words, a treaty less favorable to Panama than the one Colombia had rejected. The Panamanians were scarcely overjoyed at his handiwork but, given their dependence upon the United States for protection against Colombia, had little choice except to swallow what had been foisted upon them. On February 26, 1904, Ambassador Bunau-Varilla and Secretary Hay solemnly exchanged ratifications of the canal pact.

For Cromwell and Bunau-Varilla the climax of their long campaign was at hand—payment of the $40,000,000 due the New Canal Company. As previously arranged, the United States Treasury turned over that amount to the J. P. Morgan Company in its capacity as financial agent for the French combine. What happened to the money after that remains a mystery. Neither Congressional investigations, newspaper reporters, nor historians have been able to do more than speculate. All agree that a large portion of the money was siphoned off before the ordinary French shareholder received payment. Some estimate that Bunau-Varilla and his associates pocketed as much as $16,000,000 and one historian who has studied the subject guesses that perhaps $25,000,000 never left the United States. Who shared in this bonanza can only be imagined. Cromwell, for example, submitted for his services a bill of $800,000, a handsome fee even for a lawyer of his undeniable talents. He and Bunau-Varilla each penned recollections of their participation in the canal affair; neither shed any light on this aspect of it.

WORK on the canal began in a matter of months as Roosevelt announced his determination to "make the dirt fly on the isthmus." A healthy amount of bungling occurred at first but, after a justly proclaimed effort against adverse conditions such as the heat and yellow fever, the canal was completed and officially opened in 1914. That same year President Woodrow Wilson sent to the Senate a treaty with Colombia which expressed "sincere regrets" on the part of the United States and provided for a cash indemnity of $25,000,000 for "past actions." Angry Republicans, led by Henry Cabot Lodge, defeated the treaty while expressing their outraged horror at the slur upon Roosevelt's honor. By 1921 enough of these same Senators, still led by Henry Cabot Lodge, reversed their vote to pass the treaty after removing the expressed apology. That the discovery of highly desirable oil deposits in Colombia influenced their behavior, all stoutly denied. One wag accurately dubbed the cash settlement "canalimony."

Arrangements over the canal strip have been revised periodically but the basic fact of American control over it has constituted a permanent affront to Panamanian nationalists, an affront often manifested in violence. That the Panamanians are fully aware of the circumstances surrounding the original agreement helps matters not at all. "If I had followed traditional, conservative methods," Roosevelt boasted some years after the revolution, "I would have submitted a dignified State paper of probably 200 pages to Congress and the debates on it would have been going on yet; but I took the Canal Zone and let Congress debate; and while the debate goes on the Canal does also." From a longer view, the fact that he saved perhaps a year or two by his actions seems far less praiseworthy than he thought.

6 Inside Twentieth America

Century

The popular coffee table version of American experience since the end of World War I subscribes to a sort of roller coaster theory of history. This notion has it that first there were the roaring twenties, then the grim, depression-ridden thirties, followed in the forties by the glorious drama of World War II, which led to the prosperous fifties, followed by the coming-apart tailspin of the sixties. Doubtless there is some truth to this picture, but such a view fails to recognize that throughout this sixty-year period the United States has been faced by ongoing challenges such as rapid technological innovation, racial tension, and urban growth. Thus, it is not surprising that historians have noted the continuities as well as the discontinuities and have qualified the labels of coffee table history.

In "Red Summer: 1919," William Tuttle recalls the gruesome outburst of racial violence with which the post–World War I era began. Clearly the racial violence of the fifties and sixties are not without antecedents.

"The decade of the nineteen twenties was at one and the same time the gaudiest, the saddest, and the most misinterpreted era in modern history," writes Bruce Catton in "The Restless Decade." Looking beneath the surface glitter created by the flapper, the speakeasy, the gangster, and the speculator, Catton finds that an uneasy materialism was replacing more work-oriented values.

Surely one of the most significant aspects of the fifties and the sixties has been the growing concern about racial equality. The crucial problem for historians has not been so much to record the marches, assassinations, and riots—television and the daily newspaper have seen to that—but rather to determine what it all adds up to. In "The 1950's: Racial Equality and the Law," Norman Amaker seeks to evaluate both the steps that led to the Supreme Court's 1954 decision that separate schools were inherently unequal and those that precipitated "The Movement" that followed that decision.

By 1970 the attention given to the plight of non-white Americans had helped prompt other groups to protest what they considered to be unadmitted inequities. "White Ethnic" by Michael Novak is a jarring reminder of the almost infinite complexity of American pluralism. "I am born of PIGS," begins Novak, "those Poles, Italians, Greeks, and Slavs, non-English-speaking immigrants, numbered so heavily among the workingmen of this nation. Not particularly liberal, nor radical, born into a history not white Anglo-Saxon and not Jewish—born outside what in America is considered the intellectual mainstream. And thus privy to neither power nor status nor intellectual voice."

The late sixties and early seventies saw "sexism" join "racism" as yet one more charge that inequities still flourished in democratic America. In "The Feminists: A Second Look," Gerda Lerner contends that "male supremacy has had a devastating effect on the self-consciousness of women; it has imbued them with a deep sense of inferiority, which has stunted their development and achievements."

This section ends with two articles devoted to assessing the political trends and the presidential administrations of Lyndon Johnson and Richard Nixon. In "The Vantage Point," David Halberstam discusses the Johnson years, and in "From the New Frontier to the New Revolution," Emmet John Hughes focuses on the rhetoric and meaning of Nixon's pronouncements and policies.

Urban racial violence is hardly a new phenomenon in America but, until recent times, it never struck with quite the force of the hot . . .

"Red Summer" 1919

By WILLIAM M. TUTTLE, Jr.

William M. Tuttle, Jr., formerly Senior Fellow in Southern and Negro History at Johns Hopkins, is now at the University of Kansas. His book on the "Red Summer," "Race Riot: Chicago in the Red Summer of 1919," was recently published by Atheneum, and is recommended for those wishing to read more on the subject.

"The parks and bathing beaches," Chicago's leading black newspaper, the *Defender,* reminded its readers in July 1919, "are much more inviting these warm days than State Street. A hint to the wise should be sufficient." Specifically, the *Defender* recommended Lake Michigan's 25th Street beach, where there were free towels and lockers and where "every precaution is being taken to safeguard the interests of the bathers." The *Whip*, another of the city's black newspapers, also boosted the attractions to be found at the 25th Street beach. There were not only bathing beauties there but even a black lifeguard; so come to 25th Street, the *Whip* urged, and help Chicago's black people "make this beach [their] Atlantic City."

The temperature that Sunday, July 27, soared into the 90's. The heat was already stifling by early afternoon when 14-year-old John Harris and four other

From *American History Illustrated*, July 1971. Reproduced through the courtesy of The National Historical Society, publishers of AMERICAN HISTORY *Illustrated*, 206 Hanover Street, Gettysburg, Pa. 17325. Published 10 times a year.

black teenagers hopped on a produce truck driving north on Wabash Avenue. At 26th Street, the truck slowed down to cross the streetcar tracks, and the boys alighted. They walked seven blocks to the lake. Perspiring freely and carrying their rolled-up swimming trunks, they were naturally eager to get to the cooling water and to a homemade raft at the beach, and to hurry past the hostile domain of an Irish gang that had attacked them with rocks several times before.

The boys were not headed for the black-patronized 25th Street beach; nor did they intend to try to swim at the white beach at 29th Street. They were going to their own, very private spot, in between, a little island which the boys called the "hot and cold." Located behind the Keeley Brewery and Consumers Ice, the "hot and cold" got its name from the effluence discharged by these companies. The waters of Lake Michigan could be as cold as the melting ice from Consumers, but the run-off from the vats at the brewery was not only hot but chemically potent as well. It could even temporarily bleach a black person white. "It was hot as Jesus," John Harris recalled, "I would be as white [as a white man] when I got done—so actually no women or nothing ever come through, so we [often] didn't even wear a suit, just take our clothes off and go down to the bank. . . ."

Tied up at the "hot and cold" was the raft the boys had built: "a tremendous thing," fully fourteen by nine feet, with a "big chain with a hook on one of the big logs. . . ." Harris and his friends could hang onto the raft and propel it by kicking. The goal of the youths that Sunday was a marker nailed on a post several hundred yards from shore. At about 2 o'clock, the boys pushed off, angling their raft south toward the post—and toward 29th Street.

Meanwhile, at the 29th Street beach, the fury of racial hatred had just erupted. Defying the unwritten law that the beach was for whites, several black men and women had strolled to 29th Street to enter the water there. Curses, threatening gestures, and rocks had frightened the intruders away. Minutes later, however, their numbers reinforced, the blacks reappeared, this time hurling rocks. The white bathers fled. But the blacks' possession of the beach was only temporary; behind a barrage of stones white bathers and numerous sympathizers returned. The battle that ensued was frightening in its violence but it was merely Act One in Chicago's long-feared race war.

Innocently unaware of the savage exchange of projectiles and angry words at 29th Street, the five boys continued to "swim, kick, dive, and play around." Then, as they passed the breakwater near 26th Street, a white man began hurling rocks at them. It was simply "a little game," the boys thought. "We were watching him," said Harris. "He'd take a rock and

throw it, and we would duck it—this sort of thing. . . . As long as we could see him, he never could hit us, because after all a guy throwing that far is not a likely shot. And you could see the brick coming. . . ."

The head of one of the boys, Eugene Williams, had just bobbed out of the water when one of the others diverted his attention. "And just as he turned his head this fellow threw [the rock] and it struck him . . . on the . . . forehead." John Harris could tell that Eugene was injured, for he slid back into the water; not diving, "he just sort of relaxed." Harris dived down to try to help, but, as he remembered, Eugene "grabbed my right ankle, and, hell, I got scared. I shook him off." By that time the boys were in about fifteen feet of water. Gasping for breath and panic-stricken, Harris surfaced, and "began to shudder." "I shook away from him to come back up, and you could see the blood coming up, and the fellows were all excited. . . ."

The man on the breakwater ran toward 29th Street. "Let's get the lifeguard," shouted Harris as he pushed off from the raft. Dog paddling and swimming underwater, Harris reached shore and dashed to the 25th Street beach to tell the head lifeguard, who "blew a whistle and sent a boat around." But by that time there was nothing that anybody could do. Thirty minutes later, divers recovered Eugene's body.

Also by that time, anger had begun to replace the panic and the awe of the black boys. With a black policeman from the 25th Street beach, they marched to 29th Street and pointed out the alleged rock-thrower to the white policeman on duty, who not only would not arrest the man, but refused to permit the black policeman to arrest him. As the policemen argued, Harris and his friends ran back to 25th Street, and "told the colored people what was happening, and they starting running this way," to 29th Street.

The argument at 29th Street raged on. And in the midst of it, the white officer, while continuing to ignore the exhortations of blacks to arrest the accused murderer, arrested a black man on the complaint of a white. In the meantime, distorted rumors of the brawl and drowning had engulfed the South Side. Whites told each other that a white swimmer had drowned after being struck with a rock thrown by a black. A rumor in the nearby "black belt" was that the policeman had not only caused Williams' death by preventing expert swimmers from rescuing him but that he had even "held [his] gun on [the] colored crowd and permitted white rioters to throw bricks and stones at [the] colored." Hundreds of angry blacks and whites swarmed to the beach, filling the streets

White children and adults cheering outside Negro residence which they have set afire. (United Press International, Inc.)

approaching it. The crowd was tumultuous when a patrol wagon pulled up at 29th Street to put the arrested man in custody. Volleys of bricks and rocks were exchanged. Then a black man drew a revolver and fired into a cluster of policemen, wounding one of them. A black officer returned the fire, fatally injuring the Negro. Suddenly, there was the reverberation of other pistol shots. The restless onlookers, many of them armed, had heard their cue, the gunfire that signaled the beginning of a race war.

Once ignited on July 27, the rioting raged virtually uncontrolled for the greater part of five days. Day and night white gangs assaulted isolated blacks, and teenage blacks beat white peddlers and merchants in the black belt. As rumors of atrocities circulated through the city, members of both races sought vengeance. White gunmen in automobiles sped through the black belt shooting indiscriminately as they passed, and

black snipers fired back. Roaming mobs shot, beat, and stabbed to death their victims. The undermanned police force was an ineffectual deterrent to the waves of violence which soon overflowed the environs of the black belt and flooded the North and West Sides and the Loop, Chicago's downtown business district. Only six regiments of state militiamen and a cooling rain finally quenched the passions of the rioters, and even then sporadic outbursts occurred for another week. The toll was awesome. Police officers had fatally wounded seven black men during the riot. Mobs and lone gunmen had brutally murdered an additional sixteen blacks and fifteen whites, and well over 500 Chicagoans of both races had sustained injuries.

The bloodshed inflicted an ineradicable scar on the city's reputation, and it outraged the sensibilities of countless Americans, black and white. But the Chicago race riot of 1919 should not have been altogether surprising to men and women who had read the

chronicle of America's past, with its history of racial violence in the 18th and 19th centuries. There was a notable burgeoning of urban racial violence North as well as South in the first decades of the 20th century, with riots in New York City in 1900; Springfield, Ohio in 1904; Atlanta, Georgia, in 1906; and Springfield, Illinois, in 1908.

Clearly urban racial violence was more than a regional problem. White Northerners could no longer scoff at the barbarity of their Southern countrymen, as the bloodshed of the East St. Louis, Illinois, riot so vividly illustrated. Fueled by economic, political, and social tensions, the smoldering fires of antagonism between blacks and whites burst into furious rioting in Juy 1917. When the smoke from the burning boxcars and houses of East St. Louis lifted, nine whites and about forty blacks were dead, many of them the **victims of unspeakable horrors.** A white reporter

counted six black corpses lying near the corner of Fourth and Broadway. "I think every one I saw killed had both hands above his head begging for mercy." He had heard one moan, "My God, don't kill me, white man." Whites put torches to the homes of black people, leaving them with the choice of burning alive or fleeing and chancing death by gunfire. Some blacks were hanged, including men who were already practically dead from injuries. One black man had suffered severe head wounds; but, as he was not dead yet, the mob decided to hang him. "To put the rope around the negro's neck," noted a reporter, "one of the lynchers stuck his fingers inside the gaping scalp and lifted the negro's head by it, literally bathing his hand in the man's blood." Whites did not allow their black victims "to die easily"; when "flies settled on their terrible wounds the dying blacks [were warned not] to brush them off." Law enforcement was worse than nonexistent. Many police and militiamen, instead of trying to quell the violence, worked

A detail of mounted police in Chicago escort a Negro to a safety zone. (Photograph, United Press International, Inc.)

in collusion with the white mobs in their quest to "get a nigger." State troops fraternized and joked with lawbreaking whites, and many were seen helping in the murders and arson.

The factors that had caused East St. Louis to explode were evident in varying degrees in other American cities in 1919 two years later. It seemed, in fact, that the atmosphere during the first year of peace after World War I was even more conducive to racial violence than that during the war itself. When black intellectual and civil rights leader James Weldon Johnson originated the title the "Red Summer," he was referring to the race riots that bloodied the streets of twenty towns and cities in the six-month period from April to early October 1919. One of these riots was a massacre, with an indeterminate number of black people slaughtered in rural Phillips County, Arkansas, and it is thus impossible to determine ex-

actly how many died in race riots that summer. But the number of blacks and whites killed must have exceeded 120.

The Red Summer was consistent with the nation's history of racial violence. Yet it was also part of a generalized climate of violence in 1919, and this helps to account for the great number of race riots that year. It is thus not coincidental that the summer of 1919 also marked the beginning in the United States of the xenophobic and hysterically antiradical "Red Scare." Both phenomena were the ugly offspring of some of the same unrest, anxieties, and dislocations that plagued America and, indeed, the immediate postwar world. Mankind's values, attitudes, and expectations were in disarray in 1919, and the resultant violence was worldwide.

In the United States, the "search for the 'inner enemy,'" bolstered as it was by the force of law and the nation's mores, became institutionalized in 1919;

Ruins of homes in Chicago stockyard district, blamed on Negro incendiaries. The destruction left 3,000 homeless. (UP Int.)

and then, as the sociologist Georg Simmel observed, "instead of being disapproved by members of one's group for being prejudiced, one was punished for not being prejudiced." Although the motives for and the manifestations of race prejudice in 1919 were somewhat different, this statement was as true of race relations as it was of antiradicalism and the treatment of the foreign-born. For the most highly susceptible objects of prejudice in postwar America were its black men and women, not because they were radicals but because they threatened the accommodative race system of white superordination and black subordination.

During World War I white hostility became more intense as upwards of 450,000 Southern blacks migrated to the North. There, in crowded cities, they met in bitter competition with whites over jobs, housing, political power, and facilities for education, transportation, and relaxation. Moreover, black people, visibly distinct and with behavior patterns that were alien to whites, were convenient scapegoats for people who feared that their status had dropped because of the influx from the South. The employment of a new black worker in the shop or the arrival of a black family on the block only heightened the anxieties of status deprivation, often prompting whites to drag out once again the ancient shibboleth that blacks were grasping not for material improvement, but for "social equality." For their part, black men and women entered 1919 with aspirations for a larger share of both the nation's democracy and its wealth. In 1919, racial uneasiness was evident in cities and towns throughout the country. And there seemed to be a threshold of tension above which racial violence was almost bound to occur, spurred by a precipitating incident and in the absence of external controls of law enforcement to discourage potential rioters and lynchers. These various factors coalesced time and time again in 1919, and an unparalleled outburst of racial violence struck the United States.

Lynch mobs murdered seventy-eight black people in 1919, an increase of fifteen over 1918 and thirty over 1917, and contemporaneous with the lynchings, of course, were the race riots of the Red Summer. The first of the major disruptions struck Charleston, South Carolina. It was Saturday night, May 10, when the black man doubled up in pain and slumped to the street. There had been an argument, and the bullet wound inflicted by the white sailor had been fatal. Hundreds of other sailors were also on liberty that night; hearing rumors of a racial altercation involving a Navy man, they began to swarm angrily into the city's black district. Augustus Bonaparte, a black man, was having his hair cut at the time. Startled by shouts, he looked out of the barbershop window

to see a mob of sailors dash by and into a nearby shooting gallery, which they proceeded to loot for rifles. Automobiles filled with sailors soon crowded the streets. "Get a nigger," was the angry cry. James Frayer, a black cobbler, saw frightened black men and boys running toward his shop, shouting that the sailors were coming. Quickly, he shut his door and latched it. "Open the door," yelled a voice. When nobody moved, the sailor outside fired his weapon at random through the door, wounding Frayer's apprentice in the back.

Unable to subdue the rioters, the city police asked the Navy to order Marines with fixed bayonets into the streets. Although the presence of troops aided in restoring calm, certain of these men continued the terrorization that the sailors had begun. T. B. Nelson, for example, darted from his house upon hearing moaning in the street. Lying there wounded was a black youth, who pleaded with the Marines who hovered over him. "What are you shooting me for, I was not doing anything." "Why didn't you halt when we told you to?" demanded one of the men. The boy gasped that he had not been ordered to stop. "Hush your mouth or we'll give you some more." When Isaac Moses also told Marines that he had not heard their command to halt, they responded by calling him a "damned liar," knocking him in the head, stealing five dollars, and stabbing him through the leg with a bayonet. The death toll from that night of rioting in Charleston was two black men. Wounded were seventeen blacks, seven sailors, and a white policeman.

Racial violence next exploded in Longview, Texas in a county of 8,500 whites and 8,200 blacks. Longview had been uneasy with racial tension. Members of the local chapter of the Negro Business League had established black cooperative stores which sold products at lower prices than did white merchants. For another, these same black leaders—men such as Dr. C. P. Davis, a physician, and S. L. Jones, a high school teacher—had urged black farmers to avoid the white cotton brokers in Longview by selling direct to the buyers in Galveston.

Then, on June 17, there was a lynching. Lemuel Walters had allegedly been discovered in a white woman's bedroom. The next day his nude body was found lying near the railroad tracks at a desolate spot known as Foote's Switch, four miles south of Longview. Fear and apprehension swept the black community, and a delegation of eleven men led by Davis and Jones made a call on the county judge. The judge advised silence, saying that "there [should] be no talking as talking would interfere with locating the culprits." Days passed, but no arrests were made, and it appeared to the black men that local officials not only were not investigating the lynching but that they were even using this time to destroy evidence which would prove the guilt of the murderers. The men returned to the judge, who told them that he had informed the district attorney of their suspicions. Again the judge advised "no talking."

A Saturday morning event in Longview's black district was the arrival on the train of the weekly Chicago *Defender*. And the issue of the newspaper that July 5 was of special interest, for it had a story about Longview. Lemuel Walters, read the article, "was taken from the Longview jail by a crowd of white men when a prominent white woman declared she loved him, and if she were in the North would obtain a divorce and marry him." His only offense, the *Defender* added, was having had a white woman love him, and the penalty he had paid was death.

Chicago race riots. Typical hit-and-run tactics of a group of whites. Note man with bricks in foreground. (UP Int., Inc.)

S. L. Jones, who was also the local *Defender* agent, drove his automobile to the downtown business district the following Thursday, July 10. There he encountered three white men, who brusquely demanded that he come with them. Jones refused and tried to pull away from one of the men who had grabbed him. Another of the men struck Jones a heavy blow on the head with a wrench. Other blows followed. Jones fell to the pavement, struggled to get up but fell again. Since he had written the *Defender* article, his attackers insisted, it would be much easier if he simply admitted it. When Jones denied that he had, they beat him again. Finally, the pummeling stopped, and Jones dragged himself to Dr. Davis' office.

Meanwhile, there was talk of impending "trouble that night." If Jones were still in Longview by midnight, according to one rumor, he would be lynched. Mayor G. A. Bodenheim sent a messenger to Davis to warn him and Jones to leave town at once. But Davis sent word back that he was staying. Davis also learned that the mayor and other city officials were

meeting in emergency session at city hall, and he decided to join them. When he arrived at city hall, however, all that the white authorities would tell him was to take off his hat. "Yes!" Davis replied heatedly. "That's all 'you all' say to a colored man who comes to talk serious business to you: 'Take off your hat.' I am not going to do it. I want to know what protection we colored citizens are going to have tonight." "You will have to take your chances," the mayor replied.

As darkness settled on Longview, black volunteers met at Davis' house, "pledging their lives in his defense." The doctor assumed command of the men, posting them "where they could safeguard every side from which an attack could be made," and instructing them not to fire before he did and "under no circumstances to shoot into white people's houses." At about 11 p.m., Dr. Davis sneaked through alleys and dark streets to within eyeshot of the city hall. It was just as he had feared; white men were gathering, using the fire department as their command post. Returning to his house, he told his troops what the prospects were, and "offered to allow any of them who did not feel like risking his life . . . to retire. . . . Every man stayed and said he was prepared to take what might come." About midnight, Davis and Jones recalled, "the mob came down through a back street." The black men crouched quietly, waiting in ambush until Jones's house was "approached or attacked. Four white men came on the back porch of the house and called to Jones to come out." There was no answer. "When it became evident that they intended to force their way in, Davis fired the first shot and the melee began." Over 100 shots were fired in a half-hour, and four whites fell with fatal wounds, causing the rest of the mob of about a dozen whites to retreat to the town square. Minutes later, and one at a time, automobiles sped down the street leading to Jones's house, white men hopped out, picked up the dead and wounded, and sped away.

Throughout the night, a fire bell was sounded, eventually summoning about 1,000 white men to the town square. Until almost daybreak the leaderless crowd simply milled around; then, as if suddenly energized by the first shafts of daylight, men began smashing their way into the hardware store and helping themselves to rifles, pistols, and ammunition. Thus armed, a mob headed back to Jones's house. By then, however, Jones and Davis were in hiding, and the mob occupied itself by dousing their homes with kerosene and igniting them, along with the homes of four other of the "principal" black residents. The next day, police officers, aided by bloodhounds, tracked down Marion Bush, the 60-year-old father-in-law of Davis, and shot him dead in a cornfield three miles south of town.

Davis and Jones succeeded in escaping from Longview. Dressed in a soldier's uniform and improvised leggings, Davis boarded a train a few miles from town; and knowing that authorities searching for him would be looking for a doctor, he "bought some popcorn, some red pop and some other refreshment and walked around . . . throwing the bottle in the air, drinking from it ostentatiously and eating and singing, like a simple 'darky.'" Fearing worse violence, the governor of Texas declared martial law in Longview and ordered the state militia and Texas Rangers into the town. Yet there was no more bloodshed. Certain white citizens of the community even adopted a resolution deploring the "scurrilous [*Defender*] article" about "a respectable white lady." That day and night of rioting, however, had left five dead, a score wounded, and many homeless.

Washington, D.C., in 1919, was a city where lurid tales of black rapists seemed to gain front-page coverage day after day. In June and July four women allegedly were assaulted in Washington, and three in the portion of Maryland contiguous to the District of Columbia. The press featured emotional accounts of these attacks, imputing them all without substantive evidence to blacks. One alleged victim claimed that she had been sexually assaulted by "two young negroes . . . wearing white shirts, no coats, tan or yellow hats." Two weeks later she admitted that she had not been attacked by black youths, or indeed attacked at all. But the denial received miniscule coverage compared to the initial accusation. Such inflammatory journalism aroused the ire of whites, especially of military personnel stationed in or near the Capital, and racial tension mounted.

On Saturday, July 19, the *Washington Post* ran headlines telling of another sexual assault: "NEGROES ATTACK GIRL . . . WHITE MEN VAINLY PURSUE." The next night the volcano of race hatred erupted in Washington, following a minor white-black dispute on Pennsylvania Avenue. Roaming bands of soldiers, sailors, and Marines began to molest any black person in sight, hauling them off streetcars and out of restaurants, chasing them up alleys, and beating them mercilessly on street corners. With ineffectual police restraint, violence reigned for three days as white mobs ran amuck through the streets. Finally, on the fourth day, blacks retaliated when threatened by fires to their residences. Having witnessed the helplessness of the Washington police, Secretary of War Newton D. Baker ordered in 2,000 Regular Army soldiers. On the evening of July 22, with Federal troops and a downpour of rain deterring would-be rioters, the violence subsided, leaving six dead in the streets and upwards of 100 injured.

During the riot, further irresponsible journalism, both by the white and the black press, heightened the anger of the mobs. On the first day of bloodshed, the *Bee,* a black newspaper, declared: "A RIOT IS AL-MOST CREATED: A Texan in the War Risk Bureau Assaults a Colored Female." The article beneath the headline told that the "assault" was actually a verbal insult. Two days later the *Washington Post* notified the aroused armed servicemen of a "Mobilization for Tonight." "It was learned," the *Post* noted, "that a mobilization of every available service man . . . has been ordered for tomorrow evening near the Knights of Columbus hut. . . . The hour of assembly is 9 o'clock and the purpose is a 'clean-up' that will cause the events of the last two evenings to pale into insignificance." Thus the *Post* had not only inflamed the passions of the rioters, it had even furnished them with a battle plan.

After the bloodshed in Washington, the New York *Times* consoled itself that, "painful as it is to say," a race riot such as the one in the nation's Capital "could not have arisen in any Northern city where the police had been trained to expect riot duty." The *Times* displayed little prescience on this occasion, however. For in a northern city, just four days later, John Harris and his four young black friends hopped on the back of a produce truck, dreaming about the Lake Michigan beach at the foot of Chicago's 26th Street, and about their homemade raft and all the excitement that awaited them in the water. Obviously, the Red Summer of 1919 knew no bounds, North or South. It was a national disaster.

Chicago race riots. A detachment of the Illinois National Guard on duty in Negro section. (Chicago Historical Society)

THE RESTLESS DECADE

All the old rules seemed to be vanishing in the Twenties.

In exchange came a strange new world both gaudy and sad

BRUCE CATTON

The decade of the nineteen twenties was at one and the same time the gaudiest, the saddest, and the most misinterpreted era in modern American history.

It was gaudy because it was full of restless vitality burgeoning in a field where all of the old rules seemed to be gone, and it was sad because it was an empty place between two eras, with old familiar certainties and hopes drifting off like mist and new ones not yet formulated. It was misunderstood because so many of its popular interpreters became so fascinated by the things that floated about on the froth that they could not see anything else.

Most of the tag lines that have been attached to it are wrong. It was, we are assured, the period when *everybody* did fantastic things. Everybody detested Prohibition, patronized bootleggers, made atrocious gin in the bathtub and worse beer in the basement, and, inspired by the products of these activities, danced the Charleston. Everybody bought stocks on margin or Florida lots on binder clauses and confidently expected to become rich before old age set in. Everybody put his moral standards away in moth balls, so that neither the scandalous doings in Washington nor the murderous forays of the Chicago gangsters seemed very disturbing. Everybody, in short, was off on a prolonged spree, and the characteristic figure of the era was the Flapper, the girl who bobbed her hair and wore short skirts with nothing in particular beneath them and put in her time piling in and out of open cars populated by collegians in coonskin coats.

It makes an entertaining picture—it made one at the time, in a way, for the people who were in it—but it is at best only a partial picture.

The first thing to remember is that the word "everybody" is much too inclusive. There were a great many people in the United States in the nineteen twenties, and most of them were serious, hard-working people who did their best to earn a living, bring up their children, live decently by the best light they had, and lay away a few dollars for their old age. Most of them never saw the inside of a speakeasy, most never really tried to make gin or beer at home, and anyone over the age of twenty-six who danced the Charleston regretted it immediately—it was an exercise in all-out acrobatics rather than a dance, and only the young could manage it. Acceptance of the Prohibition law was so widespread that repeal of the Eighteenth Amendment was not voted, or ever seriously considered, until after the decade had ended. Certainly the vast majority bought neither stocks, bonds, nor Florida real estate and never had the faintest notion that with a little luck they could soon stroll down Easy Street. They were just as deeply disturbed by Teapot Dome and Al Capone as anyone would be today, and if these and other phenomena helped to destroy confidence in public leadership, it ought to be added that the kind of leadership that was given to the American people in those years was pretty poor.

Nevertheless, the decade did have its own peculiar character—because it was a time of unending change.

It was a hollow time between wars. The 1914–18 war, which had been ever so much more cataclysmic than anybody had imagined any war could be, was over, but it had left smouldering wreckage all over the landscape; and if the next war was not yet visible, there was ominous heat lightning all along the horizon to warn that there had been no real break in the weather. The certainties the adult American was used to, in 1920—the basic assumptions about world society which he had always taken for granted—were obviously either gone forever or rapidly going. Europe, which had always seemed to be the very center of stability, had collapsed. Of the great empires which had maintained order and set standards, some had vanished without trace and the survivors were mortally injured; Europe was a center of disorder, with monstrous doctrines either being followed or vigorously preached; and the one certainty was that things would get worse before they ever got better.

There was an immense, all-pervading disillusionment. The nation's highest ideals had been appealed to during the war, so that to win the war seemed the holiest of causes; the war had been won, but it was hard to see that anything worth winning had been gained; the idealism had been used up, and people had an uneasy feeling that they had been had. The Prohibition act contributed to the letdown. Here was a social experiment which, as President Herbert Hoover correctly said, had been adopted with the noblest of motives, but nothing was working out as had been anticipated, and the problems the law was supposed to solve seemed to have been made worse; the majority was not yet ready to discard the law, but it was beginning to see that something somewhere was awfully wrong with it.

So lots of people became materialists. The light of faith was flickering low; the average citizen had his own, private faith in the relationship between himself and his Maker, but his faith in the world itself and in the values on which it operated was not robust. It was easier, indeed it was almost necessary, to center one's attention on the material things that were going on in this country.

A great deal was going on, and it was immensely stimulating. The world was in the act of shifting gears —not without grating—starting to move with bewildering speed, and if the destination was wholly unclear, the speed itself was exhilarating.

The age of the automobile was arriving. In 1920 the average American did not own an automobile and did not suppose that he ever would; by 1930 the automobile was a necessity of daily life, and the incalculable change it was going to inflict on America—change for city, town, and countryside, for ways of living and habits of thought—was already visible. At the same time the era of mass production was coming into full effect, and mankind (most especially in America) was beginning to lay its hands on the fabulous capacity to solve any problem on earth so long as the problem was purely material. This of course was most unsettling, because it brought with it the uneasy awareness that the real problem was going to be man himself and not his ability to reshape his environment, and no one was ready to tell people what they ought to do about themselves. But it was a miraculous age. The instruments, skills, and techniques—airplanes, electronics, automation—that would change the world forever were appearing. Albert Einstein, who was known to the few Americans who had ever heard of him as an oddball professor type who thought that space was curved, had already published the formula that was to lead to the atomic age.

It was an exciting decade; in many ways a good time to be alive. If the spirit of the nineteen twenties took on a materialistic cast, nobody can be blamed. It was good simply to look at the surface and enjoy it.

The surface contained elements of sheer fantasy. Along with everything else, the age of mass communications was here, in exuberant, uninhibited blossoming, and the public ear could be reached as never before. In some ways those were the years of the sportswriter, the press agent, and the newspaper columnist —not the purveyor of gossip, but the man who found amusement and a large audience by discussing the items that floated about on the froth. It was the time of the big headline and the loud-speaker, which were reserved for the purely spectacular.

So the most famous people in America were a strange assortment—movie stars, gangsters, Channel swimmers, professional athletes, imaginative amateur murderers, and eccentrics of high and low degree. Before 1920, moving-picture actors and actresses were outsiders; now they were at the top of the ladder, living in the limelight as no one ever did before or since. Before 1920 prize fighting had been disreputable, outlawed in most states, tolerated in a few; now the heavyweight champion was a hero, an ideal for American youth, a man whose performances could command a box-office sale of a million dollars or more. Once in the mid-Twenties the author of a quiz program played a sly trick: by posing two innocent questions he showed that although every adult American could name and identify the star halfback at the University of Illinois, no one outside of the academic profession knew the name of that university's president.

As Westbrook Pegler said, this was the Era of Wonderful Nonsense. Publicity was the thing, and it had no standards of value except pure sensation. An American girl swam the English Channel, nonstop; the mayor of Chicago ran for re-election with the promise that he would hit the King of England on the nose if chance allowed; the President of the United States, asked how such nations as England and France could ever repay their enormous war debts without coming to utter ruin, replied drily: "They hired the money, didn't they?" A countrywoman who tended pigs was carried into court on a stretcher to testify in an earth-shaking murder trial, and for a few days everybody in the country (well, a lot of people, if not quite everybody) was talking about the Pig Woman . . . and all of these things were of equal weight, they made the headlines for a few days, and then life went on as before.

Stock prices went up and up, Florida real-estate prices did likewise; supposedly realistic analysts said that this was only natural because "everybody" was in the market, and the happy theory that everybody in the United States had plenty of money overlooked the fact that farmers and wage earners were being caught in a terrible squeeze in which their bitterest protests went unheeded. A conservative senator announced that congressmen who protested about this situation were simply "sons of the wild jackass" whose cries need not be noticed, and one of the country's best-known economists said that inflated stock prices need worry no one because the nation had reached a new, permanently high plateau in which all of the old standards could be ignored.

If all of this was exciting it was not really satisfying, and people knew it. They were hungry for something they were not getting—an appeal to idealism, to the belief that the greatest values cannot be expressed in cash or set forth in headlines. The amazing response to Charles A. Lindbergh's flight proves the point.

Lindbergh flew from New York to Paris in 1927. The Atlantic had been flown before, it was obviously going to be flown again—two or three highly publicized expeditions were poised at New York, getting ready, while the nation waited—but what he did seemed like nothing anyone had ever imagined before. He was young, boyish, unspoiled, the kind of youth people had stopped believing in, a young man nobody had heard of before, and he came to New York, waited for a good weather report, and then took off, unaided by any of the elaborate devices that would make such a flight routine nowadays. When he landed in Paris it seemed as if mankind had somehow triumphed over something that greatly needed to be beaten. After he had vanished into the over-ocean midnight, and before any word of him had come back, people waited in an agony of suspense, and when it was announced that he had indeed landed in Paris, unharmed and on schedule, there was literally rejoicing in the streets.

It was odd, and revealing. After years in which it seemed as if everybody who got any kind of fame was on the make, here was a young man who apparently had done something great for nothing. Lindbergh became the hero of the decade. We have not felt quite that way about anybody since; he lifted up the heart, and all of a sudden it was possible to believe in something once more. The response to what he did was a perfect symbol of what everybody had been lacking.

It seemed like a miracle . . . but at last the glitter faded, and like everything else, this bright deed was buried under a spate of words. There were too many words in those years. Everybody listened, and nobody got much out of it. Much of the talk came from men who were not qualified to address a large audience. At the beginning of the decade, radio had been nothing much more than a useful device by which a sinking ship could call for help; in a very few years it was central to the mass-communications business, and the man who spoke into the microphone was suddenly a power in the land. E. B. White summed it up by remarking that man's "words leap across rivers and mountains, but his thoughts are still only six inches long."

It was a time for long thoughts, but long thoughts were not often being thought, and when they were it was hard to find an audience for them. The world was passing across one of the significant watersheds in human history and the crest of the pass seemed to be situated right in the United States, but it was hard to think about anything except that, for the moment, the path led upward. The people of the nineteen twenties really behaved about the way the people of all other decades have behaved. They did a great deal of hard work, doing some of it extraordinarily well, when you stop to think about it; they carried their own individual loads of worry and aspiration and frustration along with them; and if they did some foolish things, they precisely resembled, in the doing of them, both their ancestors and their descendants.

Yet the essential point about the Twenties, the thing that makes us think of the decade as a separate era, was its curious transitional character, which was not like anything ever seen before—or since. The Twenties were years that no one who lived through them can ever forget, and they were also a time nobody in his senses would care to repeat, but you do have to say one thing for them: when the great catastrophe came, one decade after the Twenties had ended, the generation the Twenties had raised proved to be strong enough to stand the shock.

The 1950's: Racial Equality and the Law

". . . the Brown decision . . . affected the development of legal rules in all areas of race relations . . . and started a chain reaction . . . affecting . . . the action of Congress and the Executive as well as that of the states and local governments."

Norman C. Amaker

First Assistant Counsel, NAACP Legal Defense and Educational Fund, Inc.

Norman C. Amaker joined the staff of the Legal Defense and Educational Fund in 1960. Among his cases have been many in defense of civil rights demonstrators. He is a member of the Bar of the Supreme Court of the United States and the bars of various lower federal courts.

The SCHOOL SEGREGATION Cases decided by the United States Supreme Court a decade and a half ago[1] marked a watershed in the development of United States law on race relations, a development which in the American context has principally meant the treatment of blacks before the law and the concomitant attitude of whites (as well as blacks and other Americans) of what that treatment should be. The decision, of course, affected the principal subject with which it dealt—what the Constitution required of the former slave states in affording equal educational opportunities to black children descended from their slave ancestors.

The Court unanimously held that those states which had maintained by law a dual system of public education—one for the whites, the other for the blacks—were now obliged to operate only one school system for all children. The legal duty to integrate the schools arose, said the Court, because as a matter of law separate educational systems were inherently unequal.

But the *Brown* decision was of far greater significance than the mere pronouncement in a group of cases[2] of a legal rule albeit of constitutional dimension relating to the public schools. It affected the development of legal rules in all areas of race relations—indeed, its impact is still felt in these areas as well as

in the continuing effort to implement its specific prescriptions.[3] It started a chain reaction in society equivalent to that of nuclear fission, affecting not only subsequent decisions of the courts, but eventually the action of Congress and the Executive as well as that of the states and local governments. Attitudes of other Americans toward the Negro and of Negroes toward themselves began to undergo change. And in its repudiation of the "separate-but-equal" doctrine of *Plessy* v. *Ferguson*,[4] a case decided by the Supreme Court in 1896, it represented a sharp break with the American past, a past in which society's assumption of the racial inferiority of black people was written into law.

THE LAW'S CONTRIBUTION TO RACIAL INEQUALITY

In historical perspective, the law contributed as much as anything else to the attitude of American society toward the Negro. The incorporation of notions of black inferiority—and hence of racial inequality—began very early in our history as a nation with the deletion of Thomas Jefferson's antislavery section from the proposed Declaration of Independence. This was followed by the approval by the Constitutional Convention of three clauses protecting the institution of slavery.[5] More laws followed, e.g., the Fugitive Slave Law and the Black Codes.

Then, too, the courts of the land, theoretically the ultimate repositories of equal justice under law, contributed to the rule-making process which made notions of the black man's inferiority a part of the national character. In 1857, the United States Supreme Court, in the *Dred Scott* case,[6] held that

Negroes were not citizens of the country, that the framers of the Declaration of Independence and the Constitution never intended black men to share in the fruits of the new democracy, and that it had been clear

for more than a century before these documents were written that blacks were regarded as beings of an inferior order; . . . altogether unfit to associate with the white race . . . so far inferior, that they had no rights which the white man was bound to respect.

After the Constitution's Fourteenth Amendment had presumably administered the *coup de grace* to the *Dred Scott* decision and the reformist zeal of the Reconstruction Congresses had attempted to reverse the long-standing national process of weaving attitudes of racial inferiority into the fabric of law by the enactment of a succession of civil rights laws, the Supreme Court in the last three decades of the century revived the process by a series of rulings on the meaning of the Fourteenth Amendment. In the first of these, in 1873, the Court held that the clause of the first section of the amendment forbidding any state to make or enforce a law abridging the privileges or immunities of citizens of the United States did not mean that the states were required to make any efforts to protect the fundamental rights and liberties of their citizens which, of course, included the newly freed slaves.[7] A decade later, the Court held that the amendment proscribed only racially discriminatory action by the states, not by individuals.[8] And, in 1896, the *Plessy* case with its ruling that the states could separate whites from blacks on public conveyances embodied the separate-but-equal doctrine which firmly embedded the notion of a racial caste system into law.

Thus, before the *Brown* case was decided, for well over a century the nation's lawmakers had contrived a set of legal rules which erected a superstructure of racial inequalities of formidable proportions. Whether social attitudes create law or whether law creates social attitudes is a debate without real substance. Unmistakably, the truth is that each contributes to the other. It was clear, however, at the time of *Brown* and before, that

---

[1] *Brown* v. *Board of Education*, 347 U.S. 483 (1954). For excerpts, see p. 297.

[2] The other cases decided with *Brown* (which arose from Kansas) were: *Briggs* v. *Elliott* (S.C.); *Davis* v. *School Board of Prince Edward County* (Va.) and *Gebhart* v. *Belton* (Del.). Public school segregation in the District of Columbia was outlawed simultaneously. *Bolling* v. *Sharpe*, 347 U.S. 497 (1954).

[3] The controversy over school desegregation guidelines fashioned as a result of the 1964 Civil Rights Act is a ready example. An equally obvious reaction to the decision is the current school decentralization process occurring in our large cities.

[4] 163 U.S. 537 (1896).

[5] The so-called "three-fifths" clause of Article I, Section 2 for apportioning representatives to the House; the provision of Article I, Section 9 allowing the slave trade until 1808; Article IV, Section 2 providing for the return of fugitive slaves.

[6] *Scott* v. *Sanford*, 19 How. (60 U.S.) 393 (1857).

[7] *The Slaughter-House Cases*, 16 Wall. (83 U.S. 36 (1873).

[8] *The Civil Rights Cases*, 109 U.S. 3 (1883).

so long as the face of the law remained set against equality of treatment for the Negro, so long as the legal structure of injustice remained, there was no hope of making the necessary changes in attitude essential to the eventual eradication of the racial caste system.

The school cases, then, were the first step of major significance in eradicating the legal underpinnings of the caste system and in changing (however slowly) the notions of generations of Americans about the innate inferiority of black people. In this regard, *Brown* is unquestionably the most important legal decision of this century. It did not, however, spring forth full grown like Athena from the head of Zeus; its antecedents are discernible, its gestation period of fairly long duration. Perspective on *Brown's* impact on the law and the nation is gained by an understanding of what led up to the decision.

THE ANTECEDENTS OF BROWN

Plessy was the apotheosis of the incorporation into law of the idea of Negro racial inferiority. The judgment, as a matter of constitutional doctrine, that black people should be separated from white people was a cruel, positive, razor-sharp statement, however denied,[9] of the society's deeply held conviction of the Negro's inferiority. That the case involved intrastate transportation was purely incidental. No one, black or white, was misled: the nation's highest court, the ultimate interpreter of the law, had plainly said that blacks and whites must be separated because blacks were not fit to associate with whites. Clearly, more than private social relations (which the Court took pains to point out were not affected by the amendment) were involved: separation meant no participation for Negroes except as subservients in all the community's affairs; no voice in government, no voice in how society was to be arranged, no voice in where one lived or how one's children were educated, no voice in where one worked or under what conditions, no voice in how one was dealt with at the hands of the law. In short, no power, no manhood.

Obviously, in the twentieth century, a major effort was required to bring about a change in the posture of the law. The effort began with the courts. They were ultimately responsible for saying not only what the law was but what it should be. By the turn of the century, black people had no effective voice in the nation's legislatures or its executive branches. Only by persuading the courts to alter their rulings, to change their interpre-

tations of law, was it possible to set in motion the process, culminating in *Brown*, by which the features of the law's stone face so firmly set against black people began to crumble.

The cases leading up to *Brown* were brought by lawyers acting at the behest of the NAACP,[10] which was formed in 1909. The first cases were responses to situations as they arose, not the result of the planned systematic effort that occurred in the 1930's and 1940's when first the NAACP and later the NAACP Legal Defense Fund[11] took to the United States Supreme Court the graduate school cases that were the direct precursors of *Brown*. Each of these early cases, however, as seen now in the afterlight of legal history, contributed—to continue the metaphor—to the chipping away of the features of the stone face of the law.

The first case concerned the right to vote. In a 1915 decision,[12] the Supreme Court outlawed the so-called "grandfather clause" of Oklahoma's constitution which established a literacy test for prospective voters but exempted persons whose forebears were eligible to vote prior to January 1, 1866. This, of course, effectively disfranchised black voters. Two years later, the Court held a residential segregation ordinance of Louisville, Kentucky, unconstitutional.[13] The first important case—resulting from a famous race riot in eastern Arkansas in 1919—guaranteeing some semblance of due process in the courts to black people was decided by the Supreme Court in 1923[14] and the first of the so-called Texas "white primary" cases[15] was decided in 1927. In this case the Court ruled that a Texas statute making blacks ineligible to participate in a Democratic primary election violated the Fifteenth Amendment to the Constitution which had been passed after the Civil War to guarantee the Negroes' right to vote.

But the major cases resulting in the *Brown* decision were the cases begun in the 1930's seeking the admission of Negroes to all-white college and graduate school facilities. As described in the 1934 Annual Report of the NAACP, "the major emphasis [was] placed upon education inequalities" and the undertaking was a campaign "carefully planned . . . to secure decisions, rulings and public opinion on the broad principle instead of being devoted to merely miscellaneous cases." The first decision involved a black man,

Lloyd Gaines, who sought admission to the University of Missouri Law School. He was denied admission because of his race and was offered a scholarship to a law school outside the state. In its 1938 decision, the Supreme Court ruled that Gaines was not required to leave the state to attend law school when there was an existing facility in Missouri, and ordered his admission.[16]

A decade later, the second graduate school case reached the high Court. A black woman, Ada Sipuel, sought admission to the law school of the University of Oklahoma. Oklahoma, following the usual pattern, offered her aid to attend law school outside the state; if she refused, the state argued, it was not obliged to establish a separate law school for her. The Supreme Court held that Oklahoma was required to provide a legal education for the plaintiff "as soon as it does for applicants of any other group," thus requiring her admission.[17] The separate-but-equal canard remained intact but the principles of these cases (1) that blacks need not leave their home state to get an education and (2) that they need not wait for a black school facility to be established had diminished its force.

The final two graduate school cases went to the threshold of *Brown*. They came respectively from Texas and again from Oklahoma and were decided by the Court on the same day in 1950.[18] *Sweatt*, as did *Gaines* and *Sipuel*, involved the admission of a Negro to law school. The decisions in the earlier cases had made it clear that Negroes could no longer be barred from entrance simply because there was not a Negro law school in the state. But the University of Texas, rather than admit the plaintiff to its law school, first established makeshift facilities for the plaintiff, then undertook to build a law school for blacks. These efforts failed. In the *McLaurin* case, the plaintiff had actually been admitted to the University of Oklahoma but, once admitted, had been segregated in the instruction he received.

When the cases reached the Supreme Court, the Court was urged to overrule the separate but equal doctrine. However, it declined, ruling in *Sweatt* that "substantial equality" could only be gained through admittance to the University of Texas Law School, and in *McLaurin*, that the test of substantial equality was not met through internal segregation within the school. But certainly it was clear from these decisions that at least on the level of graduate and professional education, separation did not provide the equality required by the Constitution. It remained to adapt this prin-

---

[9] "We consider the underlying fallacy of the plaintiff's argument to consist in the assumption that the enforced separation of the two races stamps the colored race with a badge of inferiority. If this be so, it is not by reason of anything found in the act [La. statute providing for separate railway coach facilities] but solely because the colored race choses [sic] to put that construction upon it" (163 U.S. at 551).

[10] This very familiar abbreviation is for National Association for the Advancement of Colored People.

[11] The Legal Defense Fund was formed in 1939 as a separate corporation to carry on as its exclusive function the work begun by the legal committee of the NAACP. The two organizations are often confused because the Fund (LDF) took as part of its corporate title the abbreviation of the Association's corporate name. However, despite the obvious fatherhood, the two organizations function as entirely separate entities.

[12] *Guinn v. United States*, 238 U.S. 347.

[13] *Buchanan v. Warley*, 245 U.S. 60.

[14] *Moore v. Dempsey*, 261 U.S. 86.

[15] *Nixon v. Herndon*, 273 U.S. 536.

[16] *Missouri ex rel. Gaines v. Canada*, 305 U.S. 337 (1938).

[17] *Sipuel v. University of Oklahoma*, 332 U.S. 631 (1948).

[18] *Sweatt v. Painter*, 339 U.S. 629; *McLaurin v. Oklahoma State Board of Regents*, 339 U.S. 637.

ciple to the public elementary and secondary schools in the School Segregation Cases which were the predictable outcome of the development of the law in the graduate school cases.

Thus, at the time of *Brown*, the seeds for reversing the incorporation into law of the idea of the black man's inferiority had been sown for several decades by an evolving series of judicial decisions. It had been a long, tortuous road back from the nadir of *Plessy*. Social developments had undoubtedly played a role—the revulsion in many parts of the country against lynching and other forms of overt brutality practiced against blacks, the effect of two world wars with the unmistakable changes they wrought in the society, changes of personnel on the Court, and the work of established civil rights groups like the NAACP and Urban League. These developments contributed to the maturing of a philosophy that found its quintessential expression in *Brown*. Add to this the skill and dedication of the lawyers who implemented the strategy devised in the 1930's, and the evolution of the law from *Plessy* to *Brown* can be understood. With the recognition by the nation's highest Court that segregation inevitably meant discrimination and with the replacement in law of the principle of racial inferiority by that of racial equality, the stage was set for subsequent developments in law and in society.

THE CHANGES WROUGHT BY BROWN

With the law no longer an obstruction, some communities, including the defendants in the Delaware, Kansas and District of Columbia cases, began desegregating their schools immediately. Others were defiant; in this group were South Carolina and Virginia, the other states directly involved in the decision. Before acting, ostensibly (though not actually), they were awaiting the Court's decision in the second *Brown* case a year later. For the Court, recognizing the import of its decision, had ordered the cases restored to its docket for reargument on the question of how its decision should be implemented. After reargument, the Court adopted a "with all deliberate speed" formulation of the defendants' duty to begin desegregation, i.e., the states were to be given time to effect the transition but "a prompt and reasonable start toward full compliance" had to be made.[19]

This decision, however, prompted not only outright defiance (which was predictable), but what was to emerge as a greater problem: evasive tactics and delay. The decision also fostered attempts to misapply its doctrine. When the first *Brown* decision was announced, an appeal from a Florida court which had

refused to admit a Negro to the University of Florida's Law School was pending. After the Court's decision, it ordered the lower court to reconsider the case. The Florida Supreme Court, however, interpreted the direction to reconsider the case as encompassing the second *Brown* decision as well as the first and accordingly delayed the applicant's admission. Nearly a year after the second *Brown* decision, the Supreme Court ruled that in higher education "all deliberate speed" was inapplicable, that the admission of blacks to graduate schools was to be accomplished immediately.[20]

Another test of this principle that occurred shortly after *Brown* was the attempt of Autherine Lucy to gain admission to the University of Alabama. The local Alabama District Court, following the *Brown* decision, ordered her admission. But in this instance, occurring so soon after *Brown*, the changes in attitude just beginning to evolve had not developed sufficiently to provide the climate necessary to assure her attendance. Consequently, despite the Court's order, Autherine Lucy was thwarted in her attempt to enroll as a student. However, almost eight years later, in 1963, conditions had changed. Two other black students were admitted to this state university and by this time blacks had been admitted to other formerly all-white state universities, including the admission of James Meredith to the University of Mississippi in 1962.

The effects of the *Brown* decision were seen soon in other areas. Legal decisions began to emerge, establishing the principle of nondiscrimination in the use of all governmentally connected facilities. The extension of the rule of *Brown* to public transportation was an apparent and logical step. The separate but equal doctrine had been transposed to public schools from the public transportation case of *Plessy*. Its repudiation in *Brown* obviously signaled an end to discrimination in transportation, particularly since *Plessy*, in fashioning the separate but equal doctrine, relied upon decisions upholding school segregation. Even before *Brown*, inroads had been made on the *Plessy* doctrine with regard to segregated travel. In a 1946 case, the Supreme Court had outlawed segregation in interstate travel.[21] After *Brown*, two decisions of the Interstate Commerce Commission relied heavily on its doctrine in declaring carrier discrimination violative of the Interstate Commerce Act.[22]

Prior to *Brown*, the Court, following *Plessy*, had held that state laws requiring

segregation in intrastate travel were constitutional. But in a 1956 case which affirmed the decision of a Montgomery, Alabama, district court in the case growing out of the Montgomery bus boycott (which catapulted the late Martin Luther King, Jr., to national prominence) the Court held that segregation on intrastate buses was also forbidden by the Fourteenth Amendment.[23]

Another problem connected with the right to travel was that of the use of terminal facilities. The City of Birmingham, Alabama, in the late 1950's, attempted to maintain racial segregation at its railroad terminal facilities by distinguishing between interstate and intrastate passengers. Negroes who could not produce a ticket showing that they were passengers on an interstate journey were not permitted to use the waiting room available to all white passengers whether or not on an interstate journey. This practice too was stopped by a judicial decision relying heavily on the doctrine of *Brown*.[24] At about the same time, a young black Howard University law student was arrested in a Richmond, Virginia, bus terminal on a journey from Washington, D. C., to his home in Alabama because he insisted on service at the terminal's lunch counter. In a 1960 case (the first "sit-in" case in the Supreme Court), the Court held that passengers had a right to use any facilities that were an integral part of a carrier's operation.[25]

Notwithstanding this principle, most bus terminals throughout the South continued to segregate their facilities. Because of this, the Congress of Racial Equality (CORE), one of the direct action groups which began to emerge after the *Brown* decision, sponsored the "freedom rides" in the spring of 1961. The freedom rides, like the growth of the direct action movement in the late 1950's and early 1960's generally, demonstrated the interlocking nature of the development of legal rules and the direct action protests set in motion by the *Brown* principle. For what emerged from this series of demonstrations in 1961 was not only a judicial declaration of the right of people to use transportation terminal facilities on an integrated basis,[26] but also principles of judicial protection for the expression of protest designed to remove the vestiges of the racial caste system.[27]

Absorption of the newly enunciated rule of the *Brown* cases occurred even more quickly in the area of public recreation than in that of public transportation. Pending at the

[19] *Brown* v. *Board of Education*, 349 U.S. 294 (1955).

[20] *Florida ex rel. Hawkins* v. *Board of Control*, 350 U.S. 413 (1956). In *Watson* v. *City of Memphis*, 373 U.S. 526 (1936), the Supreme Court aborted a similar attempt to delay integration of public parks.

[21] *Morgan* v. *Virginia*, 328 U.S. 373.

[22] *NAACP* v. *St Louis-S.F. Ry. Co.*, 297 ICC 335 (1955); *Keys* v. *Carolina Coach Co.*, 64 MCC 769 (1955).

[23] *Browder* v. *Gayle*, 352 U.S. 903 (1956).

[24] *Baldwin* v. *Morgan*, 287 F.2d 750 (1961).

[25] Two cases decided by lower federal courts in 1960 outlawed discrimination at airport terminals. *Henry* v. *Greenville Airport Commission*, 284 F.2d 631 (4th Cir. 1960) (waiting rooms); *Coke* v. *City of Atlanta*, 184 F.Supp. 579 (N.D. Ga. 1960) (restaurants).

[26] *Lewis, et al.* v. *Greyhound Corporation*, 199 F.Supp. 210 (1961).

[27] *United States* v. *U. S. Klans, Knights of the Ku Klux Klan Inc.*, 194 F.Supp. 897 (1961).

time of the decision were three cases filed earlier in Baltimore seeking an end to racially segregated bathing facilities in that city and its environs which were to become the landmark cases in the field. After the decision was rendered, a federal district court in Baltimore rejected the argument that the rule of *Brown* should be extended to public recreation. However, this decision was overturned on appeal by a federal appeals court which held that racial segregation in recreational activities could not be sustained as a proper exercise of the state's police power.[28] This decision was later upheld by the Supreme Court.[29]

Numerous other cases in the years of the *Brown* decade established the right of Negroes to use a variety of public recreational and other facilities. In some instances, municipalities opted to close the facility in question rather than to permit use by Negroes, as did Montgomery, Alabama, in 1959. But whatever the response of the governmental unit involved, the clamor of black people for the right to use whatever facilities were open to other citizens became increasingly insistent and—as the number of lawsuits that were filed during this period attests—there was considerable resistance to overcome.

BEGINNING OF "THE MOVEMENT"

A major task still remained. *Brown* and the cases following it were decided on the ground that the Fourteenth Amendment proscribed discriminatory treatment that could fairly be said to be the action of the state. However, given the American economic system, the majority of facilities held out to

[28] *Dawson v. Mayor and City Council of Baltimore,* 220 F.2d 386 (4th Cir. 1955).
[29] *Baltimore City v. Dawson,* 350 U.S. 877 (1955).

public use are privately owned. The remedy for continuing racial exclusion from these facilities was a combination of direct protest action and legal action. This combined effort which came to be known as "the movement" marked the major legal battleground of the period from *Brown* into the early 1960's.

With the change in the climate of law created by *Brown,* the seeds for the direct action protest movement were planted. As long as *Plessy* remained the law, it was difficult for these kinds of protest to occur. But with *Brown* on the books, the protest movement grew in confidence; the law could now be used to vindicate the claim to racial equality. Thus it was no accident—because of the nexus between law and social attitudes—that prominent leaders such as King emerged on the American scene, and civil rights groups other than the NAACP and the Urban League began to proliferate. King founded the Southern Christian Leadership Conference, an association of black Southern ministers. He was instrumental in organizing the Student Nonviolent Coordinating Committee, which grew out of the Nashville student movement. As previously indicated, the Congress of Racial Equality (CORE) was revivified with its sponsoring of the freedom rides in 1961.

These groups soon began to occupy the direct action field. Because the state action concept was inapplicable to privately owned facilities open to the public, protests in the form of sit-ins, marches and other demonstrations were necessary to establish the right of black people to use all facilities open to the public generally, without racial discrimination. Because of the judicial decisions, increasing in number, which were slowly leveling the barriers to the open society, protest action became increasingly more effective.

The "movement" was able to mount successful assaults on the total segregation practices of many cities throughout the country.

But the protest movement created new legal problems. The ingenuity of lawyers in protecting the right to protest was tested. Lawyers, however, proved fit for the task. In a series of cases beginning in 1960, lawyers from the NAACP Legal Defense Fund were able to convince the Supreme Court that the arrests of persons taking part in sit-in demonstrations were illegal. And these cases prior to the passage of the 1964 Civil Rights Act served in part as the legal justification for that legislation, which guaranteed to blacks access to privately owned facilities open to the public. Legal decisions arising from such major battlegrounds of the civil rights movement of the early 1960's as Albany, Georgia, and Birmingham, Alabama, helped to establish the principles that have been used throughout this decade in protecting peaceful civil rights demonstrations and demonstrations of other sorts as well.

Unquestionably, the major outpouring of support for the cause of civil rights under law was the 1963 March on Washington, which occurred soon after the Birmingham demonstrations, and largely in response to them. The process of change initiated by *Brown* and continued through a series of judicial decisions building on that base (which had in turn stimulated protest activity) culminated in the major demonstration in the nation's capital in the summer of 1963. For the first time, many segments of white America joined the black protest movement. The March on Washington was the high water mark of a concept of black and white brotherhood which had been fostered by the development in law of the idea of racial equality.

WHITE ETHNIC

The anger of a man disinherited by the authorized American fantasy

Michael Novak

Michael Novak teaches "social ethics" at the State University of New York at Old Westbury. His most recently published book is The Experience of Nothingness. *This article is from his book about the rise of the ethnics, to be published next spring by Macmillan.*

GROWING UP IN AMERICA has been an assault upon my sense of worthiness. It has also

been a kind of liberation and delight.

There must be countless women in America who have known for years that something is peculiarly unfair, yet who have found it only recently possible, because of Women's Liberation, to give tongue to their pain. In recent months, I have experienced a similar inner thaw, a gradual relaxation, a willingness to think about feelings heretofore shepherded out of sight.

I am born of PIGS—those Poles, Italians,

Greeks, and Slavs, non-English-speaking immigrants, numbered so heavily among the workingmen of this nation. Not particularly liberal, nor radical, born into a history not white Anglo-Saxon and not Jewish—born outside what in America is considered the intellectual mainstream. And thus privy to neither power nor status nor intellectual voice.

Those Poles of Buffalo and Milwaukee—so notoriously taciturn, sullen, nearly speechless. Who has ever understood them? It is not that Poles do not feel emotion: what is their history if not dark passion, romanticism, betrayal, courage, blood? But where in America is there anywhere a language for voicing what a Christian Pole in this nation feels? He has no Polish culture left him, no Polish tongue. Yet Polish feelings do not go easily into the idiom of happy America, the America of the Anglo-Saxons and, yes, in the arts, the Jews. (The Jews have long been a culture of the word, accustomed to exile, skilled in scholarship and in reflection. The Christian Poles are largely of peasant origin, free men for hardly more than a hundred years.) Of what shall the man of Buffalo think, on his way to work in the mills, departing from his relatively dreary home and street? What roots does he have? What language of the heart is available to him?

The PIGS are not silent willingly. The silence burns like hidden coals in the chest.

All four of my grandparents, unknown to one another, arrived in America from the same county in Slovakia. My grandfather had a small farm in Pennsylvania; his wife died in a wagon accident. Meanwhile, a girl of fifteen arrived on Ellis Island, dizzy, a little ill from witnessing births and deaths and illnesses aboard the crowded ship, with a sign around her neck lettered "PASSAIC." There an aunt told her of the man who had lost his wife in Pennsylvania. She went. They were married. Inheriting his three children, each year for five years she had one of her own; she was among the lucky, only one died. When she was twenty-two, mother of seven, her husband died. And she resumed the work she had begun in Slovakia at the town home of a man known to us now only as "the Professor": she housecleaned and she laundered.

I heard this story only weeks ago. Strange that I had not asked insistently before. Odd that I should have such shallow knowledge of my roots. Amazing to me that I do not know what my family suffered, endured, learned, hoped these past six or seven generations. It is as if there were no project on which we all have been involved. As if history, in some way, began with my father and with me.

Let me hasten to add that the estrangement I have come to feel derives not only from a lack of family history. All my life, I have been made to feel a slight uneasiness when I must say my name. Under challenge in grammar school concerning my nationality, I had been instructed by my father to announce proudly: "American." When my family moved from the Slovak ghetto of Johnstown to the WASP suburb on the hill, my mother impressed upon us how well we must be dressed, and show good manners, and behave —people think of us as "different" and we mustn't give them any cause. "Whatever you do, marry a Slovak girl," was other advice to a similar end: "They cook. They clean. They take good care of you. For your own good."

When it was revealed to me that most movie stars and many other professionals had abandoned European names in order to feed American fantasies, I felt only a little sadness. One of my uncles, for business reasons and rather late in life, changed his name too, to a simple German variant. Not long, either, after World War II.

Nowhere in my schooling do I recall an attempt to put me in touch with my own history. The strategy was clearly to make an American of me. English literature, American literature; and even the history books, as I recall them, were peopled mainly by Anglo-Saxons from Boston (where most historians seemed to live). Not even my native Pennsylvania, let alone my Slovak forebears, counted for very many paragraphs. I don't remember feeling envy or regret: a feeling, perhaps, of unimportance, of remoteness, of not having heft enough to count.

The fact that I was born a Catholic also complicated life. What is a Catholic but what everybody else is in reaction against? Protestants reformed "the Whore of Babylon," others were "enlightened" from it, and Jews had reason to help Catholicism and the social structures it was rooted in to fall apart. My history books and the whole of education hummed in upon that point (during crucial years I attended a public, not a parochial, school): to be modern is decidedly not to be medieval; to be reasonable is not to be dogmatic; to be free is clearly not to live under ecclesiastical authority; to be scientific is not to attend ancient rituals, cherish irrational symbols, indulge in mythic practices. It is hard to grow up Catholic in America without becoming defensive, perhaps a little paranoid, feeling forced to divide the world between "us" and "them."

We had a special language all our own, our own pronunciation for words we shared in common with others (Augustine, contemplative), sights and sounds and smells in which few others participated (incense at Benediction of the Most

"Nowhere in my schooling do I recall an attempt to put me in touch with my own history. The strategy was clearly to make an American of me."

Blessed Sacrament, Forty Hours, wakes, and altar bells at the silent consecration of the Host); and we had our own politics and slant on world affairs. Since earliest childhood, I have known about a "power elite" that runs America: the boys from the Ivy League in the State Department, as opposed to the Catholic boys from Hoover's FBI who, as Daniel Moynihan once put it, keep watch on them. And on a whole host of issues, my people have been, though largely Democratic, conservative: on censorship, on Communism, on abortion, on religious schools ... Harvard and Yale long meant "them" to us.

The language of Spiro Agnew, the language of George Wallace, excepting its idiom, awakens

CHARLES GATEWOOD

childhood memories in me of men arguing in the barbershop, of my uncle drinking so much beer he threatened to lay his dick upon the porch rail and wash the whole damn street with steaming piss—while cursing the niggers in the mill, below, and the Yankees in the mill, above: millstones he felt pressing him. Other relatives were duly shocked, but everybody loved Uncle George: he said what he thought.

We did not feel this country belonged to us. We felt fierce pride in it, more loyalty than anyone could know. But we felt blocked at every turn. There were not many intellectuals among us, not even very many professional men. Laborers mostly. Small businessmen, agents for corporations perhaps. Content with a little, yes, modest in expectation. But somehow feeling cheated. For a thousand years the Slovaks survived Hungarian hegemony, and our strategy here remained the same: endurance and steady work. Slowly, one day, we would overcome.

A special word is required about a complicated symbol: sex. To this day my mother finds it hard to spell the word intact, preferring to write "s--." Not that much was made of sex in our environment. And that's the point: silence. Demonstrative affection, emotive dances, exuberance Anglo-Saxons seldom seem to share; but on the realities of sex, discretion. Reverence, perhaps; seriousness, surely. On intimacies, it is as though our tongues had been stolen. As though in peasant life for a thousand years the context had been otherwise. Passion, yes; romance, yes; family and children, certainly; but sex, rather a minor part of life.

Imagine, then, the conflict in the generation of my brothers, sister, and myself. (The book critic for the *New York Times* reviews on the same day two new novels of fantasy: one a pornographic fantasy to end all such fantasies [he writes], the other about a mad family representing in some comic way the redemption wrought by Jesus Christ. In language and verve, the books are rated even. In theme, the reviewer notes his embarrassment in reporting a religious fantasy, but no embarrassment at all about the preposterous pornography.) Suddenly, what for a thou-

sand years was minor becomes an all-absorbing investigation. It is, perhaps, one drama when the ruling classes (I mean subscribers to *The New Yorker*, I suppose) move progressively, generation by generation since Sigmund Freud, toward consciousness-raising sessions in Clit. Lib., but wholly another when we stumble suddenly upon mores staggering any expectation our grandparents ever cherished.

YET MORE SIGNIFICANT in the ethnic experience in America is the intellectual world one meets: the definition of values, ideas, and purposes emanating from universities, books, magazines, radio, and television. One hears one's own **voice echoed back neither by spokesmen of "Middle America" (so complacent, smug, nativist, and Protestant), nor by "the intellectuals."** Almost unavoidably, perhaps, education in America leads the student who entrusts his soul to it in a direction that, lacking a better word, we might call liberal: respect for individual conscience, a sense of social responsibility, trust in the free exchange of ideas and procedures of dissent, a certain confidence in the ability of men to "reason together" and to adjudicate their differences, a frank recognition of the vitality of the unconscious, a willingness to protect workers and the poor against the vast economic power of industrial corporations, and the like.

On the other hand, the liberal imagination has appeared to be astonishingly universalist, and relentlessly missionary. Perhaps the metaphor "enlightenment" offers a key. One is initiated into light. Liberal education tends to separate children from their parents, from their roots, from their history, in the cause of a universal and superior religion. One is taught, regarding the unenlightened (even if they be one's Uncles George and Peter, one's parents, one's brothers perhaps), what can only be called a modern equivalent of *odium theologicum*. Richard Hofstadter described anti-intellectualism in America, more acurately in nativist America than in ethnic America, but I have yet to encounter a comparable treatment of anti-unenlightenment among our educated classes.

In particular, I have regretted and keenly felt the absence of that sympathy for PIGS that simple human feeling might have prodded intelligence to muster: that same sympathy that the educated find so easy to conjure up for black culture, Chicano culture, Indian culture, and other cultures of the poor. In such cases, one finds, the universalist pretensions of liberal culture are suspended: some groups, at least, are entitled to be both different and respected. Why do the educated classes find it so difficult to want to understand the man who drives a beer truck, or the fellow with a helmet working on a site across the street with plumbers and electricians, while their sensitivities race easily to Mississippi or even Bedford-Stuyvesant?

There are deep secrets here, no doubt, unvoiced fantasies and scarcely admitted historical resentments. Few persons, in describing "Middle Americans," "the Silent Majority," or Scammon and Wattenberg's "typical American voter," distinguish clearly enough between the nativist American and the ethnic American. The first is likely to be Protestant, the second Catholic. Both may be, in various ways, conservative, loyalist, and unenlightened. Each has his own agonies, fears, betrayed expectations. Neither is ready, quite, to become an ally of the other. Neither has the same history behind him here. Neither has the same hopes. Neither is living out the same psychic voyage. Neither shares the same symbols or has the same sense of reality. The rhetoric and metaphors differ.

There is overlap, of course. But country music is not a polka; a successful politician in a Chicago ward needs a very different "common touch" from the one used by the county clerk in Normal; the urban experience of immigration lacks that mellifluous, optimistic, biblical vision of the good America that springs naturally to the lips of politicians from the Bible Belt. The nativist tends to believe with Richard Nixon that he "knows America and the American heart is good." The ethnic tends to believe that every American who preceded him has an angle, and that he, by God, will one day find one too. (Often, ethnics complain that by working hard, obeying the law, trusting their political leaders, and relying upon the American Dream they now have only their own naïveté to blame for rising no higher than they have.)

It goes without saying that the intellectuals do not love Middle America, and that for all the good warm discovery of America that preoccupied them during the 1950s, no strong tide of respect accumulated in their hearts for the Yahoos, Babbitts, Agnews, and Nixons of the land. Willie Morris, in *North Toward Home*, writes poignantly of the chill, parochial outreach of the liberal sensibility, its failure to engage the humanity of the modest, ordinary little man west of the Hudson. The intellectual's map of the United States is succinct: "Two coasts connected by United Airlines."

Unfortunately, it seems, the ethnics erred in attempting to Americanize themselves, before clearing the project with the educated classes. They learned to wave the flag and to send their sons to war. (The Poles in World War I were 4 per cent of the population but took 12 per cent of the casualties.) They learned to support their President—an easy task, after all, for those accustomed abroad to obeying authority. And where would they have been if Franklin Roosevelt had not sided with them against established interests? They knew a little about Communism, the radicals among them in one way, and by far the larger number of conservatives in another. Not a few exchange letters to this day with cousins and uncles who did not leave for America when they might have, whose lot is demonstrably harder and less than free.

Finally, the ethnics do not like, or trust, or even understand the intellectuals. It is not easy to feel uncomplicated affection for those who call you "pig," "fascist," "racist." One had not yet grown accustomed not to hearing "Hunkie," "Polack," "Spic," "Mick," "Dago," and the rest. At no little sacrifice, one had apologized for foods that smelled too strong for Anglo-Saxon noses, moderated the wide swings of Slavic and Italian emotion, learned decorum, given oneself to education American style, tried to learn tolerance and assimilation. Each generation criticized the earlier for its authoritarian and European and old-fashioned ways. "Up-to-date" was a moral lever. And now when the process nears completion, when a generation appears that speaks without accent and goes to college, still you are considered pigs, fascists, and racists.

Racists? Our ancestors owned no slaves. Most of us ceased being serfs only in the last 200 years —the Russians in 1861. What have we got against blacks or blacks against us? Competition, yes, for jobs and homes and communities; competition, even, for political power. Italians, Lithuanians, Slovaks, Poles are not, in principle, against "community control," or even against ghettos of our own. Whereas the Anglo-Saxon model appears to be a system of atomic individuals and high mobility, our model has tended to stress communities of our own, attachment to family and relatives, stability, and roots. We tend to have a fierce sense of attachment to our homes, having been homeowners less than three generations: a home is almost fulfillment enough for one man's life. We have most ambivalent feelings about suburban assimilation and mobility. The melting pot is a kind of homogenized soup, and its mores only partly appeal to us: to some, yes, and to others, no.

It must be said that we think we are better people than the blacks. Smarter, tougher, harder working, stronger in our families. But maybe many of us are not so sure. Maybe we are uneasy. Emotions here are delicate. One can understand the immensely more difficult circumstances under which the blacks have suffered, and one is not unaware of peculiar forms of fear, envy, and suspicion across color lines. How much of all this we learned in America, by being made conscious of our olive skin, brawny backs, accents, names, and cultural quirks, is not plain to us. Racism is not our invention; we did not bring it with us; we found it here. And should we pay the price for America's guilt? Must all the gains of the blacks, long overdue, be chiefly at our expense? Have we, once again, no defenders but ourselves?

TELEVISION ANNOUNCERS and college professors seem so often to us to be speaking in a code. When they say "white racism," it does not seem to be their own traditions they are impugning. Perhaps it is paranoia, but it seems that the affect accompanying such words is directed at steelworkers, auto workers, truck drivers, and police—at us. When they say "humanism" or "progress," it seems to us like moral pressure to abandon our own traditions, our faith, our associations, in order to reap higher rewards in the culture of the national corporations—that culture of quantity, homogeneity, replaceability, and mobility. They want to grind off all the angles, hold us to the lathes, shape us to be objective, meritocratic, orderly, and fully American.

In recent years, of course, a new cleavage has sprung open among the intellectuals. Some seem to speak for technocracy—for that alliance of science, industry, and humanism whose heaven is "progress." Others seem to be taking the view once ascribed to ecclesiastical conservatives and traditionalists: that commitment to enlightenment is narrow, ideological, and hostile to the best interests of mankind. In the past, the great alliance for progress sprang from the conviction that "knowledge is power." Both humanists and scientists could agree on that, and labored in their separate ways to make the institutions of knowledge dominant in society: break the shackles of the Church, extend suffrage to the middle classes and finally to all, win untrammeled liberty for the marketplace of ideas. Today it is no longer plain that the power brought by knowledge is humanistic. Thus the parting of the ways.

Science has ever carried with it the stories and symbols of a major religion. It is ruthlessly universalist. If its participants are not "saved," they are nonetheless "enlightened," which isn't bad. And every single action of the practicing scientist, no matter how humble, could once be understood as a contribution to the welfare of the human race; each smallest gesture was invested with meaning, given a place in a scheme, and weighted with redemptive power. Moreover, the scientist was in possession of "the truth," indeed of the very meaning of and validating procedures for the word. His role was therefore sacred.

Imagine, then, a young strapping Slovak entering an introductory course in the Sociology of Religion at the nearby state university or community college. Is he sent back to his Slovak roots, led to recover paths of experience latent in all his instincts and reflexes, given an image of the life of his grandfather that suddenly, in recognition, brings tears to his eyes? Is he brought to a deeper appreciation of his Lutheran or Catholic heritage and its resonances with other bodies of religious experience? On the contrary, he is secretly taught disdain for what his grandfather *thought* he was doing when he acted or felt or imagined through religious forms. In the boy's psyche, a new religion is implanted: power over others, enlightenment, an atomic (rather than a communitarian) sensibility, a contempt for mystery, ritual, transcendence, soul, absurdity,

> "The ethnic tends to believe that every American who preceded him has an angle, and that he, by God, will one day find one too."

and tragedy; and deep confidence in the possibilities of building a better world through scientific understanding. He is led to feel ashamed for the statistical portrait of Slovak immigrants which shows them to be conservative, authoritarian, not given to dissent, etc. His teachers instruct him with the purest of intentions, in a way that is value free.

To be sure, certain radical writers in America have begun to bewail "the laying on of culture" and to unmask the cultural religion implicit in the American way of science. Yet radicals, one learns, often have an agenda of their own. What fascinates *them* among working-class ethnics are the traces, now almost lost, of *radical* activities

GEORGE GARDNER

among the working class two or three generations ago. Scratch the resentful boredom of a classroom of working-class youths, we are told, and you will find hidden in their past some formerly imprisoned organizer for the CIO, some Sacco/Vanzetti, some bold pamphleteer for the IWW. All this is true. But supposing that a study of the ethnic past reveals that most ethnics have been, are, and wish to remain, culturally conservative? Suppose, for example, they wish to deepen their religious roots and defend their ethnic enclaves? Must a radical culture be "laid on" them?

America has never confronted squarely the problem of preserving diversity. I can remember hearing in my youth bitter arguments that parochial schools were "divisive." Now the public schools are attacked for their commitment to homogenization. Well, how *does* a nation of no one culture, no one language, no one race, no one history, no one ethnic stock continue to exist as one, while encouraging diversity? How can the rights of all, and particularly of the weak, be defended if power is decentralized and left to local interests? The weak have ever found strength in this country through local chapters of national organizations. But what happens when the national organizations themselves—the schools, the unions, the federal government—become vehicles of a new, universalistic, thoroughly rationalized, technological culture?

Still, it is not that larger question that concerns me here. I am content today to voice the difficulties in the way of saying what I wish to say, when I wish to say it. The tradition of liberalism is a tradition I have had to acquire, despite an innate skepticism about many of its structural metaphors (free marketplace, individual autonomy, reason naked and undisguised, enlightenment). Radicalism, with its bold and simple optimism about human potential and its anarchic tendencies, has been, despite its appeal to me as a vehicle for criticizing liberalism, freighted with emotions, sentiments, and convictions about men that I cannot bring myself to share.

In my guts, I do not feel that institutions are "repressive" in any meaning of the word that leaves it meaningful; the "state of nature" seems to me, emotionally, far less liberating, far more undifferentiated and confining. I have not dwelt for so long in the profession of the intellectual life that I find it easy to be critical and harsh. In almost everything I see or hear or read, I am struck first, rather undiscriminatingly, by all the things I like in it. Only with second effort can I bring myself to discern the flaws. My emotions and values seem to run in affirmative patterns.

My interest is not, in fact, in defining myself over against the American people and the American way of life. I do not expect as much of it as all that. What I should like to do is come to a better and more profound knowledge of who I am, whence my community came, and whither my son and daughter, and their children's children, might wish to head in the future: I want to have a history.

More and more, I think in family terms, less ambitiously, on a less than national scale. The differences implicit in being Slovak, and Catholic, and lower-middle class seem more and more important to me. Perhaps it is too much to try to speak to all peoples in this very various nation of ours. Yet it does not seem evident that by becoming more concrete, accepting one's finite and limited identity, one necessarily becomes parochial. Quite the opposite. It seems more likely that by each of us becoming more profoundly what we are, we shall find greater unity, in those depths in which unity irradiates diversity, than by attempting through the artifices of the American "melting pot" and the cultural religion of science to become what we are not.

There is, I take it, a form of liberalism not wedded to universal Reason, whose ambition is not to homogenize all peoples on this planet, and whose base lies rather in the imagination and in the diversity of human stories: a liberalism I should be happy to have others help me to find.

THE FEMINISTS: A SECOND LOOK

GERDA LERNER

■ *Gerda Lerner, who has a Ph.D. degree in History from Columbia University, teaches at Sarah Lawrence College and has for many years been active in women's organizations. She is the author of* The Grimké Sisters from South Carolina: Rebels Against Slavery *(Houghton Mifflin, 1967) and the soon to be published* The Woman in American History *(Addison-Wesley). Her current projects include a documentary history of black women in America, under a grant from the Social Science Research Council, and a re-evaluation of the role of women in United States history.*

I ask no favors for my sex. All I ask our brethren is that they will take their feet from off our necks and permit us to stand upright on the ground which God designed us to occupy.
　　　　　　　　　　　　　　—Sarah Grimké, 1838

Women are the best helpers of one another. Let them think; let them act; till they know what they need. . . . But if you ask me what offices they may fill, I reply— any. . . . Let them be sea-captains if you will.
　　　　　　　　　　　　　　—Margaret Fuller, 1845

Within the past three years a new feminism has appeared on the scene as a vigorous, controversial, and somewhat baffling phenomenon. Any attempt to synthesize this diffuse and dynamic movement is beset with difficulties, but I think it might be useful to view it in historical perspective and to attempt an evaluation of its ideology and tactics on the basis of the literature it has produced.

Feminist groups represent a wide spectrum of political views and organizational approaches, divided generally into two broad categories: the reform movement and the more radical Women's Liberation groups. The first is exemplified by NOW (National Organization of Women), an activist, civil rights organization, which uses traditional democratic methods for the winning of legal and economic rights, attacks mass media stereotypes, and features the slogan "equal rights in partnership with men." Reform feminists cooperate with the more radical groups in coalition activities, accept the radicals' rhetoric, and adopt some of their confrontation tactics; yet essentially they are an updated version of the old feminist movement, appealing to a similar constituency of professional women.

Small, proliferating, independent Women's Liberation groups, with their mostly youthful membership, make up a qualitatively different movement, which is significant far beyond its size. They support most of the reform feminist goals with vigor and at times unorthodox means, but they are essentially dedicated to radical changes in all institutions of society. They use guerrilla theater, publicity stunts, and confrontation tactics, as well as the standard political techniques. Within these groups there is a strong emphasis on the reeducation and psychological reorientation of the members and on fostering a supportive spirit of sisterhood.

What all new feminists have in common is a vehement impatience with the continuance of second-class citizenship and economic handicaps for women, a determination to bring our legal and value systems into line with current sexual mores, an awareness of the psychological damage to women of their subordinate position, and a conviction that changes must embrace not only laws and institutions, but also the minds, emotions, and sexual habits of men and women.

An important parallel exists between the new feminism and its nineteenth-century counterpart. Both movements resulted not from relative deprivation but from an advance in the actual condition of women. Both were "revolutions of rising expectations" by groups who felt themselves deprived of status and frustrated in their expectations. Education, even up to the unequal level permitted women in the 1830s, was a luxury for the advantaged few, who found upon graduation that except for school-teaching no professions were open to them. At the same time, their inferior status was made even more obvious when the franchise, from which they were excluded, was extended to propertyless males and recent immigrants.

The existence of the early feminist movement depended on a class of educated women with leisure. The women who met in 1848 at Seneca Falls, New York, did not speak for the two truly exploited and oppressed groups of women of their day: factory workers and black women. Mill girls and middle-class women were organizing large women's organizations during the same decade, but there was little contact between them. Their life experiences, their needs and interests, were totally different. The only thing they had in common was that they were equally disfranchised. This fact was of minor concern to working women, whose most urgent needs were economic. The long working day and the burdens of domestic work and motherhood in conditions of poverty gave them not enough leisure for organizing around anything but the most immediate economic issues. Except for a short period during the abolition movement, the interests of black women were ignored by the women's rights movement. Black women had to organize separately and, of necessity, they put their race interests before their interests as women.

Unlike European women's rights organizations, which were from their inception allied to strong socialist-oriented labor movements, the American feminist movement grew in isolation from the most downtrodden and needy groups of women. William O'Neill, in his insightful study, *The Woman Movement: Feminism in the United States and England* (Barnes & Noble, 1969), describes the way the absence of such an alliance decisively affected the composition, class orientation, and ideology of the American women's rights movement. Although there were brief, sporadic periods of cooperation between suffragists and working women, the feminists' concentration on the ballot as the cure-all for the ills of society inevitably influenced their tactics. Despite their occasional advocacy of unpopular radical causes, they never departed from a strictly mainstream, Christian, Victorian approach toward marriage and morality. By the turn of the century feminist leadership, like the male leadership of the Progressives, was nativist, racist, and generally indifferent to the needs of working women. (Aileen Kraditer demonstrates this well in *The Ideas of the Women Suffrage Movement: 1890-1920,* Columbia University Press, 1965.) Suffrage leaders relied on tactics of expediency. "Give us the vote to double your political power," was their appeal to reformers of every kind. They believed that once enacted, female suffrage would promote the separate class interests since women, as an oppressed group, would surely vote their common good. Opportunist arguments were used to persuade males and hostile females that the new voters would be respectable and generally inoffensive. A 1915 suffrage banner read:

For the safety of the nation to
Women give the vote
For the hand that rocks the cradle
Will never rock the boat

Not surprisingly, after suffrage was won, the women's rights movement became even more conservative. But the promised block-voting of female voters failed to materialize. Class, race, and ethnic, rather than sex, divisions proved to be more decisive in motivating voting behavior. As more lower-class women entered the labor market and participated in trade-union struggles with men, they benefited, though to a lesser extent, where men did. Middle-class women, who now had free access to education at all levels, failed to take significant advantage of it, succumbing to the pressure of societal values that had remained unaffected by the narrow suffrage struggle. Thus, at best, the political and legal gains of feminism amounted to tokenism. Economic advantages proved illusory as well, and consisted for most women in access to low-paid, low-status occupations. The winning of suffrage had failed to emancipate women.

If the new feminism did not appear on the scene in the 1930s or forties, this was because the war economy had created new job opportunities for women. But at the end of World War II, returning veterans quickly reclaimed their "rightful places" in the economy, displacing female workers, and millions of women voluntarily took up domesticity and war-deferred motherhood. The young women of the forties and fifties were living out the social phenomenon that Betty Friedan called the "feminine mystique" and Andrew Sinclair the "new Victorianism." Essentially it amounted to a cultural command to women, which they seemed to accept with enthusiasm, to return to their homes, have large families, lead the cultivated suburban life of status-seeking through domestic attainments, and find self-expression in a variety of avocations. This tendency was bolstered by Freudian psychology as adapted in America and vulgarized through the mass media.

It was left to the college-age daughters born of the World War II generation to furnish the womanpower for the new feminist revolution. Like their forerunners, the new feminists were, with few exceptions, white, middle class, and well educated. Raised in economic security—an experience quite different from that of their Depression-scarred mothers—they had acquired an attitude toward work that demanded more than security from a job. They reacted with dismay to the discovery that their expensive college educations led mostly to the boring, routine jobs reserved for women. They felt personally cheated by the unfulfilled promises of legal and economic equality.

Moreover, they were the first generation of women raised entirely in the era of the sexual revolution. Shifting moral standards (especially among urban professionals), increased personal mobility, and the availability of birth control methods, afforded these young women unprecedented sexual freedom. Yet this very freedom led to frustration and a sense of being exploited.

Many of these young women had participated, with high hopes and idealism, in the civil rights and student movements of the fifties and sixties. But they discovered that there, also, they were expected to do the dull jobs—typing, filing, housekeeping—while leadership remained a male prerogative. This discovery fueled much of the rage that has become so characteristic of the Women's Liberation stance, and turned many of these young women to active concern with their identity and place in society.

They continued in the nineteenth-century tradition by emphasizing equal rights and accepting the general concept of the oppression of women. The reformists have adopted, also, the earlier conviction that what is good for middle-class women is good for all women. Both branches, reform and radical, learned from the past the pitfalls of casting out the radicals in order to make the movement more respectable. Until now, they have valiantly striven for unity and flexibility. They have jointly campaigned for childcare centers, the equal rights amendment, and the abolition of abortion legislation. They have organized congresses to unite women and a women's strike, and they have shown their desire for unity by accepting homosexual groups into the movement on the basis of full equality. But the radicals in Women's Liberation have gone far beyond their Victorian predecessors.

Radical feminism combines the ideology of classical feminism with the class-oppression concept of Marxism, the rhetoric and tactics of the Black Power movement, and the organizational structure of the radical student movement. Its own contribution to this rich amalgam is to apply class-struggle concepts to sex and family relations, and this they have fashioned into a world view. On the assumption that the traditional reformist demands of the new feminist are eminently justified, long overdue, and possible of fulfillment, the following analysis will focus on the more controversial, innovative aspects of radical theory and practice.

The oppression of women is a central point of faith for all feminists. But the radicals do not use this term simply to describe second-class citizenship and discrimination against women, conditions that can be ameliorated by a variety of reforms. The essence of their concept is that all women are oppressed and have been throughout all history. A typical statement reads:

Women are an oppressed class. Our oppression is total, affecting every facet of our lives. . . . We identify the agents of our oppression as men. Male supremacy is the oldest, most basic form of domination. All other forms of oppression (racism, capitalism, imperialism, etc.) are extensions of male supremacy: men dominate women, a few men dominate the rest. . . . *All men* receive economic, sexual, and psychological benefits from male supremacy. *All men* have oppressed women. (Redstockings Manifesto, *Notes From the Second Year: Women's Liberation*)

Actually opinions as to the source of the oppression vary. Some blame capitalism and its institutions, and look to a socialist revolution for liberation, while others believe that all women are oppressed by all men. Where socialist governments have failed to alter decisively the status of women, the socialists say, it is because of the absence of strong indigenous Women's Liberation movements.

If what they mean by oppression is the suffering of discrimination, inferior rights, indignities, economic exploitation, then one must agree, undeniably, that all women are oppressed. But this does not mean that they are an oppressed class, since in fact they are dispersed among all classes of the population. And to state that "women have always been oppressed" is unhistorical and politically counterproductive, since it lends the authority of time and tradition to the practice of treating women as inferiors.

In fact, in the American experience, the low status and economic oppression of women developed during the first three decades of the nineteenth century and was a function of industrialization. It was only *after* economic and technological advances made housework an obsolete occupation, only *after* technological and medical advances made all work physically easier and childbearing no longer an inevitable yearly burden on women, that the emancipation of women could begin. The antiquated and obsolete value system under which American women are raised and live today can best be fought by recognizing that it is historically determined. It can therefore be ended by political and economic means.

The argument used by radical feminists that the essential oppression of women occurs in the home and consists in their services as housewives is equally vague and unhistorical. The economic importance of housework and the status accorded the housewife depend on complex social, demographic, and economic factors. The colonial housewife, who could be a property-holding freeholder in her own right and who had access to any occupation she wished to pursue since she lived in a labor-scarce, underdeveloped country with a shortage of women, had a correspondingly high status, considerable freedom, and the knowledge that she was performing essential work. A similar situation prevailed on the Western frontier well into the nineteenth century.

The movement's oversimplified concept of class oppression may hamper its ability to deal with the diverse interests of women of all classes and racial groups. No doubt all women are oppressed in some ways, but some are distinctly more oppressed than others. The slaveholder's wife suffered the "disabilities of her sex" in being denied legal rights and educational opportunities and in her husband's habitual infidelities, but she participated in the oppression of her slaves. To equate her oppression with that of the slave woman is to ignore the real plight of the slave. Similarly, to equate the oppression of the suburban housewife of today with that of the tenant farmer's wife is to ignore the more urgent problems of the latter.

New feminists frequently use the race analogy to explain the nature of the oppression of women. A collectively written pamphlet defines this position:

For most of us, our race and our sex are unequivocal, objective facts, immediately recognizable to new acquaintances. . . . Self-hatred in both groups derives not from anything intrinsically inferior about us, but from the treatment we are accustomed to. . . . Women and Blacks have been alienated from their own culture; they have no historical sense of themselves because study of their condition has been suppressed. . . . Both women and Blacks are expected to perform our economic function as service workers. Thus members of both groups have been taught to be passive and to please white male masters in order to get what we want. (*I am Furious—Female*, Radical Education Project, Detroit, n.d.)

This analogy between Blacks and women is valid and useful as long as it is confined to the psychological effect of inferior status, but not when it is extended to a general comparison between the two groups. Black women are discriminated against more severely than any other group in our society: as Blacks, as women, and frequently as low-paid workers. So far, radical feminists have failed to deal adequately with the complex issues concerning black women, and the movement has generally failed to attract them.

There is a segment of the radical feminist movement that sees all men as oppressors of all women and thinks of women as a caste. The minority group or caste analogy was first developed by Helen Hacker in her article, "Women as a Minority Group" (*Social Forces,* 1951), which has greatly influenced Women's Liberation thinking. Hacker posited that women, although numerically a majority, are in effect an oppressed caste in society and show the characteristics of such a caste: ascribed attributes, attitudes of accommodation to their inferior status, internalization of the social values that oppress them, etc.

This analogy has since been augmented by a number of psychological experiments and attitude studies, which seem to confirm that women, like men, are socially and culturally prepared from early childhood for the roles society expects them to play. Social control through indoctrination, rewards, punishments, and social pressure, leads to the internalization of cultural norms by the individual. Women are "brainwashed" to accept their inferior status in society as being in the natural order of things. It is, in fact, what they come to define as their femininity. There is increasing experimental evidence that it is their acceptance of this view of their femininity that causes women to fall behind in achievement during their high school years and to lack the necessary incentives for success in difficult professions. And this acceptance creates conflicts in the women who do succeed in business and the professions. Mass media, literature, academia, and especially Freudian psychology, all contribute to reinforce the stereotype of femininity and to convince women who feel dissatisfied with it that they are neurotic or deviant. It is a process in which women themselves learn to participate.

Radical feminists see this system as being constantly reinforced by all-pervasive male supremacist attitudes. They regard male supremacy, or sexism —a term the movement coined—as the main enemy. They claim that like racism, sexism pervades the consciousness of every man (and many women), and is firmly entrenched in the value system, institutions, and mores of our society. Attitudes toward this adversary vary. Some wish to change *institutionalized* sexism; others believe that all men are primarily sexist and have *personal* vested interests in remaining so; still others see a power struggle against men as inevitable and advocate man-hating as essential for the indoctrination of the revolutionists.

In viewing the oppression of women as caste or minority group oppression, one encounters certain conceptual difficulties. Woman have been at various times and places a majority of the population, yet they have shared in the treatment accorded minorities. Paradoxically, their status is highest when they are actually a minority, as they were in colonial New England. Caste comes closest to defining the position of women, but it fails to take into account their uniqueness, as the only members of a low-ranking group who live in more intimate association with the higher-ranking group than they do with their own. Women take their status and privilege from the males in their family. Their low status is not maintained or bolstered by the threat of force, as is that of other subordinate castes. These facts would seem to severely limit the propaganda appeal of those radical feminists who envision feminine liberation in terms of anti-male power struggles. The ultimate battle of the sexes, which such a view takes for granted, is surely as unattractive a prospect to most women as it is to men. This particular theoretical analysis entraps its advocates in a self-limiting, utopian counterculture, which may at best appeal to a small group of alienated women, but which can do little to alter the basic conditions of the majority of women.

The attack on sexism, however, is inseparable from the aims of Women's Liberation; in it means and ends are perfectly fused. It serves to uncover the myriad injuries casually inflicted on every woman in our culture, and in the process women change themselves, as they are attempting to change others. Male supremacy has had a devastating effect on the self-consciousness of women; it has imbued them with a deep sense of inferiority, which has stunted their development and achievements. In fighting sexism, women fight to gain self-respect.

In attempting to define the nature of the oppression of women, radical feminism reveals little advance over traditional feminist theories. All analogies—class, minority group, caste—approximate the position of women, but fail to define it adequately. Women are a category unto themselves; an adequate analysis of their position in society demands new conceptual tools. It is to be hoped that feminist intellectuals will be able to develop a more adequate theoretical foundation for the new movement. Otherwise there is a danger that the weaknesses and limitations of the earlier feminist movement might be repeated.

Largely under the influence of the Black Power movement, Women's Liberation groups have developed new approaches to the organizing of women that include sex-segregated meetings and consciousness-raising groups. Various forms of separatist tactics are used: all-female meetings in which men are ignored; female caucuses that challenge male domination of organizations; outright anti-male power struggles in which males are eventually excluded from formerly mixed organizations; deliberate casting of men in roles contrary to stereotype, such as having men staff childcare centers while women attend meetings, and refusing to perform the expected female services of cooking, serving food, typing.

These tactics are designed to force men to face their sexist attitudes. More important still is their effect on women: an increase in group solidarity, a lessening of self-depreciation, a feeling of potential strength. In weekly "rap" sessions members engage in consciousness-raising discussions. Great care is taken to allow each woman to participate equally and to see that there are no leaders. Shyness, reticence, and the inability to speak out, soon vanish in such a supportive atmosphere. Members freely share their experiences and thoughts with one another, learn to reveal themselves, and develop feelings of trust and love for women. The discovery that what they considered personal problems are in fact social phenomena has a liberating effect. From a growing awareness of how their inferior status has affected them, they explore the meaning of their femininity and, gradually, develop a new definition of womanliness, one they can accept with pride. Women in these groups try to deal with their sense of being weak, and of being manipulated and programmed by others. Being an emancipated woman means being independent, self-confident, strong; no longer mainly a sex object, valued for one's appearance.

The effect of the group is to free the energies of its members and channel them into action. This may largely account for the dynamic of the movement. A significant development is that the group has become a *community*, a substitute family. It provides a noncompetitive, supportive environment of like-minded sisters. Many see in it a model for the good society of the future, which would conceivably include enlightened men. It is interesting that feminists have unwittingly revitalized the mode of cooperation by which American women have traditionally lightened their burdens and improved their lives, from quilting bees to literary societies and cooperative childcare centers.

From this consciousness-raising work have come demands for changes in the content of school and college curricula. Psychology, sociology, history have been developed and taught, it is claimed, from a viewpoint that takes male supremacy for granted. Like Blacks, women grow up without models from the past with whom they can identify. New feminists are demanding a reorientation in the social sciences and history; they are clamoring for a variety of courses and innovations, including departments of feminist studies. They are asking scholars to reexamine their fields of knowledge and find out to what extent women and their viewpoints are included, to sharpen their methods and guard against built-in male supremacist assumptions, and to avoid making generalizations about men and women when in fact they are generalizing about men only. Feminists are confident that once this is done serious scholarly work regarding women will be forthcoming. Although one may expect considerable resistance from educators and administrators, these demands will undoubtedly effect reforms that should ultimately enrich our knowledge. In time, these reforms could be more decisive

than legal reforms in affecting societal values. They are a necessary precondition to making the full emancipation of women a reality.

Radical feminists have added new goals to traditional feminist demands: an end to the patriarchal family, new sexual standards, a reevaluation of male and female sex roles. Their novel views regarding sex and the family are a direct outgrowth of the life experiences and life styles of the younger, or "pill," generation, the first generation of young women to have control over their reproductive functions, independent of and without the need for cooperation from the male. This has led them to examine with detachment the sexual roles women play. One statement reads:

The role accorded to women in the sexual act is inseparable from the values taught to people about how to treat one another. . . . Woman is the object; man is the subject. . . . Men see sex as conquest; women as surrender. Such a value system in the most personal and potentially meaningful act of communication between men and women cannot but result in the inability of both the one who conquers and the one who surrenders to have genuine love and understanding between them.

The question of sexual liberation for both men and women is fundamental to both the liberation of women and to the development of human relationships between people, since the capacity for meaningful sexual experience is both an indication and an actualization of the capacity for love which this society stifles so successfully. (*Sisters, Brothers, Lovers. . . . Listen,* Judy Bernstein, *et al,* New England Free Press)

Female frigidity is challenged as a male-invented myth by at least one feminist author, Anne Koedt, in her article "The Myth of the Vaginal Orgasm" (*Notes From the Second Year: Women's Liberation*). She explains that the woman's role in the sexual act has been defined by men in such a way as to offer *men* the maximum gratification. She exposes the way in which women fake sexual pleasure in order to bolster the male ego. It is a theme frequently confirmed in consciousness-raising groups.

Radical feminists speak openly about sex and their "hang-ups" in regard to it. This in itself has a liberating effect. Although they take sexual freedom for granted, they challenge it as illusory and expose the strong elements of exploitation and power struggle inherent in most sexual relationships. They are demanding instead a new morality based on mutual respect and mutual satisfaction. This may seem utopian to some men, threatening to others—it is certainly new as raw material for a revolutionary movement.

In America, femininity is a commodity in the marketplace. Women's bodies and smiling faces are used to sell anything from deodorants to automobiles. In rejecting this, radical feminists are insisting on self-determination in every aspect of their lives. The concept that a woman has the right to use her own body without interference and legislative intervention by one man, groups of men, or the state, has already proved its dynamic potential in the campaign to abolish abortion legislation.

But it is in their rejection of the traditional American family that radical women are challenging our institutions most profoundly. They consider the patriarchal family, even in its fairly democratic American form, oppressive of women because it institutionalizes their economic dependence on men in exchange for sexual and housekeeping services. They challenge the concept that children are best raised in small, nuclear families that demand the full- or part-time services of the mother as housekeeper, cook, and drudge. They point to the kibbutzim of Israel, the institutional childcare facilities of socialist countries, and the extended families of other cultures as alternatives. Some are experimenting with heterosexual communal living; communes of women and children only, "extended families" made up of like-minded couples and their children, and various other innovations. They face with equanimity the prospect of many women deliberately choosing to live without marriage or motherhood. The population explosion, they say, may soon make these choices socially desirable. Some feminists practice voluntary celibacy or homosexuality; many insist that homosexuality should be available to men and women as a realistic choice.

Not all radical feminists are ready to go that far in their sexual revolution. There are those who have strong binding ties to one man, and many are exploring, together with newly formed male discussion groups, the possibilities of a new androgynous way of life. But all challenge the definitions of masculinity and feminity in American culture. Nobody knows, they say, what men and women would be like or what their relations might be in a society that allowed free rein to human potential regardless of sex. The new feminists are convinced that the needed societal changes will benefit men as well as women. Men will be free from the economic and psychic burdens of maintaining dependent and psychologically crippled women. No longer will they be constantly obliged to test and prove their masculinity. Inevitably, relations between the sexes will be richer and more fulfilling for both.

What is the long-range significance of the new feminist movement? Judging from the support the feminists have been able to mobilize for their various campaigns, it is quite likely that significant changes in American society will result from their efforts. In line with the traditional role of American radical movements, their agitation may result in the enactment of a wide range of legal and economic reforms, such as equal rights and job opportunities, vastly expanded childcare facilities, and equal representation in institutions and governing bodies. These reforms will, by their very nature, be of greatest benefit to middle- and upper-class women and will bring women into "the establishment" on a more nearly egalitarian basis.

The revolutionary potential of the movement lies in its attacks on the sexual values and mores of our society and in its impact on the psychology of those women who come within its influence. Changes in sexual expectations and role definitions and an end to "sexual politics," the use of sex as a weapon in a hidden power struggle, could indeed make a decisive difference in interpersonal relations, the functioning of the family, and the values of our society. Most important, the new feminists may be offering us a vision for the future: a truly androgynous society, in which sexual attributes will confer neither power nor stigma upon the individual—one in which both sexes will be free to develop and contribute to their full potential.

The official portrait of President Johnson is taken by photographer Arnold Newman in the White House, December, 1963.

The Vantage Point

Perspectives of the Presidency 1963-1969.
By Lyndon Baines Johnson.
Illustrated. 636 pp.
New York: Holt, Rinehart and Winston. $15.

DAVID HALBERSTAM

David Halberstam is a former New York Times and Harper's Magazine reporter who is now completing a book, "The Best and the Brightest," how and why we went to war in Vietnam, to be published next spring. He is currently a fellow of the Adlai Stevenson Institute in Chicago.

The literature on him has always been surprisingly thin, considering the scope, force and range of his life, its sheer excitement and unpredictability. He is after all, a figure worthy of a very great book; nothing about him was simple, nothing about him was boring. Yet the Kennedy literature is thick, and his is thin; magazines soon learned that Kennedy covers, any Kennedy would do, sold extra copies. Johnson covers hurt sales. Rowland Evans, co-author of "Lyndon Johnson and the Exercise of Power," is reputed to

have said, after sales proved disappointing, that he and Robert Novak should have called their book "Between Two Kennedys."

Yet he was a politician and a force the like of which I doubt we shall see again in this country, a man whose life began with earthy frontier attitudes and yet took us to the very edge of the moon. The texture of his life is far more interesting than that of either Kennedy, both of whom were comets who flashed before us, filled with light and promise, quickly extinguished. Johnson was real; his highs were higher and his lows were lower than any major figure in recent time, and as a study in political psychopathology, he is probably without peer.

There are only two books of excellence on him so far. One is the Evans-Novak book, a fine political study that explains with considerable insight the seeming contradictions of Lyndon Johnson, changing as his constituency changed and as his ambitions expanded, going from the straight hill-country New Dealer to

the more conservative Senator who provided Texas with more than its share of defense contracts. And finally in the late fifties, as he thought of national office, changing from Southerner to Westerner. The other book is Bill Brammer's "The Gay Place," a novel and an American classic in which a Johnsonian figure named Arthur "Goddam" Fenstemaker strides through the pages, large, earthy, intelligent, threatening, working it seemed, more often on the side of the angels than against them.

Now he comes to us in his own writ, his autobiography of those years in the Presidency, "The Vantage Point," having signed a contract that any author would envy. It should be said of Johnson the book writer that Johnson the politician was never much of a book reader; he was action-oriented, a memo reader and a newspaper reader because papers and memos could be of immediate help. He was not a reflective man and he believed that there was not much you could learn from books; that which existed and happened in real life, and that which books claimed had happened were quite different. Real stories were to be told mostly in the back room of Sam Rayburn's office, where the boys talked over what had in fact happened, and good writers were men who, being privy to these stories, did not print them.

Thus the real story of the Johnsonian Presidency is not to be found in this book. It is his story as he would have it, his view of how he would like things to be. It is straightforward enough from that viewpoint, and the writing is good, simple expository prose. But where Lyndon Johnson was filled with human juices, this book is almost totally devoid of them. It is all tidied up, antiseptic, ordered, very calm; there are no villains, no personal opinions on people, no judgments, there is no anger, precious little intimacy. It fails as a book in the same way that he failed in part as a politician.

As a politician, he was a man of almost primal force, driven, restless, brilliant, shrewd, ruthless, insecure, clever, a great mimic, a knowing and yet surprisingly subtle man. He knew the weaknesses and strengths of everyone around him, how much pressure to apply, how much flattery to use, how to extract the last ounce of human energy from those around him. In private meetings he was a man of stunning capability, knowing when to overpower, when to wait and when to listen. But all of this was in private; to those outside, he was quite different. We saw him as he should be seen. Haunted as he was—and still is—by a sense of regional pre-

judice, he did not think we would accept him or tolerate him as he really was. The result was an imitation Lyndon Johnson, the force and the power and the earthiness replaced by fake humility and an aggressive piety. The people around him pleaded with Johnson to be himself, but he did not think he could. He misread our capacity to appreciate him as a man, which was our loss and his too. If that were a problem with him as a politician, it is similarly a problem with his book. It is Lyndon Johnson deciding what he should look like (above the

fray, the statesman, the man who did the best he could with what God gave him) and excising all his real feelings and judgments from the book.

Thus it is very carefully sanitized. All of the real Johnson is missing. The Johnson who could say of the literati protesting his White House Festival of the Arts in 1965 that "half of those people are trying to insult me by staying away and half of them are trying to insult me by coming." The Johnson who, resigning himself to the difficulty of firing J. Edgar Hoover, could say, "Well, it's probably better to have him inside the tent pissing out, than outside pissing in." The Johnson who on meeting Henry Kissinger with President Nixon during the transition period repeatedly kept calling him "Dr. Schlesinger." The Johnson who referred to Senator Fulbright as "the stud duck of the opposition." The Johnson promising a great friendship to Russell Baker, about to cover him for the first time for The Times, "For you I'll leak like a sieve." Oh to have his real book, his real judgments (has McNamara ever been the same since Johnson described him as the one with the Stacomb on his hair?), to sit back and hear how he felt about the men around him, about the Congress, about the war, the press, de Gaulle, Robert Kennedy (of the latter, he writes, "During the four and a half years of my Presidency I had never been able to establish a close relationship with Bobby Kennedy . . .").

None of that is here; this is the official version, and he almost succeeds in making the Presidency, his Presidency in the mid-Sixties, sound boring. And about the only touch of humanity comes in a memo written by LadyBird in 1964 on the question of whether or not he should seek re-election. She writes of the op-

tions:

"You will have various ranch lands, small banking interests and presumably the TV to use up your talents and your hours.

"They are chicken feed compared to what you are used to.

"That may be relaxing for a while. I think it is not enough for you at 56. And I dread seeing you semi-idle, frustrated, looking back at what you left, I dread seeing you look at Mr. X running the country and thinking you could have done it better.

"You may look around for a scapegoat. I do not want to be it.

."You may drink too much — for lack of a higher calling."

History, Whittaker Chambers once wrote William Buckley, hit us with a freight train. I cannot vouch for Chambers, but it surely hit Lyndon Johnson with one. It tore him apart; he was caught in an enormous change in both world forces and in American domestic attitudes. Poorly advised and served by a group of inherited national security managers he made the fatal decision to go to war in Vietnam with combat troops. He was aware of the dangers he was risking when he made that decision, he was in fact far from eager and euphoric about it. But he did, and it cost him his Presidency. Vietnam is the key to his Presidency and it is also the focus of this book.

In this Vietnam theme there are two characteristics of Johnson the politician that are reflected in Johnson the author. The first is that the consensus politician has turned out a consensus book. The second is the Johnson so eager to control everything around him (ready to cancel an appointment, if word of it leaked out), who in this book wants to show that he was always in control of every decision.

First the consensus. Everyone is signed on board: Ike, Dulles, John Kennedy, Robert Kennedy, Everett Dirksen, George Ball; every pro-intervention treatment of all those years is reflected. A steady stream of important officials march through the pages just long enough to assure him that they are with you, Mister President. Not surprisingly a good deal of this is quite selective — Fulbright's affirmative remark to a questioning John Sherman Cooper during the Tonkin debate that Yes, the resolution could potentially be used as a legal justification for war; Fulbright's statement to a querying Gaylord Nelson who wanted an amendment specifically limiting the Administration in sending combat troops to Vietnam, Fulbright saying that this was not necessary because the Administration had assured him that it shared Nelson's intent, is not included. The list of those signing on is quite thorough, but what is missing is the systematic filtering out of doubters from 1964 on. The result is a consensus book like a consensus Presidency.

The problem with the Administration's consensus on Vietnam was that it was always a false one, concealing far greater disagreement than it actually symbolized. For example, on the 1964 bombing decision, there was a surface consensus, but beneath it was a vast and truly irreconcilable disagreement. There were the civilians who thought the bombing would work; and there were the civilians who thought it probably wouldn't work, but would allow the Administration to say that it had tried everything possible. There were the generals who wanted a bombing campaign as a real and total weapon in the classic sense, and there were the generals like Westmoreland who never thought the bombing would

work but were willing to go along because the civilians said it would bring political benefits in Vietnam, and because they saw it as a brief interim measure on the way to combat troops. So if the decision making was far more complicated than one might expect, that does not surface in this book.

In the same manner all doubts and opposition within the Administration are quickly glossed over. Thus in a particularly ungenerous moment Johnson refers to George Ball as a devil's advocate. A devil's advocate is someone who presents arguments he does not personally believe in. Ball and the small group of State Department people who worked with him believed in what they were doing. Ball's case may have been a charade as far as Johnson was concerned (the evidence even here is contrary; whenever Ball presented Johnson a memo the President was able to quote it by heart, page and paragraph, the next day), but it was not a charade as far as Ball was concerned.

In his eagerness to demonstrate his control of the total situation, he goes to great lengths to show that the Tet offensive did not come by surprise, that it had long been expected. He insists that there was not a great struggle within the bureaucracy over the decision to halt the bombing in March, 1968, and that he was not forced out of the Presidential race in 1968 by a combination of the Tet offensive and domestic political repercussions. It seems in this book that if he has any regret about the war, it is his failure to warn the nation that he knew that Tet was coming. But he makes no mention of the fact that in immediately preceding months he had brought both Westmoreland and Bunker home to stiffen the morale of an increasingly dubious nation. In effect the

White House had systematically created an aura of optimism about Vietnam which Tet shattered. As for his decision whether to run or not, I would agree with what the two Democrats who ran against him probably concluded, that the combination of New Hampshire, Tet, and very poor polls from Wisconsin showed him that his consensus was all coming apart.

It is the story of the February-March 1968 events which is probably the most interesting part of the book. Certainly Johnson is still obsessed by that period; it is by far the longest and most detailed section of the book, as if he feels compelled to prove that he controlled his own destiny and his own decisions. He still resents any suggestions that Clark Clifford and a group of civilians under him played any particular role in changing and limiting the bombing policy. (Johnson, at the time, particularly detested a book by Undersecretary of the Air Force, Townsend Hoopes, "The Limits of Intervention," which made the case for the Clifford group, and he would tell people, "Hoopees. Who is this Hoopees? I took four million people out of poverty and all they ask me about is this Hoopees.") Not surprisingly those who have kept their mouths shut about their doubts, such as McNamara, are treated well in his account, and those who have gone public or semi-public, such as Clifford, have had their roles denigrated.

The formal initiative for a partial bombing is credited to Rusk, not Clifford, which technically may well be true. He claims that he himself made the decision not to send the 206,000 men requested by Westmoreland, even before The New York Times printed a story saying there was a struggle taking place over a new troop increment (which again could be true; he might have decided on this, and let the bureaucracy keep fighting over the issue). Perhaps. But we have been through this kind of thing with him before and what he does not say about that period is more important. He gives no real sense of what Clifford and his people were trying to do, which was to clamp a lid on the war, and then turn the policy around. Clifford and his aides were arguing that the ongoing policy did not work, that this country was coming apart and that we had to start limiting rather than escalating our commitment.

A truly violent bureaucratic fight raged in those months, and Clifford was the leader of the dissidents; he was sometimes, as one White House friend said, "alone in the trenches." From time to time in those months he was even cut off from important cable traffic by the White House. Rusk, whatever his memo on the bombing limit, was not an ally of Clifford, and Rusk's main deputy on the war, Bill Bundy, was regarded by the Clifford group as a major opponent in that period (they felt at times that Bundy shared some of their doubts, but that he was under orders from Rusk). To a certain degree Clifford succeeded and the war was capped; but he and Harriman did not succeed in getting to Paris without giving Thieu-Ky a veto power over our policy. But it was a beginning. There is no sense of that very real battle in this book, but rather a reinforced sense of what was projected at the time: that Johnson listened to Clifford, but eventually resented having listened to him.

The central fascination of a Johnson memoir cannot be its literary grace but rather what he says about a number of crucial points already clouded by considerable doubt, his notor-

ious "credibility gap." Did he or did he not promise in 1964 that he would not send American boys to do a job which Asian boys should be doing? What about the covert operations immediately prior to the Tonkin Gulf incident? What about the way he sliced the combat-troop commitments? Did he, as James Reston suggested, escalate by stealth? And what about the financing of the war, was the lack of a tax bill his fault or that of the Congress? The book will not satisfy old doubters.

(The book was written before the Pentagon Papers appeared, and the editor Aaron Asher assures reviewers that there were no changes made after the papers surfaced. This in itself is intriguing, since a number of crucial McNamara and Bundy memos which are in the Pentagon Papers and which were obviously classified, are declassified for this book. Since Daniel Ellsberg has been attacked by high officials for declassifying of documents, this again raises the question of who may and who may not declassify documents, and under what conditions? William Bundy, who is writing a book on the same period, has used a copy of the papers made available by his good friend Bob McNamara, long before Ellsberg surfaced with the copies. Were McNamara and Bundy violating national security by doing this after they left office?)

On his 1964 campaign promise-implication that he would not send American boys to fight a war which Asian boys should be fighting, Johnson now writes:

"On several occasions I insisted that American boys should not do the fighting that Asian boys should do for themselves. I was answering those who proposed or implied that we should take charge of the war, or carry out actions that

would risk a war with Communist China. I did not mean that we were not going to do any fighting, for we had already lost many good men in Vietnam. I made it clear that those who were ready to fight for their own freedom would find us at their side if they wanted and needed us. We were not going to rush in and take over, but we were going to live up to the commitment we had made.

"Any thinking American knew there were already many thousands of Americans in Asia, not just in Vietnam, but in Korea, Japan, Okinawa, Taiwan, the Phillipines, and Thailand. They were there for a purpose: to defend what four American Presidents and the Congress of the United States had said were vital American and world interests . . . The American people knew what they were voting for in 1964. They knew Lyndon Johnson was not going to pull up stakes and run. They knew I was not going to go back on my country's word. They knew I would not repudiate the pledges of my predecessors in the Presidency."

You can make of this what you wish, but three previous Presidents had also very carefully avoided sending combat troops to Vietnam.

On the provocative role of the 34-A harassment patrols in the Tonkin area immediately before the attack upon the two American destroyers (the North Vietnamese PT boat intercepts clearly showed that the other side linked the 34-A operations with the Maddox mission), Johnson says in the book that McNamara briefed the Senate Foreign Relations committee on these operations at the time. It is a charge which did at the time and still does bring a reaction of anger and bitterness from members of the committee. About the kindest that can be said for that McNamara testimony is that it is a study in the disingenuous; if the extent of our participation in the provocation right before the Tonkin incident had been known at the time, the entire Senate debate, which was based upon the thesis of Hanoi attacking us, instead of Hanoi responding to very specific provocations, might have been very different.

On the way in which we slipped into sending combat troops, and just how candid the White House was, the fact is (and it is never admitted in this book) that he and McNamara were always deliberately vague about the figures, as vague as they could possibly be, with the press, with the Congress, and with members of their own Government. Both Johnson and McNamara deliberately kept projected (and agreed-upon figures) as secret as long as they could in order not to give the impression of a big war, which might have panicked the public and lost the Congress for domestic reform.

Thus, late in July, 1965, when the Administration finally crossed the Rubicon and made its first major combat troop commitment, the decision was to add 100,000 troops to an existing base of 75,000 Americans (largely support and advisory troops). But it was announced to the American people as a decision to go from 75,000 to 125,000. Though the President did say in the announcement that additional forces would be needed later, and would be sent, there was an element of conscious deception here that would typify troop decisions throughout the war. In his book Johnson simply glides by it ("Our military commanders had refined

their estimates and indicated they could meet the immediate demand with 50,000 men . . ."). The best story of that particular day was written by Hanson Baldwin, The Times military writer, a man with particularly good connections to the J.C.S., who reported that the top military were surprised, indeed shocked, by the announced decision, the chopping in half of the agreed-on figure and the decision not to call up the reserves. It was to be the first sign of a bastardized war, half in, half out, the American domestic implications of Westmoreland's strategy never thought through.

On the financing of the war itself, Johnson criticizes Congress for not wanting in 1965 to move on a tax bill, which is in part true. What Johnson does not tell is the fact that he and McNamara deliberately hid from Congressional leaders — and worse, from their own economic advisers — the proposed troop levels and thus prevented a reasonably accurate projected cost of the war. The Congressional leaders, in turn, made a judgment against the tax increase based on highly fallacious information and estimates. (The Administration for instance encouraged in late 1965 its own economic advisers to project a very limited cost for the war, and to put down claims by Senator John Stennis that the war would be big and expensive. Stennis, with his excellent connections with the military, was accurate, while the Council of Economic Advisers, depending on the private statements of McNamara, were totally wrong.)

There was of course a reason for this: Johnson did not think he could get both the war and the Great Society in 1965.

He felt that if the Congress knew what the real cost of the war would be it would keep the war, and reject his Great Society. So he manipulated the Congress for the good of the people. The kindest thing that can be said about what McNamara told the Congress and the economic advisers in this period is that it was dissembling bordering on raging dishonesty. Out of this came the complete miscalculation of the budget and the virulent Johnson-McNamara inflation which is still with us. His treatment of the financing of the war will not convert many critics.

Nor in fact will the book. Credibility gap still lives. The lesson is that if you cannot control events as a politician, you cannot control them any better in your memoirs. This kind of book can only rekindle old controversies (one envisions students of the game taking the Johnson account of the February - March 1968 events and comparing them, hour by hour with the Clifford-Warnke-Hoopes accounts). Nor will the book bring any particular insight into either the author or the years during which he presided. He is, I think, somehow a more sympathetic figure than he appears in his own book: he was caught in a major switch of history, indeed his very escalation of the war accelerated domestic change. He was not particularly wise in that one fateful decision, but neither were the men around him. Indeed, one of his close associates who was there during the great days of 1965 says that of the five or six principals Johnson was the most reluctant about the escalation because he knew he had the most to lose. And he lost it. ∎

The politics of the sixties—

From the New Frontier To the New Revolution

EMMET JOHN HUGHES

EMMET JOHN HUGHES, whose books include "The Ordeal of Power," teaches at the Eagleton Institute of Politics at Rutgers University. He was an administrative assistant to President Eisenhower.

"Probe the earth and see where your main roots run."
—HENRY DAVID THOREAU

"Above all, what this Congress can be remembered for is opening the way to a New American Revolution."
—PRESIDENT RICHARD NIXON, 1971 STATE OF THE UNION ADDRESS

"If I get around to writing a general history of the recent past, I'm going to call the chapter on the sixties 'The Age of Rubbish.'"
—PROF. RICHARD HOFSTADTER

OR the whole political season—from the New Frontier through the Great Society and on to the New Revolution—could be called The Age of Outrageous Paradox. The more elaborate insult probably would be more welcome to most makers and movers of the politics of the nineteen-sixties. They relished the taste of ornate verbiage. They sadly lacked any nose for the smell of cant.

By whatever name, it was, as decades go, a muddle. The political life of a democratic society, in any age and on any continent, always seems rife with anomalies, of course. But I doubt that there have been many chapters in the story of the American Republic when the incongruous has appeared so stark, the irrational so irresistible and the clearly improbable so eventually certain.

This was the time, after all, that simultaneously witnessed two great flights by Americans: to the beckoning stars and from their crumbling cities. This was the period, too, when the nation's chosen leaders, Democratic and Republican alike, concurred that the future of American civilization depended far more urgently on the erasing of Communism in Southeast Asia than the erasing of poverty in the United States; and they wagered more than $20-billion a year—year after year—on the soundness of this judgment. Across the nation, the most stirring change of the age, the advance of black Americans toward dignity and opportunity, progressed slowly under the least likely political auspices: it was dramatically encouraged by the first Southern President since the Age of Reconstruction while "the party of Lincoln" fretted, evaded and dawdled. All the while, some 25 million needy Americans, a half on welfare rolls and a half on poverty-level incomes, stayed stoically calm as the children of the relatively more affluent, on campuses from Boston to Berkeley, violently protested *their* suffering and deprivation. Finally the peace-lovers, almost 200 million strong, divided into two armies distinguishable not by confidence in their own virtues but only by their choice of weapons: the older seekers of "peace with honor" principally relied on incantations, helicopters and a little napalm; the younger zealots of "peace and love" usually favored obscenities, bricks and a little vandalism.

The general parody of rationality found faithful recording in most of the decade's speeches, resolutions and debates. On the whole, the parody was conducted in a bipartisan spirit, as Republicans and Democrats competed to wrap old policies in new packages and to paste different slogans on the same ideas. Such was the nature of much of the national debate over Vietnam. From 1962, the Republicans collectively set the stage for travesty, of course, by abdicating any serious opposition role as they shunned the expression of any doubts, much less critiques, about the unfolding American venture in Southeast Asia. By 1964, the Tonkin Gulf Resolution, supporting further undefined military action, proved that the Senate, almost unanimously, could behave with the same mindless acquiescence as the G.O.P. By 1966, the public leaders most outraged by the consequences of that authorization included many of the same Democrats who had voted it; but by the autumn of the same year, a President no longer concerned with their counsel was himself in Vietnam, exhorting his soldiers: "Come home with that coonskin on the wall!" By 1968, in the snows of New Hampshire, the footprints of the President soon to be leaving the White House crossed the path of the candidate soon to be arriving there (or so it would later seem). President-to-be Richard Nixon avowed on nationwide radio: "It is essential that we end this war, and end it quickly, but... in such a way that we win the peace." An attentive ear would have caught the fact that the Johnsonian and Nixonian exhortations varied only in verbal style—the first command in the jargon of a Western evangelist, the second in the fuzzier idiom of an Eastern lawyer. But each was appealing to a military court for just one verdict. Both men wanted the coonskin.

The most contagious anomaly of these years, however, was the addiction of the decade to self-conscious self-esteem. While the drug habits of the younger generation alarmed much of the country, little note was taken of the uninhibited indulgence by elder statesmen in two deadly hallucinogens of politics: the fancied image of historic greatness and the revered sound of one's own voice. Thanks to such stimulants, almost all national matters appeared swollen to sizes never less than vast. A kind of innocent but indicative keynote might first have been heard in the ringing Inaugural Address by John F. Kennedy in 1960; it saluted no mere New Administration, but a whole New Generation. In like spirit, the nation's legislators and leaders in the succeeding years almost never faced anything so puny as a problem; it had to be a crisis. To despairing critics, the society was not just gravely distraught and deeply divided; it was plainly doomed.

IF an era can be thought to act like a man, the age neatly performed the old jest about human vanity — it mastered the art of strutting while sitting down. To bring off the trick, it was necessary only to appraise all items on the national agenda as not just impressively big but also profoundly *new*. Thus, for the nation's prosperity there were the New Economics; for its security there was the New Foreign Policy cannily directing the New Diplomacy, and for the general entertainment and excitement of the electorate there were the New Politics. Eventually, the escalation of rhetoric had to reach a kind of climax. This came with the call to the American people to mobilize for a New American Revolution. And who could issue the command so logically —so aptly for an age of such anomaly — as the era's most resolute antirevolutionary and the nation's 37th President, Richard Milhous Nixon?

No man could have closed out all the public speech of the last decade, all its pallid pieties and vivid hyperboles, with so fitting a peroration as the President's State of the Union address to the 92d Congress. Its timing was almost flawless; it missed by just two days the 10th anniversary of the Kennedy inaugural. It stayed faithful to the semantic fash-

ion of the nineteen-sixties, too, sprinkling the adjective "new" as if it were an indispensable mark of punctuation. And showing the sense of both history and humor so typical of both the Administration and the age, the President's chief political counselor, Attorney General John Mitchell, judged the Chief Executive's pronouncement to be "the most important document since they wrote the Constitution"—an opinion whose implied disparagement of that continuingly nettlesome Emancipation Proclamation might have been largely inadvertent.

Yet no appreciation of the President's address surpassed his own. Aloft once again on "the lift of a driving dream," he announced— —vaguely but vigorously—the end of "a long, dark night of the American spirit." He went on to set forth some substantive matters for legislative action, and the two most important were the sharing of Federal tax revenues with the beleaguered states and cities and the redrawing of the administrative frontiers of the Cabinet departments. Nonetheless, the worth and relevance of even these ideas were made only more difficult to assess by the awesome seriousness with which the President professed to view them. Again and again calling upon the Founding Fathers to anoint his proposals, he stated that their enactment called for no less than the same "vision" and "boldness" as the James Madisons and the James Wilsons had shown in their constitutional labors of 184 years ago. A general assent to all this by the members of the 92d Congress—so the President promised them — would do more than assure their perpetual remembrance for "a record more splendid than any in our history"; it would enlist them in "a revolution as profound, as far-reaching, as exciting" as the Old American Revolu-

tion. And to many a wide-eyed Senator and Representative, there appeared to be little left out of such a prospective melodrama other than a vignette of Secretary of Defense Melvin Laird kneeling in the snows of Valley Forge, a glimpse of Senator J. William Fulbright cowering in the uniform of Benedict Arnold or a vision of National Security Adviser Henry Kissinger, sashed and sworded, waving his tricorn as he sped off to take the surrender of North Vietnam's armies at some Asian Yorktown.

THE important incongruities of this study of the State of the Union, however, were more than shows of verbal extravagance. They were matters of basic substance. And two were most striking.

First, for all its ardent professing of the new, it pathetically echoed the old. Read as prologue, it could only be remembered as epilogue. For his economic prescriptions, Richard Nixon reached back to the essentially heretical practices of Franklin Roosevelt to discover anew the uses of deficit financing, now rendered orthodox by the euphemism of "a full employment budget"— the spending of Federal funds "as if we were at full employment." For his political definitions, the President described the humanity and the efficiency of local government in language that sounded as though it had been carefully culled from the most forgettable speeches of President Herbert Hoover. For his social solutions, he stayed more modern, going back only five or so years to the early days of the Presidency of Lyndon Johnson and finding there a public discussion of Federal revenue - sharing that now struck him as "historic." The steady flow of such Federal dollars to state and city would long since have started, of course, if Lyndon Johnson and Richard Nixon had not assigned a truly "historic" priority to Washington's revenue-sharing with Saigon.

Second, for lighting the path out of the "dark night" of the nineteen-sixties and into the seventies, the President held up the torch of one central doctrine. This was the faith that "local government" has been and must be "closest" and "most responsive" to the people. Such government cannot fail, he said, to be "far more intimate" with the citizenry than any "bureaucratic élite in Washington." In short, the time had come for "power" to be shipped out from the national capital and "turned back to the people."

The implications of such a homily from such a pulpit had to stun a little. No American President, probably not even Herbert Hoover, had ever stated with such seeming personal conviction that the Federal establishment over which he presided—from an office whose painful pursuit had cost this President some 20 years of fund-raising dinners and soul-searing disappointments — afforded, after all, only the least responsive and sensitive government in all the land. The notion was enough to make some citizens wonder why a politician so

patriotic and so neighborly had not spent all his energies striving to become a councilman or a mayor. And it was enough to prod others to consider whether a leadership so self-effacing had intended to call for a New American Revolution or a New American Spiral.

THE decade deplored by a Richard Hofstadter was not, of course, designed by a Richard Nixon. The President was not its masterful architect but its typical product. And the incongruities of his political life carried back to 1960, when he did something quite alien to his critics' image of him. Privately, he then yielded the office for which he had publicly fought and would fight again.

The 1960 Presidential campaign had seen John Kennedy and Richard Nixon duel each other almost to a draw. So narrow a decision—by some 118,000 votes — set political experts of all persuasions to frantic search for the tiny clue to victory. Some thought they found it in the face-to-face debates of the two candidates; the younger man had simply won by the phraser's edge. Others argued a kind of political predestination; it sufficed to look at Richard Nixon's heavy jowls or snore over his heavy platitudes to know, just absolutely know, that this man was a born loser and a natural non-President. And there were those closest to the defeated candidate who were quite certain of a less mystical explanation: that they had been cheated by the voting machines of Cook County, Ill.,

and the voting blocs of marble from the graveyards of a few counties in Texas. For these last observers, the political moment did not call for automatic congratulating of the winner; it called for absolutely raising hell.

There followed a remarkable scene. In a motel not far from Los Angeles, Richard Nixon met with a small group of his closest confidants to consider whether he should charge that he had been cheated of the Presidency. There were none present who doubted this to be the fact. He listened to all, and he overruled them. To one, he explained: "A national argument like this would make American democracy ludicrous to the whole world." To another, he added: "If this were to become a public dispute, it could conceivably carry us all toward the brink of a kind of civil war." A challenge to the election could, indeed, have embittered the nation, and the blame for the stress might have fallen on anyone. But in an era whose ironies were almost altogether melancholy, there appeared something worthy of respect and remembrance in the decision of Richard Nixon to ignore his political counselors and defer his political dreams.

Between the renunciation of 1960 and the return of 1968, there surged—or careened—across the national political scene no less than three quite distinct hosts or movements. All of them inevitably proclaimed their essential newness, of course, even as each struck out in a wholly different direction. And each deserves a quick backward glance.

THE first was the New Frontier of John F. Kennedy. Because its life — his life — would be so sickeningly short, this must remain the hardest to judge of all the larger political thrusts of the sixties. For whatever reason, an impression lingers that its style was considerably grander than its substance. Even this, however, may have been the product less of artifice than of analysis — the quite cool appraisal of J.F.K. himself. On the night of his inauguration, I happened to be in the Georgetown home of his close friend Joseph Alsop when the President startled some dozen guests by suddenly appearing for a quiet, postmidnight chat. After idle banter turned toward serious politics, he spoke one conviction categorically: "The country is going to the right, of course. We are on a conservative pendulum, no doubt." (I recall vigorously dissenting.) Shrewdly or mistakenly, the fact is that the hero of the nation's liberals, at the very moment that he assumed power, assumed not much at all about the future of American liberalism. Perhaps from this lack of faith there followed the apparent lack of zeal, over many, many months on the part of the President and his brother, the Attorney General, in pressing action to assure the civil rights of black Americans. This lack seemed so clear that one member of the civil rights commission, Father Theodore Hesburgh, the president of Notre Dame University, came close to resigning to summon public attention to what he viewed as the New Frontier's unconcern over any new frontier for

more than 20 million Americans. Some years later, there ensued one more of the happier ironies of the decade, when Robert Kennedy, well before his murder, made himself a trusted hero to the same 20 million.

The second passionately "new" political movement followed, in 1964, the leadership of another United States Senator of nearly comparable personal appeal and wholly contrary political purpose. Senator Barry Goldwater of Arizona nostalgically cherished a far older kind of "frontier": an America of mid-19th-century outposts manned by sheriffs and marshals who knew how to impose mid-20th-century law and order on Europe's foreign-aid rustlers or Asia's war-of-liberation highwaymen, so that the road of history could be kept clear for the stagecoach of American democracy speeding into the future. For millions, however, the promise of the vision was not at all old but wondrously new. Since the Senate days of Robert A. Taft, they had been waiting for a Presidential election affording them "a choice, not an echo." They got their wish. And their party barely survived their spell of joy.

And the third host of political pioneers marched in 1968 under the banner of the New Politics and behind yet another Senator, Eugene McCarthy of Minnesota. Of the three "insurrections" in the politics of the sixties, there seems little doubt that this one ignited the most intense zeal and unselfish devotion. There also seems little doubt that this movement—true to an age so anomalous—finally showed itself to be the most

self-centered and the most self-defeating. Even as it aroused the nation's conscientious dissenters and radicals, especially among the young, the New Politics of Eugene McCarthy had rather little to say ardently and persuasively about civil rights or cities' dying. Even as it pressed just one issue — the tragedy of Vietnam — with more single-minded intensity than any other national movement in a modern election, it stayed remarkably cryptic about precisely what it proposed to do to end the tragedy. Soon after it had run its course, it left a host of its disciples wondering what the din had truly meant. Perhaps they would have wondered somewhat earlier, had they known of one revealing episode midway in the 1968 primary campaigns. On this occasion, the Senator from Minnesota met in New York with an important group of editors. They asked for his choice for President, after himself, among all other candidates. He unhesitatingly answered: "Richard Nixon." One can only guess the incredulous look on the faces of his most devoted followers had they been privileged to hear such candor.

THROUGH all the decade of politics dominated by these three different sorts of insurgency, there spread a practice for which I find only one reasonably descriptive term: the politics of masturbation. These political exercises were conducted in a spirit that essentially did not care whether they created or communicated or convinced in any fruitful sense; they simply wanted to be heard or felt. Ultimately, they did not much desire to give birth; they aspired only to give pleasure. And this pleasure - seeking, too, could claim a largely bipartisan popularity.

Perhaps the American right indulged more obviously, on levels from the national to the municipal. The ascendancy of Barry Goldwater in 1964 provided an instance difficult to match in self-serving political foolishness: a national party deliberately chose a "Southern strategy" to unseat the first President in more than three generations who could himself be called "Southern." At the 1964 Republican convention in San Francisco, the ruling emotions could probably have been called less political than sensual: the revulsion toward Gov. Nelson Rockefeller, the flagellation of the news media and the adulation of a "faithful" Republican in the person of the Senator from Arizona. The prevailing passions of most delegates, moreover, had been heated by their avid reading of such political pornography as "A Choice Not an Echo" or "None Dare Call It Treason." As one despairing liberal Republican Senator grieved to me: "These people don't give a damn about ballots — they want blood." So they proceeded to design their own disaster.

As with the Western hero of American conservatism, so it would be with its Eastern oracle, William F. Buckley. A year after Goldwater's humiliation, Buckley entered the lesser but exciting arena of New York City politics. Unambitious personally for City Hall, he was nonetheless confident that his epigrams and epithets could keep so offensively liberal a Republican

Conrad in The Los Angeles Times.

"I would hope that the court
would look at the time factors involved. . . ."

as John Lindsay from becoming Mayor. The pundit enjoyed the exercise enough to write a whole book about it later. And there occurred in all this but one flaw: his intervention subtracted enough Catholic votes from normally Democratic ranks to seal victory for the Republican he had sought to rout.

Still, the American left performed almost as confoundingly. In New York four years later, a campaign by Norman Mailer in the Democratic primary discovered the same delight in self-defeat earlier enjoyed by William Buckley. Mailer's siphoning off of liberal votes from two leading

liberal contenders made possible the nomination of Mario Proccacino, the demoralization of New York liberals and the re-election of John Lindsay, who had to begin to marvel at his luck in always being challenged, rather than supported, by the community's more aggressively political intellectuals.

On a larger scene and for a longer span, the political measure of much student violence of these last years has to be taken in terms of the same contempt for consequence. Fist or oath or bomb, the resources of the movement have appeared again and again to serve less as weapons than as drugs—the paraphernalia for a "trip," as it were, but in political terms a journey to nowhere. This was the express warning of the radical priest Father Daniel Berrigan, when he wrote the Weatherman band three days before his own arrest last August: "The movement ...shows how constantly we are seduced by violence, not only as method but as an end in itself." And from all this self - thwarting confusion of angry young citizens there followed, perhaps inexorably, the inner illogic that eventually came to control the McCarthy campaign of 1968. The campaign could not have been more loudly committed to a New Politics militant enough to smash precedents and shake establishments. In immediate terms, it did shake the confidence of President Johnson. But in more fateful terms—by its nationwide sullenness toward the Democratic candidacy of Hubert Humphrey, by its encouragement of liberal apathy in such key states as California—it no less surely helped to bring about the final arrival at the White House of Richard Nixon.

SINCE the 1968 campaign closed the circle on the Presidential politics of the decade, it might be expected to afford its own study in irony. It did, indeed. Most briefly stated, the incongruity of the election may be seen in three dimensions: political, psychological and personal.

In political terms, the result for Richard Nixon could be called a victory only with some serious abuse of the word. More accurately, it amounted to an almost incredibly narrow avoiding of

an almost unbelievable defeat. Perhaps no myth of partisan politics was so religiously recited throughout the sixties as the fable of the sagacity of Mr. Nixon, the awesomely canny politician. He endured three grinding campaigns in this decade, and his progress in all three, from start to end, was consistently backward. He began his 1960 campaign with a substantial 6 per cent lead in the opinion polls over John Kennedy—and he lost it. He began his 1962 campaign for the Governorship of California with a 16 per cent lead —and he lost it. He began his 1968 campaign with the same lead of 16 per cent recorded in August — and he barely missed losing it. This kind of accomplishment in reverse can be properly appreciated only in the context of the historically extraordinary erosion in Democratic strength that had taken place after the equally extraordinary Democratic triumph of 1964, when Lyndon Johnson had won 61.3 per cent of the vote. A study of the voting swings since 1892 shows that the percentage change between 1964 and 1968 was exceeded only twice, by the swings from Wilson to Harding and from Hoover to Roosevelt. The collapse of Democratic power in 1968, in other words, had no precedent since the collapse of Republican strength in 1932; in both cases, the abrupt decline in support for the incumbent Administration exceeded 18 per cent. Yet in all such swings since 1892, there was no gain so small for the winning party as the mere 4.9 per cent recorded by the G.O.P. in 1968. As one scholar has said of the Nixon victory: "Only a political upheaval of

near-cataclysmic proportions could have created the conditions in which his election was possible at all."*

In psychological terms, the "conditions" contriving this result suggest a special irony. By the judgment of almost all veteran watchers of political omens, the fate of the Johnson Administration was decreed by one political fault: its loss of credibility as a decisive number of citizens came to feel that it was a government of double-talking and double-dealing. A citizenry so alienated had to rebel. But the curiosity of future historians surely will be stirred to wonder how the disenchanted then turned for leadership to one man whose whole political life had been shadowed (fairly or falsely) by one indictment above all: his lack of credibility.

In personal terms, a kind of mystery about the man persisted through this victory of the candidate. It was perhaps most crisply, if unintentionally, stated by Kevin P. Phillips, the author of "The Emerging Republican Majority," who served in 1968 as a special assistant to the campaign manager, Attorney-General-to-be John Mitchell. To cite Mr. Phillips's later appraisal of the campaign: "It was a catastrophe — millions of dollars spent by Madison Avenue lightweights who converted certain victory into near defeat. The soap salesmen drained all of the issues out of the campaign that would have won it big . . .

*Walter Dean Burnham, "Election 1968, The Abortive Landslide," in Trans-Action, December, 1968.

Nixon knew his campaign stunk. He wanted to be himself, and he knew he should have fought the campaign on the issues Middle America was ready for..." Such an opinion from so friendly a source raises more questions than it answers, of course. Why did not the man on his way to the White House act on what he "knew"? Could "soap salesmen" also be blamed for the defeats of 1960 and 1962? And if the President-in-the-making was not his own self, whose was he?

FROM an election decided by such anomalies, there could follow only an Administration of seemingly interminable ambivalence. This it has been. A Republican President—who probably has repeated more often than any living politician the hoary aphorism that the Government must balance its budget so that all American families can balance their budgets — has needed only two years in office to proclaim his new Keynesian faith in unbalanced budgets. A President with a mind trained in law and sensitive to the political role of the Supreme Court, Richard Nixon has managed to have his first two nominees to the Court spurned by the Senate. A President so impressed with the quality and importance of his new Cabinet that he introduced all his nominees to the people on national television, he has excelled almost any predecessor in the White House in treating the Cabinet as a kind of hopelessly vestigial organ of government. Addressing himself to the trials and problems of black Americans, he could issue in March,

1970, a command of some 10,000 words for school desegregation in the South; but nine months later he could avow on nationwide television that he would, in effect, do only what the law compelled to encourage desegregation of housing. Taking the occasion of his inauguration in 1969 to appeal to the people for a general lowering of voices, he made his own intervention in the 1970 campaign the most tasteless display in recent memory of Presidential intolerance and stridence.

To explain this disconcerting public performance, there have been varying, if not satisfying, theories over the years. Probably this President, through 20 years of American politics, has had no apologist so loyal and persuasive as Secretary of State William Rogers. And during the Eisenhower Presidency, I recall his explaining: "The trouble with Dick—and I keep telling him this—is not just that he sees both sides to every question, like a good lawyer. The trouble is that he appears in public—without meaning to—confessing that he does." It would be hard to make a more compassionate or subtle excuse for irresolution.

A more complex apologia was spoken in December, 1970, by Daniel Patrick Moynihan in his tribute to the President on leaving the White House to return to university life. He hailed the "profoundly important" leadership of Richard Nixon, while regretting that the President's "initial thrusts were rarely followed up with a sustained...second and third order of advocacy." Consequently, he said, "the impression was allowed to arise," with regard to White

66 Washington is a factory town, and the thickest gases causing the densest pollution generally belch from the tallest official chimneys. 99

House proposals like the Family Assistance Plan, that "the President really wasn't behind them." The accolade—or exoneration—carried an odd echo: Mr. Moynihan on the Nixon Presidency sounded precisely like Mr. Phillips on the Nixon campaign. The most obvious question to follow was: Who "allowed" the "impression" of Presidential uninterest to "arise"? The more important question was: Did the candidate of 1968 who could not be himself now preside over an Administration in 1971 that could not know itself?

A SEARCH for any answer has to return to the official definition of his Presidency that Richard Nixon gave in the form of his State of the Union address in January. And here it may suffice to take a quick look at one of the message's central propositions, the reliance on local government.

The President's avowed faith in government removed as far as possible from Washington, and hence made "closest" to the people, both decreed and exalted Mr. Nixon's plan for Federal revenue-sharing. While the technical merits of the fiscal formula invited legitimate debate, the political fallacies of the inspiring doctrine, as stated, are flagrant enough to

SAME OLD WAR—*The "New Revolution" includes a familiar cast: Melvin Laird, above, "kneeling in the snows of Valley Forge"; J. William Fulbright, left, "cowering in the uniform of Benedict Arnold," and Henry Kissinger, off to an Asian Yorktown.*

need but brief noting. There were three most pertinent: (1) The often clumsy centralization of powers and programs on the Federal level—far from proving the superior quality of local governments—has followed from a long history of the abdication or incompetence of government at lower-than-national levels. (2) By any comparison of national and local governments, it is the national authority that receives the more intense critical public scrutiny, while the Federal Government has also been for generations incomparably more dedicated to concern for individual freedoms and civil rights. (3) In all the American Federal structure, there are no regimes to match local governments in venality and corruption, nor political authorities with boundaries more archaic and absurd than the frontiers of most states. None of these facts, of course, is the least novel or obscure. The one remarkable fact is that few politicians in the nation are more wholly aware of them than President Nixon.

As for the President's proposal of nothing less than "a complete reform of the Federal Government itself," he here pointed to a path incredibly simple: "I propose that we reduce the present twelve Cabinet departments to eight." To be sure, a "complete reform" of the Federal establishment "to match our structure to our purposes," as Mr. Nixon urged, could refresh the whole nation's faith in its leadership. This kind of reform would have to deal with a number of grievous problems, perhaps most urgently with these: the reasonable restraint of Presidential caprice in foreign policy and military commitment, the freeing of the legislative branch from the shackles of seniority and filibuster and the restoration of the Cabinet to a level of effective responsibility.

The singular distinction of the President's call for reform was that it was "complete" in only one sense: it avoided totally the mention of any one of these issues So doing, the oration called to mind the rhetoric of Warren Harding: "not heroism but healing, not nostrums but normalcy..." And at that early date, the lasting meaning of such speech and thought was definitively described by William Gibbs McAdoo as "an army of pompous phrases moving over the landscape in search of an idea."

The Army that has moved longest and most painfully over the political landscape of the sixties has not been made of words, of course, but of men. Their terrain has been Indochina. Their search, equally unavailing, has been for a purpose whose attainment could possibly justify their presence and repay their sacrifice. And their grim pursuit has been proof that over nearly a decade the national leadership could learn, amend, repent, enlighten and progress as absurdly little in foreign policy as in national policy.

The political knack of the time—for confusing paralysis with progress—may be nowhere more obvious than here. In 1961, a serious sort of precedent was set by the naming of a special Presidential adviser to reside, with ample staff and authority, in the White House as the Chief Executive's immediate and personal counselor on foreign

policy. He was a man of talent, intelligence and persuasiveness. He came from a distinguished academic background — Harvard University. Sincerely and strongly, he believed that his own confidence and skill could impose a new kind of order on the often haphazard ways of American diplomacy. On the immediate Washington scene, he impressed diplomats and journalists alike with his articulate renderings of current events; there was almost nothing done or said by the Administration for which he could not offer either an intriguing explanation or a beguiling excuse. As for the global scene, he felt no timidity about the deployment of American power in any arena where it might bring the enhancement of American prestige. As for the specific arena of Southeast Asia, he believed firmly in the necessity for American intervention, the vulnerability of Communist forces and the reality of a democratic future. In 1961, the name of this Presidential assistant to John Kennedy was, of course, McGeorge Bundy. In 1971, this Presidential assistant, now serving Richard Nixon, had become Henry Kissinger. Aside from this change of name, all had stayed constant: the same teacher from the same campus was in the same office applying the same doctrine, dedicating it to the same ends and defending it with the same arguments.

A study of the intellectual and political odyssey of Henry Kissinger through the sixties may make the general incongruity more vivid. During the whole decade, as well as in earlier years, Dr.

Kissinger's principal employer in politics was Governor Rockefeller, who has always summed up his foreign policy views toward Communism generally and Vietnam particularly with a candor rare for the times: "I'm simply a hardliner." It was Dr. Kissinger who consistently inspired and frequently authored the Governor's public speeches in this vein—including those pronouncements during the 1964 Republican primaries arguing flatly that there could be no substitute for victory over the Vietcong. During the same years, however, the professor from Harvard quite often joined the White House councils of President Kennedy. Under the Johnson Administration, he did even more, undertaking official missions both to Vietnam and Europe and reporting all intelligence gleaned to Washington's policy-makers. It was in these years, too, that he somehow persuaded such Democratic critics of official policy as Averell Harriman that, in the forme New York Governor's words, "Henry was as much a dove as I."

With the approach of the 1968 campaign, the threads of Dr. Kissinger's beliefs and associations ramified considerably as the political scene became more tangled. On his return to Cambridge from his official missions abroad, he sought out those academic colleagues known for their closeness to Senator Robert Kennedy, generously briefing them for the Senator's benefit; as one of them has later recalled, "he gave at least the clear impression of believing Bobby the best qualified candidate for the Presidency." Meanwhile, he continued regularly to counsel Nelson Rockefeller not only on world affairs but also on national politics, urging his candidacy with special insistence on the grounds that the New York Governor quite possibly was "the only leader who could, in the final analysis, keep a lightweight like Bobby Kennedy out of the White House." When the Governor's campaign was carried to the Republican convention in Miami, Dr. Kissinger, vigorously representing Rockefeller's foreign policy views before the appropriate platform committee, voiced only scorn for those put forth in the name of Richard Nixon. Indeed, he had long since distinguished himself among all Rockefeller advisers as the one most pithy and scathing in his personal contempt for the Republican nominee. In one nicely concise and relatively temperate comment on Mr. Nixon's nomination, he observed: "The man is, of course, a disaster. Now the Republican Party is a disaster. Fortunately, he can't be elected—or the whole country would be a disaster area." And the question may fairly be asked: could so idiosyncratic an itinerary through the politics of the sixties come to any logical end except in the White House as the chief architect of Richard Nixon's world strategy?

As with Washington strategists in war and peace, so, too, with a great many of the capital's pundits and prophets; the accompanying rhythms of their commentaries have tended to change as imperceptibly as policies have changed. The case of the Alsop brothers, the veteran columnists Joseph and Stewart, may suffice to illustrate. In the Camelot of the Kennedys at the start of the sixties, no clairvoyant in the realm enjoyed greater favor with the President and Mr. Bundy than Joseph Alsop; in the Middletown of Richard Nixon, the same official favor has touched both brothers, who respond with equal appreciation of the policies of the President and Dr. Kissinger. Along the way, the journalistic accents and fortunes of the two brothers have varied slightly, of course. By the middle of the Johnson Presidency, the armies of North Vietnam had so inconsiderately refused to panic before Joseph Alsop's repeated threats of imminent American triumph—and even the American armies had so often disobeyed his military theories —that threats and theories alike became something of a journalistic jest. By the middle of the Nixon Presidency, however, the slack was taken up by the rather newly militant writings of Stewart Alsop. Few if any Washington correspondents have been led by Dr. Kissinger more frequently or more gladly into that room in the West Wing of the White House on whose door those less favored have fancied seeing the stern sign: KEEP OUT — ADMISSION ONLY TO THE ABSOLUTELY ANONYMOUS AUTHORITATIVE SOURCE AND HIS STUDENTS.

From that room few men emerge unaffected. The recent commentaries on Indochina by Mr. Alsop so attest. These have included apologies for Administration policy in terms of analogies often almost breathtakingly inappropriate. One of these recently challenged the "selectivity" of Democratic critics who deplored "the horrors of war" in Vietnam as "obscene" while failing to find anything "obscene" in the air force of Israel, which had "used their American planes" to inflict thousands of Egyptian casualties before the cease-fire in the Middle East. If a theoretical analogy itself can be called "obscene," this last would qualify. Precisely by its decrying "selectivity," of course, it argued that the "horrors" of war may not be variously judged in terms of the purposes of a people or the policies of a nation; a corpse is a corpse is a corpse; and all causes for which men suffer death, therefore, must really be pretty much the same, obscene or clean.

There follows from this a fairly critical point about the intellectual life of Washington. If the author of these improbable analogies were an innocent in journalism or a lackey of Government, the gist of them would never be worth noting. Instead, of course, he is an experienced and respected commentator as well as a perceptive and compassionate man. So the hidden commentary in such writings must apply to the atmospheric hazards of uninterrupted life in this political factory town whose one industry is Government. As in almost all such towns, the thickest gases causing the densest pollution generally belch out from the tallest official chimneys. And there are nearly none who can avoid inhaling some of them.

Into this political air, the exponents of the Nixon-Kissinger Asian strategy tried, over at least the last year, to float a half-new kind of quasi rationale for the continuing military semipresence in Vietnam. An explanation specially calculated to impress moderately liberal observers, it has been soothingly confided by the White House's Absolutely Anonymous Authority in roughly these terms "*You* know and *I* know that the President wants to withdraw from Vietnam as fast as he can. How fast should this be? It is a pace that must not provoke a wild outcry from the radical right—all the professional patriots bewailing another sellout to Communism and yelling the gospel of neoisolation. Who would want to plunge the nation into that kind of crypto-Fascist mood? So (don't you see?) he must move in your direction—but *slowly*."

To some skeptics, this sort of talk might dismayingly insinuate that just as President Lyndon Johnson thought he might sneak into Vietnam without potential critics quite noticing at all, President Richard Nixon imagines he can sneak out.

Herblock in The Washington Post.

"Don't worry, Chief—
We're going to find the radical nut
who appointed that commission."

— *copyright 1970 by Herblock in The Washington Post*

MOREOVER, this strategy by subterfuge raises a couple of harsh questions. Beneath the surface of its assurances, does there not appear an almost terrible crudity in the contention that a lower American death rate in Vietnam, for an indefinite while, is a sacrifice well worth making to deceive and to assuage America's radical right? Does not this official doctrine deliver over American soldiers to be held not as captives in Communist jails but as hostages in the hands of American fanatics? Does this not come close to

putting national policy into the stinging language of Mylai, where killing amounts only to prudent "wasting" and a few more casualties add up to "no big deal"? Finally, by what imaginable irony could Richard Nixon, whose entire political life has rung with his cries against all "appeasement" of national enemies abroad, let himself be committed, at such cost, to appeasement of potential enemies at home?

A larger mystery still—and a kind of distillate of all the politics of evasion of the sixties—has been described by

the full trajectory of Richard Nixon's views on Vietnam. These stayed clear and predictable through the middle years of the decade, with Mr. Nixon frequently visiting Vietnam and calling for a faster and larger American military buildup. On one trip to Saigon, he urged an expeditionary force of more than 500,000 men with an insistence plainly implying that such action, promptly taken, promised victory. By 1968, the Nixon formula suddenly became much less explicit. He still hailed the conflict as nothing less than "a cause fundamental to man's hope," and he deplored the "gradualism" that had kept American military involvement too slow and small. But he hastened on from these generalities, with not much explanation, to his pledge to "end" the war "quickly" and also "win the peace." Shortly thereafter, he declared for himself a "moratorium" suspending all discussion of Vietnam — a dispensation scarcely ever interrupted through primary and campaign. Thus, by 1969, he could be said to have traveled all the way to the White House in a political sort of sealed train, silently waving to the nation's crowds from behind debate-proof glass. Once installed as President, he proceeded with reasonable dispatch to press forward programs called de-escalation and Vietnamization, so that two years later he had brought American strength in Vietnam down to the level that five years earlier he had denounced as woefully inadequate to fight "a cause" so "fundamental."

What is striking in this political performance is no mere question of the candidate's or the President's consistency or sincerity; with some reason, it may be assumed that he felt equally sincere at all times. What is remarkable is that—faithfully following his own military and political maps through the years—he was able, in effect, to point to the strategic mountain, urge its swift scaling, storm to its summit and march straight down its farther side without breaking stride and without feeling at all pressed to account for any possible change of mind about the merit of the whole costly climb. In substance and in speech alike, he thus successfully managed to record the most elaborate and elusive *non sequitur* in modern American foreign policy.

A POLITICIAN capable of executing such a tour de force might be forgiven the presumption behind the President's second report to Congress on "the State of the World." The report's 65,000 words on "Building for Peace" scarcely bothered to pretend to add anything noticeable to general sum of American knowledge. Inevitably, the President's words congratulated his Administration for designing "a new foreign policy for a new era." The rhetoric about Vietnam, however, was cautious if not slightly nervous. He acknowledged "little progress toward a negotiated peace"; he foresaw "some hard choices" ahead on the battlefield, and he qualified all the hopes of "Vietnamization" by stating that the program "cannot, except over a long period, end the war altogether." Distinctly vague about the future of Laos and Cambodia, he merely remarked that "we believe that the two Governments can survive"—an affirmation that stayed as far as possible from the central question of any American action possibly necessary if such faith proved in error. In short, all the 65,000 words expounding "the new foreign policy" were unblemished by a single proposition that might not have been written some 15 years previously by the author of SEATO, John Foster Dulles.

A kind of postscript from Henry Kissinger proved a bit more revealing of official thought. In a televised interview, he observed that "all the tough decisions" by any President are "very close . . . on the basis of maybe a 55-45 balance." But he went on to assert: "Once you've made the decision, you are committed to it or you are stuck with it 100 per cent." This conveys a notion of foreign policy that would surely have stunned such figures in Western history as Metternich, much admired by Dr. Kissinger, or deGaulle, much respected by Mr. Nixon. If the French leader had been inhibited by so binding a rule of international life, the French tragedy in Algeria would even now be lasting as long as the American tragedy in Indochina. If the Soviet leaders since World War II had been inspired by such an understanding of "commitment," they long since would have been reigning in Iran, occupying West Berlin and stockpiling nuclear missiles in Cuba.

Yet the phrase itself sticks. For the nation indeed has stayed "stuck with" a long and venerable array of myths and shibboleths, taboos and fantasies — snarling national purpose and wrenching national policy. Of all such myths, perhaps none guarantees larger grief than the lethal legend that America —alone of all great powers in all ages — has been destined never to know a defeat or yield an arena, commit a great blunder or confess a great wrong. And the propagating of legends of this spirit must be as wicked as the teaching of a son by his father that the sublime mark of manhood is never to cry.

WE have had occasions

during the sixties to learn anew that instant history can be a snare and prophetic history a fraud; but it is hard to resist the reckless guess that some future study of the collective leadership of the Nixon Presidency must appear under the title of "Profiles in Complacence." As its principal figures have beheld each other and their works, in any case, they have seemed almost to flush with pleasure. It has been thus whenever Attorney General Mitchell has publicly appraised Richard Nixon. "He was programed and made to be President," Mr. Mitchell recently exulted on national television. "Since he has been in office, he has always kept his cool. I've never really seen him angry at anything." This is the kind of official self-congratulation that can be almost embarrassingly self-revealing. The technology of the times supposedly serves to "program" computers and machines, not candidates or Presidents; and there have been few popular doubts more haunting to Richard Nixon over the years than the fear (reasonable or wrong) that he was altogether too much of a computer, a human calculating machine able to do no more than add ballots and divide opponents. As for a "cool" lack of "anger," this was, of course, precisely what chilled millions of citizens when they beheld a White House wholly incapable of indignation over such outrages in 1970 as the National Guard killings at Kent State or a South Carolina white mob's assault on school buses filled with black children. In all the litany of human qualities ever cited as desirable for Presidential leadership, I know of

no longing for a want of passion.

The Richard Nixon who grew to power through this age—so fittingly to preside, at last, over its politics—has excited almost endless analysis and even psychoanalysis. I distrust such studies, hostile or amiable; it is hard enough to know one's friend or neighbor, much less one's President. Usually, it is also challenging enough to dissect a President's nostrums without pretending to diagnose his neuroses. And this said, there may be perhaps only two paradoxes about this 37th President worth noting for some wiser future weighing.

The first is a matter central to his whole political career. Of the hundreds who have closely watched or worked with him for much more than a decade, there possibly is not one who has not described him as a "lonely" man. Also, there probably is none in the same ranks who would not name as his decisive political patron President Eisenhower. And thus do the masks and cosmetics of national politics sometimes, almost unbelievably, deceive. The fact is that no one in public life may have done more to seal Richard Nixon's sense of personal isolation than Dwight Eisenhower. For the General-President acted as a political father to his official successor with roughly the enthusiasm that most men show in situations of wholly unplanned paternity.

T HE record here, though not public, has been unmistakable to those knowing both men through the years. In 1952 the tension and alienation be-

gan with Eisenhower exasperating Nixon by his slow acceptance of Nixon's televised account of his controversial political fund. In 1956, the President was trying to nudge the Vice President off the Republican ticket, solicitously urging him to acquire "administrative experience" in some such office as Secretary of Defense, while explaining more softly to others that "Dick's just not Presidential timber." In 1960, the retiring Republican President earned the silent rage of the future Republican President by his casual confession at a Washington news conference that he would need some time to remember a substantial contribution by Richard Nixon to any major national decision of the Eisenhower Administration. In the ensuing Presidential campaign, Nixon clearly resolved to stand stoically alone, beyond the embracing shadow of Eisenhower. Quite possibly, this determination more than all else assured his defeat. A fortnight before the election, Eisenhower, offended by the candidate's failure to plead for all possible help, responded to one Republican leader with the icy lament: "He just seems like a loser to me. I look at those slumping shoulders and those drooping eyes, and I can tell you he'd never get a promotion in any army of mine."

Such an experience in high politics could drive almost any man into a sort of steely privacy. For this particular man, the refuge has been a room full of yellow legal pads and gray political possibilities, a place where he may follow his own thoughts, hide his own hurts, draft his own speeches, frame his own decisions and imagine his own mandates. In personal terms, all of this adds up to something easily understandable. In political terms, however, it amounts to a sum of qualities that totals not so much a President as a man in the Presidency. By force of this distinction, the great role itself becomes not "I" but "mine."

And this points straight to the other major paradox probably worth pondering by future historians: the abiding nature—the ruling temper—of the Nixon Presidency. Its sovereign spirit appears to be one that neither wholly feels, wholly enjoys nor wholly understands sovereignty itself. A distinguished Washington journalist who has closely watched the life of the White House through all the sixties recently depicted this spirit thus: "We all have seen for years the inner tensions and the outer contradictions of this man—the professional politician and the emotional hermit, the reasoning lawyer in private who becomes the inflaming orator in public. Again and again, we have seen his startling swings from reticence to militance and from near-statesmanship to super-partisanship. Now, the result is the kind of Government that deGaulle ascribed to the French Fourth Republic —the sort of leadership that is 'perpetually oscillating between melodrama and mediocrity.' Why should it be so? It was no idle sneer when Lyndon Johnson called Richard Nixon 'a chronic campaigner.' This is the serious truth. The longing of his political life has really not been

to govern but to campaign. The 'lift' of his 'driving dream' has been to win, not to lead. But having won, he finds that the very meaning of victory— the Presidency itself—eludes him. And the race that meant everything is now, alas, over."

This may not be exactly so, but it must strike exceedingly close to the political truth, for it describes a Presidency true to its times. Such a Presidency does more than capture— it almost celebrates —the political age, all the reaction on the right preached purely for the pleasure of its preachers, all the insurrection on the left never shying from the fight and never looking toward the future. As citizens of one temper came to practice national violence as an end in itself, there could be no more fitting response from citizens of a different mind than enjoyment of a national campaign as an end in itself. And what sort of sovereignty could finally crown all politics of the time so rightly as a Government not eager to govern and a leadership not ready to lead?

All this cannot, I fully believe, long serve or suffice. It cannot suffice for the Presidency. And it cannot serve the people.

THE first American President was a man of immense common sense and quite uncommon insight but not much famed for concise aphorisms. Yet he wrote one rarely remembered sentence stating a law of popular leadership with a precision that has never been surpassed. "The truth is," Washington said, "the people must *feel* before

they will *see*." The simple statement measures the problem of his 36th successor: how can the sight of the people be clarified—their support aroused and their energies enlisted—by a leadership that itself feels nothing in particular?

As for the related problem before the people . . .

"Probe the earth and see where your main roots run." The advice of Thoreau for a man is just as sound for a nation.

The political roots in question run far beneath the surface of all the politics of facile maneuver and easy answer. They mark values, not evasions. They trace firm beginnings, not fancied endings. And the purpose of their searching out is to learn, not to hide.

This is the kind of hard labor that any avowedly and seriously free people has to do for itself. It cannot be vicariously performed by politicians, professors, self-appointed prophets or even nationally elected Presidents. A people that does not too much mind being fooled some of the time will get, and perhaps deserve, a longer and falser charade than it ever imagined.

The heart of the matter has nothing to do, in short, with New politics or New economics or New diplomacy. It has only to do with concerns and convictions very, very old. It is, ultimately, a matter of whether any people or any nation can be self-governing unless it is also self-perceiving. It is a matter, quite simply, of whether a people wants to know itself badly enough to find itself and go on to be itself.

The roots are there. ■

7 The Uses of American Power in the Twentieth Century

The results of the Spanish-American War made it certain that the United States would be one of the twentieth century's great powers. Power, however, has proved to be a mixed blessing. Today the nation and its historians grope for the key to the proper use of power. Historians have sought an answer by examining the record of the last seventy years.

This section begins the inspection of that record with "Woodrow Wilson's Dirty Little War" by Jules Archer. Wilson, like many of his successors, thought largely in moral terms. "To conquer with arms is to make only a temporary conquest. To conquer the world by earning its esteem is to make *permanent* conquest." As Archer points out, such moral aspirations proved no substitute for savvy when Wilson was confronted with the intricacies and duplicities of revolutionary Mexico in 1914. The result was that moral conquest was replaced, unsuccessfully, by the heavy hand of American military might.

The hatred that such gunboat diplomacy inspired led to the search for a new policy that would prove acceptable to both North and Latin American interests. That policy is best known as "The Good Neighbor Policy" and is most frequently identified with Franklin Roosevelt. But "The Era of the Good Neighbor," according to George W. Grayson, Jr., was more a self-proclaimed title than it was an accomplishment. "While promoting American exports and security," concludes Grayson, "good neighborism served to freeze the socio-economic, political status quo. Despite its immediate success, it is difficult to perceive enduring contributions of the policy to inter-American relations or to conditions in the hemispheric republics."

In the years following World War II, "isolationism" came to be something of a dirty word. Now, after the tragedy of Vietnam, scholars such as Thomas Paterson in "Isolationism Revisited" are reviewing the isolationism of the thirties to see if it may not deserve a better reputation. Isolationism came abruptly to an end with the Japanese attack on Pearl Harbor—"The Day of Infamy," as FDR called it. However, in "Before Pearl Harbor," Walter LaFeber traces the history of American involvement in the Far East to events long preceding that attack. "For nearly a century before Pearl Harbor," writes LaFeber, "Americans sought riches and empire in the Far East. The events of December 7, 1941, climaxed that quest, but did not signal the denouement. The momentum of history was too strong, and the United States resumed the quest after 1945 with increased power, better strategy, and greater disasters."

"FDR: The Untold Story of His Last Year" by James MacGregor Burns is a reexamination of Roosevelt as he was in 1945 when his health—and some have claimed his mind and will—was failing him. To Burns, Yalta and other agreements were a resounding success. "He [Roosevelt] picked up Woodrow Wilson's fallen banner," writes Burns, "fashioned new symbols and programs to realize old ideals of peace and democracy, overcame his enemies with sword and pen, and died in a final exhausting effort to build a world citadel of freedom."

Next a *Time Magazine* essay by Mayo Mohs explores the intriguing question "What If Hiroshima Had Never Happened?" Harry S Truman, the tough, Missourian who made the decision to drop the bomb—he had a sign on his desk saying, "The buck stops here"—also decided to commit the United States "to support free people who are resisting attempted subjugation by armed minorities or by outside pressure." In "The Truman Doctrine," George Lewis explores the genesis of a policy that led first to the support of Greece and Turkey, then to the Marshall Plan and Point Four, and finally to the commitment of American power to the defense of Korea and Vietnam. From Truman's point of view such commitments were essential. "Isolationism," he said, "is a confession of mental and moral bankruptcy."

But when the United States military machine bogged down in Indochina and when the tonnage of American bombs dropped on that luckless part of the world had exceeded the total tonnage dropped in all of World War II, Americans began to question the effects of American power not only on other societies but also on their own. In "The New American Militarism," David M. Shoup, formerly Commandant of the United States Marine Corps, flatly asserts that "America has become a militaristic and aggressive nation."

Whatever the ultimate outcome in Vietnam or the long-term effects of Nixon's new China policy, it is clear that the United States will remain a Pacific power. In "Fateful Triangle: The United States, Japan and China," Edwin Reischauer examines the dynamics of great power relationships in that part of the world.

That there are moral dangers to the exercise of power few would question. But in the opinion of one historian, Arthur Schlesinger, Jr., it is necessary to accept the necessary amorality of foreign affairs. In "Morality and International Politics," Schlesinger writes, "Moralism in foreign policy ends up as fanaticism, and the fanatic, as Mr. Dooley put it, 'does what he thinks th' Lord wud do if He only knew th' facts in th' case.'"

Part of the argument about the place of morality in foreign affairs goes back to the Wilsonian dream of a world organization sufficiently strong to keep the peace. In "After Many a Summer Dies the Majority," Richard Walton examines what the commitment of the United States to the United Nations has been and what it ought to be now that American policies no longer can be counted on to command a majority of delegate votes. As Richard Curtis and Dave Fisher contend in "The Seven Wonders of the Polluted World," the ecological crisis is likely to force a new kind of international awareness on all the peoples of planet Earth.

Woodrow Wilson's Dirty Little War

JULES ARCHER

Jules Archer is the author of over 1000 published articles and stories as well as nine books for adults and young people. His work has been translated into twelve languages, reprinted by the State Department, adapted for television, and included in book collections. The foregoing article is an excerpt from his most recent book, World Citizen: Woodrow Wilson, published by Julian Messner, a Division of Simon & Shuster, Inc.

It is almost forgotten today how Woodrow Wilson, one of the most well meaning and erudite Presidents at the helm of American destiny, was dragged reluctantly into the civil strife of Mexico through miscalculations of foreign policy similar to those that have entangled the present occupant of the White House in the fratricide of Vietnam.

Had President Johnson made a careful study of Wilson's high-minded blunders and the painful lesson they taught, he might have been more cautious about the American "commitment" in Vietnam that has proved even more calamitous than the Wilson fiasco turned out to be half a century ago.

"It would be the irony of fate," Wilson told Ellen just before they moved into the White House, "if my Administration had to deal chiefly with foreign affairs." His burning interest was domestic reforms. Yet from his first week in office, foreign problems kept spilling into his lap from the fumbling fingers of Bryan, his inept Secretary of State.

He had inherited the gunboat diplomacy of Teddy Roosevelt, who believed that the way to deal with Latin America was to "speak softly and carry a big stick," and the dollar diplomacy of Taft, whose Secretary of State, Philander C. Knox, had used U.S. troops to prop up Latin-American dictators who were paid puppets of American big business.

Wilson was determined to write a new, more honorable chapter of Pan-American relations. He intended to export Wilson-style diplomacy to the people of Latin America so that they, too, could enjoy the New Freedom. A missionary at heart, he urged his Christian principles upon a skeptical Congress.

"To conquer with arms," he persuaded, "is to make only a temporary conquest. To conquer the world by earning its esteem is to make *permanent* conquest." That conviction became the cornerstone of his foreign policy.

War, he was convinced, was unnecessary. He set out to prove that all international disputes could be negotiated peacefully. He had Bryan negotiate treaties with thirty different nations, providing for a cooling-off period of one year during which disputes would be resolved by arbitration. Germany was one of the nations scorning such a treaty.

American businessmen were curtly advised that they could no longer expect U.S. military force to back up their foreign investments. Wilson squelched a Morgan loan to the new Republic of China under Dr. Sun Yat-sen because its terms allowed enforcement of payment of the loan, if necessary, by U.S. bayonets. Such terms, Wilson charged, were "obnoxious to the principles upon which the government of our people rests." Wall Street fumed at such "amateur" interference in the affairs of international finance. But the American people ap-

Francisco I. Madero was elected President of Mexico after his agrarian revolution in 1911. He became a martyr to "dollar diplomacy" when deposed and assassinated by the foreign-financed Victoriano Huerta (below).

plauded enthusiastically.

World powers began to sit up and take notice of this new, remarkably ethical voice in the White House. Tokyo appealed to him to interfere when the California legislature barred Japanese-Americans from land ownership. But Wilson was forced to explain that he could not interfere with a state's laws. The Japanese Government furiously hinted at war.

"Our navy's not prepared," Daniels advised glumly. "They could take the Philippines, Hawaii and Alaska."

"Maybe," Wilson mused, "but they couldn't keep them."

General MacArthur verified his prophecy twenty-eight years later.

Wanting to assure our Latin-American neighbors that the era of Yankee imperialism was dead, Wilson delivered a major policy speech at Mobile, Alabama, in October, 1913. No more, he promised solemnly, would Washington use the Monroe Doctrine as a pretext to meddle in Latin-American affairs.

"The United States will never again seek one additional foot of territory by conquest!" he vowed. Nor would Wall Street be allowed to charge ruinous interest on loans to Latin America. "I would rather belong to a poor nation that was free," he cried eloquently, "than to a rich nation that had ceased to be in love with liberty!"

Was the new *Presidente Americano* really sincere? Little Colombia tested Wilson by asking a $50 million indemnity and an American apology for ex-President Roosevelt's grab of its land to build the Panama Canal. Wilson promptly offered them an official apology and $20 million, but the Senate was outraged at the idea of allowing an American apology for *anything*. The canal opened on August 15, 1914, and the squabble persisted until Wilson had left office. Then Colombia received $25 million—but no apology.

Wilson also insisted upon behaving honorably when the British protested paying higher canal tolls than American shipping was charged, despite a 1901 treaty guaranteeing equal treatment. "If you go to Congress to correct this," Ellen worried, "won't you lose all the Irish, German and anti-British votes in the next election?"

"I can't count the cost to my political future," he replied. "Maybe we did make a bad bargain with England on Panama tolls. But it will be all the more credit to us as a nation if we stand by it, whatever the sacrifice."

Going before Congress, he told them, "We are too big, too powerful, too self-respecting a nation to find loopholes in promises just because we have power enough to give us leave to read them as we please." Congress

Venustiana Carranza (above) swore to return constitutional government to Mexico.

reluctantly raised U.S. tolls in Panama to equal those charged Britain.

Wilson's tendency to oversimplify complex Latin-American problems surfaced when revolutionary turmoil broke out in the corrupt "banana republics"—Nicaragua, Haiti and Santa Domingo. Intelligence reports hinted that European creditor nations were planning to invade these bankrupt countries with occupation forces. Wilson squirmed in an agony of indecision. He finally felt compelled to forestall this possibility by sending in U.S. Marines backed by warships. An American occupation, he told Bryan hopefully, would at least give him a chance to bring law, order, democracy, and prosperity to the wretched people of those misruled little countries.

But what really happened was bluntly revealed to a Congressional investigating committee years later by Major General Smedley Butler, twice awarded the Congressional Medal of Honor during his long career as a combat Marine commander. "I spent 33 years being a high-class muscle man for Big Business, for Wall Street and the bankers," he told a *New York Times* reporter acidly on August 21, 1931. "I helped purify Nicaragua for the international banking house of Brown Brothers. . . . I brought light to the Dominican Republic for American sugar interests. . . . I helped make Haiti and Cuba a decent place for the National City (Bank) boys to

A cornerstone of Wilson's foreign policy lay in his own words: "To conquer the world by earning its esteem is to make a permanent conquest." Yet in the spring of 1914 Wilson lifted a self-imposed embargo of Mexico and sent a landing force to the port of Vera Cruz to prevent unloading of European munitions en route to Huerta. The American flag was raised in the harbor after a bloody battle at the customhouse and U.S. sailors patroled the city's streets (left).   American marines died (above) but the "speak softly and carry a big stick" policy held firm. Defending Mexicans (below left) became victims of U.S. arrogance.

In July, 1914, Huerta's support crumpled and he fled to Spain. Wilson grudgingly recognized Carranza, but civil war broke out again in Mexico when one of Carranza's supporters, Pancho Villa (right), struck out as a bandit hoping to inflame a resurgence of anti-Americanism and gain control of a united country. Above Villa gallops alongside one of his raiding columns.

collect revenue in. I helped in the rape of half a dozen Central American republics for the benefit of Wall Street."

It was in Mexico, however, that Wilson's naivete about the realities of life south of the border had the most disastrous consequences. The Mexicans had elected Francisco Madero as their President in 1911, following the overthrow of dictator Porfirio Diaz by revolution. Wilson knew Madero to be sincerely dedicated to curbing foreign exploitation of Mexico's resources and people, and to relieving the harsh life of its peons and Indians.

But two weeks before Wilson assumed office, bandit general Victoriano Huerta had overthrown Madero, who had then been arrested and murdered. Strong evidence linked foreign oil, railroad, mining and land-owning interests to the plot. America's investment-minded Ambassador in Mexico City, Harry Lane Wilson, urged immediate recognition of Huerta.

Woodrow Wilson refused indignantly. Not only would such recognition dignify a usurper and murderer, but it would crush the hopes of the Mexican people, who were struggling to free themselves from enslavement by a rich, brutal feudal class. He labeled Huerta "the bitter, implacable foe of everything progressive and humane in Mexico," and insisted that "just government rests always on the consent of the governed." He warned Huerta and all Latin-American bandit chiefs that, "the Government of the United States will refuse to extend the hand of welcome to anyone who obtains power in a sister republic by treachery and violence." He told Congress, "We shall yet prove to the Mexican people that we know how to serve them without first thinking how we shall serve ourselves!"

In his apostolic zeal, it never occurred to him for a moment that the Wilson brand of democracy might be neither welcome nor practical in Latin America, where the cultural heritage was so different. "I am going to teach the South American republics to elect good men!" he assured Sir William Tyrell, an attache of the British Embassy. He laid down conditions of U.S. recognition to Huerta—a genuine election in which Huerta must not be a candidate, followed by U.S. help in stabilizing the newly elected government.

Huerta scornfully rejected this attempt to control Mexican affairs by a messianic American President. British recognition strengthened his hand. American businessmen protested bitterly to Wilson that his stubbornness was letting the practical British win the inside track with Huerta on foreign concessions. He replied coldly, "Wherever I look—China, Mexico, Nicaragua, Santo Domingo—I see always the same enemy." Big business had no doubt whom he meant.

Wilson pinned his hopes in the Mexican dilemma on a rival to Huerta—General Venustiano Carranza, Governor of Coahuila, whose Constitutionalist followers were sworn to avenge the overthrow and murder of Madero. As fighting began, the President declared a hands-off policy, asking all Americans to leave Mexico and banning arms shipments to either side. He dispatched a fleet to cruise significantly in the Gulf of Mexico, and settled down to "watchful waiting."

Huerta proved strong enough to entrench himself in power as an absolute dictator, and began importing arms from Europe to crush Carranza. Dismayed, Wilson scrapped his own embargo and rushed U.S. arms to the Carranza forces. Full-scale civil war broke out all over Mexico. Carranza was joined by Francisco ("Pancho") Villa, a powerful bandit chief.

In the savage fighting American industrial property was destroyed, and U.S. businessmen were forced to flee by outrages committed against them by both sides. They stormed to Washington to protest the lack of military protection. Wilson told Navy Secretary Daniels, "I sometimes have to pause and remind myself that I am the President of the whole United States, and not merely of a few property-holders in the Republic of Mexico." He asked Daniels to make it clear to them that the day of gunboat diplomacy was over; U.S. bayonets would *not* protect private investments in foreign countries.

Receiving them, Daniels demanded, "Why did you leave the United States and go to Mexico? You went there because you preferred to invest there rather than in the United States, to make more profit. Isn't that so? Well, then, you must take the risk of losing your property. . . . You must not expect the people of the United States to pay taxes for the support of an army to protect your property in Mexico!"

Harvard's ex-President Charles Eliot expressed his delight: "America has now turned her back on the familiar policy of Rome and Great Britain of protecting or avenging their wandering citizens by force of arms."

On April 9, 1914, a U.S. naval shore party was sud-

Pancho Villa and General Pershing pose happily at a meeting in Mexico before Villa turned against Carranza (above). A cartoon of the times, Sweet Land of Liberty, *spoofs Huerta's tyranny.*

denly arrested in Tampico by Huerta's soldiers. They were soon released with an expression of regrets over a misunderstanding of orders. But granite-faced U.S. Admiral Henry T. Mayo issued an outraged ultimatum to the local Huerta general. He demanded punishment for the arresting officer, a formal apology, a twenty-one gun salute to the American flag and compliance within twenty-four hours—or else!

Washington and Mexico City buzzed with alarm. Would this mean war? Huerta proudly defied Mayo's demands. Dismayed, Wilson felt that he had been left no choice but to back up his fiery naval commander. Disdaining to give ear to old Mexican hands in the State Department who sought to caution him, he made an emotional appeal to Congress on April 20 for approval to use whatever armed forces were needed to bring Huerta to terms. He emphasized that his quarrel was not with the Republic of Mexico, but with Huerta alone.

Next day he ordered U.S. Marines to land in Vera Cruz and prevent the unloading of munitions for Huerta from the German steamer *Ypiranga*. Any uneasiness he felt was soothed by Colonel House, who assured him, "If a man's house was on fire he should be glad to have his neighbors come in and help him put it out, provided they did not take his property. It should be the same with nations. If Mexico understands that our motives are unselfish, she should not object to our helping adjust her unruly household."

"Your praise of anything I do or say is always sweet to me," Wilson replied gratefully. "I would rather have your judgment than that of anybody I know." His high esteem for his affable silent partner was not shared by those of the Cabinet whom the Colonel had intrigued against. "House was an intimate man," Daniels said, "even while cutting a throat."

Wilson was confident that his occupation of the port of Vera Cruz would be met only with a Mexican shrug. How could Huerta hope to oppose the great naval might of the United States? But when Marines and some U.S. soldiers tried to take the Vera Cruz custom house, Mexican troops opened fire from housetops. In the battle that developed, nineteen servicemen and several hundred Mexicans were killed.

The news stunned Wilson. Deeply depressed, he told Dr. Grayson, "The thought haunts me that it was I who ordered those young men to their deaths." He gloomily insisted upon leading the funeral procession of the fallen servicemen in New York. When the Secret Service discovered a plot to assassinate him, New York's Mayor Mitchel begged him not to march, pleading

"The country cannot afford to have its President killed!"

"The country," Wilson replied tersely, "cannot afford to have a coward for President." His funeral oration reflected his suffering over the tragic developments in Mexico. "We do not want to fight the Mexicans," he cried in anguish. "We want to serve the Mexicans if we can." There was self-pity: "It is just as hard to do your duty when men are sneering at you as when they are shooting at you. When they shoot at you, they can only take your natural life. When they sneer at you, they can wound your living heart."

He made it clear that he was looking to history to vindicate him: "The cheers of the moment are not what a man ought to think about, but the verdict of his conscience and of the consciences of mankind."

The A.B.C. powers of South America—Argentina, Brazil, Chile—offered to mediate the trouble in Mexico. Hard-pressed by Wilson in front, and the armies of Carranza and Villa behind, Huerta agreed. So did Wilson, hoping to reassure Central and South America that his intentions were not imperialistic. But the A.B.C. Conference failed when Wilson made it clear that he expected to mediate only between Huerta and Carranza —not between Huerta and Wilson.

He kept the Marines on in Vera Cruz, grimly determined that Huerta must go, at all costs. What had begun for him as a matter of high principle had become, although he would not admit it, a personal vendetta between himself (hero) and a Mexican usurper (villain). The outcome was inevitable.

In July, 1914, Huerta's support finally crumbled and he fled to Spain. A year later he was found in Texas and arrested on suspicion of plotting a military expedition to regain power in Mexico. He died in an El Paso prison, as much a martyr to American "missionary diplomacy" as Madero before him had been to the plotters behind dollar diplomacy.

But Wilson's troubles in Mexico did not end with the coming to power of Carranza. Civil war promptly broke out between Carranza and Villa. Both turned a deaf ear to Washington. Both committed fresh outrages against American property and lives, reflecting the anger in Mexico over the U.S. troops kept on in Vera Cruz. "The soil of the *patria* is defiled by foreign invasion!" protested a Mexico City newspaper, *El Imparcial*. "We may die, but let us kill!" Headlines in *La Patria* demanded: VENGEANCE! VENGEANCE! VENGEANCE!

A statue of George Washington was toppled in Mexico City by angry mobs shouting, "Death to the gringos!"

Wilson finally withdrew the Marines from Vera Cruz

in October, and gave gloomy recognition to the Carranza government. An outlaw bandit once more, Villa set about trying to provoke Wilson into intervening in Mexico again. If Mexicans were inflamed into a fresh burst of anti-Americanism, they might sweep Carranza—Wilson's choice—out of power.

So in March, 1916, Villa led his forces across the border and attacked Columbus, New Mexico, killing twenty Americans.

This was too much for Wilson. Calling out the National Guard, he sent an expeditionary force under Brigadier General John G. Pershing into Mexico to capture Villa. At the same time, he assured Carranza that the punitive columns on Mexican soil were "in no sense intended as an invasion."

But Carranza was indignant at Wilson's temerity in violating Mexican sovereignty. He sent his own troops against Pershing, who, for fear of being cut off and wiped out, was forced to retreat after penetrating 200 miles into Mexico.

The unsuccessful expedition, costing $150,000,000, succeeded only in illuminating further the bankruptcy of Wilson's perplexed and desperate Mexican policy. Everything he had done out of high purpose had boomeranged and intensified Latin suspicions of Yankee imperialism.

In vain he swore, "I am more interested in the fortunes of oppressed men and pitiful women and children than in any property rights whatever. Mistakes I have no doubt made in this perplexing business, but not in purpose or object!"

Day after day outraged Senators stormed into his office to demand full-scale intervention south of the border to "clean up" Mexico once and for all, and handpick some safe Mexican aristocrat as its new President.

"I happen to know that you have two sons," Wilson told one Senator. "If I take steps to mobilize the young of America for a Mexican war, will you promise me that *your* sons will be among the first to enlist?"

He was also importuned by Tumulty, who had been swept up by the war fever raging in the Senate. Wilson replied firmly, "There won't be any war with Mexico if I can prevent it, no matter how loud the gentlemen on the hill yell for it. I came from the South and I know what war is, for I have seen its wreckage and terrible ruin. It is easy for me as President to declare war. I don't have to fight, and neither do the gentlemen on the hill. It is some poor farmer's boy who will have to do the fighting and dying!"

Jingoist newspapers called him cowardly and jeered at his "Hesitation Waltz—one step forward, two steps backward, then sidestep!" Eyes flashing, he faced reporters at the New York Press Club. "Do you think the glory of America would be enhanced by a war with Mexico?" he demanded indignantly. "Do you think that any act of violence by a powerful nation like this

against a weak and distracted neighbor would reflect distinction upon the annals of the United States?"

There was no war with Mexico. Yet if Wilson deserved credit for that, and for his sincere concern for "poor Mexico, with its pitiful men, women and children, fighting to gain a foothold in their own land," his conviction that he knew what was best for them had proved a fatal error. His sanctimonious interference had alienated Latin America.

Worse, the militarists of Germany had been scornfully studying his indecision, his scruples, his "watchful waiting." They grew confident that they could pluck the tail of the American eagle as arrogantly as they liked, and Wilson would not unsheath its claws. When that miscalculation made war with Germany inevitable, only one South American country, Brazil, offered to fight at the side of the United States.

The others shed no tears over the plight of the Colossus of the North. South of the border, cynical Juan had suffered equally under gunboat diplomacy, dollar diplomacy, and missionary diplomacy. To him they had all added up to the same old thing—Yankee intervention in his affairs.

Why should one risk his life for *that*, senor? ✤

The Era of the Good Neighbor

"The seeds of this country's massive military involvement in Latin America in the 1950's and 1960's were sown during the Good Neighbor period."

GEORGE W. GRAYSON, JR.

George W. Grayson, Jr., has made four trips to Latin America in the past four years, and has written for several publications on Latin American topics. His study of the Chilean Christian Democratic party appeared as *El Partido Democrata Cristiano Chileno* (Buenos Aires: Editorial Francisco de Aguirre, 1968).

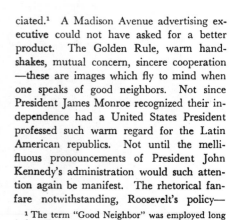

I N HIS INAUGURAL speech of March 4, 1933, President Franklin Roosevelt departed long enough from domestic concerns to articulate a basic precept of his foreign policy:*

In the field of world policy I would dedicate this nation to the policy of the good neighbor—the neighbor who resolutely respects himself, and, because he does so, respects the rights of others —the neighbor who respects his obligations and respects the sanctity of his agreements in and with a world of neighbors.

The following month, in a Pan American Day message, the President made it clear that the above principle was to apply specifically to the Western Hemisphere:

The essential qualities of a true Pan Americanism must be the same as those which constitute a good neighbor, namely, mutual understanding, a sympathetic appreciation of the others' point of view. It is only in this manner that we can hope to build up a system of which confidence, friendship and good will are the cornerstones.

The Good Neighbor policy was thus enun-

------

* For research and typing assistance, I wish to express my appreciation to Betty Orr and Barbara Batson.

ciated.[1] A Madison Avenue advertising executive could not have asked for a better product. The Golden Rule, warm handshakes, mutual concern, sincere cooperation —these are images which fly to mind when one speaks of good neighbors. Not since President James Monroe recognized their independence had a United States President professed such warm regard for the Latin American republics. Not until the mellifluous pronouncements of President John Kennedy's administration would such attention again be manifest. The rhetorical fanfare notwithstanding, Roosevelt's policy—

------

[1] The term "Good Neighbor" was employed long before Roosevelt gave it currency. Elihu Root, Charles Evans Hughes, Herbert Hoover and other Republicans had used it, and the phrase appeared, apparently at the instance of Mexico's Commissioners, in the preamble to the 1848 Treaty of Guadalupe Hidalgo, which concluded the Mexican-American war. See Bryce Wood, *The Making of the Good Neighbor Policy* (New York: W. W. Norton and Co., 1961), p. 124.

From *Current History*, June 1969. Copyright © Current History, Inc.

some say policies[2]—toward the hemispheric nations was (1) essentially negative, with a few exceptions, (2) largely unilateral, despite lavish references to multilateralism, and (3) the genesis of a significant United States military involvement with the nations of the Americas. Above all, good neighborism was aimed at furthering the immediate interests of the United States, namely, trade expansion and the security of the Hemisphere against Axis aggression and subversion.

A NEGATIVE POLICY

To be a good neighbor, the United States would have to lay aside the "big stick" which the President's cousin Teddy (President Theodore Roosevelt) had fashioned for handling unruly Latin American states. As early as 1928, Franklin Roosevelt had insisted that: "Single-handed intervention by us in the internal affairs of other nations must end; with the cooperation of others we shall have more order in this Hemisphere and less dislike."[3] This idea found its way into the 1932 Democratic platform which called for "no interference in the internal affairs of other nations. . . ."

By the time Roosevelt entered the White House, intervention no longer constituted an efficient instrument for dealing with republics south of the Río Grande. Although private United States firms occasionally benefited, sending Marines abroad was expensive, and democratic governments failed to blossom in their wake as President Woodrow Wilson had hoped. Ill will sprang up instead. The supremacy of the United States in the region was now unchallenged: war and economic collapse constrained extra-continental expansion by European nations, and major Latin American states—Argentina and Brazil, for example—were trapped in the vortex of the great depression. In the Caribbean, domestic guardians of order had been groomed: the *Guardia Nacional* of Anastasio Somoza in Nicaragua, Rafael Leonidas Trujillo's army in the Dominican Republic, and the Haitian constabulary under the political control of Sténio Vicent. How could Washington voice moral indignation at Japanese imperialism if the United States were dispatching troops to the Americas?

An opportunity to jettison this bankrupt policy soon emerged. In December, 1933, representatives from the American republics converged on Montevideo for the Seventh International Conference of American States. There the *latinos* planned to find out whether Roosevelt's Good Neighbor talk was substance or shadow. Specifically, the delegates considered a Convention of the Rights and Duties of States, Article VIII of which stated

that: "No state has the right to intervene in the internal or external affairs of another." Article XI contained the provision that: "The territory of a State is inviolable and may not be the object of military occupation nor of other measures of force imposed by another state directly or indirectly or for any motive whatever, even temporarily."

Secretary of State Cordell Hull, chief of the United States delegation, ardently desired clarification of the convention's language. Rather than give the appearance of hedging, however, he signed the document with the stipulation that the United States reserved its rights by "the law of nations as generally recognized."[4] Whereas President Herbert Hoover had expressed disenchantment with military intervention, the Roosevelt administration renounced such action, a position reiterated three years later at the Buenos Aires conference.

Cuba provided the first trial of the non-intervention principle. President Gerardo Machado, legally elected in 1925, altered the constitution three years later to extend his term of office. As resistance snowballed, the dictator resorted to Gestapo-like suppression and lawlessness swept the country. What should the United States do? Didn't the 1901 Platt Amendment authorize intervention "for the preservation of Cuban independence, the maintenance of a government adequate for protection of life, property, and individual liberty. . . ?" Despite mounting pressures—Ambassador Sumner Welles three times urged Roosevelt to send in a military force—Washington eschewed armed intervention. Not only were troops withheld, but the Platt Amendment was abrogated in 1934, although Washington held fast to its Guantánamo base.

Military inaction did not mean that the United States avoided interference in Cuban affairs. To the contrary, Ambassador Welles coaxed, cajoled and hectored Machado to vacate the presidency. When the dictator finally fled, Welles persuaded the State Department to withhold recognition from a new regime headed by Ramón Grau San Martín, a fiery social reformer who urged land reform, higher wages, shorter working days and increased taxes on foreign holdings. This pressure, accompanied by the presence of 30 United States warships off the Cuban coast, hastened Grau's overthrow, and Washington speedily recognized the new government

headed by a puppet of army boss Fulgencio Batista, whom Welles described as an "extraordinarily brilliant and able figure." For the United States ambassador, this regime represented "the first step in the long process of Cuba's return to constitutional government, economic prosperity, and normal social stability."[5]

Still, the real test of non-interventionism occurred in Mexico. In 1938, President Lázaro Cárdenas expropriated the holdings of foreign oil companies which opposed a labor settlement decreed by the Mexican Supreme Court. United States firms valued (perhaps extravagantly) at $260 million numbered among the properties seized. At no time did the State Department contest the expropriation rights of a sovereign government. What concerned Washington was that, in accordance with international law, prompt, adequate and effective compensation must be made. The oil companies howled in anger at Mexico's move and Secretary of State Cordell Hull, his "Tennessee temper" boiling, referred privately to Cárdenas and his associates as "Communists,"[6] but the cool diplomacy of Ambassador Josephus Daniels rejected highhanded bullying, preserved diplomatic relations and paved the way for an understanding. Though the Mexican government suffered harassment,[7] a peaceful solution was reached whereby a joint commission of experts decided upon fair compensation for the United States companies. Two important factors motivated Washington to press for an amicable settlement: fear of antagonizing the country which flanked this nation's southern border, and alarm at the growing interest of Germany, Japan and Italy in Mexican petroleum. Thus the episode revealed an emerging tenet of good neighborism, e.g., that United States national interests would henceforth supersede those of private firms.

Other examples of Roosevelt's non-interventionism are readily found. The final detachment of Marines left Nicaragua in 1933, and the following year the President ordered them out of Haiti, which they had occupied for 19 years. For the first time since 1915, no United States troops were stationed in Latin America (and none intervened there until President Johnson dispatched the Marines to the Dominican Republic in 1965). Under the 1936 Hull-Alfaro Treaty, ratified in 1939, the United States foreswore its "right to intervene" in Panama, though the canal remained under United States control. The 1937 seizure by the Bolivian government of

---

[2] Wood argues that three policies—"nonintervention," "noninterference," and "reciprocity"—made up good neighborism. See *ibid., passim.*

[3] "Our Foreign Policy: A Democratic View," *Foreign Affairs,* Vol. 6, No. 4 (July, 1928), p. 585.

[4] Samuel Flagg Bemis, *The Latin American Policy of the United States* (New York: W. W. Norton and Co., 1967), p. 274.

[5] By rather opaque reasoning, the ambassador argued that the U. S. government would have been "derelict in its obligations to the Cuban people" in recognizing the unpopular and "disastrously incompetent" Grau regime; see Sumner Welles, *The Time for Decision* (New York: Harper and Brothers, 1944), pp. 196–199. An excellent discussion of this episode is offered by E. David Cronon, "Interpreting the New Good Neighbor Policy: The Cuban Crisis of 1933," *The Hispanic American Historical Review,* November, 1959, pp. 538–567.

[6] Wood, *op. cit.,* p. 217.

[7] The U. S. Treasury temporarily suspended purchases of Mexican silver and the State Department supported a boycott of Mexican oil. See Lloyd C. Gardner, *Economic Aspects of New Deal Diplomacy* (Madison: The University of Wisconsin Press, 1964), p. 116. U. S. Government lending agencies made no loans to Mexico between August, 1937, and November, 1941. See Wood, *op. cit.,* p. 233.

Standard Oil Company holdings was settled through diplomacy and economic enticements, not by armed force, and by 1941 the United States had ceased collecting customs in Haiti and the Dominican Republic.

All of these cases underscore the negative character of good neighborism. The United States was saying, in effect, that it would *not* send troops to collect debts; it would *not* seize customs houses; it would *not* intervene militarily in political affairs; it would *not* rush to the rescue of private United States firms.

On the positive side, the Roosevelt administration sought to boost trade to pull the country from the depths of the Great Depression. Secretary Hull, architect of the program, proposed bilateral trade liberalization to the 1933 Montevideo conference. The following year Congress passed the Reciprocal Trade Agreements Act, which authorized the President to negotiate tariff cuts of up to 50 per cent with countries prepared to reciprocate. The reductions, based on the extremely high schedules set by the 1930 Smoot-Hawley tariff, failed to tumble the high wall encircling the United States market, and protectionism persisted in Latin America. Nevertheless, United States-Latin American trade shot up 302 per cent between 1933 and 1942. The value of United States exports to the Hemisphere increased from $244 million to $871 million, while United States imports from Latin American nations expanded from $335 million to $1,045 million. In spite of the oil controversy, imports from Mexico increased from $31 million to $124 million, and United States exports to its southern neighbor rose from $38 million to $148 million in the ten-year period.[8]

To spur trade, Congress in 1934 created the Export-Import Bank, which made a number of loans to United States exporters operating in Latin America. Once war broke out, the bank became an important supplier of credit to hemispheric governments. It also assumed a political role. The multimillion dollar Volta Redonda steel complex, the bank's most dramatic project, was undertaken to preempt Brazil's steel industry from German and Japanese interests. Similarly, other credits helped to circumscribe Axis influence in the Americas. The bank initiated United States foreign aid to Latin America, which has continued under Point IV and the Alliance for Progress.

UNILATERAL POLICY

During the 1930's, United States representatives turned the air blue with talk of the Good Neighbor policy's multilateral character. Alarmed by the aggressive posture of Benito Mussolini and Adolph Hitler, Roose-

velt sought hemispheric unity against possible European threats to the New World. In personal letters to the heads of Latin American states, he invited them to send delegations to an extraordinary inter-American conference, convened in Buenos Aires in December, 1936. Despite his crippled condition which required a heavy steel brace, the President voyaged 7,000 miles to attend this special meeting. In an opening speech, he stressed the importance of social and political justice in the Hemisphere, extolled the equality of the American states, and emphasized the need to maintain peace.

The diplomatic adroitness of Argentine Foreign Minister Saavedra Lamas, convinced that his country's interests lay principally with Europe, not the Americas, prevented the creation of machinery for joint action; however, the delegates adopted a "Consultative Pact," which called for consultation among the American states in the event of direct or indirect threats to hemispheric security. Another article, unanimously adopted, stipulated that "every act susceptible of disturbing the peace of America affects each and every American republic and justifies the initiation of the procedural consultation provided for. . . ." According to one scholar, this agreement constituted the "Pan-Americanization of the Monroe Doctrine."[9] In truth, this "Pan-Americanization" received only lip-service.

Representatives to the Eighth International Conference of American States, meeting in Lima three months after the September, 1938, Munich debacle, continued this verbal cooperation. They unanimously approved the "Declaration of Lima," which reiterated support both for hemispheric solidarity and for consultation in the face of outside dangers. Though opposition from Argentina chilled United States efforts to forge a front against totalitarian expansion and Nazi-Fascist subversion, Secretary Hull settled for an agreement that all the foreign ministers would "meet upon the call of any one of them."

This machinery soon spun into action. In the aftermath of Germany's rape of Poland in September, 1939, the American foreign ministers gathered in Panama. There they proclaimed a "safety belt" around the Americas south of belligerent Canada, ranging from 300 to 1,000 miles in width. The foreign ministers thus warned the European combatants to steer clear of the Western Hemisphere, an act nearly as brazen as the assertion of the Monroe Doctrine over a century before. The American republics were seeking to avoid war, but they lacked the collective means or will to enforce their neutrality zone. (A flagrant violation of this zone, sometimes derisively called a "chastity belt," occurred when British warships at-

tacked the *Graf von Spee*, a German "pocket" battleship, off the Uruguayan coast.)

Two permanent standing committees emerged from the Panama conference: the Inter-American Financial and Economic Advisory Committee, which initiated a study of financial and economic matters affecting the interests of the hemispheric states; and the Inter-American Neutrality Committee, which attempted to devise a code of conduct for the neutral American nations.

Following the *Wehrmacht's* onslaught into West Europe, the foreign ministers assembled in Havana to decide the status of French and Dutch colonies in the Western Hemisphere after Hitler had overrun their mother countries. The upshot was the "Act of Havana," which asserted that one or more American republics would temporarily administer colonies that were in danger of changing hands, until their previous status or independence was attained. Though a convention embodying its principles was ratified by two-thirds of the signatory states early in 1942, the Act of Havana was never invoked. The Havana conference also adopted a reciprocal assistance declaration providing that an attack by a non-American state on any hemispheric republic would be treated as an attack on all and joint consultation would begin immediately.

Inter-American meetings from Buenos Aires to Havana evidenced increasing United States-Latin American cooperation. Despite frequent allusions to multilateralism, however, responsibility for implementing policies adopted at these sessions rested with Washington. What country had armed forces sufficiently powerful to threaten retaliation against European incursions into the Hemisphere? Whose navy could patrol the seas that washed the American republics? Who was strong enough to take control of European colonies—in the face of an Axis threat—and administer them for the duration of hostilities? In every case, the answer was clear—the United States.

The United States military never seriously considered multilateral defense of the Hemisphere. A Joint Planning Committee of the Army and Navy prepared a series of in-depth reports on the alternative responses this country could make to a violation of the Monroe Doctrine. Called the "Rainbow Plans," these studies assigned primary defense responsibilities to United States forces in the event of an Axis attack. The Latin American nations were relegated to a minor supporting role because of their low military capability.[10]

Following the collapse of France, United States military officers entered into extended conversations with their Latin American counterparts. These so-called "Staff Agree-

[8] U. S. Department of Commerce, *Historical Statistics of the United States, Colonial Times to 1957* (Washington: Government Printing Office, 1960), pp. 550, 552. These figures are not corrected for changes in the price level.

[9] Edwin Lieuwen, *U. S. Policy in Latin America* (New York: Frederick A. Praeger, 1965), p. 72.

[10] J. Lloyd Mecham, *A Survey of United States-Latin American Relations* (Boston: Houghton Mifflin Company, 1965), p. 132.

ments" concerned American access to land, sea, and air bases in the Hemisphere. The American representatives impressed upon the Latins that they were to hold off external aggressors until United States forces could rush to the rescue. The Latin Americans were not allies, in the sense that they would share decision-making on defense questions, as seen in the commitment they would have to make for United States aid:

1. To call on the United States for armed assistance in event of actual or threatened attack.
2. To report to the United States any non-American attack.
3. To explain, via radio, to the rest of the world, and especially to Latin America, the reason for a request of United States assistance.
4. To permit the transit of United States forces going to the aid of a neighbor.
5. To develop and maintain an effective and complete interchange of intelligence relating to continental security.
6. To develop and maintain an adequate and efficient secret service in order to keep under surveillance aliens and subversive groups.
7. To eliminate anti-United States propaganda in terms of emergency.[11]

GROUNDWORK FOR MILITARY INVOLVEMENT

The seeds of this country's massive military involvement in Latin America in the 1950's and 1960's were sown during the Good Neighbor period. On May 19, 1926, Congress passed an enabling act permitting officers of the United States Army, Navy and Marine Corps to assist certain Hemisphere governments in military and naval matters.[12] Taking advantage of this legislation, the Roosevelt administration concluded a number of "Military Mission Agreements" with South and Central American countries. The President was anxious to send missions to Latin America to prepare local officers for hemispheric defense and to offset the influence of Germans and Italians, long involved in training Latin American armies, who intermingled Nazi and Fascist propaganda with their instruction.

A pact establishing a United States mission in Brazil typified these bilateral accords. Negotiated for a two-year period and subject to extension, this agreement called for five United States officers to set up a coast artillery instruction center, to formulate the curriculum and to assist in teaching. This mission would also lend a hand to the military's tech-

nical school in courses dealing with fortification, ordnance and chemical warfare. The Brazilian government, which agreed to pay the salaries of the United States personnel, pledged not to engage "any Mission or personnel of any foreign government" for the project undertaken by the Americans as long as the pact remained in effect.

These and similar accords enabled the United States to supplant Italy and Germany in advising Latin American armies (United States Naval missions replaced those of France and England in training hemispheric navies). In November, 1938, nine United States, four German and eleven Italian missions were operating in Central and South America. Three years later not a single German or Italian advisory unit remained, and the United States boasted air, naval or army groups in nearly every Latin American country. One reason for this shift was Washington's readiness to underbid its Axis rivals and offer quality technical assistance at bargain basement prices.[13] Latin Americans were also invited, in increasing numbers, to study at West Point, Annapolis and other special military schools in this country. Today, as an outgrowth of its efforts in the 1930's, the United States maintains Military Advisory Assistance Groups in a dozen Hemisphere republics, shores up the Inter-American Defense Board, directs the Inter-American War College, and annually trains hundreds of Latin officers and prospective officers.

Military materiel flowed into the Hemisphere on the heels of United States advisors. Senate haggling over payments delayed sending obsolete surplus weapons to Latin America, as requested by the War, Navy and State Departments. However, the 1941 passage of the Lend Lease bill, symbolically numbered 1776, furnished a means of making munitions available to allies.

Washington sought bases in exchange for its missions and aid. The War Department expressed special concern over protecting the Brazilian "hump," fearing that Hitler might leap from Dakar onto the back of the sleeping Portuguese-speaking giant. In addition, Japan's alignment with Germany and Italy exposed the Panama Canal's Pacific approaches to potential danger. At first, the Latins rebuffed demands for base facilities, but after Pearl Harbor and the advent of Lend Lease, resistance melted. By 1942, Brazil, Mexico, Cuba, Panama and Ecuador had provided bases, causing one pundit to suggest that while Columbus discovered America in 1492, the United States discovered Latin America in 1942.[14]

In its quest for security against the virus of

Axis "isms," the United States embraced several of the twentieth century's most venal dictators. Lest he become "a victim of totalitarian influences," Fulgencio Batista was invited to Washington where Roosevelt, Hull and others lavished attention on him. There the Cuban strong-man promised to "cling to democratic principles."[15] When President Somoza of Nicaragua arrived in Washington in 1939, Roosevelt himself went to Union Station to greet the visiting dignitary, for whom a military parade was held. A year later, the red carpet was rolled out for General Trujillo, the Dominican despot, whose ventures included bribery, murder and graft. Although the President also welcomed democratic leaders to the White House, the *abrazos* tendered Batista, Somoza and Trujillo suggested that the United States government was allergic only to European and Asian totalitarianism, and Haya de la Torre barbed Roosevelt as "The Good Neighbor of tyrants." The truth was that the Axis dictators posed a menace to the United States; the strutting generals of the Hemisphere did not.

The Good Neighbor policy succeeded with flying colors in attaining its principal objective: the promotion of immediate United States economic and security interests. Despite several oil disputes and the renunciation of armed intervention to protect private firms, United States investors found manifold opportunities in Latin America. Moreover, reciprocal tariff reductions and Export-Import Bank credits stimulated North-South commerce. Vital raw materials flowed to the United States from Latin America following the outbreak of World War II.

At the same time, political advantages accrued to Washington in return for unequivocal abandonment of military intervention and liberalized trade policies. Whereas only eight Latin American nations declared war on the central powers in 1917–1919 and none dispatched troops to Europe, the situation would change radically during World War II.

Though it advanced United States interests to speak, temporarily at least, of the "equality of American states and multilateral policy-making," no institutions developed to achieve these goals. Decisions emanated from Washington, and Uncle Sam remained a Gulliver amid the Latin Lilliputians. Nor was attention focused on the internal problems besetting each hemispheric state—gross income inequities, feudalistic social structures, lopsided development, predatory militarism. While promoting American exports and security, good neighborism served to freeze the socio-economic, political status quo. Despite its immediate success, it is difficult to perceive enduring contributions of the policy to inter-American relations or to conditions in the hemispheric republics.

---

[11] *Ibid.,* p. 137.

[12] This legislation was required to overcome the prohibition set forth in the last paragraph of Article I, Section 9, of the U. S. Constitution, which reads:
"No Title of Nobility shall be granted by the United States: And no Person holding any Office of Profit or Trust under them, shall, without the Consent of the Congress, accept of any present, Emolument, Office, or Title, of any kind whatever, from any King, Prince, or foreign State."
See S. S. Jones and D. P. Myers, *Documents on Foreign Policy* (Boston: World Peace Foundation, 1939), p. 59.

[13] Edwin Lieuwen, *Arms and Politics in Latin America* (Rev. ed.; New York: Frederick A. Praeger, 1965), p. 191.

[14] Thomas A. Bailey, *A Diplomatic History of the American People* (7th ed.; New York: Appleton-Century Crofts, 1964), p. 753.

[15] Wood, *op. cit.,* p. 117.

ISOLATIONISM REVISITED

THOMAS G. PATERSON

Mr. Paterson is assistant professor of history at the University of Connecticut. He is now completing for publication next year three books on American foreign political and economic relations since the beginning of the cold war.

In his June speech at the Air Force Academy, President Nixon branded critics of his military and foreign policies "new isolationists," and suggested that they were turning their backs on the world. A few weeks before leaving office, Secretary of State Dean Rusk had similarly warned Americans away from a return to "isolationism." The Johnson administration had occasionally labeled as "isolationist" those foreign policy dissidents who asked for limited American commitments abroad and a retrenchment from empire. It is a label meant to discredit. It conjures up the specter of the 1930s, when the United States allegedly shirked international responsibility and thus unleashed mad dictators and Japanese imperialists. The label further summons the memory of America's rise to world eminence after World War II, throwing off its isolationism and assuming its rightful first rank in world affairs. Today, then, "isolationism" is a pejorative term connoting weakness, appeasement, surrender, mindless idealism and a retreat from the obligations of international leadership.

Scholars have also dealt critically with the noninterventionists of the 1930s, in part because most historians and political scientists today endorse internationalism and what they might call nonimperialist intervention. Historians have complained that the isolationists ignored the threat of totalitarianism, helped bring on World War II, left the United States militarily unprepared, even courted fascism, and in general nurtured a wrongheadedness which restrained America from influencing international events. Prof. Selig Adler has written that the "Congressional isolationists, so anxious to keep out of war, actually helped invite a foreign catastrophe of such immense proportions that no nation could have escaped its consequences." The eminent diplomatic historian Dexter Perkins has concluded that "time has placed their arguments in perspective, revealing that they were largely unsound."

But the isolationist movement was notably diverse. Nazis, Communists, pacifists, defeatists like Charles Lindbergh, "fortress America" types like Herbert Hoover, anti-Semites like Father Charles E. Coughlin, liberal reformers, thoughtful intellectuals—all adhered to it at one time or another. Because the isolationist America First Committee housed some unprogressive businessmen and because many isolationists, especially late in the 1930s, were opposed to the New Deal, isolationism has often been linked to conservatism, or at the extreme, with self-serving American proponents of German totalitarianism.

Historians have thus accurately found isolationists whom we cannot admire. It is also true that the isolationist Ludlow Amendment, which would have required a public referendum on all war decisions, was ill-advised. The isolationists sometimes imagined war plots and conspiracies. The isolationist or "revisionist" histories of World War I written by men like Charles Beard and Charles Tansill have been less than scholarly and too polemical. Above all else, the isolationists were wrong in the 1930s to believe that the United States could avoid any involvement in the developing crises in Europe through the Neutrality Acts, which prohibited America from punishing the aggressor. Their formula for American foreign policy did not fit the diplomacy of the depression thirties.

What scholars and politicians alike have obscured, however, is the long-term and constructive isolationist criticism of many facets of American foreign policy. Even in their failure the isolationists left an intelligent critique from which we can profit today. Those isolationists who were domestic liberal reformers especially deserve attention, for their assessment of foreign policy was the best articulated, the least rigid, and the most meaningful for the 1960s and the 1970s. Conservative isolationists did not dominate isolationism, and Prof. Manfred Jonas, in his excellent study of isolationism, has suggested that the historical treatment of the subject has been somewhat unbalanced and inaccurate: "To regard isolationism as pure obstructionism . . . is unfruitful and misleading." Such men as Sen. Gerald P. Nye, Norman Thomas, Charles Beard, John Bassett Moore and Sen. William Borah "did not approach American foreign policy from a purely negative and obstructionist viewpoint." Isolationism "was the considered response to foreign and domestic developments of a large, responsible, and respectable segment of the American people."

Indeed, unlike today, the term "isolationist" was not a label of reproach, and was respectably worn by many leading Americans, including perhaps even President Franklin D. Roosevelt for a time. Isolationism did not mean isolation. Most isolationists desired foreign trade, continued immigration and cultural exchange, and diplomatic intercourse with other nations. Senator Borah, for example, favored international action to promote dis-

From *The Nation*, September 1, 1969.

armament and in 1933 led the fight for American recognition of the Soviet Union. Nor was isolationism the phenomenon of one region, one political party, one ethnic group, or one socioeconomic rank. It was national, and had three basic strains of thought which attempted to answer the question, isolation from what?

The first strain was a profound abhorrence of war, a fear of war and militarism. Isolationists disliked not only the bloodshed of war and the utter waste of total mobilization but also the detrimental effects of war on domestic reform and civil liberties. The second ingredient of isolationism was nonintervention—that the United States should avoid interference in the affairs of other nations, should be selective in its foreign involvement, and disengage from empire. The third strain was unilateralism or independence. That is, the United States should preserve its freedom of choice in foreign relations by avoiding binding and restrictive alliances or commitments.

With these three core ideas, the isolationists dissected, studied and influenced American foreign policy in the 1930s. Their assessment showed them to be aware of some of the realities of world power politics and capable of compromise. We must credit many of them, too, with changing their minds in the last few years before American entry into World War II. Most important, the three ideas of freedom of action, nonintervention and abhorrence of war have a potent relevance for our views of American foreign relations today. Thus we should take another look at isolationism in the 1930s.

The isolationists were intense in their fear of war. The National Farmers Union in 1936 argued that "war is an utter negation of civilization. It is a relic of barbarism, regimenting mankind in organized murder, starvation, disease, and destruction. It is incompatible with every moral and Christian teaching." Writing in 1937, Congressman Louis Ludlow declared that the "science of slaughter has advanced with vast strides during the last twenty years. . . . The art of killing people en masse and maiming and wrecking human bodies has been perfected until it is impossible to imagine the next large-scale war being anything less than a vast carnival of death. . . ."

Many isolationists believed that the United States had been drawn unnecessarily into World War I, that civil liberties had been blatantly curtailed at home, and that in general the war was not the noble crusade President Woodrow Wilson said it was. Oswald Garrison Villard summed up the isolationist memory of World War I when he wrote in 1935 that "you cannot advance the welfare of the world by wholesale slaughter."

Every nation needs its internal critics—especially those countries which have had a long record of war and foreign interventions. The isolationists of the 1930s accepted measured appropriations for national defense, but they tried to twinge the American conscience to the horrors of war and the futility of military escalation. At times their thinking was wishful, and their ideas inapplicable to the trend of international affairs. But as Norman A. Zucker, biographer of George Norris, put it: "If, like Isaiah, he

longed for a civilization in which nation no longer warred against nation . . . he held a vision worth dreaming." And Prof. Arthur Ekrich, Jr., recently observed: "As some of the isolationists of the 1930s warned, the pursuit of power may seduce and corrupt even the most liberal and idealistic of statesmen and nations."

Isolationists with a commitment to reform were part of a tradition of opposition to intervention and war in favor of attention to domestic priorities. The anti-imperialists of the 1890s and the opponents of war in 1917-18 preceded them. The moderate Socialist leader Norman Thomas asked the question which troubled some Americans after World War I: "If we go into the [second] war, what will happen to the things we prize? What will happen to decency and tolerance, to morality and culture, to democracy and civil liberty . . . ?" Thomas agreed with Charles Beard and several Congressmen who suggested that America put its own house in order, to stand as an example to the world of social progress. Only a viable social democracy could combat the evils of fascism. Senator Nye called for "correcting our own ills . . . saving our own democracy rather than soliciting the trouble to come from any move to police and doctor the world."

Liberal isolationists emphasized the social problems created by the depression, and envisioned the death of the New Deal and a denial of civil liberties. William Henry Chamberlin argued that war would bring "universal regimentation, hysterical intolerance, and physical and intellectual goose-stepping." The most pessimistic of all, perhaps, was Stuart Chase, who saw "the liquidation of political democracy, of Congress, the Supreme Court, private enterprise, the banks, free press and free speech; the persecution of German-Americans and Irish-Americans, witch hunts, forced labor, fixed prices, rationing, astronomical debts, and the rest." Although Chase's forecast was obviously exaggerated, it is clear in 20th-century American history that war and intervention help to undermine domestic reform movements and create an atmosphere for the abridgment of civil liberties.

The isolationists could remember World War I very well. As Prof. William Shannon recently wrote: "No other American President ever left office with as poor a civil-liberties record as Woodrow Wilson." Norman Thomas remarked in 1938 that "the last war almost cost America what liberty she had." Then, too, the isolationists were experiencing the Un-American Activities Committee of Martin Dies, who condemned people for their ideas rather than for their actions. Nye, opposing conformity of thought, reminded Americans that there was a distinction between "unity" and "disloyalty."

The record of World War II demonstrated that the isolationist alarm was well founded. The removal of Japanese-American citizens to concentration camps in the deserts and swamps of America marred an otherwise fair Roosevelt record. The injustice, however, is too obvious and damaging for us to dismiss this episode as an aberration. And we should remember that World War II was followed by a Red scare initiated by the Truman administration's loyalty program and carried forth by

Joseph McCarthy. Today the eternal J. Edgar Hoover runs the FBI, the CIA functions as an almost independent and uncontrolled agency, the draft is used as a punishment, Thomas Dewey talks about abolishing the Fifth Amendment, the Attorney General supports wire tapping, war protesters are indicted for conspiracy, 41 per cent of the budget goes to the military and the cry is for law and order at any cost. It behooves us to read more closely what the isolationists said about the impact of war upon domestic America.

Believing in nonintervention, many isolationists catalogued the long history of American armed and subtle intervention in Latin America. In 1930, the United States had troops in Nicaragua and Haiti, and held protectorates over the Dominican Republic, Cuba and Panama. The anti-imperialist isolationists questioned official Washington's assertion that the United States was backing "democracy" in Latin America. At least twelve of the twenty Latin American nations were ruled in 1938 by dictators supported by Washington. "It would seem," concluded Beard, "that the rhetoric of democratic solidarity in this hemisphere does not get very far below the surface of things." Nye condemned the intervention of the Marines in Nicaragua in 1927 and their presence there until 1933 "to crucify a people . . . merely because Americans have gone there with dollars to invest and we have made it our policy to give whatever protection is possible to those dollars." Others complained that the Good Neighbor Policy was window dressing.

Isolationists also opposed unlimited arms sales abroad. Prof. John Wiltz, who has studied the isolationist Congressional investigating committee headed by Nye, noted that the committee "proved . . . that most munitions sales to Latin America, China, and the Near East depended upon bribery. . . . It established that munitions firms sometimes played one belligerent off against another. . . . The Committee exhibited documents which shocked many Americans into the realization that there was a difference between selling instruments of human destruction and selling sewing machines and automobiles." With the encouragement of isolationists, Roosevelt banned all arms shipments to Bolivia and Paraguay in the Chaco war. The isolationists may also have stimulated the partial American retrenchment from Latin America under Roosevelt. The questions of arms sales to Latin America and of armed intervention there are relevant today, and have been seriously studied by Sen. J. William Fulbright, among others.

In pointing out that the United States itself often acted like an imperialist, the isolationists also inspected quite closely the foreign relations of one of America's "natural allies," Great Britain. Believing that all nations act in self-interest, that no nation has a monopoly on virtue and morality, the isolationists asked Americans to stop applying an international double standard: one set of rules for themselves and the British and another for other nations. Robert Hutchins, the young chancellor of the University of Chicago, looked at the reality: "Mr.

Roosevelt tells us we are to save the democracies. The democracies are presumably England, China, Greece, and possibly Turkey. Turkey is a dictatorship. Greece is a dictatorship. China is a dictatorship." He went on: "And what do we do about countries which were victims of aggression before 1939? . . . What do we do about Hong Kong, the Malay States, the Dutch East Indies, French Indo-China, Africa, and above all, India?" Isolationists compared Italy's subjugation of Ethiopia to Britain's role in India.

In short, the isolationists condemned all imperialist nations, but unfortunately they often refused to make the choice of the lesser of two evils, as all men must, and thus did not focus their criticism entirely on the most brutal: Germany. What is important and lasting for us, even in this failure, is their cutting through the camouflage, rhetoric and clichés to define international relations in terms of power and self-interest. Today many Americans too have begun to ask for more precise use of words like "peace," "security," "democracy," "aggression."

The rhetoric of the American business community has preached that American businessmen have always served the national interest. Isolationists examined instances of business diplomacy in Latin America and protested the sale of arms to Japan and Germany in the 1930s. Such munitions businessmen were called "merchants of death," participating in "rotten commercialism" with an "inhumane, immoral, and un-Christian" behavior. This view was derived in part from the reform zeal of isolationists who wanted to abolish child labor, improve factory safety conditions, pass anti-trust legislation, curtail monopolies and the misuse of America's natural resources, and lift the living standards of the disadvantaged. They logically asked: If we are fighting big business at home, why help to extend its power overseas? Those parts of the Neutrality Acts which curtailed loans and arms shipments to belligerents, then, reflected parts of the reform movement of the 1930s. The Nye committee revealed much questionable activity on the part of American companies in international cartels, but did not prove the claim of some isolationists that American business drew the United States into World War I.

Senate investigations during World War II indicated that the isolationists had indeed been partially correct in their suspicions that some businesses were compromising the national interest for profit in the 1930s. The American business press was overwhelmingly anti-Fascist. But as Prof. Gabriel Kolko has demonstrated, twenty-six of the top 100 American corporations of 1937 were involved in significant cartel and contractual agreements with Nazi Germany. And fifty-six American companies were connected with the backbone of Hitler's war machine, the I. G. Farben Company. Standard Oil helped Germany develop both synthetic rubber and 100-octane aviation fuel. Bendix Aviation, controlled by General Motors, as late as 1940 provided a German company (Robert Bosch) with complete data on aircraft and diesel engine starters in return for royalties. As an official of the Dow Chemical Company boldly remarked in the 1930s: "We do not inquire into the uses of the products. We are interested in selling them." This attitude was made clear too by the businessmen who continued to ship scrap metal and oil to Italy, even though the President asked for a voluntary embargo in 1935. In fact, in the last three months of 1935, American oil shipments to Mussolini's Italy tripled. The isolationists were important watchdogs over American business. We have few watchdogs today, and have moved into the era of conglomerates, with some companies dependent upon military orders and contributing through lobbies to the world's arms race.

Some critics of the isolationists have incorrectly interpreted isolationism to mean friendliness toward fascism, or at least a condoning of fascism. The isolationist camp did attract Fascists, but they did not constitute the movement. Indeed, numerous liberal isolationists were early and vociferous in their denunciation of Hitlerism and the persecution of the Jews. Oswald Garrison Villard, for example, in 1933 and 1935 urged Western Europe to boycott Hitler's Germany and Mussolini's Italy, and in 1936 appealed to the League of Nations to act against Hitler. Villard became despondent, as did many isolationists, when the other European nations themselves would do nothing to contain the dictators. "The overwhelming majority of all isolationists," Jonas has written, "had no desire to see the Axis Powers gain their ends."

The Spanish Civil War was particularly agonizing for liberal isolationists, and the response of many of them suggests their flexibility and their opposition to fascism. How can one be committed to both peace and liberty? Many isolationists chose liberty, and encouraged the Roosevelt administration to aid the anti-Franco Loyalists. But to their dismay and surprise, the President and Secretary of State Cordell Hull performed like strict isolationists by imposing an arms embargo on Spain. Furthermore, Roosevelt followed the lead of the European nonintervention committee, which proved unworkable in the face of German, Italian and Russian intervention.

If some isolationists demonstrated that they would accept selective intervention, as in the Spanish Civil War, others later showed themselves capable of changing their minds over the question of aiding Britain against the rising Germany. Many liberals quit the isolationist ranks in 1939-41, leaving conservatives there, and thus contributing to the notion that conservatism and isolationism were linked. It should be stated, too, that the isolationists cannot be blamed for the coming of World War II. Germany did not depend upon American isolationism in making its plans. Britain and France let Germany nibble for a number of years, conceding to Fascist demands. Not until April of 1939 did France and Britain guarantee the independence of Poland. The League of Nations was moribund in the 1930s, its members unwilling to take decisive action. The Soviet Union was excluded from membership until 1934 and then ousted in 1939. Germany was admitted to the League in 1926 and departed in 1934. Both Japan and Italy withdrew in the mid-thirties. Britain was more interested in balance of power than collective security. As Robert A. Divine has suggested, European appeasers co-authored the American Neutrality Acts, because some Americans concluded that we had better steer clear of the chaos in Europe.

Scholars and politicians have distorted isolationism and confused a useful heritage. We cannot accept the notion of Fortress America; we reject strict unilateralism and the idea of a foreign policy conspiracy. But there is much value in the isolationist argument for freedom of action and limited commitments in foreign relations. This does not mean a rejection of international cooperation and the United Nations. It means simply independence and freedom of choice. Our alliance arrangements may drag us clumsily into wars. As someone has put it, we have constructed Pearl Harbors throughout the world. We cling to obsolete agreements like NATO which tie us to collapsing military alliances and impede East-West relations. We should give more attention, too, to the isolationist call for nonintervention and self-determination.

The isolationist critique is relevant to the senseless war in Vietnam which, among other detriments, has crippled a domestic reform movement. As America moves to the political right, the isolationist warning of war's effect on civil liberties is imposing. We might recall, too, that the isolationists worried about the growing and somewhat independent role of the President in foreign affairs. Today Congressmen are questioning the evolution of Presidential commitments in Vietnam without a declaration of war. The "National Commitments Resolution," introduced by Senators Fulbright and Gore, and recently passed by a 70-to-16 vote, expressed the Senate's desire for participation in national security questions.

In this day of global diplomacy and world-wide military skirmishes, we might reflect upon the isolationist critique of the 1930s and its significance to our problems. Surely many Americans share with the isolationists the fear (in the words of Prof. Warren Cohen) "that social democracy may die in the United States if it has to be fostered abroad by force rather than by precept."

Before Pearl Harbor

WALTER LaFEBER

Walter LaFeber is chairman of the history department at Cornell University. He is the author of *America, Russia and the Cold War* (New York: John Wiley, 1967); *John Quincy Adams and American Continental Empire* (Chicago: Quadrangle, 1965); and *The New Empire: An Interpretation of American Expansion, 1860–1898* (Ithaca: Cornell University Press, 1963).

FOR NEARLY a century before Pearl Harbor, Americans sought riches and empire in the Far East. The events of December 7, 1941, climaxed that quest, but did not signal the denouement. The momentum of history was too strong, and the United States resumed the quest after 1945 with increased power, better strategy and greater disasters. The present American dilemmas in Asia, and particularly the deadlocks in the relations between the United States and China, must be explained in the context of 125 years of Sino-American relations. The burdens which that history imposes will not be easily lifted. Not even a people so favored as the Americans can begin a new day in foreign policy by pretending that the obligations, prejudices and ambitions of the day before no longer matter.

In that sense, United States involvement with the Far East can be traced back well before the 1840's when the first Sino-American treaty (the Treaty of Wanghai, July 3, 1844) was formally signed. The term "Far East," indeed, is misleading, for Americans have always regarded China as an extension of their own drive west for empire. Frederick Jackson Turner wrote in the 1890's that the interest of his countrymen in the affairs of the western Pacific was not accidental, but was the natural outcome of their settlement of the western plains.

Until the 1840's, perhaps, the use of the European view that Asia lay to the east was of some relevance to United States thinking; thereafter several events reshaped that perception. California and Oregon were settled and brought within the Union, giving the United States direct access to the Pacific. A spirit of Manifest Destiny gripped the country, allowing empire-builders to justify the war with Mexico and the taking of the West Coast as only a part of an irresistible march across the continent to the Pacific and beyond. This spirit was evident in the accelerating industrial revolution that marked the decade

and created a business complex that would view China as the last and greatest of all markets. The spirit was also embodied in the American missionaries who were the products of the nation's drive for reform and sanctity in many areas of society (particularly, of course, in regard to slavery), and who, in the century which followed, led the penetration of China for American secular as well as spiritual interests.

Perhaps these changes were best symbolized by Asa Whitney, a hard-driving entrepreneur dedicated to the building of the transcontinental railroad in the 1840's. Whitney exemplified what historian Charles Vevier has labelled American Continentalism. This philosophy held that the great Mississippi Valley must be developed for two reasons. It would provide an area of production whose immense surpluses could be marketed abroad and thus suck wealth from around the world into the United States. It would also be a bridge between east and west, the vital link of a great highway which could carry the products of Europe, the eastern United States and the valley itself to Pacific ports and hence to the fabled markets of Asia. As Missouri Senator Thomas Hart Benton bragged, the legendary "road to Cathay" would be opened through the heartland of the United States. (It is not a coincidence that the Midwest has been the most vocal section in demanding the restoration of pre-1949 China.) The first formal diplomatic step occurred in 1844, when Commissioner Caleb Cushing negotiated the Treaty of Wanghai, with China guaranteeing United States ships entry into ports which the Chinese had opened to the British the year before.

THE COURSE OF EMPIRE

These and subsequent events must also be placed in another historical context. Since at least the seventeenth century, men have argued that the course of empire has moved historically from east to west. Americans seized upon this belief, using it to justify their hope that inevitably the New World would rise as the Old World declined, and using it also to justify their involvement in Asian affairs. For if power did move westward (and a superficial reading of history seemed to indicate that the imperial centers had moved from Asia Minor to Greece to Rome to Paris to London and then to the United States), then it followed that the western Pacific would be the next cockpit of international power. This moved such Americans as historian Brooks Adams (at the turn of the twentieth century) and founder of Time-Life Inc. Henry Luce (in 1941) to conclude that the American future depended largely

on the control or at least the westernization of the Orient and especially of China.

Perhaps no American statesman held this view more strongly than William Seward. He was one of the leading Whig and Republican Senators in the 1850's, ending his public career as Secretary of State for Abraham Lincoln and for Andrew Johnson between 1861 and 1869. Seward wrote that he saw power moving east to west through precisely that nation whose foreign policies he would direct. A visit to the Seward home in Auburn, New York, is revealing for this reason. A visitor scanning the library is struck by the New Yorker's interest in British imperial events which, in the mid-nineteenth century, centered on India and China. The house also contains shelves of fine dishes and other mementos from Asia, many of which Seward obtained during his trips overseas. This was the atmosphere in which he lived.

His belief in the United States destiny in Asia became a reality when, in 1867, he negotiated the purchase of Alaska from Russia for $7.2 million. At the time this territory was called the "drawbridge to Asia," and certainly Seward viewed the triumph partially in that perspective. The following year he negotiated (with Anson Burlingame, former United States Minister to China and at that time the envoy of the Emperor of China) a treaty which enlarged United States commercial rights in China and allowed for the immigration of Chinese into the United States. Seward could look back at his accomplishments with considerable satisfaction. He had found Chinese markets for the burgeoning American industry, brought in cheap labor, removed the threat of an ambitious Russia operating on the North American continent, opened up new avenues to Asia, all this time, of course, helping Lincoln to preserve the Union, which in the future could profit from such diplomacy.

He made one further fundamental contribution to American policy. Until the 1860's, there was a question as to which diplomatic tactics would best accomplish the goals of American empire in the Far East. The choices had to be made from two sets of alternatives: the United States could cooperate with European powers in developing China or it could try to go it alone; and Americans could use force to obtain their objectives or could attempt to use non-military tactics which, hopefully, would set them apart from and above the European gunboat diplomats in the minds of Chinese officials. Seward chose to cooperate with the Europeans and to join them in their use of force, particularly in regard to affairs during the 1860's in Japan and Korea.

From *Current History*, August 1969. Copyright © Current History, Inc.

United States policies with China proceeded to move along the course which Seward had charted.[1] During the 32 years that followed the Alaska Purchase, the United States established an island chain which could be utilized by commerce or a fighting navy. Midway was obtained in 1867; then the magnificent harbor of Pago Pago in Samoa was acquired in 1878; Pearl Harbor was leased in 1887; and the entire Hawaiian chain was annexed in June, 1898. Hawaii became part of the United States during the three-month war with Spain in 1898. That conflict's primary result was the annexation of the Philippines in February, 1899. Absorbing the Philippines not only completed the island-chain of bases, but occurred within the context of an international power struggle over China. That struggle explains why the United States annexed the Philippines and opened the twentieth century by sending Marines to the mainland of China itself.

POWER STRUGGLE IN CHINA

With the defeat of China by Japan in a short struggle in 1894–1895, Japan emerged as a leading world power and the Chinese empire could finally be seen clearly as a crumbling shell. Germany, Russia, France and Great Britain entered a quick, dramatic race for supremacy in the vital market and raw material regions in and around China, threatening to lop off parts of China and close those sections to other nations, so that the victors could enjoy undisturbed exploitation of Chinese raw materials and markets.

The administration of William McKinley realized that these European policies threatened the traditional United States policy of keeping China whole and open to all powers. Americans had just endured the terrible economic depression and social instability of the 1890's, and key businessmen and public officials believed that the Chinese market was essential for long-term American prosperity. With its new industrial prowess, moreover, the United States could easily compete 'for markets in China with other powers as long as there was a "fair field and no favor," as Secretary of State John Hay phrased it. The United States wanted no part of a colonial scramble on the Asian mainland.

On September 6, 1899, Secretary Hay formally declared the Open Door policy when he asked Great Britain, Germany and Russia (and, shortly afterwards, France, Japan and Italy) to agree that in any European sphere of interest which already existed in China, equality would be guaranteed to all in the application of harbor and railroad levies and, further, that the Chinese government should be recognized as the legitimate collector of

tariffs within the government's realm.

Ten months later, Hay and McKinley confronted an anti-Western uprising in China led by a fanatical sect called Boxers. Officials in Washington correctly feared that European powers would use the rebellion as an excuse to send in troops to partition desirable parts of China. On July 3, 1900, Hay once again asked the other powers to agree to a formula which would pledge them to "preserve Chinese territorial and administrative entity" and "safeguard for the world the principle of equal and impartial trade with all parts of the Chinese Empire." On August 14, foreign troops—including United States Marines—landed to protect foreign legations, and attempted to restore order.

Seward's policies, modified by Hay and McKinley, faced grave tests from two sides. For the first time, the threat of Chinese revolution became real. The United States hurried to join the other powers in eradicating the Boxers and restabilizing parts of China, for only in a settled non-revolutionary China could the Open Door policy work. But the major powers were not united. Great Britain and Japan allied in 1902 to confront the growing Russian challenge to British control in India and Japanese interests in Manchuria and Korea. The United States favored the British and Japanese, in part because of a common hatred for and fear of the Czar's government, and also because Washington officials mistakenly assumed that Japan shared a long-run commitment to the Open Door and could be depended upon to beat off any Russian threats to the "fair field and no favor" principle. This assumed a relative balance of power between Japan and Russia. That premise was destroyed in 1905 when the Japanese defeated the Russians in a short conflict and set off the revolutionary events which would topple the Czar's regime 12 years later.

By 1907, the Japanese were the dominant power in Asia. The British empire acquiesced as Japan made a protectorate of Korea and began closing the door to Manchuria. No important American counseled the abandonment of China. The United States could either cooperate with the Japanese in Asia or attempt to contain Japan; the latter choice might ultimately mean using force to stop Tokyo from closing the door to China. Economic, missionary and international power considerations required a United States commitment. The already voluminous historical record that revealed the development of Sino-American ties could not be expunged.

The long love affair which many Americans believed they were having with China now became a three-way relationship and, as in most such love triangle situations, it could be guaranteed that at any given moment two of the participants could be counted on to hate the third. The only question was the circumstances that would dictate the pairing off.

WORLD WAR I

With the advent of World War I, the United States attempted to stand with China against Japan. Taking advantage of the European powers' determination to bleed one another thousands of miles from China, Japan conquered several German holdings on the Chinese periphery; then, in the fall and winter of 1914–1915, she attempted to put China under de facto Japanese control by handing Peking the Twenty-One Demands. These demands would have given Japan a large measure of control over Chinese police, financial and military policies and would also have given her large economic concessions.

President Woodrow Wilson's administration, after some initial and nearly fatal fumblings, vigorously protested the Japanese policy, but it was British pressure that finally forced Japan to retreat. Two years later, when the United States entered World War I, British power had greatly diminished. With American attention riveted on France, Japan was without a real power check in the Far East. In the autumn of 1917, however, the United States and Japan agreed (in the Lansing-Ishii Notes) that "Japan has special interests in China, particularly in the part to which her possessions are contiguous." In return, the Japanese promised, in a secret protocol to the agreements, that they would not take advantage of the European conflict to make new demands upon China.

The Lansing-Ishii Notes heralded a 15-year period of United States-Japanese cooperation on the problem of handling China. Differences did appear, particularly when the Japanese insisted at the Paris Peace Conference that they must retain the former German possession of Shantung, which the Chinese claimed as part of their own ancient empire. The Japanese position particularly compromised President Wilson's widely publicized policy of self-determination, and the President's failure to force Japan to return Shantung in 1919 was one reason why the United States Senate then rejected the Wilsonian settlement. The Shantung question, however, paled in significance in the light of the Russian Revolution of 1917 and the May, 1919, revolutionary movement in China itself.

Those two upheavals led the officials in Tokyo and Washington to formulate common policies to deal with China. The keynote was sounded at the Washington Naval Conference of 1921–1922. This conference laid down the guidelines which United States policy-makers, Republicans and Democrats alike, would follow throughout the entire interwar period. It also raised important questions about the so-called "isolationist" policy of the Republicans. The conference not only produced a political agreement which the United States happily signed, but created an international power alignment which the United States pledged to uphold.

The Americans scored first with the Four-Power Pact, in which the United States, Japan, France and Great Britain agreed to respect each other's rights in the Pacific and to refer disputes to a joint conference. This agreement ended the 19-year-old Anglo-Japanese alliance, thereby freeing Washington officials from the fear that in any future disputes they would have to face a formally allied British-Japanese coalition. The next victory was the Five-Power Treaty, signed February 6, 1922, by the United States, Great Britain, Japan, France, and Italy, which established a capital ship ratio of 5–5–3–1.75–1.75 among the powers. The first three nations also agreed not to construct new naval bases or fortifications west of Hawaii, north of Singapore, or south of Japan.

United States naval officers bitterly fought this agreement, for they understood that Japan would emerge as the paramount naval power in the western Pacific. Their complaints made little headway, and Secretary of State Charles Evans Hughes apparently systematically excluded military officers from any important role at the conference. Hughes was willing to accept what the Five-Power agreement implied: a tripartite division of the world, with Japan dominant in the western Pacific, the United States paramount in the Western Hemisphere, and the three victorious European powers controlling Europe. Together, the five powers would stabilize world affairs, that is, contain revolutions and make the world safe for their own methods of international development.

For China, the meaning of this pact became clear in the formulation of the Nine-Power Treaty at Washington. Signed by the five major powers plus Belgium, Portugal, China and the Netherlands, this document became the only formal, specific affirmation of the Open Door policy ever agreed upon by these major powers. The signatories agreed to respect the

sovereignty, the independence, and the territorial and administrative integrity of China, [and] to use their influence for the purpose of effectually establishing and maintaining the principle of equal opportunity for the commerce and industry of all nations throughout the territory of China.

When the Chinese delegation attempted to regain for China some control over her own tariffs and also over foreigners within China, the other powers, led by the United States, refused.

At Washington, the United States agreed to give Japan naval control of the western Pacific in return for Japan's promise to maintain the Open Door in China. Two assumptions of this agreement are crucial in understanding the 20 years between the conference and Pearl Harbor. First, both powers feared the revolution which was picking up speed in China, but they believed that they could return to the pre-Boxer China by treating the

Chinese in the traditional manner. China was viewed as passive; she was the bone in the middle, as Secretary of the Treasury Henry Morgenthau aptly characterized China a decade later. Second, the United States assumed that with the Nine-Power agreement signed and sealed, Japan could be depended upon to cooperate with and protect the historic United States interests in China. Or as a young, aspiring New York politician, Franklin D. Roosevelt, phrased the policy in the early 1920's, the United States and Japan would march shoulder to shoulder in developing Asia.

REVOLUTION IN CHINA

Both assumptions were wrecked within 10 years. By 1924, the Russian Bolshevik government was committed to aiding the Chinese revolutionaries. The Chinese needed little help. The success of their revolution was marked by intense anti-foreign outbreaks, particularly against missionaries, between 1925 and 1927. In 1927, Chiang Kai-shek emerged as the dominant figure within the Nationalist organization, broke with Russia, and drove the Chinese Communists out of the movement. The United States reaction to Chiang's triumph was confused and inconsistent, shaped no doubt by the chaos within China herself.

By 1930, President Herbert Hoover and Secretary of State Henry Stimson mistrusted the Chinese and preferred to cooperate with Japan to keep China open and as stable as possible. At the London Naval Conference of 1930, the United States agreed to grant the Japanese request for complete parity in submarines and an improved position in destroyers and cruisers. The basic assumption, that Japan could be depended upon by the United States, still prevailed. Indeed, in the context of the revolutions in Russia and China, Americans wanted to believe this more than ever before.

Consequently when the Japanese invaded Manchuria in September, 1931, the United States reaction was less than inspired. The invasion had been triggered by an explosion along the track of the Chinese Eastern Railway near Mukden where the Japanese were in control. Toyko claimed that the rails had been blown up by Chinese soldiers. With this explanation, the Japanese interpreted the incident as another anti-foreign outbreak and thereby played neatly to the fears of Stimson and Hoover—fears that unless they were brought under control the Chinese Nationalists would succeed in driving out all foreign interests from China. Indeed, in 1929, when a similar incident developed between the Russians and the Chinese, Stimson had supported the Russians (although the United States did not recognize that the Moscow government existed officially) because of his fear that to do otherwise would encourage the Chinese to undertake further actions

against foreign interests.

Trapped between this traditional fear and the growing realization that Japan was carrying out a systematic policy aimed at conquering the whole of Manchuria, Hoover and Stimson hesitated. As the President commented in one conversation with members of his Cabinet, he sympathized with the Japanese because they were confronted with a Bolshevik Russia on one flank and the possibility of a Bolshevik China on the other flank.

As the Japanese attack spread in January and February, 1932, Stimson pressed for counteraction. The President blocked any use of military or economic coercion. The use of such force might temporarily slow up the Japanese, but it would surely be double-edged, for it would declare bankrupt the assumption of United States policy which had guided American diplomats in Asian affairs since 1921 and, moreover, it could lead to war with Japan. Stimson consequently settled for an announcement on January 7, 1932, that the United States would not recognize any

situation or any treaty or agreement entered into between [Japan and China] which may impair the treaty rights of the United States or its citizens in China, including those which relate to the sovereignty, the independence, or the territorial and administrative integrity of the Republic of China, or to the international policy relative to China, commonly known as the open-door policy.

A month later this "non-recognition doctrine" was coupled with another policy, which was announced in a letter from Stimson to Senate leader William Borah. Stimson warned that the Washington Conference treaties were interrelated; that is, if Japan violated the Open Door provisions of the Nine-Power treaty, the United States would be free of the restrictions written into the naval arrangements of the Five-Power Pact.

THE POLICY OF THE 1930's

This warning had little effect, but it delineated the choice which confronted Franklin D. Roosevelt during the next nine years. In 1934, Roosevelt began a major naval building program and endorsed various kinds of economic and military aid to China. This approach contained too little and was put into effect too late. On July 7, 1937, a major conflict again broke out between Japan and China. At the Brussels Conference in November, the United States rejected Soviet suggestions that Russian-American political cooperation was needed to contain the Japanese. Again, the United States response was historically consistent: when Washington-Moscow relations were formally restored in November, 1933, the United States had refused a Soviet request for a non-aggression agreement that would indicate to the Japanese a common Russian-American concern for peace and stability in the Far East.

In 1939 and 1940, the United States used economic sanctions against Japan. It terminated the commercial treaty of 1911, imposed an embargo on exports of scrap iron and oil and, in July, 1941, froze all Japanese assets in the United States. By this time, however, these moves only sharpened the Japanese feeling that an economic sphere in Asia was necessary if Japan hoped to remain economically viable and politically stable. Japan was no longer willing to compete within an Open Door policy in order to retain such viability.

The United States policy also played into the hands of the militarists in Tokyo who were willing to use force to obtain new areas for markets, vital raw materials and the settlement of Japanese emigrants. In July, 1941, Japan completed a rapid conquest of French Indochina. In United States-Japanese negotiations which continued

through November, Tokyo agreed under certain conditions to evacuate Indochina, but refused to listen to United States demands for the abandonment of the campaign against China. To the Japanese, this was a matter to be settled between China and Japan; Tokyo would not allow United States mediation.

The tragedy that followed at Pearl Harbor can be traced back at least to the Washington Conference arrangements. The United States had had other alternatives. It could have worked with an independent, revolutionary China; cooperated with Soviet Russia as a check against Japan; built a navy which could have offset Tokyo's military supremacy in the western Pacific; or viewed United States interests in China as of too little significance to take the risks involved in keep-

ing the doors open to the Chinese market.

To understand why none of these alternatives were followed, however, the story must be taken back yet further. In 1900, the United States had committed itself to the Open Door publicly because the McKinley administration believed the Chinese consumer to be essential to United States well-being. In the 1840's, Americans had formally entered the Asian scene because of a sense of their destiny and, above all, of their needs—both secular and spiritual. The United States involvement in China was neither sudden nor accidental, nor is the current American abhorrence of the Chinese revolution. The historical record helps to explain United States involvement in Asia and continues to play an important role in shaping the American distaste for the Chinese revolution.

FDR: The Untold Story of His Last Year

Was Franklin D. Roosevelt really as sick and incompetent during his last months in office as his critics allege? This week, on the twenty-fifth anniversary of FDR's death, a distinguished historian re-examines the old charge in the light of new evidence.

JAMES MacGREGOR BURNS

JAMES MacGREGOR BURNS is Woodrow Wilson professor of government at Williams College and author of *Roosevelt: The Lion and the Fox* and many other works.

Late in March 1944, a young cardiologist at the United States Naval Hospital in Bethesda, Lt. Comdr. Howard G. Bruenn, had an emergency summons from his superiors. He was requested to conduct a heart examination the next day; his patient would be the President of the United States. The young Navy doctor was called in so hurriedly that he had no time to look over Franklin D. Roosevelt's medical records before greeting his eminent patient. He soon felt at ease, however, when the President came rolling down the corridor in his wheelchair, wisecracking with an old friend and waving genially to the nurses and patients who clustered in the hallways and peeked around corners. As the President was lifted to the examining table, he seemed to Dr. Bruenn neither disturbed by having to

undergo examination nor annoyed by it—indeed, not especially interested.

Little could the young doctor know that he was about to examine a medical case that would become a political issue in later years. As the cold war deepened after World War II, it was charged that Roosevelt was too ill during his final year to carry the burden of the wartime Presidency; that he could not make tough strategic decisions; that he was, in Ambassador Patrick Hurley's words, "already a sick man at Yalta." Until now, the truth has been elusive. At Eleanor Roosevelt's request, there was no autopsy of the President; the official medical records disappeared; and the President's physicians, including Bruenn, chose not to publish their own recollections and records. This month, however, Bruenn is furnishing a full medical report on President Roosevelt's last year in the *Annals of Internal Medicine* (April 1970). How does the old allegation about the sick, incompetent President

stand up in the light of what Bruenn discloses?

It was with mounting surprise and shock, Bruenn recently told me, that he had taken the President's blood pressure that day in March 1944; he also studied his lungs and heart, read the electrocardiogram, fluoroscopy, and X-rays, and checked the earlier records. The Commander-in-Chief was clearly an ill man. Not only was he tired and gray, slightly feverish, somewhat breathless, and coughing frequently—evidently suffering from bronchitis—but his basic condition was serious. His heart, Bruenn found, while regular in rhythm, was enlarged. At the apex, he found a blowing systolic murmur. The second aortic sound was loud and booming. Blood pressure was 186/108, compared with 136/78 in mid-1935, 162/98 two years later, and 188/105 in early 1941. Since 1941, there had been significant increase in the size of the cardiac shadow. The enlargement of the heart was evidently caused by a dilated and

FDR with Churchill and Stalin at Yalta—"Roosevelt the idealist as well as Roosevelt the Machiavellian must be brought back before the bar of history."

tortuous aorta; furthermore, the pulmonary vessels were engorged.

Bruenn's diagnosis was alarming: hypertension, hypertensive heart disease, cardiac failure.

It is not clear, though, as to just who was alarmed. Bruenn reported his findings to the Surgeon General, Adm. Ross T. McIntire, an ear, nose, and throat specialist, who was also the President's old friend and physician. Roosevelt's condition had been wholly unsuspected up to that time. Emergency conferences were now held among Admiral McIntire, Bruenn, and a half-dozen other specialists and consultants. It was evident that the President had to be put on a regimen, but how much could a President—especially *this* President —be expected to follow the ordinary heart patient's routine? One or two weeks of nursing care were suggested but rejected because of the demands on the office; the invasion of Normandy, for one thing, was only two months off. Bruenn urged that the President at least be digitalized; there was some resistance, but the young Navy officer insisted that, if that were not done, he could take no further re-

sponsibility for the case. The doctors finally agreed on a program: digitalis, less daily activity, fewer cigarettes, a one-hour rest after meals, a quiet dinner in the White House quarters, at least ten hours' sleep, no swimming in the pool, a diet of 2,600 calories moderately low in fat, and mild laxatives to avoid straining.

The crucial question during these worrisome days was who should tell the President about his condition, and how candidly. It was soon clear that Roosevelt would not raise the question himself; he did not seem curious as to why he had been examined or prescribed a new regimen. He simply followed the doctors' recommendations to the extent he could and let the matter rest there. Bruenn, a junior officer, did not feel it his right or duty to inform the President. Evidently, everyone assumed that McIntire had the responsibility and would exercise it, but there is no evidence that he did. Perhaps he lacked confidence in his own effectiveness in passing on such portentous findings to his chief, especially if he should be asked difficult

questions. Perhaps he sensed that the President would neither accept the significance of the findings nor act on them—that in a fundamental sense the President did not want to know. Perhaps he realized how fatalistic the President was, or perhaps he realized that no matter how well grounded the findings, there was a heavy psychological and political element in the situation, and that a President—especially one with Roosevelt's fortitude and self-confidence—could not be advised as authoritatively as the ordinary patient. Or perhaps, after all his optimistic reports on the President in the past, he was simply too timid.

Conceivably, he *did* tell the President, but that probably would not have made much difference. For a quarter of a century Roosevelt's health had been a personal and political issue; meantime he had become one of the most active and effective political leaders of his era. He had an enormous self-confidence in his ability to carry on, to win out. With the doctors' help, he might have reasoned, he would overcome this health problem just as he had the effects of polio. In any event, as a soldier, he would not quit while the war was still being waged.

On the face of it, Bruenn's findings would seem to support the charge that Roosevelt was an ill man at Yalta, and, indeed, during the last year or two of his life. Paradoxically, Bruenn's disclosures—which are as full and authoritative as anything we are likely to have on the matter—will force us to revise most interpretations of the significance of Roosevelt's medical condition during his final year.

For Bruenn's records indicate that during the last year the digitalis and the other ministrations seemed to work. To be sure, the President did have one heart attack—in the middle of a speech he was making at Bremerton upon return from his Pacific trip in August 1944—but he was able to finish the speech. He looked gaunt and haggard in that last year, but this was in large part because he wanted to carry out the doctors' recommendation that he lose weight. He conducted a brilliant re-election campaign against Governor Thomas E. Dewey; his "my dog Fala" speech was a virtuoso performance. If he erred later in the year in withdrawing Gen. Joseph Stilwell from China, it was not because Roosevelt lost contact with the Chinese tragedy; he was in close touch with the principals. He carefully laid the ground for American—and Soviet—acceptance of the new United Nations organization. His death on April 12, 1945, was not directly from a heart attack, but from a cerebral hemorrhage.

The crucial test of Roosevelt's last year, and of his health, was Yalta, where the great strategic questions of World War II converged. Bruenn's long-delayed report should effectively remove Roosevelt's health as a major historical factor. To be sure, the President's health was probably not good enough that last year to have enabled him to conduct a sweeping alteration of his foreign policy—for example, to shift to a hard-line strategy toward Moscow. But such a shift was virtually out of the question anyway; Roosevelt had made his commitment to a coalition strategy with Russia, and he was going to see it through, at least as long as the war lasted. In most respects, his final year was a culmination of the decisions reached earlier in the war, especially at Teheran.

But to remove Roosevelt's health as an issue in history is not to remove the historical issue. On the contrary, it is to sharpen the charge made by Roosevelt's critics after Yalta and ever since, the charge that in his last year in office Roosevelt knowingly sold his country out in a series of Munich-type appeasements of the Soviet Union. Most of the American official records are now open on this period. What today, a quarter of a century later, with all the advantages—and the humility—of hindsight, can we say about Roosevelt's decisions during that last year, especially at Yalta?

The two great assumptions made by Roosevelt's critics are that he was blind to the real history and nature of Soviet communism and hence was willing to trust it, and that as the commander of the greatest aggregation of balanced military power in history he was in a position to exact major concessions from Moscow about postwar arrangements but failed to do so.

The first assumption is not well founded. One cannot study Roosevelt's whole political and personal development without crediting him with the most realistic apperception of the ambitions and realpolitik of rival leaders and their constituencies. This was the man, after all, who had vanquished his domestic opponents, had early recognized the nature of Nazism, and had conducted a kind of cold war against the Soviet Union itself (largely because of its war on Finland) during the months before the German attack on Russia in June 1941. Roosevelt had few illusions about Soviet communism as it was. He was not totally defeatist, however, about Soviet foreign policy—as it might be. Since we still harbor some hope in the matter twenty-five years later (and about our own foreign policy, too), it would hardly seem unpatriotic for Roosevelt to have tried to make postwar arrangements that might serve to undergird a continued Anglo-American-Soviet coalition.

The second assumption compels us to look at Roosevelt's main decisions about postwar arrangements—decisions shaped throughout the war, but formalized at Yalta. The question is: Did Roosevelt have the bargaining power to compel Russia to make greater concessions to the Anglo-American position than it did?

The cardinal issue during Roosevelt's last year was Poland. In fact, by 1945, Stalin had both moral and military control of the situation. By the time of Yalta, the Red Army had overrun Poland, after having suffered frightful losses. Stalin had possession of the real estate. It was understood, of course, that questions such as the shape and future government of Poland would be decided by the Big Three, but morally that expectation rested on the assumption that the Allies jointly had regained Poland—that they had fully shared in the sacrifices of the anti-Hitler effort. And of course they had not. From Stalin's point of view, the British and Americans were in no position to claim a share of the diplomatic spoils of Poland.

The issue cuts much deeper. For three solid years, Stalin had pleaded with Roosevelt and Churchill for a major cross-Channel invasion of France, in order to take the Nazis' pressure off his troops. For three long years, Roosevelt and Churchill had responded with promises. The cross-Channel invasion of June 1944 had come too late, from Moscow's standpoint, to make much difference in eastern Europe. The Red Army had had to go it alone. Far from getting major military aid from the Allies, Stalin contended, he had had to bail them out in the Battle of the Bulge.

At Yalta, Roosevelt was under no illusion about prospects for Poland. It had long been agreed by the Big Three that the war-racked nation would be picked up like a carpetbag and set down a few hundred miles to the west, satisfying Russia's appetite, penalizing Germany's, and taming Poland's. The cardinal issue was: Who would govern Poland, the Lublin Poles, a communist-dominated group nurtured by Moscow, or a genuine coalition of Lublin Poles and "London Poles," the non-communist leadership long sponsored by Churchill? A few weeks before Yalta, the Soviets recognized the Lublin Poles in the face of Roosevelt's and Churchill's urgent pleas for delay. Roosevelt decided to be relatively flexible at Yalta about Poland's new borders—which in any event had been essentially determined by the Red Army's advance, by understandings at Teheran, and by the position of Britain's Lord Curzon a generation before—but to insist on a democratic, independent, and viable Polish government.

From the start, Stalin was absolutely obdurate on Poland. When Roosevelt led off the discussion by saying that he had "six or seven million Poles in the United States" and that "the Poles, like the Chinese, wanted to save face," the Marshal shot back, "Who will save face—the Poles in Poland or the émigré Poles?" When Churchill at his most eloquent reminded the Marshal that Britain had gone to war with Germany so that Poland would be free and independent and that "this had nearly cost us our life as a nation," the Marshal asked for an intermission—and then came back well primed. His remarks suggest the absolute stone wall Churchill and Roosevelt were up against at Yalta. Said Stalin:

"The Prime Minister has said that for Great Britain the question of Poland is a question of honor. For Russia, it is not only a question of honor but of security. . . . During the past thirty years, our German enemy has passed through this corridor twice. This is because Poland was weak. It is in the Russian interest as well as that of Poland that Poland be strong and powerful. . . .

"The Prime Minister thinks we should make a gesture of magnanimity. But I must remind you that the Curzon line was invented not by Russia but by foreigners. The Curzon line was made by Curzon, Clemenceau, and the Americans in 1918 and 1919. Russia was not invited and did not participate. . . ." Stalin was speaking with more and more heat. "Some want us to be less Russian than Curzon and Clemenceau. What will the Russians say at Moscow, and the Ukrainians? They will say that Stalin and Molotov are far less defenders of Russia than Curzon and Clemenceau.

"I cannot take such a position and return to Moscow."

By now Stalin was standing. He preferred that the war continue and let Poland get more land at the expense of Germany. As for the government, how could they set up a Polish government at Yalta without the participation of Poles, who were not there? "They all say that I am a dictator, but I have enough democratic feeling not to set up a Polish government without Poles." As a military man, he wanted peace and quiet in the wake of the Red Army. The Lublin government could maintain order, while the agents of the London government had already killed 212 Russian soldiers. The Red Army would support only the Lublin government, "and I cannot do otherwise. Such is the situation."

There was a pause, and Roosevelt suggested adjournment. During the next three days, he and Churchill and their aides waged a tough and concerted campaign to win concessions from Stalin on Polish independence. Roosevelt warned the Marshal that unless the Big Three could agree on Poland—which to the President meant not recognizing the Lublin regime—they would "lose the confidence of the world." Churchill warned that 150,000 Polish soldiers on the Italian and western fronts would feel betrayed.

The pressure on Roosevelt during this period was acute. He looked worse than ever; Churchill's physician wrote him off as a dying man. One evening, after an especially difficult discussion of Poland, the President's blood pressure for the first time showed *pulsus alternans*. Although his lungs and heart were good, Bruenn insisted on no visitors until noon and more rest. Within two days his appetite was excellent and the *pulsus alternans* had disappeared.

Step by step, Roosevelt and Churchill exacted paper concessions from the Russians: that the Lublin government be "reorganized on a broader democratic basis" with the inclusion of democratic leaders from within Poland and from without; that free and unfettered elections be held soon—perhaps within a month—on the basis of open suffrage and secret ballot; that émigré leaders could take part in them. What was really at stake, however, was not the general formula but how much opportunity London and Washington would have, in fact, to influence the reorganization of the government, and to monitor the conduct of the elections. Even on this score Stalin conceded that the American and British ambassadors to the Soviets could consult with Lublin and non-Lublin leaders in Moscow, but the specific arrangements for holding and policing the elections were left obscure.

"Mr. President," said Admiral Leahy when he saw the compromise formula, "this is so elastic that the Russians can stretch it all the way from Yalta to Washington without even technically breaking it."

"I know, Bill—I know it. But it's the best I can do for Poland at this time."

The best he could do. Roosevelt was not ill at Yalta, or befuddled, or weak, or unpatriotic. As a realist, he saw that he had reached the limit of his bargaining power. He simply did not hold the cards. He wanted far more from Stalin than Stalin wanted from him. This fact dominated settlement of the other crucial question at Yalta: the Far East.

Roosevelt had no illusions about what Stalin wanted in the Far East, for the Russians had long made this clear—chiefly the return of the Kuriles and southern Sakhalin to Russia; and special railroad and port concessions in Port Arthur, Dairen, and Harbin. The Russians had also made clear that they would enter the war against Japan some time after Germany was beaten. Some Americans naïvely wondered

whether Stalin would make good on this promise; actually, there had never been any question whether Stalin would be in on the Far Eastern kill. The American military was desperately anxious that the Soviets share the burden of the final conquest of Japan. It was expected to be very costly. One million Anglo-American casualties were forecast—and many more if the Russians did not come into the war on the continent.

But Stalin—and probably Roosevelt, too—knew that what was crucial was not the fact of Soviet participation but its timing and strength. And here Stalin was in the delicious situation of having Roosevelt and Churchill in just the position that they had had him for three long years. He could delay his Far East attack until London and Washington had suffered terrible losses in overcoming the home islands—and then he could march on the mainland against the collapsing Japanese forces there. In Europe, his allies had made the Red Army take the bloodbath; now he could let the Americans and British carry the burden of battle, and he could take his share of the spoils. It was Roosevelt's task at Yalta to induce Stalin to come into the Far Eastern war at a time that would be advantageous to the British and Americans, not just the Russians. This Stalin agreed to do —but for his price in territory and concessions.

Instead of "bribing" Russia to come into the Far Eastern war, why did Roosevelt not rely on the atom bomb to defeat Japan? Was this proof of his ebbing health? Actually, the President kept in close touch with the Manhattan Project; at the end of 1944, Secretary of War Henry L. Stimson had told him that the first bomb (but without previous full-scale testing) would be ready about August 1, 1945. There was little indication, however, that the A-bomb, even if operative, would be effective against the military situation the Allies most feared—millions of Japanese soldiers (and civilians) fanatically resisting in caves and entrenchments along hundreds of miles of Japan's coasts and mountain ranges.

So in the Far East as well as in Poland there was an imbalance between what Stalin was asking of Roosevelt and what Roosevelt wanted from Stalin. All the Marshal really sought was legitimacy for dominating territory most of which he had the military power to control anyway. A third issue at Yalta, the nature of the new United Nations organization, was another case of imbalance; Roosevelt wanted a Soviet commitment to the United States, and Stalin was playing cool. In general, Roosevelt did the best he could with the strategic resources he had.

But we cannot leave the matter there. Why was Roosevelt's bargaining position so poor? The answers to this question are multifold: the Soviets' stupendous counterattack against Hitler, the weaknesses of a coalition divided by history and ideology, and simple geography and military power. But if we ask to what extent Roosevelt was responsible for his own strategic plight during his last year, the answer lies in part in his brilliance as Commander-in-Chief as compared with his failures as grand strategist. As Commander-in-Chief he conserved the lives of American soldiers in Europe and made a deal with Stalin to conserve them in the Pacific; he presided over a series of stunning military victories after 1942; but he bought these military victories at a political price. That price was exacted at Yalta.

Yet we cannot leave the matter even there. Roosevelt was not a mere military opportunist or improviser. He had exalted political goals; few leaders in history have defined them with such eloquence and persistence. But he was a deeply divided man. His major failing was that he acted out the parts of both improviser and man of principle without always seeing the interrelation of the two. He was a practical man who proceeded now boldly, now cautiously, step by step toward immediate ends. He was also a dreamer and a sermonizer who spelled out lofty goals. He was both a Soldier of the Faith, battling with his warrior comrades for an ideology of peace and freedom, and a Prince of the State, protecting the interests of his nation in a threatening world. The fact that his faith was more a set of attitudes than a firmly grounded moral code, that it embraced hope verging on utopianism and sentiment bordering on sentimentality—all this made his credo evocative but also soft and pasty, so that it crumbled easily under the press of harsh political alternatives and strategic decisions.

For a quarter-century now, Roosevelt has been under attack for his lack of "realism" during that last year. Perhaps a new generation of scholars and students is coming along that will pay more attention to Roosevelt the idealist. Without question he acted in large part on the basis of faith rather than realpolitik. At the final banquet at Yalta, he spoke of the time in 1933 when Eleanor Roosevelt had gone to a country town to open a school and had found on a classroom wall there a map of the world with a large, empty, unnamed blank space for the Soviet Union. Roosevelt felt that great progress had been made since his recognition of the Soviet Union in 1933; he had faith that more progress would be made. He was trying always to lift people out of their narrow and short-sighted ways and attitudes, at the risk of being called a utopian, an appeaser, or a dupe.

He picked up Woodrow Wilson's fallen banner, fashioned new symbols and programs to realize old ideals of peace and democracy, overcame his enemies with sword and pen, and died in a final exhausting effort to build a world citadel of freedom. In a day when we are trying to find out where we went wrong, how we can find our way again, how we can re-establish a principled and even idealistic foreign policy—in this day Roosevelt the idealist as well as Roosevelt the Machiavellian must be brought back before the bar of history.

WHAT IF HIROSHIMA HAD NEVER HAPPENED?

Mayo Mohs

It is a hot August evening in Tokyo, just after nightfall, in the summer of 1945. Workers scurry home through darkened streets still littered with the charred rubble of the spring fire-bomb raids. The Cabinet sits late, pondering the accumulating evidence of Japan's almost certain defeat; but the diehards, led by War Minister Korechika Anami, want to fight to the last breath. Suddenly, air-raid sirens wail. In the sky, just short of the city, two Superfortresses wheel, and a single huge projectile drops through the dark toward the bay. A mile above the water, it detonates.

A blinding flash turns the night instantly, terrifyingly, into day. A pillar of fire roils up toward the sky. Windows shatter. A mighty wind whips the stunned onlookers peering upward from the streets, government buildings, the Imperial Palace. But there are few injuries, even fewer deaths. The blast, the Japanese people are told by a U.S. radio broadcast the next day, was a fearful new weapon, the atomic bomb. It had been deliberately triggered at a high altitude, offshore, to show them its power but spare them its hideous consequences. If they do not want the next Bomb on one of their cities, they must surrender within a week. Six days later, the Emperor himself breaks a Cabinet deadlock by declaring that Japan must submit.

T is one of mankind's many tragedies that the scenario is not true. The facts, so grimly and indelibly recorded a quarter-century ago this week, are quite different. Hiroshima, Aug. 6, 1945: a weapon called *Little Boy,* right on target; at least 68,000 dead. The actual number of dead may never be known; several estimates place it higher than 200,000 (*see* THE WORLD). Nagasaki, Aug. 9, 1945: a weapon called *Fat Man,* over a mile off target; at least 35,000 dead. In the face of such insistent horror, the question still haunts the mind: Was Hiroshima —and was Nagasaki—necessary?

Wishful thinking, and a good deal of armchair remorse, has compounded the question. So have the ironies of history. The Bomb was originally conceived as a counter to the threat of Hitler and the further threat that Nazi Germany might build it first. But it was not ready until after Germany had surrendered. Thus only by historical circumstance was the Bomb ever juxtaposed to an even bloodier alternative—the massive invasion of the Japanese mainland.

By the spring of 1945 the Japanese Empire was clearly sagging, blockaded from vital supplies, harassed daily by air, living precariously off a fast-decreasing cache of fuel and food. But the Japanese refused to surrender, and invasion seemed the only possible next step. A million American casualties were anticipated, including a half-million dead. Japanese casualties would certainly be in the millions.

Millions of dead and wounded on one hand. A single Bomb on the other, a Bomb that still had done nothing to justify three years of intensive work and a cost of more than $2 billion. Save one, spend the other. On the face of it, it was a simple choice. After all, even the Los Alamos laboratory chief himself, J. Robert Oppenheimer, had estimated that a reasonably sheltered population would suffer "only" 20,000 dead. Four times that number had died in a single night of fire raids in Tokyo. More B-29 incendiary raids might have caused havoc even greater than Hiroshima and Nagasaki.

At the end of May, six weeks before the critical test at Alamogordo, the Interim Committee, charged with advising the President on the Bomb and atomic energy, met in a two-day session. The committee —chaired by War Secretary Henry Stimson and including Scientists Vannevar Bush, Karl T. Compton and James B. Conant—recommended that the Bomb should be used against Japan as soon as possible. The objective, they also recommended, should be a "dual target," a military or industrial site surrounded by more lightly constructed buildings. The attack should come by surprise. The argument was that the U.S. must exhibit its new power spectacularly and decisively. "This deliberate, premeditated destruction," wrote Henry Stimson with sad conviction after the war, "was our least abhorrent choice. [It] put an end to the Japanese war. It stopped the fire raids, and the strangling blockade; it ended the ghastly specter of a clash of great land armies."

In reality, the choices were hardly so narrow. Admiral William D. Leahy, Chief of Staff, resolutely opposed invasion since Japan was "already thoroughly defeated." The Interim Committee itself was not fully convinced that the surprise bombing of a major target was the only way to use the Bomb: it asked its scientific panel to consider other alternatives. The panel ultimately endorsed the committee's decision, but others did not. From the Metallurgical Laboratory in Chicago, the cover name for the atomic research center there, came the outspoken Franck Report, formulated by Physicists James Franck and Leo Szilard and Chemist Eugene Rabinowitch. Dropping the atom bomb on Japan, the report suggested, might unleash a nuclear arms race and a period of international distrust that would far outweigh any temporary advantage the U.S. might gain.

The report was the beginning of a wave of dissent that spread among many scientists in the atomic laboratories and executives in the Government after the Alamogordo test on July 16 demonstrated what the Bomb could do. Some dissenters demanded that the enemy be warned; critics of this course objected that Allied prisoners might be placed in the target area. Still others proposed demonstrations of various kinds—perhaps before an international inspection group, or as Physicist Edward Teller seems to have suggested offhandedly, a highly visible burst right on the Emperor's front porch, in Tokyo Bay.

Convenient Pretext

Might such a demonstration have worked? Historians are divided. It is true that the one-two punch on Hiroshima and Nagasaki propelled the Japanese war party into an untenable position, gave the Emperor a convenient pretext for intervening in the crisis, and made it appear that the U.S. had Bombs to spare (in fact, there were no more immediately available). But the Nagasaki attack seems to have been lamentably premature. Hiroshima was 400 miles from Tokyo, far from the eyes of those who made national war policy. On the day *Fat Man* exploded, the Supreme Council was just getting the first fully detailed reports of damage at Hiroshima. Teller's pyrotechnical display over nighttime Tokyo, or a purely military raid on a nearby installation, might have made as much impression on the decision makers at little or no cost to civilian life.

It was not the twin bombings alone, moreover, that influenced the mode and speed of the Japanese surrender. Other factors were involved, some of them impossible to measure. The Russian entry into the war on Aug. 9 surely played a role, most importantly in convincing the Japanese that they could no longer expect mediation through Moscow. Failure of imagination on the U.S. side had prolonged the war. Old Japan hands like Joseph Grew had encouraged the U.S. to declare forthrightly that Japan could keep its Emperor, but his advice was heeded only in the final days of the war. Less reliance on the Bomb might well have produced more creative diplomacy, making a mere demonstration of the Bomb

PROTEST MARCH

HIROSHIMA

BOMB VICTIMS

more than enough to tip the balance.

If it had, and Japan had forthwith surrendered, how different would have been the shape and mood of the postwar world? The framers of the Franck Report argued that international control of nuclear armaments—such as later suggested in the Baruch Plan before the U.N. in 1946—would have been much easier to achieve, and the argument seems tenable. A humane precedent would have been set, and the U.S. would have established a standard of trustworthiness even among those who had no will to give it trust, just as later, with the Marshall Plan, it would earn a reputation for generosity even among the most cynical. The nation would be free of the guilt that has nagged at its conscience ever since.

Traumatic Terror

Most important, the new atomic generation might have grown up confident that man was the master rather than the victim of nuclear discoveries, seeing the power of the atom more as opportunity than threat —and making that opportunity flower. Quite probably Japan, for instance, freed of its traumatic terror of atomic energy, would have been among the pioneers in peaceful nuclear research. Instead, an entire generation of children, all around the globe, has reached adulthood with a constant sense of lurking terror that has all too often surfaced in nightmares, or more maturely, in peace demonstrations.

Perhaps more than many other wartime decisions, dropping the Bomb was a consciously moral decision, wrought mostly by good men, mostly for good reasons—or at least for such good reasons as can be perceived under the pressures of war. But the evidence argues that it was a mistake, simply a choice of a lesser evil over a greater one, not so much moral wisdom as moral despair. Historian Gabriel Kolko suggests a political deficiency, calling the use of the Bomb and reliance on Russian intervention "a triumph of conservatism and mechanism" in U.S. policy. Whether the failing be moral or political, however, it remains the same—a lack of imagination, an unwillingness to risk a new tactic even in a new situation.

Edward Teller, one of the inventors of the hydrogen bomb and a champion of thermonuclear deterrent, complains that atomic experience has made Americans Bomb-shy, afraid to consider any rational use of nuclear weapons—worse yet, so fatalistic about nuclear warfare that they cannot bring themselves to build an adequate civilian defense system. It is a questionable complaint; U.S. deaths in a massive nuclear exchange, even in a well-sheltered nation, could approach 40 million—an unfathomable catastrophe for any society. But, in another sense—a sense Teller undoubtedly does not intend—the fatalistic terror about nuclear warfare may indeed be a vice. Because the Bomb is so much more inhuman than conventional arms, we are hypnotized by it and tend to overlook the inhumanity of many lesser weapons, such as the napalm and cluster bombs used in Southeast Asia.

Revisionist historians have found the bombings of Hiroshima and Nagasaki sinister in another—and less persuasive—way. They see them not so much as the closing acts of the Pacific war but the opening acts of the cold war—intended primarily to impress Stalin. There was a time, indeed, Louis Halle observes in *The Cold War as History*, when the U.S. had an atomic monopoly and might theoretically have challenged Soviet expansion by interposing a threat of nuclear bombing. Stalin, of course, might have chosen to respond by dispatching the giant Red Army to overrun a then poorly defended Europe. But Halle suggests a broader pragmatism in American restraint: the U.S. could not and did not attempt any such nuclear blackmail because it might have threatened "the whole fabric of world order."

With or without the heritage of threat and distrust from Hiroshima and Nagasaki, a cold war of some kind seems to have been virtually unavoidable. In fact—and this is one of the few advantages of the Bomb's fatal use—it seems to have helped prevent the cold war from turning hot. Without Hiroshima's brutal demonstration of the Bomb's power, might not one or another of the contestants have been tempted to test it during a military action such as Korea? Perhaps on the U.N. forces streaming toward the Yalu, or the Chinese forces massed at that border river?

If such temptations have been resisted, it may be because Hiroshima and Nagasaki have assumed the proportions of myth—needed and useful myth. This fact does not justify the toll of dead and wounded, nor lay their ghosts in the national conscience. Yet it gives them meaning. Horrifying as the ghosts of those victims are, there is no comparable meaning in the 135,000 ghosts of Dresden, that totally vengeful, ultimately useless crime of conventional warfare. But Dresden was a massive effort, involving 2,750 bombers. The essential terror of the nuclear bomb is that it is so small, so sudden and so simple to deliver—with the touch of a button.

Two Thousand Hiroshimas

Given this myth, we now measure nuclear and thermonuclear weapons in Hiroshimas. "Thirty megatons" means nothing. Two thousand Hiroshimas—its ex-

plosive equivalent—does. We multiply mentally: the dead, the maimed, the burned, the merely (and mercifully) vaporized. The ever-growing sophistication of weapons appalls: a Bomb with the explosive force of *Little Boy* can now be conveniently carried in a bowling bag and left on a park bench. It is now a fortunate commonplace that nuclear war simply cannot be a rational instrument of international policy.

Once, the U.S. tried to make it so. The alternative was an invitation missed—an invitation to moral heroism and political imagination—and an opportunity forever lost. Yet tragic errors can be the beginnings of new maturity. It may be no coincidence that since Hiroshima and Nagasaki, Americans seem to have discerned a dimension of tragedy in their lives, have been more willing to admit their faults, more able to examine the darker side of their actions.

Nations are still invited by the Bomb to heroic virtue and creative politics, but now the stakes are higher, not 100,000 lives but perhaps as many as 100 million. Imagination may demand boldness and risk: such adventurous human gambles, perhaps, as graduated gestures of disarmament, to encourage the larger success of strategic arms limitation agreements and other rational attempts toward mutual reduction of terror among nuclear powers. Such options, for a free nation as for a free man, still remain open. Even with Hiroshima and Nagasaki burned forever in the memory, there persists the hope for new opportunities and fresh choices.

THE TRUMAN DOCTRINE

By 1947 Communist expansion had created a world crisis which was to lead to an entirely new United States foreign policy.

George Lewis

George Lewis is a Los Angeles editor, writer, and historian specializing in the Truman administration.

Official American behavior on the international scene continues to be based on interpretations of a philosophy born of crisis less than twenty-five years ago. To intelligently question contemporary policies it is necessary to understand the events and circumstances from which this philosophy

sprung. It may be that in the long run it is not a "new morality" questioning "decaying ideals," but rather the old American isolationism protesting a relatively new point of view.

This is the story of the development of that philosophy, of a changing world and one nation's adjustment to it.

From *Mankind*, February 1970. Reprinted from Mankind Magazine, copyright © 1970 by Mankind Publishing Co.

At ten o'clock Wednesday morning, February 27, 1947, eight of the most powerful members of the United States Congress gathered in the White House for a special meeting called by President Harry S. Truman. If these men, or the others who were there, felt any premonition of crisis or conflict, it was for good reason. A most real crisis did exist and it was to explain the situation that the President had hastily called the meeting. Conflict was present, too, for the leadership of both American political parties was there—one controlling the Legislative Branch of the government, the other commanding the Executive offices.

With the exception of the State Department representatives, Secretary of State George Marshall and Under-Secretary Dean Acheson, there were five Democrats and four Republicans present. Representative John Taber, a Republican from New York, had also been asked to attend, but he was unable to see the President until later in the day.

But the differences were deeper than just membership in opposing political parties. The newly seated Congress was, for the first time in sixteen years, controlled by the Republicans, and since the war was over, so was patriotic bipartisan unity. Already Speaker Joe Martin had announced a Republican program to cut Truman's budget by 8.5 billion dollars. This was the Eightieth Congress that was to fight Truman's programs so effectively that a year later, during his campaign for re-election, Truman was to brand it the "Do-nothing Congress."

Harry Truman understood the nature of this conflict, for there were two categories in which the President could be classified as an expert: politics and history. He had learned politics through experience and knew the American political system from the bottom (elected County Judge in 1922) to the top (Senator, Vice President, and President). Nine years in the Senate had given him an understanding of Congress that only a few Presidents ever had.

His understanding and knowledge of history is one facet of Truman that was (and still is to some degree) seldom recognized. He was well read in history and approached the subject as "solid instruction and wise teaching." He knew how to apply the lessons he had learned and he had an acute memory for historical fact. He was quite familiar with the story of another President during a post-war period, and of the defeat that Wilson had met at the hands of an unfriendly Congress. "But I always kept in mind the lesson of Wilson's failure in 1920. I meant to have legislative co-operation," he later said.

So, combining both his knowledge of history and politics, Truman recognized the problem he had to face if he was to handle the current crisis in the way he wanted. Calling in the Congressional leaders of both parties was the first political step in eliminating the problem of conflict.

The vital decision that I was about to make was complicated by the fact that Congress was no longer controlled by the Democratic party. . . . It seemed desirable, therefore, to advise the congressional leadership as soon as possible of the gravity of the situation and of the nature of the decision which I had to make.

—Truman

The President began the meeting by reading a diplomatic note from the British government—a note which brought to a critical climax a problem that had been developing for some time: What to do about Russian aggression.

Since the end of World War II, Russia had completely ignored the provisions of the Yalta Declaration pertaining to free elections for the liberated European countries. Everywhere that there were Soviet troops communist puppet governments had been installed. So far, there had been little that the rest of the Allies could, or were willing, to do about it. The United States and Britain complained and objected, but within a year of the war's end all of the nations on Russia's European border had become part of a Communist Empire.

Then in March of 1946 the nature of Soviet expansionism changed. Russia began to put belligerent pressure on the governments of Greece, Turkey, and Iran. The difference was that these "were the first states beyond the confines of the Red Army to feel the resulting expansionist pressure of the Soviet Union." Iran came first.

Russian and British troops had occupied Iran since the early years of the war. Iran, Britain, and Russia formed the Tripartite Treaty of Alliance in 1942, which stated that all foreign troops would be withdrawn from Iran within six months after the end of hostilities. At the London Conference of Foreign Ministers in 1946 this withdrawal date was set for March 2, 1946. When the time limit was up the Soviet forces still remained. Charges and counter-charges were made in the United Nations, diplomatic notes were fired back and forth, and finally strong statements were made by London and Washington (indicating that both countries would use force to remove the Russians) before the Soviets pulled out.

Still Moscow wanted a foothold in the Middle East. Economically they needed the rich oil lands; politically and militarily, this was the pivot point—across this ancient land bridge lay Africa, Asia, and Southern Europe. The communist leaders, like the czars before them, turned on Greece and Turkey.

The pressure on Turkey was diplomatic and economic. In August of 1946 the Russians sent the Turks a note proposing joint control of the Dardanelles. "Joint control," of course, meant sending Russian soldiers into Turkey to "assist" in the defense of the Straits. "This was indeed an open bid to obtain control of Turkey," Truman later said.

The Turkish government turned to the United States for help. Truman called in his Secretaries of State, Navy, and War, and asked them for recommendations concerning the situation. Four days later they returned to the President with a recommendation for the strongest possible diplomatic and military measures. Truman had already reached the same decision based on his acute understanding of the problem and its historical significance.

*Truman agreed so readily with this drastic interpretation that General Eisenhower, sitting in as Army Chief of Staff, hesitantly and anxiously raised the question of whether the President fully understood and appreciated all the implications of his decision. Dean Acheson recalls that Truman took a well-worn map of the region from his desk drawer and, using it as a guide, delivered a ten minute dissertation of the historical significance of the Dardanelles and the eastern Mediterranean, "stretching from Tamerlane to the day before yesterday."—*Cabel Phillips in *The Truman Presidency.*

The following day, five days after Turkey had asked for help, Truman sent word to the Turks to hold their position and, in a very plainly stated diplomatic note, he told the Soviet Union: "It is the firm opinion of this government that Turkey should continue to be primarily responsible for the defense of the Straits. Should the Straits become the object of attack or threat of attack by an aggressor, the resulting situation would constitute a threat to international security and could clearly be a matter for action on the part of the Security Council of the United Nations."

This statement possibly had as much effect on the Soviet decision to withdraw her demands as did the fact that by the end of the month there was a U.S. Naval Task Force holding maneuvers off the coast of Turkey.

Soviet economic pressure con-tinued. By publicly maintaining a hostile attitude toward Turkey, Russia forced the financially troubled Turkish government to maintain a sizable army on the long Turkish–Russian border.

In Greece the Kremlin's pressure was not so subtle. During the German occupation, the Greek partisan underground had divided into two factions and were actually fighting each other before the Nazis were driven out. At the end of the war the Royalists, supported by the British, took control of the government, and the communist guerrillas fled to the hills. By 1947, however, the communist units, receiving support from Bulgaria, Albania, and Yugoslavia, had thrown the country into full civil war. By February of 1947 there was a constant flow of messages from Americans in Greece indicating that a complete communist takeover was likely at any time.

To complicate the Greek situation even more, the country was on the brink of complete economic collapse. In the two years since the end of the war Britain had sent $760 million in aid without being able to stabilize the economy.

Since the days of Queen Victoria, *Pax Britannica* had ruled the waves, and Mother England—the self-appointed world policeman—had managed to maintain a balance of power between nations. The United States stepped in to assist in 1917, but gladly "re-isolated" after the war. The end of the Second World War in 1945 also saw the beginning of an American trend to hand the job back to the British, but two costly wars had broken the Empire and by 1946 the English economy began to crumble. During that summer the British had informed the United States that they were going to have to cut back on their aid to Greece.

Then, nature took a hand. A severe blizzard struck, and snow and ice paralyzed the British Isles. Before she dug out, England lost an estimated $800 million in export production. The British economy could no longer support Greece and Turkey.

This was the situation up until three weeks before the White House meeting with the Congressional leaders. On February 3, the crisis began to swell, and it came on fast. The American Ambassador in Athens notified the State Department of a rumor that the British troops were going to pull out of Greece. The rest of the month rushed at the American State Department like a bad dream. They had anticipated a problem in the Middle East, but the crisis developed at a pace much faster than they had expected.

On February 12, Secretary of State Marshall brought me a dispatch from MacVeagh [American Ambassador to Greece] urging that we give immediate consideration to supplying aid to Greece. The British, the Ambassador reported, were not able to keep up even the little they were doing. On February 18, Mark Ethridge of the U.S. Investigating Commission cabled that all the signs pointed to an impending move by the communists to seize the country. On February 20, our embassy in London reported that the British Treasury was opposing any further aid to Greece because of the precarious financial condition in which Britain found herself. In the late afternoon on Friday, February 21, the British Ambassador asked to see General Marshall. —Truman

When the request from the British Ambassador, Lord Inverchapel, was received, Secretary Marshall had left Washington to deliver a speech at Princeton, and was not expected back until Monday. Inverchapel did not feel that the message could wait that long; he arranged for his First Secretary, H. M. Sichell, to meet with the State Department's Director of Near Eastern and African Affairs, Loy Henderson, that afternoon while he waited until Monday to see Marshall. The note was delivered and the crisis was at hand.

Harry Truman decided that the

United States should assume the responsibility of supporting the governments of Greece and Turkey. His decision was based on his foresight, born of the lessons of history, and his personal convictions, including most emphatically a high degree of personal courage.

The President's major problem on the morning of February 27 was how to get Congressional approval for his decision. To save Greece and Turkey would require money, and financial expenditures came only with the approval of the Congress. He had to win the support of men who were not only his political opponents, but whose basic philosophy—isolationism—was by its very nature a contradiction of the Truman position.

He explained to them the basic implications of the British note, and then told them what he was planning to do.

I explained to them the position in which the British note on Greece had placed us. The decision of the British Cabinet to withdraw from Greece had not yet been made public, and none of the legislators knew, therefore, how serious a crisis we were suddenly facing. I told the group that I had decided to extend aid to Greece and Turkey and that I hoped Congress would provide the means to make this aid timely and sufficient.—Truman

The immediate reaction of the Congressmen was one of shock. They found it hard to believe that England had reached the end of the line. The President then turned the meeting over to the Secretary of State, who went into the details of the situation. Marshall elaborated on the problem, stressing the economic factors, the need to keep the Greek government and army going, and the need to eliminate the poverty from which the communist rebellion sprang. He concluded by making it quite clear that the United States could act and save Greece, or do nothing and lose to the communists by default.

The Isolationists were tense, the Budget-Cutters stirred; was New Deal charity being expanded to support the whole world?

Under-Secretary Dean Acheson, who, because Marshall was preparing for the upcoming Moscow Conference, was leading the State Department work on the crisis, asked to make a few remarks and proceeded to explain why this question of Greece was a crisis of the first magnitude.

It was no longer a case of losing one more country to the Soviet Empire, but rather the possibility of losing the rest of the free world. He pointed out what was to become known as the "Falling Dominoes" theory: If Greece fell, all of Italy's eastern flank would be communist, and Italy had the highest number of communists of any of the free European states. A communist Italy on the border of France also constituted a dangerous threat. France had the second highest party membership in Europe. If France fell, then West Germany would virtually be surrounded. In the other direction, if Greece became communist it was to be expected that Turkey would follow in a matter of weeks. Through Turkey lay the Arab states, India and Africa. If that much of the world became communist, then the security of the United States itself would be threatened.

The Congressmen got the point. Truman noted, "... there was no voice of dissent ... " from the men who " ... had, not so long ago, been outspoken isolationists."

Senator Arthur Vandenberg, one of the "outspoken isolationists," said afterwards, "I sense enough of the facts to realize that the problem of Greece cannot be isolated by itself. On the contrary, it is probably symbolic of the worldwide ideological clash between Eastern communism and Western democracy; and it may easily be the thing which requires us to make some very fateful and far-reaching decisions."

On the way out of the White House, Vandenberg, realizing the problem Truman would have getting the money from Congress, turned to the President and suggested that he send a personal message to Congress and go before the people and "scare the hell out of the country." Thirteen days later, that is exactly what Harry Truman did.

By Thursday, when the Congressmen came to the White House, planning and advisory committees were already at work. They had to decide what kind of aid to send, and how much. The affirmative decision to send aid was the President's; their job was to expedite his policies. These men of the State Department approached their work with new zeal; for the first time, after months of playing by ear, they were finally working together, with a unity and sense of purpose that they had not had before.

At a Cabinet meeting the amount of initial aid was decided: $2.5 million for Greece and $1.5 million for Turkey. Officials at a policy meeting of the State, War, and Navy Departments suggested that the new policy be stated in terms of "assistance to free governments everywhere." Another meeting was held with the Congressional leaders. A long-range policy planning staff was set up for the State Department. And the speech writers were called in.

Clark Clifford, the future Secretary of Defense, was given the job of putting the new policy on paper. It was his task, along with the State Department's people, to write the speech that Truman would deliver to Congress.

The first rough ideas on how the policy should be stated met Truman's approval but not the first copy of the speech. He said that there were too many details in it so that it "sound[ed] like an investment prospectus." The speech was rewritten and the final draft given to the President. Again he went through it, making what changes he felt it needed. One of the most significant was in the basic policy statement. Where the State Department's copy suggested that this new policy "should" be adopted by the government, Truman changed the word to "must." As he explained it a short while later, "I wanted no hedging in this speech. This was America's answer . . . it had to be clear and free of hesitation or double talk."

There has been some question in later years about how much of the policy was actually the idea of Truman himself. All of it was. Clifford wrote his draft of the speech only after having the policy orally explained to him. Truman directed every step of the program. There is good evidence that this type of policy had been forming in the President's mind for some time before the crisis. In his State of the Union message two months before he had said, "We have made it . . . clear that we will not retreat to isolationism." He was tired of "babying the Russians." Six days before making the speech to Congress he told an audience at Baylor University in Texas, "Times have changed . . . Isolationism after two world wars, is a confession of mental and moral bankruptcy."

Isolationism, though still a dominant factor in the American philosophy, ended as a policy of the American government around two o'clock in the afternoon of March 12, 1947, when President Truman concluded his message to a joint session of the Congress. It did not slowly die out or just give up, but was struck between the eyes with a fatal blow by the President of the United States. In its final form the Truman Doctrine was stated so strongly that many foreign diplomats considered it to be dangerously close to a declaration of war.

Two weeks after receiving the British note, on Wednesday, March 12, 1947, Truman went before a joint session of the two Houses of Congress. He began to speak at one o'clock. His words came out in a monotone, but they contained the full measure of seriousness and urgency that the subject demanded. He was interrupted three times by applause. He told them of the problem in Greece, and then explained what the new American policy was to be. He came to the climax: " . . . it must be the policy of the United States to support free people who are resisting attempted subjugation by armed minorities or by outside pressure."

He then asked them to appropriate four million dollars in aid, and when he finished, all but one man rose to applaud the speech. (The member who remained seated was Congressman Vito Marcantonio, a socialist from New York.)

Critics and historians rated the speech as one of the most important in American history. Looking back, Truman said, "This was, I believe, the turning point in America's foreign policy. . . ." Indeed it was.

Truman committed the United States to the leadership of the free world because he thought it was his duty. His foresight probably forewarned of the potential serious consequences that would follow if the United States entered the realm of of big league diplomacy. Yet, as he told Congress that afternoon, "This is a serious course upon which we embark. I would not recommend it except that the alternative is much more serious."

The Congress, though in general agreement with the new policy, thought about it, debated, and investigated until April 22, when the Senate voted 67 to 23 in favor of it, and seventeen days later the House, with a vote of 287 to 107, passed Public Law No. 75. On May 22, 1947, in Kansas City, President Truman made it official with his signature.

But a policy is just a position, a philosophy, or an idea if it is not put into effect. A series of programs were begun to carry out the new philosophy. First, aid was sent to Greece and Turkey. Next, there was the Marshall Plan, which was followed by Point Four. Finally, the policy was established permanently by the "ultimate step"—military action in Korea. American foreign policy today, over two decades later, is still fundamentally constructed on the foundation of the Truman Doctrine.

All of the original steps were taken under the leadership of President Harry Truman. The politician and historian worked well together. The broad philosophy of the man of study and the shrewd moves of the professional politician were well incorporated in the President to produce a foresighted statesman.

THE NEW AMERICAN MILITARISM

Its roots are in the experience of World War II. The burgeoning military establishment and associated industries fuel it. Anti-Communism provides the climate which nurtures it. "It" is a "new American militarism." General Shoup, a hero of the Battle of Tarawa in 1943, who rose to become Commandant of the United States Marine Corps for four years until his retirement in December, 1963, doesn't like it. He has written this essay in collaboration with another retired Marine officer, Colonel James A. Donovan.

GENERAL DAVID M. SHOUP

AMERICA has become a militaristic and aggressive nation. Our massive and swift invasion of the Dominican Republic in 1965, concurrent with the rapid buildup of U.S. military power in Vietnam, constituted an impressive demonstration of America's readiness to execute military contingency plans and to seek military solutions to problems of political disorder and potential Communist threats in the areas of our interest.

This "military task force" type of diplomacy is in the tradition of our more primitive, pre-World War II "gunboat diplomacy," in which we landed small forces of Marines to protect American lives and property from the perils of native bandits and revolutionaries. In those days the U.S. Navy and its Marine landing forces were our chief means, short of war, for showing the flag, exercising American power, and protecting U.S. interests abroad. The Navy, enjoying the freedom of the seas, was a visible and effective representative of the nation's sovereign power. The Marines could be employed ashore "on such other duties as the President might direct" without congressional approval or a declaration of war. The U.S. Army was not then used so freely because it was rarely ready for expeditionary service without some degree of mobilization, and its use overseas normally required a declaration of emergency or war. Now, however, we have numerous contingency plans involving large joint Air Force-Army-Navy-Marine task forces to defend U.S. interests and to safeguard our allies wherever and whenever we suspect Communist aggression.

We maintain more than 1,517,000 Americans in uniform overseas in 119 countries. We have 8 treaties to help defend 48 nations if they ask us to—or if we choose to intervene in their affairs. We have an immense and expensive military establishment, fueled by a gigantic defense industry, and millions of proud, patriotic, and frequently bellicose and militaristic citizens. How did this militarist culture evolve? How did this militarism steer us into the tragic military and political morass of Vietnam?

Prior to World War II, American attitudes were typically isolationist, pacifist, and generally anti-military. The regular peacetime military establishment enjoyed small prestige and limited influence upon national affairs. The public knew little about the armed forces, and only a few thousand men were attracted to military service and careers. In 1940 there were but 428,000 officers and enlisted men in the Army and Navy. The scale of the war, and the world's power relationships which resulted, created the American military giant. Today the active armed forces contain over 3.4 million men and women, with an additional 1.6 million ready reserves and National Guardsmen.

America's vastly expanded world role after World War II hinged upon military power. The voice and views of the professional military people became increasingly prominent. During the postwar period, distinguished military leaders from the war years filled many top positions in government. Generals Marshall, Eisenhower, MacArthur, Taylor, Ridgeway, LeMay, and others were not only popular heroes but respected opinion-makers. It was a time of international readjustment; military minds offered the benefits of firm views and problem-solving experience to the management of the nation's affairs. Military procedures—including the general staff system, briefings, estimates of the situation, and the organizational and operational techniques of the highly schooled, confident military professionals—spread throughout American culture.

World War II had been a long war. Millions of young American men had matured, been educated, and gained rank and stature during their years in uniform. In spite of themselves, many returned to civilian life as indoctrinated, combat-experienced military professionals. They were veterans, and for better or worse would never be the same again. America will never be the same either. We are now a nation of veterans. To the 14.9 million veterans of World War II, Korea added another 5.7 million five years later, and ever since, the large peacetime military establishment has been training and releasing draftees, enlistees, and short-term reservists by the hundreds of thousands each year. In 1968 the total living veterans of U.S. military service numbered over 23 million, or about 20 percent of the adult population.

Today most middle-aged men, most business, government, civic, and professional leaders, have served some time in uniform. Whether they liked it or not, their military training and experience have affected them, for the creeds and attitudes of the armed forces are powerful medicine, and can become habit-forming. The military codes include all the virtues and beliefs used to motivate men of high principle: patriotism, duty and service to country, honor among fellowmen, courage in the face of danger, loyalty to organization and leaders, self-sacrifice for comrades, leadership, discipline, and physical fitness. For many veterans the military's efforts to train and indoctrinate them may well be the most impressive and influential experience they have ever had—especially so for the young and less educated.

In addition, each of the armed forces has its own special doctrinal beliefs and well-catalogued customs, traditions, rituals, and folklore upon which it strives to build a fiercely loyal military character and esprit de corps. All ranks are taught that their unit and their branch of the military service are the most elite, important, efficient, or effective in the military establishment. By believing in the superiority and importance of their own service they also provide themselves a degree of personal status, pride, and self-confidence.

As they get older, many veterans seem to romanticize and exaggerate their own military experience and loyalties. The policies, attitudes, and positions of the powerful veterans' organizations such as the American Legion, Veterans of Foreign Wars, and AMVETS, totaling over 4 million men, frequently reflect this pugnacious and chauvinistic tendency. Their memberships generally favor military solutions to world problems in the pattern of their own earlier experience, and often assert that their military service and sacrifice should be repeated by the younger generations.

CLOSELY related to the attitudes and influence of America's millions of veterans is the vast and powerful complex of the defense industries, which have been described in detail many times in the eight years since General Eisenhower first warned of the military-industrial power complex in his farewell address as President. The relationship between the defense industry and the military establishment is closer than many citizens realize. Together they form a powerful public opinion lobby. The several military service associations provide both a forum and a meeting ground for the military and its industries. The associations also provide each of the armed services with a means of fostering their respective roles, objectives, and propaganda.

Each of the four services has its own association, and there are also additional military function associations, for ordnance, management, defense industry, and defense transportation, to name some of the more prominent. The Air Force Association and the Association of the U.S. Army are the largest, best organized, and most effective of the service associations. The Navy League, typical of the "silent service" traditions, is not as well coordinated in its public relations efforts, and the small Marine Corps Association is not even in the same arena with the other contenders, the Marine Association's main activity being the publication of a semiofficial monthly magazine. Actually, the service associations' respective magazines, with an estimated combined circulation of over 270,000, are the primary medium serving the several associations' purposes.

Air Force and Space Digest, to cite one example, is the magazine of the Air Force Association and the unofficial mouthpiece of the U.S. Air Force doctrine, "party line," and propaganda. It frequently promotes Air Force policy that has been officially frustrated or suppressed within the Department of Defense. It beats the tub for strength through aerospace power, interprets diplomatic, strategic, and tactical problems in terms of air power, stresses the requirements for quantities of every type of aircraft, and frequently perpetuates the extravagant fictions about the effectiveness of bombing. This, of course, is well coordinated with and supported by the multibillion-dollar aerospace industry, which thrives upon the boundless desires of the Air Force. They reciprocate with lavish and expensive ads in every issue of *Air Force.* Over

96,000 members of the Air Force Association receive the magazine. Members include active, reserve, retired personnel, and veterans of the U.S. Air Force. Additional thousands of copies go to people engaged in the defense industry. The thick mixture of advertising, propaganda, and Air Force doctrine continuously repeated in this publication provides its readers and writers with a form of intellectual hypnosis, and they are prone to believe their own propaganda because they read it in *Air Force*.

The American people have also become more and more accustomed to militarism, to uniforms, to the cult of the gun, and to the violence of combat. Whole generations have been brought up on war news and wartime propaganda; the few years of peace since 1939 have seen a steady stream of war novels, war movies, comic strips, and television programs with war or military settings. To many Americans, military training, expeditionary service, and warfare are merely extensions of the entertainment and games of childhood. Even the weaponry and hardware they use at war are similar to the highly realistic toys of their youth. Soldiering loses appeal for some of the relatively few who experience the blood, terror, and filth of battle; for many, however, including far too many senior professional officers, war and combat are an exciting adventure, a competitive game, and an escape from the dull routines of peacetime.

It is this influential nucleus of aggressive, ambitious professional military leaders who are the root of America's evolving militarism. There are over 410,000 commissioned officers on active duty in the four armed services. Of these, well over half are junior ranking reserve officers on temporary active duty. Of the 150,000 or so regular career officers, only a portion are senior ranking colonels, generals, and admirals, but it is they who constitute the elite core of the military establishment. It is these few thousand top-ranking professionals who command and manage the armed forces and plan and formulate military policy and opinion. How is it, then, that in spite of civilian controls and the national desire for peace, this small group of men exert so much martial influence upon the government and life of the American people?

THE military will disclaim any excess of power or influence on their part. They will point to their small numbers, low pay, and subordination to civilian masters as proof of their modest status and innocence. Nevertheless, the professional military, as a group, is probably one of the best organized and most influential of the various segments of the American scene. Three wars and six major contingencies since 1940 have forced the American people to become abnormally aware of the armed forces and their leaders. In turn the military services have produced an unending supply of distinguished, capable, articulate, and effective leaders. The sheer skill, energy, and dedication of America's military officers make them dominant in almost every government or civic organization they may inhabit, from the federal Cabinet to the local PTA.

The hard core of high-ranking professionals are, first of all, mostly service academy graduates: they had to be physically and intellectually above average among their peers just to gain entrance to an academy. Thereafter for the rest of their careers they are exposed to constant competition for selection and promotion. Attrition is high, and only the most capable survive to reach the elite senior ranks. Few other professions have such rigorous selection systems; as a result, the top military leaders are top-caliber men.

Not many industries, institutions, or civilian branches of government have the resources, techniques, or experience in training leaders such as are now employed by the armed forces in their excellent and elaborate school systems. Military leaders are taught to command large organizations and to plan big operations. They learn the techniques of influencing others. Their education is not, however, liberal or cultural. It stresses the tactics, doctrines, traditions, and codes of the military trade. It produces technicians and disciples, not philosophers.

The men who rise to the top of the military hierarchy have usually demonstrated their effectiveness as leaders, planners, and organization managers. They have perhaps performed heroically in combat, but most of all they have demonstrated their loyalty as proponents of their own service's doctrine and their dedication to the defense establishment. The paramount sense of duty to follow orders is at the root of the military professional's performance. As a result the military often operate more efficiently and effectively in the arena of defense policy planning than do their civilian counterparts in the State Department. The military planners have their doctrinal beliefs, their loyalties, their discipline—and their typical desire to compete and win. The civilians in government can scarcely play the same policy-planning game. In general the military are better organized, they work harder, they think straighter, and they keep their eyes on the objective, which is to be instantly ready to solve the problem through military action while ensuring that their respective service gets its proper mission, role, and recognition in the operation. In an emergency the military usually have a ready plan; if not, their numerous doctrinal manuals provide firm guidelines for action. Politicians, civilian appointees, and diplomats do not normally have the same confidence about how to react to threats and violence as do the military.

The motivations behind these endeavors are difficult for civilians to understand. For example, military professionals cannot measure the success of their individual efforts in terms of personal financial gain. The armed forces are not profit-making organizations, and the rewards for excellence in the military profession are acquired in less tangible forms. Thus it is that promotion and the responsibilities of higher command, with the related fringe benefits of quarters, servants, privileges, and prestige, motivate most career officers. Promotions and choice job opportunities are attained by constantly performing well, conforming to the expected patterns, and pleasing the senior officers. Promotions and awards also frequently result from heroic and distinguished performance in combat, and it takes a war to become a military hero. Civilians can scarcely understand or even believe that many ambitious military professionals truly yearn for wars and the opportunities for glory and distinction afforded only in combat. A career of peacetime duty is a dull and frustrating prospect for the normal regular officer to contemplate.

The professional military leaders of the U.S. Armed Forces have some additional motivations which influence their readiness to involve their country in military ventures. Unlike some of the civilian policy-makers, the military has not been obsessed with the threat of Communism per se. Most military people know very little about Communism either as a doctrine or as a form of government. But they have been given reason enough to presume that it is bad and represents the force of evil. When they can identify "Communist aggression," however, the matter then becomes of direct concern to the armed forces. Aggressors are the enemy in the war games, the "bad guys," the "Reds." Defeating aggression is a gigantic combat-area competition rather than a crusade to save the world from Communism. In the military view, all "Communist aggression" is certain to be interpreted as a threat to the United States.

The armed forces' role in performing its part of the national security policy—in addition to defense against actual direct attack on the United States and to maintaining the strategic atomic deterrent forces—is to be prepared to employ its *General Purpose Forces* in support of our collective security policy and the related treaties and alliances. To do this it deploys certain forces to forward zones in the Unified Commands, and maintains an up-to-date file of scores of detailed contingency plans which have been thrashed out and approved by the Joint Chiefs of Staff. Important features of these are the movement or deployment schedules of task forces assigned to each plan. The various details of these plans continue to create intense rivalries between the Navy-Marine sea-lift forces and the Army-Air Force team of air-mobility proponents. At the senior command levels parochial pride in service, personal ambitions, and old Army-Navy game rivalry stemming back to academy loyalties can influence strategic planning far more than most civilians would care to believe. The game is to be ready for deployment sooner than the other elements of the joint task force and to be so disposed as to be the "first to fight." The danger presented by this practice is that readiness and deployment speed become ends in themselves. This was clearly revealed in the massive and rapid intervention in the Dominican Republic in 1965 when the contingency plans and interservice rivalry appeared to supersede diplomacy. Before the world realized what was happening, the momentum and velocity of the military plans propelled almost 20,000 U.S. soldiers and Marines into the small turbulent republic in an impressive race to test the respective mobility of the Army and the Marines, and to attain overall command of "U.S. Forces Dom. Rep." Only a fraction of the force deployed was needed or justified. A small 1935-model Marine landing force could probably have handled the situation. But the Army airlifted much of the 82nd Airborne Division to the scene, included a lieutenant general, and took charge of the operation.

Simultaneously, in Vietnam during 1965 the four services were racing to build up combat strength in that hapless country. This effort was ostensibly to save South Vietnam from Viet Cong and North Vietnamese aggression. It should also be noted that it was motivated in part by the same old interservice rivalry to demonstrate respective importance and combat effectiveness.

The punitive air strikes immediately following the Tonkin Gulf incident in late 1964 revealed the readiness of naval air forces to bomb North Vietnam. (It now appears that the Navy actually had attack plans ready even before the alleged incident took place!) So by early 1965 the Navy carrier people and the Air Force initiated a contest of comparative strikes, sorties, tonnages dropped, "Killed by Air" claims, and target grabbing which continued up to the 1968 bombing pause. Much of the reporting on air action has consisted of misleading data or propaganda to serve Air Force and Navy purposes. In fact, it became increasingly apparent that the U.S. bombing effort in both North and South Vietnam has been one of the most wasteful and expensive hoaxes ever to be put over on the American people. Tactical and close air support of ground operations is essential, but air power use in general has to a large degree been a contest for the operations planners, "fine experience" for young pilots, and opportunity for career officers.

The highly trained professional and aggressive career officers of the Army and Marine Corps played a similar game. Prior to the decision to send combat units to South Vietnam in early 1965, both services were striving to increase their involvement. The Army already had over 16,000 military aid personnel serving in South Vietnam in the military adviser role, in training missions, logistic services, supporting helicopter companies, and in Special Forces teams. This investment of men and matériel justified a requirement for additional U.S. combat units to provide local security and to help protect our growing commitment of aid to the South Vietnam regime.

There were also top-ranking Army officers who wanted to project Army ground combat units into the Vietnam struggle for a variety of other reasons; to test plans and new equipment, to test the new air-mobile theories and tactics, to try the tactics and techniques of counterinsurgency, and to gain combat experience for young officers and noncommissioned officers. It also appeared to be a case of the military's duty to stop "Communist aggression" in Vietnam.

THE Marines had somewhat similar motivations, the least of which was any real concern about the political or social problems of the Vietnamese people. In early 1965 there was a shooting war going on and the Marines were being left out of it, contrary to all their traditions. The Army's military advisory people were hogging American participation—except for a Marine Corps transport helicopter squadron at Danang which was helping the Army of the Republic of Vietnam. For several years young Marine officers had been going to South Vietnam from the 3rd Marine Division on Okinawa for short tours of "on-the-job training" with the small South Vietnam Marine Corps. There was a growing concern, however, among some senior Marines that the Corps should get involved on a larger scale and be the "first to fight" in keeping with the Corps's traditions. This would help justify the Corps's continued existence, which many Ma-

rines seem to consider to be in constant jeopardy.

The Corps had also spent several years exploring the theories of counterinsurgency and as early as 1961 had developed an elaborate lecture-demonstration called OPERATION CORMORANT, for school and Marine Corps promotion purposes, which depicted the Marines conducting a large-scale amphibious operation on the coast of Vietnam and thereby helping resolve a hypothetical aggressor-insurgency problem. As always it was important to Marine planners and doctrinaires to apply an amphibious operation to the Vietnam situation and provide justification for this special Marine functional responsibility. So Marine planners were seeking an acceptable excuse to thrust a landing force over the beaches of Vietnam when the Viet Cong attacked the U.S. Army Special Forces camp at Pleiku in February, 1965. It was considered unacceptable aggression, and the President was thereby prompted to put U.S. ground combat units into the war. Elements of the 3rd Marine Division at Okinawa were already aboard ship and eager to go, for the Marines also intended to get to Vietnam before their neighbor on Okinawa, the Army's 173rd Airborne Brigade, arrived. (Actually the initial Marine unit to deploy was an airlifted antiaircraft missile battalion which arrived to protect the Danang air base.) With these initial deployments the Army-Marine race to build forces in Vietnam began in earnest and did not slow down until both became overextended, overcommitted, and depleted at home.

For years up to 1964 the chiefs of the armed services, of whom the author was then one, deemed it unnecessary and unwise for U.S. forces to become involved in any ground war in Southeast Asia. In 1964 there were changes in the composition of the Joint Chiefs of Staff, and in a matter of a few months the Johnson Administration, encouraged by the aggressive military, hastened into what has become the quagmire of Vietnam. The intention at the time was that the war effort be kept small and "limited." But as the momentum and involvement built up, the military leaders rationalized a case that this was not a limited-objective exercise, but was a proper war in defense of the United States against "Communist aggression" and in honor of our area commitments.

The battle successes and heroic exploits of America's fine young fighting men have added to the military's traditions which extol service, bravery, and sacrifice, and so it has somehow become unpatriotic to question our military strategy and tactics or the motives of military leaders. Actually, however, the military commanders have directed the war in Vietnam, they have managed the details of its conduct; and more than most civilian officials, the top military planners were initially ready to become involved in Vietnam combat and have the opportunity to practice their trade. It has been popular to blame the civilian administration for the conduct and failures of the war rather than to question the motives of the military. But some of the generals and admirals are by no means without responsibility for the Vietnam miscalculations.

Some of the credibility difficulties experienced by the Johnson Administration over its war situation reports and Vietnam policy can also be blamed in part upon the military advisers. By its very nature most military activity falls under various degrees of security classification. Much that the military plans or does must be kept from the enemy. Thus the military is indoctrinated to be secretive, devious, and misleading in its plans and operations. It does not, however, always confine its security restrictions to purely military operations. Each of the services and all of the major commands practice techniques of controlling the news and the release of self-serving propaganda: in "the interests of national defense," to make the service look good, to cover up mistakes, to build up and publicize a distinguished military personality, or to win a round in the continuous gamesmanship of the interservice contest. If the Johnson Administration suffered from lack of credibility in its reporting of the war, the truth would reveal that much of the hocus-pocus stemmed from schemers in the military services, both at home and abroad.

Our militaristic culture was born of the necessities of World War II, nurtured by the Korean War, and became an accepted aspect of American life during the years of cold war emergencies and real or imagined threats from the Communist bloc. Both the philosophy and the institutions of militarism grew during these years because of the momentum of their own dynamism, the vigor of their ideas, their large size and scope, and because of the dedicated concentration of the emergent military leaders upon their doctrinal objectives. The dynamism of the defense establishment and its culture is also inspired and stimulated by vast amounts of money, by the new creations of military research and matériel development, and by the concepts of the Defense Department-supported "think facto-

ries." These latter are extravagantly funded civilian organizations of scientists, analysts, and retired military strategists who feed new militaristic philosophies into the Defense Department to help broaden the views of the single service doctrinaires, to create fresh policies and new requirements for ever larger, more expensive defense forces.

Somewhat like a religion, the basic appeals of anti-Communism, national defense, and patriotism provide the foundation for a powerful creed upon which the defense establishment can build, grow, and justify its cost. More so than many large bureaucratic organizations, the defense establishment now devotes a large share of its efforts to self-perpetuation, to justifying its organizations, to preaching its doctrines, and to self-maintenance and management. Warfare becomes an extension of war games and field tests. War justifies the existence of the establishment, provides experience for the military novice and challenges for the senior officer. Wars and emergencies put the military and their leaders on the front pages and give status and prestige to the professionals. Wars add to the military traditions, the self-nourishment of heroic deeds, and provide a new crop of military leaders who become the rededicated disciples of the code of service and military action. Being recognized public figures in a nation always seeking folk heroes, the military leaders have been largely exempt from the criticism experienced by the more plebeian politician. Flag officers are considered "experts," and their views are often accepted by press and Congress as the gospel. In turn, the distinguished military leader feels obliged not only to perpetuate loyally the doctrine of his service but to comply with the stereotyped military characteristics by being tough, aggressive, and firm in his resistance to Communist aggression and his belief in the military solutions to world problems. Standing closely behind these leaders, encouraging and prompting them, are the rich and powerful defense industries. Standing in front, adorned with service caps, ribbons, and lapel emblems, is a nation of veterans—patriotic, belligerent, romantic, and well intentioned, finding a certain sublimation and excitement in their country's latest military venture. Militarism in America is in full bloom and promises a future of vigorous self-pollination—unless the blight of Vietnam reveals that militarism is more a poisonous weed than a glorious blossom.

The opinions contained herein are the private ones of the author and are not to be construed as official or reflecting the views of the Navy Department or the naval service at large.

Fateful Triangle— The United States, Japan and China

EDWIN O. REISCHAUER

EDWIN O. REISCHAUER, professor of East Asian studies at Harvard, was Ambassador to Japan from 1961 to 1966, is author of "Japan: The Story of a Nation."

WE Americans love surprises and daring adventure. We have always been fascinated by China — by far the largest, oldest and perhaps most mysterious country in the world. And after a quarter century of agonizing over the "loss," "containment" and bitter hostility of China, who would not welcome a step that promises to

lead toward a relaxation of tensions between us and this great nation? The announcement that President Nixon would visit Peking before next May thus produced a wave of happy excitement.

As the wave of euphoria subsided, however, some nasty rocks began to appear in its wake. The Japanese were embarrassed, perhaps even outraged, not by what we had done but by the way we had done it. And the Chinese themselves, it soon developed, were not really worrying about us so much as they were about Japan. Then President Nixon's announcement on Aug. 15 of a 10 per cent surtax on imports and the end of the dollar's convertibility into gold, both of which were aimed primarily at forcing a revaluation of the yen, sent another sharp wave of resentment through Japan. The Japanese Government, forced to explain these acts to a public disillusioned and irritated over Japan's close alignment with the United States, has wisely chosen to downplay the tensions in the situation, but the unhappy Japanese public reaction to the events of this past summer reveal that there is probably a more immediate and dangerous crisis in Japanese-American relations than in our relations with China. The great Sino-American confrontation has begun to appear as merely an aspect of two more basic problems—tensions

between China and Japan, and strains in the alliance of Japan and the U.S.

THIS is not the first time that what we have thought of as our "China problem" turned out to be in reality a problem of Sino-Japanese and Japanese-American relations. During the first four decades of this century, our Far Eastern policy, which we defined as being based on the "open door" to trade and China's "territorial integrity," actually centered around a growing confrontation between Japanese and American power, brought to a head by a shifting relationship between Japan and China. The resulting Pacific War, one

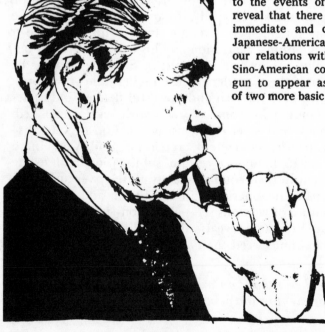

"Any strengthening of the Sino-American side of the triangle (the apexes are here represented by Mr. Nixon, Chairman Mao

of the greatest conflicts in history, was essentially a Japanese-American war, in which China played only a peripheral role. No one would predict a rerun of this sad story, which in the present age would be cataclysmic for humanity. But there are parallels. The key relationship in East Asia once again is that between China and Japan; the crucial issue is how it affects relations between the United States and Japan, the number one and number three economic powers in the world, whose hitherto close cooperation suddenly seems threatened by a number of serious problems.

This restructuring of the trans-Pacific problem, although largely ignored by Americans, has been long in the making. Japan has been racing ahead economically for 15 years. Growing roughly at more than 10 per cent annually in real terms, the Japanese economy has been doubling in productive capacity every seven years. Its productivity is already close to three times China's, and will soon equal that of all Asia put together. Japan has already passed the Soviet Union in per capita output and could exceed it in total economic power in a little over a decade. It is the chief, or at least the second, trading partner of almost every country, Communist or non-Communist, in East Asia. The explosive expansion of Japanese exports, doubling on the average every five years, constantly upsets existing economic balances in the world, thus setting off serious anxieties, not just among Japan's less industrialized neighbors, but in the United States and Western Europe. The prospect of a more than $2-billion deficit in our trade with Japan in 1971 helped trigger the President's latest economic move.

MEANWHILE, the great Sino-American confrontation has been fading rapidly in the minds of both Chinese and Americans. We have come to realize that China's supposed military aggressiveness is much less of a threat to vital American interests than our own over-involvement in the internal instabilities of Indochina. We now recognize that the Vietnam war was the product of conditions within Vietnam, not of Chinese plotting, much less ag-

gression, and that the Chinese military stance has all along been basically defensive rather than offensive. The desirability of a long-range rapprochement with China now seems to outweigh the need for short-range military containment.

To the Chinese, the Soviet Union for a decade has seemed more menacing than has the United States, and more recently worries about a militarily resurgent Japan have come to outweigh fears of an apparently tired and confused United States. Peking obviously believes that we will really wind down our war in Vietnam, if not withdraw entirely from Southeast Asia. While it views us as the chief culprit in the creation of a separatist Taiwan, it regards Japanese trade and investment in the island and the historic orientation of the Taiwanese toward Japan as the chief stimulants to continued separatism there.

It is easy to disparage Chinese fears of revived Japanese militarism and expansionism. The Japanese in their dealings with China have been circumspect and even obsequious, readily accepting insult from Peking in the hope of avoiding damage to trade relations. Few nations in the world today are more thoroughly pacifist, and no large country has devoted less of its national wealth to military power. Japanese defense expenditures are less than 1 per cent of the gross national product, as opposed to the 3 to 9 per cent range of most other large countries, including China itself, and there are no plans for an increased proportion of military spending. Perhaps most important, almost all Japanese have drawn a clear lesson from their pre-World War II travails, from the disaster of the war itself and from their postwar prosperity and contentment. Any attempt to extend Japanese military or political dominance abroad would seem to them the height of folly, and militarism also appears the greatest of domestic evils, since it was military leadership that not only got Japan into catastrophic wars, but also brought economic miseries and the suppression of personal freedoms at home.

Still, Chinese fears of Japan are very real and, when seen from a Chinese historical perspective, quite understandable. Japan, a cultural daughter of China, diverged most sharply from the Chinese pattern of civil-bureaucratic rule by developing a militarized feudal system. Through pirate marauders and a 16th-century incursion into the Chinese defense zone in Korea, the Japanese figured among the "barbarian" gadflies that harassed the great "central land" of civilization. The still feudalistic Japanese in the 19th century easily picked up the more modernized militarism of a Europe that had itself emerged from feudalism not long before. Once military, economic and political modernization had strengthened their sinews, they happily joined the late 19th-century Western game of imperialism at the expense of weaker nations, notably China. By the end of World War I, the Japanese had replaced the British as the chief economic threat to China, and the Russians as the major military menace to China's survival as an independent nation. Then, in the nineteen-thirties, under increasingly fanatical military leadership, Japan embarked upon a persistent and infinitely cruel effort to force China into complete subservience. Much of

Drawings by Robert M. Cunningham.

and Premier Sato) requires strengthening the Sino-Japanese side — and it all must rest on a strong Japanese-American base."

China had been overrun and devastated before this unwise policy eventually led to Japan's own destruction.

The memory of Japan as the chief menace to China's national existence persists in the minds of China's leaders, whose adult lives go back to World War I. To see such a Japan grown far more economically powerful than it was in the thirties is indeed frightening. Through economic dominance it seems at last to be creating the "Greater East Asian Co-Prosperity Sphere" which it set as a goal in World War II. To the Chinese it is inconceivable that the Japanese will not in time defend this economic empire by political and military means. There are many signs that a revived national self-esteem is sweeping Japan. To the Chinese this can easily appear to be a revival of Japan's militaristic expansionism of only a few decades ago. The spectacular suicide last autumn of the popular author Mishima, in which he evoked military virtues of the past, might well seem to Chinese a sign of the turning of the tide back toward militarism.

The Chinese leaders do not themselves know postwar Japan, and they are ill-prepared to understand what they may learn of it. They have the traditional Chinese contempt for Japan. Isolated from most of the world and narrowly focused on their own problems, they have little understanding of the psychological and political realities of a rapidly changing country like Japan, which is a vastly more modernized and complex society than China. The prisms of 19th-century Marxism only further distort their view of late 20th-century Japanese society. Thus it is not surprising that in Chinese eyes the Japanese leopard continues to have militaristic spots.

Japanese consternation over the President's handling of our move toward détente with China and over Japanese-American economic issues may be exaggerated. After all, most Japanese have themselves been urging us to relax tensions with China. And what right have they to complain of our methods? They have wished to remain the politically invisible country in the world, in order to concentrate on their own economic growth and foreign trade. They have accepted American defense of their islands and the surrounding seas that are so vital to their national existence, while constantly carping about American policies and making no move themselves to assume any political or military responsibilities beyond the narrowest definition of self-defense. This is the "free ride" some American critics have pointed to.

In a sense there has also been an economic "free ride." While finding some 30 per cent of its export markets in a relatively open United States, Japan has been very slow to reciprocate by opening its doors to American industrial exports and capital investments. The Japanese, through a tight coordination between Government and business that has given rise to the term "Japan, Inc.," have developed a variety of means besides tariffs for limiting imports in fields they wished to reserve for themselves. In addition to import quotas, they have endless administrative barriers which have effectively kept out imports in these fields. As a result, Japan has limited its imports from the United States largely to agricultural products and other raw materials—as if we were a less developed country — and has kept out the industrial goods that would seriously compete with Japanese products. While there is much that Japan must buy from the United States, there is practically nothing we import from Japan that we could not produce ourselves. Under these circumstances one might expect a large trade balance in America's favor. The looming $2-billion deficit in our trade with Japan suggests that there is something very much amiss. It is for such reasons that some Americans argue that if Japan chooses to disregard American favors and legitimate American interests, it should not expect the United States to consult it on China policy or refrain from economic countermeasures. As such critics would see it, the time has come for the Japanese to stop taking the United States for granted as an indulgent but rather stupid elder brother.

Viewing the problem from the Japanese perspective, however, one again comes out with a very different picture. Most older Japanese, remembering the terrible conditions of their country in the early postwar years, regard Japan as still a weak country, struggling to catch up with the United States and Western Europe. They think of themselves as relatively poor—and they are in terms of lack of space and paucity of investment in urban housing, flush toilets and some other amenities of life, though not in terms of national productivity and exports, which have an economic impact on other nations. The Japanese people have assumed that their Government's policy has been shaped, and is still circumscribed, by an overly rigid American stance in Asia. They feel that the United States is responsible for Japan's somewhat anomalous position of recognizing Taiwan, while being China's as well as Taiwan's chief trading partner. To the Japanese, China looms far larger than to Americans, because of its geographic proximity, their deep cultural affinity to the Chinese and the concentration of their economic and imperialist ambitions in the past on China. Relations with China, therefore, constitute a far more delicate and explosive political issue in Japan than in the United States.

GIVEN these attitudes, Japanese resentment over our recent moves is understandable. To many Japanese it appears that, after forcing Japan into an unsound relationship with China, the United States is blithely turning its back on her, leaving her stranded in this precarious position, while we work out an accommodation with Peking, very possibly at Japan's expense. They also see us as a giant (geographically 25 times as big as Japan and still five times larger in economic productivity) which, because of mismanagement and possibly grave moral deficiencies, has got itself into an economic fix from which it is trying to extricate itself with little concern over the damage its methods may do to a worthy, industrious and morally sound little country like Japan. The Japanese public has been given two terrible successive shocks by the President's apparent overlooking of Japan in his dealings with China and his spectacular economic measures, which have forced the Japanese against their will to let the yen float upward in value and thus increase the cost of their exports and limit their markets in the United States.

Japanese political and economic leaders are perhaps more sophisticated on these matters. They know perfectly well that for at least a decade Japan has set its own course in foreign policy. But they have found it politically expedient to let the Japanese public continue to assume that the United States dictated Japan's policy toward China. They see American and Japanese interests in China, Taiwan and East Asia as fundamentally compatible, and it has seemed to them that, at this time of obvious change in the whole situation, the safest strategy is to stay in step with the United States and to emphasize to the public the closeness of cooperation between the two countries. Under such circumstances, it has been a great public humiliation that President Nixon, when he decided on a showy new move in China relations, either forgot

to inform the Japanese, much less consult them, or else considered their interests in this matter as worth sacrificing in order to win a better rapport with Peking. Premier Eisaku Sato's personal political career has probably been damaged irreparably and the whole position of the Government party weakened.

Japan's leaders are also better informed than the public on the economic issues between the two countries. The strength of the Japanese economy and its continuing rapid growth, they realize, necessitate some adjustment in monetary and trade policies on both sides. The answer clearly is closer coordination of economic policies and greater cooperation between the United States and Japan. But the question is whether this will be possible in the political climate that is developing on both sides of the Pacific. Public fears and resentments run high. Since the democratic process in both countries is basically controlled by local political interests, popular indignation could easily overwhelm the more balanced judgment of economic experts.

It is high time for both Americans and Japanese to look carefully at what is at stake in the triangular relationships between the United States, Japan and China. Henry Kissinger's visit to Peking is, of course, a welcome symbol of relaxation in Sino-American tensions. It is comforting to know that China and the United States each seems to be reconsidering its image of the other as a major menace. Recognition of Peking as the capital of the great historic China is long overdue, as is Peking's rightful occupancy of the United Nations seats assigned to that country. China, with close to a quarter of the world's pop-

ulation, has to become engaged in what must before long be a worldwide effort to face the great problems that are fast closing in on humanity—survival in a nuclearized world, population growth, depletion of natural resources and global pollution.

OTHER gains from the new policy, however, are not likely to be great in the foreseeable future. Even at best, America's trade with China could not amount to more than a small fraction of our trade with Japan. Cultural and intellectual relations will remain an even tinier fraction. The Taiwan problem will persist, to be resolved primarily by the attitudes of the Government and the people on that island. The very dangerous Korean situation—a raw confrontation between two highly militarized, relatively powerful and extremely antagonistic regimes—will remain almost unchanged. The solution of the Indochina problem will depend basically on the attitudes and abilities of the people of that region. China's influence on other countries, even those of Southeast Asia, will not be greatly altered. Its economic leverage will remain very small compared to that of Japan or the United States. Although its basic revolutionary intent will continue, its subversive potential will probably not be great, as the failure in 1965 of the Chinese-backed Communist movement in Indonesia illustrates. In Malaysia, where the Chinese minority constitutes more than a third of the population, China's influence could be important, but elsewhere the Chinese minorities, instead of being an asset to China's foreign policy, are probably a liability. They create deep resentments and suspicions, and therefore increase resistance to Chinese influence.

On balance, a strengthening of the Sino-American side of the triangle is highly desirable—though not at the expense of the other two sides. A Sino-American deal behind Japan's back could not only sour Japanese-American relations but could increase Sino-Japanese tensions. It could trigger a series of moves and countermoves that might make Sino-Japanese relations in the future a far greater threat to the world than Sino-American relations have ever been. The deep anxiety of Peking's leaders over the possibility of revived militarism in Japan shows how great that danger is.

Most important, the Japanese - American relationship must not be weakened, for it is by far the largest of the three and is, in a sense, the base on which the other two sides of the triangle rest. President Nixon's two successive shocks to the Japanese have come at a time when there already are mounting strains in that relationship. Although Japanese - American trade, which has climbed to well over $10-billion a year, is vastly beneficial to both sides, the Japanese have fumed for years over so-called "voluntary" restrictions ("You voluntarily restrain your exports—or else") and some involuntary ones on their sales to us, while Americans have become increasingly irritated with Japan's lack of full reciprocity in opening its markets and investment opportunities to us. It would not be difficult for reciprocal acts of reprisal to set off a real trade war in which Western Europe, the third great member of the trading community of advanced industrial nations, would no doubt join. We might then see a general de-

generation of world trade, re-creating the international economic conditions that helped bring on World War II. The greatest step forward in international relations during the past quarter century has probably been the development, through relatively free trade between these industrialized nations, of a sort of economic interdependence that has made war between them unthinkable, even though not long ago they were the chief protagonists in two great world wars. It would be a tragedy if this interdependence were to start crumbling at this time, when humanity, in order to survive, must move ahead to broader levels of cooperation.

IN military matters—the area of China's greatest fears — the Japanese-American relationship is even more seriously threatened, because, although the Japanese realize that they have no alternative to a huge trade relationship with us, many of them feel that the defense relationship is quite unnecessary and even harmful. A large proportion of the Japanese look upon the presence of American military bases in Japan as basically undesirable — a quite understandable point of view — and the Japanese-American defense relationship embodied in the Mutual Security Treaty as more in America's interests than Japan's. Apparently assuming that the United States will in any case maintain more of a military presence in the Western Pacific than is actually needed, they would prefer to see it pursue its dangerous Far Eastern policies from bases outside of Japan, thus sparing Japan the possibly unhappy consequences of American adventurism. Japan's ac-

ALLIES—Sato and Nixon at the White House during the Premier's 1969 visit.

ceptance of the security treaty, they feel, is the result of its lack of independence in foreign policy and its need for American markets. Since these markets are possibly less essential to an economically restored Japan, and since such trade is threatened by American restrictionism anyway, the time has come, they feel, to wriggle out of the defense relationship.

Such attitudes have been greatly strengthened recently by uncertainties over the value of American defense commitments. Part of the problem is the ambiguity of the so-called Nixon Doctrine first enunciated by the President on Guam in the summer of 1969. The basic concept behind the doctrine, I believe, is the perfectly valid worldwide distinction between our commitments to industrialized and politically stable lands, such as Japan, Australia and the countries of Western Europe, and the necessary limitations on our defense commitments to less developed countries, which are chiefly threatened by their own internal instabilities. The latter need from us technological and economic aid rather than military involvement. Unfortunately, the doctrine has been made to sound like a concept applying only to an Asia that is so alien to the United States that it is not worthy of defense at the cost of American lives. "Asian boys" should fight "Asian wars," and presumably the Japanese should therefore not count on American defense commitments but instead become involved themselves in the defense of other Asian areas. Such a racist view seems to the Japanese plausible because of their own deeply racist attitudes. An American commitment to blood and cultural cousins in Europe seems more trustworthy to them than our commitments to a nation of a clearly different race like Japan.

The Japanese have also come to wonder if the United States has the will or ability to meet its commitments to Japan. To a homogeneous people like the Japanese, the virtues and strengths of a racially and culturally pluralistic country like the United States are much less evident than its problems and weaknesses. Under the circumstances, it is not surprising that every Japanese political party advocates a weakening of the defense bond with the United States, differing only on the speed and the com-

Drawing by Tim in L'Express, Paris

pleteness with which it should be dissolved. The blows of this past summer have certainly not increased Japanese confidence in the reliability of the United States an an ally.

As Japanese military power is gradually restored, American bases will probably disappear from Japan, and the defense relationship between the two countries might even be weakened. But any rapid motion in this direction at this time could have a catastrophic impact on East Asia and the world. Without bases in Japan and the tacit support of the Japanese, the United States would almost inevitably be forced to withdraw its military power from the whole area. In that case the Japanese—dependent as they are for their livelihood on a vast seaborne commerce, deeply feared and resented by the Chinese and their other neighbors, and surrounded by the military instability in Korea and Southeast Asia—would unquestionably feel insecure with only their present minuscule naval power. The building of a sizable fleet would seem to them only common sense. To the Chinese and other East Asians, however, such a step would appear to verify their worst fears. Tensions would mount, and hostile reactions from Japan's neighbors would spur further Japanese defense efforts. The Japanese might drift into becoming a major military power and, ultimately, a member of the nuclear club. If a trend in this direction starts, then more relaxed Sino-American relations would have been more than offset by increased Sino-Japanese strains, and even Japanese-American relations might drift back toward the suspicion and hostility that characterized them in the past—indeed a disastrous tradeoff.

THESE gloomy speculations, of course, run far ahead of present developments. There is time to avoid the abyss in our path. It is possible that President Nixon's two announcements may have shocked the Japanese out of their complacent attitude of taking the United States for granted. Possibly their anguished outcries will shock us out of our equally complacent attitude of taking Japan for granted.

The problem remains whether the interests of the two countries are really sufficiently compatible—or rather are seen by both sides to be sufficiently compatible—to permit a continuation of our close cooperation. In the nineteen-thirties our differing perceptions of the road to prosperity and security made a clash inevitable. Our concept of a desirable world order simply could not be squared with the Japanese belief that the only sure way for Japan to achieve prosperity and security was by conquering an empire comparable in economic size to those of Britain and France and to the continental expanses of the United States and the Soviet Union.

Fortunately, no such divergence of basic views separates us today. Both Americans and Japanese yearn for peace and believe that this can best be achieved in a world made up not of hegemonic blocs but of many independent states which live peacefully together under some system of international law. Their cultural and intellectual contacts are growing rapidly to their mutual advantage. Both countries, as the world's two strongest global trading nations, believe heartily in the desirability of maximizing world trade. Each finds the other its chief overseas trading partner (only with Canada do we do a greater trade than with Japan). While their massive trade contacts produce endless economic friction, both profit greatly from this relationship. Although they inevitably will compete with each other for markets and resources in much of the world, both gain in a general way from the economic stimulation the other provides the whole world, and, particularly, the less developed countries. The very presence of the other as a major competitor is in a sense a political advantage in countries that are fearful of foreign economic domination. In Southeast Asia, for example, a continued strong American economic presence would help alleviate fears in these countries that Japan will dominate them. Similarly, a strong Japanese economic presence in Latin America might ease the tensions in the relationship between that area and the United States.

Both countries share much the same hopes, reservations and fears regarding a rapprochement with China. Their relations with Taiwan are quite similar. Even though Japan is China's chief trading partner, its trade with Taiwan is still slightly larger. While the Japanese have much better prospects of expanding their trade with China than does the United States, their China trade in the predictable future is not likely to amount to more than a small fraction of its trade with the United States. The real defense interests of the U.S. and Japan in East Asia are largely identical, because America's chief strategic interest in Asia is Japan's security. Both peoples, while much aware of their own shortcomings, value highly the free and democratic societies they are trying to perfect. Even the area of basic disagreement in the past is shrinking, as the United States moves away from its overly military approach to East Asian problems, its close-in "containment" of China and its military involvement in Indochina, all of which most Japanese felt were mistaken policies. If two countries with such fundamentally compatible views of the world cannot cooperate fully and easily, the prospects for humanity are indeed bleak.

AFTER looking at the three sides of the triangle, it should be clear that any significant strengthening of the Sino-American side requires a parallel strengthening of the Sino-Japanese side—and both of these must continue to rest on a sold base of Japanese-American cooperation. The real fruits of a rapprochement with China for both the United States and Japan will develop only uncertainly and over time. The terrible dangers of a falling out between them are immediate and far greater.

Relations between the three countries cannot safely be based on the quicksand of false premises. The political leadership and peoples of both the United States and Japan must come to realize and act on the truisms that experts in the two countries have long been repeating to each other: a friendly and cooperative United States is of overwhelming importance to Japan in its foreign relations, just as a friendly and cooperative Japan is of overwhelming importance to the United States in its relations with Asia. Both sides must realize that, whatever the economic frictions and irritation between them, a trade war would be infinitely worse. They must also realize that the best way to maximize their security and minimize their military burdens is by

66There is time to avoid the abyss in our path. It is possible that the President's two announcements [of his visit to Peking and of the import surcharge] have shocked the Japanese out of their complacent attitude of taking the United States for granted. Possibly their anguished outcries will shock us out of our equally complacent attitude of taking the Japanese for granted.99

sharing the defense load, as the United States does with Western Europe. If such a relationship is to be maintained in the future, the United States must recognize that Japan, situated as it is in East Asia, is best able to determine what the defense needs may be and how they can best be shared. The United States must also clarify the Nixon Doctrine to get rid of its distressing racist overtones and make clear that American commitments to a politically stable and industrially powerful Japan are of the same order as American commitments to the similarly stable and powerful countries of Western Europe.

The United States and Japan must each realize that no permanent improvement in the relations of either with China is possible through catering to Chinese fears or prejudices toward the other. They should not play up to the hopes of the Chinese leaders that they can divide the United States from Japan or enlist American support in "containing" Japan. It is a curious situation indeed when the President of the U.S. plans a visit to the capital of what has been considered America's greatest enemy in Asia, when no President has ever visited the capital of America's chief ally. The only promising approach to China for either country would be one based on an openly acknowledged coordination of policy between the two. Both Washington and Tokyo are showing signs that they have come to understand this point. President Nixon's reception of the Japanese Emperor in Alaska next Sunday will be a courteous gesture, but coordination of policy between the two countries would best be symbolized by a Presidential visit to Tokyo well before his trip to Peking. It is encouraging that proposals for such a visit have been made. ■

Morality and International Politics

Arthur Schlesinger, Jr.

Mr. Schlesinger is Albert Schweitzer Professor of Humanities at The City University of New York.

FOR CENTURIES, theologians have distinguished between just and unjust wars, jurists have propounded rules for international conduct, and moralists have worried whether their own nation's course in foreign affairs was right or wrong. Yet the problem of the relationship between morality and international politics remains perennially unsettled. It is particularly difficult and disturbing for Americans today. The Indochina war was first widely justified on moral grounds and is now widely condemned on moral grounds. Both judgments cannot be right.

This contradiction and, even more, of course, the shame and horror of the war must surely compel us to look again at the moral question in its relation to foreign policy.

William James used to say that temperaments determined philosophies. People who respond to international politics divide temperamentally into two schools: those who see policies as wise or foolish, and those (evidently in the majority today) who see them as good or evil. One cannot claim an ultimate metaphysical difference here. No one can escape perceptions of good and evil, and no policy can achieve a total separation of political and moral principles. Nor in the impenetrability of one's heart can one easily know when political motives are moral motives in disguise or when moral motives are political motives in disguise. Still the choice of disguise reveals something about temperament and philosophy.

In this time, when both Right and Left yield with relish to the craving for moral judgment, it may be useful to set forth a minority view. Should—as both supporters and critics of the Indochina war have asserted—overt moral principles decide issues of foreign policy? Required to give a succinct answer, I am obliged to say: as little as possible. If, in the management of foreign affairs, decisions can be made and questions disposed of on other grounds, so much the better. Moral values in international politics—or so, at least, my temperament enjoins me to believe—should be decisive only in questions of last resort. One must add that questions of last resort do exist.

Individual vs. state morality

HOW TO DEFINE RIGHT AND WRONG in dealings among sovereign states? The moralist of foreign affairs relies on the moral code most familiar to him—the code that governs dealings among individuals. He contends that states should be judged by principles of individual morality. As Woodrow Wilson put it in his address to Congress on the declaration of war in 1917: "We are at the beginning of an age in which it will be insisted that the same standards of conduct and of responsibility for wrong done shall be observed among nations and their governments that are observed among the individual citizens of civilized states." John Foster Dulles said it even more bluntly, or naïvely, in the midst of the second world war: "The broad principles that should govern our international conduct are not obscure. They grow out of the practice by the nations of the simple things Christ taught."

The argument for the application of moral principles to questions of foreign policy is thus that there is, or should be, an identity between the morality of individuals and the morality of states. The issues involved here are not easy. Clearly, there are cases in foreign affairs where moral judgment is possible and necessary. But I suggest that these are extreme cases and do not warrant the routine use of moral criteria in making foreign-policy decisions. It was to expose such indiscriminate moralism that Reinhold Niebuhr wrote *Moral Man and Immoral Society* forty years ago. The passage of time has not weakened the force of his analysis.

Niebuhr insisted on the distinction between the moral behavior of individuals and of social groups. The obligation of the individual was to obey the law of love and sacrifice; "from the viewpoint of the author of an action, unselfishness must remain the criterion of the highest morality." But nations cannot be sacrificial. Governments are not individuals. They are trustees for individuals. Niebuhr quotes Hugh Cecil's argument that unselfishness "is inappropriate to the action of a state. No one has a right to be unselfish with other people's interests." Alexander Hamilton made the same point in the early years of the American republic: "The rule of morality . . . is not precisely the same between nations as between individuals. The duty of making its own welfare the guide of its actions is much stronger upon the former than upon the latter. Existing millions, and for the most part future generations, are concerned in the present measures of a government; while the consequences of the private action of an individual ordinarily terminate with himself, or are circumscribed with a narrow compass."

In short, the individual's duty of self-sacrifice and the nation's duty of self-preservation are in conflict; and this makes it impossible to measure the action of nations by a purely individualistic morality. "The Sermon on the Mount," said Churchill, "is the last word in Christian ethics. . . . Still, it is not on those terms that Ministers assume their responsibilities of guiding states." Saints can be pure, but statesmen must be responsible. As trustees for others, they must defend interests and compromise principles. In politics, practical and prudential judgment must have priority over moral verdicts.

The indifference of God

NATIONAL SOCIETIES HAVE JOINED, to a considerable degree, individual morality and political necessity. The moral sense of a community finds embodiment in positive law. But the shift of the argument from morality to law only strengthens the case against the facile intrusion of moral judgment into foreign affairs.

A nation's law can set down relatively clear standards of right and wrong in individual behavior because it is the product of an imperfect but nonetheless authentic internal moral consensus. International life has no such broad or deep moral consensus. It was once hoped that modern technology would create a common fund of moral ideas transcending the interests of particular nations—common concepts of interest, justice, and comity—either because the revolution in communications would bring people together through hope of mutual understanding or because the revolution in weapons would bring them together through fear of mutual destruction. Such expectations have been disappointed. Until nations come to adopt the same international morality, there can be no world law to regulate the behavior of states. Nor can international institutions—the League of Nations or the United Nations—produce by sleight of hand a moral consensus where none exists. World law must express world community; it cannot create it.

This is not to say we cannot discern the rudiments of an international consensus. Within limits, mankind has begun to develop standards for conduct among nations—defined, for example, in the Hague Conventions of 1899 and 1907; in the Geneva Protocol of 1925 and the Geneva Conventions of 1949; in the Charter and Covenants of the United Nations; in the Charter, Judgment, and Principles of the Nuremberg Tribunal, and so on. Such documents outlaw actions that the world has placed beyond the limits of permissible behavior. Within this restricted area a code emerges that makes moral judgment in international affairs possible up to a point. And within its scope this rudimentary code deserves, and must have, the most unflinching and rigorous enforcement.

But these international rules deal with the limits rather than with the substance of policy. They seek to prevent abnormalities and excesses in the behavior of states, but they do not offer grounds for moral judgment and sanction on normal international transactions (including, it must be sorrowfully said, war itself, so long as war does not constitute aggression and so long as the rules of warfare are faithfully observed). They may eventually promote a world moral consensus. But, for the present, national, ideological, ethical, and religious divisions remain as bitterly intractable as ever.

Moreover, few problems in international politics call for unequivocal ethical approval or disapproval. Most foreign-policy decisions are self-evidently matters of prudence and maneuver, not of good and evil. "I do not think we can conclude," George Kennan noted a decade ago, "that it matters greatly to God whether the free trade area or the Common Market prevails in Europe, whether the British fish or do not fish in Icelandic territorial waters, or even whether Indians or Pakistani run Kashmir. It might matter, but it is hard for us, with our limited vision, to know." The raw material of foreign affairs is, most of the time, morally neutral or ambiguous. In consequence, for the great majority of foreign-policy transactions, moral principles cannot be decisive.

But this is not all. It is not only that moral principles are of limited use in the conduct of foreign affairs. It is also that the compulsion to see foreign policy in moral terms may have, with the noblest of intentions, the most ghastly of consequences. The moralization of foreign affairs encourages, for example, a misunderstanding of the nature of foreign policy. Moralists tend to prefer symbolic to substantive politics. They tend to see foreign policy as a means not of influencing events but of registering virtuous attitudes. One has only to recall the attempt, made variously by Right and by Left, to make recognition policy an instrument of ethical approval or disapproval.

A deeper trouble is inherent in the very process of pronouncing moral judgment on foreign policy. For the man who converts conflicts of interest and circumstance into conflicts of good and evil necessarily invests himself with moral superiority. Those who see foreign affairs as made up of questions of right and wrong begin by supposing they know better than other people what is right for them. The more passionately they believe they are right, the more likely they are to reject expediency and accommodation and seek the final victory of their principles. Little has been more pernicious in international politics than excessive righteousness.

Moral absolutism may strike at any point along the political spectrum. From the standpoint of those who mistrust self-serving ethical stances, the heirs of John Foster Dulles and the disciples of Noam Chomsky are equal victims of the same malady. Both regard foreign policy as a branch of ethics. They end up as mirror images of each other. In the process of moral self-aggrandizement, each loses the humility which is the heart of human restraint. Sir Herbert Butterfield, after observing that "moral indignation corrupts the agent who possesses it and is not calculated to reform the man who is the object of it," makes the essential point: "The passing of what purports to be a moral judgment—particularly a judgment which amounts to the assertion that they are worse men than I am—is not merely irrelevant, but actually immoral and harmful." It is "really a demand for an illegitimate form of power. The attachment to it is based on its efficacy as a tactical weapon, its ability to rouse irrational fervour and extraordinary malevolence against some enemy."

Moralism in foreign policy ends up in fanaticism, and the fanatic, as Mr. Dooley put it, "does what he thinks th' Lord wud do if He only knew th' facts in th' case." Abroad it leads to crusades and the extermination of the infidel; at home it perceives mistakes in political judgment as evidence of moral obliquity. The issue becomes not self-delusion or stupidity but criminality and treachery; ferreting out the reprobate as traitors or war criminals becomes the goal. Those who are convinced of their own superior righteousness should recall Chekhov's warning: "You will not become a saint through other people's sins."

Losing crusades

IF MORAL PRINCIPLES have only limited application to foreign policy, then we are forced to the conclusion that decisions in foreign affairs must generally be taken on other than moralistic grounds. What are these other grounds? I believe that where the embryonic international community cannot regulate dealings among nations, the safest basis for foreign policy lies not in attempts to determine what is right or wrong but in attempts to determine the national interest.

Though the idea is an old and honorable one, "national interest," despite the valiant efforts through the years of Walter Lippmann, George Kennan, and Hans Morgenthau, has become an alarming phrase in America in the 1970s. Mention it before students, and the audience shudders. The words should alarm no one. A moment's thought will show that every nation *must* respond to some sense of its national interest, for a nation that rejects national interest as the mainspring of its policy cannot survive. Without the magnetic compass of national interest, there would be no regularity and predictability in international affairs. George Washington called it "a maxim founded on the universal experience of mankind that no nation is to be trusted farther than it is bound by its interest."

This is not to say that national interest is a self-executing formula providing an automatic answer to every perplexity of foreign affairs. Men can argue endlessly about the content of national interest. One man's national interest may be another man's poison. Still the idea is not totally open-ended. Every nation, for example, has a set of fairly definite strategic interests. One has only to reflect on the continuities of Russian foreign policy, whether directed by czars or commissars. When one moves to politics and economics, identification of national interest certainly becomes more debatable. Yet even here one notices that nations often preserve, through changes of government and ideology, an impressive amount of continuity. In any case, the idea of national interest provides the focus and framework within which the debate can take place. It is the debate itself that gives the idea its content and, in a democracy, its legitimacy.

Obviously a government can take a greedy as well as an enlightened view of its nation's interest. Greed tends to become the dominant motive when there is disparity of power between nations: thus the history of imperialism. But national interest has a self-limiting factor. It cannot, unless transformed by an injection of moral righteousness, produce ideological crusades for unlimited objectives. Any consistent defender of the idea of national interest must concede that other nations have legitimate interests too, and this sets bounds on international conflict. "You can compromise interests," Hans Morgenthau has reminded us, "but you cannot compromise principles."

This self-limiting factor does not rest only on the perception of other nations' interests. It is reinforced by self-correcting tendencies in the power equilibrium which, at least when the disparity of power is not too great, prevent national interest from billowing up into unbridled national egoism. History has shown how often the overweening behavior of an aggressive state leads to counteraction on the part of other states determined to restore a balance of power. This means that uncontrolled national egoism generally turns out to be contrary to long-term national interest. Can it be persuasively held, for example, that Hitler's foreign policy was in the national interest of Germany? The imperialist states of nineteenth-century Europe have generally been forced to revise their notions as to where national interest truly lies. In time this may even happen to the Soviet Union and the United States.

National interest, realistically construed, will promote enlightened rather than greedy policy. So a realist like Hamilton said (my emphasis) that his aim was not "to recommend a policy absolutely selfish or interested in nations; but to show, that a policy regulated by their own interest, *as far as justice and good faith permit*, is, and ought to be, their prevailing one." And a realist like Theodore Roosevelt could say: "It is neither wise nor right for a nation to disregard its own needs, and it is foolish—and may be wicked—to think that other nations will disregard theirs. But it is wicked for a nation only to regard its own interest, and foolish to believe that such is the sole motive that actuates any other nation. It should be our steady aim to raise the ethical standard of national action just as we strive to raise the ethical standard of individual action."

Double standard

BOTH HAMILTON AND ROOSEVELT thus tempered their conception of national interest with moral considerations because, as realists, they knew that national self-assertion at the expense of the value and interests of others could lead to national disaster. They did so too, no doubt, because there is something emotionally frustrating about calculations of national interest as the basis for decision. As moral men, we prefer to feel that our actions spring from profound ethical imperatives. The Anglo-American tradition, in particular, has long been addicted to the presentation of egoism in the guise of altruism. And if one has an honest sense of moral concern or moral outrage, it seems idle—indeed, false—to deny this when supporting or censuring a foreign policy. For better or worse, moreover, democratic opinion rebels at the idea of the domination of policy by self-interest. "Let the people get it into their heads that a policy is selfish and they will not follow it," A. J. P. Taylor has wisely written. ". . . A democratic foreign policy has got to be idealistic; or at the very least it has to be justified in terms of great general principles."

Nor is this cynicism. It may well be that the instinct among nearly all nations to justify their actions in terms of abstract moral principle is an involuntary tribute to the existence of a world public opinion, a latent international consensus, that we must all hope will one day be crystallized in law and institutions. This is what Jefferson had in mind when the Declaration of Independence enjoined "a decent respect to the opinions of man-

kind." It is the point made in a prescient passage in the 63rd Federalist:

> *An attention to the judgment of other nations is important to every government for two reasons: the one is, that, independently of the merits of any particular plan or measure, it is desirable, on various accounts, that it should appear to other nations as the offspring of a wise and honorable policy; the second is, that in doubtful cases, particularly where the national councils may be warped by some strong passion or momentary interest, the presumed or known opinion of the impartial world may be the best guide that can be followed. What has not America lost by her want of character with foreign nations; and how many errors and follies would she not have avoided, if the justice and propriety of her measures had, in every instance, been previously tried by the light in which they would probably appear to the unbiased part of mankind?*

Thus an irrepressible propensity to moral judgment in the field of foreign affairs exists. Nor, despite the perils of moral absolutism, is it without value. It may provide an indispensable reminder that all policies are imperfect and all statesmen capable of self-deception. Indeed, the truly Christian perspective offers the best antidote to the moralistic fallacy of transforming expedients into absolutes. John C. Bennett tells us of the meeting of a delegation from the World Council of Churches with President Kennedy in 1962. The delegation brought a message to heads of states from the New Delhi Assembly of the Council; a paragraph called for the cessation of nuclear tests. When Kennedy read this passage, he responded by discussing his own dilemma: what should the United States do to assure its own security in view of the resumption of tests by the Soviet Union? Impressed, a member of the delegation said, "Mr. President, if you do resume tests, how can we help you?" Kennedy turned to him and said, "Perhaps you shouldn't." Not all statesmen thus recognize the value of separating ultimate from immediate considerations and of preserving ideals in a world of distasteful compromise; if more did, the world would be spared much trouble.

In addition, there are certain problems in foreign policy with so clear-cut a moral character that moral judgment must control political judgment—questions of war crimes and atrocities, of the nuclear

"Most foreign- policy decisions are self-evidently matters of prudence and maneuver, not of good and evil."

arms race, of colonialism, of racial justice, of world poverty. Some have already been defined in international documents. Others define themselves when the consequences of decision transcend the interests of individual nations and threaten the very future of humanity. Modern weapons technology has notably enlarged the number of problems demanding moral priority, for the nuclear bomb, the ICBM and MIRV, by virtue of their unimaginable powers of indiscriminate destruction, have gone far beyond the limits of prudential decision. Still other essentially moral problems arise when civilized values of tolerance and human dignity are menaced by powerful armed fanaticisms whose victory would abolish intellectual and civil freedom. I have in mind such movements as Nazism and Stalinism.

These moral considerations should be brought to bear upon the idea of national interest, but they should not supersede it. Dr. Bennett in his wise and modest book, *Foreign Policy in Christian Perspective*, has made the proper distinction: "We may say that Christian faith and ethics offer ultimate perspectives, broad criteria, motives, inspirations, sensitivities, warning, moral limits rather than directives for policies and decisions." I cannot think of any recent problem in our foreign policy that could not have been adequately and intelligently disposed of on the grounds of national interest, qualified as Hamilton and Roosevelt would have us qualify it. We are asked to consider such questions as when a nation is justified in using force beyond its frontiers or in providing armed support of or opposition to revolutions in other countries. Plainly such questions cannot be answered by *a priori* moral principles but only by careful case-by-case assessment. Burke long ago pointed out the difference between the statesman and the moralist: "the latter has only a general view of society; the former, the statesman, has a number of circumstances to combine with those general ideas, and to take into his consideration. Circumstances are infinite, are infinitely combined, are variable and transient. . . . A statesman, never losing sight of principles, is to be guided by circumstances."

It is through the idea of national interest that moral values enter most effectively into the forma-

tion of foreign policy. The moral question arises particularly in a state's observance or nonobservance of its own best standards. Foreign policy is the face a nation wears to the world. If a course in foreign affairs implies moral values incompatible with the ideals of the national community, either the nation will refuse after a time to sustain the policy, or else it must abandon its ideals. A people is in bad trouble when it tries to keep two sets of books—when it holds one scale of values for its internal polity and applies another to its conduct of foreign affairs. The consequent moral schizophrenia is bound to convulse the homeland. This is what happened to France during the Algerian war. It is what is happening to the United States because of the Indochina war.

Moral slogans, Asian mud

IN ORDER TO CONDEMN THIS horrid conflict it is not necessary to deliver a moral judgment on it. If our policy had been founded on a sober and deliberate calculation of the national interest, we could hardly have sunk so deeply and unthinkingly into a situation where our commitment so far exceeds any rational involvement of that interest or any demonstrable threat to our national security. This is why the analysts who have most consistently invoked the idea of the national interest—Lippmann, Kennan, and Morgenthau—have been skeptical about the Indochinese adventure from the start.

I do not suggest that its advocates did not have a national-interest argument too. This argument in its most sophisticated version was that, with the establishment of nuclear balance between America and Russia, the main source of world instability lay in Third World wars—the kind that Khrushchev called "national liberation" wars in the truculent speech of January 1961 which had so unfortunate an effect on the Kennedy Administration. If the United States proved its ability to deal with such wars, then the world could look forward to an age of peace. Unhappily, this argument assumed that Communist activity everywhere occurred at the behest of and for the benefit of the Soviet Union. It gravely underestimated the strength of national Communism, and it wildly overestimated the capacity of the United States to win guerrilla wars.

Moreover, the argument was thereafter translated into a crude series of political propositions. Our national interest was involved, we were soon given to understand, because the Vietcong and Hanoi were the spearheads of a planned system of Chinese expansion. Therefore, by fighting in Vietnam, we were holding the line against an aggressive Red China. If we did not fight, we would, like Chamberlain at Munich, invite further aggression; and a billion Chinese armed with nuclear weapons (a specter invoked with relish by Secretary Rusk) would overrun Asia and turn the world balance of power permanently in favor of Communism. "The threat to world peace," as Vice President Humphrey summed up this fantasy as late as October 1967, "is militant, aggressive Asian communism, with its headquarters in Peking, China. . . . The aggression of North Vietnam is but the most current and immediate action of militant Asian communism."

The argument that Asian Communism was a monolithic movement run out of Peking was preposterous at the time. It is more preposterous in these days of Ping-Pong diplomacy. As even William Buckley has managed to discern, President Nixon's China policy abolishes the major strategic argument for the Indochina war.

Since it is painful to charge our national leaders with stupidity, one must suppose that this foolish analysis was only a secondary motive for our involvement in Indochina. The primary motive, it seems probable in retrospect, had little to do with national interest at all. It was, rather, a precise consequence of the belief that moral principles should govern decisions of foreign policy. It was the insistence on seeing the civil war in Vietnam as above all a moral issue that led us to construe political questions in ethical terms, local questions in global terms, and relative questions in absolute terms.

The propensity toward thinking big in foreign policy was implicit in the Wilsonian tradition. The habit of ideological escalation grew in the early years of the Cold War. It became rampant in the era of the rigidly Presbyterian Dulles. The Kennedy Administration vacillated between the impassioned rhetoric of the Inaugural Address and Kennedy's own acute sense of the limitations of American power. Then Kennedy was murdered while he was still in the process of giving American foreign policy new precision and restraint. With his successors, moralism triumphed.

Other pressures hastened the Indochina catastrophe—above all, the momentum of the military machine, with its institutional conviction that political problems have military solutions; its institutional desire to try out weapons, tactics, and personnel; and its institutional capacity for self-delusion about the ability of just one more step of escalation to assure military success. Still, the opportunity seized with such avidity by the military was created by those who believed that America was in Vietnam on a moral mission—who applauded when President Johnson cried in 1965:

> History and our own achievements have thrust upon us the principal responsibility for protection of freedom on earth. . . . No other people in no other time has had so great an opportunity to work and risk for the freedom of all mankind.

The Indochina war was a morality trip, and moral absolutism was the final stop. As early as 1965, the *New York Times* quoted an American pilot: "I do not like to hit a village. You know you are hitting women and children. But you've got to decide that your cause is noble and that the work has to be done." In this anointed spirit we conceived ourselves the world's judge, jury, and executioner and did our work in Indochina.

Grim lessons

THE MORALISTIC CANT of Presidents Johnson and Nixon helped delude a lot of pilots into supposing they were doing God's work. Unfortunately, instead of strengthening the national-interest wing of the opposition to the war, Vietnam seems to have incited an equally moralistic outburst on the part of the war's most clamorous critics. Too many people on both sides of the Indochina debate feel they know exactly what the Lord would do if He only knew the facts in the case.

Yet may not these critics, emotional and extravagant as they often are, have a point? Are not even those quite satisfied to oppose the war as contrary to our national interest still obliged to face the question of whether it may not be an immoral as well as a stupid war? I think they are, if we are ever to extract the full and awful lesson from this catastrophe.

My own answer to the question is yes, it is an immoral war, and it became so, ironically, when our moralistic zeal burst the limitations of national interest. Our original presence in South Vietnam hardly seems immoral, since we were there at the request of the South Vietnam government. Nor does it seem necessarily contrary to our national interest: conceivably it might have been worth it to commit, say, 20,000 military advisers if this could preserve an independent South Vietnam. But at some point the number of troops, and the things they were instructed to do, began to go beyond the requirements of national interest. This point was almost certainly the decision taken in early 1965 to send our bombers to North Vietnam and our combat units to South Vietnam and thus to Americanize the war.

Theologians talk about the principle of proportionality—the principle that means must have a due and rational relationship to ends. The Indochina war became, in my view, what can properly be called an immoral war when the means employed and the destruction wrought grew out of any conceivable proportion to the interests involved and the ends sought.

Enjoined by our leaders as to the sublimity of the mission, we cast ourselves as saviors of human freedom, misconceived the extremely restricted character of our national stake in Indochina, and, step by step, intensified senseless terror till we stand today as a nation disgraced before the world and before our own posterity.

"Moralists tend to see foreign policy as a means not of influencing events but of registering virtuous attitudes."

How will our descendants ever understand the mood in which ordinary GIs, inflamed with the belief that anything Americans did was right, virtuously massacred Indochinese women and children—or in which such crimes were condoned, if not concealed, by the theater command? How will they understand the mood in which some American citizens hailed an hysterical killer as a national hero and proposed that, instead of conviction by a military court-martial, he should receive the Congressional Medal of Honor? How will historians explain national decisions, piously taken by God-fearing men in air-conditioned offices in Washington, that resulted in the detonation over this weak and hapless land of six million tons of explosives—three times

as much as we dropped on Germany, Italy, and Japan during the second world war?

For years we averted our eyes from what we were doing in Indochina—from the search-and-destroy missions and the free-fire zones; from the defoliation and the B-52s; from the noncombatants slaughtered; the villages laid waste; the crops and forests destroyed; the refugees, one-third of the population of South Vietnam, huddled in unimaginable squalor; from the free and continuous' violations of the laws of war. For years we even refrained from pursuing the question of why we were fighting in Indochina—the question that will mystify future historians as they try to figure out what threat to national security, what involvement of national interest, conceivably justified the longest war in American history, the systematic deception of the American people, and the death of thousands of Americans and hundreds of thousands of Vietnamese.

The Calley trial at last compelled the nation to contemplate these questions. The days of pretending were over. No one can doubt that the ordeal of self-interrogation, however damaging it may be to our self-image and self-illusions, will be profoundly beneficial to our nation. If we have the fortitude to carry this process through, history may conclude that the brave men who died in Vietnam did not altogether die in vain.

At the very least, a full inquiry into the causes and consequences of the war, as recently suggested by the *New Republic*, would force the nation to contemplate the things we must do to provide reparation for our acts and safeguards against their repetition. But such an inquiry, one must trust, will not result in the vindication of the moral approach to foreign policy. One must hope, rather, that it would increase skepticism about moral judgments promiscuously introduced into international politics. One must hope that the Indochina experience will inoculate the nation against the perversion of policy by moralism in the future. An intelligent regard for one's own national interest joined to unremitting respect for the interests of others seems more likely than the invocation of moral absolutes to bring about greater restraint, justice, and peace among nations.

After Many a Summer Dies the Majority

RICHARD J. WALTON

RICHARD J. WALTON is former U.N. correspondent for Voice of America and author of *The Remnants of Power: The Tragic Last Years of Adlai Stevenson*.

Most Americans still believe the myth that the United States, whatever its other faults in international life, is a stanch, unswerving supporter of the United Nations. As with most myths there is some truth to this, but not complete truth. The U.N., to be sure, is an American invention with FDR the father and Wilson the grandfather. The United States has contributed as much, or more, money to the U.N. as all the other members combined. President after American President has pledged both genuine and generous support to the U.N. In short, without the U.S. there would be no U.N.

Nor is there any doubt that the U.N. has been assaulted constantly by the Soviet Union. Many would agree with the words of Professor Inis L. Claude of the University of Michigan, perhaps the pre-eminent American scholar on the United Nations: "Through the history of the United Nations, the United States and the Soviet Union have undertaken, respectively, to enhance and to frustrate the effectiveness of the United Nations as an operative mechanism." One can see the heads in Foggy Bottom nodding in agreement, for that is what the State Department has been arguing for years. But Professor Claude continues: "At one level of analysis, this might be taken to mean that the United States has been dedicated, and the Soviet Union opposed, to the development of a potent instrument of world order. At another, and deeper, level these contrasting policies might be interpreted as reflecting the differing estimates of the two major powers as to their capability for directing and controlling the activities of the organization."

This statement contrasts with the conventional view that American support of the U.N. is not merely a reflection of enlightened self-interest but a higher act in response to the higher purposes of the world organization. This impression is entirely natural and has been cultivated by successive administrations, although President Nixon has been chary of even rhetorical support, as was President Johnson toward the end of his term. But critics of present American foreign policy should not go so far as to accuse the U.S. of complete cynicism in the cultivation of this "higher purpose" belief. In the early years of the cold war Washington genuinely believed that its purposes were identical with those of the U.N. and that it was the Soviet Union which sinned against the principles of international morality embodied in the U.N. Charter.

Thus, the United States used the United Nations as an instrument in its struggle with the Soviet Union. The U.N. existed and so did the cold war, and at the time it was unavoidable that whichever country could use the U.N. would. For the next fifteen to twenty years the United States commanded an unchallengeable majority in the Security Council and the General Assembly and regarded the organization not only as the embodiment of international ideals but as a political mechanism meant to be used by those nations with the power and the skill.

The roles of the United States and Soviet Union were cast by circumstance. The Americans emerged as champions of the U.N. because they had the votes, and the Soviets, regardless of the merit or frequent lack of merit of their arguments, emerged as villains because they didn't have the votes. Therefore, Russia brandished its veto in the Security Council more than a hundred times, to the frequent condemnation, often justified, of the government and people of the United States. Yet, curious as it may seem to some, the veto saved the U.N. If the Soviet Union had not been able to gain minimal protection for its interests through use of the veto, it no doubt would have quit the organization. No Soviet Union, no United Nations, at least not in any real sense. Nor should the frequent dismay over Soviet vetoes obscure the fact that at San Francisco the United States demanded the veto fully as much as the Soviet Union.

These assertions about American use of the U.N. should be documented. Perhaps the most significant example is the familiar China question. In 1949, when the Communists gained unquestioned control of the mainland, the United States blocked its seating and preserved the representation of the Taiwan government, as it continues to do. This is not merely a matter of internal U.N. politics; it has always been a matter of profound importance to an unsettled world. There is, of course, the legal, and some would say moral, question. The government in Peking is the government of China and as a matter of course should have taken the Chinese seat in the U.N. Then there is the philosophic question. The U.N. aspires to universality, and it can hardly be universal when a nation of 700 million is not a member. There is another point that is infinitely more important: It is in the interest of the U.N. and world peace that China be a member. Both the Korean and Vietnam wars might never have occurred had China been a member, or they might have taken a less disastrous course. As for the future, progress on disarmament, nuclear testing, the spread of nuclear weapons, and a political settlement in Asia are all difficult, perhaps impossible, without Chinese participation.

Then there is the case of Korea, which is often cited as a U.N. success story. However justified President Truman's decision to intervene, it was a cold war decision, unilaterally made. Yet Washington decided that it would be politically advantageous to intervene under the U.N. flag, and it had the votes to get U.N. authorization. Thus, for use of the U.N. flag and a token number of contingents from other countries, the U.S. made the U.N. a party to the war and ruled out whatever role the organization might have played as mediator.

But the U.N. became even more involved. When Truman decided to intervene, he, as he wrote in his *Memoirs*, "wanted it clearly understood that our

From *Saturday Review*, June 27, 1970. Copyright 1970 Saturday Review, Inc.

operations in Korea were designed to restore peace there and to restore the border." In short, Truman's goal was to restore the situation as it existed before the North Korean invasion. However, once the American and South Korean armies repelled the nearly successful North Korean invasion, there was a complete turnabout and the allied armies poured northward. Truman then changed his goal and decided not to stop at the 38th parallel but to conquer North Korea. Because of American dominance in the U.N. General Assembly, he again got authorization. It was one thing for the U.N., even as a cold war partisan, to take part in an operation to restore the previous situation; it was quite another to participate in the attempted conquest of North Korea. The U.N. had shifted from defensive participation to offensive participation, and in the face of China's blunt warnings that it would intervene if American (U.N.) troops crossed into North Korea. Intervene it did, of course, and the result is basic to the continuing hostility between China on the one hand and the United States and the U.N. on the other.

All through the hottest years of the cold war, the United States used its dominance of the U.N. as a political instrument—in Iran, Greece, Czechoslovakia, Berlin, Hungary, the Congo, Cuba, the Gulf of Tonkin, or for various peacekeeping missions, and so forth. To be sure, the Russians, even without the votes to pass resolutions, often made use of the U.N. as a forum for propaganda attacks on the U.S. The point is not that the United States was wrong in these disputes with Russia, for it was very often right, but that the U.N. was immobilized when it might have had some useful effect as a mediator. To quote Claude again:

> On the one hand, leaders of the United States valued the organization, and encouraged the American public to value it, as a reliable instrument of American policy in opposition to the Soviet Union; on the other hand, they insisted that Soviet leaders should regard the United Nations as an impartial agency of the world community, ready to serve neutrally in the solution of conflicts, and entitled to the support of all states.

But by the mid-Sixties the circumstances had begun to change. Newly

independent African and Asian states had flooded into the U.N. in such numbers that they dominated voting in the General Assembly. No longer did the U.S. have its automatic majority; so, not surprisingly, the American attitude began to change. American officials, particularly in private, began to talk disapprovingly of irresponsible bloc voting and disparagingly of such nations as Chad and Gabon having the same vote in the Assembly as the United States. The eloquent advocate of majority rule began to question it, although no one could recall the U.S. ever terming the Latin American bloc irresponsible or remember the State Department disparaging the right of Paraguay or Nicaragua to have the same vote as the United States. The U.S. has also been influenced by its inability, despite several tries, to use the U.N. to lessen its responsibility for the Vietnam War.

Again, as was true decades earlier, circumstances dictated the roles. The United States, sometimes finding itself in an unaccustomed minority, particularly when the Afro-Asian bloc passed a resolution calling on the Western nations to match their words on racism with specific, concrete deeds, has discovered that the majority can be irresponsible. And the Soviet Union, finding itself, on colonial and racial questions at least, with an unaccustomed majority, sees new virtue in majority rule.

This change in the American attitude was dramatically demonstrated on March 17 of this year when the United States exercised its veto for the first time. It had always been assumed that the United States would cast its first veto only in momentous circumstances, only when paramount American interests were at stake. But the first American veto seemed unnecessary. The U.S. quite understandably shared Britain's dismay at the Security Council resolution condemning the U.K. for not using force to put down the white minority government in Rhodesia and ordering all states to cut all relations

with Rhodesia. But Britain's negative vote alone would have sufficed to kill the Afro-Asian resolution. Casting its first veto on a matter of secondary concern, the U.S. seemed to be indicating a tougher line in regard to the Afro-Asian bloc.

The erosion of American strength in the U.N.—although the U.S. remains by far the most powerful single nation—has been accompanied, quite naturally, by a de-escalation of American rhetoric. Where once every major speech by President or Secretary of State contained eloquent phrases of American support for the U.N., such language has largely disappeared in the last two or three years. Indeed, when Mr. Nixon appeared before the General Assembly last fall, he barely mentioned the U.N., even in its own house, nor did he give it more than passing attention in his recent State of the World message. It appears now that the U.S. has joined the U.S.S.R. in believing that although the U.N. certainly has its uses, it can hardly be relied on as major instrument of foreign policy. Perhaps after a while in which neither superpower can use the U.N. as the U.S. once did, both will conclude that a more neutral U.N. can serve a very real function as mediator, buffer, go-between—something less than was hoped for in San Francisco but more than the organization had been during the bitter cold war years.

And what are we to think, those millions of us who have long believed or wanted to believe that the U.N. has no better friend than the United States? Again, Professor Claude: "Most of us Americans have convinced ourselves that we are stanch and dependable supporters of international organization. The truth is, I think, that we do not yet know whether this is so—we have not had a chance to find out. The question of our attitude toward the world organization should be put to us after we have accumulated a considerable experience of losing rather than winning in the United Nations, of having it conduct programs of which we disapprove, of having it press us to pay assessments in support of activities that we think damage rather than serve our national interests. Then, and only then, shall we be able to say how deep our commitment is to the United Nations or to the principle of an organized world system."

The Seven Wonders of the Polluted World

RICHARD CURTIS & DAVE FISHER

RICHARD CURTIS is a freelance who specializes in environmental subjects. His latest book, "The Case for Extinction," a satire published under the pseudonym Professor Morton Stultifer, advocates the destruction of most living things. DAVE FISHER is a reporter for Life magazine.

RATHER than always spend your vacation seeking out virgin forests, umblemished beaches and unspoiled natural wonders, how would you like to try something downright polluted? Before you say no, stop and think for a moment. Wouldn't you appreciate the beauties of the earth more keenly after having exposed yourself to a ravaged wilderness, a fetid waterway or a decayed town?

Well, all right, if you won't actually *expose* yourself to such things, perhaps you will at least *read* about them. So come, let us take you by the hand and lead you on a modern-day Grand Tour, a globe-circling expedition to the Seven Wonders of the Polluted World.

The journey begins at Manhattan's piers. We board our cruise ship, steam

Perhaps you'll appreciate the beauties of our planet more keenly, say the authors, after you've taken their Grand Tour of the Seven Wonders of the Polluted World — from London to Tokyo, Venice to Vietnam.

out of New York Harbor toward Ambrose Point and travel a scant 12 miles before encountering our first wonder— a dead sea of sewage sludge and industrial wastes covering 20 square miles of what once was ocean.

Sludgeophiles, as authorities on this sort of thing are called, have long hailed New York as the liquid waste capital of the world. Each year, under permits issued by the Army Corps of Engineers, five million cubic yards of treated sewage are towed by barge to this site and dumped here. To this are added six million tons of dredging spoils annually and 365 million gallons of raw sewage from the Hudson River *daily.* The result is a chemical broth that has destroyed all marine life in the vicinity.

Marine biologists and Army engineers regularly lower buckets into this gunk and haul up samples. One Army man described the bottom as "a gooey mess," but the surface of the ocean out here is something to write home about, too. Depending on the season, its color ranges from phew-green to feh-brown, with odors to match. Fred Ulrich, senior sanitation engineer of the Interstate Sanitation Commission, says a catalogue of the junk floating around would awe even a seasoned garbage collector, and he concludes somewhat anticlimactically

that "the water is definitely not safe for swimming." Since "huge chunks of decayed piers" are among the more prominent detritus he mentioned, one would imagine that it's not only not safe for swimming but scarcely safe for anything smaller than dreadnought-class ships.

Like most unnatural wonders, this dead sea was not created overnight. Dumping has been going on here for at least 40 years, and there are no signs that it will end soon. But dead though it is, this titanic cube of gumbo is by no means immobile. Subject to winds and currents, it occasionally drifts toward the New York-New Jersey coastline, tantalizing residents with the prospect that the Metropolitan area may become the first excrement-locked region in the world. In fact, fringes have already brushed New Jersey and contributed, in the opinion of some scientists, to an occasional "red tide"—an invasion of highly toxic microorganisms that turn the water red and render the ocean unfit for bathing.

Should a capricious breeze or current decide to deposit even a portion of this

Sludge, Smells, Sights, Slums,

sea of goop on our doorsteps, Fun City residents might one day find themselves participating in an unscheduled summer festival. "If the bottom was ever agitated and this stuff turned up on the beaches, it would be disastrous," says Joseph L. Brown, pollution control specialist for the Army Engineers. "You couldn't possibly swim without picking up some sort of disease." Arthur Ashendorff, assistant director of the Bureau of Sanitary Engineering for the New York City Department of Health, cites typhoid and dysentery as some of the more interesting possibilities.

With a prayer of thanks that our ship's hull hasn't corroded beneath our feet, we proceed eastward to serene—and noisome—Venice. Although Europe offers plenty of contenders for odor pollution honors, the laurels must go to Venetians for stubborn resistance to the evidence of their own nostrils. Fumes from the fertilizer plants, steel mills and oil refineries in the surrounding industrial area of Mestre-Marghera mingle with noxious naphtha produced by the burning of soft coal to heat homes, then blend with sewage and garbage odors rising from the canals plus oily wastes from multitudes of *vaporetti* —motor-driven canal boats. Not wishing

to leave anything to the winds of chance, public-spirited citizens deposit their refuse in the watery streets, and drowned rats and poisoned fish lend a final exquisite touch to the fetid atmosphere of the city once called the Queen of the Adriatic.

Fouled Canals

One of the Great Moments in Pollution History took place here in midsummer, 1970. Wastes from the Marghera factories filled the water and air with such a concentration of sulphur that the canals turned dark brown, eyes bright red, and exposed silver a tarnished rust color. True, many municipalities are subject to sulphurous effluvia due to industrial activity, but the damp Venetian climate tends to trap residues close to the ground so that they form a heavy blanket over the city. Although Venetians suffer mightily, the prime victim of the virulent air is the city's fabled statuary. Marble that survived hundreds of millions of years of geological upheaval is beginning to disintegrate after a mere century of exposure to Venice's least-talked-about manufactured item—sulphuric acid, the result of rain, mist and sea spray combining with sulphurous effluents. According to Prof. Francesco Valcanover,

Superintendent of Fine Arts in Venice, more than one-third of the city's buildings and sculpture have been corroded by what locals quaintly term "marble cancer." Moreover Professor Valcanover estimates that the erosion is taking place at the rate of 5 per cent of the marble works every year, to say nothing of Venice's glorious frescoes and paintings. Luckily, for many statues, the nose is the first part to go.

From Venice we wing to London, exchanging nasal for visual pollution. London, this sublime city whose residents like to think of themselves as divinely ordained defenders of Western tradition, is rapidly yielding to a form of architectural barbarianism that has been dubbed The New Brutalism. No doubt about it, London leads the European League in historic structures batted down.

More than a quarter of Britain's capital city was leveled by the blitz in World War II, but the peacetime blitz symbolized by the wrecker's ball has proven even more effective: 14 acres are being knocked down and rebuilt every week. Bridget Cherry, an architectural historian, has actually furnished proof that more of central London is being de-

NEW YORK—A titanic cube of gumbo, the surface of which covers 20 square miles of ocean, exists just off Manhattan Island, where dumping has been going on for at least 40 years.

VENICE—"The prime victim of the virulent air is the city's fabled statuary." Sulphuric acid—the result of rain, mist and sea spray combining with sulphurous effluents—causes what the locals quaintly term "marble cancer."

Sprays, Smog and Seepage

stroyed by developers than was ever done by the Luftwaffe.

The fact is, however, that it's hard to say which is the more appalling—the widespread demolition or the quality of the new construction. The first replacement structure to horrify everyone was the 28-story London Hilton, a towering, gleamingly sterile box wedged into the genteel five-story serenity of Mayfair back in 1963. It sounded a clarion call to every mediocre architect in the city to see if he couldn't outdo it. Many succeeded. The ensuing building boom in the Mayfair area wrote finis to at least a hundred Georgian terrace houses, the famed Carlton Mews and numerous other examples of a glorious heritage.

Not content with Mayfair, developers have sought to wreak mischief elsewhere. St. Paul's, for example, is being pushed out of the picture by the 600-foot National Westminster Bank under construction a half-mile away. The Thames is the setting for the monstrous 34-story Vickers office tower overshadowing the Houses of Parliament, Westminster Abbey and Big Ben, which Britons are wryly coming to call Little Ben. Across the river stands the 24-story Shell Tower, described as "a tombstone of boardroom architecture." A new project planned for the area combines a skyscraper headquarters for the International Paper Company with a housing project and tropical resort-style hotel.

"Miami Beach" is rapidly becoming London's favorite building style, according to Ada Louise Huxtable, architecture critic of The New York Times. "There is a new London rising and all that is missing is the palm trees," she says.

For the next leg of our journey we fly southeast, and if you're the gregarious sort you'll be sublimely happy almost from the moment you touch down at the aptly named Dum-Dum International Airport in India, just outside Calcutta, for you'll never get closer to people than here. In Calcutta you may observe the ultimate fulmination of the population bomb: 7.5 million people living on the city's 135 square miles of usable land. Of course, many cities, such as Tokyo, Amsterdam, Copenhagen and even New York, are densely populated, but in the core of Calcutta roughly 100,000 people occupy each square mile, and that's a record. In addition, it must be explained that population density isn't as significant as the capacity of an area to support its inhabitants. And that's where Calcutta is really unsurpassed. Four and a half million of its residents are housed in squalid slums and nearly a quarter of a million live on the sidewalks.

To 77 per cent of Calcuttans, 40 square feet is home, a little larger than one of our king-size water beds. Indeed, it might be said that Calcutta itself becomes the world's biggest water bed whenever it rains, because the sewage system backs up. Built in 1888, it was designed for a city of no more than two million, which is why Calcutta has become the earth's permanent convention center for cholera bacilli. At least 200,000 Indians die of cholera annually, according to World Health Organization statistics.

What holds Calcutta's mass of human beings together is a stoical belief in an underpopulated afterlife plus a sense of humor. A favorite saying here is, "Calcutta would simply go down the drain—if there was one." And an Indian economist, asked what he would do if elected mayor of the city, replied, "Buy six feet of wire and hang myself." Oh, Calcutta! An absolute must for Zero Population Growth freaks!

From India to South Vietnam is a longish passage, but no tour of defiled

CALCUTTA—With 7.5 million people living on the city's 135 square miles of usable land, a favorite saying has become: "Calcutta would simply go down the drain—if there was one."

VIETNAM—The United States has defoliated one-seventh of the total area of the country. What is more, tree trunks have become so riddled with shrapnel that local sawmills regularly lose one to three hours a day repairing damage to saw blades.

areas would be complete without a visit to this masterpiece of technological desecration. In the last nine years United States "advisers" have managed to defoliate one-seventh of the total area of the country. Over four million acres have been sprayed with a variety of green-killing chemicals, converting the soil into something approaching the texture of concrete. More than one-third of the dense jungle comprising half of the country's forest land has been stripped by defoliants sprayed from planes in an enterprise appropriately named "Operation Hades." The fledgling Vietnamese timber industry has been devastated: 6.5 billion board feet have been lost.

have been burned out, some by fires purposely set by combatants, others ignited by artillery shells. Naturally the Air Force is not to be outdone by land forces. B-52 bombers have dropped over 2.5 million 500- and 750-pound bombs, leaving craters as deep as 30 feet and as wide as 35, and giving the countryside a surface-of-the-moon aspect—and one showing about as much life in many places.

Of more recent vintage is a piece of ordnance affectionately dubbed "the cheeseburger." Weighing in at 15,000 pounds, it is the world's biggest non-nuclear bomb. Because it is too heavy for a conventional bomber to carry, it

ties. . . . It is likely that the tiger population has increased, much as the wolf population in Poland increased during World War II."

To our next destination bring a gas mask. With luck and radar our plane will make it safely through the soupy air of Tokyo.

The Japanese are determined to become the most industrialized nation in the world even it kills them, and they are well on the way to fulfilling their ambition. The country's phenomenal post-war recovery has created forests of smokestacks around every major city, and some 75,000 of them around Tokyo alone daily belch hundreds of tons of

RICHLAND, Wash.—"I do not conceive of leaking tanks as acceptable storage" for radioactive wastes, one expert recently declared.

In addition, according to Time magazine, "Trees are so riddled with shrapnel that sawmills lose 1 to 3 hours a day repairing damage to saw blades."

But if recent studies are indicative, greenery may not be the only victim of this chemical warfare. In the spring of last year the United States Government acknowledged that one of the substances sprayed extensively over South Vietnam was capable of producing birth defects in rats and mice, and debate now rages in scientific circles about the future genetic effects of this spraying of 60,000 tons of a certain chemical called 2,4,5-T on Vietnamese people. As one health official laconically observed, "It can't help."

To get back to trees, chemical pollutants are not the only tools of destruction diligently applied to them here. Gigantic 38½-ton bulldozers specifically designed to ram down forests are being employed on a wide scale. Over 40 per cent of South Vietnam's pine plantations

must be borne in the bay of a giant C-13 cargo plane. The cheeseburger explodes horizontally and is capable of leveling an area the size of a football field to instantly create a landing place for helicopters. In the words of one airman, "It kills everything within a hundred yards, even the worms in the ground." People standing more than a mile from ground zero may be deafened. Judging by the effectiveness of this anti-tree campaign, it is little wonder that the fastest-growing cash crop of South Vietnam is marijuana.

Incidentally, one intriguing by-product of the war has been a probable increase in Vietnam's tiger population. Gordon H. Orians and E. W. Pfeiffer, in a recent issue of Science, reported that over the last 24 years of struggle, involving first the French and then the U.S., tigers have "learned to associate the sounds of gunfire with the presence of dead and wounded human beings in the vicinity. As a result, tigers rapidly move toward gunfire and apparently consume large numbers of battle casual-

noxious sulphur, nitrous oxides, ammonia and carbon gases into an atmosphere already saturated with chemical dust and ashes. Add emissions from the 1.5 million vehicles clogging Tokyo's streets and what do you get? Something pretty awful. On a recent summer day the density of carbon monoxide in the air rose to 74.5 on a scale where 20.0 represents serious peril.

Visibility Zero

The result of this outpouring is permanently visible air, which, unfortunately, tends to make everything else invisible. Visibility along the heavily traveled sea route between Tokyo and Yokosuka, for example, fell to zero more than 50 times during one recent 12-month period, resulting in over one hundred maritime collisions. Among the famous sights that have largely vanished is the view of Mount Fuji once so dear to postcard senders. Only one day out of every nine will get you a clear look at the mountain because of the miasma, which has also decimated

Tokyo's cherry tree population. Indeed, the cherry tree mortality rate is so high that the Japanese have asked Washington for sprigs from the very trees they bestowed on America five decades ago.

In the best tradition of devilish Oriental cleverness, however, citizens of Tokyo have taken exciting steps to adapt to their smog problem. Traffic policemen, for example, return to their headquarters several times a day for oxygen boosters. The man in the street may purchase oxygen in shops at the equivalent of two bits a whiff. Gauze surgical masks are in common use on particularly bad days. Thus, once again, the Land of the Rising Sun has pointed the way to the future—a future with no rising sun.

From Tokyo we proceed to our last stop for a look at what is probably the most attractive form of pollution from the viewpoint of those seeking to cause maximum harm with minimum effort—radioactivity. We land at the Tri-City Airport just 10 miles outside of Richland, Wash., back in the U.S.A.

Richland is the home of the Hanford atomic facilities, where 140 huge steel and concrete tanks lie buried just below the surface of the ground. They contain approximately 55 million gallons of concentrated radioactive waste, the by-product of plutonium manufactured for nuclear weapons. So intensely hot is this waste that it boils by itself for years, will be violently toxic for tens of thousands of years, and is so nasty that a few gallons released in a city's watershed might contaminate it for the indefinite future.

Risk of Disaster

It seems that some of these tanks leak a little, and there have been a few instances of near-rupture. Since they are situated only 240 feet above the water table of the Columbia River, the possibility of a Really Big Show is always imminent. In addition, the chance of tank ruptures at Hanford is enhanced by the fact that it is in a seismically unstable area that is part of the earthquake belt that rings the Pacific, the one responsible for chronic temblors in Alaska, California, South America and Japan. Some geologists have theorized that an offshoot of a major fault runs underneath the atomic facilities and it is known that there was an earthquake in the general area as little as 52 years ago.

Though a quake might not damage the tanks themselves, it could harm the elaborate cooling and stirring systems that keep the tanks from developing hot spots. A breakdown might burst the seams and release radioactive gases into the air. If atmospheric conditions were right, these gases could blanket an extremely large territory like a killer smog, only far more virulent—yea, the havoc could prove worse than that wrought by the atomic bomb over Hiroshima.

Dr. Chauncey Starr, founder and past president of the American Nuclear Society, is a great believer in the development of nuclear power, but even he admitted in a recent interview in Look magazine that "I do not conceive of leaking tanks as acceptable storage." Other experts, not given to couching their opinions quite so conservatively, have averred that the situation scares them to death.

So here we have the seventh wonder—tanks built to last 10 or 20 years but required to hold radioactive wastes for thousands, for periods "longer," to quote one Atomic Energy Commission spokesman, "than the history of most governments that the world has seen." Hanford, Wash., is future pollution at its finest, a splendid climax to a splendid tour.

8

Probing Future

Historians today are much like the adventuring mariners of the Age of Discovery. Pushing beyond their knowledge of the past, they probe the uncharted world of the onrushing future. Whether or not these intellectual voyages are accurate to the nth degree, only time will tell. Nevertheless, it would be foolish not to consider seriously their imaginative and timely insights.

John Brooks' "A Clean Break with the Past" begins this section. "A startling discontinuity, as stark as a geologic fault, has occurred in our cultural history since 1964," writes Brooks. "The trigger for the mood is harder to identify. Many would equate it with the hateful trigger of Lee Harvey Oswald's mail-order gun." Inspecting the dramatic events of our time and the corresponding attitudinal changes of millions of Americans, Brooks finds the slippage along that historical faultline so shattering that "every American except the very young, the very empty, and the very enclosed must now, to some extent, feel himself a foreigner in his native land." In our second article, "The Roots of Lawlessness," Henry Steele Commager echoes Abraham Lincoln's analysis of 1838. "If destruction be our lot," said Lincoln, "we must ourselves be its author and finisher. As a nation of free men, we must live through all time or die by suicide."

In a more partisan tone, William A. Williams, in an article entitled "The Future of American Politics," calls on the New Left to give up its doomsday prophesies and to prove to the American public why and how socialism will be "better than a capitalism without the Vietnam War and with a continuing (and improving) pattern of permissive welfarism."

In "Phase II of the Capitalist System," Robert Heilbroner explores the angry and inappropriate images that both conservatives and radicals have of present-day American capitalism. Unlike Williams, Heilbroner believes that "there seems no reason to claim that capitalism cannot cope with the problems of the 20th century, whereas socialism is able to."

Optimist or pessimist, no historian of the emerging future can afford to leave out of his calculations the accumulating and accelerating effects of technology. In "America in the Technetronic Age," Zbigniew Brzezinski recalls what the Frenchman Alexis de Tocqueville said 140 years ago: "America is the first society to live in the future." Brzezinski proceeds to describe what living in the world's first technetronic, postindustrial society means. The next three articles explore the problems and the possibilities of technology. In "Priorities for the Seventies," Robert Heilbroner argues, "What we need are technological answers to technological problems." Next, Harrison Brown explores the possiblity of "strip-city USA" in "After the Population Explosion." "Imagine the thrill," writes Brown, "of flying from Los Angeles to New York and having the landscape look like Los Angeles all the way." Technology holds the threat of nemesis, but to Ivan Illich in "The Alternative to Schooling," it also holds possibility of providing "each man with the ability to understand his environment better, to shape it with his own hands." To this end, Illich looks forward to the day when schools will have been "disestablished" and learning will be *from* the world and not *about* it.

The future success of American civilization depends largely on what happens to our cities and to race relations. In "Liveable Cities," Donald Alexander asks for a new structuring of federal, state, and urban responsibilities. In "A Century of Negro Suffrage," Henry Lee Moon examines the tortuous path that the black vote has had to travel since the ratification of the fifteenth amendment to the Constitution in 1870. In asking the question "What America Would Be Like without Blacks," a *Time* essay concludes that "the nation could not survive being deprived of their presence because, by the irony implicit in the dynamics of American democracy, they symbolize both its most stringent testing and the possibility of its greatest human freedom."

A CLEAN BREAK

JOHN BROOKS

John Brooks's disturbing article serves as a grim postscript to his book The Great Leap: The Past Twenty-Five Years in America, *published in 1966. Mr. Brooks is a staff writer for* The New Yorker, *and his most recent book is* Once in Golconda: A True Drama of Wall Street, 1920–1938.

Something very strange has happened in the United States very recently. Traditional attitudes and values

that have prevailed and come down from generation to generation in all but unbroken succession since the founding of the republic have suddenly been overturned or are in the process of being overturned. Traditional American ways of looking at things—including the traditional way of looking at our own past—have suddenly been reversed. A startling discontinuity, as stark as a geologic fault, has occurred in our cultural history since 1964.

It is a temptation, and one constantly yielded to by social commentators, to look upon these things (like the geologic fault) as having simply *happened*—as having occurred without human volition or control. The environment has changed, it is said; no wonder people and their

DRAWN FOR AMERICAN HERITAGE BY COLOS

"In terms of change in American attitudes and American values, these last five years have surely been the crucial ones in the quarter century since V-J Day. And these changes seem of such a magnitude that every American except the very young, the very empty, and the very enclosed must now, to some extent, feel himself a foreigner in his native land"

WITH THE PAST

attitudes change. The process is made to appear as inexorable as changes in the phase of the moon.

What has "happened" in America has been largely the doing of the older half of our present population—those born before the Second World War. Through their ingenuity and enterprise and with the help of their equally ingenious and enterprising predecessors of the generations before, the members of the present older generation have changed the country so radically that the old conditions under which the old values obtained are simply not there any more. True enough, the change was brought about (in traditional American fashion) entirely without planning, and, indeed, its social effects have by and large not been felt by the generation responsible.

Not really understanding what it has wrought (still quaintly anthropomorphizing computers, for example) and being beyond the age when long-held attitudes and values are easily surrendered, the older half of the country mostly clings to the old ideas. In the meantime the younger half, those born since the war, have grown up in a whole new world and, in a triumph of environment over heredity, have become a new breed. The fathers, clever enough to invent computers, jet planes, moon ships, antibiotics, and weapons of race suicide, are not wise enough to know their own sons, who are now shaping the values of America and will soon *be* America.

A quarter century ago next month, with V-J Day, the United States emerged from the war into modern times.

In the subsequent twenty years, while the nation's adults, the prewar generation, were unwittingly removing from their own and their children's lives the physical underpinnings of the old national faiths and attitudes, they were also continuing—in fact, accelerating—the long process of social amelioration that had gone on, though not uninterruptedly, since not long after the Civil War. The first postwar quarter century was one of outstanding social as well as material progress.

About five years ago, I undertook a study of social change in the United States over the twenty-five years between the outbreak of the Second World War in 1939 and the mid-sixties. I found, among other things, that the great corporations, considered so gigantic and sinister in 1939, had become many times more gigantic and —in the pretty-well-substantiated public view—a good deal less sinister. (In the late thirties the Temporary National Economic Committee had reported with awe that General Motors, perhaps the archetypical American corporation, had assets of one billion dollars; less than two decades later General Motors would have *annual profits after taxes* of one billion dollars. It would meanwhile have abandoned its former rather surly attitude toward society and become a corporation as enlightened as most in its social attitudes.) The gross national product over the period had gone from 90 billion to 630 billion dollars a year; the federal budget had swollen from around nine billion to over one hundred billion; national income per capita had risen from nine hundred to well over three thousand dollars, while the national population (in sharp contradiction to the glum demographic predictions of 1939 that the nation faced a people shortage) had risen from 130,000,000 to over 190,000,000. Taxes and other forces had brought about a vast and generally beneficent redistribution of national wealth. Computer technology, in 1939 just a gleam in a few scientists' eyes, was already on the way to bringing about a new era in science and technology and, more obviously at first, in business methods; and the initial fears that computers would throw millions of people out of their jobs were beginning to prove unfounded. Poverty had by no means been eliminated, but by almost any fair-minded standard it had been sharply reduced; indeed, my calculations showed that by the standards applied in 1964, Franklin D. Roosevelt's one third of a nation ill fed, ill housed, and ill clothed in the thirties had been a gross understatement.

I found that over the period under study there had been a vast tidal migration from farms to cities. Thirty-one million Americans, or a quarter of the population, were farmers in 1939; only thirteen million, or less than 7 per cent, were still on the farms by 1964. The effect of this influx on the cities and on the new urbanites themselves, despite crime and overcrowding and suburbia

and urban sprawl, had not proved to be all bad. I found a tremendous rise in formal education: the average American was an elementary-school graduate in 1939, a high-school graduate by 1964; 15 per cent of college-age Americans attended college in 1939, well over 40 per cent in 1964.

Further, I argued that anti-Semitism, a strong and ominous thread in our national warp in 1939, had ceased

by 1964 to be an important factor—permanently, I patriotically supposed. On the question of Negro rights and privileges the evidence of progress, though more equivocal, was nevertheless present. In 1964, in the nation's capital city, where in 1939 no black man had been suffered to eat in a public restaurant used by whites or to register in any hotel, Congress was passing a wide-ranging civil rights act, and the next year it would pass a far wider-ranging one. A long, painful campaign for civil rights in the South, beginning with the Supreme Court's first desegregation decision in 1954, had caught the national imagination and that of our Texan President himself, and as a result of increased black-voter registration Negroes were being elected to office at many levels in most parts of the country. Economically, to be

"... the national mood reversed itself as dramatically as a manic-depressive"

sure, the average black man was only slightly better off in relation to the average white man than he had been in 1939. Formerly his income had been somewhat less than half of the white man's; now it was slightly more than half. But in 1964 the country seemed to have the will to tackle even this anomaly. One felt, buoyantly, that with the political liberation of the Negro virtually accomplished, his economic liberation was next on the agenda.

In its foreign affairs I said that the United States, which with the end of the war had assumed free-world leadership for the first time, had handled this generally unwanted responsibility fairly well in spite of some spectacular bungling. There were, despite moral arguments advanced in their behalf, such egregious disasters as the Bay of Pigs, the ill-starred U-2 reconnaissance flight, the unfortunate (but then not yet overwhelmingly tragic) miscalculation of our involvement in Vietnam. But there was also the nuclear test-ban treaty of 1963, the relief programs all over the world, and, of course, the Marshall Plan, which through its backers' statesmanlike vision of where enlightened self-interest lay, had done so much to set flattened Europe back on its feet.

In sum, my research convinced me that "the quarter-century . . . had seen such rapid and far-reaching changes in many aspects of American life as are not only unprecedented in our own national experience, but may well be unprecedented in that of any nation other than those that have been suddenly transformed by . . . war or plague." And I concluded that while the enormous material gains of the quarter century had unquestionably had their moral costs, the moral loss was far less clear than the material gain. America could not patly be said to have "sold its soul for mediocrity."

So I wrote then. Between then and now, over the past five years, many but not all of the trends I noted have continued. Economic growth has gone on to the point where most economists believe that 1971 will be the year when our gross national product will pass the all but inscrutable figure of a trillion dollars a year. Our 1964 federal budget is now almost doubled. Poverty, more and more in the news, is nevertheless still decreasing in fact.

On the other hand the migration from farms to cities has slowed sharply. Anti-Semitism in a new form has made an ominous appearance among Negro militants. Racial integration of schools has failed tragically, as shown by the fact that at the beginning of 1970—sixteen years after the Supreme Court's desegregation decision—less than one fifth of southern Negro pupils and hardly more than one fourth of northern and western Negro pupils were attending predominantly white schools. The stagnation of black economic status is shown by the persistence of two familiar statistics—black income still just over half that of whites, black unemployment still double that among whites.

But statistics are not all. There exist also national moods, and they rather than statistics reflect attitudes and values. There are fashions in statistics; appropriate ones can be found to fit any mood, to buttress any conventional wisdom, and it can be argued that the moods give birth to the figures rather than vice versa. At any rate, some time recently, probably in 1965, the national mood reversed itself as dramatically as a manic-depressive patient goes from the heights to the depths, and I see my study as having been completed in the last, climactic days of a period of national euphoria.

The trigger for the mood change is harder to identify. Many would equate it with the hateful trigger of Lee Harvey Oswald's mail-order gun in Dallas in November, 1963, and contend that the accomplishments of 1964 and early 1965 were the result of accumulated momentum—that, indeed, the productive phase of the Kennedy administration was actually the year and a half after John Kennedy's death. Others would choose the Watts riots of August, 1965, the first time the murderous and suicidal rage and despair of urban blacks outside the South was revealed; perhaps the largest number would choose the escalation of the Vietnam war, which began with the bombing of North Vietnam that February. At all events the change occurred, and the nation went into the valley of a shadow from which it has not yet emerged as this is written.

In terms of inner change, of change in American attitudes and American values, these last five years have surely been the crucial ones in the quarter century since V-J Day. And these changes, which I propose to examine here as cheerfully as possible, seem of such a magnitude that every American except the very young, the very empty, and the very enclosed must now, to some extent, feel himself a foreigner in his native land.

Better than statistics, as a starting point for a study of moods, are words. The 1947 *Britannica Book of the Year* gave a list of words that, according to its authorities, "became prominent or were seemingly used for the first time" in either 1945 or 1946. Predictably enough, some of the listed words were of only ephemeral usefulness and have vanished without leaving a trace; for example, *athodyd* (a ramjet engine), *cuddle seat* (a contrivance for carrying small children, both word and device introduced by Australian war brides), and *Huff-Duff* (a navigation aid for ships and planes that was quickly superseded). But a surprising number of the new coinages survive,

A Clean Break...

and a listing of some of them gives a remarkable picture of the preoccupations of the time: *atomic cloud*, *be-bop*, *buyers' strike*, *existentialism*, *fact finder* (as in a labor dispute), *fissionable*, *gray market*, *iron curtain*, *operation* (as in Operation This-or-That), *push-button* (as a metaphorical adjective), *shock wave*, *sitter* (for babysitter), *truth serum*, *U.N.*, *UNESCO*.

Fact finder, *fissionable*, *sitter*: talismans of the time, casting strange shafts of light into the future. It was a time of getting settled. That, of course, meant more than veterans coming home; it also meant industrial workers demanding the raises that had been deferred by wartime controls, and therefore strikes. In November, 1945, there began a series of crippling strikes in key industries. Meanwhile, as the government vacillated on price controls, meat disappeared from grocery shelves for days at a time because of speculative withholding by suppliers. None of these inconveniences held back the business of nest building. The year 1946 stands out as the all-time record year for marriages in the nation's history, not only relative to population but in absolute numbers—2,291,000 marriages all told, or almost 700,000 more than in 1945, and almost twice as many as there had been in the deep Depression years before the war. The first nest in 1946 was usually an apartment rather than a house; material shortages held up the beginning of the great postwar home-building boom, but even so, construction of one-family dwellings tripled between 1945 and 1946. And whatever their nature, the new nests were quickly fruitful. The national birth rate went up 20 per cent in 1946 over 1945 (that November, New York City actually ran out of birth certificates) and another 10 per cent in 1947 over 1946, as the celebrated postwar baby boom got under way.

So the ex-serviceman, in college on the GI Bill, with his pregnant wife struggling to make a palatable dinner on short meat rations in their barracks apartment, was earnestly trying to sop up the knowledge that would get him a civilian job, with no thought farther from his mind than questioning, much less protesting against, the social framework or the institution in which he worked. Nest-building time is not a time for rebellion. Also in 1946 the government was paring back its budget from 1945's one hundred billion to sixty billion dollars, and the next year it would spend less than forty billion; the infant United Nations was trying out its unsteady legs at the optimistically named Lake Success on Long Island; there were four lynchings in the South; the Bikini bomb tests were appalling us, and the Cold War was taking shape; radio was still the great national diversion,

with Jack Benny first in the Hooperatings, Fibber McGee and Molly second, and—incredible as it now seems—Amos 'n Andy seventh. And while all these quaint happenings were in process, the word *existentialism* was coming into the American language.

Of such was the nest-building mood, the nation's first in the postwar period. There have been five more since then that I can distinguish: the Korean-war mood, the McCarthy mood, the Eisenhower-prosperity mood, the Kennedy go-go mood, and finally the present one of paralysis, gloom, and reappraisal.

Beginning with the North Korean invasion of South Korea on June 25, 1950, the Korean war was a time of nightmare. There was a kind of *déjà vu* about finding ourselves again embroiled in a war when we had just settled down to peace, and for thousands of veterans of the Second World War who had signed up for the reserves without thinking twice about it (I remember, for example, that when I was separated from the Army at Fort Dix, New Jersey, in 1945, they encouraged reserve enlistment by letting you out one day sooner if you signed up), it meant an actual return to combat. It was a new kind of war—not even officially called a war, but rather a "police action"—as frustrating as an unpleasant dream, that we could not win and apparently were not *supposed* to win. (We would learn more about that kind of war later.) The rumors we heard, later confirmed, that American prisoners were being subjected to a new and horrifying form of mental torture called brainwashing were literally the stuff of nightmare. So was the vision of an endless mass of humanity, bent on killing and seemingly unconcerned about being killed, that was embodied in the phrase "human wave," used to describe the Chinese Communist hordes that streamed south across the Yalu River in November, 1950. Finally, during the two years that the armistice talks dragged on at Panmunjom while the shooting continued, there was the nightmare sense of trying to wake up to a pleasanter reality and being unable to do so.

Shaken but relieved, the country finally awoke with the signing of the armistice on July 27, 1953—but awoke merely, as sometimes happens, from one level of nightmare to another. The time of the paid informer and the false witness had already come. As early as 1948 Whittaker Chambers had first made his charges of Communist spying against Alger Hiss, the apparently exemplary young statesman who had been a framer of the United Nations charter, and the Dreyfus case of modern America was launched. In 1949 eleven leaders of the U.S. Communist Party had been sent to prison; the following year Judith Coplon and Dr. Klaus Fuchs had been convicted of spying, the latter with reference to vital atomic secrets, and the young Senator Joseph McCarthy,

"... the word _existentialism_ was coming into the American language"

seeing his chance, had made his famous series of accusations that there were 205 (or 57 or 81 or 10 or 116) Communists in the State Department. With that, the hounds of fear and distrust slipped their leashes, and by the time of the Korean armistice Senator McCarthy had made the nightmarishly irrational term "Fifth Amendment Communist" into a household expression; hardly any professional in the country could feel his job or his way of life safe from the random malice of almost anyone, and constitutional guarantees against just this sort of mischief were becoming all but meaningless.

That nightmare almost drove us crazy—perhaps came closer than we care to admit, even now. But finally our underlying national health asserted itself, and we awoke at last, this time definitively, in December, 1954, when the Senate censured McCarthy and McCarthyism went into decline. Small wonder, after such horrors, that the next mood should have been a recessive one, one of huddling in our shells and comforting ourselves with material things while remaining heedless of the mess we were making. The essence of the Eisenhower mood was long-deferred self-indulgence. It was a time of soaring stock-market prices and soaring participation in the boodle. The members of the middle class, the hugely expanding group that dominated the country, were becoming capitalists at last and were doing very well at it. It was a time of rocketing corporate profits and resulting fat dividends —at the cost of inflation and polluted air and water. It was a time of greatly increased leisure for millions—at the cost of littered roadsides and tamed and uglified national parks and forests. It was a time of more and more automobiles for more and more people—at the cost of traffic jams, more air pollution, eyesore automobile graveyards, and neglected public transportation. It was a time of bursting cities and proliferating suburbs—at the cost of increasingly neglected slums full of explosive anger quietly ticking away. It was a time when we thought of our "race problem" as being mainly a political matter confined to the South; when, in foreign policy, we fatalistically hid behind the dangerously provocative shield of "massive retaliation" and "brinkmanship" (and meanwhile were sowing the seeds of our Asian disaster); when college students kept a low profile, politically and otherwise, so as not to jeopardize their chances of flowing smoothly onto the production line to affluence right after graduation; and when—not so paradoxically as it may seem at first glance—the federal budget grew year by year and social security and other public benefits were greatly widened. The Eisenhower era is not to be compared too closely to that of Coolidge in terms of free enterprise's running wild. In the earlier

time the country had been all too truly committed to unrestricted free enterprise, but by the late fifties, despite Fourth of July paeans to the "American system" as fulsome as ever, the notion of cradle-to-grave security _for most people_ had been thoroughly accepted and, indeed, assimilated into the system. The mood was heedless hedonism.

Next, in abrupt reaction, came the Kennedy years with their quite opposite mood of responsibility and hope. It is tempting now to think of those years as a golden age, though if we look closely we find they were scarcely that in practical terms; after all, Kennedy's domestic legislative defeats—on civil rights, on tax reform, on Medicare—far outweighed his victories, and he died leaving unsolved most of the problems he had inherited, including, of course, Vietnam. But his successful conclusion of the 1962 Cuban missile crisis, along with the limited nuclear test-ban treaty that followed the next summer, did much to allay the fear of nuclear war that had overhung the country all through the postwar period up to then. Much more important, he and his administration, through the almost magically inspiring quality of their very style, succeeded in regenerating the old American faith, not in the perfection of man or his nation but in their perfectability. No one despaired under Kennedy; somehow everything seemed possible. "I have a dream that one day this nation will rise up, [and] live out the true meaning of its creed . . ." Martin Luther King, Jr., said at the interracial March on Washington in August, 1963—a fitting epitome of the Kennedy mood, in a climax that no one could know came near the end of the last act.

Then everything went wrong. With Kennedy's death that November began an age of assassination; within five years probably the two most admired black men in the country, King and Malcolm X, and almost certainly the most admired white man, John Kennedy's brother Robert, would be dead from the same horrifying and dispiriting cause. During the same period more and more Negro leaders turned against King's dream, rejecting the American creed for a cynical, angry separatism; the hopeless war in Vietnam was escalated, and revelations about its conduct led many Americans to a similarly escalating sense of horror, disillusion, and shame; political colloquy at home became violent rather than reasonable; Americans achieved the technical masterwork of flying to the moon and back while failing to accomplish the technically simple one of giving all their citizens proper food and clothing. The sixth postwar mood was, and is, one of violence, disillusion, and doubt verging on despair such as has not been felt since the time of the Civil War.

It is my thesis, then, that while material change has generally been steady, continuous, and for the most part beneficent over the postwar period, the past five years or so have seen an explosive—and morally equivocal—increase in the rate of change in values and attitudes. It is in these last five years that most of our moral history since V-J Day has been written, and it is since 1965 that many Americans have come to feel like expatriates in America. In support of the thesis, let me tick off a few current American attitudes—now accepted widely enough among the influential, especially in the communications media, to constitute what might be called leadership opinion, if not national consensus—that would have been unthinkable not only on V-J Day but on the day of John Kennedy's death as well.

The attitude toward military affairs, and in particular toward our own military, has to a large extent undergone a reversal. My own generation, the one whose coming of age coincided with U.S. entry into the Second World War, had thought itself pacifist; we had been brought up on Dos Passos' *Three Soldiers* and Hemingway's *A Farewell to Arms* and the Nye investigation with its implication that wars are fought for the profits of munitions makers. But it turned out that our pacifism was only skin-deep; when the call to arms came, it found us full of sanguine enthusiasm. We wanted to be in it, and quickly, and we hurried to the recruiting offices; we thought of draft-dodging as contemptible and conscientious objection as respectable but, to say the least, highly eccentric. After Pearl Harbor a uniform, even that of an ordinary soldier or sailor, was a clear-cut asset in the pursuit of girls.

In the postwar period up until recently a uniform was neutral, considered neither glamorous nor unappealing. Not so now. There are no American "heroes" of Vietnam (not that there has been no actual heroism), and the sporadic efforts of the military to create some have failed utterly. On the contrary, among the heroes to today's youth, or a significant segment of it, are the evaders who are hiding out illegally in Canada or Sweden. Idealistic young people casually and openly discuss and choose among the legal and illegal ways of avoiding induction, and many of them consider the act of draft avoidance or evasion to be a *moral* one. As for the sexual aspect: the son of some friends of mine, living in a conservative eastern community, complained soon after he was drafted that girls who had formerly gone out with him would no longer do so. The old taunt of "Why aren't you in uniform?" has become the opposite: "Why aren't you in Sweden or in jail?" Soldiers on leave these days wear mufti.

Again, certain broad, vague expressions of patriotic

sentiment that in 1945 would have been considered commendable and in 1963 at least harmless have now become specifically distasteful to many as indicative of "extremist" beliefs. To a liberal—and liberals, on political record, are something like half of our voters—the display of a bumper sticker reading "Honor America" now suggests that the owner of the car is a full-fledged reactionary, ready to jail dissenters against the war and to use atomic weapons in its prosecution. "Support Your Local Police," which until a few years ago might have been an advertisement for a cake-sale benefit, now suggests racial prejudice. Even more to the point, display of the American flag itself in many unofficial settings has come to have disturbing implications. I confess, with some reluctance, that a flag decal posted in the window of a car or a barbershop now arouses in me feelings of hostility toward the owner. It would emphatically not have done so in 1945.

True enough, the practice called flag-waving has been in bad repute in sophisticated American circles for generations. But the expression was metaphorical, usually referring to overly florid oratory. That the display of the flag itself should come to suggest extremist political and social views is surely an anomaly without precedent. Try to imagine any other democratically ruled nation in which such a condition exists—or ever has existed.

"Why aren't you in Sweden or in jail?"

The reason behind these changes is hardly obscure. On V-J Day we were triumphantly concluding a war in which the moral imperative had been clear to just about everyone. On the one hand our territory had been attacked in the Pacific, and on the other a barbaric aggressor who clearly represented a threat to us as well as to our allies was at large in Europe. Now we are engaged in a military adventure in a distant country in which I believe tortuous logic is required to find the threat to ourselves and in which, threats aside, the moral imperative is certainly not clear to many millions. Is the change, then, only temporary and expedient—like, say, the 1930's pacifism of my generation? I rather think not.

The computer revolution, filtering through from technology to culture, has recently come to change ways of thinking, perhaps more than we usually realize. Norman Macrae, deputy editor of the British *Economist*, commented after a recent U.S. visit on "the greater air of professionalism which runs through all ranks of American society; the greater instinct among ordinary individuals to say 'Now here is a problem, how can I solve it by a systematic approach?'" We have learned that computers can not only imitate the human brain (play chess, choose marriage partners) but can in many ways far exceed it (retrieve material from huge library collections or scan the contents of a fat telephone book in a fraction of a second; predict election results in an instant; put men on the moon). Is it not logical, then, that we should try to improve our minds by making them as much like computers as possible? The young executive or computer programmer who has learned the meaning and value of the systems approach to problems tries to apply it in every area of his personal life—in choosing schools for his children, in mowing his lawn, in pleasing his wife. It may well be that the current cult of irrationality is partly a reaction against this computer-spawned mimicry of mechanical thinking in everyday life.

Whether or not television and its concomitants in mass communications and world travel have done what Marshall McLuhan says they have—destroyed the "linear" habit of thinking imposed by the printed page and returned the whole world to the instinctual communication methods of the primitive tribal village—they have, it seems evident enough, changed our living and thinking habits in the direction of passive receptivity. I suggest that, with the first generation of television children now coming of age, we are just beginning to feel the force of this change.

While the Negro-rights movement has passed through its various stages—full integration of the armed forces (1948), the fight for integration of schools and public facilities (1954 *et seq.*), and finally "black power"—white attitudes toward aid to the Negro cause have gone through a spectrum of changes. In 1945 the majority of us, to judge from our actions, still clung to the thought that such aid through federal intervention was unnecessary or inappropriate. During the civil-rights decade beginning in 1954 most of us permitted ourselves to think of such aid as morally commendable on our part—that is to say, to think of it as having at least a component of charity. Now, in the black-power era when integration as a goal and the possible perfectability of American society are being increasingly rejected by the more militant black leaders, it has been borne in on more and more of us that giving things to minorities is and always was at best mere political expediency and at worst blackmail. Such ideas were unthinkable for nearly everyone in 1945; for all but a few in 1964. (President Johnson, it is interesting to note, was very much in the avant-garde of American thought in 1965 when he said at Howard University, "You do not wipe away the scars of centuries by saying, 'Now, you are free to go where you want, do what you desire, and choose the leaders you please.' You do not take a man who, for years, has been hobbled by chains, liberate him, bring him to the starting line of the race, saying, 'You are free to compete with the others. . . .'" Might not those words—had they not been spoken by an American President—serve as a black-power slogan?)

Along with the change in white attitudes toward blacks is a profound and unsettling change in the attitude of liberals toward our national history. Blacks and others, but mainly blacks, have persuaded liberals that ours is in crucial ways a racist society, and that it always has been. Formerly we thought of the American past, broadly, in terms of rural individualism, fanatical independence, and anti-intellectualism combined with visceral folk wisdom and an inherent sense of fairness—thought of it, that is, in a way that was both affectionate and patronizing. We minimized or dismissed particular instances of racism (lynchings, the Scottsboro case, or the wartime detention camps for Nisei) as being confined to a particular geographical area or attributable to the bad judgment of particular leaders. Now, for many Americans, almost any tintype glimpse of the American past—the village band concert with its handful of tentatively smiling black faces in the back row, the political rally with no black faces anywhere—suggests racism. To a degree our history has been poisoned for us. And I believe that the consequences of this, in the light of our current national demoralization, can hardly be

". . . the defense of irrationality is often put on rational grounds"

overemphasized at this time in America's life.

Our leaders themselves have become demoralized to an extent surely without precedent since the Civil War. "We know our lakes are dying, our rivers growing filthier daily, our atmosphere increasingly polluted," John Gardner, former Cabinet member and more recently head of the Urban Coalition, said not long ago. "We are aware of racial tensions that could tear the nation apart. We understand that oppressive poverty in the midst of affluence is intolerable. We see that our cities are sliding toward disaster. . . . But we are seized by a kind of paralysis of the will." Does not such language, in the nation of Fourth of July oratory, and coming from not just an Establishment figure but to some *the* Establishment figure of the present moment, represent a clear break with the past, even the very recent past?

Naturally, the demoralization of the leaders is felt among the people. "Most people no longer seem to care—if, indeed, they know—what is happening to their country," Richard Harris wrote late last year in *The New Yorker* magazine. "Exhausted by the demands of modern life and muddled by the fearful discord tearing at society, they seem to have turned their common fate over to their leaders in a way that would have been inconceivable five years ago." But when the leaders talk of paralysis of the will, who will lead?

I come now to recent changes in attitudes and values among the young, where we may find a key to what is happening to the country. To review briefly, then, the most obvious manifestations of these changes:

Youth on the campus has discovered its previously unsuspected and therefore untested power to change its environment and the conditions of its life. From the Berkeley revolt (1964) to the one at Columbia (1968) to the one at Harvard (1969) we have seen the content of such campus uprisings gradually broaden from demands for the right to use dirty words to demands for changes in the course of study, insistence on sexual and other forms of personal freedom, demands for revision of admissions policies, and ultimatums about the reorganization of entire curricula. The rebels have developed their own jargon—largely mindless and question-begging like all political jargon: in pursuit of "restructuring" (getting their own way) the dissidents resort to "confrontation" (violence or the threat of it), make "nonnegotiable demands" (refuse to engage in reasonable discussion), and, if they get what they want, sometimes complain with what seems to be a certain disappointment that they have been "co-opted" (yielded to). A comical aspect of their behavior is that they frequently ask those

in authority to help them revolt against that very authority; they want, for example, to be offered formal courses in the techniques of campus disruption as well as guerrilla warfare. (A university president told me recently of a student delegation that had come to ask him, not without an attractive diffidence, that he help them by giving them the benefit of his political experience. "What they wanted me to help them rebel against was *me*," he commented.) But campus revolts are not a joke. They are evidence of an idea completely new in the United States, poles apart from the passive orthodoxy of the silent generation of a decade earlier, that teaching authority is not absolute but fluid and malleable, that the young can move the sun and the moon in their heavens if they try, that their universe in spite of its ordered surface is basically anarchic. And the authorities, by yielding to them again and again, have confirmed their most disturbing suspicions.

Recent statistics compiled by the Urban Research Corporation of Chicago give a striking picture of how widespread campus revolts have been. Covering 232 campuses over the first half of 1969, the study showed that during that period 215,000 students, or about one tenth of all those enrolled at the institutions studied, actively participated in a total of nearly three hundred major protests—all in just six months. Before the fact that only one student in ten was active in the uprisings is taken to indicate that the youth revolt is just the phenomenon of a small but visible minority, we would do well to consider that historically the passive sympathizers with new movements have usually far outnumbered the activists.

The young have turned against careers in business, particularly in big and long-established business, to such an extent that some campus recruiters have expressed concern as to where the managers of the future will come from—although up to now there have been enough exceptions to keep the business schools from being depopulated and the lower ranks of corporate management from being undermanned.

They have made a cult of irrationality, what with astrology, Oriental occultism, and above all the use of drugs. ("*We* never needed drugs to drive us crazy," the middle-aged social commentator David T. Bazelon once told me.) This tendency runs deep and wide, cutting across economic, social, and intellectual lines among the young. The sheltered, conservatively brought-up white southern darling and the would-be hippie son of liberal northern suburbanites yearn alike for the experience of New York City's East Village, and the young Harvard intellectual is almost as likely as the high-school dropout to express or imply hostility to the traditional intellectual materials, abstract ideas, and rational comment. Curiously, the defense of irrationality is often put—persuasively—on rational grounds: that logical thought in foreign policy led to Vietnam, that logical thought in economic development led to pollution, and so on.

The young are apparently in the process of radically redefining sex roles. The question of which forces (the Pill, the obscenity explosion in the media set off by the courts' anticensorship decisions, or the general air of permissiveness in the land) have brought about a radical change in sexual customs among both the young and their elders, remains undecided. No one really knows. What is much clearer, and perhaps more interesting, is that the traditional aggressiveness of the young American male about his maleness, which has so often led to anti-intellectualism, Babbittry, and cultural self-deprivation in general—for example, the American he-man's hostility to most of the arts on grounds that they are effete—seems to have been emphatically reversed. The short hair and pointedly different clothing that he always used to set himself unmistakably apart from girls are more and more being abandoned in favor of long hair, fur coats, beads, and other adornments that were formerly considered feminine. The American male's dread of appearing to be unmanly seems to be lessening. More significantly, one is struck by the new sense of community that boys and girls feel. The growing insistence of the young on coeducation is not just a matter of having sex available but one of principle, growing out of a new conviction that the sexes are not so different as American culture has decreed them to be and that the old segregation is therefore absurd.

The symptoms I have been recording are, of course, parts of a syndrome, and one that may be viewed in two diametrically opposed ways. Looked at in a favorable light, the new youth are gentle, loving, natural, intuitive, opposed only to war and obsession with money, to hypocrisy and the other agreed-upon weaknesses of modern society as organized by their elders. In a different perspective they represent progressive-school permissiveness and self-indulgence run wild: their causes are merely self-serving (opposition to the draft, for example), their attitudes are self-righteous ("Just because you are growing older do not be afraid of change," they gravely lecture their parents and teachers), their manners are deplorable or nonexistent, their minds are flabby, their herding together indicates fear of standing alone, and the manner of their protests sometimes appears ominously antidemocratic. Macrae of *The Economist* goes so far as to say that some of the actions of black-power and radical white students during the winter of 1968-69 "invited the most direct comparison with the way that Hit-

ler's brownshirts operated in the Weimar Republic." On the other hand Ralph Nader's consumer-protection crusade, which clearly appeals strongly to the brightest and most idealistic among the young, might fairly be described as passionately *pro*democratic in that its aim is to save that most characteristic democratic institution, the business corporation, from its own shortcomings. Paradoxes and contradictions, then; and it is quite possible—indeed, perhaps it is inevitable—for a liberal of the previous generation to see the young in both lights at the same time.

For such an observer, analysis is more profitable than judgment. Consider, then, the vital statistics. The median age of the American population at present is a bit under twenty-eight years. Half of us, roughly speaking, were born before the middle of World War II and half since it. Half of us were of an age to be percipient before V-J Day, and half were not. The distinction is not arbitrary, because it was with the end of the war that the new era, the modern world, began. The time has come when "over thirty" means precisely "born before the war." Only the younger half of the American people have never known the world of traditional values as it was without the disrupters of those values—television, computers, jet travel, space travel, the threat of nuclear extinction. Only the younger half truly belong to the new world—that is, accept it instinctively, without mental or emotional effort, because they have not any old world to compare it with.

And consider this: the five postwar moods before the present one were conjoined as well as consecutive—each had its roots in reaction to the previous one, as have the moods of most nations through most of past history. Wartime family disruptions led logically and naturally to early postwar domesticity. The Cold War, which really began in 1945 at Yalta, bore its bitter fruit five years later in Korea. Armed conflict with our former allies, the Communists, led logically to the era of suspicion. The eventual relaxation of that crisis cleared the way for the Eisenhower years of self-indulgence. And the new energy and responsibility of the Kennedy term was clearly enough a reaction to that. In such a linear way did our history unfold for almost two decades.

And then—snap! The chain of events seemed to be broken. Suddenly we flew off in directions that seemed to be neither a continuation of nor a reaction to anything that had gone before. Disillusion with uniform and flag did not appear to be rooted in reaction to any particular superpatriotism of the preceding period; mechanized thinking was not new, but the existence, indeed the ubiquitous presence, of actual thinking machines was; the new youth rebellion could be seen as a reaction to youth passivity a decade earlier, but the breadth and depth of the response was so far out of proportion to the

"Will the affairs of General Motors be managed by men smoking pot?"

challenge as to make such an explanation seem entirely inadequate. The present American mood, then, in many of its aspects, has had no precedents or antecedents; it represents almost a clear break; it seems to have come out of the blue. Meanwhile, let us remember, it has not been accompanied by sharp breaks in or reversals of the broad ameliorative trends that have marched through the whole postwar period. There are no jolts or breaks around 1964 or 1965 in the charts of social progress. The nation seems to have changed its mind, or to be in the process of changing its mind, on many of the most basic matters for no immediately discernible material reason. And this occurs precisely at the time when the new post-V-J Day generation is coming of age.

Can this conjunction of facts be more than coincidental? Indeed, must it not be? If so, then the new generation, the generation that is in tune with the new world because it never knew the old one, appears, for better or worse, as the basic force behind the new, unprecedented American attitudes. As for the statistical charts, their relatively smooth continuance through this period of violent cultural upheaval may be explained by the fact that the charts and the things recorded in the charts—matters of business, government, philanthropy—remain in the hands of the old postwar generation. It does not really live in the new world it has made, yet it still nervously holds all the levers of national power.

One who accepts such an analysis is Margaret Mead. In her recent book, *Culture and Commitment: A Study of the Generation Gap,* she declares that "our present situation is unique, without any parallel in the past," and that—not just in the United States but world-wide—the human race is arriving through the youth revolt at an entirely new phase of cultural evolution. Putting her argument in a context of rigorous anthropological study rather than in the familiar one of parlor sociology, she describes the new phase as a "prefigurative" society: one in which the traditional handing down of knowledge and belief from the elder generation to the younger is being reversed and in which "it will be the child and not the parent or grandparent that represents what is to come." No longer anywhere in the world, Dr. Mead says, can the elders, born before the Second World War, know and understand what the children know and understand: "Even very recently the elders could say, 'You know, I have been young and you never have been old.' But today's young people can reply, 'You never have been young in the world I am young in, and you never can be.'" The prefigurative society she sees emerging is, Dr. Mead says, the first one in human history.

It is a persuasive case, and, fitted together with the vital statistics I have cited, it leads to a persuasive explanation of why changes in our values and attitudes, after years of poking along like a donkey cart in a time of great transformation in our material situation, have recently taken off as steeply as a jet plane. So it comes about that the elders—whether they conservatively wring their hands over the new changes or liberally try to understand, absorb, and temper them—feel like expatriate visitors in their own country. Like expatriates, we of the prewar generation are inclined to spend our days wavering between wonder, exasperation, apprehension, disgust, and superiority toward what we see around us. Again like expatriates, we tend to cling together in enclaves, to propitiate our sense of loneliness by finding islands of our own within the new world that conform as closely as possible to the old one. The turned-on headlights of daytime drivers that have been so familiar a sight in many parts of the country in recent months are supposed to mean support of our Vietnam policy, but they mean more than that. They are a symbol by which the loneliest of the lonely expatriates reassure themselves that they are not wholly alone; they are the club ties of the American Club in Samarkand.

Even if the analysis is right, all of this is, of course, a change still in process, and indeed still in an early stage of process, rather than an accomplished fact. The "silent majority" apparently still *is* a majority—of poll respondents and of voters—and even if it were not, traditional methods of succession to power have survived up to now to the extent that the older generation would still hold business and government power and might be expected to continue to do so for some years to come Even among the young themselves Dr. Mead's prefigurative culture is still very far from universal. There are whole campuses in "middle America" where a long-haired boy is an object of derision, where revolt against university authority never crosses anyone's mind, where books and magazines containing four-letter words are missing from the library shelves, and where "God Bless America" is sung without irony.

But such attitudes among the postwar generation seem to represent cultural lag. They are scarcely the wave of the future. It is those older than the nation's median age who make up the bulk of the silent majority. In purely actuarial terms, this majority is living on borrowed time; it is a majority under a death sentence.

What happens next?

One line of thought holds that the strange new attitudes and values are attributable not to the influence of youth but to the Vietnam war and the disruptions, frustrations, and loss of morale attendant upon it—its ability, as James Reston of the *New York Times* has written, to "poison everything." This interpretation is reassuring to the prewar generation because it implies that when the war is over everything will revert to the way it was before. But those born in the years immediately after V-J Day, who were entering college when the Vietnam war was escalated and are leaving it now, and who have lived only in the strange new world, can scarcely be expected to go back where they have never been. I am convinced that Vietnam is not the root cause of our current malaise and that if there had been no Vietnam the young would have found plenty of other reasons to dissociate themselves violently from their elders and their elders' regime. Certainly the end of the war, when it blessedly comes, will mark the end of our current paralysis and the beginning of a seventh and more hopeful postwar mood; but I expect it to be a mood not of returning to the familiar but of pushing forward to something new and unknown. In the traditional American cultural pattern youth has always been allowed its fling with the tacit understanding between youngsters and elders that after graduation the youngsters would "put away childish things" and "settle down." The wild young buck who had been proud of his capacity for beer and beer-inspired pranks would sink quickly into sober, hard-working domesticity, and the pretty blonde who had found it amusing to flirt with Communism while in college would become his meekly Republican, upwardly mobile bride. It is impossible for me to imagine the post-V-J Day generation following this familiar pattern. One can, for example, visualize their male hairstyle going from shoulder length to shaved heads—but not to crew cuts; one can visualize their politics doing a flip-flop to dangerously radical rightist positions—but not to traditional conservatism or traditional liberalism.

How, then, can they be expected to react to being older and to assuming power and responsibility instead of defying them? Will they, in their turn, be "prefigured" by the new younger generation that will consist of their children? How will they run the Ford Foundation? the Institute for Advanced Study? the Bureau of the Census? Will they continue the broad liberal trends initiated by the older generation that they now revile—trends toward more social-minded corporations, better-distributed wealth, more general education, less pervasive bigotry? Will they bring to reality *The Economist*'s prophecy that "the United States in this last third of the twentieth century is the place where man's long economic problem is ending"? Will, say, the affairs of General Motors be managed by men (or women) wearing long hair and beads and smoking pot during sales conferences? Or will there be no General Motors?

The fact that it sounds like material for a musical-comedy skit indicates how little we know what to expect. Adolf A. Berle said recently, speaking of economic and social affairs in the United States, "We are beginning to evolve a new ball game." Whether we like it or not, the rules of the new game will not be our rules. They will be devised by those born since V-J Day.

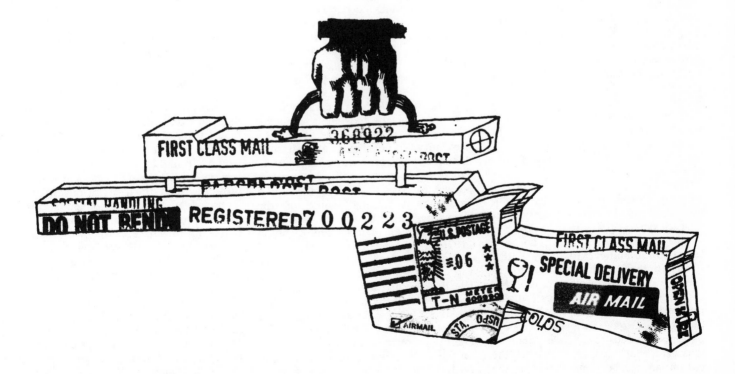

The Roots Of Lawlessness

"If destruction be our lot, we must ourselves be its author...." —ABRAHAM LINCOLN, SPRINGFIELD, 1838.

—Bettmann Archive

HENRY STEELE COMMAGER

HENRY STEELE COMMAGER, educator, historian, and man of letters, is at present writing a book on the Enlightenment in Europe and America.

It was in 1838 that the young Abraham Lincoln—he was not yet twenty-nine—delivered an address at Springfield, Illinois, on "The Perpetuation of Our Political Institutions." What he had to say is curiously relevant today. Like many of us, Lincoln was by no means sure that our institutions could be perpetuated; unlike some of us, he was convinced that they should be.

What, after all, threatened American political institutions? There was no threat from outside, for "all the armies of Europe, Asia, and Africa combined could not by force take a drink from the Ohio or make a track on the Blue Ridge in a thousand years." No, the danger was from within. "If destruction be our lot, we must ourselves be its author and finisher. As a nation of freemen, we must live through all time or die by suicide."

This, Lincoln asserted, was not outside the realm of possibility; as he looked about him, he saw everywhere a lawlessness that, if persisted in, would surely destroy both law and Constitution and eventually the nation itself. In the end, lawlessness *did* do that—lawlessness in official guise that refused to abide by the Constitutional processes of election or by the will of the Constitutional majority. It was to be Lincoln's fate to be called upon to frustrate that lawless attack on the nation, and to be remembered as the savior of the Union. And it has been

our fate to be so bemused by that particular threat to unity—the threat of sectional fragmentation—that we have failed to appreciate the danger that so deeply disturbed Lincoln at the threshold of his political career.

The explanation of our confusion is rooted in history. The United States invented, or developed, a new kind of nationalism, one that differed in important ways from the nationalism that flourished in the Old World. One difference was the enormous emphasis that Americans, from the beginning, put on territory and the extent to which American nationalism came to be bound up with the acquisition of all the territory west to the Pacific and with the notion of territorial integrity on a continental scale. The idea that a nation should "round out" its territory, or take over all unoccupied territory, was not prominent in the nationalism of the Old World. Territory there, after all, was pretty well pre-empted, and there was no compelling urge to acquire neighboring land for its own sake.

In the Old World, threats to unity had been, for the most part, dynastic or religious rather than territorial. As proximity did not dictate assimilation, distance did not require separation. But in America space and distance appeared to pose threats to the Union from the beginning. Some of the Founding Fathers, to be sure, continued to think of unity and disunion in Old World terms of interests and factions, rather than in terms of territory. This was perhaps because they had little choice in the matter or none that they could publicly acknowledge, for the United States was born the largest nation in the Western world, and the Framers had to put a good face on the matter. But Europeans generally, and some Americans, long familiar with Montesquieu's dictum that, while

a republic could flourish in a small territory, a large territory required a despotism, assumed that the new United States, with boundaries so extensive, could not survive.

Jefferson and his associates were determined to prove Montesquieu mistaken. From the beginning, they formulated a counter-argument that size would strengthen rather than weaken the nation. Brushing aside the warnings of such men as Gouverneur Morris, they boldly added new states west of the Alleghenies. They made the Louisiana Purchase, seized West Florida, and looked with confidence to acquiring all the territory west to the Pacific; thus, the Lewis and Clark expedition into foreign territory, something we would not tolerate today in our territory. Territorial expansion and integrity became a prime test of the American experiment, and within a few years what had been a test became, no less, a providential command: Manifest Destiny. From this flowed naturally the principle that the proof of union was territorial, and the threat to union territorial.

A second American contribution to the ideology of nationalism was, in time, to become its most prominent characteristic: the notion that national unity required not merely territorial unity but social and cultural. In the Old World, the only cultural unity that had any meaning was religious: The principle *Cuius regio eius religio* was dictated by the fact that the ruler's religion determined the religion of the state. But class distinctions were taken for granted, as were profound differences in cultural and social habits—in speech, for example, or in such simple things as food and drink and dress and games.

Americans changed this pattern around. They rejected the principle of religious unity—doubtless in large part because they had no alternative—and then substituted cultural for religious unity. Americans were not expected to pray alike, but they were expected to talk alike, dress alike, work alike, profess the same moral code, and subscribe to the same legal code. Eventually, as we know, they were expected to eat the same food, drink the same liquors, play the same games, read the same journals, watch the same television programs, and even have the same political ideas—expectations never seriously entertained by, say, German or Italian nationalists.

American nationalism thus became, at a very early stage, a self-conscious affair of imposing unity upon a vast territory, a heterogeneous population, and a miscellaneous culture. Because there was indeed land enough to absorb some forty million immigrants, because those immigrants were so heterogeneous that (with the exception of the Germans and, in modern times, the Negroes) they were unable to maintain a cultural identity counter to the prevailing American culture, and because, in provisions for naturalization and opportunities for active participation, the political system was the most hospitable of any in the world, an artificial unity became, in time, a real unity. Americans managed to achieve a single language with fewer deviations than were to be found in England, Germany, or Italy; to achieve a common education—not universal, to be sure, but more nearly universal than elsewhere in the nineteenth-century world; to create a common political system, each state like every other

state; and, *mirabile dictu*, to conjure up a common history and a common past.

The threat to union, as Lincoln saw it in 1838, was not sectional or economic or social or even moral; it was quite simply the "spirit of lawlessness." As early as *Notes on Virginia* (1782), Thomas Jefferson had confessed that he trembled for his country when he reflected that "God is just and his justice cannot sleep forever," and throughout his life Jefferson saw slavery as a moral threat, but in this he was more farsighted than most. The threat to union posed by slavery was unprecedented; it was a product of that elementary fact by now so familiar that we take it for granted: that deep economic, social, and moral differences assumed a geographical pattern, and that the American Constitutional system, namely federalism, permitted them to take a political pattern as well. As it happened, the sectional pattern of slavery was in mortal conflict with a very different sectional pattern, and it was this conflict that proved in the end fatal to the thrust for Southern independence: the sectionalism created by the Mississippi River and its tributaries. That, as it turned out, was the decisive fact that preserved the Union; when, in the summer of 1863, Lincoln wrote that "the signs look better," what he noted first was that "the Father of Waters goes again unvexed to the sea."

Suppose slavery had rooted itself vertically in the Mississippi Valley rather than horizontally across the South from the Atlantic to Texas. That would have given sectionalism a more rational base than it had in the South —a base that in all likelihood would have been impregnable.

Here we have one of the assumptions about American history that gets in the way of an appreciation of our distinc-

tive characteristics. Because thirteen American states, hugging the Atlantic seaboard, became a single nation spanning a continent, we either take American unity for granted or consider fragmentation only in terms of the experiment in Southern nationalism, which misfired. But there was nothing foreordained about the triumph of unity. Why did not the vast American territory between Canada and the Gulf of Mexico go the way of Latin America, which, with a common religion, language, and territory, nevertheless fragmented into numerous independent states?

The spectacular nature of the American achievement has bemused almost all students of American nationalism and dictated most interpretations of the problem of American unity. The transcendent fact of slavery and of the Negro—so largely responsible for creating a sectionalism that did not yield to the ameliorating influences of economy, social mobility, cultural uniformity, and political compromise— has distracted our attention from other threats, if not to union then to unity. Because we had a civil war, precipitated by sectional fragmentation, we did not imagine that we could have a revolution based on social fragmentation.

We are tempted to say of Lincoln's Springfield address that it was shortsighted of him not to have seen that the threats to union were slavery and sectionalism—something he learned, in time. We should say rather that he was farsighted in imagining the possibility of a very different threat to union: an internal dissension and lawlessness that bespoke a breakdown in cultural and moral unity. This is what confronts us today: blacks against whites, old against young, skinheads against eggheads, militarists against doves, the cities against the suburbs and the countryside—hostilities that more and more frequently erupt into open violence.

Two considerations warrant attention. First, that what Lincoln described was in fact normal—we have always been a lawless and a violent people. Thus, our almost unbroken record of violence against the Indians and all others who got in our way—the Spaniards in the Floridas, the Mexicans in Texas; the violence of the vigilantes on a hundred frontiers; the pervasive violence of slavery (a "perpetual exercise," Jefferson called it, "of the most boisterous passions"); the lawlessness of the Ku Klux Klan during Reconstruction and after; and of scores of race riots from those of New Orleans in the 1860s to those of Chicago in 1919. Yet, all this violence, shocking as it doubtless was, no more threatened the fabric of our society or the integrity of the Union than did the lawlessness of Prohibition back in the Twenties. The explanation for this is to be found in the embarrassing fact that most of it was official, quasi-official, or countenanced by public opinion: exterminating the Indian; flogging the slave; lynching the outlaw; exploiting women and children in textile mills and sweatshops; hiring Pinkertons to shoot down strikers; condemning immigrants to fetid ghettos; punishing Negroes who tried to exercise their civil or political rights. Most of this was socially acceptable— or at least not wholly unacceptable— just as so much of our current violence is socially acceptable: the 50,000 automobile deaths every year; the mortality rate for Negro babies twice that for white; the deaths from cancer induced by cigarettes or by air pollution; the sadism of our penal system and the horrors of our prisons; the violence of the police against what Theodore Parker called the "perishing and dangerous classes of society."

What we have now is the emergence of violence that is not acceptable either to the Establishment, which is frightened and alarmed, or to the victims of the Establishment, who are no longer submissive and who are numerous and powerful. This is the now familiar "crime in the streets," or it is the revolt of the young against the economy, the politics, and the wars of the established order, or it is the convulsive reaction of the blacks to a century of injustice. But now, too, official violence is no longer acceptable to its victims—or to their ever more numerous sympathizers: the violence of great corporations and of government itself against the natural resources of the nation; the long drawn-out violence of the white majority against Negroes and other minorities; the violence of the police and the National Guard against the young; the massive and never-ending violence of the military against the peoples of Vietnam and Cambodia. These acts can no longer be absorbed by large segments of our society. It is this new polarization that threatens the body politic and the social fabric much as religious dissent threatened them in the Europe of the sixteenth and seventeenth centuries.

A second consideration is this: The center of gravity has shifted from "obedience" to "enforcement." This shift in vocabulary is doubtless unconscious but nonetheless revealing. Obedience is the vocabulary of democracy, for it recognizes that the responsibility for the commonwealth is in the people and appeals to the people to recognize and fulfill their responsibility. Enforcement is the language of authority prepared to impose its will on the people. Lincoln knew instinctively that a democracy flourishes when men obey and revere the law; he did not invoke the language of authority. We are no longer confident of the virtue or good will of the people; so it is natural that we fall back on force. The resort to lawless force—by the Weathermen, the Black Panthers, the Ku Klux Klan, the hardhats; by the police in Chicago; by the National Guard at Orangeburg, South Carolina, and Kent, Ohio; or by highway police at Jackson, Mississippi—is a confession that both the people and their government have lost faith in the law, and that the political and social fabric that has held our society together is unraveling: "By such examples," said Lincoln at Springfield, "the lawless in spirit are encouraged to become lawless in practice."

It has long been our boast—repeated by the President's Commission on Violence—that notwithstanding our lengthy history of violence we have never had a "revolution," and that our political system appears to be more stable than those of other nations. Our only real revolution took a sectional pattern and was not called revolution but rebellion; since it was rationalized by high-minded rhetoric, led by honorable men, and fought with gallantry, it speedily took on an aura of respectability, and to this day Southerners who would be outraged by the display of the red flag of rebellion proudly wave the Stars and Bars of rebellion.

Thus, like most of our violence, violence against the Constitution and the Union, and by implication against the blacks who were to be kept in slavery, is socially approved. Where such violence has been dramatic (as in lynching or industrial warfare), it has not been widespread or prolonged; where it has been widespread and prolonged (as in slavery and the persistent humiliation of the Negro), it has not been dramatic. Where its victims were desperate, they were not numerous enough or strong enough to revolt; where they were numerous (never strong),

they did not *appear* to be desperate, and it was easy to ignore their despair. Now this situation is changing. Lawlessness is more pervasive than ever; the sense of outrage against the malpractices of those in power is more widespread and articulate; and the divisions in society are both deeper and more diverse, and the response to them more intractable.

One explanation of our current malaise is that it seems to belong to the Old World pattern rather than that of the New. Much of the rhetoric of the conflict between generations is that of class or religious wars—class war on the part of, let us say, Vice President Agnew; religious protest on the part of Professor Charles Reich and those involved in what he calls "the greening of America." If this is so, it goes far toward explaining some of our current confusion and blundering: the almost convulsive efforts to distract attention from the genuine problems of environment, social injustice, and war, and to fasten it on such phony issues as campus unrest or social permissiveness or pornography. What this implies is ominous: Our society is not prepared, either by history or philosophy, for the kind of lawlessness and violence and alienation that now afflict us.

Why is this so ominous?

Traditionally, our federal system could and did absorb regionalism and particularism, or channel these into political conduits. More accurately than in any other political system, our representatives represent geographical places—a specific Congressional district or a state—and our parties, too, are organized atop and through states. Our system is not designed to absorb or to dissipate such internal animosities as those of class against class, race against race, or generation against generation.

A people confident of progress, with a social philosophy that assumed that what counted most was children and that took for granted that each new generation would be bigger, stronger, brighter, and better educated than its predecessor, could afford to indulge the young. "Permissiveness" is not an invention of Dr. Spock but of the first settlers in America. Today, a people that has lost faith in progress and in the future, and that has lost confidence in the ameliorating influence of education, indulges instead in convulsive counter-attacks upon the young.

A nation with, in Jefferson's glowing words, "land enough for our descendants to the thousandth and thousandth generation" could indulge itself in reckless exploitation of that land—the mining of natural resources, the destruction of deer and bison and beavers, of the birds in the skies and the fish in the streams, and could even (this was a risky business from the beginning) afford to ignore its fiduciary obligations to coming generations without exciting dangerous resentment. But a nation of more than two hundred million, working through giant corporations and giant governments that ravage, pollute, and destroy on a scale heretofore unimagined, cannot afford such self-indulgence. Nor can it persist in its habit of violating its fiduciary obligations without outraging those who are its legal and moral legatees.

A nation that had more and better land available for its people than any other in history and that, for the first time, equated civilization with the pastoral life and exalted the farmer over the denizen of the city could take urban development in its stride, confident that the city would never get the upper hand, as it were. Modern America seems wholly unable to adapt its institutions or its psychology to massive urbanization, but proceeds instead to the fateful policy of reducing its farm population to a fraction and, at the same time, destroying its cities and turning them into ghettos that are breeding places for crime and violence.

A system that maintained and respected the principle of the superiority of the civil power over that of the military could afford to fight even such great conflicts as the Civil War, the First World War, and the Second World War without danger to its Constitution or its moral character. It cannot absorb the kind of war we are now fighting in Southeast Asia without irreparable damage to its moral values, nor can it exercise power on a world scale without moving the military to the center of power.

No nation could afford slavery, certainly not one that thought itself dedicated to equality and justice. The issue of slavery tore the nation asunder and left wounds still unhealed. Here is our greatest failure: that we destroyed slavery but not racism, promised legal equality but retained a dual citizenship, did away with legal exploitation of a whole race but substituted for it an economic exploitation almost as cruel. And this political and legal failure reflects a deeper psychological and moral failure.

Unlike some of our contemporary politicians, Lincoln was not content with decrying lawlessness. He inquired into its causes and, less perspicaciously, into its cure. In this inquiry, he identified two explanations that illuminated the problem. These—translated into modern vocabulary—are the decline of the sense of fiduciary obligation and the evaporation of political resourcefulness and creativity. Both are still with us.

No one who immerses himself in the writings of the Revolutionary generation—a generation still in command when Lincoln was born—can doubt that the sense of obligation to posterity was pervasive and lively. Recall Tom Paine's plea for independence: " 'Tis not the concern of a day, a year, or an age; *Posterity* are virtually involved in the contest and will be . . . affected to the end of time." Or John Adams's moving letter to his beloved Abigail when he had signed the Declaration of Independence: "Through all the gloom I can see the rays of ravishing light and glory. *Posterity* will triumph in this day's transaction." Or Dr. Benjamin Rush's confession, after his signing, that "I was animated constantly by a belief that I was acting for the benefit of the whole world and of future ages." So were they all.

The decline of the awareness of posterity and of the fiduciary principle is a complex phenomenon not unconnected with the hostility to the young that animates many older Americans today. It is to be explained, in part, by the concept of an equality that had to be vindicated by each individual; in part, by the fragmentation of the Old World concepts of family and community relationships, which was an almost inevitable consequence of the uprooting from the Old World and the transplanting to the New; in part, by the seeming infinity of resources and the seeming advantages of rapid exploitation and rapid aggrandizement; in part, by the weakness of governmental and institutional controls; in part, by the ostentatious potentialities of industry and technology, the advent of which coincided with the emergence of nationalism in the United States; and, in part, by the triumph of private enterprise over public.

However complex the explanation, the fact is simple enough: We have wasted our natural resources more recklessly than has any other people in modern history and are persisting in this waste and destruction even though we are fully aware that our children will pay for our folly and our greed.

Lincoln's second explanation—if it can be called that—was that we had suffered a decline of the creativity and resourcefulness that had been the special distinction of the Founding Fathers. "The field of glory is harvested," he said, "the crop is already appropriated." Other leaders would emerge, no doubt, and would "seek regions hitherto unexplored." At a time when Martin Van Buren was in the White House, to be succeeded by Harrison, Tyler, Polk, Taylor, Fillmore, Pierce, and Buchanan, that expectation doubtless represented the triumph of hope over history. But the decline of political creativity and leadership was not confined to this somewhat dismal period of our history; it has persisted into our own day. We can no more afford it than could Lincoln's generation. At a time when the white population of English America was less than three million, it produced Franklin and Washington, Jefferson and Madison, John Adams and Hamilton, John Jay and James Wilson, George Wythe and John Marshall, and Tom Paine, who emerged, first, in America. We have not done that well since.

Even more arresting is the undeniable fact that this Revolutionary generation produced not only many of our major leaders but all of our major political institutions, among them federalism, the Constitutional convention, the Bill of Rights, the effective separation of powers, judicial review, the new colonial system, the political party. It is no exaggeration to say that we have been living on that political capital ever since.

Here again the explanation is obscure. There is the consoling consideration that the Founding Fathers did the job so well that it did not need to be done over; the depressing consideration that American talent has gone, for the past century or so, more into private than into public enterprise; and the sobering consideration that at a time when our chief preoccupation appears to be with extension of power rather than with wise application of resources, those "regions hitherto unexplored" appear to be in the global arena rather than the domestic. Whatever the explanation, lack of leadership is the most prominent feature on our political landscape, and lack of creativity the most striking characteristic of our political life.

It is still true that, "if destruction be our lot, we must ourselves be its author"—that the danger is not from without but from within. But

    . . . passions spin the plot;
    We are betrayed by what is
      false within.

For, paradoxically, the danger from within is rooted in and precipitated by foreign adventures that we seem unable either to understand or to control. We have not been attacked from Latin America or from Asia; we have attacked ourselves by our own ventures into these areas.

The problem Lincoln faced in 1838 is with us once again: the breakdown of the social fabric and its overt expression in the breakdown of the law. Lincoln's solution, if greatly oversimplified, is still valid: reverence for the law. A people will revere the law when it is just and is seen to be just. But no matter how many litanies we intone, we will not induce our people to obey laws that those in authority do not themselves obey. The most striking feature of lawlessness in America today is that it is encouraged by public examples. It is no use telling a Mississippi Negro to revere the law that is palpably an instrument of injustice to him and his race. It is no use exhorting the young to obey the law when most of the major institutions of our society—the great corporations, the powerful trade unions, the very instruments of government—flout the law whenever it gets in their way. It is of little use to admonish a young man about to be drafted to revere the law when he knows that he is to be an instrument for the violation of international law on a massive scale by his own government. It is futile to celebrate the rule of law and the sanctity of life when our own armies engage in ghoulish "body counts," burn unoffending villages, and massacre civilians. While governments, corporations, and respectable elements in our society not only countenance lawlessness and violence but actively engage in it, violence will spread and lawlessness will flourish. We are betrayed by what is false within.

THE FUTURE OF AMERICAN POLITICS
HOW CAN THE LEFT BE RELEVANT?

William A. Williams

Mr. Williams, an American historian now teaching at Oregon State University, is the author of The Contours of American History *and* The Tragedy of American Diplomacy. *The following article, "An American Socialist Community?" is from* Liberation, *June 1969.*

In moving about the country a good bit the last four years—from the campuses to the metropolis and through the provinces—

I have repeatedly been struck by two things. The first is the accuracy of Harold Cruse's observation: "Americans generally have no agreement on who they are, what they are, or how they got to be what they are. . . . All Americans are involved in an identity crisis." The second is that the Left, or The Movement as the jargon has it, is not doing very much that is effective in dealing with that dangerous but potentially creative situation.

There is no persuasive evidence that The Movement is in the process of becoming a social movement of the kind that can generate and push through major reforms on a continuing basis—let alone institute structural changes—in American society. Whatever the victories of the Left, there are a good many indications that the activities of The Movement are increasing the concern and willingness within The Establishment to reform and rationalize the corporate system according to its own adaptation of our criticisms.

From *Liberation Magazine*, June 1969. Reprinted in *Current*, August 1969, No. 109.

And some actions of the Left are creating growing support for repressive policies (as contrasted with suppression in specific crises).

There are two orthodox comments at this point. One maintains that the revolution is being made by people doing their own thing: that if you leave the System it will collapse. If that is correct, then we either collapse with it or confront the necessity of a new ruthlessness to build the replacement. The other argument maintains that Establishment reforms will not—even cannot—go far enough quickly enough to avert a crisis that will open the way for The Movement. I do not rule out that possibility. But I do not think it is probable because the analysis overlooks, or discounts, several major considerations.

One: while American society is sick, it is not sick to the verge of rolling over dead, or even to the point that a good push will topple it into History. The will to maintain the system is real and visible and consequential. Two: an Establishment trying to reform itself will, for a long period, hold the loyalty of most of those who are reluctant to repress, as well as those who are now ready to maintain the National Guard on standby alert. This is particularly true so long as the Left makes no discriminations among and within other groups in society, makes no sustained effort to involve them as participating equals in a non-elitist movement, and offers nothing to attract them into such a venture. Three: things can not only get worse as a short run prelude to getting better, but can get worse for an indefinite period.

The New Romanticism

There simply cannot be an era of radical reform, or structural change, without a living conception of community and a clearly developed approach to alternatives to meet the needs of America in an equitable and effective manner. Much of the Left is operating—consciously or unconsciously—under the illusion that the United States today is comparable to England twixt 1660 and 1688, France in 1789, Russia in 1917, or one of the many poor and non-industrial countries of the contemporary world. It has become fashionable to call this the New Romanticism, and defend it with orthodox irrationality. It would be better, for the honor of true Romanticism, and for our own well-being (to say nothing of the millions of poor and powerless), to call it ignorance at best—innocent or arrogantly self-righteous as warranted by the specific case—and at worst the most insidious kind of anti-intellectualism.

It flatly will not do, in the last third of the 20th century, to pretend—or simply assert—that we in the United States can indulge ourselves in an indefinite period of willy-nilly-working-out-of-a-new-order. Nor is it meaningful to talk about anarchy or self-contained communes of mutually compatible couples. Or of the underground that can provide you with subsistence for a year. There is no more justification for putting people off in that fashion than there is for putting people down. Yet The Movement is doing a good deal of both.

Come the revolution

Eldridge Cleaver heated up the soul on this issue as hotly as anyone. "We start with the premise that every man, woman and child on the face of the earth deserves the very highest standard of living that human knowledge and technology is capable of providing. Period. No more than that, no less than that." That is not really enough, or at least it is seriously open to the charge of mistaking economism for socialism (or whatever other name for the new order you prefer), but it is more than sufficient to end the explicit and implicit nonsense of The Movement that mundane matters will take care of themselves come the revolution. They do not now, which is one of our criticisms, and they will not do so even ten years after the revolution if we do not see to it ourselves.

In one of his classic throw-away lines, Schumpeter once remarked that socialism was a post-economic problem. In a strict sense that is true. Socialism is, or at any rate should be, about the nature and functioning of a community, rather than about the failings of the capitalist system. And a community is not created, let alone maintained, by everyone simply doing their own thing. Adam Smith wrote that prescription for heaven on earth in 1776, and after 200 years we ought to be able to recognize the limitations. But Schumpeter's arrow did not hit the center of the bullseye. For Marx accurately noted that while capitalism created the means for solving the economic problem it could not organize and use those powers to fulfill its avowed reason for being.

Cleaver, Schumpeter, and Marx. All three were correct. Still are correct. Cleaver's proposition, explicitly expanded to include intellectual, cultural, and interpersonal matters, will stand as the "no less than that" of an American radicalism. But to get on with realizing that objective we have to deal with the implications of Schumpeter's point about socialism. We have, that is, to speak to the nature of a new economy and to the philosophic, physiological, and psychic foundations for a man who is not, as Adam Smith maintained, defined by his propensity to barter and trade in the marketplace. The Left, old or new, has yet to answer either question.

Leviathan versus community

It is no longer relevant to prove that socialists can operate (albeit more fairly and more efficiently) the centralized and consolidated economic system created by mature capitalism. That would have been very helpful if we had come to power between 1894 and 1914, but the challenge today is to maintain and increase productivity while breaking the Leviathan into community-sized elements. And while the Hippies have blasted through some of the walls that capitalism erected around true humanism, they are very largely operating as a self-defined interest group in the classic sense of 19th century capitalism. It is no answer to Smith to define individualism in Freudian terms, or some other human propensity.

So what we come down to, Cruse to the contrary notwithstanding, is Marx. It is so obvious as to be the cliché of the era: capitalism has demonstrated a congenital incapacity to use its literally fantastic powers and achievements to enable untold members of the lower and middle classes—and even many in the upper class—to live as human beings. But Marx also said that the purpose and the responsibility of The Movement was twofold: to extend, deepen, and focus the awareness of that failure, and to organize the people of the society to use the powers created by mature capitalism in humane and creative ways.

So far there is less irrelevant about Marx than there is parochial about The Movement. The issues here are not the tactics of disruption, provocation, and violence. At least not for many (including myself) who lack the training or guts to be pacifists, or feel morally queasy about righteously provoking the worst in other men we know are not prepared to transcend their prejudices in a moment of crisis, or consider non-violent revolution as a strategy appropriate only for an established socialist society. I do not think it is possible—even under the best of circumstances—to move from mature capitalism to established socialism without considerable disruption and some amount of blood.

The central matter, however, concerns when—in what context and for what purposes—we disrupt and spill blood. I think there has been a good deal of both that has not produced any *sustained* deepening and focusing of radical consciousness. It has been my observation, as well as experience, that six months of quiet work in the dormitories, or of going up to the doorbell for a half-hour conversation, has deeper and more lasting consequences than the occupation of a building or the provocation of a bust. It was, after all, the teach-ins rather than the marches that played the major role in generating the now widespread opposition to the Vietnam War. Cruse is everlastingly correct on a visceral point: we must create and generalize our conception of what it means to be an American.

And of course that brings us to the two nut-crackers. One: we do not have a meaningful conception of what it is to be an American. We have instead a collection of disjointed notes on what it does not mean, and a vague assertion that all things will be beautiful and lovely come the revolution.

Nineteenth century leftists

Two: we ought to transcend our narrowness in faulting Marx for being over 30 when we know he is over 100. Marx saw the necessity—moral and practical—for radical socialist change at a time when capitalism was plumbing the foundations for its century of great creativity. That was his genius. Our stupidity, at least so far, has been to think and talk about today and tomorrow so largely in terms of 1885. For, in an eerie way, much of the Left is still operating in terms of the 19th century world. The Hippies are almost a mirror reversal of full-blown Victorianism. The Communists are almost a mirror reversal of late 19th century corporate reformers. And there are similar comparisons with the anarchists and the Brook Farmers.

But, even though he fails to exploit it, Cruse does have a point about Marx. Taken literally, Marx is irrelevant because the only way to deepen and focus the radical social consciousness of the large numbers of women and men of our time is to tell them in concrete and specific terms how their lives can be richer and purposeful.

There is simply not any time or justification for us to be vague like Marx, technocratically optimistic like Lenin, romantically irresponsible like Trotsky, or latter-day agrarians like Mao and Castro.

If we are going to have a social movement, we will have to build it on the basis of a workable answer to the eminently fair demand from our potential constituency among the lower and middle classes. *Why and how will socialism be any better than a capitalism without the Vietnam War and with a continuing (and improving) pattern of permissive welfarism?* We have, that is, to convince those vast numbers of human beings that we can take the productive apparatus of mature capitalism and reorganize it for their benefit. That means erasing two primary lines in their image of the Left. One is the line that connects radical structural change with things getting worse than they are. The other line connects radicalism with radicals doing their own things at the expense of large numbers of other people.

I am very skeptical that we can meet that challenge through a strategy based on the declining age of the majority of the population; at least not as it is now being attempted by various campus groups. For one thing, most Americans do not define their hopes for a better society in terms of university reform. To use the jargon, that is not relevant to them. Frankly, I sympathize with that for, while it is important to me personally in the short-run and to me as a socialist in the long-run, it is not nearly as central as building an inclusive social movement capable of forcing the Establishment to give large chunks of ground on primary issues affecting the majority of my fellow citizens. Secondly, as presently organized and conducted, the campus wing of The Movement is not making any serious outreach to its own recent members— McCarthy and Kennedy are all the footnotes needed on that point.

A strategy for The Left

I think another strategy warrants serious consideration. It has three parts.

One: use the campus as a base for reaching the community. This means, in connection with campus action, preparing the ground in the city and the state for the ultimate confrontations on campus. It means, in the broader sense, using the campus as what it is—a generator of ideas—and as a center of serious intellectual activity dealing with the problems of the general society. A radical movement that weakens, or even destroys, the university to gain secondary and symptomatic reforms is not demonstrating a convincing case for general leadership of the society.

Two: stop evading the legitimate demands for clear and convincing proposals for the new American community. If we cannot meet that request, then we are irrelevant. It is at best a disingenuous way of putting people down; it is at worst hard evidence of intellectual incompetence. And, for ourselves, we ought to be able to learn from Russia and China that the lack of clear ideas and programs can lead to all kinds of serious moral and practical troubles.

Three: start dealing with large numbers of Americans, however misled or mistaken we may consider them, as human beings rather than as racists and stupids to be jammed up against the wall. For the self-righteous arrogance in The Movement is at least as dangerous to its future as The Establishment.

Phase II of the Capitalist System

Neither the conservative nor the radical perception of American capitalism sheds much light on our current economic reality.

ROBERT L. HEILBRONER

ROBERT L. HEILBRONER is Norman Thomas professor of economics at the New School.

CONSIDER the following day in the life of a conservative-minded New York businessman we will call Smith:

Arising early one morning, Smith glances at the headlines that feature the Government's latest excursion into price controls, and groans: They are out to destroy the business system. As he reads the details of this latest Government foray, he is moved to reflect on the importance of Government in the private economy. Even his breakfast is touched by Government—the orange-juice container, the wrapper on his loaf of bread, the tin that holds his coffee all bear descriptive labels that are imposed by Government decree.

Indeed, it seems to Smith, as he goes about his day, that Government is everywhere. The taxi he takes to Penn Station charges a fare set by Government. The train he boards for Washington (Government city) is owned and operated by the Government. Once in Washington, Smith learns that a proposed merger in which his company is interested will be forbidden by Government ruling. Telephoning the news to New York, at rates set by a Government agency, he decides to return immediately, boarding an aircraft whose route, maintenance, equipment, operating procedures and fare have all been Government determined. On the trip home Smith figures how much of his anticipated year-end bonus will go to the Government in taxes, ruefully calculating the rate at more than 50 per cent; and then even more ruefully, he recalls that it is up to Government whether or not he will be allowed to get a bonus in the first place.

Home again, he relaxes in his apartment, whose construction was partly subsidized by Government, and idly watches a Government-licensed television station that is dutifully complying with a Government regulation to devote a portion of its prime time to public-interest programing. His son, who attends a Government-supported university, comes in to borrow the family's car, which has been designed to meet certain Government specifications. Before retiring, Smith looks over his mail, which includes a bill from the Government for the Social Security payments he must make for his maid. Switching off the lights, for which he has been paying at Government-established rates, he settles onto his bed, from whose mattress still dangles the Government-decreed tag ("Do Not Remove Under Penalty of Law)," and as he finally dozes off, asks himself: "Is this still capitalism?"

THIS is the sort of scenario that delights the guardians of economic conservatism, some of whom will no doubt find use for the foregoing paragraphs in a speech entitled "We Are Drifting into Socialism." But consider the scenario again, this time from the point of view of another Smith, say a professor of radical political leanings. Reading the news of the Government's most recent moves in the area of wage and price controls, Radical Smith notes that once again Government has failed to match its restraints on labor with corresponding restraints on capital: Where is the needed excess-profits tax? Eating his breakfast, Smith observes the compulsory labels on his food, but reflects on how little faith one can repose in them, given the sorry record of the Food and Drug Administration's responsiveness to industry pressure. Paying his cab fare, Radical Smith regrets that the taxi industry is controlled by a public agency readier to boost fares than to increase the number of licensed cabs. Boarding the Amtrak train, he recalls that the railway was taken over by Government only as a last resort to shore up a sagging industry. Arriving in Government city, he is struck by the ease with which Government energies can be marshaled for such purposes as the $5-billion import quota and tax-depletion subsidy for the oil industry, and with how much difficulty they are marshaled for such matters as school lunch programs or Model Cities.

Moreover, Radical Smith is not much impressed by a single merger that fails, since he knows that we have gone through the greatest merger boom in history: The top 100 industrial corporations today own a larger percentage of total corporate assets than did the top 200 corporations 20 years ago. So too, Smith is less impressed by the fact that airlines are regulated than the fact that the result of regulation has been

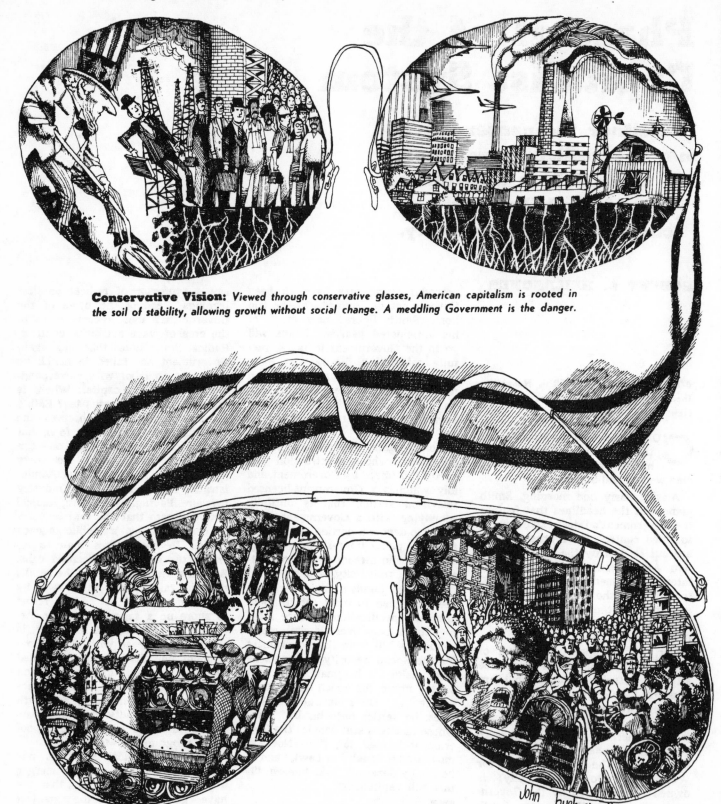

Conservative Vision: *Viewed through conservative glasses, American capitalism is rooted in the soil of stability, allowing growth without social change. A meddling Government is the danger.*

Radical Vision: *American capitalism, through radical spectacles, contains inherent contradictions that give rise to imperialist war, racism, sexual exploitation and widespread alienation.*

to prevent the formation of even a single competitive new trunk line since regulation began in 1938. Radical Smith would not worry about Conservative Smith's tax burden, since he knows that the top 1 per cent of taxpayers (with incomes of roughly $45,000 and up) have paid an average of only 26 per cent of their total incomes, including capital gains, to the Internal Revenue Service in recent years. He would point out as well that the expensive apartment house in which the other Smith lives was built with money provided for "low cost" housing, and that the safety specifications on the other Smith's car were generally regarded as inadequate, thanks to industry protestations. As for Social Security going to the maid, he would note that it was insufficient to support her above the poverty level, whereas the electric-light rates established by Government were high enough to permit Consolidated Edison a profit of 10 per cent on sales. "Is this capitalism?" asks Radical Smith. "Of course. What else?"

Thus both Smiths would impatiently dismiss the question "Is this capitalism?" although both would answer it differently. Nevertheless, I intend to ask the question in all seriousness. For implicit in the answers of both Smiths is the presumption that each clearly knows what capitalism is, or at least what it ought to be. At the risk of irritating both Smiths, I am inclined to think that neither the conservative nor the radical conception of capitalism sheds light on the economic reality that surrounds us, much less on the destination to which it may be headed.

LET me begin with the conservative's picture of capitalism. Like the radical's, it is founded on what we might call a minimal structural definition: Capitalism is an economic system in which the means of production—factories, farms, mines, etc.—are owned by private individuals or firms rather than by the state, and in which the primary method of distributing incomes is the competitive marketplace. We shall have an opportunity later to discuss how useful this minimal definition is. But also like the radical, the conservative sees more in capitalism than a bare institutional structure. Basically he sees capitalism as a static social

system. By this he does not rule out the possibility of economic growth—indeed, this becomes one of his main arguments in favor of the system. But it is growth without social change, growth in which magnitudes become larger but in which fundamental social relationships remain unaltered.

In this vision of a fundamentally static society, one obdurate fact bedevils the conservative. It is the steadily growing presence of Government. From decade to decade the Government looms ever larger within the economic framework. No wonder, then, that the conservative pictures the intrusion of Government as disruptive—even subversive—of the stable social condition that capitalism implies to him.

HAS the steady entry of Government meant the subversion of capitalism? Let us try to answer that question by dividing the long history of Government intervention into the American economy into three distinct, although overlapping, periods. The first can be traced back to colonial America and probably reaches its heyday in the early to middle decades of the 19th century. This is the period in which Government directly intervened in the economy as a direct stimulus for economic expansion itself. Here is the era in which Federal and state money made possible the network of early roads, canals and railroads (not to mention public schools) that played an important role in imparting the momentum of growth to the formative system. To be sure, it is difficult to measure exactly the contribution made by Government, but it seems probable that undertakings such as the Erie Canal, the transcontinen-

tal railroads, or, later, the Panama Canal, were at least as important for the expansion of capitalism in their time as the Federal highway system, the airline network or the armaments industry have been for the growth of the economy in our own time—evidence, I need hardly add, that the propulsive role of Government has not come to an end.

A second phase of Government's relation to capitalism begins after the Civil War and peaks during the New Deal. This is the phase in which the main form of Government intervention appears in the proliferation of agencies such as the Interstate Commerce Commission, the Federal Trade Commission, the Federal Reserve System and the New Deal alphabet array that began to supervise the operation of agriculture, the securities industry, utilities, transportation in virtually all fields and the like.

What was the common element in this new insinuation of Government power? I think most historians would agree that it was the regulation of markets. In one manner or another, the new agencies sought to bring orderliness to markets in which the competitive process was threatening to bankrupt an industry (farming), or to undermine its reliability (banking), or to demoralize its operation (utilities or transportation). Indeed, one of the insights that "revisionist" historians have given us is the recognition of the role played by leading businessmen in actively promoting regulation in order to stave off cutthroat competition and other evils that they were unable to police by themselves. In 1911, Judge Elbert Gary, the arch-conservative head of United States Steel, actually told a dumfounded Congressional committee that "I believe we must come to enforced publicity and Government control . . . even as to prices . . ." —a proposal dismissed by the committee as "semisocialistic."

Whatever the responsibility of the business community in originating the legislation controlling its own operations, there is little doubt that, once enacted, the regulatory laws were used to "stabilize" industrial operations, as witness the long solicitous history of I.C.C. railroad rate-setting, or the aforementioned refusal of the C.A.B. to license an additional competitive trunk line. This does not mean that business has "liked" being regulated, or that regulation has not to some extent served the public as well as the private interest. But the history of regulation makes it difficult to contend that the power of Government has been used to "destroy" any sector over which it was appointed to keep order. On the contrary, the evidence is that regulation has almost invariably been used to protect that sector against competition, from within or without, or against abuses that were threatening to undermine it.

A THIRD phase of Government-business interaction opens with the New Deal and is still with us. This is the active use of central Government powers to bring the economy to an acceptable level of employment, growth and welfare.

Of all changes in business-Government relations, this was probably the one most attended with feelings of "socialistic" betrayal on the part of conservatives—indeed, in the late nineteen-thirties, one of the less adaptive Roosevelts even formed the Veritas Society, whose main purpose was to expunge the teaching of Keynesian economics from the Harvard curriculum. I suspect that the Veritas Society is now defunct, for with Milton Friedman and Richard Nixon both professing their subscription to the principles of Keynesianism there is no longer any respectable conservative opposition to the use of the Government's fiscal and monetary powers to counteract a deficiency in aggregate demand, or to bring individual incomes above some minimum poverty line. But just as the dust has settled in this area of Government intervention, it is stirred up in another. Do wage and price controls betoken a fourth phase of Government-business relation? Is this phase—as Milton Friedman warns—potentially subversive for the system as a whole?

I presume it will not come as a surprise if I opine that, like the previous exercise of Government power, wage and price controls are measures undertaken to enhance, rather than to weaken, the viability of the capitalist system as a whole. For behind the promulgation of wage and price controls, we find the same motivations as those which underlay earlier changes in the role of Government. These motives were, and still are, a conscious effort to adapt the operation of the market system to a changing techno-

logical, social and political environment.

Certainly the use of Government as an expansive force has always been recognized as a deliberate effort to strengthen the economic underpinnings of the nation in those areas that technology opened up, but in which private enterprise, for whatever reasons, was unable to advance alone. In much the same manner, technology was the source of the changed environment that brought Government regulation. New modes of transport, manufacture and distribution gave rise, in the eighteen-seventies and eighteen-eighties, to nation-spanning enterprises serving nationwide markets. Disruption and disorganization on these markets threatened far more serious consequences than in the "atomized" economy of pre-Civil War days, as no one understood better than the businessmen in those industries themselves.

The introduction of Keynes-

> **66Wage and price controls are yet another defensive Government attempt to restore something like stability to the system.99**

ian policies also represented a defensive reaction to another change in the environment. The clear lesson of the nineteen-thirties was that capitalism could not cope with mass unemployment, in large measure because an urbanized society could no longer expect its needy to fend for themselves by going back to the family farm. In retrospect

I believe few would deny that the gradual acceptance of Government responsibility for maintaining high employment and minimal standards of welfare was a profoundly conservative, rather than a revolutionary, turn of events.

From this point of view, the latest phase of Government intervention takes its place as yet another defensive adaptation to environmental change. Since World War II, capitalist governments all over the world have put to vigorous use the lesson of the nineteen-thirties, and are actively promoting economic growth and maintaining a (rising) floor of social well-being. As a result, the insecurity of economic life has greatly lessened for the great majority of people. In this new milieu of modest affluence and sanguine expectations, both industry and labor found their bargaining power enhanced—industry by the presence of a Government commitment to continuous expansion, labor by the much greater staying power of its individual members in case of strikes. In this altered setting the competitive mechanism no longer brings a stable over-all equilibrium, but a continuous upward pressure on prices, requiring the intervention of Government to restore something like stability to the system. Thus the emergence of "income policies" of one sort or another in virtually every capitalist nation abroad, and the recourse to wage and price controls at home.

IS the conservative wholly wrong, then, in his conception of capitalism? It must be clear that I think he is quite mistaken with regard to the "subversive" role of Government. Yet, oddly enough, I believe the conservative is right in his underlying picture of capitalism as a static social system. Only it is not the institutional framework that is static. It is the social core of the system, its structure of privilege.

The most obvious and important form that this privilege takes is the continuous creation and allocation of a highly disproportionate share of income to two groups within capitalist society—those who own substantial quantities of property and those who man the command posts within the business world. Capitalism has always rewarded these strata generously. Going back to 1910 (admittedly on the basis of somewhat shaky data), we find that the top 10th of income recipients got just over one-third of total income. In 1968 the top 10th of family units (not quite the same measure as "income recipient") received 30 per cent of all income. The change, if any, has been small. Moreover, on the basis of much firmer data, it seems likely that the share accruing to the top 10th has increased since 1960.

Unfortunately, income distribution statistics are deceptive because changes in the tax laws cause upper-income receivers to rearrange the manner in which they get income — swapping capital gains for outright compensation, or causing large payments to be deferred into installments over future years. However, when examining more substantial data with respect to the ownership of wealth, we find that here, too, the overwhelming impression is one of stability rather than change. Estimates based on studies by Robert Lampman and others indicate that the share of private wealth held by the top 2 per cent of all families declined from 33 per cent in 1922 to 25 per cent in 1949, and thereafter rose again to about 32 per cent in 1958. Perhaps even more striking are the figures regarding the ownership of corporate stock, by far the most strategic form of wealth in a capitalist system. According to Lampman's findings, the top 1 per cent of adults owned 61.5 per cent of all corporate stock in 1922 and 76 per cent in 1953.

The point of these statistics is obvious and irrefutable. Despite 50 years of increased Government intervention, supposedly "confiscatory" taxation, welfare statism and the rest, nothing like a dramatic change in the concentration of wealth or income has taken place within capitalism. This in no way denies that the system has generated a steadily rising standard of living for most of the population. But there remains a vast gulf between the quality of life of the "middle" classes (let us say the 15 million American families that in 1968 enjoyed incomes of more than $8,000 but less than $15,000), and the very small group of Americans—perhaps some 200,000 families in all—who enjoyed an annual income of $100,000 or more. It is this stratum of privilege that capitalism protects, and whose persistent presence confirms, albeit from an unexpected angle, the conservative's view of capitalism as a system that grows but does not fundamentally change.

NOT surprisingly the radical sees things from a diametrically opposite vantage point. Like the conservative, the radical also fastens on the pillars of private property and the market as the critical and distinctive institutions of capitalism. But unlike the conservative, who sees in these institutions the foundation for a static social system, the radical sees in them the source of a pervasive and ultimately irresistible social dynamics. Indeed, to the radical the most striking attribute of capitalism is precisely its inherent tendency for revolutionary change.

By far the most powerful dynamic conception of capitalism as a system wracked by unavoidable change is the classic Marxian view in which a working class is first immiserated, then disciplined, finally goaded beyond endurance by a system that systematically exploits and deceives it. That drama has now lost its convincing ring for most radicals. Marxian theorists such as Ernest Mendel or Paul Sweezy no longer anticipate the clear-cut class polarization foreseen by Marx. In their eyes, the dynamics of capitalism continue to undermine the system, but in a more complex way, expressing the contradictions—the inherent incompatible tendencies—of the system in the rise of an unstable policy of imperialist hegemony on the one hand, and an inner decay on the other, visible in racism, sexism and widespread alienation.

TWO problems remain unexamined in this latter-day interpretation of capitalist dynamics. The first is the dangerous question of whether the United States, with all its problems, is to be taken as the archetype — the ideal expression of capitalism. Most radicals would answer that question unquestionably in the affirmative, claiming that America is imperialist, racist, sexist and alienated *because* it is a capitalist society.

But here is where the question gets dangerous. For suppose one turned the tables and asked whether the Soviet Union, which is also imperialist and racist and alienated, were the archetype of Socialist society, and its evils therefore inherent to Socialism? Most radical critics would recoil at the suggestion. Yet, if the United States, as the largest and most powerful capitalist system *is* archetypal, why is not the Soviet Union? And if the Soviet Union is *not* archetypal, but is instead to be "explained" by the special circumstances of its national heritage and traditions, why should not the excesses of the United States be explained in the same way? In a word, why are not Norway or Sweden—both societies also built on private property and the market system—models of "pure" capitalism, and the United States only a sorry case of a capitalism come to maturity in a land cursed with slavery (not a capitalist institution) and formed in the peculiar mold of an exacerbated frontier individualism?

To this perplexing and difficult problem let me add another that also sheds doubt on the radical view of capitalist dynamics. It is that the same basic economic structure can give rise to such different results in different settings.

When we say the word "capitalism," we include societies as different in their social, political and economic institutions as Japan, where the large corporations guarantee lifetime employment to their workers—and the Republic of South Africa, where something very close to indentured labor is an essential part of the system; New Zealand, with its virtual absence of unemployment—and the United States, with its nagging problem of unemployment; Norway, with its severe taxation of upper incomes—and Italy, with its *dolce vita*; Denmark, with its long tradition of political security—and France, with its equally long tradition of insecurity. All these nations have economic structures built on private property and a market mechanism, and all display certain economic tendencies and problems typical of these systems, such as instability, inflation, economic concentration, etc. But the manner in which they cope with these problems, and the social and political superstructures they erect on their common economic base, display an extraordinary variety.

It is difficult to maintain in the face of this diversity that imperialism (Norway?), racism (Denmark?), a widening gap between rich and poor (Sweden?) or other such problems are inherent in "capitalism." To put it differently, it is hard to explain how capitalism can assume so many shapes and forms unless we are willing to admit that factors of a noneconomic kind —geographic position, size, racial mixtures, political institutions, "national character" or whatever—are critical in determining the outcome of capitalist dynamics in each case. But to do that is to abandon the Marxist belief in the ultimate hegemony of the economic forces of history, and to admit on an equal footing the forces of politics and social institutions. And once we do that, it becomes impossible to maintain that capitalism has a predictable future determined by the one thing that sets it apart from other kinds of societies—its economic institutions.

IS the radical view of capitalism as deficient, therefore, as the conservative? Clearly I reject its mechanical linkage between economic forces and social and political consequences, and its easy assumption that every evil visible in America is a direct expression of pure capitalism at work. Yet, just as I believe that the conservative view correctly emphasizes the presence of a static core within capitalism, so I think the radical view equally correctly stresses the presence of continuous stresses — "contradictions" if you will—within the system. Indeed, I believe it is in the complex interaction between the effort to preserve the static core, and the strains imposed by a relentlessly changing environment, that we find the best means of making general prognostications as to the future of capitalism. With all diffidence let me venture two:

1. *There will be a further substantial increase in the intervention of Government.*

The reasons for this are implicit in our previous discussion: capitalist economies throughout the world stand at

STOPGAPS—New and growing social problems force Government to greater rescue efforts to maintain economic viability.

the threshold of an era in which new environmental and social problems will require new rescue efforts to maintain their viability.

Some of these problems are now familiar — pollution, urban decay, population growth. Others are still novel, such as the recent discovery of the extreme vulnerability of advanced service-oriented societies to labor stoppages. In "old-fashioned" capitalism one could buffer the effects of a strike by living off inventories of coal and steel while labor and management fought it out. But there are no inventories of garbagemen's or teachers' or flight controllers' services. An urbanized economy is critically dependent upon the regular performance of its service tasks; and to secure this performance it must rely on every governmental power at hand.

From many parts of the environment, then, strains and stresses are arising that will most probably be met by an increasing intervention of Government. The main drift of institutional change over the next generation is virtually certain to be toward planning, although probably not toward the kind of massive central planning typical of contemporary East-European Socialism. Will this planning be subversive for capitalism? I shall answer the question only by mentioning that Thomas J. Watson of I.B.M. has called for "national goal-setting and planning" before the New York Bond Club; that Robert Sarnoff of R.C.A. has echoed his call before the National Industrial Conference Board; and that "Counter-budget," an ambitious outline of greatly enlarged Govern-

ment participation in an ordered economy, bears the signatures of such revolutionaries as David Rockefeller, James Roche, chairman of G.M., and H. I. Romnes, chairman of A. T. & T.

2. In the advanced capitalist nations, new élites based on science and technology are gradually displacing the older élites based on wealth.

It is much too early to declare capitalism "obsolete," and if the last hundred years tell us anything, it is that the structure of privilege characteristic of capitalism will not be quickly altered. Nevertheless, there seems to be a shift of power within all capitalist nations (and to some extent within Socialist ones as well) into the hands of a professional, science-based and technology-oriented group. The rise of this new élite has been observed by many, including John Kenneth Galbraith, Daniel Bell, and Zbigniew Brzezinski; in my own case (in "The Limits of American Capitalism") I have likened it to the process of displacement by which the medieval merchant, at first dependent upon and subservient to the feudal lord, gradually came to rival and then to usurp his place. In the same fashion, I suspect, there is deep-rooted change occurring now in which the scientific and technological élites, although still dependent upon and subservient to the controllers of wealth, are slowly detaching themselves from this position of subordination and becoming themselves the architects of a new social order. Here is a process that truly is subversive for capitalism, at least in the long run.

By this I do not mean to imply that a formal power struggle now impends between the old élites and the new. Much more likely is a gradual fusion and metamorphosis—the old élites taking on the scientific-technological outlook, with its natural propensity for planning and for consciously directed social change; and the new élites enjoying more and more of the privileges that formerly accrued to ownership rather than to expertise. Even so did the merchants marry aristocrats' daughters, and did aristocrats learn to carry on commercial pursuits.

NONE of this allows us to make easy predictions with regard to the future of *American* capitalism. If any conclusion seems clear, it is that different capitalisms will deal with the problems of the environment and of the internal shift in power in different ways. But there seems no reason to claim that "capitalism" cannot cope with the problems of the 20th century, whereas "Socialism" is able to. Can one really predict that Sweden must fail and Poland succeed? If the basic institutions of capitalism—private property and the market mechanism—seem in many ways ill-adapted to the problems of our age, one cannot say that the core institutions of Socialism—collective ownership and centralized planning—have yet shown themselves much better adapted. I believe that for a long period of time all advanced nations, whether Socialist or capitalist, will have to improvise and experiment to make their social systems operate effectively in a world in which technology and bureaucracy present overwhelming challenges for which we have discovered no adequate responses as yet.

There is no reason to believe that all societies will discover adequate responses: that will depend on institutional inertia, ideology, political genius, tradition. Where answers are not found we can expect increasing dysfunction, a deterioration of social morale, perhaps eventually violent political change. I suspect that how well America will fare in this long-drawn-out and cru- cially important struggle will depend less on those elements in America that are capitalist than on those elements in capitalism that are American. ■

Drawings by JOHN HUEHNERGARTH

America in the Technetronic Age

Zbigniew Brzezinski

Zbigniew Brzezinski is Professor of Government and Director of the Research Institute on Communist Affairs of Columbia University. On leave during the years 1966 and 1967, he has been serving as Member of the Policy Planning Council of the Department of State. He is also a member of the American Academy's Commission on the Year 2000. His works include, among others, *The Soviet Bloc—Unity and Conflict* and *Alternative to Partition.*

Ours is no longer the conventional revolutionary era; we are entering a novel metamorphic phase in human history. The world is on the eve of a transformation more dramatic in its historic and human consequences than that wrought either by the French or the Bolshevik revolutions. Viewed from a long perspective, these famous revolutions merely scratched the surface of the human condition. The changes they precipitated involved alterations in the distribution of power and property within society; they did not affect the essence of individual and social existence. Life—personal and organized—continued on much as before, even though some of its external forms (primarily political) were substantially altered. Shocking though it may sound to their acolytes, by the year 2000 it will be accepted that Robespierre and Lenin were mild reformers.

Unlike the revolutions of the past, the developing metamorphosis will have no charismatic leaders with their strident doctrines, but its impact will be far more profound.

Most of the change that has so far taken place in human history has been gradual—with the great "revolutions" being mere punctuation marks to a slow, eludible process. In contrast, the approaching transformation will come more rapidly and will have deeper consequences for the way and even perhaps for the meaning of human life than anything experienced by the generations that preceded us.

America is already beginning to experience these changes and in the course of so doing it is becoming a *"technetronic"* society: a society that is shaped culturally, psychologically, socially, and economically by the impact of technology and electronics, particularly computers and communications. The industrial process no longer is the principal determinant of social change, altering the mores, the social structure and the values of society. This change is separating America from the rest of the world, prompting a further fragmentation among an increasingly differentiated mankind, and imposing upon America a special obligation to ease the pains of the resulting confrontation.

The Technetronic Society

The far-reaching innovations we are about to experience will be the result primarily of the impact of science and technology on man and his society, especially in the developed world. Recent years have seen a proliferation of exciting and challenging literature on the future. Much of it is serious, not mere science-fiction. Moreover, both in the United States and, to a lesser degree, in Western Europe a number of systematic, scholarly efforts have been designed to project, predict and possess what the future

Reproduced from the Series of Occasional Papers, School of International Affairs, 1967, subsequently adapted and expanded in *Between Two Ages: America's Role in the Technetronic Era,* Viking Press, New York, 1970.

holds for us. Curiously, very little has been heard on this theme from the Communist World, even though Communist doctrinarians are the first to claim that their nineteenth century ideology holds a special passkey to the twenty-first century.

The work in progress indicates that men living in the developed world will undergo during the next several decades a mutation potentially as basic as that experienced through the slow process of evolution from animal to human experience. The difference, however, is that the process will be telescoped in time—and hence the shock effect of the change may be quite profound. Human conduct will become less spontaneous and less mysterious—more predetermined and subject to deliberate "programming." Man will increasingly possess the capacity to determine the sex of his children, to affect through drugs the extent of their intelligence and to modify and control their personalities. The human brain will acquire expanded powers, with computers becoming as routine an extension of man's reasoning as automobiles have been of man's mobility. The human body will be improved and its durability extended: some estimate that during the next century the average life-span could reach approximately 120 years.

These developments will have major social impact. The prolongation of life will alter our mores, our career patterns and our social relationships. New forms of social control may be needed to limit the indiscriminate exercise by individuals of their new powers. The possibility of extensive chemical mind control, the danger of loss of individuality inherent in extensive transplantation, and the feasibility of manipulation of the genetic structure will call for a social definition of common criteria of restraint as well as of utilization. Scientists predict with some confidence that by the end of this century, computers will reason as well as man and will be able to engage in "creative" thought; wedded to robots or to "laboratory beings," they could act like humans. The makings of a most complex—and perhaps bitter—philosophical as well as a political dialogue about the nature of man are self-evident in these developments.

Other discoveries and refinements will further alter society as we now know it. The information revolution, including extensive information storage, instant retrieval and eventually push-button visual and sound availibility of needed data in almost any private home, will transform the character of institutionalized collective education. The same techniques could serve to impose well-nigh total political surveillance on every citizen, putting into much sharper relief than is the case today the question of privacy. Cybernetics and automation will revolutionize working habits, with leisure becoming the practice and active work the exception —and a privilege reserved for the most talented. The achievement-oriented society might give way to the amusement-focused society, with essentially spectator spectacles (mass sports and TV) providing an opiate for increasingly purposeless masses.

But while for the masses life will grow longer and time will seem to expand, for the activist elite time will become a rare commodity. Indeed, even the elite's sense of time will alter. Already now speed dictates the pace of our lives—instead of the other way around. As the speed of transportation increases—largely by its own technological momentum—man discovers that he has no choice but to avail himself of that acceleration, either to keep up with others or because he thinks he can thus accomplish more. This will be especially true of the elite, for whom an expansion in leisure time does not seem to be in the cards. Thus as speed expands, time contracts—and the pressures on the elite increase.

By the end of this century the citizens of the more developed countries will live predominantly in cities—hence almost surrounded by man-made environment. Confronting nature could be to them what facing the elements was to our forefathers—meeting the unknown and not necessarily liking it. Enjoying a personal standard of living that in some countries may reach almost $10,000 per head, eating artificial food, speedily commuting from one corner of the country to work in another, in continuous visual contact with their employer, government, or family, consulting their annual calendars to establish on which day it will rain or shine, our descendants will be shaped almost entirely by what they themselves create and control.

But even short of these far-reaching changes, the transformation that is now taking place is already creating a society increasingly unlike its industrial predecessor.* In the industrial society, technical knowledge was applied primarily to one specific end: the acceleration and improvement of production techniques. Social consequences were a later by-product of this paramount concern. In the technetronic society, scientific and technological knowledge, in addition to enhancing productive capabilities, quickly spills over to affect directly almost all aspects of life.

This is particularly evident in the case of the impact of communications and computers. Communications create an extraordinarily interwoven society, in continuous visual, audial and increasingly close contact among almost all its members—electronically interacting, sharing instantly most intense social experiences, prompting far greater personal involvement, with their consciousnesses shaped in a sporadic manner fundamentally different, as McLuhan noted, from the literate (or pamphleteering) mode of transmitting information, characteristic of the industrial age. The growing capacity for calculating instantly most complex interactions and the increasing availability of bio-chemical means of

* My thinking on this subject has been much stimulated by Daniel Bell's pioneering "Notes on the Post-Industrial Society," *Public Interest*, Nos. 6 and 7, 1967.

human control increase the potential scope of self-conscious direction, and thereby also the pressures to direct, to choose and to change.

The consequence is a society that differs from the industrial one in a variety of economic, political and social aspects. The following examples may be briefly cited to summarize some of the contrasts:

1) In an industrial society, the mode of production shifts from agriculture to industry, with the use of muscle and animals supplanted by machine-operation. In the technetronic society, industrial employment yields to services, with automation and cybernetics replacing individual operation of machines.

2) Problems of employment and unemployment—not to speak of the earlier stage of the urban socialization of the post-rural labor force—dominate the relationship between employers, labor and the market in the industrial society, while assuring minimum welfare to the new industrial masses is a source of major concern. In the emerging new society, questions relating to skill-obsolescence, security, vacations, leisure, and profit-sharing dominate the relationship, with the matter of psychic well-being of millions of relatively secure but potentially aimless lower-middle class blue-collar workers becoming a growing problem.

3) Breaking down traditional barriers to education, thus creating the basic point of departure for social advancement, is a major goal of social reformers in the industrial society. Education, available for limited and specific periods of time, is initially concerned with overcoming illiteracy, and subsequently with technical training, largely based on written, sequential reasoning. In the technetronic society, not only education has become universal but advanced training is available to almost all who have the basic talents. Quantity-training is reinforced by far greater emphasis on quality-selection. The basic problem is to discover the most effective techniques for the rational exploitation of social talent. Latest communication and calculating techniques are applied to that end. The educational process, relying much more on visual and audial devices, becomes extended in time, while the flow of new knowledge necessitates more and more frequent refresher studies.

4) In the industrial society social leadership shifts from the traditional rural-aristocratic to an urban "plutocratic" elite. Newly acquired wealth is its foundation, while intense competition the outlet—as well as the stimulus—for its energy. In the post-industrial technetronic society, plutocratic pre-eminence comes under a sustained challenge from the political leadership which itself is increasingly permeated by individuals possessing special skills and intellectual talents. Knowledge becomes a tool of power, and the effective mobilization of talent an important way for acquiring power.

5) The university in an industrial society—rather in contrast to the medieval times—is an aloof ivory-tower, the repository of irrelevant, even if respected, wisdom, and, for only a brief time, the watering fountain for budding members of the established social elite. In the technetronic society, the university becomes an intensely involved think-tank, the source of much sustained political planning and social innovation.

6) The turmoil inherent in the shift from the rigidly traditional rural to urban existence engenders an inclination to seek total answers to social dilemmas, thus causing ideologies to thrive in the industrial society. (The American exception to this rule was due to the absence of the feudal tradition, a point well developed by Louis Hartz.) In the technetronic society, increasing ability to reduce social conflicts to quantifiable and measurable dimensions reinforces the trend towards a more pragmatic problem-solving approach to social issues.

7) The activization of hitherto passive masses makes for intense political conflicts in the industrial society over such matters as disenfranchisement and the right to vote. The issue of political participation is a crucial one. In the technetronic age, the question increasingly is one of ensuring real participation in decisions that seem too complex and too far-removed from the average citizen. Political alienation becomes a problem. Similarly, the issue of political equality of the sexes gives way to a struggle for the sexual equality of women. In the industrial society, woman—the operator of machines—ceases to be physically inferior to the male, a consideration of some importance in rural life, and begins to demand her political rights. In the emerging society, automation discriminates equally against males and females, intellectual talent is computable, while the pill encourages sexual equality.

8) The newly enfranchised masses are coordinated in the industrial society through trade unions and political parties, and integrated by relatively simple and somewhat ideological programs. Moreover, political attitudes are influenced by appeals to nationalist sentiments, communicated through the massive growth of newspapers, relying, naturally, on native tongues. In the technetronic society, the trend seems to be towards the aggregation of the individual support of millions of uncoordinated citizens, easily within the reach of magnetic and attractive personalities, effectively exploiting the latest communication techniques to manipulate emotions and control reason. Reliance on TV—and hence the tendency to replace language with imagery, with the latter unlimited by national confines and including also coverage for such matters as hunger in India or war scenes—tends to create a somewhat more cosmopolitan, though highly impressionistic, involvement in global affairs.

9) Economic power in the industrial society tends to be personalized, either in the shape of great entrepreneurs as Henry Ford or bureaucratic industrializers as Kaganovich,

or Minc (in Stalinist Poland). The tendency towards depersonalization of economic power is stimulated in the next stage by the appearance of a highly complex interdependence between governmental institutions (including the military), scientific establishments and industrial organizations. As economic power becomes inseparably linked with political power, it becomes more invisible and the sense of individual futility increases.

10)   Relaxation and escapism in the industrial society, in its more intense forms, is a carry-over from the rural drinking bout, in which intimate friends and family would join. Bars and saloons—or fraternities—strive to recreate the atmosphere of intimacy. In the technetronic society, social life tends to be so atomized, even though communications (especially TV) make for unprecedented immediacy of social experience, that group intimacy cannot be recreated through the artificial stimulation of externally convivial group behavior. The new interest in drugs seeks to create intimacy through introspection, allegedly by expanding consciousness.

Eventually, these changes and many others, including the ones that affect much more directly the personality and quality of the human being itself, will make the technetronic society as different from the industrial as the industrial became from the agrarian.

The American Transition

America is today in the midst of a transition. American society is leaving the phase of spontaneity and is entering a more self-conscious stage; ceasing to be an industrial society, it is becoming the first technetronic one. This is at least in part the cause for much of the current tensions and violence.

Spontaneity made for an almost automatic optimism about the future, about the "American miracle," about justice and happiness for all. This myth prompted social blinders to the various aspects of American life that did not fit the optimistic mold, particularly the treatment of the Negro and the persistence of pockets of deprivation. Spontaneity involved a faith in the inherent goodness of the American socio-economic dynamic: as America developed, grew, became richer, problems that persisted or appeared would be solved.

This phase is ending. Today, American society is troubled and some parts of it are even tormented. The social blinders are being ripped off—and a sense of inadequacy is becoming more widespread. The spread of literacy, and particularly the access to colleges and universities of about 40% of the youth, has created a new stratum—one which reinforces the formerly isolated urban intellectuals—a stratum not willing to tolerate either social blinders nor sharing the complacent belief in the spontaneous goodness of American social change.

Yet it is easier to know what is wrong than to indicate what ought to be done. The difficulty is not only revealed by the inability of the new social rebels to develop a concrete and meaningful program. It is magnified by the novelty of America's problem. Turning to nineteenth century ideologies is not the answer—and it is symptomatic that the "New Left" has found it most difficult to apply the available, particularly Marxist, doctrines to the new reality. Indeed, its emphasis on human rights, the evils of depersonalization, the dangers inherent in big goverment—while responsive to the felt psychological needs—contain strong parallels to more conservative notions about the place and sanctity of the individual in society.

In some ways, there is an analogy here between the "New Left" and the searching attitude of various disaffected groups in early nineteenth century Europe, reacting to the first strains of the industrial age. Not fully comprehending its meaning, not quite certain where it was heading—yet sensitive to the miseries and opportunities it was bringing—many Europeans strove desperately to adapt earlier, eighteenth century doctrines to the new reality. It was finally Marx who achieved what appeared to many millions a meaningful synthesis, combining utopian idealism about the future of the industrial age with a scorching critique of its present.

The search for meaning is characteristic of the present American scene. It could portend most divisive and bitter ideological conflicts—especially as intellectual disaffection becomes linked with the increasing bitterness of the deprived Negro masses. If carried to its extreme, this could bring to America a phase of violent, intolerant and destructive civil strife, combining ideological and racial intolerance.

However, it seems unlikely that a unifying ideology of political action, capable of mobilizing large-scale loyalty, can emerge in the manner that Marxism arose in response to the industrial era. Unlike even Western Europe or Japan—not to speak of Russia—where the consequences and the impact of the industrial process are still reshaping political, social and economic life, in America science and technology, particularly as socially applied through communications and increasingly computarization, both offsprings of the industrial age, are already more important in influencing the social behavior of a society that has moved past its industrial phase. Science and technology are notoriously unsympathetic to simple, absolute formulas. In the technetronic society, there may be room for pragmatic, even impatient, idealism, but hardly for doctrinal utopianism.

At the same time, it is already evident that a resolution of some of the unfinished business of the industrial era will be rendered more acute. For example, the Negro should have been integrated into American society *during* the American industrial revolution. Yet that revolution came before America, even if not the Negro, was ready for full integra-

We want your advice

What do you think of this book?

Any anthology can be improved. And this one will be. Annually.
But how we improve it depends on the guidance we get from you.
We're only publishing the book, after all. You're actually using it.
What things do you like about it — and what should be changed?
Which articles did you like most? What articles have you read that
should be in our next edition?

```
Comments




















```

Name. . . . . School . . . .

Term used . . . . Date . . . .

Address . . . .

City . . . . State . . . . Zip . . . .

Would you like a copy of the next edition? Yes ☐ No ☐
Would you like to know about Annual Editions in other fields? Yes ☐ No ☐
If so, make sure that your name is typed or printed clearly here and
that you've given us a mailing address that'll be good for at least a
year. When information is available, we'll send it to you and you can
order then if there's something you want.

tion. If the Negro had been only an economic legacy of the preindustrial age, perhaps he could have been integrated more effectively. Today, the more advanced urban-industrial regions of America, precisely because they are moving into a new and more complex phase, requiring even more developed social skills, are finding it so difficult to integrate the Negro, both a racial minority and America's only feudal legacy. Paradoxically, it can be argued that the South today stands a better long-range chance of fully integrating the Negro: American consciousness is changing, the Negro has stirred, and the American South is beginning to move into the industrial age. The odds are that it may take the Negro along with it.

Whatever the outcome, American society is the one in which the great questions of our time will be first tested through practice: can the individual and science co-exist, or will the dynamic momentum of the latter fundamentally alter the former; can man, living in the scientific age, grow in intellectual depth and philosophical meaning, and thus in his personal liberty too; can the institutions of political democracy be adapted to the new conditions sufficiently quickly to meet the crises, yet without debasing their democratic character?

The challenge in its essence involves the twin dangers of fragmentation and excessive control. To take again just a few examples: Symptoms of alienation and depersonalization are already easy to find in American society. Many Americans feel less free; this feeling seems to be connected with their loss of purpose; freedom implies choice of action, and action requires an awareness of goals. If the present transition of America to the technetronic age achieves no personally satisfying fruits, the next phase may be one of sullen withdrawal from social and political involvement, a flight from social and political responsibility through inner emigration. Political frustration could increase the difficulty of absorbing and internalizing rapid environmental changes, thereby prompting increasing psychic instability.

At the same time, the capacity to assert social and political control over the individual will vastly increase. As already noted in the introductory pages, it will soon be possible to assert almost continuous surveillance over every citizen and to maintain up-to-date, complete files, containing even most personal information about the health or personal behavior of the citizen, in addition to more customary data. These files will be subject to instantaneous retrieval by the authorities.

Moreover, the rapid pace of change will put a premium on anticipating events and planning for them. Power will gravitate into the hands of those who control the information, and can correlate it most rapidly. Our existing post-crisis management institutions will probably be increasingly supplanted by pre-crisis management institutions, the task of which will be to identify in advance likely social crises and to develop programs to cope with them. This could encourage tendencies during the next several decades towards a technocratic dictatorship, leaving less and less room for political procedures as we now know them.

Finally, looking ahead to the end of this century, the possibility of bio-chemical mind-control and the genetic tinkering with man, including eventually the creation of beings that will function like men—and reason like them as well—could give rise to the most difficult questions: according to what criteria can such controls be applied; what is the distribution of power between the individual and society with regard to means that can altogether alter man; what is the social and political status of artificial beings, if they begin to approach man in their performance and creative capacities? (One dares not to ask, what if they begin to outstrip man—something not beyond the pale of possibility during the next century?)

Yet it would be highly misleading to construct a one-sided picture, a science-fiction version of the *Animal Farm*. Many of the changes transforming American society argue well for the future and allow at least some optimism about this society's capacity to adapt to the requirements of the metamorphic age.

Thus in the political sphere, the increased flow of information and more efficient techniques of coordination need not necessarily prompt greater concentration of power within some ominous control agency located at the governmental apex. Paradoxically, these developments also make possible greater devolution of authority and responsibility to the lower levels of government and society. The division of power has traditionally posed the problems of inefficiency, coordination and dispersal of authority, but today the new communications and computer techniques make possible both increased authority at the lower levels and almost instant national coordination. It is very likely that state and local government will be strengthened in the next ten years, and many functions currently the responsibility of the Federal government will be assumed by them. (It is noteworthy that the US army has so developed its control-system that it is not uncommon for sergeants to call in and coordinate massive air-strikes and artillery fire—a responsibility of colonels during World War II.) The devolution of financial responsibility to lower echelons may encourage both the flow of better talent and greater local participation in more important local decision-making. National coordination and local participation could thus be wedded by the new systems of coordination. This has already been tried successfully by some large businesses. This development would also have the desirable effect of undermining the appeal of any new integrating ideologies that may arise, for ideologies thrive only as long as there is an acute need for abstract responses to large and remote problems.

It is also a hopeful sign that improved governmental performance, and its increased sensitivity to social needs is being stimulated by the growing involvement in national affairs of what Kenneth Boulding has called the Educational and Scientific Establishment (EASE). The university at one time, during the Middle Ages, was a key social institution. Political leaders leaned heavily on it for literate confidants and privy councillors, a rare commodity in those days. Later divorced from reality, academia in recent years has made a grand reentry into the world of action.

Today, the university is the creative eye of the massive communications complex, the source of much strategic planning, domestic and international. Its engagement in the world is encouraging the appearance of a new breed of politicians-intellectuals, men who make it a point to mobilize and draw on the most expert, scientific and academic advice in the development of their political programs. This, in turn, stimulates public awareness of the value of expertise—and, again in turn, greater political competition in exploiting it.

A profound change in the intellectual community itself is inherent in this development. The largely humanist-oriented, occasionally ideologically-minded intellectual-dissenter, who saw his role largely in terms of proffering social critiques, is rapidly being displaced either by experts and specialists, who become involved in special governmental undertakings, or by the generalists-integrators, who become in effect house-ideologues for those in power, providing over-all intellectual integration for disparate actions. A community of organization-oriented, application-minded intellectuals, relating itself more effectively to the political system than its predecessors, serves to introduce into the political system concerns broader than those likely to be generated by that system itself and perhaps more relevant than those articulated by outside critics.*

The expansion of knowledge, and the entry into sociopolitical life of the intellectual community, has the further effect of making education an almost continuous process. By 1980, not only will approximately two-thirds of US urban dwellers be college-trained, but it is almost certain that systematic elite retraining will be standard in the political system. It will be normal for every high official both to be engaged in almost continuous absorption of new techniques and knowledge, and to take periodic retraining. The adoption of compulsory elementary education was a revolution brought on by the industrial age; in the new technetronic society, it will be equally necessary to require everyone at a sufficiently responsible post to take, say, two years

of retraining every ten years. (Perhaps there will even be a constitutional amendment, requiring a President-elect to spend at least a year getting himself educationally up-to-date.) Otherwise, it will not be possible either to keep up with, or absorb, the new knowledge.

Given diverse needs, it is likely that the educational system will undergo a fundamental change in structure. Television-computer consoles, capable of bringing most advanced education to the home, will permit extensive and continuous adult re-education. On the more advanced levels, it is likely that government agencies and corporations will develop—and some have already begun to do so—their own advanced educational systems, geared to their special needs. As education becomes both a continuum and even more application-oriented, its organizational framework will be redesigned to tie it directly to social and political action.

It is quite possible that a society increasingly geared to learning will be able to absorb more resiliently the expected changes in social and individual life. Mechanization of labor and the introduction of robots will reduce the chores that keep millions busy with doing things that they dislike doing; the increasing GNP, which could permit approximately $10,000 income per capita per year, linked with educational advance, could prompt among those less involved in social management and less interested in scientific development a wave of interest in the cultural and humanistic aspects of life, in addition to purely hedonistic preoccupations. But even the latter would serve as a social valve, reducing tensions and political frustration. Greater control over external environment could make for easier, less uncertain existence.

But the key to successful adaptation to the new conditions is in the effective selection, distribution and utilization of social talent. If the industrial society can be said to have developed through a struggle for survival of the fittest, the technetronic society—to prosper—requires the effective mobilization of the ablest. Objective and systematic criteria for the selection of those with the greatest gifts will have to be developed—and the maximum opportunity for their training and advancement provided. The new society will require enormous talents—as well as philosophical wisdom—to manage and integrate effectively the expected changes. Otherwise, the dynamic of change could chaotically dictate the patterns of social change.

Fortunately, American society is becoming more conscious not only of the principle of equal opportunity for all but of special opportunity for the singularly talented few. Never truly an aristocratic state—except for some pockets such as the South and New England—never really subject to ideological or charismatic leadership—gradually ceasing to be a plutocratic-oligarchic society, the US is becoming something which may be labeled the meritocratic democracy. It combines continued respect for the popular will with an increasing role in the key decision-making institutions of

---

* However, there is a danger in all this that ought not to be neglected. Intense involvement in applied knowledge could gradually prompt a waning of the tradition of learning for the sake of learning. The intellectual community, including the university, could become another "industry," meeting social needs as the market dictates, with the intellctuals reaching for the highest material and political rewards. Concern with power, prestige and the good life could mean an end to the aristocratic ideal of intellectual detachment and search for truth.

individuals with special intellectual and scientific attainments. The educational and social systems are making it increasingly attractive and easy for the meritocratic few to develop to the fullest their special potential. The tapping and advancement of social talent is yet to extend to the poorest and the most underprivileged, but that too is coming. No one can tell whether this will suffice to meet the unfolding challenge, but the increasingly cultivated and programmed American society, led by a meritocratic democracy, may stand a better chance.

Fragmentation and the Trauma of Confrontation

For the world at large, the appearance of the new technetronic society could have the paradoxical effect of creating more distinct worlds on a planet that is continuously shrinking because of the communications revolution. While the scientific-technological change will inevitably have some spill-over, not only will the gap between the developed and the underdeveloped worlds probably become wider—especially in the more measurable terms of economic indices—but a new one may be developing within the industrialized and urban world.

The fact is that America, having left the industrial phase, is today entering a distinct historical era, a different one from that of Western Europe and Japan. This is prompting subtle and still indefinable changes in the American psyche, providing the psycho-cultural underpinnings for the more evident political disagreements between the two sides of the Atlantic. To be sure, there are pockets of innovation or retardation on both sides: Sweden shares with America the problems of leisure, psychic-wellbeing, purposelessness, while Mississippi is experiencing the confrontation with the industrial age in a way not unlike some portions of South-Western Europe. But the broad generalization still holds true: Europe and America are no longer in the same historical era.

What makes America unique in our time is that it is the first society to experience the future. The confrontation with the new—which will soon include much of what has just been outlined—is part of the daily American experience. For better or for worse, the rest of the world learns what is in store for it by observing what happens in the USA: be it the latest scientific discoveries in space, in medicine or the electric toothbrush in the bathroom; be it pop art or LSD; air conditioning or air pollution; old-age problems or juvenile delinquency. The evidence is more elusive in such matters as style, music, values, social mores, but there, too, the term "Americanization" obviously implies a particular source. Today, America is *the* creative society; the others, consciously and unconsciously, are emulative.

American scientific leadership is particularly strong in the so-called "frontier" industries, involving the most advanced fields of science. It has been estimated that approximately eighty percent of all scientific and technical discoveries made during the last few decades originated in the United States. About seventy-five percent of the world's computers operate in the United States. American lead in lasers is even more marked. Examples of American scientific lead are abundant.

There is every reason to assume that this leadership will continue. America has four times as many scientists and research workers as the countries of EEC combined; three and a half times as many as the Soviet Union. The brain-drain is almost entirely one-way. The United States is also spending more on research: seven times as much as the EEC countries, and three and a half times as much as the Soviet Union. Given the fact that scientific development is a dynamic process, it is likely that the gap will widen.*

On the social level, American innovation is most strikingly seen in the manner in which the new meritocratic elite is taking over American life, utilizing the universities, exploiting the latest techniques of communications, harnessing as rapidly as possible the most recent technological devices. Technetronics dominate American life, but so far nobody else's. This is bound to have social and political—and therefore also psychological—consequences, stimulating a psycho-cultural gap in the developed world.

At the same time, the backward regions of the world are becoming more, rather than less, poor in relation to the developed world. It can be roughly estimated that the per capita income of the underdeveloped world is approximately ten times lower than of America and Europe (and twenty-five times that of America itself). By the end of the century, the ratio may be about fifteen to one (or anywhere around 30 to one in the case of the US), with the backward nations *at best* approaching the present standard of the very poor European nations but in many cases—including India—probably not even attaining that modest level.

The social elites of these regions, however, will quite naturally tend to assimilate and emulate, as much as their means and power permit, the life-styles of the most advanced world, with which they are, and increasingly will be, in close vicarious contact through global television, movies, travel, education, and international magazines. The international gap will thus have a domestic reflection, with the masses, given the availability even in most backward regions of transistorized radios (and soon television), becoming more and more intensely aware of their deprivation.

It is difficult to conceive how in that context democratic institutions (derived largely from Western experience—but typcal only of the more stable and wealthy Western nations) will endure in a country like India, or develop elsewhere. The foreseeable future is more likely to see a turn towards personal dictatorships and some unifying doctrines, in the hope that the combination of the two may preserve the

---

* In the Soviet case, rigid compartmentalization between secret military research and industrial research has had the particularly sterile effect of inhibiting spill-over from weapons research into industrial application.

minimum stability necessary for social-economic development. The problem, however, is that whereas in the past ideologies of change gravitated from the developed world to the less, in a way stimulating imitation of the developed world—as was the case with Communism—today the differences between the two worlds are so pronounced that it is difficult to conceive a new ideological wave originating from the developed world, where the tradition of utopian thinking is generally declining.

With the widening gap dooming any hopes of imitation, the more likely development is an ideology of rejection of the developed world. Racial hatred could provide the necessary emotional force, exploited by xenophobic and romantic leaders. The writings of Frantz Fanon—violent and racist—are a good example. Such ideologies of rejection, combining racialism with nationalism, would further reduce the chances of meaningful regional cooperation, so essential if technology and science are to be effectively applied. They would certainly widen the existing psychological and emotional gaps. Indeed, one might ask at that point, who is the truer repository of that indefinable quality we call human? The technologically dominant and conditioned technetron, increasingly trained to adjust to leisure, or the more "natural" and backward agrarian, more and more dominated by racial passions and continuously exhorted to work harder, even as his goal of the good life becomes more elusive?

The result could be a modern version on a global scale of the old rural-urban dichotomy. In the past, the strains produced by the shift from an essentially agricultural economy to a more urban one contributed much of the impetus for revolutionary violence, as Barrington Moore, Jr. documents in his pioneering study *Social Origins of Dictatorship and Democracy*. Applied on a global scale, this division could give substance to Lin Piao's bold assertion that: "Taking the entire globe, if North America and Western Europe can be called 'the cities of the world', then Asia, Africa and Latin America constitute 'the rural areas of the world' . . . . In a sense, the contemporary world revolution also presents a picture of the encirclement of cities by the rural areas."

In any case, even without envisaging such a dichotomic confrontation, it is fair to say that the underdeveloped regions will be facing increasingly grave problems of political stability and social survival. Indeed, to use a capsule formula, in the developed world, the nature of man as man is threatened; in the underdeveloped, society is. The interaction of the two could produce chaos.

To be sure, the most advanced states will possess ever more deadly means of destruction, possibly even capable of nullifying the consequences of the nuclear proliferation that appears increasingly inevitable. Chemical and biological weapons, death rays, neutron bombs, nerve gases, and a host of other devices, possessed in all their sophisticated variety, it seems likely, only by the two superstates, may impose on the world a measure of stability. Nonetheless, it seems unlikely, given the rivalry between the two principal powers, that a fool-proof system against international violence can be established. Some local wars between the weaker, nationalistically more aroused poorer nations may occasionally erupt, resulting perhaps even in the total nuclear extinction of one or several smaller nations, before greater international control is imposed in the wake of the moral shock thereby generated.

The underlying problem, however, will be to find a way of avoiding somehow the widening of the cultural and psycho-social gap inherent in the growing differentiation of the world. Even with gradual differentiation throughout human history, it was not until the industrial revolution that sharp differences between societies began to appear. Today, some nations still live not unlike the pre-Christian times, while many no better than in the medieval age. Yet soon a few will live in ways so new that it is now difficult to imagine their social and individual ramifications. If the developed world takes a leap—as seems inescapably the case—into a reality that is even more different from ours today than ours is from that of an Indian village, the gap, and its concomitant strains, will not narrow.

On the contrary, the instantaneous electronic intermeshing of mankind will make for an intense confrontation, straining social and international peace. In the past, differences were livable because of time and distance that separated them. Today, these differences are actually widening, while technetronics are eliminating the two insulants of time and distance. The resulting trauma could create almost entirely different perspectives on life, with insecurity, envy and hostility becoming the dominant emotions for increasingly large numbers of people. A three-way split into rural-backward, urban-industrial and technetronic ways of life can only further divide man, intensify the existing difficulties to global understanding, and give added vitality to latent or existing conflicts.

The pace of American development both widens the split within mankind and contains the seeds for a constructive response. However, neither military power nor material wealth, both of which America possesses in abundance, can be used directly in responding to the onrushing division in man's thinking, norms and character. Power, at best, can assure only a relatively stable external environment—the tempering or containing of the potential global civil war; wealth can grease points of socio-economic friction, thereby facilitating development. But as man—especially in the most advanced societies—moves increasingly into the phase of controlling and even creating his environment, increasing attention will have to be given to giving man meaningful content—to improving the quality of life for man *as man*.

"Man has never really tried to use science in the realm of his value systems. Ethical thinking is hard to change, but history demonstrates that it does change. . . . Man does, in limited ways, direct his very important and much more rapid psychosocial education. The evolution of such things as automobiles, airplanes, weapons, legal institutions, corporations, universities, and democratic governments are examples of progressive evolution in the course of time. We have, however, never really tried deliberately to create a better society for man *qua* man. . . ."*

The urgent need to do just that may compel America to redefine its global posture: during the remainder of this century, given the perspective on the future outlined here, America is likely to become less concerned with fighting Communism or creating "a world safe for diversity" as with helping to develop a common response with the rest of mankind to the implications of a truly new era. This will mean making the massive diffusion of scientific-technological knowledge a principal focus of American involvement in world affairs.

To some extent, the US performs that role already—simply by being what it is. The impact of its reality and its global involvement prompt emulation. The emergence of vast international corporations, most originating in the United States, makes for easier transfer of skills, management techniques, marketing procedures, and scientific-technological innovations. The appearance of these corporations in the European market has done much to stimulate Europeans to consider more urgently the need to integrate their resources and to accelerate the pace of their own research and development.

Similarly, returning graduates from American universities have prompted an organizational and intellectual revolution in the academic life of their countries. Changes in the academic life of Germany, the United Kingdom, Japan, and more recently France, and even to a greater extent in the less developed countries, can be traced to the influence of US educational institutions. Indeed, the leading technological institute in Turkey conducts its lectures in *American* and is deliberately imitating, not only in approach but in student-professor relationships, American patterns. Given developments in modern communications, it is only a matter of time before students at Columbia University and, say, the University of Teheran will be watching, *simultaneously*, the same lecturer.

The appearance of a universal intellectual elite, one that shares certain common values and aspirations, will somewhat compensate for the widening differentiation among men and societies. But it will not resolve the problem posed by that differentiation. In many backward nations tension between what is and what can be will be intensified. Moreover, as Kenneth Boulding observed: "The network of electronic communication is inevitably producing a world superculture, and the relations between this superculture and the more traditional national and regional cultures of the past remains the great question mark of the next fifty years."* That "superculture," strongly influenced by American life, with its own universal electronic-computer language, will find it difficult to relate itself to "the more traditional and regional cultures," especially if the basic gap continues to widen.

To cope with that gap, a gradual change in diplomatic style and emphasis may have to follow the redefined emphasis of America's involvement in world affairs. Professional diplomacy will have to yield to intellectual leadership. With government negotiating directly—or quickly dispatching the negotiators—there will be less need for ambassadors who are resident diplomats and more for ambassadors who are capable of serving as creative interpreters of the new age, willing to engage in a meaningful dialogue with the host intellectual community and concerned with promoting the widest possible dissemination of available knowledge. Theirs will be the task to stimulate and to develop scientific-technological programs of cooperation.

International cooperation will be necessary in almost every facet of life: to reform and to develop more modern educational systems, to promote new sources of food supply, to accelerate economic development, to stimulate technological growth, to control climate, to disseminate new medical knowledge. However, because the new elites have a vested interest in their new nation-states and because of the growing xenophobia among the masses in the third world, the nation-state will remain for a long time the primary focus of loyalty, especially for newly liberated and economically backward peoples. Predicting loudly its death, and acting often as if it were dead, could prompt, as it did partially in Europe, an adverse reaction from those whom one would wish to influence. Hence regionalism will have to be promoted with due deference to the symbolic meaning of national sovereignty—and preferably also by encouraging those concerned themselves to advocate regional approaches.

Even more important will be the stimulation, for the first time in history on a global scale, of the much needed dialogue on what it is about man's life that we wish to safeguard or to promote and on the relevance of existing moral systems to an age that cannot be fitted into the narrow confines of fading doctrines. The search for new directions—going beyond the tangibles, such as economic development—could be an appropriate subject for a special world congress, devoted to the technetronic and philosophical problems of the coming age. To these issues no one society, however advanced, is in a position to provide an answer.

---

* H. Hoagland, "Biology, Brains, and Insight," *The Columbia University Forum*, Summer 1967, p. 29.

* K. Boulding, "Expecting the Unexpected," *Prospective Changes in Society by 1980*, Denver, Col., July, 1960, p. 209.

PRIORITIES FOR THE SEVENTIES

*Our needs are as simple as they are
compelling. But will we attend to them?*

ROBERT L. HEILBRONER

ROBERT L. HEILBRONER teaches at the New
School in New York. Among his books
are *The Worldly Philosophers, The Future
as History,* and *The Great Ascent.* The
above article is adapted from a lecture
presented in cooperation with the Fund
for New Priorities in America.

To talk about national priorities
is to talk about precedence, the
order in which things are ranked.
It is not difficult to establish what that
order is in America today. Military
needs rank above civilian needs. Private interests rank above public interests. The claims of the affluent take
precedence over those of the poor.
This is all so familiar that it no longer
even has the power to rouse us to indignation. There is no shock value left
in saying that we are a militaristic
nation, or a people uninterested in the
elimination of poverty, or a citizenry
whose only response to the decay of
the cities is a decision to move to the
suburbs. To get a rise out of people,
these days, one has to say something
really outrageous, such as that the
main cultural effect of advertising on
television is to teach our children that
grown-ups tell lies for money.

But I do not want to expatiate on
the present order of things. For I
presume that to talk of priorities is to
determine what they *should* be. What
should come first? What ought to be on
top of the agenda?

To ask such questions is to invite
pious answers. I shall try to avoid the
pieties by grouping my priorities into
three categories. The first has to do
with our immediate survival—not as a
nation-state, but as a *decent* nation-
state. The second has to do with our
ultimate salvation. The third with our
moving from survival to salvation.

The initial set of priorities is simple

to specify. It consists of three courses
of action necessary to restore American society to life. The first of these is
the demilitarization of the national
budget. That budget now calls for the
expenditure of $80-billion a year for
military purposes. Its rationale is that
it will permit us to fight simultaneously two "major" (though, of course,
non-nuclear) wars and one "minor" or
"brushfire" war. This requires the
maintenance of eighteen army divisions, as against eleven in 1961; of
11,000 deliverable nuclear warheads,
compared with 1,100 in 1961; of a naval
force far larger than that of any other
nation in the world.

Politically, economically—even militarily—this budget is a disaster for
America. It has sucked into the service
of fear and death the energies and resources desperately needed for hope
and life. Until and unless that budget
is significantly cut, there will be little
chance of restoring vitality to American society.

By how much can it be cut? The
Nixon administration proposes to reduce it by $4- to $6-billion by June 1971,
and by an equivalent amount each year
for another four years. *Fortune* magazine claims it can be cut faster—
$17.6-billion less by June 1972. Seymour
Melman, professor of industrial engineering at Columbia University, has
stated that it can be slashed by over
$50-billion—and his reduced budget
would still leave 2,300,000 men under
arms, an obliterative power aimed at
156 Soviet cities, and an air and naval
armada of staggering dimensions.

This conflicting testimony suggests
that the question of how much the
budget can be cut depends not on expertise alone, but on outlook—on how
much one wants to reassign into other
channels the resources absorbed by the
military. Here let us make a first approximation as to how much the military budget can be cut by determining
how large are the life-giving aims to
which we must now give priority. I see

two of these as being essential for the
attainment of decency in American society. One is the long overdue relief of
poverty. In 1967, 10 per cent of all
white families, 35 per cent of all black
families, and 58 per cent of all black
families over age sixty-five, lived in
poverty—a condition that we define by
the expenditure for food of $4.90 per
person per week. *Per week.* To raise
these families to levels of minimum
adequacy will require annual transfer
payments of approximately $10- to $15-
billion. This is half the annual cost of
the Vietnam war. I would make this
conversion of death into life a first
guide to the demilitarization of the
budget.

A second guide is provided by the remaining essential priority for American decency. This is the need to rebuild
the cities before they collapse on us.
This means not only replacing the
hideous tenements and junkyards and
prison-like schools of the slums, but
providing the services needed to make
urban living tolerable—regular garbage
collection, dependable police protection, and adequate recreational facilities.

It has been estimated that New York
City alone would need $4.3-billion per
year for ten years to replace its slums.
To provide proper levels of health and
educational services would add another
billion. And then there are Chicago and
Newark and Washington and Los Angeles. It would take at least $20- to
$25-billion a year for at least a decade
to begin to make the American city viable.

These objectives are minimal requirements for America. Fortunately,
they are easy to accomplish—at least
in a technical sense. There will be no
problem in cutting the military budget
by the necessary $30- to $40-billion once
that task is entrusted to men who are
not prisoners of the military-industrial
superiority complex. There are no great
problems in the alleviation of poverty
that the direct disbursement of money
to the poor will not tolerably remedy.

And whereas I do not doubt that it will be hard to build new cities handsomely and well, I do not think it will be difficult to tear down the rotten hulks that now constitute the slums, and to replace them with something that is unmistakably better.

Thus the essential priorities have the virtue of being as simple as they are compelling. This does not mean, however, that we will therefore attend to them. On the contrary, the chances are good that we will not do what must be done, or at best will act halfheartedly, in token fashion. The power of the vested interests of business and politics and labor in the preservation of military spending is enormous. The unwillingness of the American upper and middle classes to assist the less fortunate is a clear matter of record. The resistance to the repair of the cities is too well documented to require exposition here. Hence, we may never rise to the simple challenge of making America viable. In that case it is easy to make a prognosis for this country. It will be even more than it is today a dangerous, dirty, and depressing place in which to live. There will be an America, but it will not be a civilized America.

There is, however, at least a fighting chance that we *will* cut the military budget, that we *will* declare poverty to be an anachronistic social disease, that we *will* begin to halt the process of urban deterioration. Let me therefore speak of another set of priorities—one that many people would place even higher on the list than my initial three. They are, first, the elimination of racism in the United States, and second, the enlistment of the enthusiasm—or at least the tolerance—of the younger generation.

I have said that these priorities have to do with our salvation rather than with our survival. This is because their achievement would lift the spirit of America as if a great shadow had been removed from its soul. But like all salvations, this one is not near at hand. For unlike the first set of priorities, which is well within our power to accomplish, this second set lies beyond our present capabilities. Even if we manage to cut the military budget, to end poverty, to rebuild the cities, the bitter fact remains that we do not know how to change the deep conviction within the hearts of millions of Americans that blackness spells inferiority. Neither do we know how to win the enthusiasm of young people—and I mean the best and soberest of them,

not the drop-outs and the do-nothings —for a society that is technocratic, bureaucratic, and depersonalized.

Thus the second set of priorities is considerably different from the first. It constitutes a distant goal, not an immediate target. Any projection of what America should try to become that does not include the goals of racial equality and youthful enlistment is seriously deficient, but any projection that does not expect that we will be a racist and alienated society for a long while is simply unrealistic.

What then are we to do in the meantime? How are we to set for ourselves a course that is within the bounds of realism and that will yet move us toward the long-term goals we seek? This brings me to my third set of priorities—a set of tasks neither so simple as the first, nor so difficult as the second. I shall offer four such tasks—not in any particular order of urgency—as exemplifying the *kinds* of priorities we need in order to move from mere survival toward ultimate salvation.

I begin with a proposal that will seem small by comparison with the large-scale goals discussed so far. Yet, it is important for a society that seeks to lessen racial tensions and to win the approbation of the young. It consists of a full-scale effort to improve the treatment of criminality in the United States.

No one knows exactly how large is the criminal population of the United States, but certainly it is very large. Two million persons a year pass through the major prisons and "reformatories," some 300,000 residing in them at any given time. Another 800,000 are on probation or parole; a still larger number lurk on the fringes of serious misbehavior, but have so far escaped the law. Our response to this core of seriously disturbed and dangerous persons is to send a certain number, who are unfortunate enough to get caught, to prison. These prisons include among them the foulest places in America—charnel houses comparable to Nazi concentration camps. At Tucker State Farm in Arkansas, inmates have been reported to be forty to sixty pounds underweight, and have been subjected to acts of unspeakable cruelty, and even to murder. The sadistic practices in military stockades have become notorious. But even the more humane institutions largely fail in their purposes. In New York State the rate of recidivism for crimes of comparable importance is 50 per cent.

A recent FBI study of 18,000 federal offenders released in 1963 showed that 63 per cent had been arrested again five years later.

Indeed, as every criminologist will testify, prisons mainly serve not to deter, but to confirm and train the inmate for a career in criminality. These institutions exist not for the humanization but for the brutalization of their charges.

What is to be done? One inkling of the course to be followed is provided by reflecting on the statistics of prison care. In federal adult institutions we average one custodial person per seven inmates; one educational person per 121 inmates; one treatment person per 179 inmates. In local institutions and jails the ratio of educational or treatment personnel to inmates broadens to one to 550. In some state correctional institutions the ratio is as high as one to 2,400.

Another clue is suggested by the fact that work-release camps, widely used abroad to bridge the gap between prison and normal life, are available here in only four states. Still another is the clear need for the early detection of asocial behavior among school children, and for the application of therapy before, not after, criminality has become a way of life.

It must be obvious that an all-out effort to lessen criminality is not nearly so simple to achieve as slicing the military budget or tearing down the slums. But neither is it so difficult to achieve as racial tolerance. I suggest it is an objective well worth being placed high on the list of those "middle" priorities for which we are now seeking examples.

Recently, the Administration has declared the reform of prisons to be a major objective. Let us now see if this rhetoric will be translated into action.

My second suggestion is not unrelated to the first. Only it concerns not criminals, but those who represent the other end of the spectrum—the symbols of law and order, the police forces of America. I propose that an important item on the agenda must be an effort to contain and control a police arm that is already a principal reason for black anger and youthful disgust.

First, a few words to spell out the problem. In New York City, the Patrolmen's Benevolent Association, itself a potent force for reaction (as witness its key role in the defeat of the Civilian Review Board), is now outflanked on the right by "law enforcement" groups of super-patriot vigilantes who on several occasions have taken the law into their own hands. The actions of the Chicago police force as seen on national television during the Democratic convention do not require further comment here. In Detroit the United Press reports "open hostility" between the city's mainly white police force and the city's 40 per cent black population. At Berkeley, Harvard, and Columbia we have witnessed the dreadful spectacle of policemen smashing indiscriminately at students and using tear gas and Mace.

There is no simple cure for this ugly situation. Police forces are recruited largely from the lower middle class; they bring with them deeply ingrained attitudes of racial contempt and envious hostility to privileged youth. But there are at least a few measures that can be taken to prevent what is already a dangerous rift from widening further. To begin with, one way to minimize police abuse of Negroes is to minimize occasions for contact with them. The obvious conclusion is that black ghettos must be given the funds and the authorization to form their own police forces. Another necessary step is to lessen the contact of police forces with college youth; the legalization of marijuana would help in this regard. So would the training of special, highly paid, *unarmed*, elite police forces who would be used to direct all police actions having to do with civil demonstrations.

I do not doubt that there are many other ways to attack the problem. What is essential is to take measures now that will prevent the police from driving a permanent wedge between white and black, between student and government. Mace, tear gas, and billy clubs are weapons of repression, not of order. Few steps would contribute more to the return of American self-respect than those that would assist the growth of law and order among the forces of law and order.

Here, too, the report of the Eisenhower Commission signals an overdue awakening of public consciousness. But here again we shall have to see whether this awareness will be translated into action.

My third suggestion seemingly departs markedly from the first two. It concerns a wider problem than criminality or police misbehavior, but not a less pressing problem. It is how to rescue the environment from the devastating impact of an unregulated technology.

I need mention only a few well-known results of this ferocious process of destruction. Lake Erie is dead. The beaches at Santa Barbara are deserted. The air in New York is dangerous to breathe. We are drowning in a sea of swill; in a normal year the United States "produces" 142 million tons of smoke and fumes, seven million junked cars, twenty million tons of waste paper, forty-eight billion used cans, and fifty trillion gallons of industrial sewage. And presiding over this rampant process of environmental overloading is the most fearsome reality of all—a population that is still increasing like an uncontrollable cancer on the surface of the globe. I know of no more sobering statistic in this regard than that between now and 1980 the number of women in the most fertile age brackets, eighteen to thirty-two, will double.

Aghast at this terrific imbalance between the power of technology and the capacity of society to control and order the effects of technology, some people are calling for a moratorium on technology, for a kind of national breathing space while we decide how to deal with such problems as the sonic boom and the new supertankers. But this approach ignores the fact that it is not new technology alone that breeds trouble, but the cumulative effect of our existing technology; perhaps no single cause is more responsible for air pollution than the familiar combustion engine.

Hence, I call for a different priority in dealing with this crucial question—not for less technology, but for more technology *of a different kind*. For clearly what we need are technological answers to technological problems. We need a reliable method of birth control suitable for application among illiterate and superstitious peoples. We need an exhaustless automobile, a noiseless and versatile airplane. We need new methods of reducing and coping with wastes—radioactive, sewage, gaseous, and liquid. We need new modes of transporting goods and people, within cities and between them.

The priority then is technological research—research aimed at devising the techniques needed to live in a place that we have just begun to recognize as (in Kenneth Boulding's phrase) our Spaceship Earth. There is a further consideration here, as well. Many people wonder where we can direct the energies of the engineers, draftsmen, scientists, and skilled workmen who are now employed in building weapons systems, once we cut our military budget. I suggest that the design of a technology for our planetary spaceship will provide challenge enough to occupy their attention for a long time. We have not hesitated to support private enterprise for years while it devoted its organizational talents to producing instruments of war. We must now begin to apply equally lavish support while private enterprise perfects the instruments of peace. There would be an important side effect to such a civilian-industrial complex. It is that young people who are bored or repelled by the prospect of joining an industrial establishment, one of whose most spectacular accomplishments has been the rape of the environment, will, I believe, feel differently if they are offered an opportunity to work in research and development that has as its aim the enewal and reconstitution of this planet as a human habitat.

The items I have suggested as middle priorities could be extended into a long list. But what I am suggesting, after all, are only the *kinds* of tasks that cry out for attention, not each and every one of them.

But to speak of priorities without mentioning education seems wrong, especially for someone in education. The question is, what is there to say? What is there left to declare about the process of schooling that has not been said again and again? Perhaps I can suggest just one thing, aimed specifically at the upper echelons of the educational apparatus. It is a proposal that the universities add a new orientation to their traditional goals and programs. I urge that they deliberately set out to become the laboratories of applied research into the future. I urge that they direct a major portion of their efforts toward research into, training for, and advocacy of programs for social change.

It may be said that there is no precedent for such an orientation of education toward action, and that the pursuit of such a course will endanger the traditional purity and aloofness of the academic community. The reply would be more convincing did not the precedent already exist and were not the purity already sullied. Scientists of all kinds, in the social as well as in the physical disciplines, have not hesitated to work on programs for social change—financed by the Department of Defense, the Office of Naval Research, NASA, etc.—programs designed to alter the world by high explosives in some cases, by cooptation or skillful propaganda in others.

Some members of the academic community, aware of the destruction they have helped to commit, have now begun to withdraw from contact with the war machine. That is to their credit. But what is needed now is for them to redirect their energies to the peace machine. We live in a time during which social experimentation—in the factory, in the office, in the city; in economic policy, in political institutions, in life-styles—is essential if a technologically dominated future is not simply to mold us willy-nilly to its requirements. The forces of change in our time render obsolete many of the institutions of managerial capitalism and centrally planned socialism alike; new institutions, new modes of social control and social cohesion now have to be invented and tried.

In part the university must continue its traditional role, studying this period of historic transformation with all the detachment and objectivity it can muster. But that is not enough. As Marx wrote: "The philosophers have only *interpreted* the world; the thing, however, is to change it." As the last item on my agenda, I would like to make the university the locus of action for the initiation of such change.

After the Population Explosion

"Imagine the thrill of flying from Los Angeles to New York and having the landscape look like Los Angeles all the way."

HARRISON BROWN

HARRISON BROWN, an *SR* editor-at-large, is a professor of geochemistry, science, and government at the California Institute of Technology.

At one time or another almost all of us have asked: How many human beings can the Earth support? When this question is put to me, I find it necessary to respond with another question: In what kind of world are you willing to live? In the eyes of those who care about their environment, we have perhaps already passed the limits of growth. In the eyes of those who don't care how they live or what dangers they create for posterity, the limits of growth lie far ahead.

The populations of all biological species are limited by environmental factors, and man's is no exception. Food supplies and the presence of predators are of prime importance. When two rabbits of opposite sex are placed in a fenced-in field of grass, they will go forth and multiply, but the population will eventually be limited by the grass supply. If predators are placed in the field, the rabbit population will

either stabilize at a new level or possibly become extinct. Given no predators and no restrictions on food, but circumscribed space, the number of rabbits will still be limited, either by the psychological and biological effects of overcrowding or by being buried in their own refuse.

When man, endowed with the power of conceptual thought, appeared upon the Earth scene, something new was introduced into the evolutionary process. Biological evolution, which had dominated all living species for billions of years, gave way to cultural evolution. As man gradually learned how to control various elements of his environment, he succeeded in modifying a number of the factors that limited his population. Clothing, fire, and crude shelters extended the range of habitable climate. Tools of increasing sophistication helped man gather edible vegetation, hunt animals more effectively, and protect himself from predators.

But no matter how effective the tools, there is a limit to the number of food gatherers who can inhabit a given area of land. One cannot kill more animals than are born or pick more fruit than trees bear. The maximum population of a worldwide food-gathering society was about ten million persons. Once that level was reached, numerous cultural patterns emerged that caused worldwide birth rates and death rates to become equal. In some societies, the natural death rate was elevated by malnutrition and disease; in others, the death rate was increased artificially by such practices as infanticide or the waging of war. In some cases, certain sex taboos and rituals appear to have lowered the birth rate. But, however birth and death rates came into balance, we can be confident that for a long time prior to the agricultural revolution the human population remained virtually constant.

With the introduction of agriculture about 10,000 years ago, the levels of population that had been imposed by limited supplies of food were raised significantly. Even in the earliest agricultural societies, several hundred times as much food could be produced from a given area of fertile land than could be collected by food gatherers. As the technology of agriculture spread, population grew rapidly. This new technology dramatically affected the entire fabric of human culture. Man gave up the nomad life and settled in villages, some of which became cities.

Sufficient food could be grown to make it possible for about 10 per cent of the population to engage in activities other than farming.

The development of iron technology and improved transportation accelerated the spread of this peasant-village culture. Indeed, had new technological developments ceased to appear after 1700, it is nevertheless likely that the peasant-village culture would have spread to all inhabitable parts of the Earth, eventually to reach a level of roughly five billion persons, some 500 million of whom would live in cities. But long before the population had reached anything close to that level, the emergence of new technologies leading up to the Industrial Revolution markedly changed the course of history. The steam engine for the first time gave man a means of concentrating enormous quantities of inanimate mechanical energy, and the newly found power was quickly applied.

During the nineteenth century in western Europe, improved transportation, increased food supplies, and a generally improved environment decreased the morbidity of a number of infectious diseases and virtually eliminated the large fluctuations in mortality rates that had been so characteristic of the seventeenth and eighteenth centuries. As mortality rates declined and the birth rate remained unchanged, populations in these areas increased rapidly. But as industrialization spread, a multiplicity of factors combined to lessen the desirability of large families. After about 1870, the size of families decreased, at first slowly and then more rapidly; eventually, the rate of population growth declined.

During the nineteenth and early twentieth centuries, some of the new technologies were gradually transplanted to the non-industrialized parts of the world, but in a very one-sided manner. Death rates were reduced appreciably, and, with birth rates unchanged, populations in these poorer countries increased rapidly and are still growing.

In spite of the fact that the annual rate of population growth in the industrialized countries has dropped to less than 1 per cent, the worldwide rate is now close to 2 per cent, the highest it has ever been. This rate represents a doubling of population about every thirty-five years. The human population is now 3.5 billion and at the pres-

cnt rate of increase is destined to reach 6.5 billion by the turn of the century and ten billion fifty years from now. Beyond that point, how much further can population grow?

An analysis of modern technology's potential makes it clear that from a long-range, theoretical point of view, food supplies need no longer be the primary factor limiting population growth. Today nearly 10 per cent of the land area of the Earth, or about 3.5 billion acres, is under cultivation. It is estimated that with sufficient effort about fifteen billion acres of land could be placed under cultivation— some four times the present area. Such a move would require prodigious effort and investment and would necessitate the use of substantial quantities of desalinated water reclaimed from the sea. Given abundant energy resources, however, it now appears that in principle this can be done economically.

Large as the potential is for increasing the area of agricultural land, the increases in yield that can be obtained through fertilizers, application of supplementary water, and the use of new high-yielding varieties of cereals are even more impressive. Whereas in the past the growth of plants was circumscribed by the availability of nutrients and water, this need no longer be true. Using our new agricultural technology, solar energy can be converted into food with a high degree of efficiency, and even on the world's presently cultivated lands several times as much food can be produced each year than is now being grown.

To accomplish these objectives, however, an enormous amount of industrialization will be required. Fertilizers must be produced; thus, phosphate rock must be mined and processed, and nitrogen fixation plants must be built. Pesticides and herbicides are needed; thus, chemical plants must be built. All this requires steel and concrete, highways, railroads, and trucks. To be sure, the people of India, for example, might not need to attain Japan's level of industrialization in order to obtain Japanese levels of crop yield (which are about the highest in the world), but they will nevertheless need a level of industrialization that turns out to be surprisingly high.

Colin Clark, the director of the Agricultural Economics Research Institute of Oxford and a noted enthusiast for large populations, estimates that, given this new agricultural land and a level of industrialization sufficiently high to apply Japanese standards of farming, close to thirty billion persons could be supported on a Western European diet. Were people to content themselves with a Japanese diet, which contains little animal protein, he estimates that 100 billion persons could be supported.

To those who feel that life under such circumstances might be rather crowded, I should like to point out that even at the higher population level, the mean density of human beings over the land areas of the Earth would be no more than that which exists today in the belt along the Eastern Seaboard between Boston and Washington, D.C., where the average density is now 2,000 persons per square mile and where many people live quite comfortably. After all, Hong Kong has a population density of about 13,000 persons per square mile (nearly six times greater), and I understand that there are numerous happy people there.

Of course, such a society would need to expend a great deal of energy in order to manufacture, transport, and distribute the fertilizers, pesticides, herbicides, water, foodstuffs, and countless associated raw materials and products that would be necessary.

In the United States we currently consume energy equivalent to the burning of twelve-and-a-half short tons of coal per person per year. This quantity is bound to increase in the future as we find it necessary to process lower-grade ores, as we expend greater effort on controlling pollution (which would otherwise increase enormously), and as we recover additional quantities of potable water from the sea. Dr. Alvin Weinberg, director of the Oak Ridge National Laboratory, and his associates estimate that such activities will cost several additional tons of coal per person per year, and they suggest that for safety we budget twenty-five tons of coal per person per year in order to maintain our present material standard of living. Since we are a magnanimous people, we would not tolerate a double standard of living (a rich one for us and a poor one for others); so I will assume that this per capita level of energy expenditure will be characteristic of the world as a whole.

It has been estimated that the world's total usable coal reserve is on the order of 7,600 billion tons. This amount would last a population of thirty billion persons only ten years

and a population of 100 billion only three years. Clearly, long before such population levels are reached, man must look elsewhere for his energy supplies.

Fortunately, technology once again gets us out of our difficulty, for nuclear fuels are available to us in virtually limitless quantities in the form of uranium and thorium for fission, and possibly in the form of deuterium for fusion. The Conway granite in New Hampshire could alone provide fuel for a population of twenty billion persons for 200 years. When we run out of high-grade granites, we can move on to process low-grade granites. Waste rock can be dumped into the holes from which it came and can be used to create new land areas on bays and on the continental shelf. Waste fission products can be stored in old salt mines.

Actually, a major shift to nuclear fuel might well be necessary long before our supplies of fossil fuels are exhausted. The carbon dioxide concentration in our atmosphere is rapidly increasing as a result of our burning of coal, petroleum, and natural gas, and it is destined to increase still more rapidly in the future. More than likely, any such increase will have a deleterious effect upon our climate, and if this turns out to be the case, use of those fuels will probably be restricted.

Thus, we see that in theory there should be little difficulty in feeding a world population of thirty billion or even 100 billion persons and in providing it with the necessities of life. But can we go even further?

With respect to food, once again technology can come to our rescue, for we have vast areas of the seas to fertilize and farm. Even more important, we will be able to produce synthetic foods in quantity. The constituents of our common oils and fats can already be manufactured on a substantial scale for human consumption and animal feeds. In the not too distant future, we should be able to synthetically produce complete, wholesome foods, thus bypassing the rather cumbersome process of photosynthesis.

Far more difficult than the task of feeding people will be that of cooling the Earth, of dissipating the heat generated by nuclear power plants. It has been suggested that if we were to limit our total energy generation to no more than 5 per cent of the incident solar radiation, little harm would be done.

The mean surface temperature of the Earth would rise by about 6 degrees F. A temperature rise much greater than this could be extremely dangerous and should not be permitted until we have learned more about the behavior of our ocean/atmosphere system.

Of course, there will be local heating problems in the vicinity of the power stations. Dr. Weinberg suggests a system of "nuclear parks," each producing about forty million kilowatts of electricity and located on the coast or offshore. A population of 333 billion persons would require 65,000 such parks. The continental United States, with a projected population of close to twenty-five billion persons, would require nearly 5,000 parks spaced at twenty-mile intervals along its coastline.

Again, I want to allay the fears of those who worry about crowding. A population of 333 billion spread uniformly over the land areas of the Earth would give us a population density of only 6,000 persons per square mile, which, after all, is only somewhat greater than the population density in the city of Los Angeles. Just imagine the thrill of flying from Los Angeles to New York and having the landscape look like Los Angeles all the way. Imagine the excitement of driving from Los Angeles to New York on a Santa Monica Freeway 2,800 miles long.

A few years ago Dr. J. H. Fremlin of the University of Birmingham analyzed the problem of population density and concluded that several stages of development might be possible beyond the several-hundred-billion-person level of population. He conceives of hermetically sealing the outer surface of the planet and of using pumps to transfer heat to the solid outer skin from which it would be radiated directly into space. Combining this with a roof over the oceans to prevent excessive evaporation of water and to provide additional living space, he feels it would be possible to accommodate about 100 persons per square yard, thus giving a total population of about sixty million billion persons. But, frankly, I consider this proposal visionary. Being basically conservative, I doubt that the human population will ever get much above the 333-billion-person level.

Now some readers might be thinking that I am writing nonsense, and they are right. My facts are correct; the conclusions I have drawn from those facts are correct. Yet, I have truthfully been writing nonsense. Specifically, I have given only *some* of the facts. Those facts that I have omitted alter the conclusions considerably.

I have presented only what is deemed possible by scientists from an energetic or thermodynamic point of view. An analogy would be for me to announce that I have calculated that in principle all men should be able to leap ten feet into the air. Obviously, such an announcement would not be followed by a sudden, frenzied, worldwide demonstration of people showing their leaping capabilities. Some people have sore feet; others have inadequate muscles; most haven't the slightest desire to leap into the air. The calculation might be correct, but the enthusiasm for jumping and the ability to jump might be very low. The problem is the behavior of people rather than that of inanimate matter.

We are confronted by the brutal fact that humanity today doesn't really know how to cope with the problems presented by three-and-a-half billion persons, let alone 333 billion. More than two-thirds of the present human population is poor in the material sense and is malnourished. The affluent one-third is, with breathtaking rapidity, becoming even more affluent. Two separate and distinct societies have emerged in the world, and they are becoming increasingly distinct and separated. Numerically the largest is the culture of the poor, composed of some 2,500 million persons. Numerically the smallest is the culture of the rich, composed of some 1,000 million persons. On the surface, the rich countries would appear to have it made; in historical perspective, their average per capita incomes are enormous. Their technological competence is unprecedented. Yet, they have problems that might well prove insoluble.

The most serious problem confronting the rich countries today is nationalism. We fight among each other and arm ourselves in order to do so more effectively. The Cold War has become a way of life, as is reflected in military budgets. Today the governments of the United States and the Soviet Union spend more on their respective military establishments than they do on either education or health—indeed a scandalous situation but, even worse, an explosive one.

All of the rich countries are suffering from problems of growth. Although the rates of population proliferation in these areas are not large, per capita consumption is increasing rapidly. Today an average "population unit" in the United States is quite different from one in the primitive world. Originally, a unit of population was simply a human being whose needs could be met by "eating" 2,500 calories and 60 grams of protein a day. Add to this some simple shelter, some clothing, and a small fire, and his needs were taken care of. A population unit today consists of a human being wrapped in tons of steel, copper, aluminum, lead, tin, zinc, and plastics. This new creature requires far more than food to keep it alive and functioning. Each day it gobbles up sixty pounds of coal or its equivalent, three pounds of raw steel, plus many pounds of other materials. Far from getting all of this food from his own depleted resources, he ranges abroad, much as the hunters of old, and obtains raw supplies in other parts of the world, more often than not in the poorer countries.

Industrial societies the world over are changing with unprecedented speed as the result of accelerated technological change, and they are becoming increasingly complex. All of them are encountering severe problems with their cities, which were designed within the framework of one technology and are falling apart at the seams within the framework of another.

The technological and social complexities of industrial society — composed as it is of vast interlocking networks of mines, factories, transportation systems, power grids, and communication networks, all operated by people—make it extremely vulnerable to disruption. Indeed, during the past year we have seen that the United States is far more vulnerable to labor strikes than North Vietnam is to air strikes. This vulnerability may eventually prove to be our undoing.

A concomitant of our affluence has been pollution. That which goes into a system must eventually come out; as our society has consumed more, it has excreted more. Given adequate supplies of energy and the necessary technology, such problems can be handled from a technical point of view. But it is by no means clear that we are about to solve these problems from a social or political point of view.

Although we know that theoretically we can derive our sustenance from the leanest of earth substances, such as seawater and rock, the fact remains that with respect to the raw materials needed for a highly industrialized society the research essential to the development of the necessary technology has hardly begun. Besides, it is less expensive for the rich countries to extract their sustenance from the poor ones.

As to the poor countries with their rapidly increasing populations, I fail to see how, in the long run, they can lift themselves up by their own bootstraps. In the absence of outside help commensurate with their needs, I suspect they will fail, and the world will become permanently divided into the rich and the poor—at least until such time as the rich, in their stupidity, blow themselves up.

One of the most difficult problems in the poor countries is that of extremely rapid population growth. If an economy grows only as fast as its population, the average well-being of the people does not improve—and indeed this situation prevails in many parts of the world. Equally important, rapid growth produces tremendous dislocations—physical, social, and economic. It is important to understand that the major population problem confronting the poor countries today is not so much the actual number of people as it is rapid growth rates. Clearly, if development is to take place, birth rates must be reduced.

Unfortunately, it is not clear just how birth rates can be brought down in these areas. Even with perfect contraceptives, there must be motivation upon the part of individuals, and in many areas this appears to be lacking. Some people say that economic development is necessary to produce the motivation, and they might be right. In any event, the solution will not be a simple one.

Although I am pessimistic about the future, I do not consider the situation to be by any means hopeless. I am convinced that our problems both here and abroad are soluble. But if they are ever solved, it will be because all of us reorient our attitudes away from those of our parents and more toward those of our children. I am convinced that young people today more often than not have a clearer picture of the world and its problems than do their elders. They are questioning our vast military expenditures and ask whether the Cold War is really necessary. They question the hot war in which we have become so deeply involved. They are questioning our concepts of nationalism, materialism, and laissez faire. It is just such questioning on the part of the young that gives me hope.

If this questioning persists, I foresee the emergence of a new human attitude in which people the world over work together to transform anarchy into law, to decrease dramatically military expenditures, to lower rates of population growth to zero, and to build an equitable world economy, so that all people can lead free and abundant lives in harmony with nature and with each other.

The Alternative to Schooling

IVAN ILLICH

IVAN ILLICH is director of the Center for Intercultural Documentation (CIDOC) in Cuernavaca, Mexico, an educational organization devoted to discussion of ways for improving the cultural and social environment of the Latin American people. His most recent book, *Deschooling Society*, is being published this month by Harper & Row. Mr. Illich's first writing on education was published in *SR* (April 20, 1968). He considers this article the final formulation of his ideas in the field.

For generations we have tried to make the world a better place by providing more and more schooling, but so far the endeavor has failed. What we have learned instead is that forcing all children to climb an open-ended education ladder cannot enhance equality but must favor the individual who starts out earlier, healthier, or better prepared; that enforced instruction deadens for most people the will for independent learning; and that knowledge treated as a commodity, delivered in packages, and accepted as private property once it is acquired, must always be scarce.

In response, critics of the educational system are now proposing strong and unorthodox remedies that range from the voucher plan, which would enable each person to buy the education of his choice on an open market, to shifting the responsibility for education from the school to the media and to apprenticeship on the job. Some individuals foresee that the school will have to be disestablished just as the church was disestablished all over the world during the last two centuries. Other reformers propose to replace the universal school with various new systems that would, they claim, better prepare everybody for life in modern society. These proposals for new educational institutions fall into three broad categories: the reformation of the classroom within the school system; the dispersal of free schools throughout society; and the transformation of all society into one huge classroom. But these three approaches —the reformed classroom, the free school, and the worldwide classroom— represent three stages in a proposed escalation of education in which each step threatens more subtle and more pervasive social control than the one it replaces.

I believe that the disestablishment of the school has become inevitable and that this end of an illusion should fill us with hope. But I also believe that the end of the "age of schooling" could usher in the epoch of the global schoolhouse that would be distinguishable only in name from a global madhouse or global prison in which education, correction, and adjustment become synonymous. I therefore believe that the breakdown of the school forces us to look beyond its imminent demise and to face fundamental alternatives in education. Either we can work for fearsome and potent new educational devices that teach about a world which progressively becomes more opaque and forbidding for man, or we can set the conditions for a new era in which technology would be used to make society more simple and transparent, so that all men can once again know the facts and use the tools that shape their lives. In short, we can disestablish schools or we can deschool culture.

In order to see clearly the alternatives we face, we must first distinguish education from schooling, which means separating the humanistic intent of the teacher from the impact of the invari-

—*Cass Haber (New Schools Exchange)*

"Properly controlled, technology could provide each man with the ability to understand his environment better, to shape it with his own hands. . . . Such a use of technology constitutes the central alternative in education."

ant structure of the school. This hidden structure constitutes a course of instruction that stays forever beyond the control of the teacher or of his school board. It conveys indelibly the message that only through schooling can an individual prepare himself for adulthood in society, that what is not taught in school is of little value, and that what is learned outside of school is not worth knowing. I call it the hidden curriculum of schooling, because it constitutes the unalterable framework of the system, within which all changes in the curriculum are made.

The hidden curriculum is always the same regardless of school or place. It requires all children of a certain age to assemble in groups of about thirty, under the authority of a certified teacher, for some 500 to 1,000 or more hours each year. It doesn't matter whether the curriculum is designed to teach the principles of fascism, liberalism, Catholicism, or socialism; or whether the purpose of the school is to produce Soviet or United States citizens, mechanics, or doctors. It makes no difference whether the teacher is authoritarian or permissive, whether he imposes his own creed or teaches students to think for themselves. What is important is that students learn that education is valuable when it is acquired in the school through a graded process of consumption; that the degree of success the individual will enjoy in society depends on the amount of learning he consumes; and that learning *about* the world is more valuable than learning *from* the world.

It must be clearly understood that the hidden curriculum translates learning from an activity into a commodity —for which the school monopolizes the market. In all countries knowledge is regarded as the first necessity for survival, but also as a form of currency more liquid than rubles or dollars. We have become accustomed, through Karl Marx's writings, to speak about the alienation of the worker from his work in a class society. We must now recognize the estrangement of man from his learning when it becomes the product of a service profession and he becomes the consumer.

The more learning an individual consumes, the more "knowledge stock" he acquires. The hidden curriculum therefore defines a new class structure for society within which the large consumers of knowledge—those who have acquired large quantities of knowledge stock—enjoy special privileges, high income, and access to the more powerful tools of production. This kind of knowledge-capitalism has been accepted in all industrialized societies and establishes a rationale for the distribution of jobs and income. (This point is especially important in the light of the lack of correspondence between schooling and occupational competence established in studies such as Ivar Berg's *Education and Jobs: The Great Training Robbery*.)

The endeavor to put all men through successive stages of enlightenment is rooted deeply in alchemy, the Great Art of the waning Middle Ages. John Amos Comenius, a Moravian bishop, self-styled Pansophist, and pedagogue, is rightly considered one of the founders of the modern schools. He was among the first to propose seven or twelve grades of compulsory learning. In his *Magna Didactica*, he described schools as devices to "teach everybody everything" and outlined a blueprint for the assembly-line production of knowledge, which according to his method would make education cheaper and better and make growth into full humanity possible for all. But Comenius was not only an early efficiency expert, he was an alchemist who adopted the technical language of his craft to describe the art of rearing children. The alchemist sought to refine base elements by leading their distilled spirits through twelve stages of successive enlightenment, so that for their own and all the world's benefit they might be transmuted into gold. Of course, alchemists failed no matter how often they tried, but each time their "science" yielded new reasons for their failure, and they tried again.

Pedagogy opened a new chapter in the history of Ars Magna. Education became the search for an alchemic process that would bring forth a new type of man, who would fit into an environment created by scientific magic. But, no matter how much each generation spent on its schools, it always turned out that the majority of people were unfit for enlightenment by this process and had to be discarded as unprepared for life in a man-made world.

Educational reformers who accept the idea that schools have failed fall into three groups. The most respectable are certainly the great masters of alchemy who promise better schools. The most seductive are popular magicians, who promise to make every kitchen into an alchemic lab. The most sinister are the new Masons of the Universe, who want to transform the entire world into one huge temple of learning. Notable among today's masters of alchemy are certain research directors employed or sponsored by the large foundations who believe that schools, if they could somehow be im-

—*Photos by Photo Trends*

Surgical equipment (left); language laboratory (right)—"The technocrat's claim to power is the stock he holds in some scarce and secret knowledge."

proved, could also become economically more feasible than those that are now in trouble, and simultaneously could sell a larger package of services. Those who are concerned primarily with the curriculum claim that it is outdated or irrelevant. So the curriculum is filled with new packaged courses on African Culture, North American Imperialism, Women's Lib, Pollution, or the Consumer Society. Passive learning is wrong—it is indeed—so we graciously allow students to decide what and how they want to be taught. Schools are prison houses. Therefore, principals are authorized to approve teach-outs, moving the school desks to a roped-off Harlem street. Sensitivity training becomes fashionable. So, we import group therapy into the classroom. School, which was supposed to teach everybody everything, now becomes all things to all children.

Other critics emphasize that schools make inefficient use of modern science. Some would administer drugs to make it easier for the instructor to change the child's behavior. Others would transform school into a stadium for educational gaming. Still others would electrify the classroom. If they are simplistic disciples of McLuhan, they replace blackboards and textbooks with multimedia happenings; if they follow Skinner, they claim to be able to modify behavior more efficiently than old-fashioned classroom practitioners can.

Most of these changes have, of course, some good effects. The experimental schools have fewer truants. Parents do have a greater feeling of participation in a decentralized district. Pupils, assigned by their teacher to an apprenticeship, do often turn out more competent than those who stay in the classroom. Some children do improve their knowledge of Spanish in the language lab because they prefer playing with the knobs of a tape recorder to conversations with their Puerto Rican peers. Yet all these improvements operate within predictably narrow limits, since they leave the hidden curriculum of school intact.

Some reformers would like to shake loose from the hidden curriculum, but they rarely succeed. Free schools that lead to further free schools produce a mirage of freedom, even though the chain of attendance is frequently interrupted by long stretches of loafing. Attendance through seduction inculcates the need for educational treatment more persuasively than the reluctant attendance enforced by a truant officer. Permissive teachers in a padded classroom can easily render their pupils impotent to survive once they leave.

Learning in these schools often remains nothing more than the acquisition of socially valued skills defined, in this instance, by the consensus of a commune rather than by the decree of a school board. New presbyter is but old priest writ large.

Free schools, to be truly free, must meet two conditions: First, they must be run in a way to prevent the reintroduction of the hidden curriculum of graded attendance and certified students studying at the feet of certified teachers. And, more importantly, they must provide a framework in which all participants—staff and pupils—can free themselves from the hidden foundations of a schooled society. The first condition is frequently incorporated in the stated aims of a free school. The second condition is only rarely recognized, and is difficult to state as the goal of a free school.

It is useful to distinguish between the hidden curriculum, which I have described, and the occult foundations of schooling. The hidden curriculum is a ritual that can be considered the official initiation into modern society, institutionally established through the school. It is the purpose of this ritual to hide from its participants the contradictions between the myth of an egalitarian society and the class-conscious reality it certifies. Once they are recognized as such, rituals lose their power, and this is what is now beginning to happen to schooling. But there are certain fundamental assumptions about growing up—the occult foundations—which now find their expression in the ceremonial of schooling, and which could easily be reinforced by what free schools do.

Among these assumptions is what Peter Schrag calls the "immigration syndrome," which impels us to treat

TV studio (left) and mobile video-tape equipment in use (right)—"We must work toward a society in which scientific knowledge is incorporated in tools and components small enough to be within the reach of all."

all people as if they were newcomers who must go through a naturalization process. Only certified consumers of knowledge are admitted to citizenship. Men are not born equal, but are made equal through gestation by Alma Mater.

The rhetoric of all schools states that they form a man for the future, but they do not release him for his task before he has developed a high level of tolerance to the ways of his elders: education *for* life rather than *in* everyday life. Few free schools can avoid doing precisely this. Nevertheless they are among the most important centers from which a new life-style radiates, not because of the effect their graduates will have but, rather, because elders who choose to bring up their children without the benefit of properly ordained teachers frequently belong to a radical minority and because their preoccupation with the rearing of their children sustains them in their new style.

The most dangerous category of educational reformer is one who argues that knowledge can be produced and sold much more effectively on an open market than on one controlled by school. These people argue that most skills can be easily acquired from skill-models if the learner is truly interested in their acquisition; that individual entitlements can provide a more equal purchasing power for education. They demand a careful separation of the process by which knowledge is acquired from the process by which it is measured and certified. These seem to me obvious statements. But it would be a fallacy to believe that the establishment of a free market for knowledge would constitute a radical alternative in education.

The establishment of a free market would indeed abolish what I have previously called the hidden curriculum of present schooling—its age-specific attendance at a graded curriculum. Equally, a free market would at first give the appearance of counteracting what I have called the occult foundations of a schooled society: the "immigration syndrome," the institutional monopoly of teaching, and the ritual of linear initiation. But at the same time a free market in education would provide the alchemist with innumerable hidden hands to fit each man into the multiple, tight little niches a more complex technocracy can provide.

Many decades of reliance on schooling has turned knowledge into a commodity, a marketable staple of a special kind. Knowledge is now regarded simultaneously as a first necessity and also as society's most precious currency. (The transformation of knowledge into a commodity is reflected in a corresponding transformation of language. Words that formerly functioned as verbs are becoming nouns that designate possessions. Until recently dwelling and learning and even healing designated activities. They are now usually conceived as commodities or services to be delivered. We talk about the manufacture of housing or the delivery of medical care. Men are no longer regarded fit to house or heal themselves. In such a society people come to believe that professional services are more valuable than personal care. Instead of learning how to nurse grandmother, the teen-ager learns to picket the hospital that does not admit her.) This attitude could easily survive the disestablishment of school, just as affiliation with a church remained a condition for office long after the adoption of the First Amendment. It is even more evident that test batteries measuring complex knowledge-packages could easily survive the disestablishment of school—and with this would go the compulsion to obligate everybody to acquire a minimum package in the knowledge stock. The scientific measurement of each man's worth and the alchemic dream of each man's "educability to his full humanity" would finally coincide. Under the appearance of a "free" market, the global village would turn into an environmental womb where pedagogic therapists control the complex navel by which each man is nourished.

At present schools limit the teacher's competence to the classroom. They prevent him from claiming man's whole life as his domain. The demise of school will remove this restriction and give a semblance of legitimacy to the life-long pedagogical invasion of everybody's privacy. It will open the way for a scramble for "knowledge" on a free market, which would lead us toward the paradox of a vulgar, albeit seemingly egalitarian, meritocracy. Unless the concept of knowledge is transformed, the disestablishment of school will lead to a wedding between a growing meritocratic system that separates learning from certification and a society committed to provide therapy for each man until he is ripe for the gilded age.

For those who subscribe to the technocratic ethos, whatever is technically possible must be made available at least to a few whether they want it or not. Neither the privation nor the frus-

"Technological progress provides most people with gadgets they cannot afford and deprives them of tools they need."

THE ENGINE. 140 CID-OHC4 AND OTHER MYSTERIES.

tration of the majority counts. If cobalt treatment is possible, then the city of Tegucigalpa needs one apparatus in each of its two major hospitals, at a cost that would free an important part of the population of Honduras from parasites. If supersonic speeds are possible, then it must speed the travel of some. If the flight to Mars can be conceived, then a rationale must be found to make it appear a necessity. In the technocratic ethos poverty is modernized: Not only are old alternatives closed off by new monopolies, but the lack of necessities is also compounded by a growing spread between those services that are technologically feasible and those that are in fact available to the majority.

A teacher turns "educator" when he adopts this technocratic ethos. He then acts as if education were a technological enterprise designed to make man fit into whatever environment the "progress" of science creates. He seems blind to the evidence that constant obsolescence of all commodities comes at a high price: the mounting cost of training people to know about them. He seems to forget that the rising cost of tools is purchased at a high price in education: They decrease the labor intensity of the economy, make learning on the job impossible or, at best, a privilege for a few. All over the world the cost of educating men for society rises faster than the productivity of the entire economy, and fewer people have a sense of intelligent participation in the commonweal.

A revolution against those forms of privilege and power, which are based on claims to professional knowledge, must start with a transformation of consciousness about the nature of learning. This means, above all, a shift of responsibility for teaching and learning. Knowledge can be defined as a commodity only as long as it is viewed as the result of institutional enterprise or as the fulfillment of institutional objectives. Only when a man recovers the sense of personal responsibility for what he learns and teaches can this spell be broken and the alienation of learning from living be overcome.

The recovery of the power to learn or to teach means that the teacher who takes the risk of interfering in somebody else's private affairs also assumes responsibility for the results. Similarly, the student who exposes himself to the influence of a teacher must take responsibility for his own education. For such purposes educational institutions—if they are at all needed—ideally take the form of facility centers where one can get a roof of the right size over his head, access to a piano or a kiln, and to records, books, or slides. Schools, TV stations, theaters, and the like are designed primarily for use by professionals. Deschooling society means above all the denial of professional status for the second-oldest profession, namely teaching. The certification of teachers now constitutes an undue restriction of the right to free speech: the corporate structure and professional pretensions of journalism an undue restriction on the right to free press. Compulsory attendance rules interfere with free assembly. The deschooling of society is nothing less than a cultural mutation by which a people recovers the effective use of its Constitutional freedoms: learning and teaching by men who know that they are born free rather than treated to freedom. Most people learn most of the time when they do whatever they enjoy; most people are curious and want to give meaning to whatever they come in contact with; and most people

are capable of personal intimate intercourse with others unless they are stupefied by inhuman work or turned off by schooling.

The fact that people in rich countries do not learn much on their own constitutes no proof to the contrary. Rather it is a consequence of life in an environment from which, paradoxically, they cannot learn much, precisely because it is so highly programed. They are constantly frustrated by the structure of contemporary society in which the facts on which decisions can be made have become elusive. They live in an environment in which tools that can be used for creative purposes have become luxuries, an environment in which channels of communication serve a few to talk to many.

A modern myth would make us believe that the sense of impotence with which most men live today is a consequence of technology that cannot but create huge systems. But it is not technology that makes systems huge, tools immensely powerful, channels of communication one-directional. Quite the contrary: Properly controlled, technology could provide each man with the ability to understand his environment better, to shape it powerfully with his own hands, and to permit him full intercommunication to a degree never before possible. Such an alternative use of technology constitutes the central alternative in education.

If a person is to grow up he needs, first of all, access to things, to places and to processes, to events and to records. He needs to see, to touch, to tinker with, to grasp whatever there is in a meaningful setting. This access is now largely denied. When knowledge became a commodity, it acquired the protections of private property, and thus a principle designed to guard personal intimacy became a rationale for declaring facts off limits for people without the proper credentials. In schools teachers keep knowledge to themselves unless it fits into the day's program. The media inform, but exclude those things they regard as unfit to print. Information is locked into special languages, and specialized teachers live off its retranslation. Patents are protected by corporations, secrets are guarded by bureaucracies, and the power to keep others out of private preserves—be they cockpits, law offices, junkyards, or clinics—is jealously guarded by professions, institutions, and nations. Neither the political nor the professional structure of our societies, East and West, could

withstand the elimination of the power to keep entire classes of people from facts that could serve them. The access to facts that I advocate goes far beyond truth in labeling. Access must be built into reality, while all we ask from advertising is a guarantee that it does not mislead. Access to reality constitutes a fundamental alternative in education to a system that only purports to teach *about* it.

Abolishing the right to corporate secrecy—even when professional opinion holds that this secrecy serves the common good—is, as shall presently appear, a much more radical political goal than the traditional demand for public ownership or control of the tools of production. The socialization of tools without the effective socialization of know-how in their use tends to put the knowledge-capitalist into the position formerly held by the financier. The technocrat's only claim to power is the stock he holds in some class of scarce and secret knowledge, and the best means to protect its value is a large and capital-intensive organization that renders access to know-how formidable and forbidding.

It does not take much time for the interested learner to acquire almost any skill that he wants to use. We tend to forget this in a society where professional teachers monopolize entrance into all fields, and thereby stamp teaching by uncertified individuals as quackery. There are few mechanical skills used in industry or research that are as demanding, complex, and dangerous as driving cars, a skill that most people quickly acquire from a peer. Not all people are suited for advanced logic, yet those who are make rapid progress if they are challenged to play mathematical games at an early age. One out of twenty kids in Cuernavaca can beat me at Wiff 'n' Proof after a couple of weeks' training. In four months all but a small percentage of motivated adults at our CIDOC center learn Spanish well enough to conduct academic business in the new language.

A first step toward opening up access to skills would be to provide various incentives for skilled individuals to share their knowledge. Inevitably, this would run counter to the interest of guilds and professions and unions. Yet, multiple apprenticeship is attractive: It provides everybody with an opportunity to learn something about almost anything. There is no reason why a person should not combine the ability to drive a car, repair telephones and toilets, act as a midwife, and function as an architectural draftsman. Special-interest groups and their disciplined consumers would, of course, claim that the public needs the protection of a professional guarantee. But this argument is now steadily being challenged by consumer protection associations. We have to take much more seriously the objection that economists raise to the radical socialization of skills: that "progress" will be impeded if knowledge—patents, skills, and all the rest—is democratized. Their argument can be faced only if we demonstrate to them the growth rate of futile diseconomies generated by any existing educational system.

Access to people willing to share their skills is no guarantee of learning. Such access is restricted not only by the monopoly of educational programs over learning and of unions over licensing but also by a technology of scarcity. The skills that count today are know-how in the use of highly specialized tools that were designed to be scarce. These tools produce goods or render services that everybody wants but only a few can enjoy, and which only a limited number of people know how to use. Only a few privileged individuals out of the total number of people who have a given disease ever benefit from the results of sophisticated medical technology, and even fewer doctors develop the skill to use it.

The same results of medical research have, however, also been employed to create a basic medical tool kit that permits Army and Navy medics, with only a few months of training, to obtain results, under battlefield conditions, that would have been beyond the expectations of full-fledged doctors during World War II. On an even simpler level any peasant girl could learn how to diagnose and treat most infections if medical scientists prepared dosages and instructions specifically for a given geographic area.

All these examples illustrate the fact that educational considerations alone suffice to demand a radical reduction of the professional structure that now impedes the mutual relationship between the scientist and the majority of people who want access to science. If this demand were heeded, all men could learn to use yesterday's tools, rendered more effective and durable by modern science, to create tomorrow's world.

Unfortunately, precisely the contrary trend prevails at present. I know a coastal area in South America where most people support themselves by fishing from small boats. The outboard

motor is certainly the tool that has changed most dramatically the lives of these coastal fishermen. But in the area I have surveyed, half of all outboard motors that were purchased between 1945 and 1950 are still kept running by constant tinkering, while half the motors purchased in 1965 no longer run because they were not built to be repaired. Technological progress provides the majority of people with gadgets they cannot afford and deprives them of the simpler tools they need.

Metals, plastics, and ferro cement used in building have greatly improved since the 1940s and ought to provide more people the opportunity to create their own homes. But while in the United States, in 1948, more than 30 per cent of all one-family homes were owner-built, by the end of the 1960s the percentage of those who acted as their own contractors had dropped to less than 20 per cent.

The lowering of the skill level through so-called economic development becomes even more visible in Latin America. Here most people still build their own homes from floor to roof. Often they use mud, in the form of adobe, and thatchwork of unsurpassed utility in the moist, hot, and windy climate. In other places they make their dwellings out of cardboard, oildrums, and other industrial refuse. Instead of providing people with simple tools and highly standardized, durable, and easily repaired components, all governments have gone in for the mass production of low-cost buildings. It is clear that not one single country can afford to provide satisfactory modern dwelling units for the majority of its people. Yet, everywhere this policy makes it progressively more difficult for the majority to acquire the knowledge and skills they need to build better houses for themselves.

Educational considerations permit us to formulate a second fundamental characteristic that any post-industrial society must possess: a basic tool kit that by its very nature counteracts technocratic control. For educational reasons we must work toward a society in which scientific knowledge is incorporated in tools and components that can be used meaningfully in units small enough to be within the reach of all. Only such tools can socialize access to skills. Only such tools favor temporary associations among those who want to use them for a specific occasion. Only such tools allow specific goals to emerge in the process of their use, as any tinkerer knows. Only the

combination of guaranteed access to facts and of limited power in most tools renders it possible to envisage a subsistence economy capable of incorporating the fruits of modern science.

The development of such a scientific subsistence economy is unquestionably to the advantage of the overwhelming majority of all people in poor countries. It is also the only alternative to progressive pollution, exploitation, and opaqueness in rich countries. But, as we have seen, the dethroning of the GNP cannot be achieved without simultaneously subverting GNE (Gross National Education—usually conceived as manpower capitalization). An egalitarian economy cannot exist in a society in which the right to produce is conferred by schools.

The feasibility of a modern subsistence economy does not depend on new scientific inventions. It depends primarily on the ability of a society to agree on fundamental, self-chosen anti-bureaucratic and anti-technocratic restraints.

These restraints can take many forms, but they will not work unless they touch the basic dimensions of life. (The decision of Congress against development of the supersonic transport plane is one of the most encouraging steps in the right direction.) The substance of these voluntary social restraints would be very simple matters that can be fully understood and judged by any prudent man. The issues at stake in the SST controversy provide a good example. All such restraints would be chosen to promote stable and equal enjoyment of scientific know-how. The French say that it takes a thousand years to educate a peasant to deal with a cow. It would not take two generations to help all people in Latin America or Africa to use and repair outboard motors, simple cars, pumps, medicine kits, and ferro cement machines if their design does not change every few years. And since a joyful life is one of constant meaningful intercourse with others in a meaningful environment, equal enjoyment does translate into equal education.

At present a consensus on austerity is difficult to imagine. The reason usually given for the impotence of the majority is stated in terms of political or economic class. What is not usually understood is that the new class structure of a schooled society is even more powerfully controlled by vested interests. No doubt an imperialist and capitalist organization of society provides the social structure within which a minority can have disproportionate influence over the effective opinion of the majority. But in a technocratic society the power of a minority of knowledge capitalists can prevent the formation of true public opinion through control of scientific know-how and the media of communication. Constitutional guarantees of free speech, free press, and free assembly were meant to ensure government by the people. Modern electronics, photo-off-set presses, time-sharing computers, and telephones have in principle provided the hardware that could give an entirely new meaning to these freedoms. Unfortunately, these things are used in modern media to increase the power of knowledge-bankers to funnel their program-packages through international chains to more people, instead of being used to increase true networks that provide equal opportunity for encounter among the members of the majority.

Deschooling the culture and social structure requires the use of technology to make participatory politics possible. Only on the basis of a majority coalition can limits to secrecy and growing power be determined without dictatorship. We need a new environment in which growing up can be classless, or we will get a brave new world in which Big Brother educates us all.

Liveable Cities

"... We find the federal government ... controlling hour-to-hour details in carrying out individual local programs, we find responsibility for dealing with certain urban problems thrust upon states which have neither experience nor interest in urban affairs ... and we find individual cities struggling vainly to make their own complicated financing structures squeeze out a few more dollars for urgently needed improvement programs because assistance is not available from any other level of government."

DONALD G. ALEXANDER

Donald G. Alexander is legislative counsel for the National League of Cities and the U.S. Conference of Mayors. He has been deeply involved in development of federal grant-in-aid legislation and has directed and written several follow-up studies on the effectiveness of specific legislation relating to city problems. He has also written magazine articles on urban problems and prepared many statements on urban problems which have been presented to congressional committees.

THE DECADE OF THE 1970's is certain to be a watershed in the development of America's cities. Programs to improve cities, which were pursued with vigor in the 1950's and 1960's, must be vastly expanded in the 1970's to preserve our cities as places of enjoyment for the great majority of Americans who will be living or working in them by 1980.

The expansion process will take place through an institutional structure involving many decisions by governments, private businesses and agencies and individual citizens. All their decisions will affect the nature of the urban environment, and because of the complicated interrelationships among them, no single sector—government, business or in-

dividual citizen—will be able to achieve a development process and results entirely in accord with its desires.

Within this structure, one of the most significant influences in upgrading urban life will be public decision-making in such areas as land-use planning, transportation system development and the construction of public facilities. The President's Committee on Urban Housing has estimated that to house our population satisfactorily, a national goal of 26 million new and rehabilitated housing units, including at least 6 million subsidized units for low-income families, will be required by 1978.[1] To achieve this, we must double our current annual housing production rate of 1.4 million units. The construction rate has slowed in 1970 because of a severely restricted money supply and the high costs of inflation. Similar increased efforts must be made to provide improved public facilities —schools, parks, water supplies, sewers— which are vital but often forgotten elements in neighborhood development programs.

Numbers alone, however, tell little of the future direction of urban development. Without proper planning, these 26 million new units and their supporting facilities could be produced in a manner resembling the dull and now decaying developments which sprang up in the years following World War II. For planning to be effective it must have credibility and for planning to have credi-

[1] "A Decent Home," *Report of the President's Committee on Urban Housing* (Washington, D.C.: U.S. Government Printing Office, 1969), p. 3.

bility sufficient public and private resources must be available to carry out the plans. Today, there is a huge gap between the needs identified in local plans and the resources available to fill these needs. For urban renewal alone, nearly $3 billion worth of projects in excess of available resources are ready to be started when funding is provided. In water pollution control, over $2 billion in local projects have been planned and are awaiting funds.

The total cost required to improve the liveability of cities will be enormous, certainly approaching $1 trillion; and such a budget requires a firm commitment of public and private resources. This commitment is lacking today. In the area of housing, for example, the Housing and Urban Development Act of 1968 set a goal of 26 million new housing units by 1978, yet to date neither Congress nor the administration has backed an appropriation of sufficient funds to develop publicly supported housing at the rate necessary to meet the goal of 6 million subsidized units by 1978.

IN-MIGRATION

Local officials recognize the urgency with which massive improvement programs must be initiated to maintain and improve urban living. But although they have the responsibility and are expected to deal with the immediate crisis, city officials have startlingly little control over the conditions that create the most severe urban problems. City officials are not responsible for the economic,

From *Current History*, August 1970. Copyright © Current History, Inc.

social and cultural proverty of rural America, particularly in the South, which has led to the great in-migration of the poor and unskilled to the central cities. People come to the cities with the full knowledge that the streets are not paved with gold—but they come, for in the cities there is still hope. A detailed examination of migration problems in *Fortune* magazine noted:

Most of the migrants know that what awaits them in the urban North.is little better than a rattlesnake's hole . . . [but despite the bleak prospects] most often, the migrant heads North, where there is at least a chance of a job, no men in hoods ride the streets, and there is a welfare payment to keep the migrant alive.[2]

Though the influences come from the outside, it falls to city officials to deal with the problems which such in-migration creates. City officials often lack access to the resources necessary to cope with problems of such magnitude. Local revenue-raising capability and, to some extent, local spending choices are severely constricted by state law:

States tell cities what taxes they may raise, and in some cases how high they may raise them.
States designate who may and who may not be taxed.
States set limits on how much debt may be incurred and what interest rates may be paid, and
States sometimes mandate services which must be performed and dictate what people must be paid to perform them.

From this constricted local revenue base, demands for the full variety of municipal services must be met, and demands for increased commitments from local resources have never been greater.

The only significant revenue source which most cities are free to manipulate to gain greater revenue on their own is the property tax but, because of the high property taxes already imposed in many cities, further increases tend to discourage physical improvements and to drive out both industry and individuals able to pay, thus aggravating the very problems the city is seeking to solve. Outside help in the form of grants-in-aid or assignment of greater authority to cities to raise their own revenue through local sales or income taxes will be needed before any major improvement programs can be undertaken.[3]

Despite nationwide recognition of the urban crises, other levels of government have been slow to provide direct assistance or to loosen the legal straitjacket in which city officials must act to control problems or develop solutions.

State governments have been particularly derelict in this regard. William G. Colman, until recently the executive director of the prestigious Advisory Commission on Intergovernmental Relations, has observed, "As the road to the present urban hell was paved, many major sins of omission and commission can be ascribed to the States."[4] Nor does it appear that most states, even in 1970, are yet ready to reorient themselves to lend city officials a hand in combating the urban crisis. The impact of the crime problem is particularly concentrated in the urban areas, and the urgent needs of cities for assistance in controlling crime are great and obvious. Yet a 1970 study of state-controlled allocation of federal crime funds under the Omnibus Crime Control and Safe Streets Act of 1968, concluded with dismay:

The states, in distributing funds entrusted to them under the block grant formula of the Safe Streets Act, have failed to focus these vital resources on the most crucial urban crime problems. Instead, funds are being dissipated broadly across the states in many grants too small to have any significant impact to improve the criminal justice system and are being used in disproportionate amounts to support marginal improvements in low crime areas.[5]

The response of the federal government to the problems of urban areas has improved markedly in recent years. Federal aid outlays in urban areas grew from $3.9 billion in 1961 to $14 billion in 1969, though actual direct grants to cities were much lower than this. A much larger commitment of federal assistance is needed, and a restructuring of systems and resource allocation practices is a prerequisite to solving urban problems, if the dollars committed to such efforts are to be used effectively.

GOVERNMENTAL ROLES

An important element of this restructuring must be a clearer definition of the roles of the federal, state and local governments in urban problem solving. Currently, governmental roles in urban programs tend to be what the individual governmental units choose to make them or must make of them out of necessity.

Thus, today we find the federal government in Washington controlling particular hour-to-hour details in carrying out individ-

ual local programs; we find responsibility for dealing with certain urban problems thrust upon states which have neither experience nor interest in urban affairs but seek only to increase their political power through control of funds; and we find individual cities struggling valiantly to make their own complicated financing structures squeeze out a few more dollars for urgently needed improvement programs because assistance is not available from any other level of government. For a truly coordinated and efficient system backing the national effort, responsibilities must be more rationally related to interest, experience and resource-collecting capacity.

In this effort, city governments have a major role to play. Cities are the level of government closest to the people, and it is city government to which the people turn first when they have problems, regardless of the control which the city can exercise over the solutions. Mayors and other locally elected officials will be most responsive to the needs and problems of the community, for their jobs depend on continued progress towards satisfying local needs in a manner acceptable to their electorate. Thus, in any rational urban improvement system major responsibility for planning urban improvements and the day-to-day operation of local programs should be assigned to city governments.

States also have a significant role to play in support and oversight of urban improvement efforts. Overall goals must be set at the state level in key areas which have application beyond individual jurisdictional boundaries such as education, highway system development, water resources and land-use planning. Development of individual local programs can be coordinated with these state goals which set general direction and assure that local efforts do not work at cross purposes. State planning structures which are established must, however, reflect local determinations of need. To govern urban living, states can impose and enforce laws and regulations which individual cities could not set because of the potential confusion of varying regulations and the difficulties of local enforcement. In addition, states can provide facilities and technical assistance which many localities could not develop on their own. Such facilities and services might include state-wide crime laboratories, the higher educational systems, training for municipal personnel and counsel in the planning and development of local improvement efforts.

Great economies and efficiencies in revenue collection and distribution can also be achieved at the state level. Income and sales taxes have great potential as revenue sources which can be cultivated without an adverse impact on urban development. These can be effectively collected at the state level and

[2] "The Southern Roots of Urban Crises," *Fortune*, August, 1968, p. 80.
[3] A panel of urban financing experts convened by the National League of Cities and other groups concluded:
"Central cities should not kid themselves that the state or federal governments or the suburbs can or will come through with enough aid and relief to close the whole gap between local spending at the present rate of increase and local revenue from today's local tax practice.
"At today's growth rates of city spending vs. city tax revenue plus state and federal aid, the urban deficit for the next 10 years is estimated by the National League of Cities at $262 billion plus." "Financing Our Urban Needs," *Nation's Cities* (Washington, D.C.: The National League of Cities, March, 1969), p. 19.

[4] William G. Colman, "Making Our Federal System Work: A Challenge for the 70's," *The Urban Lawyer* (Chicago, Illinois: American Bar Association, Fall, 1969), p. 304.
[5] "Street Crime and the Safe Streets Act: What Is The Impact," A Special Research Report by the National League of Cities and the U.S. Conference of Mayors (Washington, D.C., February, 1970), p. 28.

redistributed to local governments by means of revenue-sharing formulas. Such formulas must make an adequate share of funds available to urban areas, reversing the traditional state pattern of favoritism to non-urban areas. If such a reversal of patterns can be achieved and an adequate share of funds can be made available to urban areas, the adverse impact on local development currently resulting from the heavy burdens necessarily imposed by local property taxes may be eased.

The federal government can make three vital contributions to improve urban areas. First of all, it can distribute resources to state and local governments for urban improvement programs. The federal income tax is certainly the most efficient revenue collection device and currently appears to be the fairest. Because of the overbearing influence it exercises on the national economy and the heavy burden it imposes on individual and corporate incomes, state and local governments find it difficult to establish comparably efficient and fair revenue structures.

Federal assistance for urban programs from this revenue source is currently provided through categorical grants-in-aid aimed at individual improvement projects. The present aid programs have been valuable in providing necessary support for local efforts, though they have not realized their full potential because the funds appropriated for them are meager. Categorical grants also have several drawbacks. The administrative costs of such programs are very high in relation to payoff. Grant applications sometimes resemble the Manhattan Telephone Directory; scores of federal-level checkoff points can delay approval of grants so that local programs depending upon them are severely hindered; and, once grants are approved, oversight functions sometimes severely limit local flexibility to deal with particular local conditions and add further administrative costs which divert funds. In addition, such grants make a coordinated local improvement effort supported by federal assistance extremely difficult because of uncertainty as to when funds will be available, and because the wide variety of cost-matching ratios and compliance requirements are difficult to integrate into one comprehensive urban improvement package. In addition, categorical grant programs seldom provide assistance for operation and maintenance.

To avoid these problems, to encourage comprehensive local development programs supported by federal assistance, and to make effective use of federal aid in action programs without heavy administrative costs, the National League of Cities and the U.S. Conference of Mayors are urging adoption of a revenue-sharing plan that would allow an automatic distribution of a set percentage of federal income tax receipts to cities for unrestricted use. Such a plan would greatly improve the positive role of the federal government in providing assistance for local improvement programs.

A NATIONAL URBANIZATION POLICY

The second major contribution which the federal government can make toward speeding the progress of urban improvement is the development and implementation of a national urbanization policy. This policy would set the goal of improvement of urban life as a priority concern of the federal government and would coordinate federal programs toward that common objective. At present, federal programs often work at cross purposes, some stimulating improvement in urban areas and others frustrating these efforts. For example, while the Department of Housing and Urban Development works to establish stability and to improve home ownership in underprivileged neighborhoods, federal tax laws stimulate rapid turnover of property with a resulting instability in the neighborhood structure, and the home mortgage insurance protection of the Federal Housing Administration strongly encourages the flight to the suburbs. While major federal efforts are undertaken to feed hungry people in both urban and rural areas, the Department of Agriculture spends $4 billion a year to subsidize farmers not to grow food to keep prices high, thus limiting the availability of food to the poor. A national urbanization policy would avoid such incongruities, providing the direction which all federal programs would follow.

The third major contribution which the federal government can make is the effective use of federal laws and regulatory powers when local or state action alone would be inadequate to protect and improve the quality of urban life. While it is impossible in this article to discuss the many federal laws affecting urban life, two areas can be noted where more effective federal controls are urgently needed. The first is in the area of pollution abatement. Cities, and even states, have a difficult time developing and enforcing pollution regulations because of the interstate nature of much of the activity creating the pollution and the national nature of problems such as oil spills, auto exhausts or disposable packaging. These can be controlled only by strong regulations at the national level.

The second area is organized crime and the derivative problem of drug abuse. It is estimated that as much as $30 billion passes through the hands of the crime syndicate each year. Most of this money comes from urban areas. Further, it is estimated that up to 50 per cent of the street crime in some cities is committed to support drug habits and other organized-crime-related activities. The heavy costs and high crime rates spawned by organized crime have an obvious degrading effect upon the quality of urban life. Because the problem is interstate and even international in nature, federal action is required.

NATIONAL PRIORITIES

Changes in federal, state and local systems to improve program operations and coordination and to provide greater focus for urban problems alone will not be sufficient. A major reordering of national priorities is also required to provide the resources necessary for programs of physical development and social improvement which can provide a healthier urban environment.

At present, Americans invest approximately $25 billion annually in housing construction and rehabilitation. To reach the goal of 26 million new and rehabilitated housing units set by the President's Committee on Urban Housing, an investment of $500 billion to $600 billion, about 5 per cent of the annual Gross National Product, will be required.

The United States Department of Interior has estimated that public expenditures ranging from $45 billion to $65 billion and additional private outlays of up to $6.5 billion are required for construction of facilities to control water pollution in the first part of the 1970's.[6] The present annual rate of public investment is less than $2 billion. A doubling and perhaps tripling of this is required.

Secretary of Transportation John A. Volpe has noted studies which set the necessary capital investment for public transportation system improvements as high as $30 billion in the next decade.[7] This rate is certain to be exceeded if use of the automobile in central city areas is substantially curtailed. Further, the growing trend toward government subsidy of part or all of the costs of operating public transportation indicates that a greater cost burden must be born by the taxpayers, in addition to the necessarily substantial share of the projected $30 billion capital investment.

These are the projected costs in a few programs to provide improvements in the physical environment of cities. But there are many more areas of need—schools, hospitals, airports, highways, parks, offices and stores. Exact cost estimates projected ten years ahead are nearly meaningless and the strong likelihood exists that new technology and new lifestyles will radically change many of the projected needs before the end of the decade. Still it can still be stated with some assurance that an investment of at least $1 trillion during the next decade will be neces-

[6] "The Cost of Clean Water and its Economic Impact," U.S. Department of Interior, Federal Water Pollution Control Administration (Washington, D.C.: U.S. Government Printing Office, 1969.)

[7] Statement of John A. Volpe, Secretary, U.S. Department of Transportation, before the Senate Committee on Banking and Currency, October 14, 1969.

sary to provide the physical facilities for liveable cities.

Great care will have to be taken to make sure that this huge capital investment is spent effectively. Many of the major capital investments of the 1950's and 1960's only aggravated the problems they were designed to solve. Urban highways built to end traffic problems often created additional congestion and pollution. Public housing projects built to replace slums have often become huge vertical slums into which even the police fear to venture. In his book, *Urban Dynamics,* Jay Forrester argues persuasively that public housing and other subsidy programs designed to help the poor and end poverty may have really increased poverty and despair in the central cities by creating greater concentrations of poor and unskilled than can be served by subsidy programs, at the same time raising municipal costs and undercutting the local economic base, thus further aggravating poverty conditions. Forrester observes:

> The pervasive sense of failure and frustration among men concerned with management of urban affairs points to the likelihood that inherent behavior of complex systems defies the intuitively "obvious" solutions of the past. Among political leaders, managers of redevelopment activity, and political scientists interviewed in connection with this study, there was the overwhelming opinion that the problems of the urban areas remain severe in spite of the variety of programs that have been tried over the last three decades.

> Contributing to the selection of ineffective programs is the nature of the conflict between short-term and long-term considerations in complex systems. Very often the actions that seem easiest and most promising in the immediate future can produce even greater problems at a later time. Humanitarian impulses coupled with the short-

[8] Jay W. Forrester, *Urban Dynamics* (Cambridge, Massachusetts: The M.I.T. Press, 1969), p. 10.

term political pressures lead to programs whose benefits, if any, evaporate quickly, leaving behind a system that is unimproved or in worse condition. Job-training programs, low-cost housing programs, and even financial aid, when used alone without improvements in the economic climate of a city, can fall into this same category of short-term promise followed by detrimental long-term change.[8]

SIMPLISTIC "SOLUTIONS"

New programs to improve urban life will be complicated, involving long months of often frustrating planning to make sure that all variables are considered. Simplistic solutions should be avoided. One simple "solution" currently in vogue must be viewed with particular care. It states that the key to the urban crisis is density and congestion and suggests that to solve urban problems, people, industry and federal aid should be redistributed to non-urban areas. This approach contains two serious flaws. First and foremost, there is no evidence that density, by itself, is a major contributor to America's urban problems. Many United States cities are less densely populated than major cities in Canada and Europe. Yet the difficulties of crime and physical blight are much worse in the United States because of such factors as poverty, racial discrimination and unstructured and uncontrolled development. Second, there is no guarantee that social and cultural conditions in non-urban areas would suddenly improve to satisfy today's more cosmopolitan population. The technological growth of our society, exemplified by the pervasive influence of television, has greatly altered people's expectations and aspirations. The vast range of services and the availability of public facilities staffed by highly trained specialists (which urban citizens expect) and the wide range of social and cultural facili-

ties, stores and so forth available from the private sector in urban areas precisely because they are places of highly concentrated population could not be duplicated in little centers of dispersed population all around the country. Personnel is not there to staff them; money is not there to build them; and, if it were, there would not be sufficient people to make efficient use of them.

The key to avoiding misadventures is comprehensive planning, which ties physical improvements into overall community growth patterns, coordinating transportation, housing, industry and other public facility development in one closely knit growth plan which features the needs of individual citizens for a better urban existence. Neglect of individual needs is a glaring failure of too many recent physical development efforts.

The frustrations arising from racial discrimination, hunger, sickness and poverty can negate any of the improvements gained from upgrading physical facilities. For this reason, the current preoccupation with improvement of the physical environment should be viewed with some misgiving. There is no question that massive efforts to improve our environment are necessary today to assure a pleasant, healthy tomorrow. But present efforts in the environmental field resemble too closely the preoccupation with buildings and highways in the late 1950's and early 1960's. Efforts to upgrade job opportunities, to end hunger, to improve education and to control disease among the poor cannot take a back seat to environmental improvement now as they took a back seat to building construction a decade ago. With a national commitment we can upgrade the environment and improve the prospects of all our citizens. Both are necessary if the dream of beautiful, liveable cities is to become a reality.

A Century of Negro Suffrage

1. The right of Negro citizens of the United States to vote shall not be denied or abridged by the United States or by any State on account of race, color or previous condition of servitude.

2. The Congress shall have power to enforce this article by appropriate legislation.

—FIFTEENTH AMENDMENT TO THE CONSTITUTION
OF THE UNITED STATES

HENRY LEE MOON

RATIFICATION of the Fifteenth Amendment 100 years ago, March 30, did not initiate Negro voting in this nation. The Amendment, as intended, established the right of non-white citizens to vote as a federally-protected right throughout the nation. Prior to ratification of this, the last of the three War Amendments, the determination of voter qualifications was regarded as being strictly within the domain of the several states to grant or to withhold the privilege of the franchise as each state saw fit. As a result, not only Negroes, but also women, Indians and non-Christians were barred from voting by some of the colonies and, later, by many of the states.

Negro voting in the territory which became the United States of America is older than the nation, dating back to the colonial period. South Carolina, where free Negroes first voted, was also the first colony, in 1716, to restrict suffrage to "every white man . . . professing the Christian religion." The color ban was later imposed by Georgia, 1761, and Virginia, 1762. By the time of the Revolutionary War, free Negroes were voting in 10 of the original 13 colonies including North Carolina which did not outlaw black suffrage until 1835. In the years between the end of the Revolution and the beginning of the Civil War, the number of states permitting Negro men to vote dwindled to six—Maine, Massachusetts, New Hampshire, Rhode Island, Vermont and, with special requirements not demanded of white men, New York.

The escalating economic returns from the slave system, the rising tide of racism and the ever-present fear of slave rebellions spurred a cutback in Negro voting not only in the South but also in such commonwealths as Connecticut, Delaware, Maryland, New Jersey and Pennsylvania and in the new states of the expanding West. Disfranchisement of Pennsylvania Negroes in 1838 followed the near election of a Bucks County black candidate to the state legislature.

To the Freedmen, ratification of the Fifteenth Amendment meant new hope for fulfillment of one of their three major goals—land, education and the ballot. These represented to black folk the essential tools to enable them to secure and make real their newly-achieved freedom for themselves and their children. To the former slaveholders the Amendment represented a dire threat to their dream of restoring the old order under some new name.

IN THE North ratification settled the issue of Negro suffrage. After 1870 the relatively small Negro vote was eagerly sought in the remaining non-southern states which had previously held the black population in political serfdom. Negroes were elected to public office in Massachusetts, Minnesota, Ohio and Illinois, often with the support of a sizeable white electorate.

In the South, the Amendment validated the suffrage provisions of the Reconstruction acts of 1867 which sustained, for a brief period, the new governments set up with large-scale Negro participation as voters, candidates for office, and office-holders. But the white South never accepted the new regime.

The history of Reconstruction has been systematically distorted by southern writers and politicians and their northern allies. The South bitterly complained of corruption, as if political graft had

push
me,
mister...

...register and
vote

been an invention of the new Negro voters. The regional spokesman bemoaned the alleged ignorance and incompetency of the black office-holders despite the high quality of many of them. Men of education, intelligence, poise and principle like Francis L. Cardoza and Robert Elliott Brown of South Carolina; Hiram Revels, B. K. Bruce and John R. Lynch of Mississippi; George W. White of North Carolina; Norris Wright Cuney of Texas; Jonathan Gibbs of Florida; Henry Turner of Georgia and others were certainly no less able than their white slave-holding predecessors.

At least two historians of the period—one white and the other black—saw through the sham of the unreconstructed rebels. Said William A. Dunning in his book, *Reconstruction:* "The Negroes were disliked and feared almost in exact proportion to their manifestation of intelligence and capacity." W. E. B. Du Bois, in *Black Reconstruction,* agreed: "If there was one thing South Carolina feared more than bad Negro government, it was good Negro government."

With the restoration of the Confederacy following the election of Rutherford B. Hayes and the Compromise of 1877, the Dixie subversion of the Fifteenth Amendment was intensified and continues, though with vastly diminished force and effectiveness, until this day, as witness the strong southern support of the Nixon Administration's effort to dilute the impact of the Voting Rights Act of 1965. That this resistance to the fundamental right to vote has persisted for a full century is a major American tragedy.

To maintain the right to vote as the exclusive privilege of white men, the South developed a sordid assortment of devices ranging from bold and unabashed refusal to register black citizens, regardless of their individual qualifications, to murder, and including tricky registration requirements, threats, intimidation, the poll tax and economic pressures. The white supremacists were motivated not only by stark racism, but also by a grim and defiant determination to retain political power in the hands of the ruling clique. To this end they sought not only the exclusion of Negroes from the polls but also the restriction of the voting rights of poor whites. The result was the complete negation of the "one man, one vote" doctrine and swollen power for the few southerners who did

vote. It took as many as ten times the number of votes to elect a Congressman in New York or Illinois as it did in South Carolina or Mississippi, all because of the disfranchisement of Negro voters and the discouragement of the poor whites.

THE long, hard struggle to regain the vote for black citizens in the South was spearheaded, certainly during the last half-century, by the National Association for the Advancement of Colored People. The Association intervened in the successful suit to ban the notorious "grandfather clause" in 1917 and proceeded to secure invalidation by the United States Supreme Court of the Democratic "white" primary in 1944. Other barriers to the ballot box were stricken down by court decisions and Federal legislation—the poll tax by a Supreme Court ruling in 1966, and other restrictions including, ultimately, the literacy tests by a series of Congressional enactments in 1957, 1964 and 1965.

The "white" primary was the real stumbling block. With education, a black man could pass the literacy test, when fairly administered. With money, he could pay the poll tax. He could qualify under any reasonable character test. But there was no way for him to pass the acid color test of the "white" primary. With the development of the one-party system in the South, the Democratic "white" primary became, in the words of the late Judge J. Waties Waring, "the only material and realistic election." The decisions were made in the primary and merely ratified in the general election.

The Court's decision banning the "white" primary was accepted in the more enlightened southern communities and as a result there was an upsurge of Negro voting strength in the region. For the first time since Reconstruction there was mass voting by Negro citizens. In 1940, Ralph J. Bunche estimated fewer than 250,000 Negro voters in the southern states. By 1948, four years after the court's ruling, there were 750,000 colored persons registered to vote in 12 southern states, according to an NAACP estimate. The Negro returned to the political arena not only as a voter but also as a successful candidate for office on the local level. His return was welcomed by the southern white "liberals" who, as William G. Carleton pointed out, at that time, saw in the increasing Negro vote "a boon to liberals in their fight within the [Democratic] party to gain and keep party control."

This reaction, however, was not universal throughout the South. There were then as now, after the school desegregation decree, widespread efforts to evade and circumvent the High Court's decision. New laws were passed and old measures revived. Attempts were made in South Carolina and elsewhere to declare the Democratic party a "private" white man's association operating without state authority. This move was promptly squelched by Federal Court judges, notably Judge Waring of South Carolina.

Following the 1944 court decision, Alabama, Georgia, South Carolina and Mississippi moved to tighten their registration and voting requirements with a view to making it more difficult for Negroes to qualify. In 1946, Alabama voters ratified the restrictive Boswell amendment only to have it rejected by the Federal courts because of arbitrary powers vested in the registrars. A new version of this amendment was ratified in 1951 by the narrow margin of 369 votes in a statewide referendum. A Georgia law enacted in 1949, requiring complete re-registration, created chaos and imperiled more white voters than Negro. Compliance with the law was suspended. Other means, developed in South Carolina and Mississippi, required voters to pledge that they were opposed to Federal legislation for civil rights. A common practice in southern states required applicants to pass literacy tests and to answer, to the satisfaction of the local election officials, any questions put to them.

Not only were the registration laws in the southern states generally designed to restrict voting, but the administration of the laws was frequently biased. Negroes, when permitted to vote, were usually compelled to meet the strictest requirements of the law whereas great leniency was, in many cases, granted white applicants. In some places a few Negroes were permitted to register, but not to vote. To aid Negroes in preparing for registration, the NAACP, the CIO and later, the Student Nonviolent Coordinating Committee, Southern Christian Leadership Conference, CORE and other organizations gave instructions on how to register and vote and designated persons to accompany applicants to the places of registration. The NAACP also provided legal counsel for persons who sought such assistance in cases involving their political rights.

In Virginia, certain information—name, age, address, occupation, date and place of birth, etc.—was required. In some areas of the state the applicant was handed a blank card, with no indication of what information was required, and asked to write down the necessary facts without any assistance from the registrar. In common practice the registrar, particularly in the "black belt" counties, assisted white applicants who needed direction. With Negro applicants he was apt to abide strictly by the law.

Down in Louisiana they refined the art of deception. The simple question of age was used to snare the unwary. One was required to put down his age to the day. Not simply Joe Doaks, 27; but Joe Doaks, 27 years, 5 months and 19 days. A day off was sufficient to disqualify the black applicant.

Alabama required applicants for registration to answer a list of 21 questions prepared by the State Supreme Court in compliance with a provision of the Voter Qualification Amendment. The questions, clearly designed to restrict registration, were tricky and difficult enough in themselves. However, the Jefferson County (Birmingham) board of registrars added other questions over and beyond those required by law. A Negro voter-registration committee listed 41 of these extra-legal questions.

Donald S. Strong in his 1956 study of registration in Alabama revealed a similar list of questions asked of white CIO members, indicating a desire to keep the labor vote down also. In asking these questions, Strong said, "Jefferson County imposes a requirement for which there is no legal justification."

As usual Mississippi stooped the lowest in the absurdity of the questions put to the would-be Negro registrant. Consider this classic irrelevancy: How many bubbles are there in a bar of soap? Nine Hattiesburg Negroes filed affidavits with the U.S. Department of Justice in 1953 swearing that they had been asked this and similar questions as a prerequisite for registration.

THE abolition of the "white" primary paved the way for the return of the Negro as a positive factor in southern politics. He had always been the dominant political issue in the region, but chiefly as a negative catalyst, absorbing the regional pas-

sions and retarding the intellectual development of a people who permitted the enslavement of their minds in order to keep another people in subjection. It was a massive tragedy which exacted its toll from black and white alike. The 1944 Supreme Court decision banning this iniquitous subversion of the Fifteenth Amendment afforded the opportunity for the beginning of a new emancipation for both races.

There was an immediate expansion of the Negro vote particularly in the more progressive of the southern cities—Atlanta, Memphis, Houston, Charlotte, Norfolk, Richmond and others. The smaller cities and rural areas were little affected by the ruling. Despite continuing resistance and cutbacks in some areas during the 1950s and early Sixties, there was, overall, a steady increase in the number of registered black voters in the eleven states of the late Confederacy. At least 16 persons, nine of them in Mississippi, were murdered primarily because of their voter registration activity during the 20-year period, 1946-1966. Nevertheless, the upward trend in the southern Negro vote was irreversible.

Between 1948 and 1960, the black vote in the region more than doubled to about 1,500,000. Following enactment of the Voting Rights Act of 1965 there was a spectacular increase in this vote to more than 3,000,000 by the end of the decade. In Mississippi, which had offered the most desperate resistance to Negro participation in politics, Negro registration soared from about 25,000 in 1965 to more than 250,000. There were also sharp increases in Alabama, South Carolina and Virginia. Under this law literacy tests were suspended and Federal registrars assigned to supervise registration and voting in counties where Negro electors had been kept to a minimum.

On the centennial of the ratification of the Fifteenth Amendment a survey released by the Metropolitan Applied Research Center of New York and the Voter Education Project of the Southern Regional Council in Atlanta revealed that 1,500 black men and women now hold elective office in the United States, one third of them in the South. The positions range from United States Senator to justice of the peace. As reported in *The New York Times,* March 31, the list, admittedly incomplete, showed nine members of the House of Representatives, one state treasurer, 48 mayors, 575 other

city officials, 362 school board members, 168 state legislators, 114 judges and magistrates, and 99 other law enforcement officers.

In light of the long denial of Negro political rights, the list looms impressively. But, the survey indicates the 1,500 elected black officials represent only three tenths of one per cent of the national total of more than 500,000. The Negro population currently represents about 11 per cent of the national total.

THE NATION's black people are still a long way from political parity. The sometimes strident demands made upon the Democratic party, particularly, for nomination and election of more Negroes to higher offices, heretofore regarded off-limits to blacks, is not only understandable but also justifiable if the nation is to have equality of representation at all levels of the political structure for all segments of the population. In raising this demand, however raucously, the Negro politicians, backed overwhelmingly by the black community, are following a well-established American pattern.

The attempt at this late date to discount the reality of ethnic considerations in American politics is, at best, incredible naivete and, at worst, raw racism. The minorities in our body politic have been compelled to struggle for full political recognition and participation. The Germans, the Irish, the Italians, the Poles, the Catholics and the Jews all followed this pattern. Had they failed, all major political offices in the country would still be in the hands of Anglo-Saxon Protestants with the non-WASP segments of the population contained in political serfdom. It is all right to maintain that the office should go to the "best qualified" candidate. But is this rating always to be reserved for whites only? Not in a truly democratic society.

As we celebrate the centennial of the Fifteenth Amendment it is well to recognize that the ballot, as powerful an instrument as it is, will not alone solve the Negro's problem. In the North, where black folk have enjoyed the right to vote, with little or no hindrance, for 100 years, their basic social and economic problems remain unsolved. Conditions in the North are not as bad as in the South, as some contend; but racial barriers are everywhere apparent to the naked eye and no black person is permitted, for long, to forget his racial origin and the melancholy legacy of slavery.

WHAT AMERICA WOULD BE LIKE WITHOUT BLACKS

What would America have been without the Negro? The question, however farfetched, periodically rises to the surface of the American imagination. For a discussion of the mystery and meaning of that question, TIME *turned to Black Novelist Ralph Ellison, author of* The Invisible Man *and* Shadow and Act.

THE fantasy of an America free of blacks is at least as old as the dream of creating a truly democratic society. While we are aware that there is something inescapably tragic about the cost of achieving our democratic ideals, we keep such tragic awareness segregated to the rear of our minds. We allow it to come to the fore only during moments of great national crisis.

On the other hand, there is something so embarrassingly absurd about the notion of purging the nation of blacks that it seems hardly a product of thought at all. It is more like a primitive reflex, a throwback to the dim past of tribal experience, which we rationalize and try to make respectable by dressing it up in the gaudy and highly questionable trappings of what we call the "concept of race." Yet, despite its absurdity, the fantasy of a blackless America continues to turn up. It is a fantasy born not merely of racism but of petulance, of exasperation, of moral fatigue. It is like a boil bursting forth from impurities in the bloodstream of democracy.

In its benign manifestations, it can be outrageously comic —as in the picaresque adventures of Percival Brownlee who appears in William Faulkner's story *The Bear.* Exasperating to his white masters because his aspirations and talents are for preaching and conducting choirs rather than for farming, Brownlee is "freed" after much resistance and ends up as the prosperous proprietor of a New Orleans brothel. In Faulkner's hands, the uncomprehending drive of Brownlee's owners to "get shut" of him is comically instructive. Indeed, the story resonates certain abiding, indeed tragic themes of American history with which it is interwoven, and which are causing great turbulence in the social atmosphere today. I refer to the exasperation and bemusement of the white American with the black, the black American's ceaseless (and swiftly accelerating) struggle to escape the misconceptions of whites, and the continual confusing of the black American's racial background with his individual culture. Most of all, I refer to the recurring fantasy of solving one basic problem of American democracy by getting "shut" of the blacks through various wishful schemes that would banish them from the nation's bloodstream, from its social structure, and from its conscience and historical consciousness.

Sick to Prosper

This fantastic vision of a lily-white America appeared as early as 1713, with the suggestion of a white "native American," thought to be from New Jersey, that all the Negroes be given their freedom and returned to Africa. In 1777, Thomas Jefferson, while serving in the Virginia legislature, began drafting a plan for the gradual emancipation and exportation of the slaves. Nor were Negroes themselves immune to the fan-

tasy. In 1815 Paul Cuffe, a wealthy merchant, shipbuilder and landowner from the New Bedford area, shipped and settled at his own expense 38 of his fellow Negroes in Africa. It was perhaps his example that led in the following year to the creation of the American Colonization Society, which was to establish in 1821 the colony of Liberia. Great amounts of cash and a perplexing mixture of motives went into the venture. The slaveowners and many Border-state politicians wanted to use it as a scheme to rid the country not of slaves but of the militant free Negroes who were agitating against the "peculiar institution." The abolitionists, until they took a lead from free Negro leaders and began attacking the scheme, also participated as a means of righting a great historical injustice. Many blacks went along with it simply because they were sick of the black and white American mess and hoped to prosper in the quiet peace of the old ancestral home.

Such conflicting motives doomed the Colonization Society to failure, but what amazes one even more than the notion that anyone could have believed in its success is the fact that it was attempted during a period when the blacks, slave and free, made up 18% of the total population. When we consider how long blacks had been in the New World and had been transforming it and being Americanized by it, the scheme appears not only fantastic, but the product of a free-floating irrationality. Indeed, a national pathology.

Plan to Purge

Nevertheless, some of the noblest of Americans were bemused. Not only Jefferson but later Abraham Lincoln was to give the scheme credence. According to Historian John Hope Franklin, Negro colonization seemed as important to Lincoln as emancipation. In 1862, Franklin notes, Lincoln called a group of prominent free Negroes to the White House and urged them to support colonization, telling them: "Your race suffers greatly, many of them by living among us, while ours suffers from your presence. If this is admitted, it affords a reason why we should be separated."

In spite of his unquestioned greatness, Abraham Lincoln was a man of his times and limited by some of the less worthy thinking of his times. This is demonstrated both by his reliance upon the concept of race in his analysis of the American dilemma and by his involvement in a plan of purging the nation of blacks as a means of healing the badly shattered ideals of democratic federalism. Although benign, his motive was no less a product of fantasy. It envisaged an attempt to relieve an inevitable suffering that marked the growing pains of the youthful body politic by an operation which would have amounted to the severing of a healthy and indispensable member.

Yet, like its twin, the illusion of secession, the fantasy of a benign amputation that would rid the country of black men to the benefit of a nation's health not only persists; today, in the form of neo-Garveyism, it fascinates black men no less than it once hypnotized whites. Both fantasies become operative whenever the nation grows weary of the struggle toward the ideal of American democratic equality. Both would use the black man as a scapegoat to achieve a national catharsis, and both would, by way of curing the patient, destroy him.

What is ultimately intriguing about the fantasy of "getting shut" of the Negro American is the fact that no one who entertains it seems ever to have considered what the nation would have become had Africans *not* been brought to the New World, and had their descendants not played such a complex and confounding role in the creation of American history and culture. Nor do they appear to have considered with any seriousness the effect upon the nation of having any of the schemes for exporting blacks succeed beyond settling some 15,000 or so in Liberia.

We are reminded that Daniel Patrick Moynihan, who has recently aggravated our social confusion over the racial issue while allegedly attempting to clarify it, is co-author of a work which insists that the American melting pot didn't melt because our white ethnic groups have resisted all assimilative forces that appear to threaten their identities. The problem here is that few Americans know who and what they really are. That is why few of these groups—or at least few of the children of these groups—have been able to resist the movies, television, baseball, jazz, football, drum-majoretting, rock, comic strips, radio commercials, soap operas, book clubs, slang, or any of a thousand other expressions and carriers of our pluralistic and easily available popular culture. And it is here precisely that ethnic resistance is least effective. On this level the melting pot did indeed melt, creating such deceptive metamorphoses and blending of identities, values and life-styles that most American whites are culturally part Negro American without even realizing it.

If we can resist for a moment the temptation to view everything having to do with Negro Americans in terms of their racially imposed status, we become aware of the fact that for all the harsh reality of the social and economic injustices visited upon them, these injustices have failed to keep Negroes clear of the cultural mainstream; Negro Americans are in fact one of its major tributaries. If we can cease approaching American social reality in terms of such false concepts as white and nonwhite, black culture and white culture, and think of these apparently unthinkable matters in the realistic manner of Western pioneers confronting the unknown prairie, perhaps we can begin to imagine what the U.S. would have been, or not been, had there been no blacks to give it—if I may be so bold as to say—color.

For one thing, the American nation is in a sense the product of the American language, a colloquial speech that began emerging long before the British colonials and Africans were transformed into Americans. It is a language that evolved from the king's English but, basing itself upon the realities of the American land and colonial institutions—or lack of institutions, began quite early as a vernacular revolt against the signs, symbols, manners and authority of the mother country. It is a language that began by merging the sounds of many tongues, brought together in the struggle of diverse regions. And whether it is admitted or not, much of the sound of that language is derived from the timbre of the African voice and the listening habits of the African ear. So there is a *de'z* and *do'z* of slave speech sounding beneath our most polished Harvard accents, and if there is such a thing as a Yale accent, there is a Negro wail in it—doubtlessly introduced there by Old Yalie John C. Calhoun, who probably got it from his mammy.

Whitman viewed the spoken idiom of Negro Americans as a source for a native grand opera. Its flexibility, its musicality, its rhythms, freewheeling diction and metaphors, as projected in Negro American folklore, were absorbed by the creators of our great 19th century literature even when the majority of blacks were still enslaved. Mark Twain celebrated it in the prose of *Huckleberry Finn*; without the presence of blacks, the book could not have been written. No Huck and Jim, no American novel as we know it. For not only is the black man a co-creator of the language that Mark Twain raised to the level of literary eloquence, but Jim's condition as American and Huck's commitment to freedom are at the moral center of the novel.

In other words, had there been no blacks, certain creative ten-

BY THOMAS HART BENTON—STATE CAPITOL, JEFFERSON CITY, MO.

HUCK & JIM

sions arising from the cross-purposes of whites and blacks would also not have existed. Not only would there have been no Faulkner; there would have been no Stephen Crane, who found certain basic themes of his writing in the Civil War. Thus, also, there would have been no Hemingway, who took Crane as a source and guide. Without the presence of Negro American style, our jokes, our tall tales, even our sports would be lacking in the sudden turns, the shocks, the swift changes of pace (all jazz-shaped) that serve to remind us that the world is ever unexplored, and that while a complete mastery of life is mere illusion, the real secret of the game is to make life swing. It is its ability to articulate this tragic-comic attitude toward life that explains much of the mysterious power and attractiveness of that quality of Negro American style known as "soul." An expression of American diversity within unity, of blackness with whiteness, soul announces the presence of a creative struggle against the realities of existence.

Without the presence of blacks, our political history would have been otherwise. No slave economy, no Civil War; no violent destruction of the Reconstruction; no K.K.K. and no Jim Crow system. And without the disenfranchisement of black Americans and the manipulation of racial fears and prejudices, the disproportionate impact of white Southern politicians upon our domestic and foreign policies would have been impossible. Indeed, it is almost impossible to conceive of what our political system would have become without the snarl of forces—cultural, racial, religious—that makes our nation what it is today.

Absent, too, would be the need for that tragic knowledge which we try ceaselessly to evade: that the true subject of democracy is not simply material well-being but the extension of the democratic process in the direction of perfecting itself. And that the most obvious test and clue to that perfection is the inclusion—*not* assimilation—of the black man.

Since the beginning of the nation, white Americans have suffered from a deep inner uncertainty as to who they really are. One of the ways that has been used to simplify the answer has been to seize upon the presence of black Americans and use them as a marker, a symbol of limits, a metaphor for the "outsider." Many whites could look at the social position of blacks and feel that color formed an easy and reliable gauge for determining to what extent one was or was not American. Perhaps that is why one of the first epithets that many European immigrants learned when they got off the boat was the term "nigger"—it made them feel instantly American. But this is tricky magic. Despite his racial difference and social status, something indisputably American about Negroes not only raised doubts about the white man's value system but aroused the troubling suspicion that whatever else the true American is, he is also somehow black.

Geared to What Is

Materially, psychologically and culturally, part of the nation's heritage is Negro American, and whatever it becomes will be shaped in part by the Negro's presence. Which is fortunate, for today it is the black American who puts pressure upon the nation to live up to its ideals. It is he who gives creative tension to our struggle for justice and for the elimination of those factors, social and psychological, which make for slums and shaky suburban communities. It is he who insists that we purify the American language by demanding that there be a closer correlation between the meaning of words and reality, between ideal and conduct, our assertions and our actions. Without the black American, something irrepressibly hopeful and creative would go out of the American spirit, and the nation might well succumb to the moral slobbism that has ever threatened its existence from within.

When we look objectively at how the dry bones of the nation were hung together, it seems obvious that some one of the many groups that compose the U.S. had to suffer the fate of being allowed no easy escape from experiencing the harsh realities of the human condition as they were to exist under even so fortunate a democracy as ours. It would seem that some one group had to be stripped of the possibility of escaping such tragic knowledge by taking sanctuary in moral equivocation, racial chauvinism or the advantage of superior social status. There is no point in complaining over the past or apologizing for one's fate. But for blacks there are no hiding places down here, not in suburbia or in penthouses, neither in country nor in city. They are an American people who are geared to what *is* and who yet are driven by a sense of what it is possible for human life to be in this society. The nation could not survive being deprived of their presence because, by the irony implicit in the dynamics of American democracy, they symbolize both its most stringent testing and the possibility of its greatest human freedom.

CREDITS AND ACKNOWLEDGMENTS

1. New Directions for History

4—Newsweek photo by Wally McNamee. Copyright Newsweek, 1970. 6—The Picture Decorator, Inc. New York City. 7(*top*)—Pictorial Parade. 7(*bottom right*)—United Press International. 7(*bottom left*)—Culver Pictures. 8—Courtesy of the New York Public Library—Astor, Lenox and Tilden Foundations. 9—United Press International. 10—Newsweek photo by Wally McNamee. Copyright Newsweek, 1970. 11 —Charles Phelps Cushing. 12—Authenticated News International. 13(*top*)—Culver Pictures. 13(*bottom*)—Newsweek photo by Wally McNamee. Copyright Newsweek, 1970. 14 —Culver Pictures. 15—Bob Fitch—Black Star. 16(*left*)— Newsweek photo by Jeff Lowenthal. Copyright Newsweek, 1970. 17, 18—The Bettmann Archive. 19(*top*)—Culver Pictures. 19(*bottom*)—United Press International. 21—Wide World Photos. 22 (*top*)—Daniel Bernstein. 22(*bottom*)— Wide World Photos. 23, 25—Marty Norman © 1970 by The New York Times Company. Reprinted by permission. 42 (*top*)—© 1970, Alan Copeland/Photon West. 42(*bottom*)—© 1971, Stephen Shames/Photon West.

2. Early America

50, 51—The Bettmann Archive. 52, 54, 55—Culver Pictures. 58, 59, 60, 61, 62—AMERICAN HISTORY *Illustrated*. 64— The Picture Decorator, Inc. New York City. 67—By courtesy of Liverpool City Libraries. 69(*bottom*)—*History Today*. 74—Courtesy, American Antiquarian Society. 76— From the Collections of the Maryland Historical Society. 78 —Courtesy of the New York Historical Society. 79—Historical Society of Pennsylvania.

3. National Consolidation and Expansion

84—The Bettmann Archive. 86(*left*)—Culver Pictures. 86 (*right*)—The New York Stock Exchange, Inc. 93—Courtesy of Mankind Magazine. 95—United Press International. 97— Courtesy of the Library of Congress. 100—Culver Pictures. 102—Courtesy of Mankind Magazine. 105—Culver Pictures. 107—The Bettmann Archive. 109—Anne S. K. Brown Military Collection, Brown University Library. 113—Courtesy of Mankind Magazine.

4. Civil War and Reconstruction

123—Culver Pictures. 124, 125—Courtesy of Mankind Magazine. 127, 129—Culver Pictures. 131—Courtesy Chicago Historical Society. 137(*left*)—Kean Archives, Phila. 137 (*right*)—U. S. Signal Corps Photo No. 111-B-2778 in the National Archives. 138—AMERICAN HISTORY *Illustrated*. 139, 140, 141—Courtesy of the Library of Congress. 142, 143(*top*)—Courtesy of the National Archives. 142, 143(*bottom*), 144—Courtesy of the Library of Congress. 145— AMERICAN HISTORY *Illustrated*. 146, 147—CIVIL WAR TIMES *Illustrated*. 148—Kean Archives, Phila. 149—Courtesy of the Library of Congress. 150, 151—CIVIL WAR TIMES *Illustrated*. 152—Kean Archives, Phila. 153—Courtesy of the Library of Congress. 154—CIVIL WAR TIMES *Illustrated*. 155—M. and M. Karolik Collection, Museum of Fine Arts, Boston.

5. Industrialization, Empire, and Argument

171—Courtesy of the Library of Congress. 172—AMERICAN HISTORY *Illustrated*. 173, 174, 175, 177—Courtesy of the Library of Congress. 179, 180, 181, 182—Courtesy of the General Library, University of California, Berkeley. 185 —Reis Library, Allegheny College. 187—Culver Pictures. 188 —Drake Well Museum. 190—Reprinted, courtesy of the Chicago Tribune. 192—Drake Well Museum. 193—Courtesy of the Library of Congress. 196—The Harry T. Peters Collection, Museum of the City of New York. 198, 199—Courtesy of the Library of Congress. 201—Culver Pictures. 203, 204—Courtesy of Carnegie Library of Pittsburgh—Neg. P2487; Neg. P1135; Neg. P1259. 205(*top*)—Brown Brothers. 205(*bottom*)—Courtesy of Carnegie Library of Pittsburgh —Neg. P2490. 206(*top*)—Courtesy of the Library of Congress. 206(*center*)—Courtesy of Carnegie Library of Pittsburgh—Neg. P2489. 206(*bottom*)—United Press International. 207—Brown Brothers. 211—Culver Pictures. 212— Brown Brothers. 215, 217, 218, 219—Courtesy of the Library of Congress. 220—Reprinted by permission of the publisher, from *T. A. Bailey: The American Pageant 3rd Ed.* (Lexington, Mass.: D. C. Heath and Company, 1966). 221— Keystone View Co. Photo. 222—Courtesy of the Library of Congress.

6. Inside Twentieth-Century America

226—Courtesy Chicago Historical Society. 229, 230, 231, 233—United Press International. 235—Courtesy Chicago Historical Society. 244—Charles Gatewood. 248—George W. Gardner. 256—Nan Lurie. 257—Y. R. Okamoto, courtesy L. B. J. Library. 266—Paul Conrad's cartoon reproduced courtesy of the Register and Tribune Syndicate, Inc. 269— Julio Fernandez © 1971 by the New York Times Company. Reprinted by permission. 272—*copyright 1970 by Herblock in The Washington Post.*

7. The Uses of American Power in the Twentieth Century

278, 279, 280(*top*)—Culver Pictures. 280(*bottom*)—Brown Brothers. 281(*top and right*)—Culver Pictures. 281(*bottom*), 282, 283(*top*)—The Bettmann Archive. 283(*bottom*)—Historical Pictures Service—Chicago. 285—The Bettmann Archive. 286—Culver Pictures. 298—United Press International. 303(*top left*)—Gerald R. Brimacombe. 303(*top right*) —K. Tatushi. 303(*bottom*)—*Time Magazine*, Time Inc. Brian Brake 1970. 305—From the Kansas City Star. 316, 317— Robert M. Cunningham © 1971 by The New York Times Company. Reprinted by permission. 320—Pictorial Parade —Washington Bureau. 321—Tim in L'Express, Paris. © 1971 by The New York Times Company. Reprinted by permission. 332—Copyright 1970 Saturday Review, Inc. 333—Saul Lambert © 1971 by The New York Times Company. Reprinted by permission. 334(*right*)—United Press International. 334(*left*)—Patrick A. Burns/THE NEW YORK TIMES. 335(*left*)—Sidney Schanberg/THE NEW YORK TIMES. 335 (*right*)—Ralph Blumenthal/THE NEW YORK TIMES. 336— Wide World Photos.

8. Probing the Future

340, 341, 342, 346, 351—Drawings by Colos. 352—The Bettmann Archive. 353—Copyright 1971 Saturday Review, Inc. 360, 365—John Huenergarth © 1971 by The New York Times Company. Reprinted by permission. 379—Monkmeyer Press. 383—Cassie Haber. 384—Photo Trends. 385(*left*) —Burk Uzzle/Black Star. 385(*right*)—Photo: Winston Vargas. 386(*top*)—The Bettmann Archive. 386(*bottom*)—Copyright 1971 Saturday Review, Inc. 394, 397—NAACP posters by C. R. Read, reprinted from *The Crisis*. 400—Thomas H. Benton.